But ah I feel in

a blessing never m

Thou art too lik

For earthly love to merit thee

Thou see; May, I have

not forgotten you

The Letters of
Mary Wollstonecraft
Shelley

Percy Byphe Shelley

THE LETTERS

of

MARY
WOLLSTONECRAFT
SHELLEY

VOLUME II

"Treading in
unknown paths"

Edited by Betty T. Bennett

THE JOHNS HOPKINS UNIVERSITY PRESS
BALTIMORE AND LONDON

The publication of this volume has been aided by
a grant from The Carl and Lily Pforzheimer Foundation, Inc.

The Johns Hopkins University Press, Baltimore, Maryland 21218
The Johns Hopkins Press Ltd., London

Library of Congress Cataloging in Publication Data
Shelley, Mary Wollstonecraft Godwin, 1797–1851.
The letters of Mary Wollstonecraft Shelley.
Bibliography: v. 1, pp. xxix–xxxvi
v. 2, pp. xxxiii–xli
Includes indexes.
CONTENTS: v. 1. "A part of the elect."—v. 2.
"Treading in unknown paths."
1. Shelley, Mary Wollstonecraft Godwin, 1797–1851—
Correspondence. 2. Authors, English—19th century—
Correspondence. I. Bennett, Betty T.
PR5398.A4   1980 vol 2 823'.7   [B]   79-24190
ISBN 0–8018–2275–0 (v. 1)
ISBN 0–8018–2645–4 (v. 2)

Frontispiece: Mary Shelley's sketch of Percy Bysshe Shelley, courtesy of the Humanities
Research Center, University of Texas at Austin.

End papers: Double-page opening of the inside back cover of the copy of *Queen Mab*
given to Mary Shelley by Shelley, courtesy of the Huntington Library.

To My Family

Contents

LIST OF ILLUSTRATIONS

Acknowledgments

IN PREPARING the second volume of *The Letters of Mary Wollstonecraft Shelley*, I have again received various forms of assistance from an international community dedicated to literary and historical studies, to which I am grateful. I wish especially to express my deep gratitude to Professors Alice G. Fredman and Charles E. Robinson, who read and reacted to the first draft of this volume, supplied me with materials not readily available, and continued to steadfastly encourage me, making my steps lighter as I tread in unknown paths; and to Dr. Donald H. Reiman, for his reading of the first draft of this volume and other generous assistance.

For the use of their manuscripts, as well as other assistance, I continue indebted to Lord Abinger, The Carl and Lily Pforzheimer Foundation, John Murray, and Professor Jean de Palacio.

For answering innumerable questions, tirelessly aiding in the search for the data that give context to the letters, and providing other assistance in the preparation of this volume I am deeply grateful to Robert Yampolsky, of the Pforzheimer Library. So, too, am I grateful to Mihai H. Handrea, of the Pforzheimer Library, who called to my attention pertinent material and provided translations and other assistance; to John P. Collela, of the Pforzheimer Library, who shared his expertise in Italian; and to Doucet D. Fisher, of the Pforzheimer Library, for various forms of assistance. I continue grateful to Professors Kenneth Neill Cameron and Leslie A. Marchand for their guidance and their example.

Among those who have helped in the search for letters, illustrations, or supplemental material or have otherwise assisted in the preparation of this edition are Bruce Barker-Benfield, Alan S. Bell, Powell A. Benedict, Jr., I. G. Brown, John Clubbe, Ian C. Copland, Peter J. Croft, Dennis R. Dean, Wilfred S. Dowden, Clement Dunbar, Ellen S. Dunlap, Celia Eckhardt, Herb and Merrilyn Edelman, Sibylla Jane Flower, Christina Gee, Rosemary Graham, Theodore Grieder, Gene De Gruson, Ricki B. Herzfeld, Joseph C. Hickerson, L. R. Hoare, Berti Jones, Nicholas A. Joukovsky, Stephen S. Kaagan, Philip Kelley, Ruby Levesque, William T. Little, George Lowy, Claire McCann, Josephine McSweeney, Fairlie Arant Maginnes, John Manners, Sandra Mitlas, Virginia Murray, William J. Novak, Cecilia Payne-Gaposchkin, W. Hugh Peal, Burton Pollin, Gordon N. Ray, Val Rosenquist, William St. Clair, J. N. Sene, Bruce Sharpe, David and Marion Stocking, Emily W. Sunstein, Duncan Torbet, Lynnette T. Walker, Janet Wallace, Gay Wilmerding, Clifford Wurfel, and Paul M. Zall.

Permissions to publish manuscript letters, as well as other courtesies regarding them, were given by: Alabama Department of Archives & History; Avon County Library (Bath Reference Library); Barring Brothers; Henry W. and Albert A. Berg Collection, The New York Public Library, Astor, Lenox, and Tilden Foundations; William K. Bixby Papers, Washington University Libraries, St. Louis, Missouri; Bodleian Library; Boston Public Library; Brigham Young University; The British Library; The Brotherton Collection, University of Leeds; Brown University; Chapin Library, Williams College; Trustees of the Estate of Lord Charnwood; Columbia University Library; Cornell University Library; Duke University; Dundee Central Library; Provost and Fellows of Eton College; Fales Library, New York University; Fitzwilliam Museum; Furman University; Greater London Record Office; Harkness Collection (#12), Manuscripts and Archives Division, The New York Public Library, Astor, Lenox, and Tilden Foundations; Harrow Education Department; Haverford College; The Historical Society of Pennsylvania; The Houghton Library, Harvard University; Humanities Research Center, University of Texas at Austin; The Huntington Library, San Marino, California; University of Illinois; Indiana State Library; India Office Library and Records; The Honorable Society of the Inner Temple; University of Iowa Libraries; The Johns Hopkins University Press; University of Kansas; London Borough of Camden, from the collections at Keats House, Hampstead; Keats-Shelley Memorial House, Rome; Keele University Library; University of Kentucky; William Luther Lewis Collection, Texas Christian University; The Library of Congress; The Library of Scotland; Lilly Library, Indiana University, Bloomington, Indiana; Lockwood Memorial Library, State University of New York at Buffalo; McGill University; George S. MacManus Co.; Maggs Bros.; Massachusetts Historical Society; Mitchell Library, Sydney; John Murray; Museum Calvet; National Library of Ireland; National Library of Scotland; National Portrait Gallery, London; National Portrait Gallery, Washington, D.C.; The Carl and Lily Pforzheimer Foundation; The Pierpont Morgan Library; Princeton University Library; Public Record Office, Kew Richmond; The Rosenbach Museum and Library; Royal Academy of Arts; Royal Literary Fund; The John Rylands Library; Scottish Record Office; Smith College Library; The Robert H. Taylor Collection, Princeton University; Alexander Turnbull Library, Wellington, New Zealand; Messrs. Josiah Wedgwood & Sons; Wellesley College Library; The Archives Department, Westminster City Libraries; Dr. Williams Library.

Permission to publish the illustrations, as well as other courtesies regarding them, were given by: Bibliothèque National; University of California Press; Humanities Research Center, University of Texas at Austin; Huntington Library; John Murray; National Portrait Gallery, London; and National Portrait Gallery, Washington, D.C.

Grants from the American Philosophical Society and the Carl and Lily Pforzheimer Foundation allowed me to travel abroad to work firsthand with manuscripts of the letters and other pertinent material.

I thank Joanne Allen for her concern and expertise in copy-editing volumes I and II, and Donald S. Owings, of Pratt Institute, for developing a computer program to make indexing more accurate and efficient. To my colleague Janice Ragland Klinzing I am deeply grateful for all her generous activities that helped so materially in the assembly of this volume.

I am ever grateful to my parents, Jennie and Mayer Edelman, the children Peter and Matthew Bennett and Katelin, Ellie, and Derek Thomas for their love and encouragement and to my husband Gary Thomas, who has read and responded to different phases of this project and participated in the long search for manuscripts with love and enthusiasm.

Introduction

ON 3 OCTOBER 1835, Mary Shelley wrote to Sir John Bowring: "The best is that the very thing which occasions the difficulty makes it interesting—namely—the treading in unknown paths and dragging out unknown things." Although this remark alludes to the challenge of doing research for a literary project, it may serve equally to characterize Mary Shelley's personal life and career from 1827 to 1840, years in which she successfully fulfilled the three major goals of her life: she provided a gentleman's education for her son, continued to write and publish, and collected and published Shelley's works in the monumental 1839 editions.

After Shelley's death until the summer of 1827, Mary Shelley remained deeply rooted in the world they had shared. Jane Williams, whose husband had drowned with Shelley, was her most important link to that past. Perhaps on one level Mary Shelley identified with Shelley through a new-found love for his "dearest friend" (Shelley to Jane Williams, *PBS Letters*, #721). Mary Shelley's letters of 1822–28 demonstrate that she has envisioned a future of mutual affection and support between herself and "the partner of her miseries" (14 February 1828). Jane Williams, however, was not like-minded; her commitment limited, she even spread malicious tales about Mary Shelley. Mary Shelley's discovery of this duplicity, in the summer of 1827, brought on an emotional crisis almost as intense as the one she experienced at Shelley's death. Her feelings of loss were renewed and in a sense made more final, as she was again deprived of a trusted confidante and companion and denied the solace of shared memories. It was at this point that Mary Shelley turned outward from reliance on the circle of "the elect" to create an independent life for herself.

The years 1827–40 were Mary Shelley's most prolific as an author and editor. She wrote three more full-length novels, bringing her total to six. The first of these, *Perkin Warbeck* (1830), is a historical novel in the style of Sir Walter Scott, but from a quite different political perspective. She rejected Scott's support for the status quo, advancing instead a staunchly anti-monarchical reformist point of view. Using Godwin's approach of carefully researching historical material, she based *Perkin Warbeck* on wide reading and consultation: she wrote to Thomas Crofton Croker for Irish sources (30 October 1828); to Sir Walter Scott for references to Scottish source material (25 May 1829); to Godwin and others for additional factual details that she could distill into her fiction. Her next novel, *Lodore* (1835), in the silver-fork genre, stresses a theme found in all of her novels: the importance of love and the necessity to set aside self-interest in favor of serving others.

Her correspondence about *Lodore* is concerned mostly with efforts to find a publisher, negotiate a contract, and see the book through publication. New letters, however, reveal that a section of *Lodore* was lost, presumably in the mail or at the publishers, and that Mary Shelley was required to rewrite a considerable part of the novel. Her final novel, *Falkner* (1837), is in theme and style akin to *Lodore*. On 8 November 1835 she confided to Maria Gisborne that she looked on fidelity as the first of human virtues and would write a novel to display that conviction. Her feelings may have been an outgrowth of her disappointment with Jane Williams Hogg; they may as well have been an outgrowth of her need to bolster her own courage and continue to pursue her objectives during years in which she was particularly lonely. Whatever the source of inspiration, *Falkner* portrays a woman's heroic loyalty, and although Mary Shelley could "see its defects," it was one of her favorite works.

These last two novels are particularly illuminating because they move the female characters from secondary roles to center-stage. The titles notwithstanding, neither Lodore nor Falkner is heroic. Both are self-willed to the point of indifference to needs other than their own and thereby cause considerable unhappiness. Moreover, Lodore dies on p. 120 of the first volume of a two-volume, 396-page novel; and Falkner's life is one of guilt and repentance. The actual main characters are two young women: Ethel Lodore and Elizabeth Raby, who are delineated as strong, sensitive, intelligent, loyal, and heroic. Their feelings and actions, which bear more than a passing resemblance to those of Mary Shelley, reflect the author's self-respect and her respect for other women. Beginning with her admiration for Mary Wollstonecraft, she early recognized the important contribution women could make to society. As she grew older, and was no longer under the strong influence of either father or husband, she more frequently voiced her feelings of esteem for women in her fiction and her correspondence. Further, the concern in her letters for these later books and her pride in *Falkner* reflect the seriousness of her commitment to her subject and her art.

During these same years, Mary Shelley also wrote three volumes of Lardner's *Lives* (see MWS, *Lives* [1835–37]; and MWS, *Lives* [1838–39]). These studies of significant French, Spanish, Portuguese, and Italian literary and scientific figures occasioned many letters from her to famous contemporaries, such as Sir John Bowring and Gabriele Rossetti, from whom she sought accurate and learned sources of biographical, historical, and critical material. These letters also indicate her delight in learning and research; indeed the subtitle of this volume of her letters is taken from a reference she made to her search for sources for her Spanish *Lives*.

Other letters refer to Mary Shelley's many short stories, poems, reviews, and essays and suggest that more of her shorter works have been published than have been identified as hers. She deals with questions of appropriate length of story, deadlines, payments, competing journals, contents, and editors and thereby affords considerable insight into contemporary publishing procedures. Her opinions of contemporary authors are derived from two sources: from her book reviews, but far more extensively from her letters, in which she mentions, among others, Jane Austen, Edward Bulwer, Thomas Campbell, Benjamin Disraeli, Catherine Gore, Leigh Hunt, Washington Irving, Letitia Elizabeth Landon (L.E.L.), Harriet Martineau, Thomas Moore, Caroline Norton, John Howard Payne, Edward John Trelawny, and William Wordsworth.

Of those closest to her, she writes of Shelley and his works throughout her letters, reviews, and fiction, finally synthesizing her opinions in the introductions and notes to her 1839 Shelley editions. She also continues to comment on Byron, often in relation to Thomas Moore's Byron editions. Her letters to Moore seem not to be extant, but his to her and hers to those who might assist Moore (including Teresa Guiccioli and Sir John Bowring) illustrate how material a contribution she made to Moore's editions. Her judgments of Godwin's works she expressed in letters and in her laudatory memoir of him for the Colburn and Bentley 1831 reprint of *Caleb Williams* (written simultaneously with her new introduction for the revised 1831 *Frankenstein*) and in her review of *Cloudesley* in *Blackwood's Magazine* (see 4 May [1830]).

In addition, her letters furnish a list of suggested topics for books and essays, mostly addressed to publishers, as Mary Shelley sought further means through her journalism to support herself, her son, her father, and her friends. The proposed projects, either not undertaken or not completed, include: full-length biographies of Mahomet, Josephine, Madame de Staël (about whom a chapter was included in *Lives*); a history of manners and literature; lives of the English philosophers; a geological history of the earth; a collection of the lives of celebrated women or a history of women; and regular articles for the *Court Journal*. Her willingness to write on this diversity of subjects demonstrates a degree of self-confidence not generally recognized in Mary Shelley.

Among projects left unfinished was her life of Godwin, who died on 7 April 1836. His will appointed Mary Shelley his literary executor and requested that she determine which of his papers and letters should be posthumously published (see 20 April 1836). She accordingly signed an agreement with Colburn to publish his memoirs and correspondence, for the benefit of his widow, whom, despite their differences over the years, she greatly assisted after Godwin's death. In the course of preparing Godwin's manuscripts, Mary Shelley began to annotate his early memoirs (now on deposit at the Bodleian Library) and to solicit his letters from friends and acquaintances, including Bulwer, Josiah Wedgwood, Thomas A. Cooper, William Hazlitt, Jr. (for letters to his father), and Henry Crabb Robinson. She also attempted to enlist Robinson's aid in obtaining letters from Wordsworth and from Coleridge's executors. On 26 January 1837 she informed Trelawny that her "sense of duty towards my father, whose passion was posthumous fame," had readied her "to meet the misery that must be mine" should the edition cause her to "become an object of scurrility & attacks." She was determined to defer publication, however, until the completion of arrangements for Percy Florence's matriculation at Trinity College, Cambridge, that following spring, so that "a cry raised against his Mother" would not harm his career. She expected criticism not on the basis of politics but on that of religion, a subject that might well elicit public attack and scandal. Perhaps for this reason, the work was never completed. Or perhaps it was set aside in favor of first completing the Shelley editions and then was not resumed because she was unwilling to undergo again the physical and psychological stress that she endured in the preparation of her editions of Shelley's poetry and prose in 1838–39.

Her intention to gather, preserve, and publish Shelley's works is repeatedly expressed in her letters, beginning almost immediately after his death. The first phase of this project, leading to the 1824 *Posthumous Poems*, is described in volume I of this edition; the 1827–40 letters detail the subsequent history of her plans that culminated in the 1839 editions. After *Posthumous Poems*, her next major involvement with publishing Shelley was in 1829, when she assisted Cyrus Redding in editing Galignani's pirated *Poetical Works of Coleridge, Shelley, and Keats*. Prohibited by an agreement with Sir Timothy Shelley from bringing Shelley's name before the public, she obviously believed she could aid this French publication with impunity and thereby keep both her commitments: *she* would not bring Shelley forward, yet his works would be kept in the public notice. New letters and evidence supply fuller information than has formerly been available about the important contributions she made to the Galignani edition.

Ten years elapsed between the Galignani edition and Mary Shelley's 1839 editions. We have information now, however, from a previously unpublished letter that negotiations for her edition began at least as early as 22 January 1834, when she informed Edward Moxon of her willingness to publish with him once "family reasons" no longer prevented her. Mary Shelley's letters between 1834 and 1839, record the development of this project. They provide a wealth of information about the problems, constraints, editorial decisions, and exhaustive labor, as well as the ideals and objectives that shaped the volumes. These letters also provide a far more accurate depiction than heretofore available of Mary Shelley's motives and actions and of contemporary publishing processes. For instance, Mary Shelley has been attacked almost universally for her omissions of the atheistical passages of *Queen Mab* in the four-volume *Poetical Works* (1839) (see 11 December 1838). The letters disclose, however, that although she disagreed with atheism and believed that Shelley himself had changed his mind about this subject, she was persuaded by the publisher Edward Moxon to omit those passages to protect his copyright, which he could lose if found guilty of publishing a work containing blasphemy. Nor was her omission of the dedication to Harriet in *Queen Mab* the result, as critics have suggested, of her reluctance to display Shelley's feelings for his first wife; rather, it was made on the reasonable editorial principle of authorial intent. Years before, she had had decisive evidence that Shelley himself preferred the omission (see 11 February [1839]).

The letters reveal her as a more than responsible editor: she sought first editions from which to publish and to correct proofs; she inquired after additional manuscripts of Shelley's works and letters; she asked advice and guidance from friends, including Leigh Hunt and Hogg. Her letters tell of her efforts in "turning over manuscript books—scraps—half illegible—unfinished" (11 November [1839]); the questions of her claim to copyright (12 January 1839); her impatience with the frustrations of the work; the injunction of her father-in-law, Sir Timothy Shelley, that she not include a biography of Shelley, which she circumvented through the notes she appended to the poems that trace their origins and history; the severe illness caused by all the editorial and personal strains of preparing Shelley's manuscripts in context. Her labors resulted in the 1839 publication of the four-volume *The Poetical Works of Percy Bysshe Shelley*, the two-volume *Essays, Letters from Abroad, Translations and Fragments by Percy Bysshe Shelley*, and the one-volume *The Poetical Works of Percy Bysshe Shelley* (with the complete *Queen Mab* and other poems added). This achievement was not merely the work of a wife seeking posthumous fame for the writings of a beloved husband, as has been suggested or implied by many critics; she approached her commitment as a professional, deliberate editor, capable of making the most difficult kinds of editorial decisions.

Subsequent editors have acknowledged their indebtedness to Mary Shelley for her arduous labors in transcribing Shelley's manuscripts, which generally appear to be illegible and undecipherable. So, too, have Shelley scholars looked to her notes and her introductions as an invaluable source of biographical and critical detail. As is true for all editors, some decisions she made are open to criticism. But the letters show that even her most serious error, the failure to use first editions consistently as copy-text when manuscripts were not available, was not the result of amateurishness or indifference. In fact, Mary Shelley's letters reveal that her editorial principles, stated or implied, stand up well even by modern standards. As editor, Mary Shelley became Shelley's collaborator, returning more than in kind the guidance he had given her when she wrote *Frankenstein* and other early works. She gathered and preserved his writings. She brought the experience of a professional author to the editing of his works. Finally, biographers and critics agree that Mary Shelley's commitment to bring Shelley the notice she believed his works merited was the single, major force that established Shelley's reputation as a poet during a period when he almost certainly would have faded from public view.

But however significant writing and editing were in her life, Mary Shelley's daily responsibilities were centered on the welfare of the Shelleys' one surviving child, Percy Florence. In September 1827, at the age of eight, he was a day boarder at a school in Arundel. He next attended Mr. Slater's School in London, then Harrow, and finally, in 1836, Trinity College, Cambridge. Mary Shelley found the means to provide this traditional gentleman's education from two sources: her income as an author and an allowance elicited from Sir Timothy Shelley. The letters record her continual negotiations with Sir Timothy, conducted on his behalf by his attorneys, William Whitton and then John Gregson, because their client was determined never to communicate directly with his daughter-in-law. Though the funds allowed by Sir Timothy were not gifts but advances repayable to his estate, he remained reluctant throughout his long life to assist Mary Shelley. Because her own means were extremely limited and were frequently strained to assist Godwin and others, she was placed in the position of constantly importuning for increases in allowance as Percy Florence's education expenses mounted. Although the "Struldbrugg" (as she called Sir Timothy in 1840) never agreed to meet her, he was induced by her efforts to allow her the funds she required for Percy Florence and, on rare occasions, even deigned to see his grandson.

Whereas Sir Timothy's contributions towards Percy Florence's education were no strain on the considerable Shelley fortune, Mary Shelley's resolve to raise her son suitably for his eventual station unquestionably exacerbated her already straitened circumstances. To better meet her financial obligations, she decided to move from London to Harrow so that Percy Florence could be enrolled as a day student rather than as a boarder. This move had been encouraged by the presence there of friends, Sir John Dean Paul and Lady Paul, who had promised to aid her. Lady Paul's sudden death, however, left Mary Shelley alone, with little money and no acquaintances within the community. Except for holidays and brief, infrequent visits to London, she remained at Harrow from 1833 through 1836, years in which she often characterized herself as acutely isolated and depressed but consoled by her pleasure in Percy Florence as he grew into early manhood. From her letters we learn that Percy Florence's main interests were music, theater, and, to his mother's consternation, sailing. She depicts him as exceptionally kind and sensitive but lacking in social grace or ambition. She describes how, most important to her, her burdens are eased by his love and concern for her. The reciprocal feelings of mother and son are typified by his invitation to her to accompany him and several of his friends on their 1840 journey to the Continent. She joyfully accepted, afterwards making this tour the topic of the first volume of her last full-length work, *Rambles in Germany and Italy* (see 6 June [1840] to Marianne Hunt).

In addition to family and career, politics continued to play an important part in the life of Mary Shelley. The 1827–40 letters testify to her active concern with political conditions and her strong opposition to despotic government in England and on the Continent. Disproving the notion that Mary Shelley's interest in politics died with Shelley, her letters contain a political as well as a social record of the transitional years between post-

Napoleonic unrest and economic depression and the emergence of Victorian attitudes and standards. For example, in her 11 November 1830 letter to General Lafayette congratulating him and France on the successful July revolution, she comments: "May England imitate your France in its moderation and heroism." Her 27 December 1830 letter to Trelawny speaks of the burnings and alarms in England, as well as her belief that "the Autocrats would have the good sense to make the necessary sacrifices to a starving people." Her 30 December 1830 letter to Frances Wright celebrates the triumph of "the <u>Cause</u>" in Europe that is expected to quell tyrants. Of England she says: "The people <u>will</u> be redressed—will the Aristocrats sacrifice enough to tranquillize them—if they will not—we must be revolutionized." Her letters of 1831 describe political unrest and her own excitement about, and support of, the impending Reform Bill. Of a threatened war in America in 1833 she says: "I am truly sorry—Brothers should not fight for the different & various portions of their inheritance. . . . War is the companion & friend of Monarchy—if it be the same of freedom—the gain is not much to Mankind between a Sovereign & a president" (16 January 1833). In 1834 she attended Parliament to hear the debates on the Irish tithe issue and the revised Poor Laws, and she was angered at Lord Brougham for his support of these measures, which increased the plight of the poor (see 19 August [1834]). A sophisticated observer of the political scene, Mary Shelley was aware of the influence of politics in almost every aspect of life. When she wrote her introductions to the 1839 editions, she indicated that Shelley's works had been treated with extreme hostility by critics because of his support of political reform. In 1839, however, in a new climate of moderation and reform, she anticipated a reception that would appreciate his genius, which proved to be the case.

Although on a number of occasions Mary Shelley wrote kindly about or to members of the Tory party, this should not be taken to mean that she had become a political conservative. Her positive references to Tories were almost always directed towards individuals, not the party, except when the Tories, rather than the Whigs, ensured Godwin's sinecure in 1835. For the most part, her friends were supporters of reform, and it was generally the political interests of her friends that determined whether she wrote to them about politics. For example, she wrote to Trelawny, Frances Wright, and Maria Gisborne about political events, knowing they shared a mutual interest, whereas she made no reference to politics in her letters to Jane Williams Hogg.

As her ardor for political reform remained strong, so did her deep love of the natural scene and her antipathy for London. Her letters as well as her fiction reflect her view of nature as sublime and restorative. She often describes the English country landscape and the peacefulness she finds there, and also recalls Italian landscapes, which become almost Edenic in her memories. Financial pressures compelled her to reside for the most part in London and its environs in 1827–40, except when she economized further by living in Harrow. This reinforced her early dislike of London, and she often mentions her ambition to purchase a country home for herself and Percy Florence. In 1839, able to fulfill this dream through funds earned from the Shelley editions, she rented, for one year, Layton House, Putney, where she enjoyed both the country and a circle of friends.

Despite her preference, however, her letters show that she did derive some pleasures from living in London. There she could often visit with Godwin. She could also attend a large number of cultural events, the frequency of her attendance determined mainly by her ability to pay her way or obtain free passes. The letters in which she arranged for tickets, extended invitations to friends to join her, and wrote about the events to correspondents offer a valuable contemporary view of the opera, theater, concert hall, and art.

Although her activities during the years 1827–40 were similar to those just after her return to England, the context of these activities was considerably altered. The breach of her intimacy with Jane Williams Hogg in July 1827 led Mary Shelley into a social and literary world far different from the Pisan circle. During the dozen years after 1827, her closest friends were the young daughters of Joshua Robinson, first Isabella, then Julia and Rosa (see vol. I, [19 February 1827]). These sisters lived in Mary Shelley's home at times; she, in turn, often stayed with them at their father's home. In effect, she became as involved with their lives as she had earlier been with Jane Williams Hogg's or, in Italy, with the Gisbornes'. The most startling aspect of these new friendships, revealed through the letters and supplemented by other evidence, was the role Mary Shelley played in assisting Isabella Robinson's charade as the wife of "Sholto Douglas." The letters of the summer of 1827 indicate that Mary Shelley, Isabella Robinson Douglas, and their entourage were then in the south of England, awaiting Isabella Robinson Douglas's husband before finalizing the Douglases' plans to go abroad. The fact is that the "husband" they waited for was actually "Doddy," identified in the first volume of these letters as Mary Diana Dods, who wrote pseudonymously as David Lyndsay (see vol. I, 30 October [1826] to Alaric A. Watts, n. 2). The letters narrate the strange story of Mary Diana Dods's transition into the role and attire of a man called Sholto Douglas, who traveled with Isabella Robinson Douglas as her husband and as the father of her infant daughter and who was accepted in French society as a man (see 17 September [1827]).

Mary Shelley not only was aware of this scheme but aided it by looking after Isabella Robinson Douglas, who was quite ill in the summer of 1827, by obtaining passports for the group through John Howard Payne, and by securing letters of introduction for them to French society from Frances Wright. Mary Shelley's feelings for Isabella Robinson Douglas proved to be misplaced. Isabella Robinson Douglas maligned her even in the very social set she met through Mary Shelley's kindness (see [27 April 1828]). Until Mary Shelley learned of her friend's deceit, she retained deep affection for Isabella Robinson Douglas; but her place in Mary Shelley's daily life was soon filled by Julia Robinson, her companion almost throughout the 1827–40 period.

Mary Shelley reported of herself that "during this period I was apt to be tousy-mousy over women" (12 October 1835). Unquestionably, she established deep and enduring friendships not only with the Robinsons but with other women as well. This was not a new pattern, but one continued from her early attachments, first to Isabel Baxter Booth, then to Maria Gisborne, and then to Jane Williams. In addition to these closer ties, Mary Shelley became the friend of a number of other women, including two of the most prominent literary and social figures of the day: Caroline Norton and Lady Sydney Morgan. Mary Shelley's letters to Caroline Norton have not been located, but Norton's letters supply considerable information about their friendship. They show that Mary Shelley stood by Caroline Norton during the period when the latter was socially ostracized because of her husband's divorce suit against her; that Norton assisted in obtaining funds for the widowed Mary Jane Godwin; that Mary Shelley was Norton's confidante about her children, her unhappy marriage, and her efforts, finally successful, to change the child-custody laws in England to obtain more justice for mothers (see [26 January 1837]). Mary Shelley's friendship with Lady Morgan seems not to have been so intimate, but it endured until Mary Shelley's death, and the letters indicate that Mary Shelley had become a welcome member of Lady Morgan's circle.

One of the most extraordinary women Mary Shelley met during these years was the Scottish-born Frances Wright, who dedicated most of her life to the cause of political and social justice in America. In August 1827 Frances Wright, an ardent disciple of Mary Wollstonecraft and William Godwin, sent Mary Shelley a letter introducing herself and her cause. Mary Shelley responded that she was honored to be addressed "on the score of my relations" and that "the memory of my Mother has always been the pride & delight of my life; & the admiration of others for her, has been the cause of most of the happiness ⟨of my life⟩ I have enjoyed" (12 September 1827). Frances Wright wanted not only to meet the daughter of Wollstonecraft and Godwin but also to persuade Mary Shelley to accompany her on her return to Nashoba, her experimental plantation in America. Though Mary Shelley declined, Wright was sufficiently attracted to her after their initial meeting in the fall of 1827 to form a friendship. Through Frances Wright, Mary Shelley was eventually introduced to a circle of French society that included General Lafayette, Mérimée, Stendhal, and the Garnett family.

These letters further disclose that Frances Wright also introduced Mary Shelley to her own dear friend Frances Trollope, who did accompany Frances Wright to America. Frances Wright's letters written after their departure from England send love from herself and Frances Trollope to Mary Shelley. Their acquaintance, however brief, leads one to speculate that the reason there was no contact between Mary Shelley and Frances Trollope when the two lived in Harrow in 1833 and had sons attending Harrow may have been Trollope's bitter attack on Frances Wright in *The Domestic Manners of the Americans*, which was published in 1832, shortly after her return to England after four disastrous years in America.

Mary Shelley invested a great deal of her emotional life in her friendships with women. She valued them in themselves and because she was basically unwilling or unprepared for anyone to take Shelley's place in her life (though she was on a few occasions after Shelley's death attracted to another man). This may be one of the reasons that she was not interested in men who pursued her but rather was drawn to men who did not reciprocate her feelings. Thus, after her return to England, she was courted by John Howard Payne, whose suit she rejected, but was interested in Washington Irving, who lived mostly on the Continent and only occasionally visited England during these years. In the period 1827–40, three men, for a variety of reasons, fit into this pattern of ensured singleness. She firmly rejected Trelawny, who romantically commented that his and Mary Shelley's fates might still be intertwined. His suggestion and her response became a topic of repartee in their letters (see 14 June 1831). More serious was her relationship with Prosper Mérimée, whom she met in Paris in the summer of 1828. Only one of her letters to him has been located, but that one seems to return to him his written marriage proposal. In her letters to friends, she alluded to this talented author and his interest in her. But most of the information about their interaction is contained in Mérimée's letters written to Mary Shelley in 1828–29, first published in 1977 (Bennett and Little, "Seven Letters from Mérimée to Mary Shelley"). The letters reveal that they shared confidences about their personal lives as well as their careers and that they fully expected to see each other within months of their initial meeting, either through another visit to Paris by Mary Shelley or one to London by Mérimée. The more pressing Mérimée's letters, however, the more distant was Mary Shelley. He was gratified by her willingness to assist his career by reviewing his latest work in the *Westminster Review*, but he complained of her melancholy, of her failure to write often enough, of rumors that she had married Trelawny, of her insistence that they keep their correspondence secret. Mérimée, ever consolable, soon turned his attentions elsewhere, and there seems to be nothing in the letters or her journal to suggest a sense of loss on her part.

Far different, it has been conjectured, were her feelings for Major Aubrey Beauclerk, brother of her beloved friend Georgiana Beauclerk Paul (see 16 January 1833). On the basis of evidence in her Journal, it has been argued that Mary Shelley was in love with him from the early 1830s until the early 1840s. The letters make no explicit reference to her feelings about Beauclerk, though it is possible to attribute some of the melancholy she experienced in the mid-1830s to her disappointment at Beauclerk's marriage in February 1834 to Ida Goring, daughter of Sir Charles Foster Goring.

Given his social status, one might well have expected him to marry, as he did, within the moneyed and titled class. Beauclerk's first wife died in 1838. In December 1841 he married Rosa Robinson, who was probably introduced to the Beauclerks by Mary Shelley. Claire Clairmont described Rosa Robinson as having been selected by Beauclerk because he needed a wife young and energetic enough to take care of the four young children born of his first marriage. The full story of Mary Shelley and Beauclerk is yet to be told. On the face of it, however, it appears that one of his attractions to her may have been the unlikelihood of a fulfilled relationship.

In addition to those already mentioned, Mary Shelley's "unknown paths" brought her into the circles of many other prominent literary, political, and social figures of the day. Her friendship with Thomas Moore grew as she assisted him with his editions of Byron's life and works. She became acquainted with Bulwer, Disraeli, Samuel Rogers, and Abraham Hayward, around whom so much of literary London revolved. Letters of this period are written, or refer, to a vast number of those with whom she was acquainted who had achieved distinction in their own right, such as Speaker of the House Sir Charles Manners-Sutton; the geologist Roderick Impey Murchison; the authors Maria and Geraldine Jewsbury and John Bowring; the artist Richard Rothwell; the publisher John Murray. She was also well-received by those who claimed family distinction, such as the Beauclerks and the Pauls.

While the letters introduce new friends and activities, they also chronicle the lives of her earlier circle. References to Shelley and Byron are a leit-motif. Of Godwin, we learn that his habits of writing and reading went uninterrupted, his last published book appearing in 1834, two years before his death at the age of eighty. His old age brought him not only financial assurance in the form of a government post but new attention, as members of the emerging Victorian literary world, including Bulwer and Disraeli, came to pay him homage. During these years Claire Clairmont became confirmed in the governess career she would pursue for many long, unhappy years. She traveled where employment necessitated—Russia, Austria, Italy, with the occasional visit to England. She and Mary Shelley maintained their contact, and though Mary Shelley wrote of her "we were never friends" ([14 May 1836]), she respected, pitied, and when she could, aided her. Thomas Love Peacock, well established at India House, fulfilled his role as executor of Shelley's will and was thereby one of the people Mary Shelley most relied on in financial matters. We hear more of Peacock towards the close of this era through Mary Shelley's correspondence with Peacock's eldest daughter, Mary Ellen, whom Mary Shelley seemed especially to like. There is a renewal of correspondence with Maria Gisborne, ending only with her death in 1836, which provides some of the frankest and most detailed reports of Mary Shelley's personal and professional life. Another continuing friendship begun in Italy was with Margaret Mason, who was closer to Claire Clairmont but also highly regarded by Mary Shelley. Prior to her death in 1835, both of Mason's daughters had married. Claire Clairmont and Mary Shelley maintained ties to the daughters, and Mary Shelley's letters of the 1840s describe her visit to them in Italy, their lives, and their circumstances.

The letters also supply a good deal of information about Leigh Hunt and his family: his continued financial tribulations; Marianne Hunt's alcoholism; the family's frequent change of residence because of their shortage of funds; the early adult life of some of the Hunts' children, including Thornton Hunt's career and his marriage to Katherine Gliddon and Mary Hunt's marriage to John Gliddon. Moreover, the letters refer to Hunt's literary projects, a number of which were quite successful during this period, particularly his highly lauded play *A Legend of Florence*, presented at Covent Garden in February 1840. If their friendship had drifted apart somewhat over the years, they were reunited when Mary Shelley called on him for advice about her Shelley editions, and he generously responded. In the same spirit, she offered to assist him in revising *A Legend of Florence* when the management of Covent Garden requested changes in his script.

Of all of her friendships within the Shelley circle, the one that altered most dramatically during the 1827–1840 period was that with Trelawny. In 1828, elated over Trelawny's return to England from Greece, Mary Shelley referred to him as "dear dear darling once again to find the true good one" ([5 June 1828]). After a brief stay in England, Trelawny went to Italy, where he remained for a few years and wrote *Adventures of a Younger Son*. He then returned briefly to England before departing for America, where he traveled for several years. His activities in these years included making arrangements for others to take care of his daughters. He also developed any number of attachments to women, including Caroline Norton and Fanny Kemble; in 1838 he formed a liaison with Augusta Goring, a friend of Mary Shelley's, and married her in 1840, after her divorce (see [?19 March 1838]). On 20 July 1839, Mary Shelley ironically wrote of him: "We are good friends & never see each other."

A number of events led to the break in their friendship, which appears to have been more the result of Trelawny's wishes than hers. Though he claimed that he disapproved of her because she had become conservative and wasted her time in the company of such friends as the Robinsons, the crux of his argument with her seems to stem from her refusal to assist him in writing a biography of Shelley (see April 1[829]). From this point, his letters to her, and to Claire Clairmont about her, take on a new tone of critical sharpness. This, however, did not prevent him from asking her to assume the responsibility of arranging for the publication of his *Adventures of a Younger Son*, negotiating the contract, and seeing it through press while he remained in Italy. Her letters to him, and on his behalf, show that she expended a great deal of time and energy in attempting to fulfill this voluntary obligation to Trelawny's best advantage. Instead of closing the gap that had begun to separate the friends, however, Mary Shelley's involvement in the *Adventures* added to it. Trelawny complained that she had not obtained enough money for him for the book; that she was overfastidious in her judgment that parts of the book would be unacceptable to publisher and public (though he acceded when Horace Smith gave the same opinion); that she did not title the book as he had wished. In 1835, when the publishers took advantage of a verbal rather than a written agreement and reneged on their promise to give Trelawny one hundred pounds if another edition were published, he found new cause to complain, suggesting that the error on her part was the result of indifference. He responded to the first-edition deletions in *Queen Mab* by returning his copy of the book to Moxon with a rude note (see 11 February [1839]). In his revised edition of *Records of Shelley, Byron, and the Author* (1878), he entirely forgot the "dear Mary" to whom he had so often pledged his love and friendship and instead vilified her.

If this break in friendship seems out of proportion to the events that precipitated it, her continued friendship with Jane Williams Hogg seems even more paradoxical. Mary Shelley had not only to overcome her acute anguish and disappointment when she discovered her friend's disloyalty, she had also to adjust to the fact that Jane Williams united herself to Thomas Jefferson Hogg, with whom, after their initial intimacy of 1814–15, Mary Shelley did not get along with very well. Despite this, the somewhat shadowed friendship between the two women endured. There are fewer letters and references to Jane Williams Hogg, but consistent with those in their early widowed years, they are always to "dearest Jane" in loving and sympathetic terms. The letters of this era tell of friendship injured and reestablished; the Hoggs' relationship; the two daughters born to the Hoggs; the growth to young adulthood of Edward and Dina Williams; Mary Shelley's attempts to help Hogg publish a novel (4 November 1830) or find a job ([?18 January–2 April 1836]); Hogg's assistance to Mary Shelley in matters of law. Moreover, they show that Jane Williams Hogg and Mary Shelley continued to come to each other's aid in times of distress. For example, Mary Shelley wrote of her severe illness in 1835: "I can never forget nor cease to be grateful to Jane, for her excessive kindness to me when I needed it most, confined as I was to my sopha, unable to move" ([?12 June–July 1835]). But that she never forgot Jane Williams Hogg's disloyalty is underscored by her ironic response of 11 February [1839] to Hogg's criticism of her omission of the dedication to *Queen Mab*: "I thank you for your kindly expressed insinuations. I began to be fed on poison at Kentish Town—it almost killed me at first—now I am used to it."

After the poison of Kentish Town, Mary Shelley was never again emotionally dependent on either a person or a memory. Released, however unwillingly, from the past, she shaped her personal life and her career on a new plane of self-reliance. The letters of 1827–40 record that portion of Mary Shelley's adult life from just after her thirtieth birthday until just before her forty-third. During this period she established new friendships, through which she entered the circles of some of the most prominent cultural and political figures of early Victorian society. At the same time, increased literary productivity extended her contacts within the literary and publishing world. The 453 letters in this volume, 225 of them previously unpublished, provide details about a segment of her life that has been more hypothesized about than documented. As varied in subject matter as her earlier letters and equally frank in tone, they considerably add to, amplify, and correct past depictions of Mary Shelley. In this setting, she emerges, despite her self-doubts, as a woman of determination and accomplishment rather than as the chronically mournful widow presented in biographies. Indeed, her achievements are all the more notable in the context of a society far from hospitable to a female, "treading in unknown paths" on her own.

Editorial Notes

MARY SHELLEY'S known extant letters date from October 1814, two months after her seventeenth birthday, through September 1850, one month after her fifty-third birthday and five months before her death, on 1 February 1851. The earliest collection of her letters is *Shelley Memorials* (1859); the most complete collection is *MWS Letters* (1944), edited by Frederick L. Jones, which numbers 705 letters. Many of these letters, however, are brief summaries, simple citations of dates and recipients, or material taken from imperfect copies. A major difficulty—then and now—was locating the letters, which are widely scattered throughout the world. To find them, I wrote hundreds of letters of inquiry to libraries, collectors, dealers, and colleagues in Africa, Australia, Europe, New Zealand, and North America. I also placed advertisements in journals and newspapers and searched through old auction records and dealers' catalogues. This process yielded more than thirteen hundred letters, several hundred of which were previously published. The total is an approximation because new letters keep turning up. (Even as this volume was going to press, a previously unpublished letter was located.)

The Carl H. Pforzheimer Library, the Bodleian Library, The Huntington Library, Lord Abinger, John Murray, the British Library, and Professor Jean de Palacio hold the largest collections of Mary Shelley's letters; the rest are in the hands of diverse collectors and libraries. Since Jones's pioneer work, much of the correspondence that he had to take from copies has been made accessible, including the 118 letters formerly owned by Sir John Shelley-Rolls, now at the Bodleian Library. And most important, significant collections of previously unpublished letters have been made available for this edition, including the letters of Lord Abinger, John Murray, and The Carl H. Pforzheimer Library. In the interest of presenting the letters as faithfully as possible, I have newly transcribed almost all of the unpublished and previously published letters from manuscript (exceptions are noted).

Mary Shelley's letters are consistent primarily in their inconsistency. Spelling and punctuation are irregular and variable; dates are often omitted, partial, or incorrect. Errors in words, phrases, and sentences are largely uncorrected. The variety of subject matter, together with the irregularities of writing style, creates an impression of haste, unselfconsciousness, and spontaneity, which reveals as much about the author as the words themselves. Rather than follow the tradition of past editors who silently corrected these irregularities, with some minor exceptions explained herein, I have reproduced the letters as Mary Shelley wrote them, adding bracketed material for clarification when the original might cause unnecessary distraction.

The letters are arranged in chronological order; letters to the same person on the same day are distinguished by letters after the date. Almost all letters in this edition are from manuscript, indicated by MS. in the textual notes. If, however, a letter is from a copy, it is taken from the earliest copy or printed form of the letter. If a later publication of a printed text is substantially superior, it is cited along with the first publication.

Following is a description of editorial principles, including minor exceptions to the original manuscript:

1. The name of the addressee is given at top left. The names of addressees identified but not given appear in square brackets: [   ]. A name in square brackets that is preceded by a question mark indicates editorial conjecture. Unidentified addressees are represented by square brackets containing only a question mark: [?   ].

2. In previously unpublished letters an asterisk precedes the addressee's name. Partially published letters that omit a significant portion of the original manuscript are treated as unpublished; however, they are cited.

3. The place of writing is given at top right, although Mary Shelley sometimes gave this information at the close of letters. If a letter was written from several places, the first and last place are given at top right (the latter appears in the body of the letter as well). Place of writing is supplied in square brackets when no place is given in the manuscript. A place in brackets preceded by a question mark indicates editorial conjecture.

4. The date of writing also is given at top right, although Mary Shelley sometimes dated letters at their close. Dates in square brackets are taken from postmarks, context, or information other than the original manuscript. Questionable dates are explained in footnotes. Conjectural dates are bracketed and preceded by a question mark. Letters written over a number of days are placed under their earliest date, but the last possible date of writing is also cited. Letters that I have been unable to date I place at their earliest possible date, the conjectural date (or dates) preceded by a question mark and in brackets. Editorial references to dates give the day, the month, and then the year.

5. The complimentary close is separated from the letter except when followed by additional text or when so informal as to be considered part of the text.

6. Postscripts appear in Mary Shelley's letters on envelopes, address sheets, and in margins; and at times they are cross-written (see below). In this edition, all postscripts follow the signature. Postscripts written any-

where except after the letter are preceded by an editorial note (in square brackets) indicating their place in the manuscript.

7. As much as possible of the following information appears after each letter (superior letters, such as in M^{rs} and 30th, are regularized):
   a. Address of recipient
   b. Postmarks
   c. Endorsement
   d. Indication that the letter is unpublished or a citation to previous publication. Letters published in *MWS Letters* and elsewhere are cited to Jones's edition. Otherwise, earliest publication is cited.
   e. Source of text. Letters from original manuscripts are indicated by MS. preceding name of present holder.
   f. Translator, if other than editor.

8. Footnotes are numbered for each letter.

9. I have made countless corrections of previously published letters; however, only corrections of particular significance are called to the reader's attention.

10. Although Mary Shelley's irregularities have been retained, *sic* has been avoided. Easily understood irregularities, such as a word or even a name spelled differently in the same letter or the substitution of *you* for *your*, are left as given, unless context requires clarification. Questionable spellings caused by uncrossed *t*'s, undotted *i*'s, and partial letters have been silently corrected. Words that might cause the reader difficulty are followed by a square bracket containing the intended word in italics, and when necessary, omitted letters of words have been inserted in the text in curly brackets: { }. Where omission of entire words proves distracting, a curly bracket has been inserted. Occasionally, based on context, I venture an editorial conjecture within those brackets.

The following is a list of Mary Shelley's common mispellings: aboutt, abroard, ach, agreably, adjustment, ammeliorated, appartments, arrisen, asortment, assylum, atatch, atmospher, bankrupcy, befal, carrige, cathederal, centinels, chamberi, comming, concious, consolotary, contemtible, corteous, cotons, craked, credibilty, crost, dayly, dicision, delettanti, demonination, descicion, desart, develope, devision, dipt, disagreable, disipated, dispair, dissappoint, docter, embarassing, enclined, evedently, exageration, exersize, exhiliarating, exiliarating, exitement, hacnied, headach, herse, hypoccrisy, immagination, immagine, impassable, improvisaing, independant, indicision, indure, insuferably, intirely, invelloped, irrisistibly, jiwellers, labratory, lodgeings, Medames, medecines, meer, negociations, occurences, orriginal, parr, patrole, peice, phisical, precipieces, prest, privarications, publickly, quarelled, reatreat, reccommended, releive, sciszars, scolars, seige, seing, seperated, shiped, sincerly, skrewing, somthing, staid, stile, stopt, synonimous, synomimies, takeing, teusday, threatning, toothach, tost, untill, upolsterer, verry, violance, walzing, witnissed.

11. Abbreviations remain, followed, when necessary, by the complete word italicized in brackets. For example, w^d is not spelled out, but *T—y* [*Trelawny*] is. Abbreviated names are followed by the full name italicized in brackets only the first time they are used in a letter unless context requires additional clarification. *S.* for Shelley and *LB* or *Lord B* for Byron appear frequently and are spelled out only if confusion might arise in a particular context.

12. False starts or obvious slips have been silently omitted. Deleted words that have significance are enclosed in angled brackets: ⟨ ⟩. A variety of means, including ultraviolet and infrared light, have been used to rescue these words. Even partial readings of such passages are given, in the hope that future readers may be able to fill in or correct material.

13. Words missing due to holes, torn seals, or deterioration of the man-uscript are treated as follows: If enough of a partial word remains to suggest the full word, the remainder is supplied in square brackets. Wholly con-jectural words are given in square brackets, italicized and followed by a question mark. Uncertain readings are given in square brackets, italicized and preceded by a question mark. Missing words that offer no sound basis for conjecture are represented by empty square brackets. Words torn from manuscripts that can be read on fragments adhering to the seals, unless they are of particular significance, have been silently inserted.

14. Mary Shelley's punctuation conforms to no system. She generally uses a dash instead of a period or comma (though at times she uses a dash in addition to other punctuation), and she usually omits end punctuation. A double space has been left after an apparent sentence ending without punctuation that is followed by a sentence beginning with a capital letter. Unpunctuated sentences run on unless clarity requires emendation, in which case punctuation will be supplied in curly brackets. Paragraphing has been added to avoid unclear, run-on postscripts. The length of dashes has been standardized.

15. Like many of her contemporaries, Mary Shelley was inconsistent in her use of capitalization. These inconsistencies have been retained.

16. Words or phrases written between lines, unless unusual in content or placement, have been silently inserted into the line. An asterisk is sub-stituted for Mary Shelley's footnote indication *x* when confusion may arise.

17. Portions of letters that contain cross-writing—that is, horizontal writing crossed by vertical writing, giving a gridlike effect—are preceded by the indication [*cross-written*].

18. Superior letters (such as in M^{rs} and 30th) are retained, but the dash or dot below is omitted: & and &c are also retained.

19. Not represented are underscorings in addresses, dates, and signatures or punctuation following addresses and dates.

20. Letters in French and Italian are followed by translations. Errors or variants in Mary Shelley's French and Italian are not corrected. Foreign words and phrases are translated in footnotes unless they are cognates or are clear by their context.

21. Persons included in the list entitled "Biographical Names" in *Webster's Seventh New Collegiate Dictionary* are not identified unless context requires additional information.

The first two volumes of this edition contain indexes of proper names. A complete index will be given in volume three. Volume three will also contain letters located too late for inclusion in their appropriate chronological order and a list of letters unlocated but noted from auction records and other sources.

EDITORIAL SYMBOLS

[?]	Unidentified addressee
[London]	Non-given but certain addressee, place, date
[?London]	Editorial conjecture of addressee, place, date
[ ]	Word torn from text or otherwise obliterated
mo[on]	Editorial conjecture of word torn from text or otherwise obliterated
[*moon?*]	Uncertain editorial conjecture of word torn from text or otherwise obliterated
[*?moon*]	Uncertain reading
[*P. 1, top*]	Editorial information
M^{rs} G [*Godwin*]	Abbreviated name supplied
and [*an*]	Clarification of word
{ }	Word or letter omitted
{moon}	Editorial conjecture of omitted word or letter
⟨ ⟩	Deletion restored

Abbreviations

Abinger MSS.	The manuscripts and letters of William Godwin, Mary Wollstonecraft Shelley, Percy Bysshe Shelley, and others in the possession of Lord Abinger (many of which are now on deposit at the Bodleian Library).
Altick, *The Cowden Clarkes*	Richard D. Altick. *The Cowden Clarkes*. London: Oxford University Press, 1948.
Alumni Cantabrigienses	*Alumni Cantabrigienses*. Edited by John Venn and J. A. Venn. 10 vols. Cambridge: At the University Press, 1922–47.
Alumni Oxonienses	*Alumni Oxonienses*. Edited by Joseph Foster. 4 vols. Oxford: Parker & Co., 1888–91.
Angeli, *Shelley and His Friends in Italy*	Helen Rossetti Angeli. *Shelley and His Friends in Italy*. London: Methuen & Co., 1911.
Annual Register	*The Annual Register, or a View of the History, Politics, and Literature*. London: Baldwin, Cradock, and Joy [various dates].
Beavan, *James and Horace Smith*	Arthur H. Beavan. *James and Horace Smith*. London: Hurst and Blackett, 1899.
Beddoes, *Letters*	*The Letters of Thomas Lovell Beddoes*. Edited by Edmund Gosse. London: Elkin Mathew & John Lane, 1894.
Bennett and Little, "Seven Letters from Mérimée to Mary Shelley"	Betty T. Bennett and William T. Little. "Seven Letters from Prosper Mérimée to Mary Shelley." *Comparative Literature* 31 (Spring 1979): 134–53.
Blunden, *"Examiner" Examined*	Edmund Blunden. *Leigh Hunt's "Examiner" Examined*. London: Cobden-Sanderson, 1928.
Blunden, *Leigh Hunt*	Edmund Blunden. *Leigh Hunt, A Biography*. London: Cobden-Sanderson, 1930.
Boyle's Court Guide	*Boyle's Fashionable Court and Country Guide*. London: Eliza Boyle & Son. Published under various titles throughout the nineteenth century and continued into the twentieth century.
Brewer, *The Holograph Letters*	*My Leigh Hunt Library, the Holograph Letters*. Edited by Luther A. Brewer. Iowa City: University of Iowa Press, 1938.
Brown, *Godwin*	Ford K. Brown. *The Life of William Godwin*. London: J. M. Dent & Sons, 1926.
Brown, *Letters*	*The Letters of Charles Armitage Brown*. Edited by Jack Stillinger. Cambridge, Mass.: Harvard University Press, 1966.

Burke's Landed Gentry	John Burke *et al.*, eds. *Genealogical and Heraldic History of the Landed Gentry.* London [various dates].
Burke's Peerage	John Burke *et al.*, eds. *Genealogical and Heraldic History of the Peerage, Baronetage and Knightage.* London [various dates].
Byron, *Correspondence*	*Lord Byron's Correspondence.* Edited by John Murray. 2 vols. London: John Murray, 1922.
Byron, *Letters and Journals* (Marchand)	*Byron's Letters and Journals.* Edited by Leslie A. Marchand. 12 vols. Cambridge, Mass.: The Belknap Press of Harvard University Press, 1973–82.
Byron, *Letters and Journals* (Moore)	*The Letters and Journals of Lord Byron: with Notices of His Life.* Edited by Thomas Moore. 2 vols. London: John Murray, 1830.
Byron, *Poetry*	*The Works of Lord Byron: Poetry.* Edited by Ernest Hartley Coleridge. 7 vols. London: John Murray, 1898–1903.
Byron, *Works*	*The Works of Lord Byron: Letters and Journals.* Edited by Rowland E. Prothero. 6 vols. London: John Murray, 1898–1901.
Cameron, *The Golden Years*	Kenneth Neill Cameron. *Shelley: The Golden Years.* Cambridge, Mass.: Harvard University Press, 1974.
Cameron, *The Young Shelley*	Kenneth Neill Cameron. *The Young Shelley: Genesis of a Radical.* New York: Macmillan Co., 1950.
CC Journals	*The Journals of Claire Clairmont, 1814–1827.* Edited by Marion Kingston Stocking with the assistance of David Mackenzie Stocking. Cambridge, Mass.: Harvard University Press, 1968.
Charnwood, *Call Back Yesterday*	Dorothea Charnwood. *Call Back Yesterday.* London: Eyre and Spottiswoode, 1937.
Clarke, *Recollections of Writers*	Charles Cowden Clarke and Mary Cowden Clarke. *Recollections of Writers.* London: Low, 1878.
Cline, *Pisan Circle*	C. L. Cline. *Byron, Shelley and their Pisan Circle.* London: John Murray, 1952.
DNB	Edgar Williams and Helen M. Palmer, eds. *The Compact Edition of the Dictionary of National Biography.* 2 vols. Oxford: Oxford University Press, 1975.
Donner, *The Browning Box*	H. W. Donner, ed. *The Browning Box; or, The Life and Works of Thomas Lovell Beddoes.* London: Oxford University Press, 1935.
Dowden, *Shelley*	Edward Dowden. *The Life of Percy Bysshe Shelley.* 2 vols. London: Kegan Paul, Trench & Co., 1886.
Dunbar, *PBS Bibliography*	Clement Dunbar. *A Bibliography of Shelley Studies: 1823–1950.* New York: Garland, 1976.
Ebers, *The King's Theatre*	John Ebers. *Seven Years of the King's Theatre.* London: William Harrison Ainsworth, 1828.

Fenner, *Leigh Hunt and Opera Criticism*

Theodore Fenner. *Leigh Hunt and Opera Criticism: The "Examiner" Years, 1808–1821.* Lawrence: University Press of Kansas, 1972.

Galignani, *Poetical Works of Coleridge, Shelley, and Keats*

The Poetical Works of Coleridge, Shelley, and Keats. Edited by Cyrus Redding. Paris: A. and W. Galignani, 1829.

Garnett Letters

Cecilia Payne-Gaposchkin, ed. *The Garnett Letters.* Privately printed, 1979.

Genest, *English Stage*

John Genest, ed. *Some Account of the English Stage from the Restoration in 1660 to 1830.* 10 vols. Bath, 1832.

Gisborne, *Journals and Letters*

Maria Gisborne & Edward E. Williams, Shelley's Friends, Their Journals and Letters. Edited by Frederick L. Jones. Norman: University of Oklahoma Press, 1951.

Godwin, Journal

Manuscript journal of William Godwin, 1788–1836 (Abinger MSS.).

Grylls, *Clairmont*

R. Glynn Grylls. *Claire Clairmont: Mother of Byron's Allegra.* London: John Murray, 1939.

Grylls, *Mary Shelley*

R. Glynn Grylls. *Mary Shelley: A Biography.* London: Oxford University Press, 1938.

Haydon, *Diary*

The Diary of Benjamin Robert Haydon. Edited by Willard Bissell Pope. 5 vols. Cambridge, Mass.: Harvard University Press, 1960–63.

Hogg, *Shelley*

Thomas Jefferson Hogg. *The Life of Percy Bysshe Shelley.* In *The Life of Percy Bysshe Shelley . . .,* edited by Humbert Wolfe. 2 vols. London: J. M. Dent & Sons, 1933.

Hunt, *Autobiography*

The Autobiography of Leigh Hunt. Edited by Roger Ingpen. 2 vols. New York: E. P. Dutton & Co., 1903.

Hunt, *Correspondence*

The Correspondence of Leigh Hunt. Edited by Thornton Hunt. 2 vols. London: Smith, Elder and Co., 1862.

Hunt, *Lord Byron and Some of His Contemporaries*

Leigh Hunt. *Lord Byron and Some of His Contemporaries.* London: Henry Colburn, 1828.

Ingpen, *Shelley in England*

Roger, Ingpen. *Shelley in England: New Facts and Letters from the Shelley-Whitton Papers.* 2 vols. London: Kegan Paul, Trench, Trubner & Co., 1917.

Irving, *Journals and Notebooks*

Washington Irving. *Journals and Notebooks.* Edited by Henry A. Pochmann. Vol. I, *1803–1806,* edited by Nathalia Wright (Madison: University of Wisconsin Press, 1969–70); vol. II, *1807–1822,* edited by Lillian Schlissel and Walter A. Reichart (Boston: Twayne Publishers, 1981); vol. III, *1819–1827,* edited by Walter A. Reichart (Madison: University of Wisconsin Press, 1969–70).

Johnstone's Guide

Johnstone's *London Commercial Guide,* August 1817.

Jones, "New Letters"

Frederick L. Jones, ed., "Mary Shelley to Maria Gisborne:

New Letters, 1818–1822." *Studies in Philology* 52 (January 1955): 39–74.

Lamb, *Letters* (Lucas)   *The Letters of Charles Lamb to Which Are Added Those of His Sister Mary Lamb*. Edited by E. V. Lucas. 3 vols. London: J. M. Dent & Sons, 1935.

Lamb, *Letters* (Marrs)   *The Letters of Charles and Mary Anne Lamb*. Edited by Edwin W. Marrs, Jr. 3 vols. to date. Ithaca: Cornell University Press, 1975–.

Locke, *Godwin*   Don Locke. *A Fantasy of Reason: The Life and Thought of William Godwin*. London: Routledge & Kegan Paul, 1980.

Lovell, *Medwin*   Ernest J. Lovell, Jr. *Captain Medwin: Friend of Byron and Shelley*. Austin: University of Texas Press, 1962.

Lucas, *Charles Lamb*   E. V. Lucas. *The Life of Charles Lamb*. London: Methuen & Co., 1905.

Lyles, *MWS Bibliography*   W. H. Lyles. *Mary Shelley: An Annotated Bibliography*. New York: Garland, 1975.

McAleer, *The Sensitive Plant*   Edward C. McAleer. *The Sensitive Plant: A Life of Lady Mount Cashell*. Chapel Hill: University of North Carolina Press, 1958.

Marchand, *Byron*   Leslie A. Marchand. *Byron: A Biography*. 3 vols. New York: Alfred A. Knopf, 1957.

Marshall, *Mary Shelley*   Mrs. Julian [Florence A.] Marshall. *The Life and Letters of Mary Wollstonecraft Shelley*. 2 vols. London: Richard Bentley & Son, 1889.

Marshall, *The Liberal*   William H. Marshall. *Byron, Shelley, Hunt and the Liberal*. Philadelphia: University of Pennsylvania Press, 1960.

Medwin, *Conversations*   *Medwin's Conversations of Lord Byron*. Edited by Ernest J. Lovell, Jr. Princeton: Princeton University Press, 1966.

Medwin, *Shelley*   Thomas Medwin. *The Life of Percy Bysshe Shelley*. Edited by H. Buxton Forman. London: Oxford University Press, 1913.

Merriam, *Moxon*   Harold G. Merriam. *Edward Moxon: Publisher of Poets*. New York: Columbia University Press, 1939.

Moore, *Accounts Rendered*   Doris Langley Moore. *Lord Byron: Accounts Rendered*. London: John Murray, 1974.

Moore, *Journal*   *The Journal of Thomas Moore*. Edited by Wilfred S. Dowden. 6 vols. Newark: University of Delaware Press, forthcoming.

Moore, *The Late Lord Byron*   Doris Langley Moore. *The Late Lord Byron*. New York: Harper & Row, 1961.

Moore, *Letters*   *The Letters of Thomas Moore*. Edited by Wilfred S. Dowden. 2 vols. Oxford: Clarendon Press, 1964.

Moore, *Memoirs*   Thomas Moore. *Memoirs, Journal and Correspondence*. Edited by Lord John Russell. 8 vols. Boston: Little, Brown and Co., 1853.

MWS, *Collected Tales*	Mary Wollstonecraft Shelley. *Collected Tales and Stories*. Edited by Charles E. Robinson. Baltimore: Johns Hopkins University Press, 1976.
MWS, *Falkner*	Mary Wollstonecraft Shelley. *Falkner: A Novel*. 3 vols. London: Saunders and Otley, 1837.
MWS, *Frankenstein*	Mary Wollstonecraft Shelley. *Frankenstein; or, The Modern Prometheus*. 3 vols. London: Lackington, Hughes, Harding, Mayor, & Jones, 1818.
MWS Journal	Manuscript journal of Mary Shelley (Abinger MSS.).
MWS *Journal*	*Mary Shelley's Journal*. Edited by Frederick L. Jones. Norman: University of Oklahoma Press, 1947.
MWS, *The Last Man*	Mary Wollstonecraft Shelley. *The Last Man*. 3 vols. London: Henry Colburn, 1826.
MWS Letters	*The Letters of Mary W. Shelley*. Edited by Frederick L. Jones. 2 vols. Norman: University of Oklahoma Press, 1944.
MWS, *Lives* (1835–37)	Mary Wollstonecraft Shelley (with others). *Lives of the most Eminent Literary and Scientific Men of Italy, Spain, and Portugal*. The Cabinet of Biography, edited by the Rev. Dionysius Lardner, vols. 86–88. London: Longman, Orme, Brown, Green, & Longman; and John Taylor, 1835–37.
MWS, *Lives* (1838–39)	Mary Wollstonecraft Shelley. *Lives of the most Eminent Literary and Scientific Men of France*. The Cabinet of Biography, edited by the Rev. Dionysius Lardner, vols. 102 and 103. London: Longman, Orme, Brown, Green, & Longman; and John Taylor, 1838–39.
MWS, *Lodore*	Mary Wollstonecraft Shelley. *Lodore*. 3 vols. London: Richard Bentley, 1835.
MWS, *Matilda*	Mary Wollstonecraft Shelley. *Mathilda*. Edited by Elizabeth Nitchie. Chapel Hill: University of North Carolina Press, 1959.
MWS, *Midas*	Mary Wollstonecraft Shelley. *Midas*. In *Proserpine & Midas. Two Unpublished Mythological Dramas by Mary Shelley*, edited by A[ndré] [Henri] Koszul. London: Humphrey Milford, 1922.
MWS, *Perkin Warbeck*	Mary Wollstonecraft Shelley. *The Fortunes of Perkin Warbeck, A Romance*. 3 vols. London: Henry Colburn and Richard Bentley, 1830.
MWS, *Proserpine*	Mary Wollstonecraft Shelley. *Proserpine, a Mythological Drama in Two Acts*. In *The Winter's Wreath*. London: G. and W. B. Whittaker, 1832 [1831].
MWS, *Rambles in Germany and Italy*	Mary Wollstonecraft Shelley. *Rambles in Germany and Italy, in 1840, 1842, and 1843*. 2 vols. London: Edward Moxon, 1844.
MWS, *Six Weeks' Tour*	Mary Wollstonecraft Shelley with Percy Bysshe Shelley. *History of a Six Weeks' Tour through a Part of France, Switz-*

| | erland, Germany, and Holland: with Letters Descriptive of a Sail round the Lake of Geneva, and of the Glaciers of Chamouni. London: T. Hookham, Jun. and C. and J. Ollier, 1817. |

MWS, *Valperga* — Mary Wollstonecraft Shelley. *Valperga: or, the Life and Adventures of Castruccio, Prince of Lucca*. 3 vols. London: G. and W. B. Whittaker, 1823.

New Grove Dictionary of Music and Musicians — Stanley Sadie, ed. *The New Grove Dictionary of Music and Musicians*. 20 vols. London: Macmillan, 1980.

Nicoll, *English Drama* — Allardyce Nicoll. *A History of English Drama, 1660–1900*. Vol. IV, *Early Nineteenth Century Drama, 1800–1850*. London: Cambridge University Press, 1960.

Nitchie, *Mary Shelley* — Elizabeth Nitchie. *Mary Shelley*. New Brunswick: Rutgers University Press, 1953.

Norman, *After Shelley* — *After Shelley: The Letters of Thomas Jefferson Hogg to Jane Williams*. Edited by Sylva Norman. London: Oxford University Press, 1934.

Norman, *Flight of the Skylark* — Sylva Norman. *Flight of the Skylark: The Development of Shelley's Reputation*. London: Max Reinhardt, 1954.

Origo, *The Last Attachment* — Iris Origo. *The Last Attachment*. London: Jonathan Cape & John Murray, 1949.

Overmyer, *America's First Hamlet* — Grace Overmyer. *America's First Hamlet*. New York: New York University Press, 1957.

Owen, *Threading My Way* — Robert Dale Owen. *Threading My Way: An Autobiography*. 1874. Reprint. New York: Augustus M. Kelley, 1967.

Palacio, *Mary Shelley* — Jean de Palacio. *Mary Shelley dans son oeuvre: Contributions aux études shelleyennes*. Paris: Editions Klincksieck, 1969.

Paul, *Godwin* — C. Kegan Paul. *William Godwin: His Friends and Contemporaries*. 2 vols. London: Henry S. King & Co., 1876.

Payne, Letterbook — Manuscript letterbooks of John Howard Payne. Columbia University Library [various dates].

PBS Letters — *The Letters of Percy Bysshe Shelley*. Edited by Frederick L. Jones. 2 vols. Oxford: Oxford University Press, 1964.

Peacock, *Memoirs* — "Memoirs of Percy Bysshe Shelley." In *The Works of Thomas Love Peacock*, vol. VIII, edited by H. F. B. Brett-Smith and C. E. Jones (Halliford Edition). London: Constable & Co., 1934.

Peacock, *Works* — *The Works of Thomas Love Peacock*. Edited by H. F. B. Brett-Smith and C. E. Jones. (Halliford Edition). 10 vols. London: Constable & Co., 1924–34.

Perkins, *Mrs. Norton* — Jane Gray Perkins. *The Life of the Honourable Mrs. Norton*. New York: Henry Holt & Co., 1909.

Perkins and Wolfson, *Frances Wright* — A. J. G. Perkins and Theresa Wolfson. *Frances Wright: Free Inquirer*. New York and London: Harper & Brothers, 1939.

Redding, *Fifty Years' Recollections*	Cyrus Redding. *Fifty Years' Recollections: Literary and Personal.* 3 vols. London: Charles J. Skeet, 1858.
Reiman, *The Romantics Reviewed*	Donald H. Reiman, ed. *The Romantics Reviewed: Contemporary Reviews of British Romantic Writers.* 9 vols. New York: Garland, 1972.
Rennie, *Traits of Character*	Eliza Rennie. *Traits of Character; Being Twenty-Five Years' Literary and Personal Recollections By A Contemporary.* 2 vols. London: Hurst and Blackett, 1860.
Robinson, *Diary*	*Diary, Reminiscenses, and Correspondence of Henry Crabb Robinson.* Edited by Thomas Sadler. 3 vols. London: Macmillan, 1869.
Robinson, *On Books*	Henry Crabb Robinson. *On Books and Their Writers.* Edited by Edith J. Morley. 3 vols. London: J. M. Dent & Sons, 1938.
The Romance	*The Romance of Mary W. Shelley, John Howard Payne and Washington Irving.* With remarks by F. B. Sanborn. Boston: Boston Bibliophile Society, 1907.
St. Clair, *Trelawny*	William St. Clair. *Trelawny: The Incurable Romancer.* London: John Murray, 1977.
S&M	*Shelley and Mary.* 4 vols. London: privately printed, 1882.
SC	Kenneth Neill Cameron and Donald H. Reiman, eds. *Shelley and his Circle, 1773–1822.* 6 vols. Cambridge, Mass.: Harvard University Press, 1961–73.
Scott, *Hogg*	Winifred Scott. *Jefferson Hogg: Shelley's Biographer.* London: Jonathan Cape, 1951.
Scott, *New Shelley Letters*	*New Shelley Letters.* Edited by W. S. Scott. New Haven: Yale University Press, 1949.
Shelley, *Complete Works*	*The Complete Works of Percy Bysshe Shelley.* Edited by Roger Ingpen and Walter E. Peck (Julian Edition). 10 vols. London and New York: E. Benn, 1926–30.
Shelley, *Essays, Letters*	*Essays, Letters from Abroad, Translations and Fragments by Percy Bysshe Shelley.* Edited by Mary W. Shelley. 2 vols. London: Edward Moxon, 1840 [1839].
Shelley Memorials	*Shelley Memorials: From Authentic Sources. Edited by Lady Shelley. To Which is Added An Essay on Christianity, By Percy Bysshe Shelley: Now First Printed.* Edited by Lady [Jane] Shelley. London: Smith, Elder and Co., 1859.
Shelley, *Poetical Works* (1839)	*The Poetical Works of Percy Bysshe Shelley.* Edited by Mary W. Shelley. 4 vols. London: Edward Moxon, 1839.
Shelley, *Poetical Works* (Forman)	*The Poetical Works of Percy Bysshe Shelley.* Edited by Harry Buxton Forman. 4 vols. London: Reeves & Turner, 1876–77.
Shelley, *Poetical Works* (OSA)	*The Complete Poetical Works of Percy Bysshe Shelley.* Edited by Thomas Hutchinson. Oxford: Oxford University Press, 1960.

Shelley, *Poetry and Prose*   *Shelley's Poetry and Prose.* Edited by Donald H. Reiman and Sharon B. Powers. New York: Norton & Co., 1977.

Shelley, *Posthumous Poems*   *Posthumous Poems of Percy Bysshe Shelley.* Edited by Mary W. Shelley. London: John and Henry L. Hunt, 1824.

Shelley's Prose Works   *The Prose Works of Percy Bysshe Shelley.* Edited by Harry Buxton Forman. 4 vols. London: Reeves & Turner, 1880.

Smiles, *John Murray*   Samuel Smiles. *A Publisher and His Friends: Memoir and Correspondence of the Late John Murray.* 2 vols. London: John Murray, 1891.

Smith, *A Sentimental Library*   Harry B. Smith. *A Sentimental Library.* Privately printed, 1914.

Steffan, *Byron's Don Juan*   Truman Guy Steffan. *Byron's Don Juan.* 2d ed. 4 vols. Austin: University of Texas Press, 1971.

Tatchell, *Leigh Hunt*   Molly Tatchell. *Leigh Hunt and His Family in Hammersmith.* London: Hammersmith Local History Group, 1969.

Taylor, *Early Collected Editions*   Charles H. Taylor, Jr. *The Early Collected Editions of Shelley's Poems.* New Haven: Yale University Press, 1958.

Trelawny, *Adventures*   Edward John Trelawny. *Adventures of a Younger Son.* Edited by William St. Clair. London: Oxford University Press, 1974.

Trelawny, *Letters*   *Letters of Edward John Trelawny.* Edited by H. Buxton Forman. London: Oxford University Press, 1910.

Trelawny, *Recollections*   *Trelawny's Recollections of the Last Days of Shelley and Byron.* With an Introduction by Edward Dowden. London: Humphrey Milford, 1931.

Trelawny, *Records*   Edward John Trelawny. *Records of Shelley, Byron, and the Author.* 2 vols. London: Basil Montagu Pickering, 1878.

Van Doren, *Peacock*   Carl Van Doren. *The Life of Thomas Love Peacock.* London: J. M. Dent & Sons, 1911.

Walling, *Mary Shelley*   William A. Walling. *Mary Shelley.* New York: Twayne Publishers, 1972.

Wardle, *Hazlitt*   Ralph M. Wardle. *Hazlitt.* Lincoln: University of Nebraska Press, 1971.

Wheatley, *London*   Henry B. Wheatley. *London Past and Present: Its History, Associations, and Traditions.* 3 vols. London and New York: John Murray and Scribner & Welford, 1891.

White, *Shelley*   Newman Ivey White. *Shelley.* 2 vols. London: Secker & Warburg, 1947.

White, *Unextinguished Hearth*   Newman Ivey White. *The Unextinguished Hearth: Shelley and His Contemporary Critics.* Durham: Duke University Press, 1938.

Williams, *Journals and Letters*   *Maria Gisborne & Edward E. Williams, Shelley's Friends, Their Journals and Letters.* Edited by Frederick L. Jones. Norman: University of Oklahoma Press, 1951.

Wise, *Shelley Library*   Thomas James Wise. *A Shelley Library: A Catalogue of Printed Books, Manuscripts and Autograph Letters by Percy Bysshe Shelley, Harriet Shelley and Mary Wollstonecraft Shelley*. London: privately printed, 1924.

Wollstonecraft, *A Short Residence*   Mary Wollstonecraft. *Letters Written during a Short Residence in Sweden, Norway, and Denmark*. London: Joseph Johnson, 1796.

Wollstonecraft, *Posthumous Works*   Mary Wollstonecraft. *The Posthumous Works of the Author of a Vindication of the Rights of Woman*. Edited by William Godwin. 4 vols. London: Joseph Johnson, 1798.

List of Letters

The Letters of
Mary Wollstonecraft
Shelley

To WILLIAM WHITTON   Sompting—2 September 1827

Sir

I am very sorry to be obliged to annoy you by another letter—but having
been obliged to yield my lodgings to some other persons I must send you
my new address—I remove to Arundel tomorrow—and my direction will
be at Mrs Cooper's Tarrant St. Arundel.[1]—This unexpected circumstance
will render any delay of my allowance doubly distressing to me. Meanwhile
permit me to apologize for the trouble I occasion you—Percy is perfectly
well, & if there be any good school in Arundel he will go to it.—

I am Y^s Obediently,
MaryW. Shelley

ADDRESS: To be forwarded / William Whitton Esq / 3 Kings Road / Bedford Row / London.
POSTMARKS: (1) Shoreham / Penny Post; (2) A / 3 SE 3 / 1827. ENDORSED: 2nd Sept 1827 /
Mrs Shelley. PUBLISHED: Jones, #286. TEXT: MS., Bodleian Library (MS., Shelley, Adds.,
c. 6, ff. 47–48).

1. Mary Shelley, Isabel Douglas, and their party were forced to move by the people they
were lodging with because "they are grasping people, & will gain by these latter about four
times as much as they do by us" (see vol. 1, 26 August [1827], for further details).

To WILLIAM WHITTON   Arundel—7th September 1827

Sir

I have received and must thank you for the cheque for £62—10—I should
not have troubled you, but that it was necessary I should inform you of my
address. When I return to town I will communicate my arrival to you.

I am, Sir
Your Ob^t Servant
MaryW. Shelley

ADDRESS: W. Whitton Esq / Stone Wall / Tonbridge. POSTMARKS: (1) Arundel / 0620; (2) F /
8 SE 8 / 1827. ENDORSED: 7th Septr 1827 / Mrs Shelley. PUBLISHED: Jones, #287. TEXT:
MS., Bodleian Library (MS., Shelley, Adds., c. 6, ff. 49–50).

*To JANE WILLIAMS HOGG   Mrs Cooper's—Tarrant St. Arundel 7.
September [1827]

Dearest—I send you the £10[1] as you asked, the moment it has been in my
possession—What I should have done without it God knows! Of course I

had ten thousand times rather have had it from your tiny store, than from one of the fellows—but am vexed to have inconvenienced you—however here it is—pray write to tell me that you receive it safely—

Tell me also that you are recovered[2]—these continual attacks on your delicate constitution are frightful—the irksomeness of ill health alone is a precipizio—and pain is a woeful thing in all its branches—as our friend says "I can bear any thing but pain"—I have quite an invalid to nurse in poor darling Isabel—she suffers much—if she had remained at Highgate, I cannot think she would have been alive now—since even the peace she enjoys here, hardly benefits her—The symptoms of asthma are so confirmed & acute that I would give the world that she could see & consult some good physician—she herself prophecies that death must ensue from the overpowering pain she at times feels—I do not fear this—asthma is a long lived disease, & besides the light of air of France, which I trust she will breathe this winter, will I hope ammeliorate the disease itself.

We have divine harvest weather—living in a town, we have lost some of our perfectly rural delights—but they are compensated to us by the beauty of the scenery of Arundel—The park is all that is lovely—& the beech woods—the streams & woodland glades, are sources of never ending pleasure—poor Isabel can hardly enjoy these—walking hurts her if she do more than stroll at the slowest pace—As yet we have not seen the Castle[3]—as the Duke is here & it is only shewn in his absence; but it is picture{s}que & crowns with romantic beauty the wooded hills.

I write in haste to save the post—How are your darlings? with the S's [Shorediches] while at Ham{p}stead? is not that expression of evil import to your sister[4]—is Hamstead to imbibe les restes of the fertilizing stream that keeps his purse not quite dry?—How is Mamina?[5]—Remember me to her— & kiss noble Med & pretty Dina for me—No letter from Trelawny! I shall write to him now that I have money

Adieu Brightest Beauty—God bless & preserve thy loveliness

Your

MS.

They gave the note at the bank thus divided—the cui bono[6] I understand non

---

ADDRESS: Mrs Jefferson Hogg / 8 Mrs Wilson / Maida Place / Paddington—London. POST-MARKS: (1) ARUNDEL / 0620; (2) F / 8 SE 8 / 1827; (3) 10. F.NOON. 10 / SP. 8 / 1827. UNPUBLISHED. TEXT: MS., Abinger MSS., Bodleian Library.

1. Repayment of the loan Mary Shelley had urgently required in order to move to Arundel (see vol. 1, 26 August [1827]).

2. Jane Hogg's illness was a result of pregnancy (see vol. 1, 28 July 1827, n. 2).

3. Arundel Castle, a historic seat of the dukes of Norfolk. The incumbent then was Bernard Edward, twelfth duke of Norfolk (1765–1842) (Burke's Peerage).

4. Sarah Shorediche, identified in volume I as a friend of Jane Williams Hogg, was in fact her sister. The evidence for this is provided by Claire Clairmont's letter to Jane Hogg of February 1830, in which she discusses the discomfort caused Jane Hogg by her sister (Abinger MSS., Bodleian Library. See also Lovell, Medwin, p. 225, n. 53; and vol. 1, 19–20 February

[1823], 15 August 1827 to Jane Williams Hogg, and 22 August 1827 to Jane Williams Hogg).
The Shorediches were in dire financial straits.

    5. Jane Williams Hogg's mother, Mary Cleveland (first name identified in Edmund Blunden, "The Family of Edward Williams," *Keats-Shelley Memorial Bulletin* 4 [1952]: 49).

    6. "For whose good." Notes were often cut in half and sent separately to prevent pilfering from the mails.

To John Howard Payne   Arundel. 9. September [1827]

What will you say, dear Friend, that I take you at your word, and give you another commission? Did I not believe that you would forgive me readily—& indeed not be angry at all, I should not have the courage to ask as it is I am more than half ashamed. The matter is simply this—I understand that the Countess Guiccioli has sent me some papers[1] thro' the principal servant of Mr Lambton[2]—which I have never received, & I want to write about them, but do not know where—Would you permit your Mercury to call at Mr Lambton's 6 Cleveland Row, St. James and to ask whether that gentleman is in town, & where he is—send immediately as he may any or every day return to the Continent—but let your person simply ask the above questions, & on no account mention my name—I have a very particular reason for this—it would annoy me greatly, if my name were mentioned.—

    A thousand apologies are due to you—I have not time for one—only this—come & receive them here—come to the sweet woods of Arundel and come and see her who is always

Yours truly & obliged
MS.

ADDRESS: J. Howard Payne Esq / 29 Arundel St. / Strand—London. POSTMARKS: (1) ARUNDEL / 0620; (2) F / [1]o SE 10 / 1827; 3 [   ] / SE 10 / 1827. PUBLISHED: Jones, #288.
TEXT: MS., Huntington Library (HM 6828).

    1. Material for Thomas Moore's biography of Byron (see vol. I, 3 July 1827, 20 August 1827; Moore, *Letters,* II, 576). From 17 August through 29 October 1827, Moore received at least seven packets containing memorabilia from Mary Shelley and/or Teresa Guiccioli. Moore acknowledges Mary Shelley's further assistance in 1828 in obtaining material from John Bowring and Teresa Guiccioli (see Moore, *Letters,* II, 603–4, 606, 612. See also 2 April [1828] to [John Bowring]; 1 May 1828; and 11 June [1828]).

    2. Perhaps Hedworth Lambton, Esq., 36 Part St., Grosvenor Square (*Boyle's Court Guide*).

To Frances Wright[1]   Arundel. 12 Sepr 1827

    You confer on me a very high honor by forgetting for a moment your high & noble views to interest y^r self in me; and in addressing me rather on the score of my relations, than myself you touch the right chord to win my ⟨affection⟩ attention, & excite my interest. The memory of my Mother has been always been the pride & delight of my life; & the admiration of others for her, has been the cause of most of the happiness ⟨of my life⟩ I have enjoyed. Her greatness of soul & my father high talents have perpetually reminded me that I ought to degenerate as little as I could from those from whom I derived my being. For several years with Mr Shelley I was blessed with the companionship of one, who fostered this ambition & inspired that of being worthy of him. He who was single among men for Philanthrophy—devoted generosity—talent & goodness.—yet you must not fancy that I am what I wish I were, and my chief merit must always be derived, first from the glory these wonderful beings have shed [?*around*] me, & then for the enthusiasm I have for excellence & the ardent admiration I feel for those who sacrifice themselves for the public good.

If you feel curiosity concerning me—how much more in the refined sense of the word, must I not feel for y^r self . . a woman, young rich & independant. quits the civilization of England for a life of hardship in the forests of America that by so doing she may contribute to the happiness of her species— Her health fails in the attempt, yet scarcely restored to that, she is eager to return again to the scene of her labours, & again to spend the flower of her life in arduous struggles & beneficent, self sacrificing devotion to others. Such a tale cannot fail to inspire the deepest interest & the most ardent admiration. You do honour to our species & what perhaps is dearer to me, to the feminine part of it.—and that thought, while it makes me doubly interested in you, makes me tremble for you—women are so per{pet}ually the victims of their generosity—& their purer, & more sensitive feelings render them so much less than men capable of battling the selfishness, hardness & ingratitude w^h is so often the return made, for the noblest efforts to benefit others.—But you seem satisfied with y^r success, so I hope the ill-fortune w^h too usually frustrates our best views, will spare to harm the family of love, w^h you represent to have assembled at Nashoba.

My absence from London prevented me probably from seeing Mr Owen.[2] it has also hindered me from receiving y^r printed papers. I have therefore only y^r letter to guide me to a knowledge of y^r settlement. Is it all you wish? Do you find the motives you mention sufficient to tame that strange human nature, w^h is perpetually the source of wonder to me? It takes a simpler form probably in a forest abode—yet can enthusiasm for public good rein in passion motive benevolence, & unite families? ⟨Nashoba⟩ it were a divine sight to behold the reality of such a picture.—

Yet do not be angry with me that I am so much of a woman, that I am far more interested in you than in (except as it is yours) your settlement. Do not excite my interest to disappoint it—Why cannot you come to England? I am near the coast—& if you crossed to Brighton, I c^d see you—At least I pray you write again—write about y^{r}self—tell me whether happiness & content repay y^r exertions. I have found that the first of these blessings can only be found in the exercise of the affections—Yet I have not found mine there—for where moral evil does not interfere—dreadful Death has come to deprive me of all I enjoyed. My life has been not like yours publicly active, but it has been one of tempestuous suffering.—now in a quiet seclusion with my boy & with the companionship of a beloved friend I repose for a few months—& such has been the uncertainty of my fate, that these seem a mighty good torn from cruel destiny & I live in perpetual fear that I shall not be permitted to enjoy it even so long.—

I fully trust that I shall hear from you again[3]—Do not, public [?spirited] as you are, turn from me, because private interests too much opress me. At least tho' mine be a narrow circle, yet I am willing at all times to sacrifice my being to it, & derive my only pleasure from contributing to the happiness & welfare of others. My sympathy is yours—let me also claim some from you that thus we may establish between us the name of friend.

With the most lively admiration I am yours

Mary Shelley

P.S.   I must not forget to say, that I only received y[r] letter today.—I answer it on the instant.

PUBLISHED: *Garnett Letters*, pp. 97–99. TEXT: Copy of MS. by Julia Garnett, on deposit at Houghton Library by heirs of Cecilia Payne-Gaposchkin.

1. Frances Wright Darusmont (1795–1852), philanthropist, author, and social reformer, was born in Scotland but was raised in England after the death of her parents in 1798. In 1818, accompanied by her younger sister Camilla (?1797–1831), she traveled to the United States, where she began her lifelong association with reform movements in America. In 1824 she and her sister established the Nashoba settlement in Tennessee, a community in which slaves could earn funds through their labors to buy their own liberty. Although Nashoba failed, Frances Wright continued to involve herself in other means of social and political reform. In 1831 she married Phiquepal Darusmont (1797–1855), a French educational theorist, from whom she was divorced in 1850 (for a full biography see Perkins and Wolfson, *Frances Wright*). In the summer of 1827 she had returned to Europe to recover from a serious illness and to enlist new members for the Nashoba colony. These facts and others pertaining to her antislavery position Frances Wright had written to Mary Shelley in her letter of 22 August 1827 from Paris (see *S&M*, IV, 1092–95).

2. Frances Wright's letter of 22 August had been hand-delivered by Robert Dale Owen (1801–77), eventually a U.S. politician and social reformer, who was the eldest son of Scottish socialist reformer Robert Owen (1771–1858). In 1826 the younger Owen had gone to New Harmony, the experimental socialist village founded by his father in Indiana. When New Harmony ceased to be a community in 1827, Owen returned to Europe with Frances Wright, whom he had met in 1826, with the plan of returning with her and others to Nashoba (see Owen, *Threading My Way*, pp. 227, 298, 302–3). The elder Owen was a supporter of Godwin's ideals and had introduced his son to Godwin in 1826 (Owen, *Threading My Way*, p. 207). It was probably Robert Dale Owen, who praised Mary Shelley in *Threading My Way* (pp. 321–24), who suggested that Frances Wright contact Mary Shelley (Perkins and Wolfson, *Frances Wright*, p. 176).

3. On 15 September 1827, Frances Wright wrote an enthusiastic response in which she set out her schedule. It would include a visit to England around 28 September, at which time she promised to meet Mary Shelley (*Garnett Letters*, pp. 99–100; *S&M*, IV, 1096–98).

Our fates seem going on pretty equally in the crab-style, my prettiest little Girl—Since I last wrote, Isabel has been very very ill—& one day especially, endured such intense pain, accompanied by fever, that I became alarmed— she is now, I trust, convalescent—but so weak & cut up, that she requires perpetual care—surely if she had remained at Highgate, she would have died. I cannot guess at what her complaint is—but it is some real disease, of which this last is a severe attack—kept off long by quiet and care—& these two will I hope soon restore her—Our lodgings here are uncomfortable enough—& the trouble I had to prevent thunder-sound, when the dropping of a pin was agony to my poor <u>patient</u> patient was infinite—there are seven children in the house! another coming next month!—Fortunately the day before her attack I had arranged Percy as day boarder at the only decent school here, where they have no day scholars.

The weather is favourable to my invalid—& infinitely pleasant—very fine, the English call it, though my Italian prejudice will hardly permit me to call a libeccio[1] agreable—yet it is—in spite of prejudice. Our beech woods are becoming yellow, and the Autumnal tints are decorating the woodland scenery of this lovely spot—I cannot prefer autumn to the genial birth of life & beauty in spring—yet as a Menlancholy [*Melancholy*] tale as Niobe,[2] or a martyred saint, can be sublimely beautiful & interesting, so is the sear Autumn. The country is filling with people but there are no sportsmen here—for the Duke[3] preserves the game carefully—it is killed by the keeper & sent to Lord Scarey—so we have seen no short coated-Joe Manton[4] bearing divinities, from whom to obtain thro' love, what we excessively <u>wish</u> for, yet cannot get for money—pheasants & partridges.

And what are you doing, my poor darling? How are your babes? Have you moved?—how do you pass your time?—<u>al solito</u>?[5]—Now there are no courts, does the duteous Jeff. plod to temple[6] each day—and back again to his fairy-girl at five?—have you no news for me?—I have written to Trelawny & to Tom[7]—how I wish I could learn anything of the former, for I get more & more anxious about him—I hear absolutely from no one—save poor dear Papa—The Hunts never write—We do not know yet when to expect Doddy. I hope Isabel will be a little in good looks for the Sposo[8]— she is pale & ill now & after all I am afraid that she wi[ll] hardly recover, till some first rate Medical person discover her ill—there is one somewhere—but what I cannot ⟨guess⟩ divine.—

You may guess how my time is taken up—I steal an hour for writing[9] in the morning, & another for a walk at night—in truth I began to suffer in health also, but am better now—The day & night of her extreme illness shook me a good deal—poor child how very much she suffered—in her head principally—is it not strange—passing strange, Janey sweet, that when her agony almost forced screams—and her chest & head were both suffering the excess of anguish—my hand on either soothed her immediately—what would Tom say to this?—I do not believe in Magnetism[10] beyond this power, which we have exercised too often & in too flagrant cases, not to force us to ⟨believe⟩ credit it—and I think that such as it is, the power ought to be known—for no fancy gave quiet to Isabel in the midst of agony—it was a real alleviation that she felt.

I wish very much to hear how you are now, you & your darlings. Take care of yourself   God bless you   Ever Yours

MS.

ADDRESS: Mrs Jefferson Hogg / 8 Mrs Wilson / Maida Place—Paddington / London. POST-MARKS: (1) ARUNDEL /0620; (2) 10. F.NOON. 10 / SP. 18 / 1827; (3) F / 18 SE 18 / 1827. UNPUBLISHED. TEXT: MS., Abinger MSS., Bodleian Library.

1. "Southwest wind."

2. After Niobe's excessive pride in her children provoked Apollo and Artemis to kill them, she was transformed by Zeus into stone, forever remembering her sorrow. The sculpture of Niobe and her children, at the Uffizi Gallery, Florence, was one of Shelley's favorite works of art (*PBS Letters,* #560).

3. See 7 September [1827] to Jane Williams Hogg, n. 3.

4. Joseph Manton (?1766–1835; *DNB*), celebrated London gunsmith.

5. "As usual."

6. A reference to Hogg's law career (see vol. I, 30 August [1824], n. 2).

7. Thomas Medwin.

8. "Husband." Volume I of this edition revealed that Mary Diana "Doddy" Dods, illegitimate daughter of George Douglas, fifteenth earl of Morton, had published under the pseudonym David Lyndsay and that her life and that of Isabel Robinson Douglas were closely connected (see vol. I, 30 October [1826] to Alaric A. Watts, 28 July 1827, and ff.). Subsequent research, which will be detailed in this volume, gives evidence of an extraordinary arrangement between these two women. The "sposo" whom Isabel Robinson Douglas awaited was in fact Doddy. That is, Mary Diana Dods, who was masculine in appearance and who earlier had written under a male name, now took on a male guise, changed her name to Walter Sholto Douglas (the name Sholto Douglas is found in a number of Scottish families, including that of Dods's father), and proceeded to live in Europe as the purported husband of Isabel Robinson. A 13 November 1827 description of Mr. Douglas as "a little deformed but clever" (MS., Harriet Garnett to Julia Pertz, Garnett letters, Houghton Library) may be compared with Rennie's description of Mary Diana Dods as someone who was extremely intelligent and whose "figure was short and, instead of being in proportion, was entirely out of all proportion" (*Traits of Character,* I, 207).

The decision to play this role may well have been reflected in Mary Shelley's comment to Jane Hogg: "I am glad for pretty Isabel's sake that D. [*Doddy*] now seriously thinks of les culottes" (see vol. I, 28 August 1827). While the motivations for this charade are not fully known, one reason may have been to give legitimacy to Isabel Robinson Douglas's apparently illegitimate infant daughter. There is only an oblique mention of this child in Mary Shelley's letters. On 26 August 1827, in writing of her own and Isabel Douglas's distress at their sudden eviction from their Sompting lodgings, she complains: "In consequence we must go tomorrow to look for lodgings, & remove without milk—can any thing be so orribile, scelerato [*horrible, villainous*] & all that?" Confirmation of the existence of an infant who would have needed milk is provided by an entry in the *DNB* and the General Register's Office. The former indicates that Henry Drummond Wolff (1830–1908) married Adeline Douglas, the daughter of Walter Sholto Douglas. In 1909 she was awarded a civil list pension of £100. The latter records that Adeline Drummond Wolff died in the second quarter of 1916, at the age of 89. This would place her birth sometime between July 1826 and June 1827. (I am indebted to Emily W. Sunstein for the General Register information.)

The legitimacy given to the daughter was shared by the mother as well: she and her "husband" were accepted in a number of social circles in France. And the *DNB* reports that in 1840 the Rev. William Falconer (1801–85) married Isabella, widow of W. S. Douglas, and that she died at St. Alessi, Italy, in 1869. When Mary Diana Dods, alias Walter Sholto Douglas, died is still unknown. Her sister, Georgiana Dods Carter, who accompanied the Douglases to Paris, remained there and died in August 1842 (Préfecture du Département de la Seine, Acte de Décès, Paris). Whether Dods also remained and died in Paris is difficult to ascertain because many French records were destroyed in World War II. The only person in the extant records who might be Dods is listed as a male with the family name Douglas, born in Scotland, unmarried, who died on 13 August 1845 and who had lived in the same arrondissement as Georgiana Dods Carter.

On 26 September 1827 Mary Shelley wrote in her Journal: "how utterly have I shaken off the dead calm of my life—interesting myself deeply for one whose destiny is so strange." Mary Shelley's letters make it quite clear that she was an active participant in her friends' complex scheme and served to chart partially the course of their lives.

9. Her novel *Perkin Warbeck* (see vol. I, [?11 January 1827], n. 1). On 26 September 1827, obviously in response to a request, Godwin sent her an account of the children of Edward IV for the novel (*S&M*, IV, 1106c–d).

10. Franz Anton Mesmer (1734–1815), Austrian mystic and physician, based on his belief in the healing and magnetic power in his own hands, developed a treatment that he named "animal magnetism" but that came to be called mesmerism. This forerunner of modern hypnosis was extremely popular for a while, although medical authorities labeled Mesmer a charlatan. Thomas Medwin introduced mesmerism to the Shelley circle at Pisa in 1820. First he, and then Jane Williams and Mary Shelley, mesmerized Shelley in order to alleviate his physical suffering from what Medwin believed to be nephritis (Medwin, *Shelley,* pp. 269–70).

*To Jane Williams Hogg   Arundel.   23. September [1827]

I am glad to hear that the sweet Loveliness is nichèe,[1] albeit in a narrow nest—but you can make a paradise of a garret, and therefore I expect to find a perfect Eden at your cottage—the fairy has a wand, with which she performs miracles:—with what admiration have I not regarded its wonders— sometimes trying to imitate—& though I was so far behind my original that she must have smiled at my attempts—yet common mortals could trace her influence even in their dim reflection of her perfection.—

D. [*Doddy*] is come & sends ten thousand kind & admiring messages to you—Mrs Carter is at Little Hampton four miles off—They are all in the greatest anxiety to get away—but alas! for your reading, that they ought to go while they have quattrini,[2]—they are forced to substitute, when they have that necessary machine for locomotion. They are moving heaven & earth to get it, & by the first week in October I think will be on the wing. D. as usual, is the most delaying. Isabel—who is better at the bare idea— & Mrs Carter, are burning with eagerness. They will proceed to Paris, & then pause & reflect. Nothing can be better than the arrangements[3] here. Our friend is absolutely fascinating. Mary Hunt is quite delighted—& Percy entertains great respect & great wish to please his new friend. All this is good. I all [*am*] still very anxious concerning Isabel's health—but physicians at Paris are good & she can consult them.—

What a ridiculous person Finch is—he is a great antipathy of mine.—I have not heard from the Hunt's D tells me that it is probable that Swinburne is dead,[4] as the house was shut up—but would they do that on such an occasion?—you may remember such was not the case at Holly Terrace.—for myself, I have in my own mind, bid adieu to the coterie you mention. I love the Gliddons for their extreme goodness—but cannot continue the up hill visiting up the hill, always seeking—never sought—no—no—in all praticareing[5] with one's kind there must be some shew of equality—& no longer for the sake of the past, can I fight so hard to link it with the present.—I have been a good, yielding, obedient, much enduring young person—but I am now ahime![6] thirty—I mean to assume dignity on the occasion—to stay home & let the world come to me—I will not go to the world. What is worth any trouble, except one look of love & true sympathy? which in spite of my being thirty, I would travel an hundred miles to seek—do not make [   ] saucy remarks on this—I was not thinking of the wro[   ] side of Bond St[7]–but of friendship love—for tho the other be [?désirer]—yet that must come, I cannot go for it—unless it were it to seek that sweet Conjunction, whom I die to see again. I hope the incongruity & folly of all this will please you but for woman's sake, being a woman—let not the sight of such trash draw Jeff's mouth into a sarcastic smile—

Adieu, beauty of the World—You at least are now safe from tempests—take care of yourself let me know how your children are and keep up your strength & courage—God bless the Fairy Girl!

ADDRESS: Mrs Jefferson Hogg / 22 Devonshire Place / Edgware Road / London. POSTMARKS: (1) ARUNDEL / 0620; (2) [10] F.NOON. 10 / SP. 24 / 1827; (3) F / 24 SE 24 / 1827. UNPUBLISHED. TEXT: MS., Abinger MSS., Bodleian Library.

1. "Settled."

2. "Money."

3. The "arrangements" and the following reference to "our friend" strongly indicate that by the time she arrived at Arundel, Doddy had assumed the role of Walter Sholto Douglas.

4. Swinburne Hunt had died on 22 September 1827.

5. "To converse, to keep company with."

6. "Alas!"

7. Bond Street was regarded as representative of fashionable habits (Henry B. Wheatley, *London Past and Present,* 3 vols. [London: John Murray, 1891], I, 218–21).

*To John Howard Payne   Arundel—23 September. [1827]

Your little note, my dear friend, is a melancholy & a painful one—you do not complain but I see all is not well with you—how hard this is! You who are so good & kind—I trust however that you are not ill[1]—with health one can struggle with much—I am afraid you work too hard & try yourself too much—let me hear that you are better, and I shall be delighted—Surely I need not make professions to you—I believe that you know me, & know that a spirit of politeness merely, would not make me write what I do not feel—and if I did not feel deep regard for you—I could not even ask you to do me services. Do not reproach me therefore for my apologies, they do not arise from any doubt concerning you—as if I felt that I could not apply to you—but kindnesses make a lively impression on me, I feel grateful, & you would not I am sure, deny me the pleasure of expressing my feelings.—

To shew you that I believe that you like to serve me, I am about to send you another commission. My friends here mean in a few days to cross the channel—they will go by Brighton & Dieppe & want a passport[2]—could you, if I sent up their names, procure it?—by so doing you would oblige me greatly. I have heard that they wont give passports in London except to the persons themselves—& that in procuring them at the Port from which they sail, it is necessary to pay—what in this case is the expence,— & will one passport, & consequently one expence, serve various members of a party travelling together?—if you could answer these questions by return of post, you would be of great service to me.

The rain is drear—Arundel is still beautiful, yet I repine at the loss of my adored summer. Adieu my dear Payne—Would I could force heaven to cause all your projects to succeed

Yours ever most truly.
MShelley

Arundel does not contain a Court Guide[3]—so will you look in one & send me Sir William Knighton's[4] address in town when you next write

ADDRESS: J. Howard Payne Esq / 29 Arundel St. / Strand / London. POSTMARKS: (1) ARUNDEL / 0620; (2) F / 24 SE 24 / 1827. UNPUBLISHED. TEXT: MS., Brown University Library.

1. Payne had been seriously ill in the spring (Mary Jane Godwin to Payne, 17 March 182[7], MS., Houghton Library; Overmyer, *America's First Hamlet*, p. 268).

2. Obtaining passports through John Howard Payne rather than in person protected the "Douglases" from discovery (see 25 September [1827] to John Howard Payne, 1 October [1827], and 13 October [1827] to John Howard Payne).

3. *Boyle's Court Guide.*

4. Perhaps Isabel Douglas's poor health was the reason that Mary Shelley wanted to consult this prominent physician, whom she knew through the Hunts (see vol. I, 10 October [1824], n. 7).

*TO ALARIC A. WATTS   Arundel.   25 September [1827]

My Dear Sir

I am sorry that delays of all kinds have prevented any writing of mine from appearing in your Souvenir.[1] I wish the "Lover's Leap"[2] would have been inserted, for it is a most beautiful story, & not known in English. Some time ago you asked me for two little mythological dramas of mine[3]— Do you still wish for them?   as if they suited you, they are at your service.   I have besides two or three short poems which you might have for your present volume if they pleased you.

I forward with this note a packet from Mrs Douglas. This Lady has transmitted to me your print of the Spanish story from Stothard,[4] asking me to write for it—I fear I should now be too late—if you desire it I will write a slight sketch for it, & send it to you in the course of the week.

Permit me to thank you for the elegant Volume you have sent me—I anticipate with great pleasure the Souvenir of the present year which you speak of surpassing those which have already appeared

I am, my Dear Sir,

Your Ob^t Servant

MaryShelley

UNPUBLISHED. TEXT: MS., Allison-Shelley Collection, The University Libraries, The Pennsylvania State University.

1. Watts noted in the introduction of the *Literary Souvenir* for 1827 that among items reaching him too late for that issue were those by David Lyndsay and the authors of *Frankenstein* and "A Traveller's Tale." Both "A Traveller's Tale" and "Lover's Leap," referred to in this letter, were the works of the Scottish author Leitch Ritchie (1800–1865). Perhaps Ritchie's work was introduced to Mary Shelley by his compatriot Mary Diana Dods. I have found no other reference to a connection between Mary Shelley and Ritchie, though Godwin knew him.

2. Published in *Friendship's Offering, 1830,* edited by Ritchie.

3. Mary Shelley had offered *Proserpine* and *Midas* in 1826 (see vol. I, 30 October [1826], to Alaric A. Watts, 9 May [1824], n. 1).

4. Thomas Stothard (1755–1834; *DNB*), painter and book illustrator.

To JOHN HOWARD PAYNE ⟨Arundel⟩ Brighton—25 September [1827]

My dear Payne

You will be surprised to hear that I make one of the party in question—My friends remain at Dieppe a month before they proceed to Paris, and they have persuaded me to pass that month with them—Say nothing of all this to my people[1]—& if they tell you any thing let it pass current—

Our party consists—of Mrs Shelley & child—which fair person I need not describe to you & whose signature will accompany this letter but lest you should beleive that so divine a being could not be personated[2] by another I subjoin two other signatures for your choice Mrs Douglas is short, i.e. an atom shorter than I—dark, pretty with large dark eyes & hair curled in the neck—Mr Douglas is my height—slim—dark with curly black hair[3]—the passport must be drawn out for M^r & Mrs Sholto Douglas—Mrs Carter & her two children—boys one ten the other nine—Mrs Percy Shelley and boy[4]—

We go early next week—Monday if possible from Brighton—to Dieppe—if there is any trouble about the passport let me know directly as in that case we will procure it here—send it to me to Arundel where we shall be till the day of our departure perhaps you had better send it pr [by] coach—the Royal Sussex sets off at half past eight on Monday Wednesday & Friday from the Silver Cross Charing Cross—it ought to come to us on Friday—Other Arundel {coaches} (Little Hampton or Bognor, passing thro' Arundel) go from other places I doubt not daily—Our address is at Mrs Cooper's Tarrant St. Arundel—Send me a letter the evening before by post to say I must expect it—but if the letter passport enclosed w^d only be charged double—or even treble send it by post.—

We shall meet again in November—& I shall be delighted to think that I can bestow a little pleasure where so much is so due—You are the most disenterested of persons the rarest & best praise—

Ever Yours
Mary Shelley

Isabel Douglas.—Sholto Douglas.[5]
I return to [Arund]el tonight

ADDRESS: J. Howard Payne Esq /29 Arundel St. London / Strand. POSTMARKS: (1) BRIGHTON / SE 25 / 1827 / 55; (2) A / 26 SE 26 / [182]7. PUBLISHED: Jones, #289. TEXT: MS., Historical Society of Pennsylvania.

1. Godwin's letter of 9 October 1827 mentions that Mary Shelley had written to him on 1 October (letter unlocated) "announcing a trip to the Continent, without the least hint when you should return" (see Marshall, *Mary Shelley,* II, 182–83). He explains that these plans have induced him to give her the details of his straitened circumstances and his unsuccessful attempts to borrow money.

2. The group planned to travel with one passport (see 23 September [1827] to John Howard Payne), but Payne obtained separate passports (see 13 October [1827] to John Howard Payne). Perhaps through his theater connections, Payne got two or more people to impersonate the travelers at the passport office (see 1 October [1827]).

3. Compare this description with that of vol. I, 30 October [1826] to Alaric A. Watts, n. 2.

4. Probably Adeline Douglas is not listed because infants in arms could travel without passports (see 17 September [1827], n. 8). Mary Hunt was not to be included (see 13 October [1827] to Jane Williams Hogg; [28–29 June 1828], n. 10).

5. The signatures are appended so that the Douglas impersonators could accurately forge their names. Sholto Douglas's signature provides further proof that this was Mary Diana Dods, as the signature is clearly in her handwriting.

TO JOHN HOWARD PAYNE   Arundel—1 October—[1827]

My friends entreat you, dear Payne, to accept their thanks[1]—they feel that I am the person who ought to be most pleased by your kindness—but they hope nevertheless that you will permit them to be grateful to you for your politeness. All seems admirably managed—and the double of my pretty friend deserves infinite praise—the signature alone is a miracle & whoever she is, pray say that we are all endebted to her.

You have written to me several times about these commissions of mine—but besides this you owe me a letter concerning yourself. Your health—your plans—your successes—do not omit to inform me of all—you are so good that you have many friends—yet not one who sympathizes more truly than I in your pleasures & sorrows.

Percy has been indisposed, so we have deferred our voyage until next Saturday. God grant us a quiet passage—Once you called me an heroine in friendship—now I am one indeed—to cross the odious sea for the sake of my pretty Isabel—sacrifices have been made—as for instance by Damon & Pythias[2]—but this in my tablets will stand above all the rest—a matchless example of fortitude, generosity—friendship and undaunted courage—pray praise me for I deserve it

Adieu believe me Affectionately Yours

MaryShelley

ADDRESS: John Howard Payne Esq / 29 Arundel St. / Strand. POSTMARKS: (1) T.P / DRURY LANE; (2) 12. NOON. 12 / 2. OC / 1827. PUBLISHED: Jones, #290. TEXT: MS., Historical Society of Pennsylvania.
    1. For the passports he had obtained for them.
    2. In c. the fourth century B.C. in Greece, Pythias, condemned to die, asked leave to arrange his affairs, and his friend Damon pledged his own life to guarantee Pythias's return. Phythias did return, and Dionysius of Syracuse (405–367 B.C.) freed them both.

*To John Howard Payne   Arundel   13 October [1827]

My dear Payne

I am not at Dieppe—I have not been there—and it is uncertain whether I shall go—Your kind offices have not been vain & the separate passports were a great good, as a part of our party has crossed to France—and another part will probably sail next week.—

Meanwhile I am anxious to know how you are—what doing—what hoping—what achieving—I cannot help thinking that at last you will reap the harvest you patient labours and goodness so well deserve—tell me if your book[1] proceeds—and whether you still think of going to America—I have seen this summer one who makes me wish to see that country—one you must have heard of, Miss Wright[2] of Nashoba—the most wonderful & interesting woman I ever saw

—Do you think of visiting Brighton—shall you come over to Arundel?— Let me hear from you at any rate

Affectionately yours
MS.

ADDRESS: J. Howard Payne Esq / 29 Arundel St. / Strand. POSTMARKS: (1) T.P. / [D]evon. St Mbne; (2) [10] F.NOON. 10 / 17. OC /1827. UNPUBLISHED. TEXT: MS., Pforzheimer Library.
    1. Perhaps the script for a play; there is no record of a book by Payne.
    2. Frances Wright's 4 October 1827 letter to Mary Shelley from London indicates that they had not yet met, and on 7 and 8 October Frances Wright was in Harrow (S&M, IV, 1099–

1100; *Garnett Letters,* pp. 101–4). We may assume, therefore, that their meeting took place between 9 and 13 October. At the same time, Frances Wright met Isabel and Walter Sholto Douglas and provided "a letter introducing a Mr. and Mrs. Douglas, friends of Mrs. Shelley" (*Garnett Letters,* pp. 108–9). The introduction was to the Garnett family, whom Frances Wright had met in 1818 on a trip to America. After John Garnett (?1749–1820) died, his wife Maria (b. 1763) and two of their daughters, Julia Philippa (1793–1852) and Harriet (1794–1874), returned to Europe, living first at Le Havre and by 1827 in Paris. The Garnett social circle included General Lafayette (1757–1834); Prosper Mérimée (1803–70); Stendhal [Marie Henri Beyle] (1783–1842); Benjamin Constant (1767–1830), Franco-Swiss politician and author, and his wife Charlotte von Hardenberg; Claude Fauriel (1772–1844), French critic and historian. All these met and accepted Mr. and Mrs. Walter Sholto Douglas, whom the Garnetts in particular befriended. In September 1827 Julia Garnett married the German historian Heinrich Pertz (1795–1876) and went with him to live in Hanover. Thereafter she kept up an almost weekly correspondence with her friends and family, which she preserved and passed on to her heirs. In 1979 Cecilia Payne-Gaposchkin, great-granddaughter of Julia Garnett Pertz, published a large portion of the correspondence in the *Garnett Letters.* The original manuscripts are now on loan at the Houghton Library. These manuscripts contain detailed information about a large number of figures, including Frances Wright; Frances Trollope (see [29 October 1827], n.3); Mérimée; Stendhal; Fauriel; Lafayette; Mr. and Mrs. Sholto Douglas; "Mr. Douglas' sister" Mrs. Carter; and Mary Shelley.

*To Jane Williams Hogg   Arundel. 13 October [1827]

I am still in the land of the living, sweet Janey, though my long long silence may well induce a belief that I had visited the tomb of the Capulets[1]— which I am sorry to say is not the case. Nor will I fill a page with excuses— for excuses I have none—save that each day I have intended to write—& each day has slipt away without my being able to command thoughts & time together. Our friends are still here, in spite of every exertion made to facilitate their voyage—the struggle is not yet over, and we are still in the most unsettled state possible. Percy has been very ill—but is now recovered—Isabel is much better—She saw the country Doctor I called in for Percy—who gave her a preparation of the Blue pill[2] which has worked miracles on her—still I find no vacancey in my office of nurse—which though it be no sinecure—is adapted to me, and as far as I am personally concerned I do not murmur

But from all clouds & uncertainty, I turn with truest congratulation on the sunshine you have reached—long may you bask in peace prosperity & happiness—Now that you have your Dina with you I do not fear that you will suffer from ennui—the absence of your children made me fear for your spirits—but where is my favorite Med?—is he with his uncle? His disposition & talents are so excellent, that I auger a brilliant career for him—if fortune be not too unkind—But surely Fate has spent her shafts upon the parents—& will spare the children of both of us.—

Winter has now come in good earnest—but we need not complain this summer—I say nothing at this moment of my return, for in about a week I suppose I shall be able to decide how things are, & to write a better detail to you—Mary Hunt has returned to town[3]—a thousand things necessitated this—The wet we have had has spoiled our walks which else were divine perhaps we shall have a little frost soon to restore us to terra firma—

I fancy your nest & all its comforts & adornments lucky girl! You have your temple & your worshipper your haven—your (o blessed word) peace! While I tempest tost—look forward with daily encreasing horror to the future—Cosa, o dio, mai Sara![4]

No letter from Claire—from Trelawny—from anyone   My time of luck is gone for the year—but were not my prophesies of last year strange & true?—Now in vain would I exert my Sibylline propensities—all seems so dark—so rayless—so very comfortless—but that the fortunate hour is gone is too certain—a kind of quiet vacancy all the winter—a teazing annoyance in the Spring till July bring its mighty good or evil to bring up the account for the year—

So I go on talking about my stupid self, of whom I am infinitely weary, when in very truth I only intended to talk of your happiness—your prospects—your health—Take care of yourself   And God preserve you—My friends are sempre a letto[5]—but you will give them credit for their saying an heartfelt amen to every blessing I invoke for you—I kiss your pretty eyes—& thank Jeff—for every hour of satisfaction you enjoy

Amica Bellissima Adio[6]
MS.

[*P. 1, top*]   Excuse this slovenly mode—I did not at first perceive the division of the sheet.—

ADDRESS: Mrs Jefferson Hogg / Devonshire Place / Edgware Road / London. POSTMARKS: (1) ARUNDEL / 0620; (2) 10. F.NOON. 10 / OC. 15 / 1827; (3) F / 15 [OC] 15 / 1827. UNPUBLISHED. TEXT: MS., Abinger MSS., Bodleian Library.

1. A reference to *Romeo and Juliet*.

2. A mercury compound used as a purgative and cholagogue; an alterative in chronic inflammations; an antisyphiletic; a parasiticide (George M. Gould, *Gould's Medical Dictionary*, ed. R.J.E. Scott, 3d ed. [Philadelphia: P. Blakiston's Son & Co., 1931], p. 782).

3. See 25 September [1827] to John Howard Payne, n. 4.

4. "What, O God, could it be!"

5. "Still in bed."

6. "Beautiful Friend Goodbye."

TO JOHN HOWARD PAYNE   Harrow—Monday   [?29 October 1827]

My dear Payne

Me voila en Londres—et me voila encore[1] troubling you—Will you direct the enclosed to the American Consul General in London (is it not Col. Aspinall) & send it to him by the 2[d] post—au plus vite possible[2]—

I am as yet at a friend's house,[3] wholly unsettled—the moment I have a roof of my own over my head, I trust you will call, for I long to see you, & thank you for all your kindness

Yours Ever

MaryShelley

Direct to me at

29 Northumberland St. <u>New Road</u>

PUBLISHED: Jones, #291. TEXT: MS., Houghton Library.

   1. "Here I am in London—and here I am again." Godwin's Journal indicates that Mary Shelley dined with him in London on 26 October and went to Harrow the next day. On 31 October Mary Shelley, Frances Wright, and Robert Dale Owen called on Godwin. After that, the frequency of visits between Mary Shelley and Godwin demonstrates that she had returned permanently to London.

   2. "As quickly as possible."

   3. Frances Wright's Harrow address (see 9 November [1827]; S&M, IV, 1104). Wright had gone to Harrow to visit her friends Thomas Anthony Trollope (1774–1835), attorney and farmer; Frances Milton Trollope (1780–1863), not yet an author; and their six children, among them the future authors Anthony Trollope (1815–82) and Thomas Adolphus Trollope (1810–92). Because Thomas Trollope senior had been financially straitened for some time, it was decided that Frances Trollope and three of her children, Cecilia (b. 1816), Emily (b. 1818), and Henry (b. 1811), would accompany Frances Wright to Nashoba to try their fortune, to be joined later by the rest of the family. On 4 November 1827 the party, which also included Auguste Jean Jacques Hervieu (b. 1794), a French artist and friend of the Trollopes', boarded the *Edward* at the Thames River landing and were seen off by Mary Shelley (Johanna Johnston, *The Life, Manners, and Travels of Fanny Trollope* [New York: Hawthorn Books, 1978], pp. 24, 47, 49, 52; Thomas Adolphus Trollope, *What I Remember* [New York: Harper & Brothers, 1888], pp. 106–8; Frances Wright to Mary Shelley, 9 November 1827 [S&M, IV, 1103–4]). Frances Trollope, immediately disappointed with Nashoba, left there almost at once. In 1831 she returned to England, where she compiled her recollections of her experiences in *Domestic Manners of the Americans* (London: Whittaker, Treacher & Co., 1832), illustrated by Hervieu, in which she severely criticized the Americans and Frances Wright. The letters written by Frances Wright to Mary Shelley during this period send messages of love and regards from herself and Frances Trollope to Mary Shelley, thus bringing to light an acquaintance heretofore unnoted in biographies of either Frances Trollope or Mary Shelley (S&M, IV, 1102–6).

TO ROBERT DALE OWEN 51 George St.   Portman Sq[1]   9 Nov. [1827]

Dear Nashobite—I send you a letter for our admirable & dear Fanny.[2] As this is foreign post day, a letter may arrive for her at N. [*Northumberland*] St.—which I will either send to you at Bedford Square—or to Liverpool—so pray, Owen, do not forget to call at the Post Office Liverpool, both tomorrow & on Sunday, for I shall direct there any thing I have to send for you.[3]—

   Take care of our Fanny, dear Dale—she is neither so independant or so fearless as you think—A thousand painful circumstances may surround her, in which you may be useful to her, and which you will not discover unless you rouse yourself to perpetual attention, & resolve to devote yourself to those minute cares for her, which will win her confidence. You will say perhaps that if she confide not in you, the secretiveness is hers.—not so— we must all be sure of sympathy before we confide at all—& a woman must very highly esteem & love a man before she can tell any of her heart's secrets to him. We have no very excessive opinion of men's sympathetic and self sacrificing qualities—make yourself an exception—Inspire a belief in your lively & active interest for her—You are not in love now—one day you will be again—and the time may come when in spite of self-esteem you may fear that you are not loved in return—Now then practise yourself in such lessons as may make you <u>loveable</u>, if I may so express myself—& therefore the more likely to make a favourable impression—Nothing is better calculated to instil sweetness of disposition, & that best & most endearing of qualities—tenderness, than constant attention to a woman, with whom if you are not in love, yet for whom you have affection and kindness—Study to please Fanny in all minutia—divine her uneasinesses, & be ever ready at her side with brotherly protection—Do not imagine that she is capable always of taking care of herself:—she is certainly more than any woman, but we have all in us—& she is too sensitive & feminine not largely to partake in this inherent part of us—a desire to find a manly spirit where on {to} lean—a manly arm to protect & shelter us—The time perhaps is not far off when Fanny may find in a lover these necessities better supplied than you can supply them—but till then, no man need be nearer—dearer or more useful to her than yourself—and every smile of thanks & appro- bation you win from her sweet lips, will not only be in itself a dear reward— but will assure you that you are becoming more & more capable of inspiring the best being that exists—a lofty minded, sensitive and talented woman— with love & devotion for you. I trust that that you will find such an one & that thus your happiness will be secured—Sœur prêcheuse thus finishes her sermon[4]—God bless you—May you have favourable Winds and a pleasant passage—speak of me at Nashoba—& do not let Fanny forget me

Your sincere Friend
Mary Shelley

Have you called at Power's[5] for me?—Mention again to Mr Walker the book for Papa

PUBLISHED: Jones, #292. TEXT: MS., Historical Society of Pennsylvania.

    1. Mary Shelley's residence in London until her departure for Paris on 11 April 1828.

    2. Frances Wright.

    3. Robert Dale Owen, his father, and their party left from Liverpool for America shortly after this letter was written. It was arranged that Mary Shelley would collect and forward Frances Wright's letters to him to ensure their receipt (see Frances Wright to Mary Shelley, S&M, IV, 1102–5).

    4. "Teacher sister." "Sœur . . . sermon" was omitted in Jones.

    5. James Power (1766–1836), music publisher at 34 Strand. Power and his brother William were Thomas Moore's music publishers (New Grove Dictionary of Music and Musicians, XV, 174).

*To JOHN HOWARD PAYNE 51 George St. Portman Sq.
Saturday [10 November 1827]

My dear Payne
Will you drink tea with me on Sunday Evening—or when shall I have the pleasure of seeing you

Y^s Affectionalely
MS.

ADDRESS: J. Howard Payne / 29 Arundel St / Strand. POSTMARKS: (1) T.P. [Bland]ford St; (2) 7. NIGHT. 7 / 10. NO / 1827. UNPUBLISHED. TEXT: MS., Pforzheimer Library.

To WILLIAM WHITTON 51 George St. Portman Sq
3 December 1827

Dear Sir
I returned to town about a month ago. I am happy to inform you that my Son is quite well—and both improved & grown since Sir Timothy saw him

I am Sir
Your Ob^t Servt
Mary Shelley

ENDORSED: 3rd Decr 1827 / Mrs Shelley. PUBLISHED: Jones, #293. TEXT: MS., Bodleian Library (MS., Shelley, Adds., c. 6, ff. 51–52).

*To TERESA GUICCIOLI Londra. 51 George St. Portman Square.
4 10bre [December] 1827

Cara Contessina
Che destino vuol che tanto tempo s'intermette fra le nostre lettere? Nella tua ultima che ricevei nel Agosto passato mi prometteste un'altra al prossimo ordinario, ed eccoci al Decembre. Povero Moore s'impazienta—e vi ha scritto—per consolarlo gli dico, che sicuramente il vostro proponimento di scrivere per lui la storia degli amori di Voi e di Bÿron non è stata compiuta cosi presto che pensavate—che sia tirato in lungo—e poi che abbiate cercato altra via che quella della posta per spedirla. Intanto, Mia Cara Amica, son io inquieta, sopra il vostro silenzio—Dio vuole que niente di funesto lo cagiona. Il Moore era grato quanto mai per la vostra promessa—s'augurio il maggior bene per la sua opera e per il carattere dell'Amico nostro—Vi prego, adunque, mia Cara, di non mutare il proponimento, e di scrivermi subito cosicchè potessi ridare a Moore l'animo che ha perduto.—
Cosa avete fatto, Cara Guiccioli, tutta questa state?—Siete stato ai Bagni di Lucca? Avete veduto Medwin costà?—o altro delle conoscenze nostre?

Che bel posto è quello! con piacere mi rammento dei mesi ivi passati col mio marito[1]—Le belle montagne—quel bisbiglio eterno del Serchio—i tuoni magnifici, che fanno parere meschini ogni altro dopo aver sentito il lungo e terribili fracasso di quelli, raddoppiati dal eco—Ma non vi siete più—siete à Ravenna—à Roma? Ah! dite mi un poco come sta il stimat[mo] Conte Ruggiero—è egli sempre a Ferrara—ed il Governo del Santo Padre non diverra mite verso al buon padre di famiglia—il caro ed eccellente Pappa vostro?—Quanto è crudele questo mondo!

La state passava in un modo per me assai dolce. Stetti con una diletta ed amabile Amica, in una villeggiatura solitaria, si—ma bella—Vicino al mare; si vedeva ogni sera il bel sole sul tramontare spargere del oro sopra lo zafiro delle acque immense e poi sorgere la luna—la cui luce d'argento, piu dolce che quel del sole, era anche più piacevole—Vicino ci era la chiesa del paese, che portava segni della religione dei nostri padri, e la S. M. col Gesu Bambino in grembo mi fece ricordare tante cose, per me care, come legate coll'idea della mia Italia. Da questo paese adavamo a Arundel—paese conosciuto dal Castello che qui si trova, possessione dei duche di Norfolk—famiglia Cattolica.—Il parc è bellissimo—i boschi, i fiumicelli e la veduta lontana del mare formavano quaddri sempre variabili, ma sempre l'un più romanzesco che l'altro—Alfine eccomi quà, oime! in Londra, che odio. La mia Amica, Madama Douglas, è ita col marito a Parigi, ed io sento amarissimamente la mancanza della sua cara amicizia.—Non saprei pur troppo cosa fare—È cosi difficile muoversi senza motivo—ma non amo la Città, ed amo la campagna—poi vorrei andare à Parigi quest'altra state far visita alla mia Amica—intanto staro qui mi pare tutto l'inverno.—

Spero, mia Cara, che pur sempre mi conservi la preziosa vostra amicizia— più si avanza nella vita, meno si può risparmiare l'affezione di quelle che ci amavano nei più bei giorni della medesima—e più si soffre dalla crudeltà della fortuna, e la poca bontà del mondo, più si trova legata à quelle anime ben nate che sono come le stelle nella notte della Vita—come le lucciole in un bosco oscuro nella bella vostra patria. Per altro ho poche notizie a darvi sulle nostre conoscenze—se non che la Hogg ha fatta una bella bimba,[2] e che il padre si trova il più felice di tutti gli uomini—Dio gli facesse sempre felice alpare—e faccia che lei godesse della pace dopo tanto soffrire—Per me, sono assaissima lontana dal posto ove lei ora s'è stabilita—E di più non spero—posso adoperare quella parola—non aspetto mai trovare uno con cui legarmi—la ricordanza delle virtù di Shelley si renda impossibile il farmi la sposa di nuovo—Almeno cosi mi pare—Il mio figlio sta benissimo—è bello, grande—forte—buono—e di talento sufficiente.

Scrivetemi, mia Cara Amica—Mi sara sempre carissima le vostre lettere— Mi ripeto pur sempre

Vo[ra] Aff[ma] Amica
Mary Shelley

Se la Signora Contessa non si trova à Ravenna, che si spedisca questa lettera a Roma.

Dear Contessina

What destiny wills that so much time should elapse between our letters? In your last, which I received last August, you promised me another by the next regular courier, and here we are in December. Poor Moore grows impatient—and has written to you—in order to console him I tell him that surely your resolution to write the love story of yourself and Byron for him has not been completed as soon as you thought—that it may be delayed—and then that you may have sought another means than that of the post for sending it. In the meantime, My Dear Friend, I myself am uneasy about your silence—God grant that nothing distressing is causing it. Moore was as grateful as ever for your promise—it augurs the greatest good for his work and for the character of our Friend—I beg you then, my Dear, not to alter your resolution, and to write me immediately in order that I might give back to Moore the courage that he has lost.—

What have you done, Dear Guiccioli, all this summer?—Were you at the Baths of Lucca? Did you see Medwin there?—or other of our acquaintances? What a beautiful spot that is! I recall with pleasure the months passed there with my husband[1]—The beautiful mountains—the eternal whisper of the Serchio—the magnificent thunderbolts, which make every other seem meager after having heard the long and terrible uproar of those, redoubled by the echo—But you are no longer there—are you at Ravenna—at Rome? Ah! tell me a little about how the most esteemed Count Ruggiero is—is he still at Ferrara—and doesn't the Government of the Holy Father grow lenient towards the good father of the family—your dear and excellent Father?—How cruel this world is!

The summer passed in a very amiable way for me. I stayed with a dear and charming Friend, in a summer holiday place, solitary yes—but beautiful—Near the sea; every evening one would see the beautiful setting sun scattering gold on top of the sapphire of the immense waters and then the rising of the moon—whose silver light, more gentle than that of the sun, was even more pleasing—Nearby was the village church, which bore signs of the religion of our fathers, and the Blessed Mother with the Infant Jesus in her lap made me remember many things, dear to me, since they are tied to the idea of my Italy. From this village we went to Arundel—a village known for the Castle that one finds here, the possession of the dukes of Norfolk—a Catholic family.—The park is very beautiful—the woods, the streams and the far-off view of the sea formed ever-changing pictures, but always one more romantic than the other—In the end here I am, alas! in London, which I hate. My friend, Madame Douglas, has gone to Paris with her husband, and I bitterly feel the loss of her dear friendship.—Unfortunately I would not know what to do—It is so difficult to move oneself without a motive—but I do not love the City, and I do love the country—then I would like to go to Paris this next summer to pay a visit to my Friend—meanwhile it seems I shall stay here all winter long.—

I hope, my Dear, that you will always keep your precious friendship for me—the more one advances in life, the less one can spare the affection of those who loved us in the best days of the same—and the more one suffers from the cruelty of fortune, and the little goodness of the world, the more one finds oneself bound to those good souls who are like the stars in the night of Life—like the fireflies in a dark wood in your beautiful homeland. Otherwise I have little news to give you about our acquaintances—other than that Signora Hogg has given birth to a beautiful baby girl,[2] and that the father feels himself to be the happiest of all men—May God make him always this happy—and grant that she might enjoy peace after so much suffering—For myself, I am very very distant from the situation in which she is now established—And furthermore I do not hope—I can use that word—I do not expect ever to find one with whom to bind myself—the recollection of Shelley's virtues makes it impossible for me to marry again—At least it seems this way to me—My son is very well—he is handsome, large—strong—good—and of sufficient talent.

Write to me, my Dear Friend—Your letters will always be very dear to me—I repeat myself always

Your most affectionate friend
Mary Shelley

If the Signora Contessa is not at Ravenna, send this letter to Rome.

ADDRESS: Alla Sua Eccelenza / La Contessa Teresa Guiccioli Gamba / a Ravenna / Romagna negli Stati Pontefici. POSTMARKS: (1) Catherine St / Strand; (2) F 27 / 294; (3) ANGLETERRE; (4) CORRISP DA ESTERA [   ]; (5) BE[AUVOISIN]; (6) M[   ] / BOLOGNA / DELLE POSTEPONT. UNPUBLISHED. TEXT: MS., Pforzheimer Library. TRANSLATION: Ricki B. Herzfeld.

1. The Shelleys were at the Bagni di Lucca from 11 June to 31 August 1818 (see vol. I, 14 June 1818, n. 2, and [c. 13] September 1818, n. 1).

2. See vol. I, 28 July 1827, n. 2.

*TO JOHN HOWARD PAYNE   [?51 George Street]
                                         Tuesday [12 December 1827]

My dear Payne

Take places for me, nevertheless—and if you can get an order for two—from any of the New{s}paper persons or in any way for Saturday, pray do—

Yours Ever
MS.

ADDRESS: J. Howard Payne Esq. / 29 Arundel St. / Strand. POSTMARKS: (1) T.P. / Blandford St; (2) 2. A.NOON. 2 / 12. DE / 1827. UNPUBLISHED. TEXT: MS., Haverford College.

*To John Howard Payne   [?51 George Street]   1828–9 *(a)*
                                                 Thursday Night[1]

Will you my dear friend forgive my caprice & come to me on Sunday instead
of Monday evening. If this is not convenient to you write by return of post
that you come on Monday—If I do not hear from you I will expect you at
7—on Sunday

                                                          Yours Ever
                                                          MS.

Postmark: Blandford 19–. Unpublished. Text: Payne, Letterbook, 1815–33.
    1. The date and postmark are taken from Payne's Letterbook copy.

*To John Howard Payne   [?51 George Street   ?1828–29] *(b)*[1]

I don't go tonight—it is too bad to stir from ones fire side
                                         a thousand thanks
                                         Yours
                                         MS

Address: J. Howard Payne. Unpublished. Text: MS., Pforzheimer Library.
    1. A copy of this letter is placed in Payne, Letterbook, 1815–33, under 1828 or 1829.

To [?James Robins][1]   51 George St.   Portman Sq
                                          Saturday   5 Jan[y]   [1828]

Dear Sir
    I am sorry on your account that I cannot comply with the polite request
of the ⟨Editors of⟩ Proprietors of the Ladies Museum. It has been my
constant endeavour to withdraw myself personally from public notice—and
I flatter myself that I have so far succeeded as to be quite sure that the
portrait of so insignificant a person would possess no attraction for the
numerous readers of the Magazine. As to a Memoir, as my sex has precluded
all idea of my fulfilling public employments, I do not see what the public
have to do with me—I am a great enemy to the prevailing custom of dragging
private life before the world, taking the matter generally—and with regard
to myself there be no greater ⟨misfortune⟩ annoyance than in any way to
be brought out of my proper sphere of private obscurity. You say you will
be gratified in meeting my wishes on the occasion—I should consider myself
very greatly obliged to you if you would use your influence to prevent my
name from appearing at all in print
    I thank you for your politeness & am

                                          Your Ob[t] Servant
                                          MaryShelley

PUBLISHED: Jones, #294. TEXT: MS., Pforzheimer Library.

1. James Robins (d. 1836), publisher of the *Ladies Museum* and author (C. H. Timperley, *Encyclopedia of Literary and Typographical Anecdote*, with new introduction by Terry Belanger, 2d ed., 2 vols. [1842; reprint ed., New York: Garland Publishing, 1977], II, 945). This letter was published by Jones as addressed to George W. Portman, a misreading of Mary Shelley's address for the name of the addressee.

*To John Howard Payne   51 George St   Portman Square
Wednesday Eveng   18 Jan 1828

I am very sorry that I have been so unluckily out when you called—I had hoped to have met you at Papa's today but you disappointed us—Will you call on me on Wednesday morning—? I have intended writing you about play-going for Percy—But this vile weather spoils all.

very truly yrs
Mary Shelley

UNPUBLISHED. TEXT: Payne, Letterbook, 1815–33.

*To John Howard Payne   51 George St
Thursday [7 February 1828] (*a*)

Dear Payne
   Would you take 4 or 6 places for Tuesday in the first tier. The dress circle being unfavorable to secure—& meet me also there if it pleases you
Yours ever M.S.

POSTMARK: Feb 8, 1828. UNPUBLISHED. TEXT: Copy, Payne, Letterbook, 1815–33.

To John Howard Payne   51 George St. Thursday Ev^g
[?7 February 1828] (*b*)

   Your heart, my most kind friend, is quick in making discoveries—and it is beyond measure generous in its sympathies—the feeling is delicate that dictated your note, and I am truly sensible to all its demonstrations—alas, mine are not <u>fresh</u> bad spirits—the same cause that ⟨caused⟩ occasioned me such dejection last summer[1] is now operating in full force—It is little to tell you (tho' this is true) that I am much better tonight than yesterday—for tomorrow—I dread tomorrow—some day I may tell you the cause of my sorrow, but I shrink from talking of it—& would fain bury it in oblivion—It is now approaching a crisis, and I expect to experience great agitation—

I know not whether agitation is to others what it is to me—to me it is bodily torture—I writhe—& long for physical pain as an antidote—to be sure I now get that as a surcroit[2]—for, what was not the case a few years ago, my mind diseased diseases my luckless framework—

All this, dear Payne, will make you wonder—pity—& love me—would you could do me any good—for then I should get rid of a part of my evils—but it cannot be—I must bear alone—

I will write to you soon again to let you know how I am—meanwhile you need not be jealous, no man-person occasions my annoyance—but I believe I was born to run through every key of sorrow—and my heart fails me both in retrospect & anticipation

I will write very soon again—a thousand heart felt thanks for your affectionate attentions

Ever Yours
MS.

PUBLISHED: Jones, #295. TEXT: MS., Huntington Library (HM 6827).
  1. See vol. I, 22 August [1827] to John Howard Payne.
  2. "Addition."

To JOHN HOWARD PAYNE   [51 George Street ?8 February 1828][1]

Detestable as your annoyances are, My dear Friend, I shall hail them as fortunate (when over) if they free you from the discomfort of avoiding them for ever—I shall be anxious, very anxious, to hear the result of your endeavours—pray let me know—

I should like to go to Otello—if you can manage orders—but do not teaze yourself—Are you half laughing at me when you speak of my "elegant & distressing note"—I would willingly bid farewell to such elegance for ever—Like all human things (unlike romantic sorrows) there is no finale to put an end at once to my annoyance—I look forward with fear & pain—but cannot see the remedy

Let me hear concerning your affairs the moment you have news to communicate—

I should like to receive the yes or no of the tickets as soon as possible for the arrangement of those who are to go with me

Affectionately Y[s]   MS.

PUBLISHED: Jones, #296. TEXT: MS., Huntington Library (HM 6825).
  1. This date is based on the reference in the letter to Mary Shelley's "elegant & distressing note" (see [?7 February 1828] [b] and her statement that the situation (which came to a head on 11 February, according to her letter of [?14 February 1828]) was still unresolved. Also, her request for tickets for Otello supports a date of 8 February, since Rossini's Otello was given at the King's Theatre on 9 February and not again until 8 March.

To Jane Williams Hogg[1]   [?51 George Street]   Thursday
                            Morning   [?14 February 1828][2]

Since Monday, I have been ceaselessly occupied by the scene, begun &
interrupted, which filled me with a pain, that now thrills me as I revert to
it. I then strove to speak, but your tears overcame me, while the struggle
must have given me an appearance of coldness—Often—how often have I
wept at instances of want of affection from you, and that you should complain of me, seemed the reproach of a benefactress to an ingrate.

If I revert to my devotion to you it is to prove that no worldly motives
could estrange me from the partner of my miseries—the sweet girl whose
beauty grace & gentleness were to me so long the sole charms of my life—
Often leaving you at Kentish Town I have wept from the overflow of
affection—Often thanked God who had given you to me—Could any but
yourself have destroyed such engrossing & passionate love?—And what are
the consequences of the change?—When I first heard that you did not love
me, ⟨I felt⟩ every hope of my life deserted me—the depression I sunk
under, and to which ⟨in consequence⟩ I am now a prey, undermines my
health—How many many hours this dreary winter, I have paced my solitary
room, driven nearly to madness as I could not expel from my mind the
⟨circumstances⟩ Memories of harrowing import that one after another in-
truded themselves. It was not long ago that eagerly desiring death—tho'
death should only be oblivion, I thought that how to purchase oblivion of
what was revealed to me last July, a torturous death would be a bed of
Roses. At least, most lovely One, my love for you was not unworthy of its
object—I have committed many faults—the remorse of love haunts me
often & brings bitter tears to my eyes—but for four years I committed not
one fault towards you—In larger, in minute things your pleasure and satisfaction were my objects, & I gave up every thing that is all the very little
I could give up to them—I make no boast, heaven knows had you loved
me you were worth all—more than all the idolatry with which my heart so
fondly regarded you.

Do not ask me, I beseech you, a detail of the revelations made me—
Some of those most painful, you made to several—others of less import,
but which tended more perhaps than the more important to shew that you
loved me not, were made only to two. I could not write of these, far less
speak of them. If any doubt remain on your mind as to what I know, write
to Isabel[3] and she will ⟨tell⟩ inform you of the extent of her communications
to me. I have been an altered being since then—long I thought that almost
a death blow was given so heavily & unremittingly did the <u>thought</u> press
on & sting me—but one lives on through ⟨such⟩ all, to be a wreck—

Though I was conscious that having spoken of me as you did, you could
not love me, I could not easily detach myself from the atmosphere of light
& beauty that for ever surrounds you—I tried to keep you, feeling the

while that I had lost you—but you penetrated the change, and I owe it to you not to disguise its cause—What will become of us, my poor girl—you say you love me—I heard you say so—such a speech a year ago would have been Elysium—then your expressions concerning me had not love in them. ⟨I cannot see a happy termination—some things might be explained—but—⟩

Do not think that I am not fully aware of the defects on my part that might well call forth your reprehension—or that I even do not appreciate your motives in trying for my sake to be my friend, when I really believe I was a burthen to you—Nay I see your natural goodness in the very shew of love towards me that you designed to assume—but the veil is torn now[4]— I believe you still and forever to be all that man or woman could desire as a lover or a friend, if you loved them, your very merits make my unhappiness—my sole claim on you was the entireness of my affection for you.

This explains my estrangement—how hateful I must have appeared to you all this time—While with you I was solely occupied by endeavouring not to think or feel—for had I done either—I should not have been so calm as I dare say I appeared—My first wish is to get out of a world where I have fabricated only misery for myself—my next to withdraw myself from all society—Nothing but my father, after the news of your safe accouchment, could have drawn me to town again—his claims only prevent me now from burrying myself in the country—I have known no peace since July—I never expect to know it again.

Were I to say, forget me—What would you reply? I cannot forget you; your form, in all its endearing grace is now before me—but more than ever I can only be an object of distaste to you, is it not best then that ⟨I should be forgotten⟩

you forget the Unhappy MS.

PUBLISHED: Jones, #297. TEXT: MS., Bodleian Library (MS., Shelley, Adds., c. 6, ff. 53–54).

1. This letter tells of the open confrontation between Mary Shelley and Jane Williams Hogg over the latter's betrayal of friendship (see vol. I, 22 August [1827] to John Howard Payne). There exist two originals of this letter in Mary Shelley's handwriting, one in the Abinger MSS., the other formerly held by Sir John Shelley-Rolls, both now at the Bodleian Library. The Shelley-Rolls letter, the text of which is given here, has many more deletions and almost certainly precedes the Abinger letter. The letters, however, are essentially the same. Previous publications of this letter have been either incomplete or from Sir Shelley Rolls's copy of the original.

2. On 12 February 1828 Mary Shelley wrote in her Journal: "Moore is in town—by his advice I disclosed my discoveries to Jane—How strangely are we made—She is horror struck & miserable at losing my friendship & yet how unpardonably she trifled with my feeling & made me all falsely a fable to others." Since Moore called on Mary Shelley on 9 February (Moore, *Journal*), the Monday of the confrontation was 11 February.

3. Isabel Robinson Douglas.

4. An echo of a number of Shelley's poems, including *The Revolt of Islam* 5. 38 and 9. 7; *Prometheus Unbound* 1. 539–40.

TO JOHN MURRAY   51 George St.   Portman Sq   19 Feby 1828

Dear Sir

I beg to acknowledge with many thanks the advance of £100[1] I have received from you through Mr Marshall. With regard to my novel[2] I shall be much pleased if you undertake its publication—An historical subject of former times must be treated in a way that affords no scope for <u>opinions,</u> and I think you will have no reason to object to it on that score.

Mr Marshall mentioned to me that you asked whether I understood Italian & its patois, saying that you had a view in asking this—I lived nearly six years in Italy & its language is perfectly familiar to me—and I should not hesitate to undertake a work that required an intimate acquaintance with it.—I should be very glad if you would communicate your ideas to me on this subject and happy to comply with your suggestions as far as my abilities permit—Shall I call again in Albemarle St. I shall be earnest to acquit myself of my debt to you

I am Sir
Your Ob^t Servt
MaryShelley

I received Mr Gifford's edition of Ford[3] and Lord Byron's works for which I beg sincerely to thank you—

ENDORSED: Feby. 19. 1828 / Shelly Mary. PUBLISHED: Jones, #298. TEXT: MS., John Murray.

1. Thomas Moore interceded with John Murray to induce him to lend Mary Shelley the £100 (see Moore, *Journal*, 16, 17 February 1828; Moore, *Letters*, II, February or March 1828). For the settlement of this debt see 12 November 1829.

2. *Perkin Warbeck.* Mary Shelley hoped the £100 was an advance rather than a loan and over a period of years offered Murray a number of prospective projects, all of which he declined.

3. *The Dramatic Works of John Ford,* ed. William Gifford, 2 vols. (London: John Murray, 1827).

TO ISABELLA BAXTER BOOTH   3 March 1828   51 George St.
                                                Portman Sq

You must be in ill spirits, love, when you would raise sorrow out of so trivial a thing as my signature—I very seldom except to absolute strangers sign more—

Perhaps you would like to bring Jessy[1] with you on Friday—I shall be very glad to see her—As to my piano I <u>must</u> contrive to move from these lodgings next week & then I shall send it away & not have one again—I merely got it for the sake of one Evening.

I am very very sorry for Catharine's[2] sake, for this interruption to her music—⟨perhaps⟩ but in talking it over with you I do not think it impossible that means might be found to continue her instruction   I wish I could contrive with you to give her a year's schooling—but this may be done a year hence if God is good—cheer up, dear girl—I am afraid my narrow means appears sometimes narrow will—when the one is enlarged you will find the other grow broad I assure you

I shall be at a very stageable distance from you as I think I shall be at Paddington

Adieu—Would that my best good & ardent wishes could bring their own fulfillment to you prays (at full length{)}

Y^r Affectionate
MaryW. Shelley

ADDRESS: Mrs Booth / &c &c &c. PUBLISHED: Gay Wilmerding, *A Prediction?* (Northampton, Mass.: Catawba Press, 1979). TEXT: MS., Smith College Library Rare Book Room.

1. Jessie Baxter, Isabella Booth's half sister (*SC*, II, 559).

2. David Booth had three children: Isabella Booth (with Margaret Baxter Booth); Catherine Booth (with Isabella Baxter Booth); and a son, about whom no details have been located except that in 1842 he was abroad. Records of the Royal Literary Fund in 1845 state that all three were more than thirty years of age at that time (vol. I, [3 November 1814], n. 2; chart of the Baxter family by George Sandeman, Central Library, The Wellgate, Dundee; application form, Royal Corporation of the Literary Fund). Mary Shelley's "old friend Izy" in her letter of 4 November 1817 (vol. I) probably refers to Isabella Booth rather than Isabella Baxter Booth. One may speculate that since no mention is made in the correspondence of Mary Shelley and Isabella Baxter Booth of a son, and his being more than thirty in 1845, he may have been David Booth's child by a union previous to his marriage to Margaret Baxter Booth.

To WILLIAM WHITTON

51 George St   Portman Sq.
Monday—10 March 1828

Mrs Shelley will do herself the pleasure of calling on Mr Whitton with her Son on Wednesday Morning at twelve o'clock—

ADDRESS: W. Whitton Esq / Kings Road / Bedford Row.   POSTMARKS: (1) T.P. / [Bland]ford St; (2) 2. A.NOON. 2 / 11. MR / 1828. ENDORSED: 10th March 1828 / Mrs Shelley. PUBLISHED: Jones, #299. TEXT: MS., Bodleian Library (MS., Shelley, Adds., c. 6, ff. 55–56).

To VINCENT NOVELLO

[?51 George Street]   11 March 1828

Tempo fà, mio caro Vincenzo, vi promisi questa treccia dei capelli della mia Madre—non mi son scordata della mia promessa e voi non vi siete scordato di me—sono sicurissima. Il regalo presente adunque vi farà rammentare piacevolmente lei chi ama per sempre i suoi amici—fra di quali crederà di sempre trovarvi quantunque le circonstanze ci dividono.

State felice—e conservatemi almeno la vostra stima, vi prega la vostra amica vera,

Mary Shelley

[Translation]

Sometime ago, my dear Vincenzo, I promised you this tress of my mother's hair—I have not forgotten my promise, and you have not forgotten me—I am very sure. This gift then will remind you pleasantly of her who loves her friends forever—among whom she trusts always to find you although circumstances may divide us.

Your true friend prays you to be happy and to preserve at least your esteem for

Mary Shelley

PUBLISHED: Jones, #300. TEXT: Clarke, *Recollections of Writers,* p. 42. TRANSLATION: John P. Colella.

TO WILLIAM WHITTON   14 March 1828   51 George St.   Portman Sq.

My dear Sir,

I walked over to Kensington today to see Mr Slater's school.[1] From all I have heard of it & from personal inspection, I am inclined to select it for my son. The terms are 45£ per ann. There will be a few extras, books &c.— & some things I must provide for him before he goes—His present school is by no means an inexpensive one—I trust therefore I am not indiscreet is [*in*] asking you to represent this Sir Timothy, and to mention that I shall find difficulty in making the present arrangement.[2] At the same time present my acknowledgements for his kindness to Percy, & for the provision with which he is good enought to supply me

I am, d^r Sir
Your Ob^t Servt
MaryShelley

ENDORSED: 14th March 1828 / Miss Shelley. PUBLISHED: Jones, #301. TEXT: MS., Bodleian Library (MS., Shelley, Adds, c. 6, ff. 57–58).

1. Percy Florence Shelley entered Edward Slater's Gentlemen's Academy, Church Street, Kensington, on 25 March (see 8 April [1828]). The school building is now the priory to the Carmelite Church, 41 Kensington Church Street.

2. Sir Timothy Shelley did not comply with Mary Shelley's request for an increased allowance (see 5 September 1828).

TO [ANNE MATHEWS][1]   Thursday Ev^eg [26 March 1828]
51 George St.   Portman Sq

My dear Madam—

I was delighted to see by the papers that Mr Mathews[2] was recovered and was about to write to ask you when we might come, when your kind note arrived. I shall be happy to avail myself of you politeness between the hours you mention on Tuesday next

I am, Dear Madam,
Yours truly
MaryShelley

UNPUBLISHED. TEXT: MS., Pforzheimer Library.

    1. Anne Jackson (d. 1869), actress and author, married the actor Charles Mathews in 1803 (see *DNB*, S. V. "Mathews, Charles").

    2. The *Morning Chronicle* of Thursday, 26 March 1828, announced that Charles Mathews had recovered from the sudden illness he had suffered en route to Edinburgh.

*TO JOHN HOWARD PAYNE   [?51 George Street 26 March 1828]

My dear Payne

    I remember now that next Monday is in Passion Week[1]—⟨So instead of going⟩ Will you—can you arrange for the French Theatre for Friday next—(the 28th) let me know immediately

Yours (in haste)
MS.

ADDRESS: John Howard Payne Esq—/ 29 Arundel St. / Strand. POSTMARKS: (1) [T.P] / Blandford St; (2) 10. F.Noon. 10 / 26. MR / 1828. UNPUBLISHED. TEXT: MS., Peal MS., University of Kentucky Libraries.

    1. The law required theaters to be closed during Holy Week and on Whitsun Eve, Christmas Eve and Christmas night, 30 January (the anniversary of the beheading of Charles I), and Ash Wednesday. Also, only oratorios could be produced on Wednesdays and Fridays during Lent. These restrictions were not abolished until the middle of the nineteenth century (Charles Beecher Hogan, *The London Stage, 1776–1800* [Carbondale: Southern Illinois University Press, 1968], p. cxxxi).

*TO JOHN HOWARD PAYNE   [?51 George Street] Friday Night

[28 March 1828][1]

I trust, My dear Friend, that you know me sufficiently to be quite sure that I could not be guilty of intentional rudeness—and I am sure you will believe that I never was more mortified than now—This is my simple history—I learnt there was no French play tonight—and I had tickets sent me for the Oratorio as circumstances obliged me to have companions this evening   I thought you would be as well pleased to join us at the theatre as at my house—I meant to have left a note telling you Where we were gone asking you to come—& I forgot

    Will you forgive me? I am sure you will, you are so good, & this makes me worse—I shall be at the Opera—either in the pit or a box I dont know

—◄{ 30 }►—

which tomorrow will you look for me & join us—this will be kind—if not pray call some morning before two (not Tuesday morning)   I want to see you because my days are few—is not this awful—but in truth I meditate a trip to Paris (mention it not) in a fortnight[2]

Yours Affectionately
MS.

ADDRESS: J. Howard Payne Esq / 29 Arundel St. / Strand. POSTMARKS: (1) T.P / Blandford St; (2) [   ] 1828. UNPUBLISHED. TEXT: MS., Fales Library, New York University.
  1. See [26 March 1828] to John Howard Payne.
  2. See 8 April [1828], n. 1.

*TO [JOHN BOWRING][1] 51 George St. Portman Sq 2 April—[1828]

My dear Sir

  I think I saw you in a street the other day, so if not your revenant,[2] you are, I suppose returned—In a fortnight or so, I take flight to France—to Paris I mean, for a month or so it would give me pleasure before I go to have copied LB's letters for Moore[3] if you could let me have them—

  I will try to get the critique[4] written before I go but am not sure—how are you?

Yours Ever
MShelley

ENDORSED: (1) Apr 2 1828 / Mrs Shelley / 3; (2) Mrs Shelley / 2 April 1828. UNPUBLISHED. TEXT: MS., Gordon N. Ray.
  1. The endorsements on this letter, which are in the same style and handwriting as other Mary Shelley letters to Bowring, as well as its contents, indicate that it was written to John Bowring (see 11 June [1828]).
  2. "Ghost."
  3. On 1 April 1828 Moore wrote to Mary Shelley asking her to "seize Bowring, too, the moment he arrives & make him disgorge all his letters" (Moore, Letters, II, 603). On 15 April he acknowledged Bowring's agreement to furnish him with copies of Byron's letters, and by 16 April Bowring had already given copies of some of the letters to Mary Shelley (Moore, Letters, II, 606; Moore, Journal. See also 9 September [1827], n. 1).
  4. Possibly Mary Shelley's article "Modern Italy," which appeared in Westminster Review 11 (July 1829): 127–40. The article reviewed Italy As It Is (London, 1828) and J. Simond, A Tour in Italy and Sicily (London, 1828) (see 11 June [1828]).

*TO JOHN HOWARD PAYNE   [?51 George Street] Wednesday
April 2, 1828

So you will not call or write is not this reve{n}ge for C—[1] very unforgiving—I revoke what I said about being at home in the morning, as un-

fortunately I am obliged to go out—But if you will come between 8 & nine
or ten one evening you shall find me at home.

Y^{rs} truly
M.S.

POSTMARK: Ap 2 1828. UNPUBLISHED. TEXT: Copy, Payne, Letterbook, 1815–33.
  1. Unidentified. Perhaps a reference to the events described in [28 March 1828].

*TO [?   ]   Friday Ev^{eg} [?4 April 1828] 51 George St.
Portman Square

My dear Madam
    My friend, Mr Robinson, is much annoyed at having been obliged to
make a business appointment for Monday—Will you admit us on Tuesday
instead?—or will you name any other day convenient to yourself.—
    I shall be here a week or two longer, and shall be much gratified if I am
not too far out of your world for you to call on me

I am, dear Madam
Yours truly
MaryShelley

UNPUBLISHED. TEXT: MS., Pforzheimer Library.

TO WILLIAM WHITTON   51 George St. Portman Sq
Tuesday 8 April [1828]

My Dear Sir
    Percy went to school, to Mr Slater at Kensington on the 25th Ult—he is
now home for the Easter holidays—& is satisfied with his school & is both
well & happy. I trust Sir Timothy will be pleased with my attention to his
wishes & my selection for him
    A friend of mine has arrived from the South at Paris—& intends im-
mediately almost to proceed to Germany[1]—As I desire very much to profit
by this only opportunity I shall have of seeing her—I intend going to Paris
the day after I take Percy back to school (next Thursday)—as I shall be
exceedingly anxious to return to him, I shall not remain away more than
three weeks.—The opportunity is the more desirable as I join other friends
who are going.—
    I will let you know immediately on my return—which will not be pro-
tracted beyond the time I have mentioned.

I shall be very glad to hear that Percy will have an opportunity of seeing his Grandfather again

I am Dear Sir,
Y^r Ob^t Servant,
Mary Shelley

ENDORSED: 8th April 1828 / Mrs Shelley. PUBLISHED: Jones, #302. TEXT: MS., Bodleian Library (MS., Shelley, Adds., c. 6, ff. 59–60).

1. Mary Shelley wrote in her Journal on 11 April 1828: "I depart for Paris, sick at heart yet pining to see my Friend." It has previously been believed that Mary Shelley went to visit Julia Robinson, but these letters and the *Garnett Letters* make it evident that Mary Shelley traveled with Julia and Joshua Robinson to visit Isabel Robinson Douglas. Mary Shelley's strong feelings of friendship for Isabel Robinson Douglas were not reciprocated, as Frances Wright's 20 March 1828 response to a letter from Harriet Garnett indicates: "The D[*ouglases'*] account of Mary does not surprise me. She did not strike me as a person of sensibility, and my first impression was decided disappointment. I resisted and lost this, and became interested in and for herself, though the interest excited by her parentage and history has always held a large share in the interest I feel in her. The D[*ouglases'*] account may be all true (and my own recalled impressions would rather go to confirm it), but it makes much against them. Not only have I seen them evince the fondest kindness for Mary, but Isabel's letters, which I have seen, are in a strain of the fondest and most dependent friendship. Deficient sensibility is a negative quality, but hypocrisy is a positive one of the worst character" (*Garnett Letters,* p. 117).

It is possible that the Douglases had gone to the south of France after 27 February and returned by 30 March, since the *Garnett Letters* make no mention of them during this period. On 23 January 1828 Harriet Garnett wrote to Julia Pertz about Sholto Douglas: "He has hopes of obtaining a place in the diplomatic line—and said he hopes it may be at Hanover" (MS., Houghton Library). By February the Douglases planned to spend the summer at Manheim and to proceed from there to Baden (MS., Maria and Harriet Garnett to Julia Pertz, 21 February 1828, Houghton Library).

TO [?CHARLES OLLIER]^1 51 George St.   10 April [1828]

My dear Sir

I return your book with many thanks—and when I return I shall ask you, as you gave me leave, to lend me others—I am now going to Paris for two or three weeks—You have not called as you said—nor sent me the book— I will let you know where I am when I return, when I shall hope to see you

I am dear Sir
Y^r Ob^t Sv^t
MaryShelley

PUBLISHED: Jones, #303. TEXT: MS., Pforzheimer Library.

1. A letter from Mary Shelley to Charles Ollier, dated April 10, from 51 George Street is listed in the Puttick and Simpson sale catalog for Monday, 22 July 1878. Jones conjectured that the addressee might have been John Murray.

Sweetest Janey—Since I have been in Paris this is the first day I have been out of bed—no wonder that I have not written to you—I travelled in a high fever—arrived in Paris—took to my bed—& after spending two days in it symptoms of the small pox occcurred—it was kept a secret from me—I thought I had the chicken pox—it was a most virulent kind—but the journey & a warm bath on my arrival brought it out so speedily & decidedly—that the critical 7th day passed, on which I was very ill,   I became convalescent last Wednesday & have gone on getting regularly better—I am assured by my Doctors that I shall not be in the least marked—

Could any thing be more provoking—to endanger poor Julia[1] so much, to put our friends[2] wholly under interdict[3] for the Parisians are dreadfully afraid of infection—to make a sick house of it—& then the illness over to be such a fright that it will be long before I can show myself—so much for human plans & schemes—we know what we are to do as much as Pope's Lamb[4]—One's only consolation is that they tell me I should have kept it in my blood much longer & have had it much worse in London—

How are you—quite recovered & your best prettiest & sweetest of babies I am far too weak to write much embrace your children for me—Pray see Percy & let me have news of him speedily—present my remembrances to Jeff—How does John[5] [?*passa*][6] I long to know—I saw Trelawny's girl[7]— but cannot say more now than that I like her very much—she is bl[   ]

Adieu dearest—write soon & tell me all good news

Ever Aff^{ly} Yours
MS

ADDRESS: Mrs Jefferson Hogg / 22 Devonshire Place / London / Edgware Road. POSTMARKS: (1) 28 / AVRI / 1828; (2) P. PAYÉ PARIS; (3) FPO / MY. 1 / 1828; (4) 12. NOON. 12 / MY. 1 / 1828; (5) [4.] EVEN. 4 / 1. MY / 1828. UNPUBLISHED. TEXT: MS., Abinger MSS., Bodleian Library.

1. Julia Robinson.

2. The Douglases and Georgiana Dods Carter.

3. In her letter of 22 April 1828 to Julia Pertz, Maria Garnett mentioned that she had not yet met Mary Shelley because of the latter's illness. She also comments that she does "not expect to like her. Mrs D. [*Douglas*] has described her character to me & I have seen her letters to her most intimate friends" (MS., Houghton Library). On 28 April 1828 Harriet Garnett informed Julia Pertz that they still had not met Mary Shelley because her illness was smallpox (MS., Houghton Library). Maria and Harriet Garnett's joint letter of 12 May 1828 to Julia Pertz states that they had met Mary Shelley the previous night and had both found her pleasing (MS., Houghton Library).

4. Pope, *An Essay on Man,* bk. 1, lines 81–86.

5. John Wheeler Cleveland, Jane Hogg's brother, who visited England in June (see [28–29 June 1828]).

6. "Travel."

7. Maria Julia Trelawny (b. 1814), Trelawny's eldest daughter, who in 1826 or 1827 was in the care of Trelawny's mother, Maria Hawkins Brereton (1762–1851). Eliza Trelawny was with her foster parents, whom Mary Shelley did not know, and Zella was with Trelawny in Italy.

Cara Amica Mia

Ricevei l'ultima cara vostra lettera al momento che stava pensando al mio viaggio quivi—Cosi dopo aver mandato l'ambasciata vostra a Moore,[1] risolse di non rispondervi se non da qui, ove sono venuta per far una visita ad una Amica mia Carissma—Ma oime! Cara—è stato finora poco piacevole un viaggio dal quale sperava godere molto—Non stette bene avante di partire—Mi pareva pero che il cambiamento d'aria doveva farmi del bene—soffri orribilmente sul viaggiare ad appena arrivata in Parigi bisognava mettermi in letto quando non tardavano i sintomi della vaijola piccola. Figuratevi il dispiacere che sentii, nel portare il seccagine d'una ammallata—il pericolo d'una cosi grave malattia, nella casa dei miei amici—era tenuta nascosto da me cos'era veramente il mio male finche tutto pericolo era passato, ora mai sono affatto convalescente, e non v'è pericolo mica che restarano cattive traccie sulla figura—pero sono brutta assai adesso—ecco la fortuna! come poco si sa l'avenire! Come mai pensare che facessi viaggio tale solamente per mettermi a letto—Pero per consolarmi medici mi dicono che la fatica del viaggio è stato una ottima cosa—e mi consolo—come i disgraziati si consolano per forza—pensando pure, quanto peggio il male poteva aver riuscito

Mia Cara, sono qui fuore d'Inghilterra, ma pero non piu vicino a Roma che in Londra, se si contasse non la distanza ma il tempo che me ne divida—Dio sa quando ci rivedremo!—Che piacere avrei rivedendovi parlando meco voi dei tempi passati—dei piaceri fugitivi, dei guai pur troppo immoti—Lettere sono un cosi piccolo conforto, e pure esse sole ci restano—

Che siete buona, Cara Contessina, verso di Moore—lui e molto sensibile alla vostra gentilezza—e mi prega di farvi ogni ringraziamento—Dice che saranno impagabile ogni manoscritto ogni pezzetto délla scrittura del nostro Amico che gradite mandare—Non sarebbe anche possibile di darli estratti dalle lette sue a voi—estratti che indicaranno i sentimenti—i progetti—gli opinioni—Vuol saper lui (se questo senza pericolo ai vostri cari si puo narrare) esattamente quanto entrava Bÿron nelle piane dei Carbonari[2]—che pensava fare con loro—Se vi rammentate cosa diceva delle varie sue poeme al tempo che le scriveva—la storia del comminciamento delle medesime—perche sceglieva i soggetti.—ogni piccolo annedetto piacevole o romanzesco che vi rammentate come arrivato à lui—come passava il suo tempo a Ravenna—Volete dar a Moore una copia di quel che scriveva a voi, il suo amore, nella Corinna[3]—In questo momento non saprei che altre questioni farvi, ma crederei che quando una volta, facendovi sforza comminciate di scrivere—crescera il manoscritto senza pure che vi ne accorgiate—e che ogni giorno trovarete cosa da aggiungere a quel gia raccontato.

Vi assicuro, Cara Amica, che non legeva ne meno una linea del libro del Sig^{re} Hunt[4] finche era stampato già—anzi non ebbi la minima idea di quel che dovesse contenere—vi prego se mai vi cadde quel libro fra le mani, no lo leggete.—vi farebbe pena—In questo mondo ove si goda cosi poco ed ove i piaceri fuggono come la nebbia cacciata del vento, si deve pure sempre risparmiarci ogni il minimo guai.—Circondersi colle idee le sue atte a con-solarsi—Scanzare tutte quelle che sono all'anima come le tempeste al cielo sereno—ecco il solo modo di vivere senza soffrire—più che le povere donne dovrebbero—care piccinine! fatt[e] da Dio per ornare il mondo—e pur troppo spess[o] ridotte a trovare il loro destino un carico intollerabile.

[St]aro qui credo, tre settimane—se vi pare che vi sia tempo, scrivetemi qui—dite me come vi troverete—e cosa farete questo state. Il mio figlio è al colleggio—gode un'ottima salute—è felice—ed amato dai Maestri. La Hogg sta bene—e la figlia sua è la più cara bambina che vi fu mai—

Addio mia cara, se trovarete più spropositi che il solito in questa lettera scusate—che il mio capo non si regge troppo bene—e mi vuol una gran'sforza per pensare—e poi tradurre quei pensiere in Intaliana è una fatica di più—Come sta il caro e buono Conte Ruggiero?—Tita è tornato in questo paese—incontrei Fletcher poco tempo fa pareva sempre il medesimo—Mia Cara, Amatemi sempre che mi ripeto sempre   Vostra Aff^{ma} A^{ca} Mary Shelley

[*Translation*]

My Dear Friend

I received your last dear letter just at the moment that I was thinking about my departure for here—Thus after having sent your message to Moore,[1] I decided not to respond to you except from here, where I came to pay a visit to my very dear Friend—But alas! Dear—it has been up until now a not very pleasant trip from which I was hoping to benefit greatly—I was not well before leaving—It seemed to me however that the change of air would have to do me good—I suffered miserably in traveling and as soon as I arrived in Paris it was necessary to put me to bed when the symptoms of the smallpox began to develop. Imagine the chagrin that I felt in bringing the annoyance of a sick person—the danger of so serious an illness, into the house of my friends—the true nature of my illness was kept from me until all danger had passed, now I am entirely convalescent, and there is not the slightest danger of any wretched marks remaining on my body—however I am ugly enough now—what luck! how little one knows of the future! I never would have thought I'd make such a trip just to stay in bed—But to console me the doctors tell me that the weariness of the trip was a very good thing—and I am consoled—as wretches console them-selves of necessity—thinking, too, how much worse the evil might have been.

My Dear, I am here outside of England, but yet no closer to Rome than I am in London, if one counts not the distance but the time that divides me from it—God knows when we will see each other again!—What pleasure

I would have seeing you again, talking with me of times past—of fugitive pleasures, of sorrows unfortunately unmoved—Letters are such a small comfort, and yet they are all that's left to us—

How good you are, Dear Contessina, to Moore—he is very much aware of your kindness—and begs me to express to you every gratitude—He says that every manuscript, every scrap of writing of our Friend that you are obliged to send will be invaluable—Wouldn't it also be possible to give summaries of his letters to you—summaries that will point out his feelings— plans—opinions—He wants to know (if one can relate this without danger to your dear ones) exactly how much Byron entered into the plans of the Carbonari[2]—what he planned to do with them—If you recall what he said about various of his poems at the time he was writing them—the story of the beginning of the same—why he selected the subjects.—every small pleasing or romantic anecdote that you remember as touching on him— how he passed his time at Ravenna—Do you want to give Moore a copy of that which he wrote to you, his love, in Corinne[3]—At this moment I would not know what other questions to ask you, but I would think that once, having made the effort to begin to write—the manuscript will grow without you even being aware of it—and that every day you will find some- thing to add to what you have already recounted.

I assure you, Dear Friend, that I did not read even one line of Signor Hunt's book[4] until it was already published—in fact I didn't have the slight- est idea of what it would contain—I beg you if ever this book falls into your hands, do not read it.—it would cause you pain—In this world where one enjoys so little and where pleasures flee like the fog chased by the wind, it is necessary to somehow always save ourselves from every small sorrow.—Surrounding oneself with ideas capable of consoling oneself— Avoiding all those which are to the spirit as tempests are to a clear sky— this is the only way to live without suffering—more than poor women should have to—dear little ones! created by God to ornament the world—and unfortunately frequently reduced to finding that their fate is an intolerable weight.

I will be here I believe, three weeks—if it seems to you that there is time, write to me here—tell me how things are—and what you will do this summer. My son is at boarding school—he enjoys the best of health—he is happy—and loved by his Teachers. Signora Hogg is well—and her daugh- ter is the dearest baby there ever was—

Addio my dear, if you find more mistakes than usual in this letter excuse me—my head is not bearing up very well—and it requires great effort for me to think—and then to translate these thoughts into Italian is an additional labour—How is the dear and good Count Ruggiero?—Tita has returned to this country—I met Fletcher a short time ago and he seems just the same— My Dear, Love me always as I repeat myself always   Your affectionate friend   Mary Shelley

ADDRESS: Importata 6 Maggio / Alla Sua Eccellenza / La Contessa Teresa Guiccioli / a Roma [*in another hand, "Roma" is crossed out, and "Ravenna" written in*]. POSTMARKS: (1) 6 / MAI / 1828; (2) BEAUVOISIN; (3) CORRISPZA DA ESTERA; (4) 19 MAG; (5) 27. MAG. UNPUBLISHED. TEXT: MS., Pforzheimer Library. TRANSLATION: Ricki B. Herzfeld.

1. See 9 September [1827], n. 1.
2. See vol. I, 10 November [1824], n. 4.
3. See vol. I, 3 July 1827, n. 3.
4. Hunt was hostile to both Byron and Teresa Guiccioli in *Lord Byron and Some of His Contemporaries*, which also included lengthy pieces on Shelley, Keats, and Thomas Moore. The book caused a critical furor, particularly among Byron supporters (see Moore, *The Late Lord Byron*, pp. 279–90; Blunden, *Leigh Hunt*, pp. 230–47).

*TO JANE WILLIAMS HOGG   4 Rue Nueve de Berry
            Champs Elysèes. 16 May [1828]

My dearest Jane—My month has now gone past—how you may guess—since although well in health—& gaining strength every day, I continue sufficiently marked to make me wish to hide myself altogether—and seeing the people I have necessarily seen, has been mortifying enough—although I am interested in & pleased with several I see here[1]—French principally—the Constants I like much   he is a venerable benevolent looking old man—she a sentimental German with great sweetness of manner. The weather is divine—we are in the open air almost all day, beneath the fresh green chesnuts of the Tuilleries—theatres we have not been to—indeed I have had very little of sight seeing.—

Do you know I cannot persuade myself to return to town—to meet the commiseration—and wonder & talk of all who shall see my ugly face—I mean to hide myself till it is all over. This is a great self denial—& a great disappointment—for there are several persons now in town whom I wished much to see,[2] were I myself—and I wish to return to those who love me—but no—I shall hide myself till the mask that disguises me disappears from before me. You know that I consider it a duty to give Percy a little sea bathing every year—I wished much to pass his holidays with him near the sea—but feared it would prove too expensive—but as things have gone I can arrange it. In about ten days I quit Paris & I shall remain at Dover. Mr Robinson—who has business there will bring my boy down to me—I shall get some country place & be quite quiet—my writing interrupted in, under the circumstances, so frightful a manner, will go on there famously; I shall ask the Godwins to visit me—and you, if possible, may steal away for a week or two—the change will do you great good, and Dina especially will be much the better for sea breezes.—Except you do this & the G's [*Godwins*] come, I shall be wholly alone—in six weeks or two months I am promised to see something white instead of red when I look in the glass, and then I shall venture to shew myself.

I wrote to Claire with directions on the outside that the letter should follow her to Toeplitz[3] M^rs G [*Godwin*] has also had a letter from her, speaking of her arrangements as decided—so unless some occasion offers itself for her going as governess to the south with some family in the meantime, of which I suppose she would avail herself, ⟨I suppose⟩ we may expect her in the spring. Poor girl! I shall be very glad to contribute to her happiness. even at the expence of my liberty—

I leave Paris Monday week—this is Friday—as my stay has been prolonged, it is necessary for me to receive here the £5 you have of mine—I am afraid that I have delayed so long writing for it, that you may find some inconvenience in sending it. If you answered me by return of post I should get your letter next Friday—if this is possible do it—if not—send it the next day—or even the next but do not delay longer writing—& if you cannot enclose the money write to tell me so & let me find it at Dover on my arrival there, directed to the Post Office.

Will you not come to me at Dover?—I think you may contrive it—I shall return to town if things go well, with Percy at the end of his holidays.—I think the sea air after this most vile illness will do me the greatest good—& get rid of its horrid remains quickly But I do not like its dividing us so long—so pray—pray come to me if you can. Adieu sweet & lovely One—let me hear that you are well & the darlings also—for ever & ever I think of you with heartfelt interest

Yours
MS.

We are so far from the post that it is long since I called there—so perhaps I shall find a letter today there waiting for me from you—but I could not delay this a post longer—they will not give letters to servants & people—direct to me to the above address—

ADDRESS: Mrs Jefferson Hogg / 22 Devonshire Place / Edgware Road / Londres London. POSTMARKS: (1) P.PAYÉ PARIS; (2) 16 / MAI / 1828; (3) [12.] NOON. 12 / MY. 19 / 1828; (4) 4. EVEN. 4 / 19. MY / 1828. UNPUBLISHED. TEXT: MS., Abinger MSS., Bodleian Library.

1. Through the Garnetts and the Douglases, Mary Shelley met Mérimée, Fauriel, Lafayette, and the Constants (see 13 October [1827] to John Howard Payne, n. 2; MSS., Garnett letters, Houghton Library).

2. Among them was probably Lord Dillon, whose letter to Mary Shelley on 13 June 1828 expressed his disappointment that she was not coming to town. In the same letter he sent regards to Miss Robinson and asked that Mary Shelley forward to him "Miss Dodd's donation" (S&M, IV, 1111–12).

3. Claire Clairmont had traveled from Moscow to the Baths of Tuplitz, near Dresden, as companion to Madame Kaisaroff and her daughters but had quit them because of a quarrel. She found a traveling companion and proceeded to London, arriving there on 16 October 1828 (CC Journals, pp. 415–16; Claire Clairmont to Mary Shelley, 22 July 1828, Abinger MSS.).

TO [PROSPER MÉRIMÉE][1]   [Paris] Samdi Soir [24 May 1828][2]

C'est parceque je ne suis pas coquette que je vous rends votre lettre. Je ne voudrois pas garder l'expression des sentiments dont vous pourriez vous repentir apres—ni la tomoignage [*témoignage*] de ce que vous paraitra (il se peut) en reflechissant une faiblesse.

Vous demandez mon amitiè—elle est à vous. Toujours je serai votre amie, si toujours vous le desirez—si toujours (pardonnez ce façon de parler à une femme, non pas coquette mais fière) vous vous en montreriez digne. Je vous ecrirai—J'espere vous revoir à Paris—à Londres—Faites moi part de vos esperances, vos succes, votre bonheur ou si çela doit etre, de vos malheurs—vous trouverez en moi une amie simpatisante—compatisante—vraie.

Je pars Lundi. Je dois donner demain à mon amie comme le denier de mon sejour à Paris. Je suis fachèe que vous ne pourriez rester toute la soiree chez Mme Garnett.   mais je vous y verrai et encore je vous assurerai de mon Amitie

[Translation]

It is because I am not a coquette that I return your letter. I should not like to keep the expression of sentiments which you will probably repent of later—nor the evidence of what you will regard (it may be) upon reflection as a weakness.

You ask for my friendship—it is yours. Always I shall be your friend, if always you desire it—if always (pardon this woman's way of speaking, not petty but proud) you should prove yourself worthy. I shall write you—I hope to see you again in Paris—in London—Let me share your aspirations, your success, your happiness or if it must be, your unhappiness—you will find in me a friend sympathetic—tender—true.

I leave on Monday. I ought to give tomorrow to my friend as the last of my stay in Paris. I am sorry you cannot spend the whole evening at Madame Garnett's. but I shall see you there and again I shall assure you of my Friendship

PUBLISHED: Jones, #304. TEXT: MS., Museum Calvet.

1. There had long existed an unsubstantiated belief that Mary Shelley and Prosper Mérimée were romantically linked and that with this letter Mary Shelley returned to him his marriage proposal (see Dennis M. Healy, "Mary Shelley and Prosper Mérimée," *Modern Language Review* 36, no. 3 [July 1941]: 394–96). Previously unlocated letters from Mérimée to Mary Shelley, dated 5 July 1828 through 4 February 1829, document a close if temporary relationship between them (see Bennett and Little, "Seven Letters from Mérimée to Mary Shelley"). Mary Shelley's half of the correspondence has not been located, but Mérimée's provides much information about Mary Shelley and her circle, including Mérimée's suggestion that Mrs. Douglas was unworthy of Mary Shelley's friendship.

2. In her 16 May [1828] letter to Jane Hogg, Mary Shelley indicated that she would "leave Paris Monday week," that is, 26 May. Harriet Garnett's letter to Julia Pertz confirms this departure date and the date of this letter in its reference to the same Saturday gathering mentioned by Mary Shelley: "Last night we drank tea with the Douglas to take leave of Mrs. Shelley. a flirting party. Mrs. S. flirts with Mérimée, Mrs. D. [*Douglas*] with Hallam & Fauriel, and all others, and poor D. [*Douglas*] looks sick and disconsolate" (MS., 25 May 1828, Houghton Library).

To William Whitton   June 4—1828 Dover

Dear Sir

I was unfortunately delayed in Paris by illness—I took with me the small pox and was laid up immediately on my arrival there. I am ordered sea bathing for my perfect recovery—and as Percy is always recommended the sea side I intend to stay with some friends on this coast till after his holidays.

I shall remain at Dover a week and shall be much obliged to you if you will let me hear from you here. I heard with great pleasure that Sir Timothy called at Kensington to see Percy[1]—I hope he was satisfied with the school and with my boy—I shall always be happy, and I have shewn this, to attend to any suggestion of his concerning them. The question of the encrease of my allowance was left in doubt last March—when indeed I indulged the hope of reaping the benefit of it—I hope it is now decided in my favour.[2]

> I am dear Sir
> Y^r Ob^t Servant
> MaryShelley

ADDRESS: W. Whitton Esq / 3 Kings Road—Bedford Row / London. POSTMARKS: (1) DOVER / 4 JU 4 / 1828 / 72; (2) A / 5 JU 5 / 1828. ENDORSED: 4 June 1828 / Mrs Shelley. PUBLISHED: Jones, #306. TEXT: MS., Bodleian Library (MS., Shelley, Adds, c. 6, ff. 61–62).

1. William Whitton told Mary Shelley that he believed that Lady Shelley and the Miss Shelleys also had called on Percy Florence (Ingpen, *Shelley in England*, II, 600).

2. Mary Shelley's allowance was not increased until June 1829 (see 1 September 1829, n. 1).

*To Jane Williams Hogg   Snargate St. Over the Sluice Dover
                                                    [5 June 1828]

Dearest Jane—At last I am again on this side of the Channel—liking it less than ever—I was, with every disadvantage of my odious illness against me, delighted with Paris—Society is nothing as an end, but as a means it is much—the means of allowing one to know of the existence of human beings with whom one can sympathize—and of which one would otherwise remain in ignorance—I have made not only acquaintances but friendships for life—One in particular—a man neither young, handsome, rich nor of high birth—but a man of talent—a poet[1]—a creature whose nature is divine—One of those rare beings in whom sensibility is joined to activity of thought—and the softest sweetness to chivalrous daring—I shall return when I can—but God only knows when that will be—As it is I remain either here or at Hastings,[2] it is not quite decided which—You ask me why I solitudinize—my luckless disfigurement answers for me—I would not for worlds shew myself in town—besides my physician told me that sea bathing will diminish by at least a month the period of my ugliness—You would not know me—

Trelawny in England!—where?—how ardently I desire to see him—Dear dear darling—once again to find the true and good one—I shall write to Miss Trelawny[3] to learn where he is—

I am sorry you cannot join me here—I am very sorry you brood so painfully over the past—I wish I could see any possibility of bringing back a state of things gone for ever—Is it possible not to love you?—your sweetness, your grace, your ten thousand excellencies command a deep sentiment—but from the first moment we met you disliked me—apart from you your imaginations paints a being suitable to yourself, and you bestow my name on the idea—together a thousand realities that formerly disgusted you would do so again, and I, fearful of annoying by silence, by speaking, by my very looks (so was it all last winter) am any thing but myself—however we are not separated; I shall return to town after Percy's holidays & we shall see—One thing I feel—I always felt extreme difficulty in making personal confidences to you—I tried—& succeeded usually—yet in doing it I never reaped the only benefit of reposing confidence—sympathy—at least I never felt as if I did—now I cannot talk of myself to you; the being so long disfigured so long depreciated in your eey [eye] cannot pour out her heart—

Do not talk of anger & revenge—the poor child![4] her sufferings transcend all that imagination can pourtray—they may satisfy your bitterest feelings—as I consider myself as in some sort the cause, so I devote myself to extricate her we shall see whether I shall succeed—Claire's coming will be an impediment—but if it can be, it shall—

Dearest Jane accept a sentiment of admiration, of tenderness—of a love which clings to you thro' every thing—Try not I conjure you, to force, but to lead me back—Do not I earnestly pray you, allude to the past, or the change which cannot be unchanged—let us begin again;—let me love you for all you are—& where find any thing more worthy to be loved?—By the way do not imagine now that I have any thing to conceal—it is not with the small pox painting one with ugliness that one loves or is loved—if I had met any to excite that feeling which I did not—moreover I promise faithfully to let you know when I am in love—

Adieu darling—it is useless to talk of my plans—Trelawny's arrival may change them   take care of yourself

Affectionately Yours
MS.

Can Jeff. sometimes get your letters franked for me—I am ruined in postage

Remember me to the Clints—tell him that I got his blanc d'argent[5] thro' an artist so I trust it is good—I will send it to town by Mr Robinson when he comes & returns Would you send to Hardings Library[6] directed to Miss Robinson—the 2 Annuals you have of mine—I want them—& Mr R. [Robinson] w^d bring them me

My address is at Mr Dawson
       Snargate St.   Over the Sluice
     Dover

ADDRESS: Mrs Jefferson Hogg / 22 Devonshire Place—Edgware Road / London. POSTMARKS:
(1) DOVE[R] / 5 JU 5 / 1828 / 72; (2) A / 6 JU 6 / 1828; (3) 10. F. NOON. 10 / JU. 6 / 1828. UNPUBLISHED. One line is quoted in Jones, #305. TEXT: MS., Abinger MSS., Bodleian Library.

1. This appears to be a reference to Mérimée, except that Mérimée was only twenty-five at that time. In her letter of 15 June [1828], Mary Shelley again mentions her poet friend but describes him as young.

2. A seaside resort in Sussex, sixty-four miles south-southeast of London.

3. Julia Trelawny.

4. Isabel Robinson Douglas, whose "sufferings" and responsibility for informing Mary Shelley of Jane Hogg's breach of friendship are more fully referred to in Mary Shelley's letter of [28–29 June 1828].

5. Lead white oil paint.

6. Two booksellers by the name of Harding are listed in London for 1828: John Harding, 32 St. James' Street, and Thomas P. Harding, 16 Chapel Street, Edgware Road (*Pigot and Co.'s Metropolitan New Alphabetical Directory . . . for Middlesex . . .* [London, 1828]).

To William Whitton   [Dover] 6 June 1828

My dear Sir

I return the receipt as you ask. I confess I am disappointed at the amount of my cheque—I do not wish to make any claim on Sir Timothy, but in sending Percy to school I counted on an encrease of my allowance as the means of paying in part for his schooling—As he grows older and now that he is away from me, his expences encrease rapidly, and I shall find myself I fear much embarrassed if Sir Timothy is not good enough to take these circumstances into consideration. As Sir Timothy is now in town may I request you to represent to him from me respectfully my hope that I might this quarter have begun to receive an addition. You may remember that when you spoke to me in the spring of 1827 on this subject, you said, that the first idea had then been to make the allowance of 300£ p ann. but that Sir Timothy had said, that as in another year my son's expences would augment, it would be more prudent to defer till then the proposed encrease—

In all this I beg to deprecate any idea of making a claim on Sir Timothy; I am grateful to him for his kindness to my son, and it would greatly pain me if he thought me intrusive—But I find the greatest difficulty in keeping from embarrassment—and to meet the expences of the school bills will be almost impossible if I now receive no more than I did before this addition to my disbursements—

                I am dear Sir
                Your Obedient Servant
                MaryShelley

ADDRESS: W. Whitton Esq / 18 Bedford Row / London. POSTMARKS: (1) DOVER / 6 JU 6 / 1828 / 72; (2) A / 7 JU 7 / 1828. ENDORSED: 6th June 1828 / Mrs. Shelley. PUBLISHED: Jones, #307. TEXT: MS., Bodleian Library (MS., Shelley, Adds., c. 6, ff. 63–64).

*To John Howard Payne   Dover   Mr Dawson—Snargate St.
Over the Sluice   Sunday   [8 June 1828]

My dear Payne

I expected to hear from you while in Paris and was constantly disappointed—I suppose you have heard of all my misfortunes—of my being laid up immediately on my arrival with the odious small pox, of which I still bear so many traces that I intend remaining a couple of months by the sea side, when they tell me they will all disappear. Yet though I cannot make up my mind to shew myself in London, fright as I am, I actually went into society in France—I shall go over again next year to prove to the people that I am pretty—they cannot suspect it now.

I like Paris excessively—my world is enlarged by my visit there, and I have acquired new friends for life—excellent persons—who join goodness to talent—and the charm of social manners to a literary reputation—There is no town I should like to live in so well, and considering the extreme ease with which one gets at it—certainly I shall, if things go well, often return. My illness prevented my seeing many lions—and took away a good deal of the charm—but enough was left to make me fully aware of how much there might be—& then there was a piquançè in my situation, which as I did not sorrow over—amused me often—and led me into one or two certainly new & rather droll situations—

I had planned to return to town in the height of the season & to enjoy myself not a little—but now—not for ten thousand worlds—my pretty compagne de voyage[1] is still with me, & with her I shall go to Hastings & bury myself, till I am restored—So God knows when we meed [meet] again—do you? How are your affairs going on—& what new prospects have opened for you?—things so change often in a few days, that little may now be as I left it—

Unless you write immediately you had better wait till you hear that I am at Hastings—or write to me to the care of J. Robinson Esq—Park Cottage—Paddington—& it will be forwarded

I wrote to Marshall[2] on Friday on a subject of business   I had hoped to hear from him today—is he in town?—if he is out of town, let me {   } I pray you by return of post, as I must provide for the vacuum his absence will leave—if he is in town, ask him if he received a letter from me enclosing a cheque—Will you do all this speedily for me, for I want to quit this place on Wednesday, & shall be much annoyed if I do not hear on Tuesday. Not a word of all this to William[3]—nor to any one—I wrote to Marshall at 7 Hadlow St.—

No more Opera—no more—o a thousand things I hoped and desired—
I am very unlucky—Will you not pity me? Besides I dare say I shall be
marked—& that will be very amusing—Adieu—

Very sincerely yours

MShelley

If you do not write by return of post with news of Marshall's being out
of town or any embroglio [   ] about my letter—direct to me at Paddington as above—

Will you send to Power's in the Strand (34) & ask if Tom Moore is in
town & let me know

ADDRESS: John Howard Payne Esq / 29 Arundel St. / London   Strand. POSTMARKS: (1)
DOVER / 8 JU 8 / [182]8; (2) A / 9 JU 9 / 1828. UNPUBLISHED. TEXT: MS., Pforzheimer
Library.

  1. "Traveling companion," Julia Robinson.
  2. James Marshall.
  3. William Godwin, Jr.

TO JOHN BOWRING   Dover—11 June [1828]

My dear Sir

When I last wrote[1] I little foresaw all the annoyances that were to over-
throw ⟨all⟩ my plans. I took with me to France the small pox, which confined
me immediately on my arrival, and destroyed every arrangement both of
pleasure and business.

Is it now too late to write the critique I promised?[2]   if not I will set
about it instantly.—I have also a request to make you—You know and I
believe think well of two works "the Comedies of Clara Gazul" & the
"Guzla"—Merrimèe, the author of these, is now bringing out another publication,[3] which he will send me as soon as it is printed—I expect it daily[4]—
if I write an article on his works, will it prove acceptable to the W.R.
[*Westminster Review*]?—I should like very much so to do.

What about LB's letters for Moore?[5] Those you gave me are safely locked
up in town—I do not intend to return to London for some time, as sea
bathing is recommended to me for my perfect recovery—Would you send
me the letters directed to J. Robinson Esq Park Cottage, Paddington—when
they would be forwarded immediately to me—and I would return them to
you as soon as copied—or will you send them immediately to Moore 19
Bury St.   St. James'—the first arrangement would please me best—

Tell me how you are & what doing—I heard some very agreable intelligence concerning you in Paris—and shall be glad to be able to congratulate
you upon it[6]

I am Most sincerely Yours

MaryShelley

ADDRESS: John Bowring Esq / J. Bentham Esq / 2 Queen's Square Place / London / Westminster. POSTMARKS: (1) DOVER / 11 JU 11 / 1828 / 72; (2) A / 12 JU 12 / 1828. ENDORSED: (1) Dover   11 June 1828 / Mary Shelley; (2) Mary Shelley / 11 June 1828. PUBLISHED: Jones, #308. TEXT: MS., Huntington Library (HM 2759).

   1. See 2 April [1828] to [John Bowring].
   2. See 2 April [1828] to [John Bowring].
   3. Mérimée's witty hoaxes *The Comedies of Clara Gazul* (1828), *La Guzla* (1827), and *La Jacquerie* (1828) are all discussed in Mary Shelley's review "Illyrian Poems—Feudal Scenes," *Westminster Review* 10 (January 1829): 71–81 (see Bennett and Little, "Seven Letters from Mérimée to Mary Shelley," pp. 135–36).
   4. By 27 June Mary Shelley received her copy of *La Jacquerie* and began to read it (see 27 June [1828]).
   5. See 9 September [1827], n. 1; 2 April [1828] to [John Bowring], n. 3.
   6. The Chancellor of the Exchequer had appointed Bowring a commissioner for reforming the system of keeping the public accounts, but his appointment was canceled because the Duke of Wellington objected to Bowring's Benthamite politics.

To ISABELLA BAXTER BOOTH   Dover   15 June [1828]

My dear Girl   you will have heard from Mrs Godwin of my hateful illness and its odious results. Instead of returning to town as I most exceedingly desired—to join my friends there, and to see again my dear Isabel—I am fain to hide myself in the country, and as I am told sea bathing will assist materially the disappearance of the marks I remain on the coast.

   I shall long to see you again—to relate and to hear a thousand histories—if I make a longer stay in the country than I now intend perhaps you will join me—but I mean now to return with Percy at the end of his holidays, that is at the end of July.[1]

   I was sickening of my illness when I left town—my journey was so painful that I shudder at the recollection & I arrived only to go to bed. What will you say to my philosophy when at the end of three weeks, in brilliant health but as ugly as the———I went into society—I was well repaid for my fortitude, for I am delighted with the people I saw—and some I love and they merit my affection—What will you say also to the imagination of one of the cleverest men in France, young and a poet,[2] who could be interested in me in spite of the mask I wore. It was rather droll to play the part of an ugly person for the first time in my life, yet it was very amusing to be told—or rather not to be told but to find that my face was not all my fortune.[3]

   I have excellent news of my darling boy whom I long to see again—I hope you are well.   Mrs G. [*Godwin*] mentioned in her last letter that your children[4] had called there and that all seemed well wtih you. When I last saw you, dear friend I very little anticipated this long separation—not at all did I fear that I should avoid London on my return from Paris—instead of seeking it as I intended as speedily as possible—Patience! My malady has made me lose a year of my life—but in spite of the marks that still remain (I am in no danger of permanent disfigurement) I am in good health—& so different from my dreary state all last winter—and looking younger than when you saw me last—

Write to me,[5] dearest, and direct to me at J. Robinson Esq—Park Cottage, Paddington—& your letter will be forwarded—Early next week I go to Hastings.

My love to Isabel & Kate and remembrances to Mr Booth

Affectionately My Isabels
MS.

Have the goodness, love, to put the enclosed in the <u>twopenny post</u> for me.

PUBLISHED: Jones, #309. TEXT: MS., Bodleian Library (MS., Shelley, Adds., c. 6, f. 65).

   1. Percy Florence returned to London on 28 July (Godwin, Journal.)

   2. Prosper Mérimée.

   3. "My face is my fortune, Sir," from the anonymous nursery rhyme "Where Are You Going to, My Pretty Maid?"

   4. See 3 March 1828, n. 2.

   5. Isabella Booth responded to this letter on 24 June 1828. She wrote of her sad life and of her wish to reestablish her friendship with Mary Shelley: "It was by the sea coast where we first knew each other, and altho I often look back with bitterness upon the black fate which interposed to check every emotion between us, yet I bless myself that I have loved perhaps more perfectly on that account and that we are still preserved to one another" (Abinger MSS., Bodleian Library).

*To Jane Williams Hogg   Dover—20th June [1828]

I have been staying here, dearest Jane, from day to day even to weeks— I had intended to remain only 8 days—but an embroglio about money &c obliged me to remain—Mr Robinson joined us last Tuesday & brought Percy with him—he leaves us on Monday—& on the same day Julia & I depa{r}t for Hastings—we shall return at the end of his holydays—I am very well & really returning to my proper appearance—though still not fit to be seen—However in another Month I expect <u>nearly</u> to be myself again.

We have been dull enough here—nothing can be more stupid than the town—the weather has been gloomy   there are no walks—& to look at the coast of France & to wish myself in dear Paris again has been my only solace—I had hoped before I set out, to return to town, & several things promised to combine for my amusement—the exchange has been triste— but fate is to blame, not I—

I fancy your bower—sweet girl—it must be like all your homes, a little paradise—I wonder whether I shall ever have an home again—I own I do not wish for one now—for a lonely homeless home is worse than wandering—Do you remain another year where you are? And what of Jeff's professorship?[1]—How are the children?—I pity you in holiday time—for you must sacrifice quiet to elegance or elegance to quiet—and both are against your nature—How is the baby?

Where can Trelawny be?—He called before my return, on Papa[2]—got my address in Paris—said he was going to Bath for a month, & promised to write to me. I wrote to him to the post office Bath immediately on hearing this—but having had no answer; I suppose it has not reached its destination—Have you heard?—if you know his direction I pray you send it me without delay—I long, each day more to embrace the darling again— Have you heard from Claire?—She is reasonable, yes—I doubt not—but one's dear liberty—the difference of having one with whom one cannot sympathize, & being alone—But I ought not to indulge in these thoughts— I will do as I ought, & leave the rest to fate.—

Nothing can be more vile than this eternal rain which prevents one's sole amusement walking—however we read and talk—& I write—which is of most consequence of all. Julia is the most amiable little girl I ever knew— & being perfectly attached to me, I find her a very pleasing companion. We go to Hastings on Monday, so direct to me there.—If you can get hold of Count Segùr's memoirs[3] & read them they are excessively amuseing—I have tried to read Mme de Genlis' memoirs,[4] but they are one large capital I from beginning to end; this amuses at first—but tires long before we get to the end of 8 vols.—Above all, dear, get the Promessi Sposi[5]—at first you may lag a little, but as you get on the truth & perfect Italianism of the manners & descriptions—the beautiful language, which differs from all other Italian prose—being really the Tusca[n] of the day that he writes, & not a bad imitation of the [   ] trecentisti[6]—the passion & even sublimity of parts rendered it to me a most delightful book—I can imagine a person who had not been to Italy not liking it, but to us it must be delightful.

I have heard from no one—The whole Hunt faction seem lost—I shall however write to Statia[7]—for after all she & Arthur are too really good not to be loved—I get well so rapidly that I shall not prolong my absence from town beyond the end of July when I shall embrace again my graceful darling

Adieu sweetest

Affectionately Yours

MS.

ADDRESS: Mrs Jefferson Hogg / 22 Devonshire Place / Edgware Road / London. POSTMARKS: (1) DOVER / 22 JU 22 / 1828 / 72; (2) A / 23 JU 23 / 1828; (3) 10. F. NOON. 10 / JU. 23 / 1828. UNPUBLISHED. TEXT: MS., Abinger MSS., Bodleian Library.

1. Hogg was appointed to a law professorship at the newly founded University of London in 1829, but in 1831, before he began to teach, his position was canceled for financial reasons. Hogg printed his inaugural address, "An Introductory Lecture in the Study of Civil Law," in 1831 (Scott, Hogg, pp. 198–99).

2. Trelawny visited Godwin on 21 May 1828 (Godwin, Journal).

3. Louis Philippe, Comte de Ségur, Mémoires; or, Souvenirs et anecdotes, 3 vols. (Paris: A. Eymery, 1824–26).

4. Stéphanie Félicité du Crest de Saint-Aubin, Comtesse de Genlis, Mémoires inédits de madame la comtesse de Genlis (Paris and London: Colburn, 1825).

5. Alessandro Manzoni, I Promessi Sposi, 3 vols. (Milan: Presso Vincenzo Ferrateo, 1825– 26 [actually published 1827).

6. Fourteenth-century authors or artists.

7. Alistasia Gliddon.

*To [? Thomas Campbell]¹ Dover 22 June 1828

My dear Sir

I enclose One or two articles—and some verses, the productions of a gentleman now abroad who wishes to contribute to the New Monthly— He has as Mʳ David Lindsay² been the successful author of "The Dramas of the Ancient World"—He contributed at one time for Blackwood & for several of the Annuals—If the Articles I now send do not quite suit you, still if you were desirous of securing him & would make any suggestions as to subjects (he is in Paris) he would be very happy to attend to them; and his known talents certainly render him an acquisition of importance Would you have the goodness to direct your reply to me to the care of Mʳ Robinson Park Cottage Paddington—& an early one would oblige me

> I am, dear Sir
> Your Obedient Serᵗ
> MaryShelley

UNPUBLISHED. Quotation in Jones, #378. TEXT: MS., Pforzheimer Library.

1. Thomas Campbell (1777–1844; *DNB*), poet, was editor of the *New Monthly Magazine* from 1820 to 1830. Campbell was also a friend of Godwin's.

2. I.e., Mary Diana Dods, also known as Sholto Douglas.

To Venceslas-Victor Jacquemont¹ Hastings ce 27 Juin
[June 1828]

Monsieur,

Je vous donne beaucoup de la peine, j'en suis très fachée. Décachetez la lettre de Mme Douglas qui contienne un objet—faites le même de la lettre de Prosper. Si vous pouviez faire passer les simples lettres sans couper les sceau j'en serai charmée—sinon—il faut se soumettre aux stupides regles— coupez les et cachetez avant de les remettre. Je portai bien des lettre même en mes mâles, cachetées à la France, il y avait mêmes des grosses, qui contenaient des brochures et on les permettait à passer sans mot—on ne visite pas les mâles surtout d'Angleterre.

Je reçoive à l'instant une letter de Mérimée² qui demande réponse veuillez vous charger encore de celle ici. Son livre³ arriva hier. Je ne fais que le commencer.

Adieu Monsieur—encore bon voyage—encore portez vous bein. Re- tournez sauf à vos amis. Saluez les miens à Paris.

> M. S[helley]

[*Translation*]

Dear Sir,

I am causing you a great deal of trouble, I am very sorry for it. Unseal the letter of Mrs. Douglas which contains an article [*objet*]—do the same with the letter to Prosper. If you are able to pass them as plain letters without breaking the seal I shall be delighted—if not—it will be necessary to submit to the stupid regulations—break them and seal again before delivering them. I carried successfully several letters in my boxes, sealed to France, there were even some thick ones, which contained pamphlets and these were permitted to pass without examination—they do not inspect boxes, especially from England.

I have just this moment received a letter from Mérimée[2] which requires an answer—will you take charge of that one also. His book[3] has arrived yesterday. I have only begun reading it.

Adieu dear Sir—again bon voyage—again take care of yourself. Return safely to your friends. Salute mine at Paris.

M. S[helley]

PUBLISHED: Jones, #311. TEXT: Healy, "Mary Shelley and Prosper Mérimée," p. 395.

1. Jacquemont (1801–32), naturalist and voyager, was Mérimée's close friend. In June 1828 he visited London in preparation for his voyage to India. He returned to Paris on 2 July, left there for India on 26 August, and died at Bombay (Prosper Mérimée, *Correspondance Générale*, ed. Maurice Partuerier, 17 vols. [Paris: Le Divan (vols. I–VI); Toulouse: Privat (vols. VII–XVII), 1941–64], I, 14, 19, 30).

2. Mérimée's response to Mary Shelley's unlocated letter sent via Jacquemont reveals many details of what she wrote about: she advised Mérimée to care more for glory as an author than for love; she had embroidered and sent him a money pouch (perhaps the "article" referred to in her letter to Jacquemont); she asked him to keep secret their correspondence; and she spoke of her own loathing for life. By 28 July Mary Shelley had written that the *Carajal* pleased her more than *La Jacquerie* (see Bennett and Little, "Seven Letters from Mérimée to Mary Shelley," pp. 142–44).

3. *La Jacquerie.*

To JANE WILLIAMS HOGG   6 Meadow Cottages, Priory, Hastings—
            Saturday   (Sunday)   [28–29 June 1828]

I am delighted, my dear Jane, to hear of your brother's arrival,[1] and the comfort that he promises to be to you. This is a good turn of fortune—God send you many such! I am very sorry that I hurt you, yet glad I confess, that I awakened your pride—I cannot tell why, but we seem to stand more equally now. It is painful to go over old grounds—I go only on what you have allowed; long you gave ear to every idle & evil tale against me—& repeated them[2]—not glossed over—nor can I—tho' I allow myself changed, admit as just the sweeping sentence you pass over my early years—the past is dear to me—& I feel that tho' now more just to myself I was then as just to others as now   What can I say? My devotion to you was entire; the discovery caused so deep a wound, that my health sank under it—from the hour it was disclosed till my recovery from this odious illness I never knew health—You ask what good has been done—I must feel the truth a good—You speak of beings to whom I link myself—speak, I pray you, in the singular number—if Isabel has not answered your letter, she will—but the misery to which she is a victim is so dreadful and merciless, that she shrinks like a wounded person from every pang—and you must excuse her on the score of her matchless sufferings. What D. [*Doddy*] now is, I will not describe in a letter—one only trusts that the diseased body acts on the diseased mind, & that both may be at rest ere long. For the rest I look forward without hope or pleasure— it is summer weather, and so I am not often in ill spirits—I shut my eyes and enjoy—but a restless spirit stirring in my heart whispers to me that this is not life, & youth flies the while—I know the occasion and opportunity is only wanted, for me to feel some return of good—but it is vain to court these—they must come—& they will not while I am as I am now—so at least I have lost one year of my life—but I have gained so much in health—& even in good looks, when these marks disappear, that I will not too much repine,—and in a few weeks I hope not to be a fright, tho' it will take months to lose every trace.—My poor hair! it is a wonder I did not lose it all—but it has greatly suffered, and I am forced to keep it clipped still. How you would have pitied me!—

I like this place very much—the air is so pure and the sea bathing is so advantageous to Percy and myself that I earnestly desire to remain here another Month—Trelawny has written to me to return to town—I have replied by asking him to come here, and anxiously await his reply[3]—town would be odious—for I <u>will not</u> see people as I am. I had enough of that in Paris—we are as quiet as mice here—Papa is now down with us,[4] & returns to town on Monday—on which day we expect Mr Robinson—I do not find Percy altered—he is the same boy—without evil—& without sentiment—docile and querelous—self willed and yielding—unsocial yet frank—without one ill fold—and the open space apparently well fitted for culture but greatly requiring it.—

Poor Medwin![5]—from first to last—poor Medwin! I am glad he will not see me, or the Guiccioli would no longer be the ugliest woman he <u>ever saw in his life</u>[6]—I cannot say that I believe the scandal about Pierino[7]—that of the old Pope may be—but too much has been said & believed of me, for me to give ear to tales about others—I wrote to her[8] from Paris, but have had no answer—

The Hunts! how completely à la Marianne is the last procèdeur[9]—I suppose I should have had a visit—after her cutting me on Mary's account[10]—I can hardly pity her for she has her <u>consolation</u>[11]—but Hunt—What a fate—What a bitter & dread fate is his—& if we say it is partly his own fault, must one not accuse the Gods who formed him to his own ruin—it is the only comfort one has (& that a sorry one) in one's total inability to serve them, that it is impossible to render them service—I shall write to Statia—

Sontag & the Opera![12] I ought to be in London now—but that I should be as far from these delights there as here—I saw very little of these things in Paris for they were too expensive—I hope your brother will understand that happiness does not consist merely in a good dinner ⟨& g⟩ going to sleep after it—& going to bed at night,[13] but will forge amusement for his sweet sister—a brother! What a dear name if linked to affection! How I envy you—a dear Man person—on whom—the first best link not existing—one can repose as one's support in life, is a vain dream too generally. Friendships lead to love—or, quite certainly, to such scandal, as—as was my case, tarnishes the reputation and hurts the guiltless in the eyes of those with whom they would stand well—Fraternal ⟨feeli[ngs] are⟩ love is too often linked to fraternal tyranny—where it is not, it is the [   ] second blessing of life—for however devotedly one may love a woman, she can never support, defend, & protect as a Man.

Tomorrow I hope to know my fate from Trelawny—& I shall then finish this letter—God bless you, my pretty pet!—

(Sunday) No letter from our friend—I am sufficiently annoyed; the prospect of returning to town before the end of July is odious, but any thing is better than this suspense.

Dear Girl, I cannot tell you how sincerely and excessively I rejoice in the gain you have made this year. Has fortune done its worst and will it now be kind to you? To know that you are happy to see you surrounded by those who love—who worship you—to feel that your affectionate heart has a resource in this well you call it queer world is so true so real a pleasure to me that I thank our person[14] for it as good to myself—the greatest I have had this Many a day.

You perceive I cannot say when we meet—probably next week—certainly in a month.

Affectionately Yours
MS.

ADDRESS: Mrs Jefferson Hogg / 22 Devonshire Place / London / Edgware Road. POSTMARKS: (1) HASTINGS / JU 29 / 1828; (2) E / 30 JU 30 / 1828; (3) 10. F.NOON. [10] / JU. 30 / 1828. PUBLISHED: Jones, #312. TEXT: MS., British Library (Ashley 4022, ff. 1–2).

1. See [27 April 1828], n. 5.

2. See vol. I, 22 August [1827] to John Howard Payne, n. 1.

3. Mary Shelley received Trelawny's letter on 27 June 1828 (Paul, *Godwin*, II, 300). On 8 July Trelawny wrote from Southampton that he might soon visit at Hastings, but he fixed no date (Trelawny, *Letters*, pp. 111–12).

4. Godwin visited Mary and Percy Shelley from 25 June through 1 July 1828 (Godwin, Journal).

5. By mid 1828 Medwin was near financial ruin (Lovell, *Medwin*, p. 225).

6. Medwin's description of Teresa Guiccioli in a letter to Mary Shelley (Lovell, *Medwin*, p. 224).

7. Count Pietro Gamba.

8. Teresa Guiccioli (see 1 May 1828).

9. "Procedure, proceeding."

10. Perhaps a reference to Mary Hunt, who had accompanied Mary Shelley in the summer of 1827. At one time that summer Mary Shelley intended to keep Mary Hunt with her when she returned to London. However, Mary Shelley's 25 September 1827 plans to accompany the Douglases to Dieppe did not include Mary Hunt, and in all likelihood these plans caused Mary Shelley to send Mary Hunt home (see vol. I, 28 July 1827, 20 August 1827). In 1830 Hunt referred to a secret about Mary Hunt but did not reveal what it was (Brewer, *The Holograph Letters*, p. 192).

11. Marianne Hunt had become an alcoholic (Blunden, *Leigh Hunt*, p. 328; Hunt, *Autobiography*, I, 231).

12. A "Dramatic Concert" at the King's Theatre by Henriette Sontag, Countess Rossi (1806–54), had been announced for 25 June 1828 (*Morning Chronicle*, 25 June 1828).

13. An allusion to Hogg.

14. Previously published as "one person" (Jones, #312).

*To Jane Williams Hogg   Hastings   17 July [1828]

You are mistaken, dear Jane, in thinking that Trelawny is here—he is at Southampton, & I have not yet seen him—this is provoking—but time is so thick with disappointments, that it only adds one to the score—we lead here the most quiet & solitary of lives—but the place is beautiful & makes up to us for all. Our fine weather has changed to ecquinoctial gales and rains—but as each day affords many fine hours, the absence of great heat favours our expeditions—We are for ever in the open air, exploring the country and always finding our labors rewarded—The whole lan{d}scape is interspersed with hill & dale and beautiful woods—chiefly of small oak—the uplands are for the most part meadow lands which the rains keep green—sometimes we scramble among the cliffs overlooking the sea, whose ravines are cloathed with trees—sometimes we proceed inland towards the beautiful villages around. Unless we go to some regular shew place, we never meet a soul—the dear English love their cages five feet by three, and seldom quit them—except to ride & drive on the London road—which we of course cut. We remain out thus whole days—& though I am still a sad fright, my health is perfectly good—after the uncomfortable state I was in all last winter, I enjoy this extreme health to the utmost.

I had a letter today from Statia—they[1] are well and happy, they say, in the midst of all their disasters—blessed content of mind, and family union and sympathy! She says "Alas! poor Hunt!—We but know that he is more and more unfortunate—the particular embarrassment is hidden from us. They have left Highgate for Epsom, it was a hidden and mysterious movement, taking place when we were at Windsor—There is no immediate suffering however—for they have got into a nice furnished house, we hear, & could it continue it would be well—We have promised to visit them but it is now an expensive ride, Can he be happy without the society of his friends? Vincent[2] has been to see him & described him as having lost his spirits—all the family are well.—You would be delighted to see the change in Vincent—I never saw such riotous health and spirits—Mary is as feverish as ever—You saw that C.C.C. [*Charles Cowden Clarke*] had married Victoria—it has been a long time about. They are still in the country—They will continue to reside with Papa & Mama[3]—Werter[4] is now living with his father entirely."

Is not this last intelligence in strange coincidence with dear Vin's recovered health?

Your place must be very pretty now—are you not often in the ⟨pretty⟩ Kilburn[5] fields with your babes?—I suppose the pretty youngest pet can now almost speak—What a nest you have of it with your chicks about you—And your brother's children must be a resource to yours. Have you an instrument? I suppose not, though that of all others is the greatest shame in the world—I shall certainly make John (is not <u>Major</u> Cleveland his name) insist on your having one. <u>As</u> to the Shorediches,[6] what is it but a riffacciamento[7] of the Hunts—except that <u>he</u> plays the evil part—How a Man his wife & 8 can live on nothing is an enigma to poor <u>I</u> who get on so ill—Hunt finds some slight resource of course in his Companion—Good heavens! When we trudged out for furniture with Marianne, and put our little hearts into the Highgate arrangement, we did not foresee this—Of course if explained, no one w[d] be to blame—Once I should have credited a great part of such explanations—but now! Where will it end?—

Trelawny tells me that Tom[8] is in difficulties, & that he has returned to Italy—a picture speculation (witness Shorediche) is the last resort of ruin—With his palace—his horses—his routs & his passion to <u>far figura</u>,[9] I can easily believe that Tom, had he a million a year, would get incumbered. What does the <u>Countess</u>[10] say?—

I am not at all sure when I return to town—If I possib[ly] can I shall remain here during August—Every trace will not then be gone—nor for many months afterwards—but I shall be much better—& sea bathing is so strongly reccomended to me that I do not like giving it up. I had a letter from M[rs] Mason—who congratulates you & Jeff—She absolutely went to a <u>veglione</u>[11] with Laurette—her daughter—Lady Helena Robinson,[12] is at Pisa—and she is delighted with her—she says "Nothing can make M[r] T. [*Tighe*] break through his retired habits—so there is no danger of their meeting"—how queerly people arrange things—it were as well that the Dowager Countess married Signor Giorgio.[13]

If it were not too inconvenient to you I wish you would choose me a pretty coloured muslin or print—either of a lilac or green ground—it must not cost more than £1—if you could send it to the cottage by Sunday M[r] Robinson talks of coming down on Monday & would bring it—at any rate send it there, & it will reach me soon. Percy will return to town for school next week.

Remember me to Jeff—When I do come to town—I suppose it will be tolerably long before I quit it—yet—these visits of mine to the real country, make me hate it devotedly—You say nothing of the Professorship.[14] Charles Clairmont is come with his brood[15]—some planet surely causes arrivals this year—Claire will bring up the march[16]—Adieu sweetest—I hope to hear that you are in good health & spirits—remember me kindly to Mamina.

Affectionately Yours
MS.

ADDRESS: Mrs Jefferson Hogg / 22 Devonshire Place / Edgware Road. POSTMARKS: (1) HASTINGS / JY. 17 / 1828; (2) E / 18 JY 18 / 1828; (3) 10. F.NOON. 10 / JY. 18 / 1828. UNPUBLISHED. TEXT: MS., Abinger MSS., Bodleian Library.

1. The Gliddons family.
2. Vincent Novello.
3. Vincent and Mary Novello.
4. Edward Holmes.
5. Kilburn Wells, one mile northwest of Maida Hill.
6. See 7 September [1827] to Jane Williams Hogg, n. 4.
7. *Rifacimento*, "version."
8. Medwin had brought his paintings to London to sell them at Christie's on 2 July 1828—"A Sale of Italian Pictures property of a Gentleman." On 3 July 1828 he wrote to James Christie to ask how much he had gained through the sale (MS., Pforzheimer Library). The sale proved to be a major loss for Medwin (Lovell, *Medwin*, p. 223).
9. "Cut a good figure."
10. Medwin's wife.
11. "Masked ball."
12. Margaret Mason's daughter by her marriage to the earl of Mount Cashell.
13. Margaret Mason and George Tighe had married on 6 March 1826 (McAleer, *The Sensitive Plant*, p. 198).
14. See 20 June [1828], n. 1.
15. Charles Clairmont, his wife Antonie Ghi(s)lain d'Hembyze Clairmont (1800–1868), and their daughters Pauline (1825–91) and Clara (1826–55) arrived in London on 11 July 1828 (Godwin, Journal; *CC Journals*, p. 481).
16. See 16 May [1828], n. 3.

*TO JANE WILLIAMS HOGG   Park Cottage—Saturday
[9 August 1828][1]

I arrived, dear Jane, Thursday Evening, but most unhappily   I brought back my poor Julia[2] who had long been ailing so ill as to be at last delirious—you may guess how frightened I was—We sent immediately for a Doctor who feared a typhus—I sat up with her all night—yesterday we applied 16 leeches—I have not stirred from her—but now she is a little better—Tomorrow I must go to Papa who I have not seen; Monday Morning I will steal out to you for a few minutes—or longer if she continues mending—Pray dont let any one see me—I have been obliged to sacrifice the few remnants of my hair & am cropt—so my frightfulness is complete—Oh this odious illness!—

Ever Affectionately Yours
MS.

ADDRESS: Mrs Hogg / 22 Devonshire Place / Edgware Road. UNPUBLISHED. TEXT: MS., Abinger MSS., Bodleian Library.
1. Mary Shelley wrote in her Journal on 11 August 1828: "I returned here with my poor sick Julia—& remain here at peace." On 10 August Godwin recorded the visit mentioned in this letter (Godwin, Journal).
2. Julia Robinson.

To John Murray   Park Cottage—Paddington   20 August [1828]

My dear Sir

You were good enough to say that you would supply me with any book I might want for my novel. Will you let me have Leland's history of Ireland—Les Memoires de Philipe de Comines[1]—I want also some description of Cork which I suppose may be found in almost any minute travels in Ireland, but if you happened to know of one that treated more of the antiquities than as it now is, it would best suit my purpose.

I was sorry to hear from Mr Marshall that you decided against the Promessi Sposi[2]

I am dear Sir
Your Ob^t Servant
MaryShelley

ENDORSED: Augt 20 1828 / Shelley. Mrs. PUBLISHED: Jones, #313. TEXT: MS., John Murray.
1. For the parts of *Perkin Warbeck* set in Ireland, Mary Shelley requested: Thomas Leland, *The History of Ireland, from the Invasion of Henry II*, 3 vols. (London, 1773); and *Les Memoires*, published in 1524 and often reprinted.
2. Mary Shelley had probably offered to translate Manzoni's *I Promessi Sposi* (see 20 June [1828], n. 5). The work first appeared in English in 1828 as *The Betrothed Lovers* (Pisa: N. Capurro, 1828). In 1834 Richard Bentley published an anonymously translated edition.

To William Whitton Park Cottage   Paddington   1 September 1828

Dear Sir

I attend with anxiety the result of any communication you may have had with Sir Tim. Shelley on the increase of my allowance. As I remember you said, when first Sir Tim was kind enough to appoint a settled income for me, that you proposed 300£, and Sir Tim desired to delay this till Percy was older, I think you will have been good enough to represent my request aided by your influence. Now that Percy is at school the bills become heavy, and as I had hoped to have received the encreased allowance at Midsummer, I shall be embarassed from its having been refused. The school bills are above £60 p an—and his dress now is very expensive; I have not been able to pay the last quarter, and shall be seriously disappointed if Sir Tim is not good enough to consider these things and to make the advance I have been led to expect.

I had hoped to see you to explain this better in an interview, and to request your kind interference—but I was disappointed and did not find you. Percy spent his holidays with me by the seaside, and went back to school in excellent health and spirits—I have seen him since   he appears very happy, and Mr Slater is perfectly satisfied with him

Pray thank Sir Tim. for me for the kind interest he has shewn in him. It would give me great pleasure when he comes to town again if he permitted me personally to thank him.

> I am, Dear Sir
> Your Ob^t Servt
> Mary W. Shelley

ADDRESS: William Whitton Esq / Stone House / Tunbridge Kent. POSTMARKS: (1) SE / 1 / 1828; (2) 1828 / 7 / 1. SP / 7 / NIGHT. ENDORSED: 1st Sept 1828 / Mrs M. Shelley. PUBLISHED: Jones, #314. TEXT: MS., Bodleian Library (MS., Shelley, Adds., c. 6, ff. 66–67).

To WILLIAM WHITTON Park Cottage—Paddington   4 September 1828

Dear Sir

I wrote to you last Monday concerning my allowance from Sir Tim. Shelley, as this is the time when I receive a quarterly payment—I should not trouble you again but that I am fearful that I mistook your address—I directed it to you at Stone House Tunbridge Kent—As you will get this letter from the Post Office at Tunbridge if it has not been delivered, I will not repeat here what I said concerning the encrease of my allowance— become now through the expense, Percy puts me to, absolutely necessary

> I am Y^r Ob^t Ser^t
> MaryShelley

ADDRESS: William Whitton Esq / 18 Bedford Row—. POSTMARK: 7. NIGHT. 7 / 4. SP / 18[28]. ENDORSED: Sept. 4th 1828 / Mary Shelley. PUBLISHED: Jones, #315. TEXT: MS., Bodleian Library (MS., Shelley, Adds., c. 6, ff. 68–69).

To WILLIAM WHITTON   Park Cottage—Paddington
                                                         5 September—1828

Dear Sir

You will oblige me by sending me a cheque for £62-10—my quarterly allowance—

I am indeed disappointed by Sir Tim^y's refusal to encrease the payment—Percy's expenses encrease—and mine were already on the most economical footing I can devise—I have hitherto kept myself carefully free from embarassment, though with a difficulty of which you, who have never felt the extreme difficulty of living on so small an income, cannot be aware. The addition of the heavy school bills I shall be wholly unable to meet—What I am to do I cannot tell—I should like to see you first, for I think you would kindly advise me for the best; is it possible that if I wrote Sir Tim. stating the impossibility of living now that my son's expences are at least £100, on the same sum that barely sufficed when he did not cost me more than half that sum, that he would consent to make that addition which I cannot think it unreasonable in me to ask, and always trusted he would concede?

I am dear Sir—Y^r Ob^t Ser^t
MaryShelley

ADDRESS: W. Whitton Esq / Stone Wall / Tunbridge—Kent. POSTMARKS: (1) [   ]GTON / [   ] SP / [   ]; (2) 5. SP / 7. NIGHT. 7 / 1828. (3) [   ] SE / 5 / 1828 ENDORSED: 5th Sept 1828 / Mrs M. Shelley. PUBLISHED: Jones, #316. TEXT: MS., Bodleian Library (MS., Shelley, Adds., c. 6, ff. 70–71).

*To John Howard Payne   Park Cottage   Paddington   Tuesday
[9 September 1828]

My dear Payne
You have not heard from me for some time yet I have been very near town—but just now I am in no great mood to see old friends who would not recognize me—In a short time I hope—that is in the winter, to be once more visible—& myself—

After this you will think me mad to ask for orders for a theatre—but one escapes in a crowd & there are one or two things I want to see—Could you get me 3 or 4 orders (& places) for the Haymarket—If I could have them for Thursday I should like it—I want to see Miss F. H. Kelley in a good part—not melodramatic—& the Green eyed monster[1]—Can you arrange this for me—let me know soon—

I hear that all the affair of your <u>ruination</u>[2] is now well settled—tell me what your prospects & hopes are—This year, I know not why—has been unlucky to me & I long for it to be over—when I shall emerge as from a chrysalis—Believe me I am always truly & deeply interested in your projects & fortunes

Yours Ever
MS.

ADDRESS: John Howard Payne Esq / 29 Arundel St. Strand. POSTMARKS: (1) T.P [   ]; (2) 10. F.NOON. 10 / 10 SP / 1828. UNPUBLISHED. TEXT: MS., Pforzheimer Library.

1. Fanny Kelly played Julia in Sheridan's *The Rivals* on Thursday, 11 September, at the Haymarket Theatre. On 18 August Fanny Kelly appeared in the first production of James Robinson Planché's *The Green Eyed Monster*, a musical comedy, at the Haymarket. (*The Times* [London], 18–22 August, 11 September 1828; Nicoll, *English Drama*, p. 376). This letter's contents, together with an envelope sheet addressed to Payne dated Friday, 12 September 1828 (MS., Pforzheimer Library), dates a letter hitherto uncertainly dated [?February 1827–32] (vol. I) as [11 September 1828].

2. Payne's financial problems had begun in 1821 (see vol. I, [14 April 1825], n. 1).

*To [?   ]   Park Cottage   Paddington   [?1828–30][1]

My dear Sir
     Could you favor me by giving me admissions for your new Piece one evening when it shall next be played—You will very much oblige me
                                        Yours truly
                                        MaryShelley

UNPUBLISHED. TEXT: MS., Pforzheimer Library.
     1. This letter is placed here because Mary Shelley's first protracted visit to Park Cottage, the Robinsons' home, began on 9 August 1828, and her first indication that she was willing to attend the theater after her attack of smallpox was on 9 September 1828.

*To JOHN MURRAY   Park Cottage—Paddington   10 September 1828

Dear Sir
     I am obliged to you for the books you were good enough to send me—M[r] Crokers Volume[1] was quite to my purpose—Could you let me have some travels in Andalusia—descriptive of the Scenery—& if with plates they would assist me greatly—& still more if the descriptions dwelt upon the Antique Moorish remains[2]
                                        I am Dear Sir
                                        Y[r] Ob[t] Servant
                                        MaryShelley

ADDRESS: John Murray Esq / Albemarle Street. POSTMARKS: (1) 12. NOON. 12 / 10. SP / 1828; (2) [   ] / 10 SP / 1828. UNPUBLISHED: Jones, #317, in summary. TEXT: MS., John Murray.
     1. Thomas Crofton Croker (1798–1854; *DNB*), Irish antiquary and friend of Thomas Moore's, wrote a number of books about Irish folklore, his most famous being *The Fairy Legends and Traditions of the South of Ireland*, 3 vols. (London: John Murray, 1825–28).
     2. These works were for the Spanish settings in *Perkin Warbeck*.

*To John Howard Payne   [?Park Cottage]   Saturday
                      [?20 September–14 October 1828][1]

Send the orders for tonight by the bearer (3 or 4)—I shall be very glad of them—but as if I do not go to the theatre, I must make another arrangement for this evening—I must not be kept in uncertainty—So let me have them—or at least know for certain that I am to have them—the how many & when—If you get them for me tell the servant to take 6 places in my name front seats in the dress circle of the Haymarket—

Yours   MS.

ADDRESS: John Howard Payne Esq / 17 Speldhurst St. / Burton Crescent. UNPUBLISHED. TEXT: MS., Pforzheimer Library.
     1. This letter is placed here because John Howard Payne took quarters at 17 Speldhurst Street for the first time sometime in mid-September 1828 and the Haymarket season closed on 15 October 1828.

*To John Howard Payne   Tuesday   [?September 1828] (*a*)[1]
                                  44 Gower Place

May I depend on the tickets tomorrow—and what about the Lyceum Saturday—if we are to be disappointed will you if you conveniently can—send me word <u>here</u> before 8 this evening

Your^s
MS.

Looking at the bills I should prefer Friday instead of Saturday at the Lyceum—but if you have already asked for this order—it matters not

ADDRESS: J. Howard Payne Esq / 17 Speldhurst St. UNPUBLISHED. TEXT: MS., Pforzheimer Library.
     1. See the previous letter, n. 1.

*To John Howard Payne   Wednesday   [?September 1828] (*b*)
      Park Cottage—Park place near the Church   Paddington

Not hearing from you I send for the tickets—the places are secured—
Am I to have those for the Lyceum Friday or Saturday—& shall I send for them or can you dispatch them to me by the post—
You must be very good to excuse this annoyance—& yet I believe you do excuse it or I should not have the courage to inflict it—Truly Y^s MS.
[*Sideways*]   If you know any one going to Paris who w^d take charge of a letter or two & a book I should like it

ADDRESS: J. Howard Payne Esq / 17 Speldhurst St / Burton Crescent. UNPUBLISHED. TEXT: MS., Pforzheimer Library.

*To JOHN HOWARD PAYNE   [?Park Cottage   September 1828] (c)

Have you the Tickets for the Lyceum for tonight or tomorrow—can you give them to the Messenger—& will you direct her to take places or not to take them—for when & how—Arrange all this for me—or disarrange it by news that you have not the orders—but in all annoy yourself as little as you can

Adieu

ADDRESS: J. Howard Payne Esq / 17 Speldhurst St. UNPUBLISHED. TEXT: MS., Pforzheimer Library.

*To JOHN HOWARD PAYNE   Sundy   [?28 September 1828][1]
44 Gower Place

My Dr [Dear] Payne

I want very very much to oblige a friend with some orders for the Adelphi.[2]—Could you get me four for Tuesday. If you can send them to me here—If you cannot leave a line <u>here</u> on Tuesday informing me, as I shall get it earlier so—At any rate write as places must be taken.

Yrs try & obliged
Mary Shelley

UNPUBLISHED. TEXT: Copy, Payne, Letterbook, 1815–33.
    1. There was no Sunday followed by a Tuesday on which Mary Shelley was at Gower Place until 24 January 1832 (Godwin, Journal), by which time contact between Payne and Mary Shelley had diminished. I tentatively place this letter here because of Mary Shelley's letter of [29 September 1828], supposing that Payne may have written to tell her that he could get tickets for Wednesday rather than Tuesday.
    2. *Wanted a Partner,* with Charles Mathews; *My Absent Son;* and *Presumptive Evidence* played at the Adelphi Theatre on Tuesday, 30 September 1828 (*The Times* [London]).

*To JOHN HOWARD PAYNE   Park Cottage near the Church—
Paddington   [29 September 1828]

Dear Payne

Don't think me quite mad but I do <u>not</u> go to Papa's tomorrow—so the tickets must come <u>here</u>—let me have them tomorrow if you can—or as early as possible Wednesday Morning

Yours (very trouble some {)}
MS.

ADDRESS: J Howard Payne Esq / 17 Speldhurst St.   Burton Crescent. POSTMARKS: (1) T.P / Maida Hill; (2) 12. NOON. 12 / 30. SP 1828. UNPUBLISHED. TEXT: MS., Pforzheimer Library.

*To Sutton Sharpe[1]　　　　　　　　　　Park Cottage　Paddington
　　　　　　　　　　　　　Thursday Eve^g　[?October 1828] (*a*)[2]

You despair easily—Captain Parry[3] was not so easily deterred from seeking
the Norths Pole　Will you not make another attempt—Call if you can on
Saturday Morning—or fix some other day when I may have the pleasure
of seeing you

　　　　　　　　　　　　　　　　　　　　　　　I am &c &c
　　　　　　　　　　　　　　　　　　　　　　　MaryShelley

UNPUBLISHED. TEXT: MS., University College, London.
　　1. Sutton Sharpe (1797–1843), English attorney, was a close friend of Prosper Mérimée,
Stendhal, and their circles (see Doris Gunnell, *Sutton Sharpe et ses amis français* [Paris: Librairie
Ancienne Honore Champion, 1925]).
　　2. Mérimée asked Sharpe, who was about to return to London from Paris after a month's
visit, to carry two letters to Mary Shelley and to deliver them personally. One of the letters
contained some ballads by Mérimée which Mary Shelley is believed to have translated, but
the translations have not been located (Mérimée, *Correspondance générale*, I, 29–30). In his
letter of Sunday, 5 October 1828, Mérimée informed Mary Shelley that he would send her
some ballads forthwith. Mérimée's letter of 29 October 1828, in which he asks for news of
"mon ami, & le votre, j'espere Mr. S. Sharpe," indicates that by that time Sharpe had visited
Mary Shelley (Bennett and Little, "Seven Letters from Mérimée to Mary Shelley," pp. 147,
149).
　　3. Sir William Edward Parry (1790–1855; *DNB*), English admiral and arctic explorer, published a number of works describing his explorations, including *A Narrative of an Attempt to
Reach the North Pole . . . in the year 1827* (London: The Admiralty, 1828).

*To Sutton Sharpe　　Park Cottage　Thursday　[?October 1828](*b*)

Mrs Shelley will {be} very happy to see Mr Sutton Sharpe on Saturday
Morning　Mrs Shelley sends the bearings by which Mr Sharpe may be
enabled to make the Cottage, he has been unable to find[1]—Paddington
Green—the Church—cross the Church yard—the first turning to the right—
the last <u>iron</u> gate, through the garden—in at the first open door.—
　　If Mr Sharpe is engaged on Saturday on any of the succeeding mornings
he will find Mrs Shelley at home.

UNPUBLISHED. TEXT: MS., University College, London.
　　1. See the previous letter.

*To Charles Ollier　　Park Cottage　Paddington　14 October, 1826
　　　　　　　　　　　　　　　　　　　　　　[error for 1828][1]

My dear Sir
　　I do not know how far you can assist me to a few <u>old</u> & one foreign book
that I need to assist me in the work on which I am at present engage—but

you will very much oblige me if you can—the work for which I am in the greatest hurry is one of Leland's (Hist of Ireland) Authorities—he merely gives the name "Ware"[2]—I want to consult his history of the years from 1485 until 1500. I want also the Chronicles of the Abbott of Croyland[3]— there is a work called Savilles collection of the Monkish Chroncles &—the foreign work is L'histoire des Ducs de Bourgogne par M. de Barante[4]—

I believe you are good enough not to need many apologies from me and the assistance you will afford me will be great

I am dear Sir

Your Ob^t Servant
MaryShelley

ADDRESS: Charles Ollier Esq / 8 New Burlington St. POSTMARKS: (1) T.P / Maida Hill; (2) 7. NIGHT. 7 / 16. OC /1828. UNPUBLISHED. TEXT: MS., British Library (Add. 42,577, ff. 150–51).

1. See postmarks.

2. Sir James Ware (see 20 August [1828], n. 1).

3. *Ingulphi Abbatis Croylandensis Historiaram* is included in Sir Henry Saville, *Rerum Anglicarum Scriptores post Bedam praecipui* (London, 1596) (William Thomas Lowndes, *The Bibliographer's Manual of English Literature* [London: Bell and Daldy, 1869], IV, 2195).

4. Prosper Mérimée's letter of 5 October 1828 lists a number of historical works that Mary Shelley had asked for in her next to last letter to him (unlocated). Among those included are "les memoires de Ph. de Commines," which he notes she is already acquainted with, and "de l'hist. des ducs de Bourgogne par Mr. de Barante" (Amable G. P. Brugière, Baron de Barante, *L'Histoire des ducs . . . 1364–1477*, 13 vols. [Paris: Ladvocat, 1824–26]) (Bennett and Little, "Seven Letters from Mérimée to Mary Shelley," p. 146).

---

*TO [?CHARLES OLLIER]   Park Cottage   Monday   [?20 October 1828]

My dear Sir

I am very much obliged to you for the books—I still keep the O'Hara Tales,[1] not having quite finished them—I certainly exonerate the Anglo Irish from the charge of impropriety—but I do not think it as clever as the Nowlans—

If you have the set of New Monthlys & could spare me the last twelve numbers you would greatly oblige me—

Do you think that there exists in any of the libraries here a copy of the French translation of Karamsin's History of Russia[2]—Hookham has it not— has Ebers?[3]—

With many thanks—I am

Your Obed^t Servant
MaryShelley

Are there any new books come out <u>quite</u> lately, you would recommend—

UNPUBLISHED. TEXT: MS., Pforzheimer Library.

1. John Banim and Michael Banim [Barnes O'Hara and Abel O'Hara], *Tales by the O'Hara Family,* 2d ser., 3 vols. (London: Henry Colburn, 1826), which included "The Nowlans."

2. Nikolai Mikhailovich Karamsin, *Istoriya gosudarstva rossiyskogo* [History of the Russian state], 12 vols. (Saint Petersburg: Voennaia tipograffiia, 1816–29); or in French: *Histoire de l'empire de Russie, par m. Karamsin,* trans. St. Thomas and Jauffert, 11 vols. (Paris: A. Belin, 1819–26).

3. John Ebers (see vol. I, 30 May [1825], n. 3), opera manager and bookseller, whose shop was located at 27 Old Bond Street.

*TO JOHN HOWARD PAYNE   Teusday [28 October 1828] (*a*)[1]
                                                       Park Cottage

Dear Payne

I have been expecting to see you & now am about to indite a billêt on the usual <u>selfish</u> object—We want to see Othello Thursday[2] can you get us 4 orders—I am the more ready to ask as though Kean draws to the pit the boxes are nearly empty—Will you bring them & go with us—but at any rate let m[e] know—

                                                   Yours Ever
                                                   MS.

UNPUBLISHED. TEXT: MS., Pforzheimer Library.

1. Payne's Letterbook copy of this letter is dated 28 October 1828. See also the following letter.

2. *Othello,* starring Edmund Kean, played at Covent Garden on Thursday, 30 October 1828 (*The Times* [London]).

TO JOHN HOWARD PAYNE   Tuesday [28 October 1828] (*b*)
                                                       Park Cottage

I have written to you at Arundel St—but as I fear the note may miss you (remember the other note is a <u>pretty</u> one this is in haste—) I write also to your other habitation to ask you to obtain 4 orders for Thursday for Covent Garden—Kean does not draw to the boxes—pray let us know soon—& come with us if you can

ADDRESS: J. Howard Payne Esq / 17 Speldhurst St / Burton Crescent. POSTMARKS: (1) T.P / Crawford St; (2) 10. F.NOON. 10 / 28. OC / 1828. PUBLISHED: Jones, #318. TEXT: MS., Huntington Library (HM 10794).

TO THOMAS CROFTON CROKER   Park Cottage—30th October [1828]

Sir

I cannot sufficiently thank you for the politeness with which you have replied to my requests—I am very sorry that I was out yesterday evening, as then I could in person have apologized for my unceremonious application—Will you afford me another opportunity for so doing?—If you will call on Saturday Morning you will add to my other obligation by allowing me to destroy any strange impression I may have made—

By some mistake there is an error in your idea of what I want—it is the easiest way to tell you my object and then you will understand my need—I am writing a romance founded on the story of Perkin Warbeck—I have just brought him for the first time to Ireland—The Antiquary is therefore of more use to me than the historian—After all I must rest satisfied with a very imperfect sketch, as never having been in Ireland, & being very ignorant of its history, I shall fall into a thousand mistakes—to diminish this number as much as possible I have applied to you—

You seem to have imagined me employed in sober useful history instead of my usual trifling—Were I indeed the least learned I might give interest to my pages by a picture of manners & incidents little known—If I get beyond mere generalities—helped or disfigured by ⟨the⟩ my imagination I must owe it to you—

If Saturday is not convenient let it be some other day

I am, Sir

Your obedient Servt

MaryShelley

PUBLISHED: La Tourette Stockwell, "Two Unpublished Letters of Mary Wollstonecraft Shelley," *Dublin Magazine* 8, no. 2 (April–June 1933): 43–44. TEXT: MS., National Library of Ireland.

*TO JOHN HOWARD PAYNE   [?Park Cottage] Tuesday Ev^g

[4 November 1828]

Miss Robinson requests me to say that she shall be delighted to see your young friend

Yours very truly

MS.

ADDRESS: J. Howard Payne Esq / 17 Speldhurst St.   Burton Cresc[ent]. POSTMARKS: (1) T.P / Up Berkeley St; (2) 12. NOON. 12 / 5. NO / 1828. UNPUBLISHED. TEXT: MS., Washington University Library.

*TO CHARLES OLLIER   Park Cottage Monday

[?17 November 1828][1]

My dear Sir

With many thanks I return your books—The Man of two Lives[2] is founded on a good idea—treated to great degree happily—yet it strikes me to be a translation—the phrases, the thoughts—the incidents are so truly German.

I wrote to Mr Colburn the other day asking for a copy of the Last Man—
he has not replied—will you obtain one for me & get it sent directed to
E.J. Trelawny Esq Fladong's Hotel Oxford St.—

I am Dr Sir
Y^r Obt Ser^t
MaryW. Shelley

ADDRESS: Charles Ollier Esq / 5 Maida Hill. UNPUBLISHED. TEXT: MS., Pforzheimer Library.
    1. This letter is dated on the basis of its references to Trelawny. In November–December
1828 Trelawny stayed at Fladong's Hotel, 144 Oxford Street. His 14 November 1828 letter
to Mary Shelley from the hotel indicated that he wanted to read *Valperga* and *The Last Man*
(*S&M*, IV, 1118).
    2. James Boaden, *The Man of Two Lives*, 2 vols. (London: H. Colburn, 1828).

TO WILLIAM WHITTON   1 December 1828 (*a*)
                                                    Park Cottage   Paddington

Dear Sir
    I am disappointed to find that Sir Timothy has not apparently been in
town & that no opportunity has been afforded me for seeing him. I do not
know how far you will judge it right to lay the accompanying letter[1] before
him, and I beg you to use your own judgement upon it—the simple facts
I state will shew you how necessary it is for me to receive an augmentation
of income without which I cannot keep from the embarassment I have
hitherto so sedulously avoided. You will be so good as to let me hear from
you on the subject soon

I am Y^{rs} Ob^{ly}
MaryW. Shelley

ADDRESS: W. Whitton Esq. ENDORSED: 1st Decr 1828 / Mrs Shelley. PUBLISHED: Jones,
#320. TEXT: MS., Bodleian Library (MS., Shelley, Adds., c. 6, ff. 74–75).
    1. See the next letter.

TO WILLIAM WHITTON   1st December—1828 (*b*)
                                                    Park Cottage—Paddington

Dear Sir
    Now that the period of the payment of my allowance is come, I become
anxious to know whether Sir Timothy will attend to my request of augmenting it. I feel quite sure that if Sir Tim^{thy} were fully aware of the necessity
he would not refuse. I cannot charge myself with any extravagance and yet
I find the present sum quite inadequate—I do not know whether it is
understood that my visit to France occasioned _no_ additional expence to my

usual mode of living—I went with a friend, I staid with a friend during the very few weeks I remained there—it seems almost needless to assert this, as with the extreme economy I practice, I had nothing to spare for a journey of any sort. I have told you that nothing could prevent my attending to Percy's bills in the first place—a half year, which with extras cannot be less than £30, will be due this Christmas, besides his taylor's bill—how I can pay these and live for three months—six weeks of which he will be at home with me for the holydays, on the payment I have hitherto received, I am at a loss to conjecture.

Will you lay this statement before Sir Timothy. Perhaps when he again comes to town he will permit me a pleasure I have long desired, namely—of seeing him; at any rate I beg you to assure him of my respect and thanks

I am Y^r Ob^t Ser^t

MaryW. Shelley

ADDRESS: William Whitton Esq / 18 Bedford Row. POSTMARKS: (1) T.P / [   ]dal St; (2) 7. N[   ]. ENDORSED: 1st Decr 1828 / Mrs Shelley. PUBLISHED: Jones, #319. TEXT: MS., Bodleian Library (MS., Shelley, Adds., c. 6, ff. 70–71).

To WILLIAM WHITTON   Park Cottage   9 December [1828]

My Dear Sir

I trust that on Sir Timothy's visit to town I shall have the honor of seeing him—in which case I should not wish my letter to be given him. Otherwise I must rely on his kindness, on which I found my application, that he will not be displeased by a request forced from me by necessity only—and which he at one time seemed to justify by the prospect held out to me that my allowance would be encreased on Percy's going to school. If therefore I should be prevented from seeing Sir Tim^y—will you present my letter with such explanation from you as may efface any idea of my pressing too much upon him.

I forward the rece^t would you have the goodness to send me cash instead of a cheque in the city—but if this is inconvenient give the cheque unin-closed to the bearer who will go on for the money.

I am Y^s Ob^{ly}

MaryShelley

ENDORSED: 9th Decr 1828 / Mrs Shelley. PUBLISHED: Jones, #321. TEXT: MS., Bodleian Library (MS., Shelley, Adds., c. 6, ff. 76–77).

To John Howard Payne   Wednesday [10 December 1828]
                                                    Park Cottage

I hope you are alive though I begin to be a little fearful on that point—if
you are, my dear Friend, have the goodness, if you can contrive it—to send
me 2 admissions to Drury Lane for Saturday[1]—& add to the favor by being
in the theatre at 1/4 to seven to attend us to our places

                                                    Yours Ever
                                                    MS.

ADDRESS: John Howard Payne Esq / Arundel St / Strand. POSTMARKS: (1) T.P / G[   ];
(2) 12. NOON. 12 / 12. DE / 1828. PUBLISHED: Jones, #322. TEXT: MS., Huntington Library
(HM 10795).
    1. On Saturday, 13 December 1828, *Ups and Downs; Love in Wrinkles;* and *Charles the
Twelfth* played at Drury Lane (*The Times* [London]).

*To John Howard Payne   Park Cottage—Monday
                                                    [22 December 1828]

I have not seen you as you promised—are you not a wrong person? I hope
nothing disagreable has prevented you—and that I shall see you soon—
    I wish very much to see Virginius—I am afraid the Pantomime may render
this difficult—but I should be glad if you can arrange 4 orders for next
Monday[1]—
    After tomorrow I leave my present peaceful hospitable abode—you will
find me at 4 Oxford Terrace—Edgware Road[2]—you will find it by walking
to the very end of the New Road—& then it is opposite to you.

                                                    Ever yours
                                                    MS.

ADDRESS: J. Howard Payne Esq / 17 Speldhurst St.   Burton Crescent. POSTMARKS: (1) T.P /
Woo[xton]; (2) 7. NIGH[T. 7] / 22. [DE] / 1828. UNPUBLISHED. TEXT: MS., Washington
University Library.
    1. *Virginius* had been announced for Monday, 29 December 1828, but *Hamlet* was given
instead (*The Times* [London]).
    2. Mary Shelley lived at Oxford Terrace until May 1829. Claire Clairmont, who had returned
to London on 16 October 1828, went to live with Mary Shelley on 24 December 1828
(Godwin, Journal).

*To Charles Ollier   Monday [?December 1828–May 1829]
                                                    4 Oxford Terrace

My Dear Sir
    A relation of mine, Mr Clairmont, wishes to do himself the pleasure of
calling on you,[1] to converse upon some literary project—or subject—I,

supposing that the evening would suit you best, appointed him for Wednesday Evening   Shall you be at home—and disengaged to receive him—

If you can arrange to call here some morning between 12 & two this week, I shall be glad to see you

Y^r Ob^t Servant
MaryShelley

ADDRESS: Charles Ollier Esq / 5 Maida Hill. UNPUBLISHED. TEXT: MS., Pforzheimer Library.
    1. On 26 May 1829, Godwin wrote a letter introducing Charles Clairmont to Henry Colburn (MS., Victoria and Albert Museum).

*TO JOHN HOWARD PAYNE   Oxford Terrace   Saturday
                                                [3 January 1829]

Love in Wrinkles[1] is never to be played it seems—I will be content therefore with Liston & Charles XII—let us go Tuesday[2] if you can arrange it

4 Tickets you know—And then also I shall have the pleasure of seeing you

Yours Ever
MS.

ADDRESS: J. Howard Payne / 17 Speldhurst St. / Burton Crescent. POSTMARKS: (1) T.P / T[ottenham Ct]; (2) 4. EVEN. 4 / 3. JA / 1829. UNPUBLISHED. TEXT: MS., Pforzheimer Library.
    1. See [10 December 1828], n. 1. *Love in Wrinkles* played eleven times altogether, beginning with its opening performance on 4 December 1828 (Genest, *English Stage*, IX, 459).
    2. On Tuesday, 6 January 1829, *Charles the Twelfth*, with John Liston; *The Illustrious Stranger*; and *The Queen Bee* played at Drury Lane (*The Times* [London]).

*TO JOHN HOWARD PAYNE   4 Oxford Terrace.   Wednesday
                                                [7 January 1829]

My dear Payne

It was vexatious that I could not profit by your kindness on Monday—perhaps if Virginius is performed next Monday you can arrange one ticket for me—if so bring it with you when we meet at the Cottage on Saturday—I am very glad this opportunity is afforded me of seeing you

Ever yours
MS.

ADDRESS: J. Howard Payne Esq / 17 Speldhurst St. / Burton Crescent. POSTMARKS: (1) PADDINGTON / 7 JA / 1829; (2) 7. NIGHT. 7 / 7. JA / 1829. UNPUBLISHED. TEXT: MS., Pforzheimer Library.

To WILLIAM WHITTON   4 Oxford Terrace   Edgeware Road
                                                    15 Jan^{ry} 1829

Dear Sir

I inform you as you ask that the death of Mr Shelley took place on the
8th July 1822—

I do not know whether you have thought it advisable to mention the
encrease of my income to Sir Timothy—I enclose you Percy's half year's
bill, not as a thing to be presented to Sir Timothy—but merely to shew
you that my statements are not exagerated, and that with the addition of
his taylor's account, Percy costs me a sum that makes my income less than
when I had only £200 P. Ann—I hope this will be considered before next
quarter as otherwise I shall be considerably embarassed

                                        I am Y^r Ob^t Servant
                                        MaryW. Shelley

PUBLISHED: Jones, #325. TEXT: MS., Bodleian Library (MS., Shelley, Adds., c. 6, ff. 78–
79).

To JOHN BOWRING   4 Oxford Terrace   3 Feb^{ry} [1829]

I have received the cheque for £5-5[1]   I was unaware that the article[2]
was of such instant necessity—or that the W.R. [*Westminster Review*] would
appear so soon—The subject is not France but Italy—Do you intend that
I should not complete it?—At present I am too much occupied by my novel
to be able to give you much time—but if you wish for my assistance & can
think of some work which would only require a short easy notice I will
accomplish it—& do better still for the number After—

I am very glad to hear of your child's convalescence—you are better off
than poor Moore—whose only little girl will I fear hardly recover[3] & whose
long protracted suffering is a sad misfortune—

                                        I am very truly Ys
                                        MaryShelley

ADDRESS: John Bowring Esq / 7 North Place / Gray's Inn Lane. POSTMARKS: (1) T.P / Crawford
St; (2) 7. NIGHT. 7 / 4. FE / 1829. ENDORSED: (1) Feb 13 1829 / Mary Shelley; (2) Mary
Shelley / 3 Feby 1829. PUBLISHED: Jones, #326. TEXT: MS., Huntington Library (HM 2760).
    1. For Mary Shelley's January review article on Mérimée's works see 11 June [1828], n. 3.
    2. See 2 April [1828] to [John Bowring], n. 4.
    3. Anastasia Mary Moore (b. March 1813), Thomas Moore's second daughter, died on 8
March 1829 (Howard Mumford Jones, *The Harp That Once* [New York: Henry Holt and Co.,
1937], pp. 153, 268–69).

*To John Howard Payne   4 Oxford Terrace   Friday
                                        [13 February 1829]

My dear Payne

Can you get me an Opera box for Teusday[1]—considering that the audiences are not numerous—& on Tuesday—I suppose they are worse than
Saturday—perhaps you can get a <u>decent</u> one—Will you also make one of
us there—which will please us all

                                                    Adieu
                                                    Yours

(I shall sign no name pour <u>raison</u>)[2]

ADDRESS: John Howard Payne Esq / 17 Speldhurst St. / Burton Crescent. POSTMARKS: (1)
T.P / Devon St M [   ]; (2) 7. NIGHT. 7 / 13. FE / 1829. UNPUBLISHED. TEXT: MS.,
Pforzheimer Library.
    1. Rossini's *L'Italiana in Algieri* was advertised for the King's Theatre for Tuesday, 17
February 1829 (*The Times* [London]).
    2. "Raison" is underlined seven times in the manuscript.

*To John Howard Payne   Thursday   [27 February 1829]
                                    4 Oxford Terrace   Edgeware Road

My dear Payne

Could you get me four Admissions for Covent Garden for Saturday[1]—
How is your cold?—My Cottagers complain much of your stinginess in
never seeing them—for my self I do not complain—but I should be glad
to see you—will you call on Sunday

                                                    Y^s
                                                    MS.

Could you get me a gallery order for either of the theatres for a day early
next week—

ADDRESS: John Howard Payne Esq / 17 Speldhurst St. / Burton Crescent. POSTMARKS: (1)
T.P / Crawford St; (2) 4. EVEN. 4 / 27. FE / 1829. UNPUBLISHED. TEXT: MS., Pforzheimer
Library.
    1. Farquhar's *The Beaux' Stratagem* played at Covent Garden on Saturday, 28 February 1829
(*The Times* [London]).

To Edward John Trelawny   London—April—1[829]

My dear Trelawny

Your letter reminded me of my ⟨mis⟩deeds of omission and of not writing
to you as I ought—and it assured me of your kind thoughts in that happy

land, where, as Angels in heaven, you can afford pity to us Arctic islanders—
It is too bad, is it not? that when such a Paradise does exist as fair Italy—
one should be chained here?—Without the infliction of much absolutely
cold weather—I have never suffered a more ungenial winter—winter it is
still—a cold east wind has prevailed for the last six weeks, making exercise
in the open air a positive punishment—This is truly English! half a page
about the weather—but here this subject has ⟨all the⟩ every importance—
it is fine—you guess I am happy and enjoying myself—is it—as it always
is—you know that one is fighting against a domestic enemy—which saps
the very foundation of pleasure.

I am glad that you are occupying yourself—and I hope that your two
friends will not cease urging you till you really put to paper the strange
wild adventures you recount so well.[1] With regard to the other subject—
you may guess, my dear Friend, that I have often thought—often done more
than think on the subject   There is nothing I shrink from more fearfully
than publicity—I have too much of it—& what is worse I am forced by my
hard situation to meet it in a thousand ways—Could you write my husband's
life, without naming me it were something—but even then I should be
terrified at the rouzing the slumbering voice of the public—each critique,
each mention of your work, might drag me forward—Nor indeed is it
possible to write Shelley's life in that way. Many men have his opinions—
none fearlessly and conscientiously act on them, as he did—it is his act that
marks him—and that—You know me—or you do not, in which case I will
tell you what I am—a silly goose—who far from wishing to stand forward
to assert myself in any way, now than I am alone in the world, have but
the desire to wrap night and the obscurity of insignificance around me. This
is weakness—but I cannot help it—to be in print—the subject of <u>men's</u>
observations—of the bitter hard world's commentaries, to be attacked or
defended!—this ill becomes one who knows how little she possesses worthy
to attract attention—and whose chief merit—if it be one—is a love of that
privacy which no woman can emerge from without regret—Shelley's life
must be written—I hope one day to do it myself, but it must not be published
now—There are too many concerned to speak against him—it is still too
sore a subject—Your tribute of praise, in a way that cannot do harm, can
be introduced into your own life—But remember, I pray for omission—
for it is not that you will not be too kind too eager to do me more than
justice—But I only seek to be forgotten—

Claire has written to you—She is about to return to Germany[2]—She will
I suppose explain to you the circumstances that make her return to the lady
she was before with, desirable—She will go to Carlsbad and the baths will
be of great service to her. Her health is improved—though very far from
restored. For myself I am as usual, well in health—occupied—and longing
for summer when I may enjoy the peace that alone is left for me—I am
another person under the genial influence of the sun—I can live unrepining
with no other enjoyment but the country made bright and cheerful by its

beams—till then I languish. Percy is quite well—he grows very fast and looks very healthy—

It gives me great pleasure to hear from you, dear Friend—do write often—I have now answered your letter though I can hardly call this one—so you may very soon expect another—Take care of yourself—How are your dogs? & where is Roberts—have you given up all idea of shooting. I hear Medwin is a great man at Florence—so Pisa and economy are at an end[3]—Adieu

Yours
MS.

[*P. 1, above address*]   (direct to me at my Father's 44 Gower Place—Gower St. and to Claire at 5 Carmarthen St—Tottenham C^t Road {)}

ADDRESS: Edward Trelawny Esq / Ferma in Posta / La Toscane / Firenze / L'italie. POSTMARKS: (1) [?22] / G[   ] / 1829; (2) 12 / JUIN / 1829; (3) Pont / B[EAU]VOISIN; (4) GENOVA [   ]. PUBLISHED: Jones, #329. TEXT: MS., Keats-Shelley Memorial House, Rome.

1. On 11 March 1829, Trelawny wrote from Florence to inform Mary Shelley that he was writing an autobiography, for which he wished her to provide documents and anecdotes about Shelley. He also mentioned that Charles Armitage Brown and Walter Savage Landor (whom Trelawny met in 1828) were assisting him and were "to review it sheet by sheet, as it is written" (Trelawny, *Letters*, pp. 116–18). According to Brown's son, Brown's assistance extended to rewriting Trelawny's *Adventures*, which Trelawny acknowledged by sharing with him the proceeds of the 1831 and 1835 editions (Brown, *Letters*, p. 292, n.5). Although Mary Shelley declined to provide Trelawny with biographical data about Shelley, she did arrange for the publication of the *Adventures* by Richard Bentley in 1831 and saw it through the press because Trelawny was in Italy. Trelawny first intended to call his story *Treloen*, but in order to remain anonymous, he changed the title to *A Man's Life*. A misunderstanding, however, led to the publication under the title selected by Mary Shelley and the publishers, the *Adventures of a Younger Son*. Trelawny's intention to write a life of Shelley was fulfilled with his 1858 *Recollections*, in which he favorably commented on Mary Shelley, and with his revised and republished 1878 *Records*, in which he viciously maligns Mary Shelley (pp. 229–32).

2. Claire Clairmont left for Dresden to rejoin the Kaisaroffs on 18 September 1829 (Godwin, Journal).

3. By September 1829 Medwin, penniless, permanently left his wife and children. In 1830 bankers won a judgment against him for thirty thousand lire. During this period Trelawny and Brown assisted Mrs. Medwin in the tangle of financial difficulties that followed Medwin. Trelawny also provided her with funds (Lovell, *Medwin*, pp. 223–40).

TO JOHN HOWARD PAYNE [?Park Cottage] Monday [6 April 1829]

May I ask you to use your influence for an Opera box for next Thursday[1]—or an early succeeding night—You would highly oblige & please me—& also if you would accompany us—I shall be at the Cottage[2] for the next week—Where I hope to see or hear from you

I was very sorry to find you called the other day when I was from home—Will you try me again

Yours
MS.

ADDRESS: For / John Howard Payne Esq / 29 Arundel St. / Strand. POSTMARKS: (1) T.P / Crawford St.; (2) 8. MORN. 8 / 7. AP / 1829. PUBLISHED: Jones, #328. TEXT: MS., Huntington Library (HM 10796).
    1. Rossini's *La Gazza Ladra* was scheduled for the King's Theatre for Thursday, 9 April 1829 (*The Times* [London]).
    2. Park Cottage, the Robinsons' home.

To Cyrus Redding   [?Park Cottage or 33 Somerset Street
                                                    ?7 April–June 1829][1]

Dear Sir,

I am sorry to have it only in my power to reply that the portrait of Mr. Shelley, to which you allude, is by no means a good one:—it is the size of life in oil, but unfortunately very unfinished. There are, however, several very striking points of resemblance, and I indulge a hope that when I can afford it, a first-rate engraver might succeed in making a good print of it. I do not know anything so disagreeable or unjust, as the too frequent custom of prefixing prints unworthy of the persons represented, and in this case there would be great danger that even Mr. Heath[2] would not succeed. I should therefore be averse to having it done, unless by him, and unless it were in my power to cancel it altogether if I did not approve of it.

If it had been otherwise—if the picture had been one which would only have needed fidelity and care, I should have been happy to have furnished you with an opportunity of making an engraving, and be assured it is not necessary to apologise to me for an application on this subject.

I believe Mr. Leigh Hunt is our common acquaintance.

                                                          I am, yours faithfully,
                                                          Mary Shelley.

PUBLISHED: Redding, *Fifty Years' Recollections*, II, 364. TEXT: Redding, *Fifty Years' Recollections*.
    1. Cyrus Redding noted that he was "absent from London once for nine to ten days in ten years" for a visit to Amiens and Paris. Based on an unpublished letter from Horace Smith that refers to Redding's Paris journey, we may date this visit abroad in the spring of 1829 (27 June 1829, MS., Pforzheimer Library). In Paris he called on the Galignanis, whose *Messenger* he had edited from 1815 to 1818. Since 1804 the Galignanis had been "literary pirates." That is, with no international copyright laws to hinder them, they reprinted English books in France (see Giles Barber, "Galignani's and the Publication of English Books in France from 1800 to 1852," *The Library*, 5th ser., 16 [December 1961]: 267–86; and *A Famous Bookstore* [Paris: The Galignani Library, n.d.], a pamphlet kindly provided by J. M. Sene, present director of Galignani Librairie). During his 1829 visit, Redding agreed to write a number of introductory biographical sketches, including one of Shelley, for Galignani's compact edition of English works, and he asked his friend Horace Smith if he might include material from Shelley's letters to Smith. Smith declined because he believed that Shelley's letters were "too confidential" for publication and full of "such heterodox notions as might horrify many good folks" (Redding, *Fifty Years' Recollections*, II, 206–7). Smith's letter is dated 10, Hanover Crescent, 6th April. The dates and addresses of unpublished Smith letters at the Pforzheimer Library allow us to date this letter in 1829. Smith's 6 April 1829 letter suggested that Redding might

apply to Godwin, Mrs. Shelley, or Peacock for a facsimile. Whether he applied to the others is uncertain, but Redding acknowledged his indebtedness to Mary Shelley for almost all his material on Shelley (Redding, *Fifty Years' Recollections*, II, 363–66; idem, *Yesterday and To-Day*, 3 vols. [London: T. Cautley Newby, 1863], III, 108). *The Poetical Works of Coleridge, Shelley, and Keats*, with Redding's biographical essays, was published around mid-December 1829 (see Brown, *Letters*, pp. 291–92) without the frontispiece containing the poets' portraits, which, according to a notice inserted in a December copy of the book, would be ready before 15 January next (1830). For further information about the frontispiece see 15 January 1830.

2. Charles Heath (1785–1848; *DNB*), engraver and promoter of many illustrated annuals, including *Keepsake, Literary Souvenir, Book of Beauty, Picturesque Annual,* and *Amulet.*

*TO JOHN HOWARD PAYNE   Park Cottage   Teusday—28 April [1829]

We seem shut out from the Opera Alas! Which is very terrific—you will when you can, I know assist us to enter the sacred walls

Can you get me an admission or two for some one of the Theatres—I am not very particular it is for a friend but if you could send me any this week or early in the next—put them in a blank envelope directed to me to the care of A. [*Alfred*] Robinson Esq[1] 17 Orchard St. Portman Square I will not ask when I am to see you—this weather is so bad—as soon as it is decent—I shall go into town then you can see me with greater facility—

I am yours ever truly
MS.

ADDRESS: J. Howard Payne Esq / 29 Arundel St. / Strand. POSTMARKS: (1) T.P / Crawford St; (2) 2. A.NOON. [2] / 28. AP / 1829. UNPUBLISHED. TEXT: MS., Pforzheimer Library.

   1. See vol. I, [19 February 1827], n. 1.

*TO MRS. GEORGE CLINT   Park Cottage   Paddington
                                        Wednesday   [?April–May 1829][1]

My Dear Mrs Clint

A friend of mine has some thoughts of sending his two little girls[2] to the Chelly's[3] at Calais—Would you be so good as to let me know the terms and rules—You will very much oblige me—

How are you this vile weather?—it has prevented my calling as I intended, to request seeing Mr Clint's pictures before they went to Somerset House—I have also been much occupied with moving &c—but I hope soon to be settled somewhere in town & to be permitted to see you—Remember me with all kindness to Mr Clint—I do dread seeing him again—this you call vanity—so it is, mingled with a due fear of shocking his good taste—

Do be so good as to let me have all necessary intelligence about the Chelly's at your earliest convenience

I am yours very truly
MaryShelley

UNPUBLISHED. TEXT: MS., Pforzheimer Library.

1. Mary Shelley's comments about her appearance and her occupation with moving indicate that she wrote this letter after her return from Paris, which might date it as early as August 1828. The request to see George Clint's paintings "before they went to Somerset House" suggests April or May of 1829, because the exhibition of the Royal Academy of Arts, Somerset House, opened annually on the first Monday of May and ran for ten weeks (information about the opening date supplied by the Royal Academy of Art). Clint was a member of the Academy from 1821 until his resignation in 1835 (William Sandby, *The History of the Royal Academy of Arts*, 2 vols. [London: Longman, Green, Longman, Roberts, & Green, 1862], II, 66–68). In 1829 he exhibited *Rubens and the Philosopher* and *Earl Spencer* (Algernon Graves, *The Royal Academy of Arts*, 8 vols. [London: Henry Graves and Co., 1905], II, 85).

2. Perhaps the younger Robinson daughters.

3. The French ministry of culture has no record of this school. Nor have I located information about it elsewhere.

*To [Cyrus Redding]   33 Somerset St—Thursday
                                        [?14 May–August 1829]

My dear Sir
   I am exceedingly obliged to you for your very delightful present[1] which has afforded me great pleasure
   God send that the portrait[2] succeed!—Who will make the drawing?[3]—if not a very clever person I fear infinitely—I can see him if you please on Saturday at 12 or one o'clock (I shall go out [a]t two)—or on any other morning [w]hich he will appoint
   I am yours obliged &c

                                                         MShelley

UNPUBLISHED. TEXT: MS., Pforzheimer Library.

1. Possibly Redding's *Gabrielle, A Tale of the Swiss Mountains* (London: J. Ebers, 1829), a collection of miscellaneous pieces, a copy of which he sent Horace Smith on 27 June 1829 (MS., Pforzheimer Library).

2. See [?7 April–June 1829].

3. After he received Mary Shelley's letter of [?7 April–June 1829], Redding and Mary Shelley had "a conference upon the subject, and I prevailed upon Mrs. Shelley to let Mr. Davis copy the poet's head under her own superintendence" (Redding, *Fifty Years' Recollections*, II, 365; see also [?3 September 1829]). Redding gives the artist's name more fully (II, 363) as R. P. Davis, about whom I can find no information. However, J. P. Davis (d. 1862), portrait painter, was a contemporary and may possibly be the artist in question (George C. Williamson, *Bryan's Dictionary of Painters and Engravers*, 5 vols. [London: G. Bell and Sons, 1920], II, 16).

*To Teresa Guiccioli   1829 Londre—Somerset

Savez-vous que Mme B [?*Blessington*] écrit un roman[1]—et veut faire croire que votre ami—et puis Trelawny et puis tout le monde ont eté amoureux d'Elle— . . Ah! Oui amoureux—comme les lievres le sont de Chasseurs;

Elle leur faisant la chasse—mais ne put jamais assez galopper pour les rejoindre; ils lui echappaient tous

[*Translation*]

Do you know that Mme B [?*Blessington*] is writing a fiction[1]—and would have it believed that your friend—and then Trelawny and then everyone have been in love with her— . . Ah! yes in love—as rabbits are of hunters; She giving them chase—but could never run fast enough to catch up with them; they all would escape her

UNPUBLISHED. TEXT: MS., unpublished, of Teresa Guiccioli's "La vie de Lord Byron en Italie." TRANSCRIPTION: John P. Colella. TRANSLATION: William Novak.

1. See 15 August [1832] for Lady Blessington's *Conversations with Lord Byron*.

TO JOHN BOWRING   Friday [22 May 1829]   33 Somerset St.
                                                 Portman Sqr[1]

My dear Sir

Can you tell me how I can obtain a German work called "Das Bild" by Houwald[2]—we have in vain tried to get it at the foreign booksellers—if we could only have the loan of it for a short time <u>immediately</u>, you would greatly oblige me by procuring it—

I trust you & your family are well

Yours truly
MaryShelley

ADDRESS: John Bowring Esq / 7 North Place / Gray's In[n Lane]. POSTMARKS: (1) T.P / Duke St M.S; (2) 10. F. NOON. 10 / 23. MY / 1829. ENDORSED: (1) May 22 1829 / Mrs Shelley; (2) Mrs Shelley / 22 May 1829. PUBLISHED: Jones, #330. TEXT: MS., Huntington Library (HM 2761).

1. Mary Shelley recorded in her Journal on 13 May 1829 that she was settled at 33 Somerset Street, Portman Square, where she expected to remain one year.

2. Christoph Ernst Houwald, *Das Bild: Trauerspiel in fünf Akten* (Leipzig: G. J. Göschen, 1821).

TO SIR WALTER SCOTT   London—33 Somerset' St.
                              Portman Sq—25 May—1829

Sir

I have been encouraged by the kind politeness you have afforded to others, and by the indulgence with which I have been informed you have regarded some of my poor productions,[1] to ask you if you could assist me in my present task.

I am far advanced in a romance whose subject is Perkin Warbeck—Of course you know that he visited the court of James IV and married the daughter of the Earl of Huntly. In consulting our historians as to his story, I have found the earlier ones replete with interesting anecdotes and documents entirely passed over by Hume &c and in the forgotten or neglected pages of English and Irish writers of a distant date I discover a glimmering of the truth about him, even more distinct than that afforded in the dissertations of the modern writers in favor of his pretentions. Your are completely versed in the Antiquities of your country, and you would confer a high favor on me if you could point out any writer of its history—any document, anecdote or even ballad connected with him generally unknown, which may have come to your knowledge. I have consulted as yet only Buchanan & Lyndsay—(the latter does not even allude to him in his history of the James's)—and among later writers Pinkerton[2]

I hope you will forgive my troubling you—it is almost impertinent to say how ⟨incongruous⟩ foolish it appears to me that I should intrude on your ground, or to compliment one all the world so highly appretiates—but as every traveller when they visit the Alps, endeavours however imperfectly, to express their admiration in the Inn's Album,[3] so it is impossible to address the Author of Waverly without thanking him for the delight and instruction derived from the inexhaustible source of his genius, and trying to express a part of the enthusiastic admiration his works inspire

I am, Sir
Your Ob^t Servant
MaryShelley

ADDRESS: For: Sir Walter Scott, Bart. / Edinburgh. POSTMARKS: (1) MY / A 25 / 1829; (2) May [   ] 2[   ] / 1829. PUBLISHED: Jones, #331. TEXT: MS., National Library of Scotland.
   1. See vol. I, 14 June 1818.
   2. George Buchanan, *History of Scotland* (Edinburgh: Alexander Arbuthnet, 1582), written in Latin and translated several times before 1800; Robert Lindsay, *The History of Scotland (1436–1565)* (Edinburgh: Baskett Co., 1728); John Pinkerton, *The History of Scotland from the Accession of the House of Stuart to that of Mary,* 2 vols. (London: C. Dilly, 1797).
   3. This recalls Shelley's self-description in Greek as "democrat, great lover of mankind, and atheist" signed in a Swiss Inn album in 1816; the deed became quickly known and brought him under attack (White, *Shelley*, I, 455–56, 714).

TO JOHN BOWRING   Somerset St.   Monday   [1 June 1829]

My dear Sir
   I am certainly a very wrong person to have delayed answering you so long—One reason is that I was out of town for a day or two—I now send the proof[1]—Thank you for your offer to breakfast with me—May I expect you next Saturday?—It will afford me great pleasure

I am truly Yours
MaryShelley

ADDRESS: J. Bowring Esq. ENDORSED: (1) June 1, 1829 / Mary Shelley; (2) Mrs. Shelley / 1 June 1829. PUBLISHED: Jones, #332. TEXT: MS., Huntington Library (HM 2762).

1. Of "Modern Italy" (see 2 April [1828] to [John Bowring]).

TO JOHN BOWRING   Thursday [4 June 1829] Somerset St.

My dear Sir

I am so very much indisposed that with great regret I am obliged to ask you to defer your promised visit till next week—May I expect you on Wednesday?—by that time surely I shall be quite well

It is too bad to be ill in summer and so to be deprived of my best pleasure—the enjoyment of warm weather—

Yours truly
MaryShelley

ADDRESS: For / John Bowring Esq / 7 North Place—Gray's Inn Lane. POSTMARKS: (1) T.P /
[   ]; (2) 7. NIGHT. 7 / 4. JU / 182[9]. ENDORSED: (1) June 4 1829 / Mrs Shelley; (2) Mrs Shelley / 4 June 1829. PUBLISHED: Jones, #333. TEXT: MS., Huntington Library (HM 2763).

TO FREDERIC MANSEL REYNOLDS[1]   Somerset St. Tuesday
[16 June 1829]

Dear Fred—

It shall be as you please—I continue your debtor therefore until next year—

I am a great deal better than when you called—tho' not yet quite strong

Yours Ever
MaryShelley

ADDRESS: F. Mansel Reynolds, Esq / 48 Warren St. Fitzroy Sq. POSTMARKS: [10] F. NOON. 10 / 17. JU / 1829. PUBLISHED: Jones, #334. TEXT: MS., British Library (Add. 27,925, ff. 123–24).

1. Frederic Mansel Reynolds (?1801–50), author. As editor of the *Keepsake* for the years 1828–35, 1838, and 1839, Reynolds published many of Mary Shelley's short stories and poems, beginning with "The Sisters of Albano" and "Ferdinando Eboli, A Tale" in 1828 (for a comprehensive record of Mary Shelley's publications in the *Keepsake* see Lyles, *MWS Bibliography*, pp. 25–31, 32–34).

TO JOHN BOWRING   33 Somerset St. Wednesday [1 July 1829]

My dear Sir

Ever since I last wrote I have been indisposed but I am now getting better—Will you let me avail myself of my convalescence by breakfasting with me on Saturday—or some Morning next week which is convenient to you

I am Yours truly
MaryShelley

Do you know where I could get (in French) The History of the Court of Burgundy by M. de Barante[1]

I had written the enclosed when your note & cheque[2] came—so I must delay seeing you till you return—when both the weather and my health will be I hope better

I have LB's letters safe. I meant & mean to give them you when I see you here

What an excellent portrait there is of you in the Exhibition[3]

Adieu

ADDRESS: John Bowring Esq / 7 North Place—Grays Inn Road. POSTMARKS: (1) T.P / Duke St M.S; (2) 2 A.NOON. 2 / 2. JY / 1829. ENDORSED: (1) July 1. 1829 / Mrs Shelley; (2) Mary Shelley / 1 July 1829. PUBLISHED: Jones, #335. TEXT: MS., Huntington Library (HM 2764).

   1. See 14 October [1828], n. 4.

   2. For "Modern Italy" see 2 April [1828] to [John Bowring].

   3. The portrait of John Bowring exhibited at the Royal Academy in 1829 was painted by Henry William Pickersgill (1782–1875; *DNB*) (information supplied by the Royal Academy of Arts).

To [?   ]   33 Somerset St. Wednesday [?1 July 1829]

My dear Sir

   I am only now recovering from the indisposition which prevented me from seeing you when you did me the favor to call—but I am well enough to see you, and shall be very glad whenever you are good enough to spend an hour here

Yours truly
MaryShelley

PUBLISHED: Jones, #342. TEXT: MS., Pforzheimer Library.

---

*TO CHARLES OLLIER   33 Somerset St. Portman Sq Monday
[?6 July 1829]

My dear Sir

   Would you have the goodness to lend me Devereux[1]—I want it very much & you would greatly oblige me

Your O[bly]
MaryShelley

The other books you were so kind as to lend me which I still have will be returned almost immdialy [*immediately*]

ADDRESS: Charles Ollier Esq / Maida Hill. UNPUBLISHED. TEXT: MS., Pforzheimer Library.
   1. Edward Bulwer, *Devereux*, 3 vols. (London: Henry Colburn, 1829), published on 9 July. Mary Shelley may have shared *Devereux* with Godwin, who read it from 9 to 14 July 1829 (Godwin, Journal).

*To John Howard Payne   [?33 Somerset Street   23 July 1829]

I was sorry that I was out yesterday & am anxious for news of the Mill.[1]

   I want very much to see Sweethearts & Wives;[2] it is to be acted tomorrow   I fear that is too soon for you—but would you arrange orders for the next time it is acted—you need not do duty tho I hope you will join me at the theatre   I wish for 4 orders as I have promised Percy to take him—& will you secure places—

   Is there any possibility of getting four or even two orders for Astleys[3] some night next week for my boy—

   The Old story this but you are good & will excuse it & me

Yours Ever
MS.

ADDRESS: J. Howard Payne Esq / 29 Arundel St. / Strand. POSTMARKS: (1) PADDINGTON / 23 JY / 1829; (2) [   ] NIGHT [   ] / 23 / 1829. UNPUBLISHED. TEXT: MS., Pforzheimer Library.
   1. Perhaps a reference to a new production of Payne's melodrama *The Two Galley Slaves; or, The Mill of St. Aldervon*, first played at Drury Lane on 11 June 1822 (Nicoll, *English Drama*, p. 369), or to a new play by Payne (see [24 August 1829]; [1 December 1829]).
   2. Scheduled for the Haymarket Theatre for 24 July 1829 (*Morning Chronicle*; see vol. I, 18–19 August [1823], n. 4).
   3. A panorama entitled *The Battle of Waterloo*, listed as a "Juvenile Fete," was playing at Astley's Royal Ampitheatre (*The Times* [London]).

To Edward John Trelawny   33 Somerset St.   Portman Sq
27 July [1829]

I gave your letter, my dear Trelawny, to Jane who will answer it—You have been so zealous, so kind, so dear a friend that you must not wonder that she should feel hurt at being (as she was) much passed over by you;[1] the affectionate tone of your letters from Greece made her readily believe that you loved her as well as Edward—I confess I did not wonder at your not going there oftener; but the fact you had so often insisted upon to me, of your slight affection for her, was not for me to report—however—the eagerness of your defence is complimentary & I suppose she is satisfied. I once almost deified Jane; and she poor girl suffers for my folly, for finding her very human, & having reason to complain of her failure in the most obvious duties of a friend, it is with reluctance I contemplate in her the destruction of my last dream of happiness—I should love her better now, had I not loved her too well formerly.

Claire has written to you—I need say little about her—She returns to Dresden[2] to an agreable situation and I envy any one who quits this sad land too much not to congratulate her on her departure: poor herself, surrounded by needy & in some cases unamiable relatives—she finds here not one of the necessary comforts of life—she began to vegetate, & to be content with vegetation—she is torn from this, and in society of persons agreable to her in Germany, will arrange a mode of life very far to be preferred to the one she is doomed to here.

For myself—I find little in life to please me—Without exercising my affections I cannot be happy—& on every side I am disappointed—My boy grows and improves, and thus I have a consolation. But I am very weary—Thus scattered about the world, useless to others, a burthen to themselves, are human beings destined to be—who might be happy, did not a thousand circumstances—tyrannical passions, & want of sympathy prevent their ever uniting to any purpose.

You are unhappy, My dear Trelawny? How legibly was the existence of untold suffering written on your brow—and the coldness, & want of that zeal we all fondly hoped would shed forgotten sunshine over us, arose from reserve on your part—this was not well—In a mere selfish point of view I wish you had been more confiding—and now in Italy in a land where my Memory and fancy place Paradise, you are wretched—What is to be done? Once you loved me sufficiently to confide in me—that time I know and feel to be gone—at least such was the case in the winter. You distorted my motives—did not understand my position, and altogether I lost in your eyes during your last visit—You were quite in the wrong—I never was more worthy of your love and esteem—but blind miserable beings thus we grope in the dark—we depend on each other yet we are each a mystery to the other—and the heart which should be in the hand of a friend, either shuns the contact, or is disdainfully rejected. I neither like life—nor the mechanism of society—nor the modes in which human beings present themselves—but I cannot mould them to my will, & in making up my mind merely to take them as they are, enthusiasm fades, and cold reality makes me each day more willing to quite [*quit*] a scene in which I am an alien.

Can nothing be done, My friend, to diminish the causes of your unhappiness? You are occupie[d] by writing—I know too well that that excitement is the parent of pain rather than pleasure.

Did you not receive a letter from me in answer to yours concerning Shelley's life?[3] I sent one. I do not wish at present to renew the recollection of the past—Your recollections of our Lost One will be precious as a record of his Merit—but I am averse to having those mingled with a history which will be the subject of cavill. I hope one day to write his Life myself—not to be published in my lifetime or even my childs   Meanwhile we neither desire the pity nor justice of the ⟨multitude⟩ few attended as they would be by the barking and railing of his enemies, and the misjudgement of the multitude. ⟨I am eager to see you.⟩ With regard to letters it seems that an unfortunate mistake caused those I had preserved previous to our visiting Italy to be destroyed—The others are almost entirely descriptive and I mean to publish them together with the rest of his prose works at a future day. I am eager to hear of the progress of your "Life."

My very dear Friend—I wish some kind spirit would visit you with happiness—I wish that I could influence you life sufficiently to render it less painful   All this is vain—Write to me   I entreat you

Yours MS.

(*P. 1, upside-down*) The Cottage girls congratulate themselves that the kindness they were eager to shew to a friend of mine was not thrown away on an ingrate—they desire to live in your remembrance—You can partly repay their attentions to you by showing some few to their brother George who will shortly visit Florence—the sons of this family are people with whom I have little intercourse notwithstanding my affection for their sisters   still on the [*p. 4, side*] present occasion I should be glad that George met with civilities from you—

ADDRESS: Italy La Toscane / L'Italie / Edward J. Trelawny Esq / Ferma in Posta / Florence Firenze. POSTMARKS: (1) F 29 / 40; (2) PONT / BEAUVOISIN; (3) CORRISPZA ESTERA DA GENOVA; (4) 10 / AGU[ST]O / 1829. PUBLISHED: Jones, #336. TEXT: MS., Bodleian Library (MS., Shelley, Adds, c. 6, ff. 80–81).

1. On 24–26 June 1829 Trelawny wrote to Mary Shelley asking why Jane Hogg "writes me the angriest and most fierce letter" (Abinger MSS., Bodleian Library).

2. See April 1[829]. Trelawny's letter of 3 July 1829 to Claire Clairmont indicates that he had received Mary Shelley's letters and that he was angry at her refusal to aid him (Trelawny, *Letters*, pp. 126–27).

3. See April 1[829], n. 1.

*[?   ]¹   33 Somerset St.   Thursday   [6 August 1829]

My dear Sir

I should be very glad <u>now</u> to see the sketches you seemed to promise to shew me—to receive any information² you can give me—& to see you. I know that I intrude on precious time—yet your politeness before makes me believe that you will excuse me. May I expect you at any time in the course of Sunday?

Is it putting you to any inconvenience to ask you if {you} can procure a frank for me?   if you could get me one for Saturday August 8. directed to J. W. Carleton Esq³ Abbey Sq. Chester you would greatly oblige me

I am dear Sir
Yours truly
MaryShelley

UNPUBLISHED. TEXT: MS., Gordon N. Ray.

1. Mary Shelley's request in this letter for a frank suggests that the recipient was a government official or a Member of Parliament.

2. The sketches and information may have been for *Perkin Warbeck*.

3. The "JWC" referred to in Mary Shelley's Journal may be J. W. Carleton. On 29 January 1829 she records: "The story of J. R. [*Julia Robinson*] & JWC. commences—and I, as usual—absorbed by & given away to sympathy with my friend." On 28 February 1831 she records: "JWC is in town—& Julia is with me—We go to the opera & it is all an imbraglio."

*To JOHN HOWARD PAYNE   [?33 Somerset Street]   Thursday Ev^g
[13 August 1829]

My dear Payne

Could you arrange to let me have two (i.e. to admit 2 people) admissions for Vauxhall for Monday[1] or an early ensuei{n}g day—You have been very unlucky lately—Why did you not come to the Cottage yesterday?—If there is anything very amusing at the Haymarket & would first let me know in the Morning before one or 2—& secondly get tickets & places for Julia[2] & I—& be at the theatre to put us in if all this can be without inconvenience—Shall it be? & When

Y^s

MS

ADDRESS: For / J. Howard Payne Esq / 29 Arundel St.   Strand. POSTMARK: 2 A.NOON. 2 / 14. AU / 1829. UNPUBLISHED. TEXT: MS., Washington University Library.

1. On Monday, 13 August 1829, the entertainment scheduled for Royal Gardens, Vauxhall, featured Italian and French minstrels, pantomime, concerts, vaudeville, fireworks, and was highlighted by the ascension of a large, hydrogen-filled flying balloon. Weather conditions forced the postponement of this spectacle until Monday, 17 August (*Morning Chronicle*). Balloons as a means of human flight began with the hot-air balloon, invented in November 1783 and quickly superseded by the hydrogen balloon in December 1783. Balloonists were often brought to public attention. In *The Last Man*, set in the twentieth century, Mary Shelley depicted balloons as a regular mode of transportation (MWS, *The Last Man*, I, chap. 4, p. 141; II, chap. 6, p. 203).

2. Julia Robinson.

*To JOHN HOWARD PAYNE   [?33 Somerset Street]
Monday [17 August 1829]

My dear Payne

I should like to go to the Haymarket tomorrow[1] if you could arrange it without trouble

Y^s Ever

M

ADDRESS: J. Howard Payne Esq / 29 Arundel St / Strand. POSTMARKS: (1) T.P / Crawford St; (2) 8. MORN. 8 / 18. AU / 1829. UNPUBLISHED. TEXT: MS., Pforzheimer Library.

1. *Nothing Superfluous; Ups and Downs; Fish Out of Water; and Modern Antiques* played at the Haymarket on 18 August.

*To John Howard Payne   [?33 Somerset Street]
                                    Monday [24 August 1829]

My dear Payne—Will you take places at the Haymarket & if you can get tickets—At any rate take places, as if you cannot I shall try for ord{e}rs— —Can you go with us? If not <u>one</u> ticket from you will be necessary
    Une lettre au façon de toutes les autres—n'est ce pas?[1] Adieu
                                                    MS.
I do hope & very much do I wish to hear good news of the Mill[2]

ADDRESS: For / J. Howard Payne Esq / 29 Arundel St. Strand. POSTMARKS: (1) T.P / Duke St. M.S.; (2) [10.] F.NOON. 10 / 24. AU / 1829. UNPUBLISHED. TEXT: MS., Washington University Library.
    1. "A letter in the manner of all the others—isn't it."
    2. See [23 July 1829], n. 1.

To John Bowring   Somerset St.   29 August [1829]

My dear Sir
    It will give me great pleasure to prove to you that I am <u>well visible</u> & at home—will you breakfast with me on Saturday—Should you welcome an Article on the "Loves of the poets"?[1]
                                            I am truly Y^s
                                            MShelley

ADDRESS: For / John Bowring Esq / 5 Millman St. POSTMARKS: (1) T.P / Duke St M.S.; (2) [ ] A.NOON.[ ] / 1. SP / 1829. ENDORSED: (1) Sept 1 1829 / Mary Shelley; (2) Mrs Shelley / 29 Augt 1829. PUBLISHED: Jones, #337. TEXT: MS., Huntington Library (HM 2765).
    1. Mary Shelley's offer was accepted. Her review of *The Loves of the Poets* (2 vols. [London: Colburn, 1829]), by Anna Brownell Jameson, the author of the *Diary of an Ennuyée*, appeared in *Westminster Review* 11 (October 1829): 472–77. The review is of particular interest because of its reference to Shelley and its expression of Mary Shelley's own views on life and poetry.

To William Whitton   1 September 1829—33 Somerset St.

My dear Sir
    May I send the receipt for 75£[1] & have the cheque in return?—
    I was very much pleased these holydays to find Percy in every respect improved—his disposition appears to me so tractable that I think that at

no time will he occasion us any trouble—but on the contrary be every thing his family could wish. I was half in hopes that Sir Tim^{thy} might have taken more notice of him during these holydays—for he grows a big boy now— He was never in better health

I am Sir Y^s Ob^{ly}

MaryW. Shelley

ADDRESS: For / William Whitton, Esq. / 18 Bedford Row. POSTMARKS: (1) T.P / Duke St M.S.; (2) 2. A.NOON. 2 / [ ]SP / 1829. ENDORSED: 1 Sepr 1829 / Mrs Shelley. PUBLISHED: Jones, #338. TEXT: MS., Bodleian Library (MS., Shelley, Adds., c. 6, ff. 82–83).

    1. As of the June 1829 quarter, Sir Timothy Shelley had agreed to advance Mary Shelley £300 per annum to meet Percy Florence's expenses at school (Ingpen, *Shelley in England*, II, 603). Her original advance of £200, begun in 1823, had been increased to £250 in September 1827 (see vol. I, 9–11 September [1823], n. 12; Ingpen, *Shelley in England*, II, 598).

TO CYRUS REDDING   Somerset St.   Thursday [?3 September 1829][1]

My dear Sir

    I send you the Errata of the Prometheus—Some changes Mr Shelley wished made in the Adonais—and a suppressed stanza of Hellas.[2] I am tempted to offer to write a brief outline of Mr Shelleys life if Galignani chose—but then my secret must be kept religiously—& no alterrations made—it would {be} very short & its chief merit the <u>absence</u> of incorrectness—I have some hopes of the portrait—the Lady who painted it is in town & will meet Mr Davis[3] & offer her suggestions tomorrow—but I would give the world to have it engraved here—where any defect in the drawing might be corrected & we superintend the whole—At any rate it will be better than a likeness after the <u>imagination</u> of a Frenchman—that is the drollest & stupidest idea—ever Man intent on selling an edition hit upon.

I am, dear Sir

Yours truly

MaryShelley

    The drawing[4] is getting better & better—Pray keep them to their promise of letting me have it—I shall feel highly gratified

    As it is now finished and at my house perhaps you will call Come as soon after 12 as you can[5]

PUBLISHED: Jones, #323. TEXT: MS., Huntington Library (HM 13209).

    1. Godwin's Journal indicates that the only time Amelia Curran, "the Lady who painted" Shelley's portrait, was in London in 1829 and visited him and Mary Shelley was from around 19 August through 22 September. On Saturday, 19 August, and Friday, 4 September, Mary Shelley and Amelia Curran were at Godwin's. On Saturday, 12 September, Godwin dined at Mary Shelley's, and Amelia Curran called there afterwards.

    2. The corrections that Mary Shelley sent Redding, except for the errata for *Prometheus Unbound*, were incorporated into Galignani's edition. Possibly *Prometheus Unbound* had already been set before the corrections were received (Taylor, *Early Collected Editions*, pp. 21–22).

3. See [?14 May–August 1829], n. 3.

4. The drawing preliminary to an engraved portrait.

5. Redding noted, "I called & was gratified at the result of my efforts to obtain the only worthy resemblance of Shelley that is extant" (Redding, *Fifty Years' Recollections*, II, 366).

*To [Cyrus Redding]   Somerset St. Teusday
                                 [?September–November 1829]

My dear Sir

I have only made one correction in the MS—The whole tone of the Memoir[1] is to my mind inaccurate—but if this is the guise it is thought right that it should assume of course I have nothing to say—since it is favorable in its way & I ought to be content—I should have written it in a different style—but probably not so much to the Publisher's satisfaction— It is a mere outline & is as communicative as a skeleton can be—about as like the ⟨original⟩ truth as the skeleton resembles the "tower of flesh"[2] of which it is the beams & rafters—But I see no positive assertion in it that is very untrue

I am very much obliged to you for the communication & grateful to you for your reminding Galignani of his promise[3]

                                        I am truly Y[s]
                                            MS.

UNPUBLISHED. TEXT: MS., Pforzheimer Library.

1. Redding's "Memoir of Percy Bysshe Shelley" in Galignani, *Poetical Works of Coleridge, Shelley, and Keats*, pp. v–xi. The published memoir includes the facts of Shelley's marriage to Harriet Westbrook, his elopement with "Miss Godwin" while he was still married, his wife's suicide, and his subsequent marriage, "at the solicitation of her father," to "Mary Wolstonecraft Godwin, daughter of the celebrated authoress of the *Rights of Woman*" (p. vi). The memoir reprints, with some minor changes, Mary Shelley's introduction to Shelley, *Posthumous Poems*.

2. Perhaps an echo of "hill of flesh" in Shakespeare, *Henry IV, Part I* 2. 4. 243.

3. To give the drawing to Mary Shelley after it had been engraved (see the previous letter).

*To John Howard Payne   [?33 Somerset Street]   Sunday
                                        [4 October 1829]

My dear Payne

I have no bills to consult but if it is possible I should like to take Percy to the Haymarket Tomorrow[1]—Let me have four tickets & places—& you also if you please—that is as you please as I dare say C. [*Charles*] Robinson[2] can go with us if you cannot—

                                        Very truly yours
                                            MS.

Let me have the tickets as <u>early</u> in the day as you <u>possibly can</u>

[*On address flap*] You would convenience me much if you cannot send <u>five</u> admissions by letting me {   } two single orders i.e. one double 2 single [*cross-written*] admit 4 in all

ADDRESS: For / J. Howard Payne Esq / 29 Arundel St. / Strand. POSTMARKS: (1) T.P / Duke St M.[S]; (2) 10. F.NOON. 10 / 5. OC / 1829. UNPUBLISHED. TEXT: MS., Pforzheimer Library.

1. Scheduled were *The Foundling of the Forest; Sweethearts and Wives;* and *John of Paris* (*Morning Chronicle*).

2. Charles Barrington Robinson, son of Joshua and Rosetta Robinson, was christened on 24 September 1815, along with Ellen Ann Robinson (perhaps his twin), at St. Mary's Church, Paddington (information supplied by Emily W. Sunstein).

TO THOMAS CROFTON CROKER   4 Nov. 1829   33 Somerset St.

My dear Sir

You never come except when I write, so that I get afraid of intruding—I was much obliged to you for the books—I have now completed one volume[1] ready for the press in which there is one Irish Chapter—the other two I hope to have in order in two or 3 weeks at furthest—I am afraid that you will think that I have troubled you to very little purpose since there must be so little about Ireland—I had written altogether enough for five vols & am cutting down to 3—so every thing is abridged—little tho' there is it is of great care to me that it should be exact—I suppose the MS. will be in Mr Murray's hands perhaps in a few days and I believe he consults you—or if you call I will shew you the Chapter—or send it to you—or wait till the ⟨three⟩ two other Irish Chapters are concluded which will occur one in the middle of the second the other at the beginning of the 3^d vol.

One other thing: you were good enough to say that you would interest Major Elrington[2] in my behalf—Can this be done soon? After all you may be out of town—I hope not ill—the vile summer was enough to kill every body & the frightful winter comes to give the coup de grace to <u>the rest</u>

Yours very truly
& Obliged
MaryShelley

PUBLISHED: Stockwell, "Two Unpublished Letters of Mary Wollstonecraft Shelley," pp. 44–45. TEXT: MS., National Library of Ireland.

1. Of *Perkin Warbeck* (see the next letter).

2. Perhaps Major George Esdaile Elrington, in 1830 retired on full pay from the 5th Royal Veterans Battalion (*List of Officers of the Army* [London: His Majesty's Stationery Office, 1830], p. 41).

To John Murray   12 November—1829   33 Somerset St.
                                                 Portman Sq

My Dear Sir

I am sorry to hear from Mr Moore[1] that you decline my Romance—
because I would rather that you published it, than any other person.

I can assure you I feel all the kindness of your message to me through
Mr Moore. Do you remember speaking to me about a life of the Empress
Josephine Md^m de Stael[2] &c ?—When I have got free from my present
occupation, I will communicate with you on the subject, and I hope that
by some plan, either of my writing for your Family Library, or in some
other way, to liquidate my debt[3]—or I must do it even in a more usual
manner—I am aware of your kindness concerning it but I could not consent
that an act of civility on my part to Mr Moore should be brought forward
as cancelling my debt to you—besides it would make me break a vow I
made never to make money of my acquaintance with Lord Byron—his ghost
would certainly come and taunt me if I did—This does not decrease but
rather enhance the value I have for your kind intention

I am dear Sir
Yours Obliged
MaryShelley

ENDORSED: 1829—Nov. 12—/ Shelley, Mrs. PUBLISHED: Jones, #339. TEXT: MS., John
Murray.

1. Moore may have informed Mary Shelley of Murray's decision on *Perkin Warbeck* on 9
November 1829 (see Moore, *Letters*, II, 660).

2. Mary Shelley apparently wrote to Mérimée of her plan to write about either Josephine
or Madame de Staël. On 4 February 1829 he suggested that both women would be difficult
subjects because of the problems of describing their active love lives "<u>plainly</u> aux Anglais"
(Bennett and Little, "Seven Letters from Mérimée to Mary Shelley," pp. 151–52).

3. See 19 February 1828. In response to this letter, John Murray replied that Mary Shelley
had done for him the service that he had asked Thomas Moore to request of her; that in
future she could provide further information without payment according to her "honourable
feelings"; and that he regretted rejecting her novel but looked forward to conferring with her
about other projects. He also included a receipt for £100 "value received" (MS., 12 November
1829, John Murray).

*To [Henry Colburn]   13 Nov. 1829   33 Somerset St.
                                                 Portman Square.

My Dear Sir

It is now more than a year ago that I communicated to you, though M^r
Leigh Hunt, my wish to treat with you concerning a Romance on which I
was occupied on the subject of Perkin Warbeck—You asked to see the
first Volume—which I was not able to send—

I may now say that it is ready for the press; although I should not be
able to submit to inspection more than a volume and a half, you might see

the MS of the rest—requiring only to be copied by me—a thing I am now occupied in doing—and achieve with great speed—

It will give me great pleasure if you continue to be my publisher[1]—I may say that my present work promises, I think, to be far more popular than the last—that I have taken great pains with it—and that the story on which it is founded appears to me both beautiful and interesting—If it is your desire to judge for yourself, of course I will send the part I mention of the MS.—Only it is to be remarked that it improves in interest as it goes on— And also (which I do not think) if the first vol. appear scanty to you—the materials I have for the rest, are even too much, and my principal endeavour is to compress—this indeed is one of the reasons that I write just now, as I shall have your opinion as to how far I ought to abridge the original—or not—

I may add that ⟨to no person⟩ every one to whom I have mentioned my subject judges it highly interesting—I may mention My father, Sir Walter Scott & Mᵣ Thomas Moore—who have all highly encouraged me

I shall be glad from the reasons above mentioned to have an early reply

I am dear Sir

Yʳ Oblᵈ & Obᵗ

MaryShelley

UNPUBLISHED. TEXT: MS., Pforzheimer Library.

1. Colburn, who had published *The Last Man* in 1826, now in partnership with Richard Bentley published *Perkin Warbeck* in 1830 (see vol. I, 6 August 1817, n. 7; and 5 January 1830).

*To John Howard Payne   33 Somerset St. Monday
                                              [1 December 1829]

My dear Payne—Could you favor me by taking places for six for next Monday at Covent Garden[1]—If you could contrive to get me a newspaper ticket—à la bonne heure[2]—it would be very acceptable

I hope you are well & that the little Mills[3] thrive

Yours ever

MS.

if you cant six altogether divide—& so reign

ADDRESS: J. Howard Payne Esq / 17 Speldhurst St. / Burton Crescent. POSTMARKS: (1) T.P / WOOX[TON]; (2) 8. MORN. 8 / 1. DE / 1829. UNPUBLISHED. TEXT: MS., Pforzheimer Library.

1. *Romeo and Juliet* and *Black-Eyed Susan* were scheduled (*Morning Chronicle*).
2. "Early."
3. See [23 July 1829], n. 1

To WILLIAM WHITTON   33 Somerset St.   Portman Sq
                                        2 December 1829

My Dear Sir

I shall send on Friday with your permission my receipt for £75—in exchange for you cheque

I have the pleasure to tell you that Percy is quite well—I have directed that he shall attend the lessons in drilling which are given at his school—the dancing Master was not enough to cure a stoop he was getting but the sergeant has done him already a great deal of good—I think Sir Timothy would find him improved—he is really very good and above all tractable—which is not quite the virtue of his fathers family

                              I am, dear Sir, Yours obliged
                                        MaryShelley

[*P. 1, top*] I hope Sir Timothy is well—it would be very kind if he permitted me to see him when he next comes to town.

ADDRESS: For / William Whitton Esq / 18 Bedford Row. ENDORSED: 2d Decr 1829 / Mrs Shelley. PUBLISHED: Jones, #340. TEXT: MS., Bodleian Library (MS., Shelley, Adds., c. 6, ff. 84–85).

To JOHN MURRAY   Monday   [7 December 1829][1]   33 Somerset St

My Dear Sir

Permit me to ask you to lend me for a few days Washington Irving's last exquisitely written and interesting work—the Conquest of Granada—I want to consult it, and have been disappointed in having it from Hookham—No book has delighted me so much for a very long time—Your kind offer with regard to books has made me take this liberty—I hope I do not do wrong

                              Yours Obliged   MaryShelley

ADDRESS: For / John Murray Esq / 50 Albermarle St. ENDORSED: 1829 Dec 7. / Shelley, Mrs. Mary. PUBLISHED: Jones, #341. TEXT: MS., John Murray.

1. This date is written in another hand. Jones suggested that the year reads "1827," which he noted was certainly incorrect, since *The Conquest of Granada* was published by Murray in April 1829. Since the final number has a loop and in no way resembles the first 7, it is probable that it is a hastily written 9. The date 1829 is confirmed by the letter's endorsement, as well as a note indicating that John Murray presented her with a copy of the work (see [?13 December 1829]).

To HENRY COLBURN   Saturday   12 Dec. 1829
                                        33 Somerset St.   Portman Sq.

My dear Sir

You were so good as to say when you sent for my MS. that I might count upon an <u>immediate arrangement</u>—this was several weeks ago—the work is still in progress—that is—copying—it was <u>written</u> when I first communicated with you[1]—I hope no circumstances have made you hesitate about becoming my publisher—I trust there is no reason for that—One is an bad judge oneself—but I should guess that for a thousand reasons, there is a better chance for "Perkin Warbeck"—than for the "Last Man"—I am less anxious about the terms & time of payment, than to be made secure that I may depend upon you as my publisher—If you have made up your mind on that subject—and I believe that you must—& in the <u>affirmative</u>—only have the goodness to send me a line to say so—and, as such may be your wish, we will defer all consideration of price &c till the MS. is perfectly finished—which will be before long—it has been somewhat interrupted by a severe cold

I am Ys. Ob^{ly}
MaryShelley

ADDRESS: For: / Henry Colburn Esq / 8 New Burlington St. PUBLISHED: Jones, #344. TEXT: MS., Pforzheimer Library.
    1. See 13 November 1829.

To [CHARLES OLLIER]   [?33 Somerset Street]   Saturday Evening
                                                    [?12 December 1829]

My dear Sir
    After all <u>this</u> was forgotten—I am not sorry as it affords me an opportunity to say a few words—as perhaps I was misunderstood—I should certainly like to come to an <u>immediate agreement</u>[1]—indeed without that I should not have spirits to proceed but I should not desire any payment until <u>all</u> is written—nor the whole payment even then—it might be arranged as Colburn liked—
    This would make the first payment to be made I should imagine at the end of this Month—
    I must add a few words to thank you for your consideration & kindness— I am the opposite of a business person and your interesting yourself in this matter is tenfold more valuable to me—I commit it to you in the full assurance that you will do your best—<u>your</u> best being <u>the</u> best—
    Do I pay a compliment? O no! I only give trouble—But you will excuse me

Yours obliged
MShelley

PUBLISHED: Jones, #345. TEXT: MS., Keats-Shelley Memorial House, Rome.
    1. See 5 January 1830, n. 1.

To John Murray   33 Somerset St.   Sunday Evening
                                          [?13 December 1829]

My dear Sir

Will you forward this to Mr Moore—I do not know his exact address—
and you will have opportunities of sending it or getting it franked—if a
member be to be found during Christmas—I am rather in haste as it is an
answer to a question concerning <u>the</u> "Life"—Which I am delighted to hear
is on the point of appearing[1]—

I am sorry that I am at your Antipodes—especially as I do not gain in
climate—I am sure that I am at the North Pole—but the South pole is also
very cold—I would make an appointment to prevent the chance of your
finding me not at home—but it might be inconvening—as I sometimes
wander into your Antarctic region I will call and ask if you are at leisure—
After all—as I am not idle yet, except that I should be glad to see you—
nothing is lost by the "line" between us being yet uncrossed

A thousand thanks for "Granada"[2]—the world is a common place—a
buying and selling[3]—& not even a well dressed world—not to take interest
in the romantic silken-suited Cavaliers of Andalusia—

                                          I am yours obliged
                                          MaryShelley
Do you expect Mr Moore in town <u>very</u> soon again[4]—

ENDORSED: 1829 (No date) / Shelley Mrs. PUBLISHED: Jones, #347. TEXT: MS., John Murray.
    1. The first volume of Byron, *Letters and Journals* (Moore) was published by John Murray
on 18 January 1830 (Jones, *The Harp That Once*, p. 272).
    2. See [7 December 1829].
    3. "The world . . . selling" echoes Wordsworth's "The world is too much with us."
    4. Moore was in London from 20 to 24 December (Moore, *Letters*, II, 669–70; Moore,
Journal).

To Edward John Trelawny   33 Somerset St.   15 Decr 1829

My very dear Trelawny

Your letter[1] would have occasioned me a great deal of pain had it not
relieved me from my painful suspense about yourself—Is it true that I have
been remiss? I thought I had been better than you by two letters—but I
write a good deal and get so weary of the sight of a pen that I know I do
neglect writing when I ought—besides—however a page of excuses would
be ridiculous—I have ever loved—I do love you—write or not this is one
of the warmest sentiments of my heart—and it is not better to feel this than
to write twenty letters—Ah have pity on my miserable clouded faculties—
free and enjoying beneath an Italian sky you cannot participate {   }
our northern island miseries—not to talk of a climate which has outdone
itself this year in rain & fogs—the peculiar situation of my relations is heavy

on me—my spirits are depressed by care and I have no resource save in what sunshine my friends afford me—afford me you a little, Dearest friend—seal up words sweeter than vernal breezes[2]—flatteries if you will—warm totens [*tokens*] of kindliness—I need them   I have been so long accustomed to turn to you as the spot whence distant but certain good must emanate that a chill from you is indeed painful—I will be a good girl in return and write often—

Your last letter was not at all kind—you are angry with me   you speak of evasions—What do you ask, what do I refuse? let me write to you as to my own heart and do not shew this letter to any one—You talk of writing Shelley's life and ask me for materials—Shelley's life as far as the public had to do with it consisted of very few events and these are publickly know—The private events were sad and tragical—How would you relate them? as Hunt has,[3] slurring over the real truth—wherefore write fiction? and the truth—any part of it—is hardly for the rude cold world to handle—His merits are acknowledged—his virtues—to bring forward actions which right or wrong, and that would be a matter of dispute, were in their results tremendous, would be to awaken calumnies and give his enemies a voice—For myself—am I to be left out in this life?—if so half my objections, more than half, would disappear—for with me would depart that portion which is most painful—I do not see what you could make of his life without me—but if that is your intention tell me—and we will see what can be done—I have made it my earnest request to all who have meddled with our Shelley to leave me out—they have assented and I consider myself fortunate—I fear publicity—as to my giving Moore materials for LB's life I thought I think I did right—I think I have achieved a great good by it—I wish it not to be kept secret—decidedly I am averse to its being published   for it would destroy me to be brought forward in print   I commit myself on this point to your generosity—I confided this fact to you—as I would any thing I did—being my dearest friend and had no idea that I was to find in you a harsh censor and public denouncer—There was something false in our mutual position when you were in England—God knows I do not accuse you of being a wordling—but—alas! of course I know any, every fault must be mine—but are we not   shall we not ever be friends?

Did I uphold and laud Medwin?—I thought that I had always disliked him—I am sure I thought him a great annoyance and he was always borrowing crowns which he never meant to pay and we could ill spare—He was Jane's friend more than any ones—to be sure We did not desire a duel—nor an horsewhipping—and Lord Byron and Mrs Beauclerk worked hard to promote peace—Can any thing be so frightful as the account you give?[4] Poor Mrs Medwin—I shall be very glad to hear that you have done any thing for her—you if any body can—Claire is at Dresden as of course you know—she says they have had fine weather ever since her arrival—we have nothing but bad since her departure—she complains that she has not heard from you—Charles Clairmont her brother, after an unsuccessful struggle here has returned to Vienna—The Hunts are at Brumpton [*Brompton*] she has just had another child[5]—Jane went to see them the other day—& he called at ⟨Pa⟩ my father's[6]—he is out of spirits—Your love Caroline Beauclerk married the other day[7]—well I believe—The pretty Cottagers are charmed by your remembrance—The little Invisibility preserves the little red arrangements among her bijouterie[8]—Jane is well—Nothing can be more stupid than London—Miss Fanny Kemble's success[9] is our only event— twelve guineas have been offered vainly for a private box on her nights— But while fog and ennui possesses London, despair and convulsion reign over the country[10]—some change some terrible event is expected—rents falling—money not to be got—every one poor and fearful—Will any thing come of it—Was not the panic and poverty of past years as great—Yet if parlia[ment] meet, as they say it will in January[11]—something is feared— something about to be done—besides fishing in Virginia Water[12] and driving about in a pony phaeton—

I should be very glad to hear more of your child[13]—I had thoughts—I desired to make an offer—but I dread a denial—and besides Italy is better than England for a child of the south—is she not lovely, delightful full of sensibility.

Adieu—my dear friend—have we quarrelled are we reconciled?—What is it?—I know little more than that I have never ceased being ⟨enti⟩ warmly attached to you and that I am always

Affectionately Yours
MWShelley

ADDRESS: L'Italie / Edward Trelawny Esq / Ferma in Posta / Florence Firenze. POSTMARKS: (1) [   ] AL TUR[   ] (2) [CORRI]SPZA ESTERA DA GE[NOVA]; (3) 3 / FEBBRAIO. PUBLISHED: Jones, #346. TEXT: MS., Bodleian Library (MS., Shelley, Adds., c. 6, ff. 86—87).

1. Of 20 October 1829 (Abinger MSS., Bodleian Library; partially published in Lovell, *Medwin*, pp. 236–37).

2. Unidentified.

3. A reference to Hunt, *Lord Byron and Some of His Contemporaries* (see vol. I, 8 April [1825], n. 1).

4. Trelawny's letter accused Medwin of folly and villainy, gave details of Medwin's desertion of his wife and daughters, and revealed Trelawny's active role in assisting Mrs. Medwin (see April 1[829], n. 3).

5. Arrabella Hunt, born 13 November 1829, died 2 December 1830 (SC, V, 262).

6. On 7 December 1829 (Godwin, Journal).

7. Caroline Beauclerk (1804–69) had married Robert Aldridge of Horsham on 20 October 1829 (*Burke's Peerage*).

8. "Jewelry."

9. Frances Anne Kemble (1809–93), actress and author, made her stage debut as Juliet at Covent Garden on 5 October 1829; her father, Charles Kemble, played Mercutio, and her mother, Maria Therese Kemble (1774–1838), played Lady Capulet. She won immediate acclaim and was celebrated throughout her long career. In 1833 she accompanied her father to America, and during that trip she became friends with Trelawny. In 1834 she married Pierce Butler, a Southern planter, whom she divorced in 1848 (*The Times* [London], 23 and 26

October 1829; vol. I, 13–18 June [1824], n. 15; Margaret Armstrong, *Fanny Kemble* [New York: The Macmillan Co., 1938], pp. 77–101, 171–80).

10. Agitation for political reform and great economic distress, continuous since the end of the Napoleonic wars, finally culminated in a series of reforms, including the Catholic Emancipation Bill (March–April 1829) and the Reform Bill (March 1832), which redistributed parliamentary representation in favor of the industrial and commercial classes (see 22–25 March 1831).

11. Parliament opened on 4 February 1830 rather than as usual in January (*Annual Register, 1830*).

12. An allusion to George IV (see vol. I, 27 September [1825], n. 6).

13. Trelawny's letters to Mary Shelley of 24–26 June 1829 stated that Zella was already with him (Abinger MSS., Bodleian Library). In fact, she arrived in Italy around 27 July (Trelawny, *Letters*, p. 129).

*To Charles Ollier   Wednesday Evening   [16 December 1829]
                                                 33 Somerset St.

My dear Sir

Your total silence and Mr Colburn's neglect of my notes are quite inexplicable—I had hoped that you would have been enabled to give me an answer last week—receiving none, I sent to Mr Colburn last Saturday—My question simply was whether he had made up his mind to publish for me—terms I left for an after consideration—You will very much oblige me if you will represent to Mr Colburn that it is excessively inconvenient to me to wait week after week in entire uncertainty—I suppose by his delay I am not to receive a negative, or he would hardly ⟨detain⟩ think it right to add to the annoyance of a denial, the extreme discomfort of this very long delay—I am very much annoyed at being obliged to intrude upon you—But you were very kind in offering me your welcome and useful services and I take you at your word. Pray, my dear Sir, let me know <u>immediately</u> the <u>cause</u> of this dilatory mode of proceeding—and better still induce Mr Colburn to come to the conclusion I desire—At any rate let me hear from you

                                    I am dear Sir
                                    Yours obliged
                                    MaryShelley

ADDRESS: For / Charles Ollier Esq / 5 Maida Hill / Paddington. POSTMARKS: (1) T.P / Duke St M.S; (2) 10. F.NOON. 10 / 17. DE / 1829. UNPUBLISHED. TEXT: MS., Pforzheimer Library.

To John George Cochrane[1]   33 Somerset St. Teusday
                                           [22 December 1829]

My dear Sir

   I have not forgotten nor neglected my task—but M. Beyle's book[2] is so trite so unentertaining—so <u>very</u> common place that I have found it quite impossible to do any thing with it

                                    Your Ob[r] Servant
                                    MShelley

ADDRESS: ———— Cochrane Esq / 3 Soho Square. POSTMARKS: (1) T.P / Duke St M.S; (2) 8. MORN. 8 / 23. DE / 1829. ENDORSED: Mrs Shelley / Decr 22d. PUBLISHED: Palacio, *Mary Shelley*, p. 609. TEXT: MS., Jean de Palacio.

   1. John George Cochrane (1781–1852; *DNB*), bibliographer and editor, was manager of the foreign bookselling house of Treuttel, Wurtz, Treuttel junior, and Richter, publishers of the *Foreign Quarterly Review* (published from July 1827 through December 1834).

   2. M. de Stendhal [pseud.], *Promenades dans Rome*, 2 vols. (Brussels, 1830).

To Charles Ollier   Thursday [?24 December 1829] Somerset St.

My dear Sir

   Do you imagine that I have heard from M[r] Colburn or M[r] Bentley?—O, no! I hear nothing from any body—& am annoyed to death—So much to excite your good nature—to which I trust

                                      Yours obliged
                                    MS.

Is the Exclusives come out[1]

ADDRESS: For / Charles Ollier Esq / 5 Maida Hill. PUBLISHED: Jones, #348. TEXT: MS., Pforzheimer Library.

   1. Charlotte Bury, *The Exclusives*, 3 vols. (London: H. Colburn and R. Bentley, 1830).

*To John Murray   Saturday [1830]—Somerset St.

My Dear Sir

   I am so sorry that I was prevented calling this morning as I intended— I was unavoidably detained—I want to see you for three minutes, though I am not in any great hurry—so I will take my chance of finding you some morning early next week

                                      Yours obliged
                                    MShelley

ADDRESS: For / John Murray Esq / 50 Albermarle St. POSTMARKS: (1) T.P / Duke St [M.S]; (2) [   ] 7 [   ]. ENDORSED: 1830 (No date) / Shelley Mrs. UNPUBLISHED: Jones, #349, in summary. TEXT: MS., John Murray.

To [Charles Ollier]   33 Somerset St.   5 Jan. 1830

My dear Sir

You brought me two propositions from Mr Colburn concerning my book—
One concerned the dividing of profits—I confess that this does not please
me, for I am no woman of business—

The other proposal was to purchase my manuscript for £150—I accept
this proposal[1]—and wish to know how soon Mr Colburn will go to the
press—

You had better call on me to make the agreement—I should be glad that
as little delay as possible should occur—

With many excuses for the trouble I give you—

I am Yours Obliged
MaryShelley

My father has seen Mr Colburn on the subject—and he received a letter
from him about it yesterday—But the modifications occasioned by this
interview none of them please me so well as the one made through you
which I accept—

Nevertheless this one is sufficiently unfavorable—but I believe I know
Mr Colburn enough to be satisfied that if the book succeed far beyond his
expectation he will take his mistake into consideration

This will make however no part of the agreement which will simply be
for the sale of Poor Perkin Warbeck for £150—

PUBLISHED: Jones, #350. TEXT: MS., Pforzheimer Library.

1. On 21 January 1830 Mary Shelley signed an agreement that Colburn and Bentley would
publish *Perkin Warbeck* in three volumes of at least three hundred and twenty pages each, to
be ready for publication by 1 March 1830. The copyright would belong to the publishers, and
Mary Shelley would be paid £150: £50 by a bill three months from the agreement date, £50
on the publication date, and £50 nine months from the publication date (MS., Agreement,
British Library, Add. 46611).

*To John Howard Payne   Wednesday [6 January 1830]
                                        33 Somerset St—

My dear Payne—I know it is difficult, is it impossible to get me an admission
for Drury Lane for Friday[1]—a newspaper one for instance—if not to admit
two get for one—you would save me some on a two sevenshillings—go I
must

Thus at least I hope I shall hear from you—perhaps see you there—for
it is fifty ages since you have been alive to me—Y^r Ever MS.

ADDRESS: For / J. Howard Payne / 17 Speldhurst St. / Burton Crescent. POSTMARKS: (1) T.P /
Duke St M[.S]; (2) 4. N[OO]N[.4] / 6. JA / 1830. UNPUBLISHED. TEXT: MS., Pforzheimer
Library.

1. *Othello* and *Jack in the Box*, a Christmas pantomime, were scheduled for Friday, 8 January
(*The Times* [London]).

To John Bowring[1]   33 Somerset St.   [7 January 1830]

My dear Sir

I have a great horror of my name being in public—even the select public of an Album—but I could not refuse you—& to imitate your other Contributors I have added some nonsense (the addition is an imitation not the nonsense) to my sign manual

I half wished to have offered an article on Irving's Granada[2] but thought you would accomplish this—for the next number che dice?[3]   I admire it excessively

I have lost you{r} note after having glanced at it once only—but I think there was no other subject mentioned   Welcome home[4]—from the north one [cross-written] May say this—from any other part of the World What horror to return to this sejour affreux[5]

Yours Ever
MS.

ADDRESS: For / Doctor Bowring / &c &c / 2 Wellington St. POSTMARKS: (1) T.P / Duke St M.S; (2) 10. F.NOON. 10 / 8. JA / 1830. ENDORSED: (1) Jany 7. 1830 / Mary Shelley; (2) Mary Shelley / 7 Jany 1830. PUBLISHED: Jones, #351. TEXT: MS., Huntington Library (HM 2766).

1. In February 1829 the University of Groningen conferred an LL.D. on John Bowring (John Bowring, *Autobiographical Recollections of Sir John Bowring* [London: Henry S. King & Co., 1877], p. 9). Mary Shelley addressed this and subsequent letters to him "Doctor Bowring."
2. The *Westminster Review* contains no article on *Granada*.
3. "What do you say?"
4. Bowring had been on a tour of Scandinavia (MS., National Library of Scotland, 3911, f. 37; *Autobiographical Recollections of Sir John Bowring*, pp. 153–56).
5. "Frightful residence."

To William Galignani   33 Somerset St.   London   8 Jan 1829
                                                [error for 1830][1]

My dear Sir

I should have been glad to lend you a portrait of Shelley for the Paris edition of the Poems had I one to spare—but that which alone I possess—although imperfect—is far too precious to me to let it out of my hands—

Were your engraver in London I should not be disinclined to let him copy it here—but as you say this is not possible I have made a little pencil sketch which I enclose in the hope that it will serve your purpose[2]—especially as you mention that the likeness is to be very small—

I am
Yours truly
MWShelley

PUBLISHED: Jones, #324. TEXT: MS., Humanities Research Center, University of Texas at Austin.

1. Given the sequence of letters concerning Galignani's edition, and Mary Shelley's letter of 15 January 1830, "1829" must be an error for 1830. This letter, however, presents a greater difficulty. The contents of the letter seem authentic and explain the origins of Mary Shelley's signed pencil drawing of Shelley (see frontispiece), but it is not in Mary Shelley's handwriting, though it has been represented as such in past publications (including *MWS Letters*; and Walter Edwin Peck, *Shelley: His Life and Work*, 2 vols. [Boston: Houghton Mifflin Co., 1927], II, 440–42). Written on stationery watermarked "J GREEN & SON / 1827," it is at best a copy meant to imitate Mary Shelley's handwriting. It is included in this edition with the question of whether it is a copy or a forgery, unresolved as to date. Mary Shelley's letter of 15 January 1830 is also a copy or a forgery rather than an actual Mary Shelley letter, and seems to have been done by the same person. I have been unable to locate the originals of these letters (the Galignanis have not kept their correspondence), nor have I found evidence as to the origins of these two letters.

2. This would indicate that Mary Shelley did not know that the frontispiece was already finished (see 15 January 1830).

TO CHARLES OLLIER   33 Somerset St.   14 Jan[y] 1830

My dear Sir

I do not hear from you I suppose because you deem all things settled— Things have been delayed so long that I now want money—I have promised to pay a Christmas bill at the end of this week and it breaks my heart not to keep such a promise—Will you get £50 from Colburn—the Manuscript is ready for the printer—Yours obliged MShelley

ADDRESS: For / Charles Ollier Esq / 5 Maida Hill / Paddington. PUBLISHED: Jones, #352. TEXT: MS., Bodleian Library (MS., Shelley, Adds., d. 5, ff. 87–88).

TO WILLIAM GALIGNANI   33 Somerset St   London   15 Jan. 1830[1]

M[rs] Shelley is sorry she troubled M[r] Galignani about the little engraved likeness of Shelley for the Paris edition of the Poems—but she could not help thinking it would have been better to have sent her a proof of M[r] Wedgwood's[2] engraving—when she could have pointed out its defects as a likeness of her husband—

It may be that the small pencil sketch was deficient in artistic merit—but at least it bore—in her opinion a likeness to the original—

If the engraver will refer again to it he will perceive that in his copy he has closed the lips and so given them a thick appearance entirely out of character—

M[rs] S. mentions this detail particularly in order to prevent its possible repetition on a larger scale—

PUBLISHED: Jones, #353. TEXT: MS., Humanities Research Center, University of Texas at Austin.

1. See 8 January [1830], n. 1, for a discussion of the authenticity of this letter.

2. John Taylor Wedgwood (1783–1856), engraver, whose miniature portraits of Coleridge, Keats, and Shelley appear on the frontispiece of the Galignani edition (Williamson, *Bryan's Dictionary of Painters and Engravers*, V, 349).

*TO WILLIAM GODWIN   [?33 Somerset Street]   Sunday
                                              [?17 January 1830][1]

My dear Father—Can you tell me whether Marshall[2] is in town—I shall be driven to borrow[3] I fear for I cannot bring Ollier to do any thing—I shall make another effort with him tomorrow

                                                            Y^s Aff^y
                                                            MS.

ADDRESS: W. Godwin Esq / 44 Gower Place / Fitzroy Sq. UNPUBLISHED. TEXT: MS., Pforzheimer Library.
    1. The reference to Ollier suggests that this letter was written after Mary Shelley's letter of 14 January 1830 and before she signed the contract for *Perkin Warbeck*, on 21 January.
    2. Godwin's Journal records that James Marshall called on him on 31 December 1829 and 11 February 1830.
    3. Claire Clairmont wrote to Mary Shelley on 28 March 1830 that she had delayed her letter in "hope of being able to send you the money for Marshall," which suggests that Mary Shelley did borrow from Marshall at this time. Further, Claire Clairmont said that as soon as she received her salary she would send "what I owe you" (*S&M*, IV, 1124–30). Both Claire Clairmont and Charles Clairmont had borrowed money from Mary Shelley to pay for their return to the Continent (Locke, *Godwin*, p. 316).

TO JOHN MURRAY   33 Somerset St.   Portman Sq   19 Jan^y [1830]

My dear Sir
    Except the occupation of one or two annoyances, I have done nothing but read since I got Lord Byron's life[1]—
    I have no pretensions to being a critic—yet I know infinitely well what pleases me—Not to mention the judicious arrangement and happy tact displayed by Mr Moore, which distinguish this book—I must say a word concerning the style, which is elegant and forcible. I was particularly struck by the observations on Lord Byron's character before his departure to Greece—and on his return—there is strength and richness as well as sweetness—
    The great charm of the work to me, and it will have the same for you, is that the Lord Byron I find there is our Lord Byron—the fascinating—faulty—childish—philosophical being—daring the world—docile to a private circle—impetuous and indolent—gloomy and yet more gay than any other—I live with him again in these pages—getting reconciled (as I used in his lifetime) to those waywardnesses which annoyed me when he was

away, through the delightful & buoyant tone of his conversation and manners—

His own letters and journals mirror himself as he was, and are invaluable— There is something cruelly kind in this single volume   When will the next come?[2]—impatient before how tenfold now am I so.

Among its many other virtues this book is <u>accurate</u> to a miracle   [*p. 1, cross-written*]   I have not stumbled on one mistake with regard either to time place or feeling

I am dear Sir
Your Ob[t] & Obliged Servant
MaryShelley

ENDORSED: 1830 Jany 19 / Shelley Mrs. PUBLISHED: Jones, #354. TEXT: MS., John Murray.

1. Published 18 January 1830 (see [?13 December 1829], n. 1).

2. The second volume was published in late December 1830 (Oscar José Santucho and Clement Tyson Goode, Jr., *George Gordon, Lord Byron: A Comprehensive Bibliography of Secondary Materials in English, 1807–1974* [Metuchen, N.J.: Scarecrow Press, 1977], p. 277).

*To John Murray   33 Somerset St.   Wednesday
                                              [?23 January 1830][1]

My dear Sir

Am I intruding too much on your proffers of kindness?—Colburn has sent me <u>a bill</u>[2]—as if I could do any thing with a bill!—My father told me that once you said to him that you would give him money for any good bookseller's bill—is not this one & will you do the same for his daughter?

If in the slightest degree inconvenient do not scruple to reject me sans façon[3]—there is nothing I fear & detest so much as making any one's kindness to <u>me</u> an annoyance to <u>themselves</u>—

I enclose the affair; you will understand it better than I—it is the first I ever got—before he paid me in a gentlemanly way with a cheque—I mean as a gentleman should pay a <u>woman</u>—I dare say gentlemen have bills among one another

Yours Ob[ly] & Obliged
MaryShelley

I send two notes.[4] that the subject of the one may not interfere with the other—

This note was to have been sent with the other but I did not get the bill till now—

ENDORSED: 1830 Jany 23. / Shelley Mrs. UNPUBLISHED: Jones, #355, in summary. TEXT: MS., John Murray.

1. Although Mary Shelley dated this letter Wednesday, which would have been 20 January (see 25 January [1830] [*a*]), the date of endorsement is 23 January. Mary Shelley signed her contract for *Perkin Warbeck* on 21 January, and the publishers' ledger shows that the first bill

was dated 21 January (see 5 January 1830, n. 1). Since this letter states that Colburn sent the bill (rather than gave her the bill), it is most likely that 23 January is the correct date.

2. A bill was not payable until its due date (in this instance, in three months), but it could be "sold" for cash at a discount.

3. "Without ceremony."

4. The first note may have been the one enclosing a letter for Thomas Moore (see [25 January 1830] [*b*]).

TO JOHN MURRAY   Monday   25 Jan [1830] (*a*)   33 Somerset St.

My dear Sir

A thousand thanks—I return the bill—it is ridiculous that I should be so ignorant of the forms of their affairs.

My book is called "Perkin Warbeck"—I believe it will go to the press immediately—& I believe it is to appear on the first of March—at least I have {been} promised this—

I have written one or two observations on his book which I should be glad if you would forward to Mr Moore by the first occasion

I am dear Sir
Yours truly
MaryShelley

ENDORSED: 1830 Jany 25 / Shelley Mrs. PUBLISHED: Jones, #356. TEXT: MS., John Murray.

TO JOHN MURRAY   Somerset St.   Monday   [25 January 1830] (*b*)

My dear Sir

I am very sorry to trouble you but will you send me back my letter to Mr Moore—I have heard from him[1]—and do not wish it to go—send it by the 2^d post—

I am dear Sir
Yours Obliged
MShelley

ADDRESS: For / John Murray Esq / 50 Albermarle St. POSTMARKS: (1) T.P / WOOXTON [   ]; (2) 4. EVEN. 4 / 25 JA / 1830. ENDORSED: 1830 (no date) / Shelley Mrs. PUBLISHED: Jones, #357. TEXT: MS., John Murray.

1. In his letter of 24 January 1830 Moore wrote: "You really are a most unlucky <u>female</u>— considering, too, how truly you deserve to be otherwise. It is, however, not half so bad as I thought at first,—for, in my utter ignorance (thank God) of the law processes, I fancied, at the first glimpse, that it was on *you in propria persona*, that the execution was to be executed—" (Moore, *Letters*, II, 681). In the same letter Moore comments: "I did not answer your letter about Lawrence because though feeling our loss (the *general* loss) most sincerely, I knew I must fall far short of your emotion on the subject. . . ." Sir Thomas Lawrence's death on 7

January 1830 deeply affected Mary Shelley, who noted it in her Journal on 9 January 1830. Mary Shelley's letter to Moore of ?7–23 January 1830 is unlocated. I have been unable to identify the "law processes" affecting Mary Shelley at this time.

*TO JOHN MURRAY Teusday Evening [26 January 1830]
Somerset St.

My dear Sir

I am so sorry to trouble you—but my letter of Yesterday enclosed one to Mr Moore on the subject of his book which I asked you to forward— but I wish it not to be sent[1]—& I should be very glad to have it back again— & not to go—

I saw my Father today who is quite delighted with Mr Moore's book[2]— indeed who is not?—He thinks the whole sets Lord Byron in the light he best deserves—Generous open hearted and kind—He particularly thinks beautiful the account of the first acquaintance between Lord Byron & Mr Moore—

Yours Obliged
MShelley

ENDORSED: 1830. January / Shelley Mrs. UNPUBLISHED: Jones, #358, in summary. TEXT: MS., John Murray.

1. This suggests that Mary Shelley forgot that she had sent a previous note requesting the return of her letter to Moore.

2. Mary Shelley had tea with Godwin on 26 January. Godwin read Byron, *Letters and Journals* (Moore) from 21 through 27 January 1830 (Godwin, Journal).

TO WILLIAM WHITTON 1 March 1830 33 Somerset St.

My Dear Sir

I will send a receipt tomorrow in exchange for the cheque

Percy is quite well—I hope this spring he will see Sir Tim[thy] perhaps more of him—and if Sir Tim[thy] comes to town, I thrust to your kindness, if possible, to obtain an interview for me with him.

I am Sir
Ys Obliged
MaryShelley

ENDORSED: 1 March 1830 / Mrs Shelley. PUBLISHED: Jones, #359. TEXT: MS., Bodleian Library (MS., Shelley, Adds., c. 6, ff. 88–89).

*To Henry Colburn and Richard Bentley [Somerset Street
?4–11 March 1830][1]

Dear Sir

I send you nearly all the MS. of Perkin Warbeck—one Chapter is with a friend to correct some Irish localities[2]—pray let me have it back without delay—

I have just finished Cloudesley—the interest is inexpressively absorbing—there is a truth and majesty in the delineation of the passions, and a simplicity and grace in the style different from the present day—and striking one as one reads as how infinitely superior[3]—

I am Your Ob^{ly}
MShelley

ADDRESS: Mess. Colburn & Bentley / 8 New Burlington St. UNPUBLISHED. TEXT: MS., Pforzheimer Library.

1. Godwin's novel *Cloudesley*, written from 29 November 1828 through 16 January 1830, was published in three volumes by Colburn and Bentley on 4 March 1830. Godwin received £450 for *Cloudesley* (Godwin, Journal; Bentley Archives, British Library, Add. 46627, vol. 68, p. 4). This date is based on the conjecture that Mary Shelley received a copy on publication date (as did Godwin) and read quickly through it. Claire Clairmont has been credited with contributing much material to, if not actually writing some parts of, *Cloudesley* (see *CC Journals*, pp. 416–17). The fact that the manuscript of *Cloudesley* is entirely in Godwin's handwriting does not disprove this claim (MS., Pforzheimer Library).

2. Perhaps Thomas Crofton Croker.

3. Mary Shelley incorporated this viewpoint in her review of *Cloudesley* (see 4 May [1830]).

*To John Murray 33 Somerset St. 5 March [1830]

My dear Sir

I wrote after seeing you to a friend of mine in Paris[1] concerning the facilities I might procure for the "Lives" in question—She says "M. Benjamin Constant will with pleasure supply you with all the materials he possesses for the Life of Mme de Staël—he will be happy to give you in the very few moments he can snatch from his political engagements during the session any assistance he can, but his time is almost wholly absorbed—and as soon as the Chambers separate—he goes to Baden—. The very best materials you will have from him—& he will get you an introduction to the duc de Broglie—M^{m} de Staël's son.in:law for the later period Materials for the life of the Empress Josephine are so abundant that you will only have to cull the best—"

This is written under the idea that I shall visit Paris—but I trust the best part of the information will be attainable without that journey—but it gives one hopes—You said Sir James MacIntosh[2] had letters that ⟨he⟩ you thought he might supply—Other channels will of course appear as I go on.

At present after neglecting my book—Colburn is in a great hurry to get it out—so I shall be be very busy for two or three weeks after which time I will see you—

I hear eternal praises of Mr Moore's book—how impatient I am for the 2nd Vol.

I hope you are quite well
I am yours obliged
MShelley

ENDORSED: 1830 / March 5 / Shelley Mrs. UNPUBLISHED: Jones, #360, in summary. TEXT: MS., John Murray.

1. Perhaps Isabel Robinson Douglas or Mary Diana Dods.

2. Catherine Allen Mackintosh, the second wife of Sir James Mackintosh (1765–1832), philosopher and political figure (and friend of Godwin), was the sister of Jessie Allen Sismondi, the wife of Simonde de Sismondi (1773–1842), historian, and an intimate of Madame de Staël (Jean R. de Salis, "Charles Sismondi, 1773–1842," *Bibliothèque de la Revue de littérature comparée* 77 [Geneva: Slatkin Reprint, 1932]: p. 378).

*TO THOMAS CROFTON CROKER   Somerset S^t   Saturday
                                         [20 March 1830]

Mrs Shelley's Compliments to Mr Crofton Croker and requests the pleasure of his company to a small evening party on Thursday[1]—

ADDRESS: To / T. Crofton Croker Esq / Admiralty. POSTMARKS: (1) T.P / [   ]; (2) 12. NOON. 12 / 22. MR / 1830. UNPUBLISHED. TEXT: MS., Greater London Record Office.

1. I find no other record of the small party of Thursday, 25 March 1830. However, on Tuesday, 23 March, Mary Shelley "gave a soiree—which succeeded very well—Mrs Hare is going—I am very sorry—she likes me—& is gentle & good—her husband is clever & her set very agreable—rendered so by the reunion of some of the best people about town" (MWS Journal). At this gathering were many members of her new social set (MWS Journal, 22 January 1830), as well as more familiar figures, including Godwin; Moore; Washington Irving; James Kenney; the Misses Robinson; Lady Mary Shepherd (1777–1847), author; Charles William Edward Jerningham (1805–54), barrister and essayist; Roderick Impey Murchison (1792–1871; *DNB*), geologist, knighted in 1846; Edward Bulwer, in 1843 Bulwer-Lytton (he and Godwin had met in 1826 at the home of Caroline Lamb and had become friends in 1828, after her death [Locke, *Godwin*, p. 318]); Ellen Purves Manners-Sutton, nee Powers, wife of Charles Manners-Sutton (1780–1845; *DNB*), Speaker of the House of Commons, and sister of Marguerite, countess of Blessington (see 15 August [1832]; Sir John Dean Paul, 1st baronet (1775–1852); John Dean Paul (1802–68), son of Sir John Dean Paul, and his wife, Georgiana, nee Beauclerk (1805–47), Mary Shelley's close friend; Henry Bevan (1776–1860) and his wife Harriet (d. 1852), parents of Louisa Harriet Paul, nee Bevan (d. 1870), who married George Robert Paul (1803–80), son of Sir John Dean Paul, in 1828; Francis Hare (1786–1842) and his wife Anne Frances Hare, nee Paul (d. 1864) (Godwin, Journal; Moore, *Journal; Burke's Peerage;* and R. H. Super, *Walter Savage Landor* [New York: New York University Press, 1954], pp. 192, 473). The Hares left for Italy on 24 September 1830 (MWS Journal).

*[?FREDERIC MANSEL REYNOLDS][1] [?33 Somerset Street]
Thursday [?March 1830][2]

My dear Friend—I send you a cheque for a part of what I owe you—I will make no promises about the rest but be assured I shall <u>not forget it</u>

Ever yours obliged
MWShelley

UNPUBLISHED. TEXT: MS., Cornell University Library.
    1. The possibility of this letter's being to Frederic Mansel Reynolds is based on Mary Shelley's letter of [16 June 1829].
    2. I tentatively date this letter 1830 because the earliest Mary Shelley letter I have located that bears the same watermark on the same stationery used for this letter, "J GREEN & SON / 1829," is her letter dated [20 March 1830].

*To RICHARD BENTLEY   33 Somerset St   Monday [19 April 1830]

My dear Sir

    A most tiresome accident has ocurred—Copy of mine the first 44 pages of my 3ᵈ Vol.[1] was given to the Printer's boy some time back—And it seems the whole parcel is mislaid—of course were I not <u>quite certain</u> that the mistake lay with them, I should not so positively assert—that there is no doubt but that they had it—I have no other copy—And cannot imagine what is to be done—except that I do not doubt but that they will find it, if it is properly looked for—

I am Sir
Yˢ Obˡʸ
MaryShelley

ADDRESS: Richard Bentley Esq / 8 New Burlington St. POSTMARKS: (1) T.P / [N]o Oxford S[t]; (2) 7. NIGHT. 7 / 19. AP / 1830. UNPUBLISHED. TEXT: MS., Pforzheimer Library.
    1. Of *Perkin Warbeck*.

*To HENRY COLBURN AND RICHARD BENTLEY   33 Somerset St.
29 April 1830

Gentlemen

    I have a little delayed answering your note that I might see my Father concerning it.[1] I confess that it does not at all strike me as necessary to alter my title—I have a prediliction for the one I have chosen—but besides that—the book being printed—and the running title of "Perkin Warbeck" being affixed to each page I do not see how <u>it can be altered</u>.

    As far as I can pretend to judge, a rivalship is of no detriment—<u>I</u> should should imagine that merely with regard to the value of a publication, no one would dream of putting one from Mr Newman's press in competition with one issueing from Mess. Colburn & Bentley—And not of course to speak of the comparative merits of the Authors—of which I know nothing— the interest mine will excite, and the judgement to be passed on it, results from its being by "The Author of Frankenstein."—I am therefore exceedingly averse to an alteration, which must be so bunglingly made—which strikes me as a concession, we are in no way necessitated to ⟨make⟩ yield, and which must on the whole be hurtful. The immediate—the instantaneous publication of my volumes—the whole of which with preface and title page I have sent to the printer would, I should think, be a measure far more useful & certain, in securing us against any injury this other publication might occasion—Could it not come out on Monday—or at least be advertised in a way that should put the public in possession of the fact that it will very speedily ⟨come out⟩ appear?—

⟨If I⟩ [*two lines deleted*] ⟨time on Saturday or Monday⟩—

I am, Gentlemen,
Yours Ob^{ly}
MWShelley

ADDRESS: For: / Mess. Colburn & Bentley / 8 New Burlington Street. POSTMARKS: (1) T.P / Ratten Ct.; (2) 10. F.NOON. 10 / 30. AP / 1830. UNPUBLISHED. TEXT: MS., Pforzheimer Library.

1. Mary Shelley had tea with Godwin on 29 April 1830 (Godwin, Journal). At issue was whether Mary Shelley should change the title of *The Fortunes of Perkin Warbeck* because of the publication, announced for May, of Alexander Campbell's *Perkin Warbeck; or, the Court of James the Fourth of Scotland*, 3 vols. (London: A. K. Newman, 1830). Mary Shelley did not change the title, and both novels were published in May.

*TO RICHARD BENTLEY 4 May [1830] 33 Somerset St.

My dear Sir

I am very sorry that I could not see you yesterday—I am afraid I cannot call today—but tomorrow I will—between three & four.

Do you still desire—and do you at all think it practicable to change the title? It might be called "The White Rose of England; or Perkin Warbeck"— By the bye I have corrected the <u>proof</u> of the title page—but I suppose you have seen it.

I am very sorry for this contretemps. But I hope no injury will be done— You have seen of course Blackwood's review of Cloudesley[1]—

Yours obt^{ly}
MWShelley

ADDRESS: Richard Bentley Esq / 8 New Burlington St. POSTMARKS: (1) T.P / WOOX[TON]; (2) 4. EVEN. 4 / 4. MY / 1830. UNPUBLISHED. TEXT: MS., Illinois University Library.

1. A review entitled "Cloudesley; A Tale by the author of Caleb Williams," in *Blackwood's Edinburgh Magazine* 27 (May 1830): 711–16. On 24 April 1830 William Blackwood wrote

to Mary Shelley to thank her for the notice of *Cloudesley* that she sent him, and he enclosed a copy of the review printed "without omission or alteration, though a fastidious person may perhaps consider some expressions as rather a little partial." He also invited her to send further communications (Abinger MSS., Bodleian Library, Dep. b. 215/6).

To WILLIAM WHITTON   33 Somerset St   Portman Sq   24 May 1830

Dear Sir

Hearing that Sir Timothy is in town, I cannot help requesting to see him[1]—I send you my note which will you be so good as to let him have—it contains simply this request—I am sorry that Lady Shelley has not seen my son either this year or last—As Percy grows up, it would be of great benefit to him, surely, to be in more frequent communication with his father's family—He is getting a big boy now—and as it is more than probable that there will be no change in his situation for years—I feel anxious that he should not be always a stranger with those who have in reality the direction of his education.

Permit me to ask you to interfere in my favor—& if you do not find Sir Timothy wholly unwilling, to do the kind office of inducing him to receive me—

I am dear Sir
Y^s Ob^{ly}
MWShelley

PUBLISHED: Jones, #361. TEXT: MS., Bodleian Library (MS., Shelley, Adds., c. 6, f. 90).

1. This request of Mary Shelley's to meet Sir Timothy Shelley was denied, as were all her other requests to be received by him.

To SIR TIMOTHY SHELLEY   33 Somerset St.   24 May [1830]

Sir

Permit me very sincerely to thank you for your kindness to my son. Hearing that you are in town I feel as if I should fail in a duty, if I did not solicit permission to wait on you. I cannot express the pleasure it would give me to see you. It appeared to me, at one time, from something Mr Peacock said, that you were not averse to it, and indeed it is this that encourages me to make the request—for I should be very sorry to press any gratification of my own that would annoy you. It appears to me that as Percy grows older, much good would result to him from my having a more frequent communication with you about him—and I trust that since my return to England, I have proved in every way that his interests and welfare are the only objects of my life—

> I am Sir
> Your Obedient Servant
> & Daughter-in-law
> MWShelley

ADDRESS: For / Sir Timthy Shelley Bart. ENDORSED: 24 May 1830 / Mrs Shelley. PUBLISHED: Jones, #362. TEXT: MS., Bodleian Library (MS., Shelley, Adds., c. 6, ff. 91–92).

---

*TO JOHN MURRAY   33 Somerset St.   Portman Square
                                                    25 May [1830]

My dear Sir

Will you have the goodness to give the Bearer my Father's Manuscript— if you have it at hand—or will you be so good as to send it to me—He is very anxious to have it immediately.[1] I should be very glad that your long delay in answering meant an affirmative and to find that you were willing to become his publisher—Otherwise it is very necessary that he should apply immediately elsewhere.

Mr Moore told me that you would soon communicate with me on the subject of the proposed life of Mme de Staël. To make it all perfect, I should fear that a visit to Paris is almost necessary—At all events I should be very glad to hear from you about it

> I am, My dear Sir
> Yours Ob^ly & Obliged
> MWShelley

ENDORSED: 1830 May 25 / Shelley Mrs. UNPUBLISHED: Jones, #363, in summary. TEXT: MS., John Murray.

1. Godwin had sent some of the twenty-three essays that were eventually included in *Thoughts on Man* (London: Effingham Wilson), published on 22 February 1831 (Locke, *Godwin*, pp. 320, 367). Murray returned the manuscript to Godwin on 29 May 1830 (Godwin, Journal).

---

*TO CHARLES WILLIAM EDWARD JERNINGHAM   33 Somerset St.
                                            Saturday   May 28 [1830][1]

Mrs Shelley's Compliments to Mr Jerningham and requests the pleasure of his Company to a small Evening party on Monday June 7[2]

ADDRESS: Charles Edd Jerningham Esq / Windham Club / St. James's Square. POSTMARKS: (1) T.P / Up Berkeley St; (2) 10. F.NOON. 10 / 31. MY / 1830. UNPUBLISHED. TEXT: MS., Pforzheimer Library.

1. 28 May 1830 was a Friday.

2. In addition to himself, Godwin's Journal (7 June 1830) lists Mary Shelley's guests as Doyle (unidentified); two Bulwers; Lady Mary Shepherd; Frederic Mansel Reynolds; Mrs. Coates (unidentified); three Robinsons; Thomas Moore; Charles Jerningham; and Richard Rothwell (1800–1868; *DNB*), Irish artist, who in 1826 had become Sir Thomas Lawrence's chief assistant (in 1841 he painted Mary Shelley's portrait, now in the National Gallery, London). Moore described the party as an "odd assembly" (Moore, *Journal*, 7 June 1830). Washington Irving had indicated that he would attend the party (Irving to Mary Shelley, 28 May 1830, Pforzheimer Library), but his omission on Godwin's list indicates that he was not there.

To William Whitton   33 Somerset St.   2 June 1830

My dear Sir

I will send my receipt tomorrow in exchange for the Cheque for my quarter[1]

Yours Ob[ly]
MWShelley

ADDRESS: For: / William Whitton Esq / 18 Bedford Row. POSTMARK: 7. NOON. 7 / 2. JU / [   ]ct. ENDORSED: 2 June 1830 / Mrs Shelley. PUBLISHED: Jones, #364. TEXT: MS., Bodleian Library (MS., Shelley, Adds., c. 6, ff. 93–94).

1. See 14 June 1830, n. 1.

To William Whitton   33 Somerset St.   14 June 1830

My dear Sir

I am afraid by some mistake you have not received my note—My receipt has been for some time in the hands of your Clerk[1]—As I understand that you return to town tomorrow—May I ask you to send me the cheque—

My son's holydays commence on Wednesday—M[r] Lawrence[2] strongly advised me to take him to the sea side this summer, and as my time is up in my present abode, I mean next week to go to a sea port[3] for the six weeks he will pass with me—Your absence from town perhaps prevented your receiving my previous note

I am dear Sir
Y[s] Ob[ly]
MWShelley

ENDORSED: 14 June 1830 / Mrs Shelley. PUBLISHED: Jones, #365. TEXT: MS., Bodleian Library (MS., Shelley, Adds., c. 6, ff. 95–96).

1. A note on Mary Shelley's letter of 2 June 1830 reads: "Sent check for 75 in letter left by Mr. Pater 15th."

2. Dr. William Lawrence (see vol. I, [24 September 1817] [*a*], n. 2).

3. Mary Shelley recorded in her Journal on 30 June 1830: "I go to Southend for a Month with Percy coming once to town during that time to a ball at the Speaker's [*Charles Manners-*

Sutton's]." Southend is a seaside town in Essex, thirty-nine miles east of London. On 22 July 1830 Godwin refused Mary Shelley's invitation to join her there, noting that she would "quit Southend this day seven-night" (Paul, *Godwin*, II, 309). She returned to London on 5 August 1830.

To Maria Jane Jewsbury[1]   33 Somerset St.   Portman Square
                                      16 June—1830

I have been very much flattered, My dear Madam, by M[r] Rothwell,[2] who assures me that you are good enough to desire my acquaintance. As your stay in town is so short, I have been induced to beleive that you would waive ceremony, and do me the pleasure of drinking tea with me either this Evening or tomorrow. May I expect you?—I enclose the autograph of M[r] Shelley's handwriting which M[r] Rothwell tells me your sister[3] wishes to have. I hope your sister will do me the favor of accompanying you ⟨tomorrow⟩

> I am dear Madam
> Your Ob[t] Servant
> MaryW. Shelley

Address: Miss Jewesbury / &c &c &c. Published: Jones, #366. Text: MS., Historical Society of Pennsylvania.

1. Maria Jane Jewsbury (1800–1833; *DNB*), author, who married Rev. William Kew Fletcher in 1832 and went to India, where she died of cholera on 4 October 1833. Maria Jane Jewsbury noted on Mary Shelley's letter: "This interview was brought on by R— [*Richard Rothwell*] having overestimated the force of an expression—but it is only just to say the [*?annexed*] note to M[rs] Jameson [Anna Jameson (1794–1860), author] conveyed my real impression of M[rs] S—The evening was divided between them—the most interesting of my town series." Maria Jane Jewsbury's impression of Mary Shelley was written to Anna Jameson on 18 June 1830:

> As you expressed a desire to know my opinion of Mrs. Shelley, I will take the present opportunity of saying, that I rarely, if ever, met with a woman to whom I felt so disposed to apply the epithet "bewitching." I can of course merely speak of appearances, but she struck me in the light of a matured child; a union of buoyancy and depth; a something that brought to my remembrance Shelley's description of Beatrice in his preface to the Cenci. To those she loves her manners would be caressing; to a stranger they are kind and playful, less from a desire to please, than from a habit of amicable feeling. Her hilarity, contrasted with the almost sadly profound nature of some of her remarks, somewhat puzzled me. It is not the hilarity assumed by worn minds in society,—it is simple— natural—and like Spring full of sweetness, but I doubt her being a happy woman, and I also doubt her being one that could be distinctly termed melancholy. Looking over the best part of the writings of her father, mother, and husband, she is the kind of woman for them to love to describe. She reminded me of no person I ever saw, but she has made me wish the arrival of the time when I am to see her again. She is not one to sit with and think ill of, even on authority (*Anna Jameson: Letters and Friendships*, ed. Mrs. Steuart Erskine [London: T. Fletcher Unwin, 1915], pp. 89–90).

In her article "Shelley's 'Wandering Jew,' " *Athenaeum*, no. 194 (16 July 1831): 456–57, Maria Jane Jewsbury highly praised Shelley's "true, pure, beautiful poetry—poetry instinct with intellectual life—radiant, harmonious, and strong."

2. See 28 May [1830], n. 2.

3. Geraldine Endsor Jewsbury (1812–80; *DNB*), author, who subsequently became an intimate of Lady Morgan (and assisted her with her *Memoirs*) and Thomas and Jane Carlyle. In 1830 Geraldine Jewsbury, in the care of her sister, was sent from their home in Manchester to London to perfect herself in languages and drawing (Susanne Howe, *Geraldine Jewsbury* [London: George Allen & Unwin, 1935], pp. 14–15).

*To John Murray   Park Cottage—Paddington   9 August—1830

My Dear Sir

A long time ago I requested Mr Moore to communicate with you on the subject of the work it was in contemplation that I should write for the Family Library. He told me that you said that you would write to me—It is not strange that your numerous avocations should have caused you to defer this—And having been out of town, I have also delayed renewing my communication. I am now anxious to that we should agree as soon as possible on the subject—both as a means of my defraying my present debt towards you,[1] and of my earning a further sum, which from circumstances with which you are acquainted, I am very eager to do.

The subject you mentioned was the Life of Mme de Staël. On communicating with some friends of mine in Paris,[2] I was assured by M. B. [*Benjamin*] Constant, that he would most readily give me every information in his power and introduce me to such other persons as would give me a great deal more. But nothing of this sort could be done by letter, but must necessitate a journey to Paris. I remember when I mentioned this to you—you said that you did not think it worthwhile—that you wanted an amusing not a profound book. It appears to me however necessary to make the book amusing. For a bare detail of what I could collect here, would contain nothing new or interesting—it is from anecdotes—from understanding through her friends the real and minute particulars of events, and learning through them her peculiar disposition and character, that I must form the interest of this or any other biography. By letter nothing could be done; for M. Constant had so little—and now must have so much less time[3] at his disposal that it { } only in conversation that I could communicate with him. With these helps it appears to me that a most interesting, and were my ability sufficient, a most delightful work might be written.

As this may not enter into your plans, I have been meditating on other subjects to form a volume of your Library. Two or three have struck me. A Friend suggested the life of Mahomet—as not having been written for some years and therefore permitting novelty. I thought of the Conquests of Mexico & Peru as forming in some sort a continuation to a Life of Columbus. But the subject that struck me most, as affording scope for novelty and amusement, from the quantity and variety of materials we possess, was a history of the manners and ⟨history⟩ Literature of England from Queen Anne to the French Revolution—from Pope to Horace Walpole—To this even might follow another of Continental manners and literature during the same period—One other subject I heard in society the other day The lives of the English Philosophers—but this would hardly be so amusing[4]

May I request as early an answer as you can conveniently give to these subjects—as my time now is tolerably unoccupied, I could easily call in Albermarle St. I confess it would give me great pleasure for a thousand reasons to contribute a volume to Your publication—The more so, as I believe though this may be vanity—that my book while it would be conscientiously accurate, would not at all fail on the score of <u>amusement</u>, which is one of the necessary adjuncts.

I am, my dear Sir
Yours Obliged
MWShelley

Are any copies of M[r] Moores 2nd Vol. made up—You may guess that I am not a little anxious to see it.

ADDRESS: John Murray Esq / 50 Albermarle St. POSTMARKS: (1) [PA]DDINGTON / EV / 10 AU; (2) 7. NIGHT. 7 / 10. AU / 1830. ENDORSED: 1830—August 9. / Shelley Mrs. UNPUBLISHED: Jones, #367, in summary. TEXT: MS., John Murray.

    1. This suggests that Mary Shelley had further borrowed from Murray or that she did not consider her debt of £100 cleared, although Murray did (see 12 November 1829, n. 3).

    2. See 5 March [1830], n. 1.

    3. Almost certainly a reference to the political events in France. Dissatisfaction with ever more rigid governmental control by Charles X (1757–1836) had culminated in the 28–29 July revolution. Lafayette had headed the radical movement, which supported him for the presidency of a French republic. Instead, Louis Philippe (1773–1850), duke of Orleans, supported by the liberal faction, was declared lieutenant general of France (30 July) and then King of the French (7 August).

    4. Noted in an unidentified hand on Mary Shelley's letter: "The last suggestion capital, if M[rs] S—be capable of undertaking it.—"

To WILLIAM WHITTON Park Cottage Paddington 1 September 1830

My Dear Sir

I shall send tomorrow the receipt for the Cheque, which you will oblige me by giving sealed up to the bearer.

I hope you are well. Percy has come back in the best possible health from our excursion to the Sea side. You would very much oblige me by letting me know when it is probable that Sir Tim[thy] will visit town

I am Y[s] Ob[ly] MWShelley

ENDORSED: 1st Sept 1830 / Mrs Shelley. PUBLISHED: Jones, #368. TEXT: MS., Bodleian Library (MS., Shelley, Adds., c. 6, ff. 97–98).

My Dear Sir

I presume, since I have not heard from you, that you have received no communication from M[r] Murray in reply to my letter. My idea has been that he intended to delay any until his return. I find however that he is not expected back for a month. Meanwhile if M[r] Murray's silence proceeds from his deciding on declining my offers, I should be very glad not any longer to be kept in a suspense, which is very inconvenient to me.

May I request you at your earliest convenience, to make my desire known to M[r] Murray. If he desires to postpone any arrangement until his return— yet ⟨means⟩ if he considers it most probable that then one will be made, of course I shall be most happy to wait. For I own I shall have great pleasure in contributing to the Family Library—I suggested several subjects in my last letter—I almost forget now whether some I am going ⟨now⟩ to mention were included. One subject I have thought of, is an History of the Earth— in its earlier state—that is an account both of the anti diluvian remains— of the changes on the surface of the Earth, and of the relics of States and Kingdoms before the period of regular history. M[r] Murray will judge how far there is any danger of intrenching upon orthodoxy on this subject—He is aware that I have a great distaste to obtruding any opinions, even if I have any, differing from general belief, of which I am not aware—and also how far such a history would be amusing. To me these speculations have always been the source of great interest, but this may not be the public taste.

I have thought also of the Lives of Celebrated women—or a history of Woman—her position in society & her influence upon it—historically considered. and a History of Chivalry.

My friend. M[r] Marshall, mentioned some time ago the idea of writing for the Quarterly[2]—and liberal as that publication has become, and clever and distinguished as it has always been, I should be very much pleased to contribute—I wrote once a Review for the Westminster—it appeared in one of the earlier numbers I forget which—it was upon "The English in Italy"[3] and as I received a good many Compliments about it—I suppose in some degree it may be received as a specimin—if the Editor wished to have one on the subject.

I am so aware of M[r] Murray's gentlemanly feeling & I must say kindness towards me, that I am sure if you will inform him how desirous I am of some kind of answer upon all these points, that he will no longer delay to furnish me with one.

> I am Dear Sir
> Y[s] Ob[ly] &cc
> MaryW Shelley

ENDORSED: 1830 Septr 8 / Shelley Mrs. UNPUBLISHED: Jones, #369, in summary. TEXT: MS., John Murray.

1. John Murray II (1778–1843) and his wife were on an extended tour of Scotland from c. 6 August to c. 27 October 1830. In his absence, John Murray III (1808–92) managed the firm (Ben Harris McClary, *Washington Irving and the House of Murray* [Knoxville: University of Tennessee Press, 1969], pp. 137–38; Moore, *Letters*, II, 695, 701).

2. *The Quarterly Review*.

3. See 2 April [1828] to [John Bowring], n. 4.

*[?   ]   Park Cottage   Monday   [?25 October 1830][1]

Dear Sir

I feel very much obliged to you for your prompt & polite communication; I shall have great pleasure in conversing with you on the subject. My present distance from town, and the liability there always is of my being out at the hour when you might chance to call, induces me now to write to say that if it is convenient to you to call on me at 33 Somerset St. Portman Square at two o'clock on Wednesday next[2]—I shall be happy to see you there. If this appointment clashes with any engagement of yours, will you ⟨name⟩ make one when I can see you in Somerset St.—and it will in all probability be quite in my power to keep it.

My object certainly is, to make an immediate engagement—it is unecessary however to say more here, as when I have the pleasure of seeing you, we shall be enabled to explain more fully, and to ⟨divine⟩ arrange whether there is any possibility of my entering upon work suggested by me

I am, Sir,

Your Ob*t* Servant

MWShelley

UNPUBLISHED. TEXT: MS., Pforzheimer Library.

1. "25*th* Oct." is written in a hand other than Mary Shelley's at the top of page 1 of this letter.

2. That is, 3 November 1830.

*TO JOHN MURRAY   Park Cottage   Thursday   28 Octr   [1830]

My dear Sir

M*r* John Murray[1] mentioned in a note to me that on your return to town you would probably call on me—But as your time is so much taken up— & I am often in town—I think the appointment had better be made for Albermarle St.—I shall remove to Somerset St. On Monday next.[2]—

I write under the idea that some one of my propositions for the Family Library may be acceptable—& because I am very unwilling to lose more time.

I wish so very much to see Mr Moore's 2^d Vol—*Will it not come out*—nor in any way be visible until January? So your people told me—& that is a very long time to wait—

> I am Dr Sir
> Yours Obt^{ly} & Obliged
> MWShelley

ADDRESS: John Murray Esq / 50 Albermarle St. ENDORSED: 1830. Octr 28 / Shelley Mrs. UNPUBLISHED. Jones, #370, in summary. TEXT: MS., John Murray.

    1. John Murray III.

    2. That is, 1 November 1830. A note in Mary Shelley's Journal reads: "Nov 4 Somerset St. / London / I return to Somerset St."

*TO HENRY COLBURN AND RICHARD BENTLEY   33 Somerset St. Portman Sq 4 Nov. 1830

Gentlemen

I called today at the request of a friend of mine who wished to know how far you would be inclined to purchase a work of his just completed. The name of this gentleman is Mr Hogg—the Author of a tour called An hundred and sixty five days on the continent, published by Hunt & Clarke—& of several able & highly valued articles in the Edinburgh review. This present work is a Romance.[1] The wit, and talent of Mr Hogg is probably known to you by reputation, and I think you will feel desirous to become the publishers of a work which is certain of being highly amusing and doubtless popular. If it enter into your views to treat upon this subject you will perhaps be so good as to let me know, when Mr Hogg will see you on the subject himself

> I am, Gentlemen,
> Your Obt. Servant
> MWShelley.

ADDRESS: Mess. Colburn & Bentley / 8 New Burlington St. POSTMARKS: (1) T.P / Tottem C Ter; (2) 7. NIGHT. 7 / 5. NO / 1830. UNPUBLISHED. TEXT: MS., Pforzheimer Library.

    1. Hogg's romance *Leonora*, an early work, seems not to have been published and at present is unlocated (*SC*, III, 257). Mary Shelley's statement that the work being offered was "just completed" suggests that Hogg had written another romance. I have found no further information about this book.

*TO GENERAL LAFAYETTE[1]   London 33 Somerset St Portman Sq. 11 Nov. 1830

My dear General

It is with great diffidence that so humble an individual as myself addresses herself to the Hero of three Revolutions. Yet I cannot refuse myself the pleasure of congratulating that Hero on his final triumph.[2] How has France redeemed herself in the eyes of the world—washing off the stains of her last attempt in the sublime achievements of this July. How does every heart in Europe respond to the mighty voice, which spoke in your Metropolis, bidding the world be free. For that word is said—one by one the nations take up the echo and mine will not be the last. May England imitate your France in its moderation and heroism. There is great hope that any change operated among us, will originate with the Government. Our king[3] is desirous of popularity; careless of opinions, leaning through family connexions to the liberal party—He will willingly accede to any measures for the good of the people. But our position is critical and dreadful—for what course of measures can annihilate the debt? and so reduce the taxation, which corrodes the very vitals of the suffering population of this country.

Pardon a woman, my dear and most respected General, for intruding these observations. I was the wife of a man who—held dear the opinions you espouse, to which you <u>were</u> the martyr and <u>are</u> the ornament; and to sympathize with successes which would have been matter of such delight to him, appears to me a sacred duty—and while I deeply feel my incapacity to understand or treat such high subjects, I rejoice that the Cause to which Shelley's life was devoted, is crowned with triumph.

Your amiable family and yourself must have almost forgotten a stranger who came among you under disastrous circumstances,[4] for so short a time, and so long ago—I trust that one day it will be my fate to visit you again; meanwhile I feel satisfaction in remembering—that sick & unlike myself as I was when in Paris—yet then I became acquainted with its most illustrious citizen and that I can boast of having conversed with La Fayette

Most respectfully Y^{rs} MaryShelley

ADDRESS: For the / General La Fayette / &c &c &c. UNPUBLISHED. TEXT: MS., Cornell University Library.

1. See 13 October [1827] to John Howard Payne, n. 1; 16 May [1828].

2. See 9 August 1830, n. 3.

3. George IV died 26 June 1830 and was succeeded by his brother William IV (1765–1837).

4. A reference to the smallpox that attacked her during her 1828 visit to Paris.

*TO JOHN HOWARD PAYNE   [?33 Somerset Street]
                                    Tuesday [?December 1830][1]

My dear Payne

I shall be very happy to see Mr Bell & am flattered by his expressing a desire to see me. It would convenience me if you could make your visit early in the day—as I am engage later

I am happy to be reminded of your existence or rather to be assured that you remember mine

Yours truly
MWShelley

ADDRESS: For / J. Howard Payne Esq / 29 Norton Street. UNPUBLISHED. TEXT: MS., Furman University.

1. According to the addresses on Mary Shelley's and Washington Irving's letters to Payne, Payne moved to 29 Norton Street sometime after January 1830 ([6 January 1830]; and Irving, *Journals and Notebooks,* II, 509–10, 514–15). By 1 February 1831 Payne lived at 77 Margaret Street, Cavendish Square, according to Mary Shelley's letter of that date. In December 1830 Washington Irving wrote to Payne saying that he had no items for Mr. Bell's journal (Irving, *Journals and Notebooks,* II, 572–73). This is probably a reference to John Browne Bell (1779–1855), publisher, who succeeded his father John Bell (1745–1831; *DNB*), publisher of *La Belle Assemblée,* which printed Mary Shelley's "Narrative of a tour round the Lake of Geneva, and of an Excursion through the Valley of Chamouni" in 1823 (see Lyles, *MWS Bibliography,* p. 40); *Bell's Weekly Messenger; Morning Post;* and many other periodic and literary works. It is likely that the Mr. Bell whom Payne wanted to introduce to Mary Shelley was this same publisher.

TO WILLIAM WHITTON

33 Somerset St.   Portman Sq.
2nd Dec^ber 1830[1]

My dear Sir

If my messinger finds you at home, you will perhaps be so good as to give him (sealed up) the usual cheque in exchange for the receipt which I enclose. Otherwise will you have the kindness to send it to me—or I will send again for it in a day or two.

Percy, thank God, is quite well and Mr Slater informs me, improves very much. I hope you are quite well—and that Percy's family are well, and not disturbed by the frightful state of the country.

I am, dear Sir
Yours Ob^ly & Obliged
MWShelley

ENDORSED: 2d Decr 1830 / Mrs Shelley. PUBLISHED: Jones, #371. TEXT: MS., Bodleian Library (MS., Shelley, Adds., c. 6, f. 99).

1. At the top of page 1, in an unidentified hand, is written "Mrs Shelley / Robinson Esq / Park Cottage / Paddington."

TO EDWARD JOHN TRELAWNY

33 Somerset St   27 Decr 1830

My dear Trelawny

At present I can only satisfy your impatience, with the information that I have received your M.S.[1] & read the greater part of it—Soon I hope to say more—George Baring did not come to England, but after considerable delay forwarded it to me from Boulogne[2]—

I am delighted with your work, it is full of passion, energy & novelty— it concerns the sea & that is a subject of the greatest interest to me—I should imagine that it must command success—

But, my dear Friend, allow me to persuade you to permit certain omissions—In one of your letters to me you say that "there is nothing in it that a woman could not read"—You are correct for the most part & yet without the omissions of a few words here & there—the scene before you go to the school with the mate of your ship—& above all the scene of the burning of the house following your scene with your Scotch enemy—I am sure that yours will be a book interdicted to women.—Certain words & phrases, pardoned in the days of Fielding are now justly interdicted—& any gross piece of ill taste will make your bookseller draw back—I have named all the objectionable passages, & I beseech you to let me deal with them as I would with Ld Byrons Don Juan—when I omitted all that hurt my taste— Without this yielding on your part I shall experience great difficulty in disposing of your work—

Besides that I, your partial friend, strongly object to coarseness, now wholly out of date & beg you for my sake to make the omissions necessary for your obtaining feminine readers—Amidst so much that is beautiful, imaginative & exalting, why leave spots which believe me are blemishes? I hope soon to write to you again on the subject—

The burnings—the alarms—the absorbing politics of the day render booksellers almost averse to publishing at all—God knows how it will all end, but it looks as if the Autocrats would have the good sense to make the necessary sacrifices to a starving people—

I heard from Claire today[3]—She is well & still at Nice—I suppose there is no hope of seeing you here—As for me I of course still continue a prisoner—Percy is quite well & is growing more & more like Shelley— Since it is necessary to live, it is a great good to have this tie to life—but it is a wearisome affair—I hope you are happy—

Yrs my dearest friend ever
Mary Shelley

PUBLISHED: Jones, #372. TEXT: MS. (copy), Abinger MSS., Bodleian Library.

1. Trelawny, *Adventures* (see April 1[829]).

2. On 28 October 1830 Trelawny had written to inform Mary Shelley that his friend George Baring, brother of the banker, had left Florence on 25 October and would go directly to London, carrying with him Trelawny's manuscript. George Baring was the youngest son of Sir Francis Baring (1740–1810; *DNB*), founder of the banking firm of Baring Bros. and Co.

3. Claire Clairmont's letter is dated 11 December 1830 (*S&M*, IV, 1133–37).

*To Charles Ollier   33 Somerset St.   Teusday
                                       [?28 December 1830]

My dear Sir—I hope your tiresome silence is not occasioned by your being
dead. Having the responsibility of Mr Trelawny's MS. on my hands—&
wishing to have a talk with you about my own affairs—I should so like to
see you   Can you call on me tomorrow or when?—do let me see you tho'
I am so troublesome

                                       Y^s Obl^d MWShelley

Compts of the Season

ADDRESS: Chas. Ollier Esq / Frith St. Soho / 8 New Burlington St. UNPUBLISHED. TEXT:
MS., British Library (Ashley A 1587, f. 123).

*To John Murray   33 Somerset St.   Portman Sq   29 Dec. 1830

My dear Sir
    You may easily guess how anxious I am to see Mr Moore's Second Vol.[1]   I
hope I do not intrude too much in reminding you of my interest in it—
Shall I have my copy soon?
    I am so sorry that I have not been able to arrange writing for your
Library—or for any other publication of yours—If I were quite sure of a
subject that would please you, I would take my chance & try—As it is I
fear that my debt must stand over till better times—but be assured that I
shall never forget it

                                       Yours Obliged
                                       MWShelley

ADDRESS: John Murray Esq / 50 Albermarle St. ENDORSED: 1830 Dec. 29 / Shelley Mrs.
UNPUBLISHED: Jones, #373, in summary. TEXT: MS., John Murray.
    1. See 19 January [1830], n. 2.

*To John Bowring   33 Somerset St.   Wednesday
                                       [29 December 1830]

My dear Sir
    I am uncertain as to the address of the enclosed—will you rectify it &
send it for me by post—unless you are about to send a parcel when you
might include it—a few d[ays] delay is of no consequence—

                                       Yours Ever
                                       MWS

ADDRESS: Dr Bowring / 12 Wellington St / Strand. POSTMARKS: (1) T.P / Duke St M.S.;
(2) 4. EVEN. 4 / 30. DE / 1830. UNPUBLISHED. TEXT: MS., Pforzheimer Library.

*To [?Rudolph Ackermann][1]   33 Somerset St.   Portman Sq
                                         30 Dec. 1830

Dear Sir

A long time ago you asked me to contribute to your beautiful Forget me not—but I write so little that I have not been able—I have written however a short mythological comic drama in verse which I think would suit, if not your former work, your Juvenile Forget me Not—the subject is Midas.[2] I offer it with the more readiness as it has been read & liked by several persons whose judgement I value—I will send it for your approval if you desire it

                                   I am, dear Sir
                                   Yours Ob^y
                                   MShelley

Unpublished. Text: MS., Pforzheimer Library.
    1. See vol. I, [5 August 1826], n. 1.
    2. It was not accepted (see vol. I, 9 May [1824], n. 1).

To Robert Dale Owen   33 Somerset St.   Portman Sq   30 Dec 1830

My dear Dale—I am tardy in thanking you for your letter[1]—yet I have thanked you a thousand times only you do not know it—for Procrastination has stolen my expression of them. Your letter gave me the greatest pleasure— first it proved to me that I was not forgotten by Fanny nor yourself—and then it gave me tidings of the former, of her success and happiness, which delighted me.

My enclosed letter to her[2] speaks of the subject that must interest us all so highly.—the triumph of the <u>Cause</u> in Europe—I wonder if Nations have <u>bumps</u>[3] a well as individuals—<u>Progressiveness</u> is certainly finely developed just now in Europe—together with a degree of <u>tyrant quellingtiveness</u> which is highly laudable—it is a pity that in our country this should be mingled with <u>sick destructiveness</u>; yet the last gives action to the former—and without, would our Landholders be brought to reason? Yet it is very sad—the punishment of the poor men being not the least disaster attendant on it.

If you are good you will write to me again. When shall you again visit England? Will Fanny never come over?[4] Talk to her of me sometimes   Remember me yourself—

                                   I am Yours ever
                                   MWShelley

Endorsed: Mary Shelley / Decr 1830. Published: Jones, #374. Text: MS., Historical Society of Pennsylvania.

1. Robert Dale Owen's letter of 5 January 1830 did not arrive in England until 15 March 1830. In this letter he explains that Mary Shelley's letter of 19 August reached Fanny Wright on the eve of her departure for New Orleans and that he has undertaken to respond in her place (Abinger MSS., Bodleian Library). At the end of May 1828 Fanny Wright left Nashoba permanently to become a public speaker in the cause of political and religious reform and part owner, with Robert Dale Owen, and editor-in-chief of the *New Harmony* (Ind.) *Gazette*. She gave lectures in Ohio, Maryland, Pennsylvania, and New York and by January 1829 decided to settle in New York. Robert Dale Owen joined her there, and they continued their newspaper under the title *Free Enquirer* (Perkins and Wolfson, *Frances Wright*, pp. 207, 229, 231).

2. See the next letter.

3. Founded by Frans Joseph Gall (1758–1828), phrenology was a system based on the belief that thorough examination of the skull would reveal the abilities and personality of an individual. Godwin had Mary Shelley assessed by his friend William Nicholson, an amateur phrenologist, when she was nineteen days old. In 1820 Godwin was assessed by a phrenologist. However, Godwin's 1831 *Thoughts on Man* essay "On Phrenology" refuted phrenology (Locke, *Godwin*, pp. 219, 320–23). Robert Dale Owen had been introduced to phrenology in the autumn of 1827 and had been assessed by Johann Gaspar Spurzheim (1776–1832), a disciple of Gall and a famous phrenologist, and a Mr. DeVille (Owen, *Threading My Way*, pp. 331–36; Andrew Carmichael, *A Memoir of the Life and Philosophy of Spurzheim* [Boston: Marsh, Capen and Lyon, 1833], pp. 3–27).

4. In fact, Fanny and Camilla Wright had returned to Europe on 1 July 1830, first briefly to England and then to France. Shortly afterwards, they were joined in Paris by Phiquepal D'Arusmont. On 8 February 1830 Camilla Wright died. In July 1831 Fanny Wright and D'Arusmont were married. Their first daughter, born c. June 1831, died in 1832. Their second daughter was born on 14 April 1832. On 3 November 1835 the D'Arusmonts returned to America, where Fanny Wright resumed her public role. From 1840 to her death in 1852 the D'Arusmonts lived apart from each other (Perkins and Wolfson, *Frances Wright*, pp. 300, 306–7, 312–18, 326, 338–55).

*To FRANCES WRIGHT   33 Somerset St.   Portman Sq   30 Dec. 1830

My Dearest Fanny—Why have I not written to you so long? Not that I have forgotten you; O, no—that would be impossible.—but I have felt timid at the idea of intruding myself upon one, whose noble mind is filled with such vast interests—and whose time is occupied by such important plans. Yet dearest Fanny, amidst all your enthusiasm for <u>the Cause</u>,[1] there is mingled a feminine sweetness and a prompt sympathy, which, if you were nearer, would make {me} eager to claim the friendship you promised me. The Atlantic divides us[2]—Our letters can say little more than what, I trust, we feel to be true without them—that we have not forgotten each other— and that we remember with pleasure our transient intercourse. Alas! I can hardly flatter myself so far—but you I must love as a bright specimen of our sex.

Nor can I omit to congratulate you on the glorious triump{h}s achieved in Europe since you left it. France has redeemed her name. The conduct held towards the guilty ministers sets her in a bright light, and washes out the stains that Robespierre dimmed her with. Much remains to be done—

in that Country—but it is impossible not to anticipate that they will finish well what they have so gloriously begun—And our dear General—the hero of true revolutions—this is the crown of his life—& may he long survive to enjoy his victory.[3] Poor Constant is gone,[4] but he was happy in beholding his party triumph. The fire is spreading from one end of Europe to the other—Russia & Prussia would assault enfranchized Belgium, but Poland rises in their path—Austria would lend his aid to his brother Anarchs[5] but Italy "Schiavi ognor frementi,"[6] keep him in check—Will not our Children live to see a new birth for the world!

Our own hapless country—but your eager correspondants must tell you every thing about that. The case seems to stand thus—The people will be redressed—will the Aristocrats sacrifice enough to tranquillize them—if they will not—we must be revolutionized—but they intend now so to do—it remains to be seen whether the people's claims will augment with the concessions—Our sick feel themselves tottering—they are fully aware of their weakness—long curtailed as to their rents, they humble—How will it all end? None dare even presume to guess.

So much for politics—Of myself I have little to say—I have added three years to my life since I saw you—And to one as keenly alive as I am, such a fact says also that I have enjoyed & suffered many things—My enjoyments shew themselves outwardly on the surfaces of things. My son is well—developing talents and excellent qualities enough to satisfy almost my maternal desires. My Father is well—enjoying a most green old age—These are circumstances to gild my life with permanent sunshine—Yet—Ah, my Fanny,—life is a toil & a cheat[7]—I love it not. If I could live in a more genial clime, it were something—but here in in my island-prison,—I sigh for the sun, & a thousand delights associated with it, from which I am cut off for ever. My youth is wasted—my hopes die—I feel fail within me all the incentives to existence—I cling to my child as my sole tie.—

Yours is a brighter lot, a nobler career. Heaven bless you in it, dear Girl, and reward you. You have chosen the wiser path and I congratulate you. Yet I feel with Spurzheim,[8] that I am made of frailer clay—and should have sunk before difficulties,—which serve to edge your heroic spirit. I should be so glad to hear of you. To learn if your exertions are their own reward—or if you have a reward beyond—Remember that in Europe you have none who loves you better than[9]—

ADDRESS: Miss Frances Wright. UNPUBLISHED. TEXT: MS., Indiana State Library.

1. Robert Dale Owen's letter of 5 January 1830 gave details of Fanny Wright's activism.

2. See 30 December 1830 to Robert Dale Owen, n. 4.

3. Lafayette, who died 20 May 1834 (see 11 November 1830).

4. Benjamin Constant died on 8 December 1830.

5. Mary Shelley's use of *anarch* here recalls Byron's "Imperial Anarchs doubling human woes," *Childe Harold* 2. 14, and Shelley's "Chained hoary anarchs," *The Triumph of Life,* line 237, as well as his references to anarchs in *Lines written among the Euganean Hills,* line 152; *Hellas,* line 318; *Laon and Cythna* 10. 5. and 9; "Ode to Liberty," St. 12, line 10.

6. "Constant clamor of slaves."

7. Perhaps an echo of Dryden, "When I consider life, 'tis all a cheat," *Aureng-Zebe* 4. 1; or Shelley, "Of parents' smiles for life's great cheat," "Ginevra," 1. 36.

8. This suggests that Mary Shelley had been assessed by the phrenologist (see 30 December 1830 to Robert Dale Owen, n. 3).

9. Mary Shelley's signature has been cut away.

*To Charles Ollier   [33 Somerset Street]   Wednesday
                                               [January–February 1831]

My dear Sir

I have been considering what you say—and I feel sure that you will think I do wisely in giving up any idea of making a proposal[1] now. According to the account you give, things can never be <u>worse</u> than now—unless London were on fire—Meanwhile I will write the novel as I proposed—You will kindly be on the <u>look out for me</u> & if a <u>lucky moment</u> occur you may bring my book forward as being in hand—Or when it is done as you approve the plan, I shall as usual depend upon your best offices for bringing it forward, & making the requisite arrangements. Do you agree with me that this is the best way?

I am very anxious about Trelawny's—You will let me know something about it as soon as you can—

Do you think that in any arrangement for the C^t Journal[2] I could take a part?—It has struck me several times that I might do something in that way. Frankly what you tell me of the state of things, of the truth of which there are too many signs fills me with disquietude for my Father, who depends on his pen—And I should be so glad to be doing any thing that was a certain gain—If I knew <u>what was wanted</u>, if any thing is wanted, I think I could be of service—I would engage for an ⟨essay⟩ Article every week—either a light one or on any given subject that was wanted—Will you propose this to Bentley I should be very much obliged to you—

                                               Yours Ever
                                               MWShelley

Address: Chas Ollier Esq / 8 New Burlington St. Unpublished. Text: MS., Pforzheimer Library.

1. Probably for the publication of her next novel, *Lodore,* published by Richard Bentley in three volumes in 1835.

2. No works by Mary Shelley have been identified in the *Court Journal.*

Somerset St   Teusday
                                                        [?January–10 March 1831][1]

My dear Sir

I have been impatiently expecting for some time an answer concerning
Trelawny's MS. Pray let me hear as soon as possible as I write to him by
Friday's post—& <u>must</u> give some account as to what is doing with it.

                                                            Yours truly
                                                            MWShelley

I send you a paper for the C[t] Journal—or the New Monthly—if possible
let me correct the press—

ADDRESS: Chas Ollier Esq / 8 New Burlington St. UNPUBLISHED. TEXT: MS., Pforzheimer
Library.
    1. See [?10 March 1831].

To William Whitton   33 Somerset St.   1 Feb[ry] 1831

My dear Sir

I am so stupid that I am by no means sure that I have worded my receipt
properly. I shall do myself the pleasure of calling on you with Percy on
Saturday next—when it can be set right. And then (unless it is convenient
to you to forward it to me before) I can receive in exchange you cheque

                                                    I am, dear Sir
                                                    Yours Ob[t] & Obli[d]
                                                    MWShelley

ENDORSED: 1st Feby 1831 / Mrs Shelley. PUBLISHED: Jones, #376. TEXT: MS., Bodleian
Library (MS., Shelley, Adds., c. 6, ff. 100–101).

To John Howard Payne   Somerset St.   Tuesday
                                                    [1 February 1831]

My dear Payne

Parties and this weather so little suit me that I have declined M[rs] Wood's
invitation[1]—Besides I am not fond of going into crowded rooms where I
shall not know a soul scarcely. I am grown old—shy—lazy—& moreover
am giving up parties as too expensive, I being desperately poor—

Marshall having stated that he arranged the <u>grand affair</u> on the strength
of my note, I cannot help going shares with him—God send we all laugh
at such <u>magnificences</u> this time twelvemonths—it is too much to be dwelling
for ever on the minutia of trash

                                                            Yours Ever
                                                            MWS.

ADDRESS: J. Howard Payne Esq / 77 Margaret St. / Cavenish Sq. POSTMARKS: (1) T.P / Duke St [M.S]; (2) 10. F.NOON. 10 / 2. FE / 1831. PUBLISHED: Jones, #375. TEXT: MS., Huntington Library (HM 6829).

1. Mary Wood (d. 1884), fifth daughter of Charles, second earl Grey (1764–1845; *DNB*), prime minister 1830–34, and wife of Charles Wood (1800–1885; *DNB*), politician, who succeeded to his father's baronetcy in 1846 and became Viscount Halifax of Monk Bretton in 1866. Godwin's Journal notes a number of gatherings at Mrs. Wood's: 2 March 1831, attended by Godwin, Mary Shelley, Leicester Stanhope, Campbell (possibly Thomas Campbell), Holm (possibly Edward Holmes), H. Payne, Morgan (possibly Sir Thomas Charles Morgan [1783–1843], husband of Lady Morgan), Miss Spence (possibly Elizabeth Isabella Spence [1768–1832; *DNB*], author); 26 June 1832, attended by the Stanhopes, Bowring, Birkbeck (George Birkbeck, M.D. [1776–1841; *DNB*], founder of educational institutions for working men and a friend of Godwin's), Holms, Visconti (unidentified), Hutchinson (unidentified), Yg. American (unidentified), C. Jones (unidentified), Mrs. Booth, Sass (unidentified); 1 January 1833, attended by Les. Stanhopes, 3 Halls (unidentified), 3 Homs, Alkali (unidentified), Mary Shelley.

*TO MARY WOOD   Somerset St.   Teusday   [?1 February 1831]

Mrs Shelley presents her compliments to Mrs Wood and regrets that not being very well, the weather prevents her from availing herself of Mrs Wood's polite invitation.

Mrs Shelley begs to be excused—for delaying her answer. She has each day intended calling on Mrs Wood, but not having a carriage, the weather has prevented her.

UNPUBLISHED. TEXT: MS., British Library (MS., Autogr. c. 24, f. 341).

*TO CHARLOTTE MURCHISON[1]   Tuesday Morn^g
                    [? February 1831–April 1833]   Somerset St.

Dear Mrs Murchison

I send you two notes of Mr Moore—and an autograph of Shelley—it is a sonnet addressed to Lord Byron[2]—All this if I do not find you—as I fear I shall be late

I am, dear Mrs Murchison,

                                        Ever truly Yours
                                        M. Shelley

ENDORSED: Mrs P. B. Shelley. UNPUBLISHED. TEXT: MS., British Library (Add. 46.28, f. 67).

1. Charlotte Murchison, nee Hugonin (d. 1869), wife of Roderick Impey Murchison (see [20 March 1830], n. 1). Mary Shelley noted in her Journal that she was at the Murchisons' home on 30 January 1831, along with Mr. and Mrs. John Gibson Lockhart, Theodore Hook, John Murray, and others.

2. "If I esteemed you less," written in 1821.

*TO CHARLOTTE MURCHISON   33 Somerset St.   Monday
                                      [?February–May 1831][1]

Dear M[rs] Murchison

Can you tell me M[r] Hook's[2] address?—I know he has left town—I think
for Fulham—is it so?

How are you? And how is M[r] Murchison—& his Treatise?[3]—Which he
has not sent me—though he promised—I shall come and claim it some
day—

I hear M[rs] Hare[4] is quite well—They are very gay at Florence—in spite
of the disturbances round them

                                                    Yours truly
                                                    MW Shelley

ENDORSED: Mrs B. Shelley. UNPUBLISHED. TEXT: MS., Pforzheimer Library.

1. The disturbances referred to in this letter were the revolutionary activities against Austrian
rule that broke out in Italy in February 1831 and continued until May. Fresh revolts broke
out at the end of 1831 but were quelled in January 1832.

2. Theodore Hook.

3. Roderick Murchison wrote numerous geological studies.

4. Anne Frances Hare (see [20 March 1830], n. 1).

*TO CHARLES OLLIER   33 Somerset St.   Friday   [18 February 1831]

My dear Sir—

I have now arranged with my Father & you shall have the Memoir[1] in
question—but I cannot be quite so speedy as I wished & intended—You
shall have it next week—on as early a day as you can.

If M[r] Colburn desires it, my father will see him & give him every information necessary concerning M[r] Fisher,[2] so as to put a complete end to the
sale of his pirated edition—My father would prefer seeing M[r] Colburn
himself upon the subject, to explain the proceedings formerly used against
M[r] Fisher

                                                    MWShelley
Have they any idea of publishing Frankenstein in their edition?

ADDRESS: Charles Ollier Esq / 8 New Burlington St. POSTMARKS: (1) T.P / Tottenm Ct
[   ]; (2) 10. F.N[OON. 10] / 19. FE / 1831. UNPUBLISHED. TEXT: MS., Pforzheimer
Library.

1. Mary Shelley wrote the introductory memoir of Godwin's life for Colburn and Bentley's
one volume reissue of Caleb Williams, published 1 April 1831 (Lyles, MWS Bibliography, p.
41; Godwin, Journal). Godwin had sold the copyright of Caleb Williams to Colburn and Bentley
for £50 on 19 June 1830 (Bentley Archives, British Library, Add. 46627, vol. 68, p. 69).

2. In 1824 S. Fisher, book publisher, 4 Warwick Lane, Paternoster Row, had violated the
copyright laws by republishing Caleb Williams in five penny numbers before Godwin took
legal action to restrain him. (Burton R. Pollin, Godwin Criticism [Toronto: University of
Toronto Press, 1967], pp. 110–11). In 1826 Fisher had published another un authorized edition
in three volumes.

*To [CHARLES OLLIER]   [33 Somerset Street]   Wednesday
                                         [?February–10 March 1831]

My dear Sir—if there is another <u>real</u> ⟨introd⟩ edition of Frankenstein[1]—
that is if it goes to the press again—will you remember that I have a short
passage to add to the Introduction. Do not fail me with regard to this—it
will only be a few lines—& those not disagreable to C. & B. [*Colburn and
Bentley*]—but the contrary—

                                                      Yours truly
                                                      MS.

Do tell me what you have done about the MS.[2] sent you to read

UNPUBLISHED. TEXT: MS., Pforzheimer Library.
   1. Colburn and Bentley published Mary Shelley's revised *Frankenstein,* with its new introduction (dated 15 October 1831), which describes the circumstances of its composition and
attributes the 1818 preface to Shelley, c. 2 November 1831 (Lyles, *MWS Bibliography,* p. 16;
Godwin, Journal).
   2. Probably Trelawny's manuscript, although Mary Shelley had sent Ollier articles for the
New Monthly Magazine or the *Court Journal.*

*To [CHARLES OLLIER]   33 Somerset St.   Thursday Ev[g]
                                         [?10 March 1831][1]

My dear Sir—I must beg for some answer on the subject of M[r] Trelawny's
M.S. So very much time has elapsed, that I am quite annoyed at the idea
he must form of my seeming neglect—
   I wish to see you also—or to hear something about the MS. I sent you—
If my articles have been published in the N.M. [*New Monthly*] I might as
well have had a copy

                                                      Yours truly
                                                      MWShelley

UNPUBLISHED. TEXT: MS., Pforzheimer Library.
   1. "11 March 1831," which was a Friday, is written on this letter in an unidentified hand.

To [CHARLES OLLIER]   [33 Somerset Street]
                                         Teusday—[?15 March 1831]

My dear Sir
   I wish much to see you to make the final arrangements about M[r] Trelawny's MS. Can you call tomorrow at about twelve—or will you tell me
when that I may not miss you—

                                                      Your &c
                                                      MWShelley

PUBLISHED: Jones, #377. TEXT: MS., W. Hugh Peal.

TO [CHARLES OLLIER]   33 Somerset St.   16 March 1831

My dear Sir

I have received the cheque of £5-5 for the Memoir.[1] I am annoyed beyond measure at this delay about Mr Trelawny—I hope to see you tomorrow before 4 as I go out at that hour—& I shall not be at home all Friday—so there will be another delay unless I can write on Friday

Remember to learn from Colburn the fate of the two articles[2]—if accepted and it is not hors de regle[3]—it would convenience me if they were paid for now—and besides I should like to understand the terms I should write for in future—and whether, if they satisfied me, Mr Colburn wished me to continue to contribute

I hope to see you tomorrow

Yours Obliged,
MWShelley

I have not yet received the proof {   } the Memoir—

PUBLISHED: Jones, #378. TEXT: MS., Keats-Shelley Memorial House, Rome.
    1. Of Godwin (see [18 February 1831], n. 1).
    2. Unidentified.
    3. "Out of the ordinary."

TO WILLIAM BLACKWOOD   33 Somerset St.   Portman Sq
21 March 1831

My dear Sir

It is long ago that you told me that you should be willing to receive articles of mine for your Magazine.[1] Not being in the habit of writing for periodicals—I have delayed taking advantage of your desire, though I have often resolved so to do. I send now an article[2]—which I hope will appear fit for insertion—if so I shall be happy to continue to communicate with you. With regard to remuneration you know the payment given for such productions better than I—and I leave it to you—I shall be very glad if my communications form a part of your valuable & amusing work

I am Sir
Yours Ob^ly
MWShelley

PUBLISHED: Irving Massey, "Mary Shelley, Walter Scott, and 'Maga,' " Notes and Queries 207 (November 1962): 420–21. TEXT: MS., National Library of Scotland.
    1. See 4 May [1830], n. 1.

2. Unidentified. Nor is there a record of Mary Shelley as a contributor to *Blackwood's* in this period.

TO EDWARD JOHN TRELAWNY March 22—1831 (Friday 25th March)
Somerset St—

My dear Trelawny—what can you think of me and of my silence?—I can guess by the contents of your letters,[1] and your not having yet received answers—Believe me that if I am at all to blame to blame in this it arises from an error in judgement not from want of zeal—every post day I have waited for the next expecting to be able to communicate something definitive—and now still I am waiting—however I trust that this letter will contain some certain intelligence before I send it After all I have done no more than send your manuscripts to Colburn—and I am still in expectation of his answer. In the first place they insist upon certain parts being expunged—parts of which I alone had the courage to speak to you—but which had before been remarked upon as inadmissable These however (with trifling exceptions) occur only in the first volume. The task of deciding upon these may very properly be left to Horace Smith[2]—if he will undertake it—we shall see—meanwhile Colburn has not made up his mind as to the price—He will not give £500—The terms he will offer I shall hope to send before I close this letter—so I will say no more except to excuse my having conceded so much time to his dilatoriness—In all I have done I may be wrong—I commonly act from my own judgement—but alas! I have great experience—I <u>believe</u> that if I sent your work to Murray, he would return it in two months unread—simply saying that he does not print novels Your 2d part would be a temptation did not your intention to be severe on Moore make it improbable that he would like to engage in it—and he would keep me as long as Colburn in uncertainty—still this may be right to do—and I shall expect your further instructions by return of post[3]—However in one way you may help yourself—You know Lockhart—He reads and judges for Murray—write to him—your letter shall accompany the M.S. to him—Still this thing must not be done hastily—for if I take the M.S. out of Colburn's hands—and failing to dispose of it elsewhere I come back to him—he will doubtless retreat from his original proposal—There are other booksellers in the world doubtless than these two—but occupied as England is by political questions and impoverished miserably there are few who have enterprise at this juncture to offer a price. I quote examples—my father and myself would find it impossible to make any tolerable arrangement with any one except Colburn—He at least may be your guide as to what you may expect—Mr Browne[4] remembers the Golden days of authors—when I first returned to England I found no difficulty in making agreements with publishers—they came to seek me—now—money is scarce, and readers fewer than ever, I leave the rest of this page blank—I shall fill it up before it goes on Friday

(Friday 25ᵗʰ March)   At length my dear friend I have received the ultimatum of these great people   They offer you £300—and another £100—on a second edition—as this was sent me in writing—and there is no time for further communication before posthour—I cannot <u>officially</u> state the number of the edition   I should think 1000—I think that perhaps they may be brought to say £400 at once—or £300 at once and £200 on the 2ᵈ Edition. There can be no time for parleying and therefore you must make up your mind whether after doing good battle, if necessary I shall accept their terms—Believe <u>my experience</u> and that of those about me—you will not get a better offer from others—because money is not to be had, and Bulwer and other fashionable and selling authors are now obliged to content themselves with half what they got before—If you decline this offer, I will if you please try Murray—he will keep me two months at least—and the worst is if (as he is an arrant coward) he won't do anything Colburn will diminish his bargain—and we shall be in a greater mess than ever—I know that as a woman I am timid and therefore a bad negociator except that I have perseverance & zeal—& I repeat—experience of things as they are—Mʳ Browne knows what they were—but they are sadly changed—The omissions mentioned must be made but I will watch over them and the mottos & all that shall be most carefully attended to. depend on me.

Do not be displeased my dear friend that I take advantage of this enormous sheet of paper to save postage—and ask you to tear off one half sheet and to send it to Mʳˢ Hare.⁵—You talk of my visiting Italy—It is impossible for me to tell you how much I repine at my imprisonment here but I dare not anticipate a change to take me there for a long time—England, it's ungenial clime—it's difficult society, and the annoyances to which I am subjected in it weigh on my spirits more than ever—for every step I take only shows me how impossible—situated as I am, that I should be otherwise than wretched—my sanguine disposition and capacity to endure have borne me up hitherto—but I am sinking at last—but to quit so stupid a topic—and to tell you news—did you hear that Medwin contrived to get himself gazetted for full pay in the Guards⁶—I fancy that he employed his connection with the Shelleys who are connected with the King through the Fitz Clarences⁷—However a week after he was gazetted as retiring—I suppose the officers cut him at mess—his poor wife and children how I pity them—Jane is quite well—living in tranquillity—Hogg continues all that she can desire—She has no hopes of recovering her Indian money—Palmer⁸ will scarcely pay a sixpence—She lives where she did—her children are well—and so is my Percy—who grows more like Shelley—I hear that your old favorite Margaret Shelley⁹ is prettier than ever—your Miss Burdett¹⁰ is married   I have been having lithographed your letter to me about Caroline.¹¹ I wish to disperse about 100 copies among the many hapless fair who imagine themselves to have been the sole object of your tenderness—

Claire is to have a first copy—Have you heard from poor dear Claire? She announced a little time ago that she was to visit Italy with the Kaisaroffs to see you   I envied her, but I hear from her brother Charles that she has now quarelled with Madam K [*Kaisaroff*]—and that she will go to Vienna[12]— God grant that her sufferings end soon—I begin to anticipate it—for I hear that Sir Tim is in a bad way—I shall hear more certain intelligence after Easter—M[rs] Paul[13] spends her Easter with Caroline who lives in the neighbourhood & will dine at Field Place—I have not seen M[rs] Aldridge since her marriage—she has scarcely been in town, but I shall see her this Spring— when she comes up as she intends—You know of course that Elizabeth St Aubyn[14] is married—so you know that your ladies desert you sadly. If Claire & I were either to die or marry you would be left without a Dulcinea at all with the exception of the six score new objects for idolatry you may have found among the pretty girls in Florence—Take courage however—I am scarcely a Dulcinea—being your friend and not the Lady of your Love— but such as I am, I do not think that I shall either die or marry this year— whatever may happen next—as it is only spring you have some time before you—. We are all here on the qui vive[15] about the Reform Bill[16]—if it pass—and Tories and all expect it—well—if not—parliament is dissolved immediately—and they say that the new writs are in preparation. The Whigs triumphed gloriously in the boldness of their measure—England will be free if it is carried. I have had very bad accounts from Rome[17]—but you are quiet as usual in Florence—I am scarcely wicked enough to desire that you should be driven home, nor do I expect it—& yet how glad I should be to see you. You never mention Zela—adieu my dear Trelawny   I am always affectionately y[rs] Mary W Shelley

Hunt has set up a little 2[d] paper the "Tatler"[18] which is succeeding—this keeps him above water—I have not seen him lately—he lives a long way off—He is the same as ever, a person whom all must love & regret.

PUBLISHED: Jones, #379. TEXT: MS. (copy), Abinger MSS., Bodleian Library.

1. Trelawny's letter of 19 January 1831 includes further instructions about the way Mary Shelley was to arrange for the publication of his manuscript. Specifically, he did not agree with her judgment that some parts were too coarse, but he agreed to allow Horace Smith or Hogg to decide; he believed he should get £200 per volume; he wished her to fill in mottoes he omitted from chapter heads with quotations from Keats, Shelley, and Byron; he wished the book titled *The Life of a Man,* not her suggested *The Discarded Son* (Trelawny, *Letters,* pp. 139–45).

2. Smith read the manuscript and suggested some alterations to Colburn and Bentley (Trelawny, *Letters,* p. 162).

3. Trelawny received this letter 6 April 1831 and responded on 8 April. He asked Mary Shelley to try to get £400 for the first edition rather than, as she writes in this letter, £300 with an additional £100 for a second edition; he agreed to Horace Smith as reader; he again asked that the title be *A Man's Life.*

4. Charles Armitage Brown (see April 1[829], n. 1).

5. Anne Frances Hare (see [20 March 1830], n. 1).

6. Medwin had returned to England in early 1831. On 1 February he had exchanged his half-pay list commission for a lieutenancy in the exclusive 1st Life Guards; two weeks later

he had sold it and resigned from the military. Lovell suggests that this was almost certainly done for the financial gain on the sale, as one might trade on the stock market, and that there was no personal disgrace attached to it whatever (Lovell, *Medwin,* pp. 250–51).

7. Fitzclarence was the name given to the ten illegitimate children of the duke of Clarence, later William IV, and Dorothea Jordon (1762–1816; *DNB*), actress. Lady Sophia Fitzclarence married Sir Philip Charles Sidney, second baronet and first baron de L'Isle and Dudley, who was the son of Sir John Shelley-Sidney, half brother of Sir Timothy Shelley.

8. Henry Palmer, Edward Williams's banker in Calcutta (Willams, *Journals and Letters,* pp. 127, 128).

9. Margaret Shelley (1801–87), the youngest of Shelley's sisters.

10. Susannah Burdett, second daughter of Sir Francis Burdett (1770–1844; *DNB*), married J. B. Trevanion in 1830 (M. W. Patterson, *Sir Francis Burdett and His Times,* 2 vols. [London: Macmillan and Co., 1931], II, 543).

11. Caroline Aldridge (see 15 December 1829, n. 7).

12. On 13 April 1831 Claire Clairmont wrote to Mary Shelley informing her that her plan to go to Vienna was uncertain and that instead the Kaisaroffs were about to set out for Genoa and Florence. She urged Mary Shelley to quickly send letters for Anne Frances Hare and Teresa Guiccioli, in care of Margaret Mason, which Claire Clairmont would personally deliver, thereby establishing contact (*S&M,* IV, 1144).

13. Georgiana Paul, Caroline Aldridge's sister.

14. Probably one of Sir John St. Aubyn's fifteen natural children.

15. "Alert."

16. See 15 December 1829, n. 10.

17. In February 1831, inspired by the July revolution in Paris, there were widespread revolts in the Papal States. The insurrections were quelled in March with the aid of Austrian troops.

18. The *Tatler,* a daily four-page journal of literature and theater, written almost entirely by Hunt, ran from 4 September 1830 to 13 February 1832. At this point Hunt severed his connection with the *Tatler,* which continued as a tri-weekly of eight pages until 20 October 1832.

TO WILLIAM WHITTON   5 May—1831 33 Somerset St.

My dear Sir

 I am very much obliged to you for your attention and interest concerning the question of my son's school. If I still encline to Eton[1] or another public school, it arises from Percy's peculiar situation & disposition. Not noticed by his own family—and my own circumstances being so restricted as to preclude my entering much into society, the forming of friends at school is of importance to him—at the same time that I think that the bustle of a school would develop his character better than the seclusion of a private tutor—However I am not <u>obstinate</u>, if Sir Timothy positively wishes the one rather than the other.

 I suppose that Sir Tim^thy will be in town soon, when not only this question may be settled, but I shall indulge a hope of at last being permitted to see him

I am, dear Sir
Y^s Ob^ly
MaryW. Shelley

ENDORSED: 5. May 1831 / Mrs Shelley. PUBLISHED: Jones, #380. TEXT: MS., Bodleian Library (MS., Shelley, Adds., c. 6, ff. 102–3).

1. Sir Timothy Shelley's letter of 8 December 1830 to Whitton expressed his objection to Percy Florence's being sent to Eton because "his Poor Fathers being there" would make his life very unpleasant. He further commented that whatever a boy does at a public school is long remembered (Abinger MSS., Bodleian Library). Shelley had attended Eton from 1804 to 1810 (White, *Shelley*, I, 31–68).

TO WILLIAM WHITTON   33 Somerset St.   6 May 1831

My dear Sir

It seems my fate to be unlucky in my written communications with you—so much so, that I would not venture on another letter, but call myself in Bedford Row, to make my excuses & explanations, had you not intimated that you should be out of town.

It pains one very much to imagine that my letter insinuates that you have taken any part to prevent Sir Tim^thy from seeing me. Permit me to assure you, that I have always felt and feel, exceedingly obliged to you for your mediation, and perfectly satisfied with it. If, as a Mother, I regreted that Percy was not permited to visit Field Place, and expressed this regret, it arose from over anxiety for him, and certainly not under any idea of appearing ungrateful to you. Do not then, be offended with me, my dear Sir, for be assured that I disavow any expression that fell from my pen that could at all offend you. I thank you sincerely for your kind offices and should be exceedingly glad of the continuation of them—

Being always
Y^r Obligid Ser^t
MWShelley

ADDRESS: W. Whitton Esq / 18 Bedford Row. POSTMARKS: (1) T.P / Duke St M[.S]; (2) 10. F.NOON. 10 / 9. MY / 1831. ENDORSED: 6th May 1831 / Mrs Shelley. PUBLISHED: Jones, #381. TEXT: MS., Bodleian Library (MS., Shelley, Adds., c. 6, ff. 104–5).

TO CHARLES OLLIER   Somerset St.   10 May [1831]

My dear Sir

I hear nothing from you—I receive no MS. is this your haste—pray do let some thing be done without more delay—

Will you send me the Tuilleries[1]—the Young Duke[2] & the No. of the N.M. [*New Monthly*] containing Mr Bulwer's portrait[3]—& will you let me see you—Y^s MShelley

ADDRESS: Chas Ollier Esq /8 New Burlington St. PUBLISHED: Jones, #382. TEXT: MS., New York Public Library.

1. Catherine Frances Gore, *The Tuilleries,* 3 vols. (London: Colburn and Bentley, 1831), reviewed in the *New Monthly* for March 1831.

2. Benjamin Disraeli, *The Young Duke,* 3 vols. (London: Colburn and Bentley, 1831).

3. Published in the May 1831 issue of the *New Monthly.*

To John Howard Payne   33 Somerset St.   Wednesday
[?18 May 1831]

My dear Payne

Is it in your power to do me a <u>pleasure</u>? if it is I am sure you will—and it will be a <u>very</u> great one to me if you can—I am an enthusiastic admirer of Paganini[1]—& wish excessively to go to hear him but the <u>tariffe</u> they put on the boxes renders this impossible—This tariffe is arbitrary, because not half the boxes are filled—& still fewer at the stated price. Could you through your acquaintance with Laporte[2] arrange that I should have a box at a moderate price—such as I have given at the beginning of the opera season—a good box on the pit tier or the ground tier or the one above it—not higher—on taking 3 tickets at half a guinea each—If you can manage this I cant tell you how obliged I should be to you—let me know speedily yes or no—

Will you not let me see the Fricandeau?[3]

Yours truly
MWShelley

PUBLISHED: Jones, #383. TEXT: MS., Huntington Library (HM 6830).

1. Niccolo Paganini (1782–1840), the renowned Italian violin virtuoso, was scheduled to give his first public performance in London on 28 May 1831 at the King's Theatre. However, the tickets were advertised at double the usual cost—from ten guineas for a ground tier box to one-half guinea for the gallery—which provoked so strong a protest as to delay his concert until 3 June, at which time tickets were sold at regular prices. Paganini remained in England until March 1832 (Jeffrey Pulver, *Paganini* [London: Herbert Joseph, 1936], pp. 225–36, 270). Mary Shelley attended Paganini's concert on 18 July. She wrote in her Journal: "I heard Paganini today—he is divine—he had the effect of giving me hysterics—yet I could pass my life listening to him—Nothing was ever so sublime."

2. Pierre François Laporte (1799–1841), actor and manager of the King's Theatre (New York Public Library, Theater Division).

3. *Fricandeau; or, the Coronet and the Cook,* a farce attributed to Payne, played for the first time on 9 August 1831, at the Theatre Royal, Haymarket (*The Times* [London]; Overmyer, *America's First Hamlet,* pp. 272–73).

To William Whitton   33 Somerset St.   3 June 1831

My dear Sir

I enclose a receipt in the form you sent me for the last—and I will send for the usual cheque in a day or two.

I called as you desired in Bedford Row—and they promised me there to let you know that I had been. But I have not heard from you since—I shall be very glad to hear that you are better[1]—and hope for some communication about Percy who is perfectly well

> I am, dear Sir
> Y[s] Ob[d]
> MWShelley

ENDORSED: 3rd June 1831 / Mrs Shelley. PUBLISHED: Jones, #384. TEXT: MS., Bodleian Library (MS., Shelley, Adds., c. 6, ff. 106–7).

1. William Whitton's health continued to deteriorate, and he died in July 1832 (Ingpen, *Shelley in England,* II, 613).

To WILLIAM WHITTON   33 Somerset St.   Monday   [6 June 1831] (*a*)

My dear Sir

I hope the accompanying note[1] is properly worded—and I write another not to mix two distinct subjects. The result of Sir Tim[thys] determination[2] is of course that Percy should remain at his present school. This I confess much disappoints me; as for many reasons it would be more eligible that he went to an establishment more suited to his future station. At the age of twelve—at which he will soon arrive, manners and habits are formed, and at M[r] Slaters he will not acquire such as are suitable. As Sir Timothy is averse to a public school, a private tutor, where other boys of his own situation were placed, is exceedingly desirable. And I must hope that Sir Timothy has not relinquished this idea but only defers it for a short period of time

I am very sorry to hear of your indisposition—and should be very glad to see you when you can afford me an opportunity

> I am, my dear Sir
> Y[s] Obliged
> MWShelley

ADDRESS: William Whitton Esq / (To be forwarded). ENDORSED: Mrs Shelley / recd with Note of 6 June / 31. PUBLISHED: Jones, #385. TEXT: MS., Bodleian Library (MS., Shelley, Adds., c. 6, ff. 108–9).

1. See the next letter, as well as the endorsement on this letter.

2. On 29 May 1831 Sir Timothy Shelley had indicated to Whitton that he must be "firm" with Mary Shelley about her future plans and their cost. At this point, Sir Timothy Shelley expressed reluctance for Percy Florence to attend any public school (Abinger MSS., Bodleian Library).

To WILLIAM WHITTON   33 Somerset St.   6 June 1831 (b)

Dear Sir

In answer to your communication I reply that I agree to the liquidation of the balance stated in the account[1] you sent me; and that I agree to secure the amount now due on the property I possess under my husband's will

                                    I am, dear Sir
                                        Yours Ob^ly
                                            MaryShelley

ADDRESS: To / William Whitton Esq. ENDORSED: 6 June 1831 / Mrs Shelley. PUBLISHED: Jones, #386. TEXT: MS., Bodleian Library (MS., Shelley, Adds., c. 6, ff. 116–17).

1. On 25 March 1831 Mary Shelley had signed a bond which guaranteed that she would repay the estate of Sir Timothy Shelley the money he advanced her plus interest. Specifically, he agreed to give her a maximum of £6,000. She had already received and owed £4,319.0.9, plus interest. The bond was protected by a penalty debt of £12,000 for nonpayment (MS., Pforzheimer Library).

To EDWARD JOHN TRELAWNY   1831   June 14—Somerset St—

My dear Trelawny

Your work is in progress at last[1] & is being printed with great rapidity— Horace Smith undertook the revision & sent a very favorable report of it to the publishers—to me he says—"Having written to you a few days ago, I have only to annex a copy of my letter to Colburn & Bentley—whence you will gather my opinion of the M.S.—it is a most powerful, but rather perilous work, which will be much praised & much abused by the liberal & bigoted—I have read it with great pleasure, & think it admirable—in every thing but the conclusion"—by this he means as he says to Colburn & Bentley "The conclusion is abrupt & disappointing especially as previous allusions have been made to his later life which is not given—Probably it is meant to be continued—& if so it would be better to state it—for I have no doubt that his first part will create a sufficient sensation to ensure the sale of a second."—In his former letter to me H. S. [Horace Smith] says "Any one who has proved himself the friend of yourself & of him whom we all deplore, I consider to have strong claims on my regard & I therefore willingly undertake the revision of the M.S." "Pray assure the author that I feel flattered by this little mark of his Confidence in my judgement & that it will always give me pleasure to render him these or any other serv- ices"—And now my dear Trelawny, I hope you will not be angry at the title given to your book—the responsibility of doing any thing for any one so far away as you, is painful, & I have had many qualms, but what could I do? The publishers strongly objected to the "History of a Man" as being no title at all—or rather one to lead astray. The one adopted is taken from the first words of your M.S.—where you declare yourself a younger son—

words pregnant of meaning in this country—where to be the younger son of a man of property is to be virtually discarded—& they will speak volumes to the English reader—it is called therefore "The adventures of a younger son"—If you are angry with me for this I shall be sorry—but I knew not what to do—Your M.S. will be preserved for you & remember also that it is pretty well known who it is by—I suppose the persons who read the M.S. in Italy[2] have talked—& as I told you, your mother speaks openly about it—Still it will not appear in print—in no newspaper accounts over which I have any controul as emanating from the publisher—Let me know immediately how I am to dispose of the dozen copies I shall receive on your account—one must go to H. Smith—another to me—& to who else? the rest, I will send to you in Italy—There is another thing that annoys me especially—You will be paid in bills dated from the day of publication—now not far distant—3 of various dates—To what man of business of yours can I consign these—the first I should think I could get discounted at once & send you the cash—but tell me what I am to do—I know that all these hitches & drawbacks will make you vituperate womankind—& had I ever set myself up for a woman of business—or known how to manage my own affairs, I might be hurt—but you know my irremediable deficiencies on those subjects & I represented them strongly to you before I undertook my task—& all I can say in addition is, that as far as I have seen—both have been obliged to make some concessions, so be as forgiving & indulgent as you can.

We are full here of reform or revolution whichever it is to be—I should think something approaching the latter, though the first may be included in the last—Will you come over & sit for the new parliament?[3]—What are you doing?—Have you seen Claire?[4] How is she? She never writes except on special occasions when she wants any thing—tell her that Percy is quite well—

You tell me not to marry[5]—but I will—any one who will take me out of my present desolate & uncomfortable position—Any one—& with all this do you think that I shall marry?—Never—neither you nor any body else—Mary Shelley shall be written on my tomb—and why? I cannot tell—except that it is so pretty a name that tho' I were to preach to myself for years, I never should have the heart to get rid of it—

Adieu, my dear friend, I shall be very anxious to hear from you, to hear that you are not angry about all the contretemps attendant on your publication—& to receive your further directions—

Y^{rs} very truly

MWShelley

PUBLISHED: Jones, #387. TEXT: MS. (copy), Bodleian Library (Dep. c. 518).

1. The agreement between Mary Shelley, on Trelawny's behalf, and Colburn and Bentley, to publish Trelawny, *Adventures,* took place on 9 June 1831. The bills were drawn on 17

December 1831 for £100 to be paid in four, seven, and nine months, respectively (British Library, Add. 46560, vol. 1, 14; Add. 46681, vol. 122, 59–60).

2. These included Landor, Charles A. Brown, Kirkup, George Baring and Mrs. Baring, and Lady Burghersh (Trelawny, *Letters*, p. 140). Pricilla Anne Fane, Lady Burghersh (1793–1879), artist and linguist, was married to John Fane, Lord Burghersh (1784–1859), in 1841, earl of Westmoreland, soldier, diplomat, and musician. He was British minister plenipotentiary at Florence at this time, and he and Lady Burghersh were acquainted with both Medwin and Trelawny (Lovell, *Medwin*, p. 222).

3. In response to this letter, Trelawny wrote on 29 June 1831: "If I thought there was a probability that I could get a seat in the reformed House of Commons, I would go to England, or if there was a probability of revolution" (Trelawny, *Letters*, pp. 163–68).

4. Trelawny responded that Claire Clairmont, looking pale, thin, and haggard, had remained in Florence about ten days. He had seen her three or four times but was unable to assist her in finding a better position than she had with the Kaisaroffs, with whom she had returned to Russia (Trelawny, *Letters*, p. 166).

5. After Mary Shelley's letter of 22–25 March 1831 playfully listed the marriages of a number of women admired by Trelawny and noted that should she and Claire Clairmont either die or marry, he would be left without a Dulcinea, Trelawny enjoined her not to "abandon me by following the evil examples of my other ladies. I should not wonder if fate, without our choice, united us" (Trelawny, *Letters*, p. 162). Trelawny answered Mary Shelley's remarks in this letter: "I was more delighted with your resolve not to change your name than with any other portion of your letter" (Trelawny, *Letters*, p. 166). For Mary Shelley's final comment on this dialogue see 26 July 1831.

To Edward John Trelawny[1]   [?33 Somerset Street
                                               ?June–July 1831]

My whole being was an aching void which refused to give forth any fruits, the fulness of sorrow is great, but how much greater its emptiness, yet sometimes I return to conscientiousness, and lifting my head above this sea of misery, behold the fragments of my shipwrecked life floating around. It is in a pause of this kind that I now write. The huricane of dispair will soon return and I shall be swallowed up again in one abyss or misery after another. Then dear friend when will the swell and storm die away and the dead calm of this great ocean come? When shall I be given up by its depths and be borne unresistingly, upon its bosom, like a weed of the sea to the distant still shores of Eternity.

I live in total retirement, buried, where my mind is sufficiently at ease in my books? The world is now nothing more to me, I am so far from it— at least in emagination, that not even a sound of its distant turmoil and turbulence reaches my ear. I do not like professions. How many covenants equally solemn have I not seen you break—sealed with equal protestations—How strangely unwise in you to talk to me of 'sacred' ties, when I hear that word I know that every outrage of neglect, contempt and selfishness is to follow.[2]

But it is not worth while to disturb the little hour, suffering leaves, with bickerings, after all what do the wicked do to the good that merits so much reproach; They do but hasten their departure to a place of safety where their sorrows can no longer peirce.

PUBLISHED: St. Clair, *Trelawny*, pp. 130–31. TEXT: MS. (copy), Edward Williams, "Sporting Sketches," Bodleian Library.

    1. It is conjectured that this letter was written in response to Trelawny's marriage proposal, which Trelawny copied into Edward Williams's notebook, in Trelawny's possession (St. Clair, *Trelawny*, pp. 130–31, 221; see also the previous letter).

    2. The remainder of the letter heretofore has been unpublished.

To William Whitton   33 Somerset St.   22 June—1831

My dear Sir

    I have deferred several days writing that I might the more carefully consider the subject before me. One word I must premise. It is my desire to restrict any ⟨larger⟩ demand for addition to my income strictly to the question of the greater expenditure to be made for my son, without reference whatever to my own means. At the same time I must mention that Percy's encreased age requires a very great encrease of expence, so that even in the present state of things, I feel very sensibly and with no small inconvenience, the encreased demands which his bills &c make upon my income—For my own maintenance I have considered £200 a year necessary, including in that the expences occasioned by Percy's residence with me during the holydays. But the latter event now so materially adds to my expences, that I find it quite impossible to keep within that compass. To prove that my consideration is wholly turned to Percy's expences, without reference to encrease of income to myself personally, I may add that when he is settled with a tutor in the country, it is my intention to take up my residence out of town, so as much as possible to restrict my mode of life.

    The Tutors and private schools in question appear invariably to make the charge of £150 for board and education—more than £100 more than his present school—to this must be added various extras for books &c—His dress at such a place would be attended with greater expence—and it is already very considerable. I have come therefore to the conclusion that to meet the encreased demands, without spending one additional shilling on myself personally, £150 P ann. must be added to my income. If this appear much to Sir Timothy, perhaps on his side he will make enquiries—and if any Gentleman who has a son at a similar school can estimate his son's whole yearly expences taken collectively at less than £250 P annum, I shall suppose that my calculation is a false one

    With regard to the Tutor with whom he is to be placed many things are to be considered. In talking on the subject with men conversant with it, I am told that while at most of these private schools great attention is payed to the physical and moral education of the pupils, very great difference exists in the more severe branches of education—their learning being Well attended to by some & much neglected by others. I wish my son to be a good classic scholar—& above all to be educated in habits of great industry—and real attention to the acquirement of knowledge.

That I may do my best to make a good selection, it is my intention to apply to a Gentleman of my acquaintance, Mr Julius Hare,[1] a man of great literary reputation, a Clergyman, and a Professor of Trinity College Cambridge. He is in the habit of examining and attending to young men on their first entrance in College, and has the means therefore of judging accurately as to who sends the best educated, & the most moral pupils out of his hands.

I hope Sir Timothy will permit me to lay Mr Hare's answer before him—and that he will favor me with his opinion, or at least his advice as to the choice I should make.

With many thanks for the trouble you give yourself, I am, my dear Sir

Yours Obly

MaryWShelley

I arranged for Mr Amory to see the deed in question,[2] I have received no communication whatever from him on the subject. Of course I expect one daily.

Percy is now at home for the holydays—He is very well—and I should be glad that Sir Timothy saw him. Percy writes to make this request—will you be so good as to give his Grandfather his letter.

ADDRESS: W. Whitton Esq / 18 Bedford Row. POSTMARKS: (1) T.P / Duke St M[.S]; (2) 4. EVEN. 4 /22. JU / 1831. ENDORSED: 22nd June 1831 / Mrs Shelley. PUBLISHED: Jones, #388. TEXT: MS., Bodleian Library (MS., Shelley, Adds., c. 6, ff. 112–14).

1. Julius Charles Hare (1795–1855; *DNB*), clergyman and literary scholar, was a brother-in-law of Mary Shelley's friend Anne Frances Hare. His name was erroneously given as Julius Stone in Jones, #388.

2. A number of deeds and bonds were negotiated between Mary Shelley and Sir Timothy Shelley relating to her eventual inheritance of Shelley's estate and the repayment of her allowance (see 6 June 1831 [*b*], n. 1).

*TO CHARLES OLLIER   33 Somerset St.   Monday   [?July 1831][1]

My dear Sir

I do not see you as you promised—Do you think that I shall tomorrow—

You promised to lend me the Life of Lawrence & Pin Money—& will you let me have also the number of Valpy's Library of English Classics containing the Cyropedeia[2]—You can tell me the damage when I see you—which I hope will be tomorrow

Yours truly

MWShelley

ADDRESS: Charles Ollier Esq / 8 New Burlington St. UNPUBLISHED. TEXT: MS., Pforzheimer Library.

1. This tentative date is based on the books cited in the letter: D. E. Williams, *The Life of Sir Thos. Lawrence*, 2 vols., was published by Colburn in May 1831; Catherine Gore, *Pinmoney*, 3 vols., was published by Colburn and Bentley in June 1831.

2. Xenophon, *Cyropedia*, trans. Maurice Ashley Cooper (1728), reprinted in Valpy's Family Classics Library (London, 1830). Mary Shelley presented a copy of this work to "Prudentia Sarah Jefferson Hogg from her affectionate Godmother. Mary Shelley. 7 Dec. [*year deleted*]" (*The Library of Jerome Kern*, auction catalogue, The Anderson Galleries, 21–24 January 1929, pt. 2, p. 346; for Prudentia Hogg see 13 October 1835, n. 2).

To Edward John Trelawny   26 July 1831   Somerset St

My dear Trelawny

Your third volume is now printing, so I should imagine that it will very soon be published—every thing shall be attended to as you wish—

The letter to which I alluded in my former one, was a tiny one enclosed to Claire which perhaps you have received by this time—It mentioned the time of the agreement—£300 in bills of 3—6 & 8 months—dated from the day of publication & £100 more on a second edition—the mention I made of your mother was, that she speaks openly in society of your forthcoming memoirs—so that I should imagine very little real secrecy will attend them—However you will but gain reputation & admiration through them—I hope you are going on, for your continuation will I am sure be ardently looked for—I am so sorry for the delay of all last winter—yet I did my best to conclude the affair—but the state of the nation has so paralized bookselling that publishers were very backward, though Colburn was in his heart eager to get at your book—As to the price, I have taken pains to ascertain & you receive as much, as is given to the best novelists at this juncture—which may console your vanity if it does not fill your pocket—

The Reform bill will pass and a considerable revolution in the government of the Country will I imagine be the Consequence. You have powers—these, and with industry and discretion would advance you in any career—& you ought not, indeed you ought not to throw away yourself as you do—Still, I will not advise your return on the speculation, because England is so sad a place, that the mere absence from it I consider a peculiar blessing—

My name will <u>never</u> be Trelawny[1]   I am not so young as I was when you first knew me—but I am as proud—I must have the entire affection, devotion & above all the solicitous protection of any one who would win me—You belong to womenkind in general—& Mary Shelley will <u>never</u> be yours—I write in haste—but I will write soon again—more at length—You shall have your copies the moment I receive them—believe me, all gratitude & affection   Y^{rs}

MWShelley.

Jane thanks you for the book promised—I am infinitely chagrined at what you tell me concerning Claire[2]—If the Beauclerks spoke against her, that means Mrs B. [*Beauclerk*] & her stories were gathered from LB. who feared

Claire & did not spare her—& the stories he told were such as to excuse the prejudice of anyone—

PUBLISHED: Jones, #389. TEXT: MS. (copy), Abinger MSS., Bodleian Library.

  1. See 14 June 1831, n. 5.

  2. Trelawny had written of Claire Clairmont: "Mrs. Hare once saw her, but she was so prejudiced against her, from stories she had heard against her from the Beauclercs, that she could hardly be induced to notice her" (Trelawny, *Letters,* p. 167).

*To Charles Ollier   [33 Somerset Street]   Thursday
                                                   [September 1831]

My dear Sir
   When you come to the last, will you be so good as to send me the last of the proofs of Mr Trelawny's book—I have been in daily expectation of seeing you—but———alas!

                                                   Yours truly
                                                   MWShelley

ADDRESS: Charles Ollier Esq. / 8 New Burlington St. POSTMARKS: (1) [   ] SP [   ]; (2) T.P / Duke St M.S. UNPUBLISHED. TEXT: MS., Clifford Wurfel.

*To [John Murray][1]   33 Somerset St.   5 Sep. 1831

My dear Sir
   Do I trespass too much on your kindness in asking you to discount the enclosed bill for me. If not inconvenient to you, you would much oblige me.

                                                   Yours truly & Ob^d
                                                   MaryShelley

ENDORSED: 1831 Sept. 5. / Shelley Mrs. UNPUBLISHED. TEXT: MS., Fitzwilliam Museum.

  1. See the next letter.

To John Murray   33 Somerset St.   7 Sep. 1831

My dear Sir
   Not having had the pleasure of hearing from you—I ⟨suppose⟩ pray forgive my troubling you by sending to know whether you can conveniently discount the bill I inclosed to you on Monday last—I am ashamed to trouble you—but an immediate answer would gratify me very much

                                                   Y^s truly & Obliged
                                                   MWShelley

ADDRESS: John Murray Esq / 50 Albermarle St. POSTMARKS: (1) T.P / Duke St M.S.; (2) [   ] MOR[N   ] / 8. SP / 1831. ENDORSED: 1831—Sept. 7 / Shelley Mrs. PUBLISHED: Jones, #390. TEXT: MS., John Murray.

*To CHARLES OLLIER   Somerset St.   28 Sep. [1831][1]

My dear Sir—I should <u>so</u> like to know what is doing & when I am to receive the 12 copies &c if you will not call on me I must on you Which is not right

Yours truly
MShelley

ADDRESS: Charles Ollier Esq / 8 New Burlington St. POSTMARKS: (1) T.P / Bond St; (2) 7[   ]. UNPUBLISHED. TEXT: MS., McGill University Library.

1. The only books Mary Shelley published with Colburn and Bentley while she resided at Somerset Street were *Perkin Warbeck,* 13 May 1830, and the revised *Frankenstein,* c. 2 November 1831. We may assume that Mary Shelley received her copies of *Perkin Warbeck* on publication, since Godwin had his copy on 12 May 1830 (Godwin, Journal), and she undoubtedly had her copies of the Standard Authors edition of *Frankenstein* (see [?February–10 March 1831]). These twelve copies must have been those of Trelawny's *Adventures* (see also the next letter).

To EDWARD JOHN TRELAWNY   33 Somerset St.   2 Oct 1831

My dear Trelawny

[*Cross-written*]   I suppose that I have now some certain intelligence to send you—though I fear that it will both disappoint and annoy you. I am indeed ashamed that I have not been able to keep these people in better order—but I trusted to honesty when ought to have ensured it—Howe{ve}r thus it stands   Your book is to be ⟨printed⟩ published in the course of the Month of November, and then your bills are to be dated—As soon as I get them I will dispose of them as you direct—and you shall receive notice on the subject without delay. I cannot procure for you a copy until then—they pretend that it is not all printed—if I can get an opportunity I will send you one by a private hand—at any rate I shall send them by sea without delay. I will write to Smith[1] about negociating your bills—& I have no doubt that I shall be be able somehow or other to get you money on them—I will go myself to the city to pay Barff's[2] correspondant as soon as I get the cash. Thus your <u>pretty dear</u> (how fascinating is flattery) will do her best as soon as these tiresome people fulfil their engagements. In some degree they have the right on their side—as the <u>day of publication</u> is a usual time from which to date the bills and that was the time which I acceded to—but they talked of such hurry & speed that I expected that that day was nearer at hand than it now appears to be   November <u>is</u> the publishing Month & no new things are coming out now—In fact the Reform Bill swallows up every other thought.

You have heard of the Lord's majority against it[3]—much larger than was expected because it was not imagined that so many bishops would vote against Government—Lord Brougham

[*Pages 3 & 4 missing*]   the birth of her little boy[4]—Do whenever you write send me news of Claire—She never writes herself, and we are all excessively anxious about her. I hope she is better   God knows when fate will do any thing for us—I despair—Percy is very well—I fancy that he will go to Harrow in the Spring—it is not finally arranged but this is what I wish— and therefore I suppose it will be—as they have promised to encrease my allowance for him, & leave me pretty nearly free—only with Eton[5] prohib- ited—but Harrow is now in high reputation under a new head Master.[6] I am delighted to hear that Zella is in such good hands[7]—it is so necessary in this world of woe[8] that children should learn by times to yield to ne- cessity—and a girl allowed to run wild makes an unhappy woman.—

Hunt has set up a penny daily paper[9]—literary & theatrical—it is suc- ceeding very well—but his health is wretched, and when you consider that his sons, now young men—do not contribute a penny towards their own support you may guess that the burthen on him is very heavy—I see them very seldom for they live a good way off—at [*and*] when I go—he is out— she busy,—& I am entertained by the children, who do not edify me. Jane has just moved into a house about half a mile further from town, on the same road[10]—they have furnished it themselves. Dina improves—or rather she always was and continues to be a very nice child.

I think, My dear Trelawny that I have told you all the news—If you write to Claire tell her that M^r & Mrs Godwin are well—my father[11]

PUBLISHED: Jones, #391. TEXT: MS., Bodleian Library (MS., Shelley, Adds., c. 6, f. 115).

1. Horace Smith.

2. Samuel Barff (1793–1880), banker and merchant, had been Byron's agent at Zante, southernmost of the Ionian Islands, west of Greece (Byron, *Letters and Journals* [Marchand], vol. 11, p. 213).

3. The Second Reform Bill passed the House of Commons by a vote of 345 to 236 on 21 September 1831. It was defeated, however, in the House of Lords, by a vote of 199 to 158 on 22 September. The Whig ministry, led by Charles, second earl Grey, prorogued Parliament to prepare a new bill. In the wake of the defeat, agitation and riots erupted throughout England.

4. William Robert Hare, born to Anne Frances and Francis Hare on 20 September 1831 (Augustus J. C. Hare, *The Story of My Life*, 2 vols. [New York: Dodd, Mead and Co., 1896], I, 29).

5. Shelley's alma mater (see 5 May 1831, n. 1).

6. Rev. Charles Thomas Longley (1794–1868; *DNB*), archbishop of Canterbury from 1862 until his death, was headmaster at Harrow from March 1829 to October 1836.

7. Trelawny had written on 1 September 1831 that "an English lady now married to a Lucchese, the Marquis Boschella, had adopted my little Greek child Zella" (*S&M*, IV, 1151). For details of Zella's life with Jane Boccella see H. J. Massingham, *The Friend of Shelley* (New York: D. Appleton & Co., 1930), pp. 292–93.

8. Shelley, *Laon and Cythna* 1. 27. 4; *Rosalind and Helen*, line 631.

9. See 22–25 March 1831, n. 18.

10. From 22 Devonshire Place, Edgware Road, to 12 Maida Place, Edgware Road, where the Hoggs remined until 1850 (Scott, *Hogg*, p. 243).

11. The remainder of the letter is missing.

*To Thomas Jefferson Hogg and Jane Williams Hogg
[?33 Somerset Street   ?1831–33][1]

Dear Jeff—Will you help me to a little <u>law</u>. I want (in a story I am writing)[2] to make a Nobleman die having one daughter, whose eldest son is to inherit his title & possessions—meanwhile, till she has a son, his wealth goes to another branch of the family, & his title lies dormant—Is this compatible with any arrangement of succession or entail according to English law—

Yours truly
MS.

Dearest Girl—give Jeff the first half of this note to read—I am very much out of spirits & have every reason—to be so—My time has been taken up since I saw you—& moreover I strained my instep which confined me to the house for some days & still makes it difficult for me to take a long walk—Could you drink tea with me tomorrow? At any rate I will reach you one day this week. Y^s Aff^ly MS.

ADDRESS: Mrs Hogg / 12 Maida Place / Ed{g}ware Road. UNPUBLISHED. TEXT: MS., Pforzheimer Library.

1. This letter is placed here as the earliest possible date it could have been written, since the Hoggs had just moved to the address of this letter (see 2 October 1831, n. 10). Mary Shelley's remarks to Jane Williams Hogg suggest that the letter was written prior to Mary Shelley's move to Harrow in April 1833.

2. This letter may refer to Mary Shelley's story, "The Elder Son," first published in *Heath's Book of Beauty, 1835,* edited by the Countess of Blessington (London: Longman, Rees, Orme, Brown, Green, and Longman, [1834]), pp. 83–123. "The Elder Son" centers around a wealthy heiress and the entailing of English estates.

*To James Kenney   Friday   [?18 November 1831–February 1832][1]
33 Somerset St.   Portman Sq

Dear Mr Kenney

Will you be so amiable as to indulge me with a sight of your new piece. Power[2] is delighted with it—so is the public—May not I also? I have arranged to go on Saturday (tomorrow) and depend upon upon your assisting a poor penniless body with a couple of admissions—

I hope you are all well—& no more afraid of Cholera than I—I think I have had it—only without any of the symptoms which makes one less afraid

Yours Ever
MWShelley

{ 147 }

UNPUBLISHED: Quotation in Jones, #327. TEXT: MS., Pforzheimer Library.

1. The cholera epidemic referred to in this letter began on the Continent and appeared in the north of England around 26 October 1831, and it raged in England for over a year (*Annual Register, 1831*). During this period two plays by James Kenney opened in London: *The Irish Ambassador*, Covent Garden, on 17 November 1831, and *The Self-Tormentor*, Drury Lane, 16 February 1832 (Nicoll, *English Drama*, p. 337). Godwin attended *The Irish Ambassador* on opening night and *The Self-Tormentor* on 17 February 1832 (Godwin, Journal).

2. James Power (see 9 November [1827], n 5).

*TO CHARLES OLLIER   6 Dec. 1831   33 Somerset St

My dear Sir—I wrote to remind you when the 20th Nov. had come—and I have received no answer—I called in Conduit St—& could not see you. This <u>unaccounted for</u> (I ought to say unaccountable) delay is annoying to me & inconvenient to Mr Trelawny. Do have the goodness to let me see you as soon as you can.

The bills must not be drawn in Mr Trelawny's name—for he wishes them to be negotiated here—and as I can get this done for him I wish them to be in the name of the Banker[1] who is to arrange the affair for me.

Can you lend me Miss Landon's Novel.[2]

Yours truly
M W Shelley

ADDRESS: Chas Ollier Esq / 8 New Burlington St. UNPUBLISHED. TEXT: MS., Houghton Library.

1. Sir John Dean Paul (see 14 June 1831, n. 1; [?9–23 December 1831]; 14 December 1831).

2. Laetitia Elizabeth Landon (L.E.L.), *Romance and Reality*, 3 vols. (London: Colburn and Bentley, 1831).

TO EDWARD JOHN TRELAWNY   [33 Somerset Street
                                           ?9–23 December 1831][1]

[*Fragment*]   me news of Claire. She has not written for more than 2 months— she was then at Naples, having left the Kaisaroffs—and I am beyond measure anxious to learn how she is & what doing. When will her trials be over? When will independence be her lot? Time alone can answer. I am assured that my father-in-law cannot last long—and his stinginess concerning the education of my son makes me indeed wish that he was no longer the Master of our destiny. Shelley's eldest sister, Elizabeth, has just died—of a decline—but this will not soften their hearts. A few lines concerning dear Claire will relieve her friends here from infinite inquietude, so pray add them to your letter. And if you write to her tell her that I and her Mother & Jane have all written, and long for answers. Jane is not well—she has had an attack of liver—but is recovering. Her children are well—and my boy bright and gay—& the consolation of my life. How lucky you are for your Zella to be under such kind protection—you were very wise to place her under a woman. When you see Mrs Hare will you tell her that I have not heard from her for a long time—and that I beg she will write. I wrote not long ago.

(Friday)   Paul[2] promised to send me word the exact sum he has of yours in his hands—but he has omitted to do so—however calculating discount & the full sum of £100 paid to Mr Lister[3] I suppose it is about £190—for which you can draw—I will write to you again next week on the subject but I do not wish to lose this post.—

We have heard of Claire thro' her brother Charles—& learn that she is at present at Pisa—this has tranquillized us—Pray let her know that her Mother—Jane & I have written lately   Ferma in Posta Napoli—

I will write speedily again & in haste

ever Y^s MWS.

ADDRESS: John Edward Trelawny Esq / Ferma in Posta /Firenze / Florence / Italy / Florence / L'Italie / (Single Sheet) / Feuille simple / Foglio Scempio. POSTMARKS: (1) [   ] Oxford / Street; (2) F 31 / 185; (3) PONT / BEAUVOISI[N]; (4) [CORR]ISPZA ESTERA [DA GE-NOVA]; (5) 4 / GENN[AI]O / 1832. PUBLISHED: Jones, #392. TEXT: MS., Bodleian Library (MS., Shelley, Adds., c. 6, f. 116).

1. Trelawny wrote on 5 January 1832 to say that he had just received Mary Shelley's 9 December 1831 letter, and he discussed matters she raised [S&M, IV, 1154–55]. However, Mary Shelley's report in this part of the letter that Elizabeth Shelley (Shelley's oldest sister, born 10 May 1794) had just died indicates that it was written on or shortly after 17 December 1831. Her date of "Friday" within the letter but following her reference to Elizabeth Shelley, and Trelawny's receipt of the letter on 5 January, indicate that she completed the letter on 23 December 1831.

2. Sir John Dean Paul. Trelawny responded that he did "not like trusting the Pauls" (S&M, IV, 1154).

3. Trelawny identified Solly Lister Esq., Abchurch Lane, as a correspondent of Samuel Barff's (S&M, IV, 1155; 2 October 1831, n. 2).

*To Charles Ollier   33 Somerset St.   14 Dec. 1831

My dear Sir

I beg to call to your remembrance that when I saw you in October you gave me your word, that the book should be published in November—probably not before the 20th but during that month. On this I relied.

I saw Mr Paul last night & he agrees to take the bills at 4—7—& 9 months—In giving up one month—I put it to the proof of whether Mess. Colburn & Bentley have any idea of treating me in a gentlemanly way. Mr Paul leaves town at the end of the week   I wish for the bills tonight or tomorrow morning early.

After your pledging your word (as you did to me before Miss Robinson) that the day of publication should be between the 20th & 30th of November—after receiving a note from you saying that Mr Bentley promised the bills for Monday last—I think that having conceded a month—they may give up <u>the letter</u> of the agreement, and send me bills for the date I mention.

I shall expect to see you tomorrow and if I do not before one, I shall call in Burlington St. and I beg that I may see you that I may entirely understand the grounds I stand on—

I am dear Sir
Yours truly
MWShelley

ADDRESS: Chas. Ollier Esq /8 New Burlington St. UNPUBLISHED. TEXT: MS., Pforzheimer Library.

*TO CHARLES OLLIER   [33 Somerset Street]   Thursday—
                                              15 Dec. [1831]

My dear Sir

I called as I appointed & was told you wd be in at 4—I am here & learn that you had returned & are gone again & are not expected till 6. A note from you declining an interview wd have saved me considerable inconvenience

I suppose that <u>your own</u> proposition of the protracted date of the bills is also refused. The distance from Florence will make a month elapse before I can receive Mr Trelawny's instructions—this being the case it will obviate a great deal of uneasiness to me—and disagreable representation to him if Mess. Colburn & Bentley will either grant the bills at the longer date—or <u>pledge themselves</u> for a day of publication. Such a pledge must come from themselves, as they do not consider your word or writing as binding. This is the least they can do considering the great inconvenience Mr Trelawny suffers, and the extreme mistake I was led into by supposing that having <u>your word</u> was a counter balance to my signature. I beg to say that I have no agreement at all in my possession & the whole thing depending on you, was left by me in such a state as I imagined I might trust to—never having before experienced any thing but Gentlemanly treatment from your house

I hope to hear from You that the day of publication is fixed & what it is

Yours truly
MShelley

ADDRESS: Chas. Ollier Esq / &c &c &c. UNPUBLISHED. TEXT: MS., Pforzheimer Library.

*To Charles Ollier   33 Somerset St.   16 Dec. 1831 (*a*)

My dear Sir

I have received the three bills for £100 each from Mess. Colburn & Bentley as a consideration for his work entitled Adventures of a younger son—being the payment of the copy right with the exception of £100 more to be paid to Mr Trelawny on the book going to a second edition.

Y^s Ob^ly
MaryShelley

ADDRESS: Charles Ollier Esq. UNPUBLISHED. TEXT: MS., Houghton Library.

*To Charles Ollier   Friday   [16 December 1831] (*b*)[1]
33 Somerset St.

My dear Sir

I was engaged when your messenger came so I could only write the few necessary lines, I add these to tell you how much obliged I feel to you for all the trouble you have taken—& above all, for succeeding in putting an end to a suspense which was infinitely annoying to me, as I knew that Mr Trelawny had entered into certain engagements depending on my accounts, that he would be able to fulfil them. All is right now, and you have my sincere thanks.

L.E.L.'s [*Laetitia Elizabeth Landon's*] 3^d vol is very good indeed.[2] It is Romance & Sentiment; which is that in which she excells—Reality she has too much fancy & feeling for—I was deeply interested in the 3^d Vol—it does her heart & imagination both great credit. Cavendish[3] I find very amusing—Do not forget Eugene Aram[4]—every day earlier that I get it will be a debt of gratitude to you—

Yours Very truly
MWShelley

ADDRESS: Chas. Ollier Esq / 8 New Burlington St. UNPUBLISHED. TEXT: MS., Pforzheimer Library.

1. See the previous letter.

2. See 6 December 1831, n. 2.

3. William Johnson Neale, *Cavendish; or, the Patrician at Sea,* 3 vols. (London: Colburn and Bentley, 1831).

4. Edward Bulwer, *Eugene Aram,* 3 vols. (London: Colburn and Bentley, 1831) (see 16 February 1832).

To Charles Ollier   [?33 Somerset Street]   Saturday
                                     [?24 December 1831]

Dear Sir

You were kind enough to promise to lend me Eugene Aram—You would
very greatly oblige me by giving it to my servant—or leaving it out so that
she could have it on calling again—If you would lend me this week's C^t
Journal—& the New Monthly for Jany I should be exceedingly glad

                                        Yours truly
                                        MWShelley

[*Crosswritten*]   I hope you got the last note I sent you, which had been
forgotten for some days—to thank you for all the trouble you took in M^r
Trelawny's affair.

I will return Cavendish in a few days—It is very clever—but the beginning
is best—& it is immoral—why [wr]ite about certain things; it is bad enough
that they are

ADDRESS: Chas Ollier Esq / 8 New Burlington St. PUBLISHED: Jones, #393. TEXT: MS.,
Pierpont Morgan Library.

*To Leigh Hunt   [?33 Somerset Street   ?January 1832][1]

Dear Hunt

Would you dislike forwarding the enclosed to Col. T— [*Thompson*]—I
cannot tell you how utterly [?*regardly*] I am of such observations as his—
& how ready I am to agree with him—I care so little for my authorship

I shall expect you tomorrow—if it rains—come on Friday—but tomorrow
is best—in haste

                                        with thanks—Ever Y^s.

UNPUBLISHED. TEXT: MS., Keats-Shelley Memorial House, Rome.
     1. This tentative date is based on Mary Shelley's dealings with Colonel Thomas Perronet
Thompson (1783–1869; *DNB*), soldier (general in 1868), politician, and author. Thompson,
proprietor of the *Westminster Review* from 1829 to 1836, complained about Mary Shelley's
reviews of Cooper's *Bravo* (1831) and Bulwer's *Eugene Aram* (L. G. Johnson, *General T. Perronet
Thompson* [London: George Allen & Unwin, 1957], pp. 182–83). Mary Shelley accepted
Thompson's criticism of her *Bravo* article, and changed it. This letter may refer to that revision,
published in the *Westminster Review* 16 (January 1832). Her review of *Eugene Aram* was not
published in the *Westminster Review*.

To William Whitton   33 Somerset St.   Portman Sq   24 Jany 1832

My dear Sir

I am exceedingly sorry to find myself obliged to trouble you with a
request, which I assure you, were it possible, I would refrain from making.

After your last letter[1] perhaps it would be your wish that I should apply to Mr Guigson [*Gregson*][2]—but as it was to you that I mentioned the circumstance—and you gave me hopes that you would kindly mediate with Sir Timothy for me—& as I believe you have hitherto done all you can for my advantage with my father-in-law—I prefer, I confess, applying to you.

You will guess after all this preface my purpose is that you would have the goodness to forward to Sir Timothy a request that he would advance me some money, without which I shall be placed in a most difficult situation. When you asked me to write down what I required for Percy, I mentioned that I had been involved ever since he first went to school—from the circumstance of my income being then limited to £250, which could not cover his encreasing expences. Now at the complete age of twelve, his expences are so very much greater than they were—& encrease so much, that these involvements are continually added to. The only mode by which I can meet them is by retrenching my own expences—to do this I must leave my present habitation—& it is my purpose to reside in some spot in the country, where I shall be able to spend less on my own wants than in London it is possible for me to do.—But I cannot quit my present abode without a sum of money to pay off a few debts. Under these circumstances, if you will add your influence I trust Sir Timothy would not refuse me £50—without which I see no hope of extricating myself from my present situation. Excu[se] my troubling you—this £50 will not add very greatly to my debt to my father in law—and if he were to see what a fine boy his grandson has become, I scarcely think he would have the heart to refuse me a favor necessary for his comfort as well as my own.

I hope your health is better—and that it will continue to improve with the advancing season—I am Dear Sir

Yours Obliged
MWShelley

ADDRESS: William Whitton Esq / Stone Wall / Tunbridge. POSTMARKS: L.S. / [   ] 18 [   ] / L.S. PUBLISHED: Jones, #394. TEXT: MS., Bodleian Library (MS., Shelley, Adds., c. 6, ff. 117–18).

1. On 6 November 1831 Whitton wrote to say that Sir Timothy Shelley was determined not to give Mary Shelley the advance she had requested (Abinger MSS., Bodleian Library).

2. John Gregson was the successor of William Whitton, who was now in very ill health (Ingpen, *Shelley in England*, II, 613–14).

TO JOHN GREGSON   33 Somerset St.   Portman Sq—27 Jany 1832

Dear Sir

Mr Whitton has informed me that you will have the goodness to further any application of mine to Sir Tim^{thy} Shelley, and being at this moment in an embarassment that obliges me to trouble him, I shall be much obliged to you if you will communicate and second my request.

You may remember that when I signed the deed last year[1] in Bedford Row—I applied for an encrease of income that I might send my son to a school of higher qualifications than Mr Slater's—Mr Whitton gave me hopes that this request would be complied with—I mentioned then that I had been embarassed for money ever since Percy went to school, when my income had not been encreased as I had expected. Afterwards Sir Tim^thy declined making any ⟨advance⟩ addition to my allowance, saying that he hoped that I should be able to give my son a good education on the sum I at present receive.

Percy is now turned twelve years old; you may imagine that his school & taylors bills encrease every year—that his incidental expences are very great—& that to ⟨meet⟩ defray them consumes a great part of my income. To meet these calls I have but one resource which is to diminish my own personal expences as much as possible—for which purpose I have long contemplated going to a quiet spot in the country, where I could spend far less than I do now. I have been prevented, because it always demands some small command of money to make any change. I had hoped that at Xmas I might have been enabled, but found it impossible—I am forced to continue in my present abode (where I have lived nearly 3 years) my debts encreasing—and perfectly unable to change and retrench from want of such a sum as permitting me to get rid of my embarassments—would enable me to execute my economical plan. Under these circumstances I can only apply to Sir Timothy—and ask for the sum of £50, upon which I shall immediately remove—and establishing myself on the cheapest plan, continue to defray the encreasing expenses of Percy's education. If I am refused this, I am at a loss to imagine what I can do—as without an entire alteration of abode & leaving London, it is impossible for me extricate myself from my present position

Percy desires his duty & Love to Sir Tim^thy & Lady Shelley—he is a very fine boy and did his grandfather see him I am sure he would not have the heart to deny me a request which has for its ultimate object his well bringing up. I would have called on you with him, but the weather prevents my going out, & I am unwilling to delay a solicitation on which my present ⟨existence⟩ hopes of doing my duty by him depend. May I ask you therefore to forward my wishes at your earliest convenience—and I trust with success—I am d^r Sir,

                                    Your Obt. Servant
                                    MWShelley

I ought to mention perhaps that as Percy will continue with Mr Slater, my new abode will not be at <u>too great</u> a distance from town—sufficiently far only to ensure economy.

Percy was very much obliged to his Grandfather for some pocket money he was kind enough to send him last Easter thro' Mrs Paul.[2] I hope the family are well after their affliction.[3]

ADDRESS: John Gregson Esq / 18 Bedford Row. POSTMARKS: (1) T.P / Duke St M.S; (2) 4. EVEN. 4 / 27. JA / 18[32]. ENDORSED: 27 Jany 1832 / Mrs Shelley. PUBLISHED: Jones, #395. TEXT: MS., Bodleian Library (MS., Shelley, Adds., c. 6, ff. 119–20).

    1. See 6 June 1831 (*b*), n. 1.
    2. Georgiana Beauclerk Paul.
    3. See [?9–23 December 1831], n. 1.

To John Gregson   33 Somerset St.   10 Feb. 1832

Dear Sir

    I have called to ask if you have made the communication I requested to Sir Timothy Shelley—and if you have received any answer.[1] My comfort & respectability so entirely depend on having a favorable one—& on being enabled to quit town—that I am most anxious on the subject. If any explanation would facilitate my wish, I will call on you at any time you may appoint

I am [   ] Ob[t] Servant
MaryShelley

ADDRESS: John Gregson Esq / 18 Bedford Row. ENDORSED: 10 Feb. 1832 / Mrs. Shelley. PUBLISHED: Jones, #396. TEXT: MS., Bodleian Library (MS., Shelley, Adds., c. 6, ff. 121–22).

    1. On 23 February 1832 Sir Timothy Shelley wrote to John Gregson indicating his agreement to raise Mary Shelley's allowance to £400. He pointed out, however, that the deed she had signed entitled her to an advance of £6,000 in all and that this amount would soon run out (Abinger MSS., Bodleian Library).

*To John Bowring   33 Somerset St.   16 Feb[ry] 1832

My dear Sir—I was much gratified by your giving me Eugene Aram to do[1]— & then just as I was setting to it "tooth & nail"—some events in the family of a friend of mine[2] forced me to go out of town, & took all my attention forcibly away from my task.   However my article is now in full progress— & I write to tell you so that you may expect it next week. One thing I am plagued about—Colburn has been too stingy to give me a copy—& getting it from a library it is continually sent for back

    It is a wonderful & a divine book—though so very sad

I am, d[r] D[r] Bowring
Yours truly
MWShelley

ADDRESS: Dr. Bowring / 1 Queen's Sq / Westminster. POSTMARKS: (1) T.P / Duke St M.S; (2) 7. NIGHT. 7 / 15. FE / 1832. ENDORSED: (1) Feby 16 1832 / Mrs Shelley; (2) Mrs Shelley / 16 Feby 1832. UNPUBLISHED. TEXT: MS., Pforzheimer Library.

1. See [?January 1832], n. 1.

2. Georgiana Beauclerk Paul and her husband John Dean Paul separated on 18 November 1831. Mary Shelley wrote in her Journal: "After a great deal of discomfort and uncertainty I have learnt the meaning of the strange occurences at the Strand—Poor Gee is sent to Norwood—her child torn from her—cast away & deserted—My first impulse is to befriend a woman—I will do her all the good I can." On 27 February 1832 she noted that her "attention—time & feelings have been absorbed by poor Gee's misfortunes" and that she witnessed Georgiana Paul's signing of the act of separation on 6 February 1832, after which Georgiana Paul, with her son Aubrey John Dean Paul (1827–90, 3d baronet in 1868), went to live at Ardglass Castle, county Down, the home of her grandfather.

To John Gregson   33 Somerset St. 2nd March 1832 (*a*)

Dear Sir

I enclose the usual receipt—and shall be glad if you will have the goodness to give the cheque in exchange to the bearer.

The entire neglect with which my request has been met, arises, I suppose, from its being refused.[1] I was in hopes, I confess, that Sir Tim^{thy} Shelley would have viewed my motives with greater kindness—& that desirous as I am to limit my expences so as to meet the encreasing ones of my son, he would have been good enough to have assisted me—Is there no hope that Sir Tim. may yet be induced to make me an advance which need not be considered as a precedent?

Percy is quite well; and I have very good accounts of him

I am, Dr Sir

Y^r Ob^t Servant

MWShelley

ENDORSED: 2 March 1832 / Mrs Shelley. PUBLISHED: Jones, #397. TEXT: MS., Bodleian Library (MS., Shelley, Adds., c. 6, ff. 125–26).

1. This indicates that neither Gregson nor Whitton had informed Mary Shelley of Sir Timothy Shelley's decision (see 10 February 1832, n. 1).

To John Gregson   33 Somerset St. Friday [2 March 1832] (*b*)

Dear Sir—I shall do myself the pleasure of calling on you at 12 tomorrow Morning

Y^s Ob^{ly}

MWShelley

ADDRESS: John Gregson Esq / 18 Bedford Row. POSTMARKS: (1) T.P / [D]uke St M.S; (2) 7. 1832. 7 / 2. MR / NIGHT. ENDORSED: 2nd March 1832 / Mrs Shelley. PUBLISHED: Jones, #398. TEXT: MS., Bodleian Library (MS., Shelley, Adds., c. 6, ff. 123–24).

To John Gregson   33 Somerset Street   [?4–10 March 1832]

Dear Sir

I am sorry to trouble you again, but I am truly uneasy at not hearing from you—When I saw you last you asked me if the promise of an encrease of income would meet my wants. I said that it would if I received the additional £25 this quarter but that was essential to me—You appeared to think that Sir Tim^{thy} would kindly make no difficulty as to that—I would not press the point, were it not one of absolute necessity—and I should be glad to hear that Sir Tim^{thy} had given you a favorable answer—

If you could let me see you on this point soon I should be glad—I would call—but you would probably be too engaged to see me. I shall be at home at five today or any day you will please to name as convenient to yourself

I am d^r Sir Y^{rs} Ob^{ly}
MWShelley

Endorsed: March 1832 / Mrs Shelley. Published: Jones, #399. Text: MS., Bodleian Library (MS., Shelley, Adds., c. 6, ff. 131–32).

To John Gregson   33 Somerset St.   14 March 1832

Dear Sir

Your continued silence frightens me—as the £25 I was in hopes to receive through you, is beyond every thing essential—& the very delay occasions the continuance of expence of which I could otherwise get rid. Will you let me know what hopes I have.

Percy came to see me on Sunday—he is quite well—and Mr Slater gives a very good account of him. I have given notice that he will quit his present school—and am taking steps for placing him with Dr Longley (the Head Master) at Harrow[1]

I am dear Sir
Yours Ob^{ly}
MWShelley

Endorsed: 14 March 1832 / Mrs M. W. Shelley. Published: Jones, #400. Text: MS., Bodleian Library (MS., Shelley, Adds., c. 6, ff. 127–28).

1. See 2 October 1831, n. 6.

To John Gregson   Thursday Morn^g   [?15 March 1832]
                           33 S. [Somerset] St.

Dear Sir

I enclose a receipt which I hope is right. Pray when you write, tell Sir Timothy that I am very sensible of his goodness in complying with my request[1]—And if when he comes to town he will permit me to thank him in person he will add greatly to the obligation. Will you tell him also that I saw Mr Slater the other day, who praises Percy for his improvement & docility—With many thanks for the trouble you have taken I am, d^r Sir

Y^s Obe^tly MWShelley

ENDORSED: March 1832 / Mrs Shelley. PUBLISHED: Jones, #401. TEXT: MS., Bodleian Library (MS., Shelley, Adds., c. 6, ff. 129–30).

   1. See 10 February 1832, n. 1.

*TO CHARLES OLLIER   Somerset St. Wednesday [?April 1832][1]

Dear Sir

    I want to see you as soon as I can upon an important question or two concerning "The Younger Son"—Can you call tomorrow between 12 & 1? do—if you possibly can, as it is of consequence—

    Could you lend me any new publ.—you w^d eternally oblige me—not the Contrast—I have read it—But the Fair of May Fair or Arlington[2]—   Y^s

MS.

ADDRESS: Chas. Ollier Esq / 8 New Burlington St. UNPUBLISHED. TEXT: MS., Pforzheimer Library.

   1. This tentative date is based on the publication date of *The Fair of May Fair* and *The Contrast* (see n. 2).

   2. [Constantine Henry Phipps, first marquis of Normanby], *The Contrast*, 3 vols. (London: Colburn), published in April 1832; Catherine Gore, *The Fair of May Fair*, 3 vols. (London: Colburn and Bentley), published in April 1832; [Thomas Henry Lister], *Arlington*, 3 vols. (London: Colburn and Bentley, 1832).

TO ELLEN MANNERS-SUTTON   [33 Somerset Street 21 April 1832]

[*Fragment*]   for you may be sure that you do quite right in following the injunctions of the very wise & very kind Speaker.[1]

    I am quite sure your Party will be a Success—for Numbers except at a Ball, are by no means necessary—I write though I see you so soon under the idea of your going to Mistley[2] on Monday—if I am wrong in this supposition, I shall hope to attain a little chat with you next week, notwithstanding this note—

    Believe me, Dear Mrs Manners Sutton,

Ever truly Y^s
MWShelley

ADDRESS: Mrs Manners Sutton / Palace Yd / Westminster. POSTMARKS: (1) T.P / Duke St M.S; (2) 10. F.NOON 10 / 21. AP / 1832. PUBLISHED: Jones, #402. TEXT: MS., Pierpont Morgan Library.

1. Sir Charles Manners-Sutton had been Speaker of the House of Commons since June 1817.

2. Mistley Hall, Manningtree, Essex, the Manners-Sutton country home (*Who's Who of British Members of Parliament,* vol. I, *1832–1885* [Sussex: Harvester Press, 1976], p. 370).

*To John Murray   33 Somerset St.   30 April [1832]   Monday

Dear Sir

When you last did me the pleasure to call on me, you said that I should see you again—and several subjects were mentioned, which seemed to require my attention, yet concerning which I have heard nothing more—You spoke concerning notes[1] for Lord Byron's Poems—& said you would send the volumes—not having received them, I have done nothing, but it has occurred to me that you may imagine that I have been forgetful—I write therefore merely to say that I have not seen Mr Finden[2]—but if your wishes continue such as when you called, both with regard to the notes & the picture, pray let me know—that my part may not be wanting—

                    I am, dear Sir
                    Y^s Obliged
                    MWShelley

Is it true what I have heard, that the Countess Guiccioli is arrived[3]—if so, and you know where she is, will you have the goodness to let me have her address immediately.

ENDORSED: 1832—April 30— / Shelley Mrs. UNPUBLISHED: Jones, #403, in summary. TEXT: MS., John Murray.

1. Mary Shelley supplied notes for *The Works of Lord Byron: with his Letters and Journals and his Life,* by Thomas Moore, published by John Murray in seventeen volumes. Volumes 1 and 12 were published in 1835, volumes 2–11 in 1832, and volumes 13–17 in 1833.

2. William Finden (1787–1852; *DNB*), engraver, who with his brother Edward Francis Finden (1791–1857; *DNB*), engraver, did *Finden's Illustrations of the Life and Works of Lord Byron* (3 vols. [London: John Murray, 1833–34]). John Murray was arranging for an engraving to be made from Amelia Curran's portrait of Shelley (see 15 April 1833). The engraving, which appeared in volume II of *Finden's Illustrations,* was given to Mary Shelley and was used by her as the frontispiece for Shelley, *Poetical Works* (1839).

3. Teresa Guiccioli, who arrived sometime after 1 April (see 15 August [1832], n. 6), remained in England until January 1833 (see 16 January 1833). By 15 March she had reached Ravenna after a long journey through France and Italy (Teresa Guiccioli to John Murray, MS., John Murray).

To John Murray   33 Somerset St.   4 May—1832

My dear Sir

I do not know how to thank you sufficiently for the very agreable presents you have made me and my friend[1]—You are quite magnificent in your generosity—and nothing can be more welcome than your books—

I am afraid I shall scarcely meet all your wishes in the intended notes. The subject of Lord Byron's adventures is greatly exhausted—and besides the names of ladies are scarcely fair subjects for publication—However I will do what I can—of course you will take care that I am not brought forward or named, as you are aware how sedulously I try to keep in the background. By the bye I must mention that early next month I leave town for some little time—so that I should be glad that Mr Finden should see me during the course of this present one.

May I without intruding on you, mention another subject?—You apparently consider the closing of your family library as conclusive on the subject of my father's writing for you. Is this necessary? You are but too well aware of the evil days on which literature is fallen—and how difficult it is for a man however gifted, whose existence depends on his pen, to make one engagement succeed another with sufficient speed to answer the calls of his situation—Nearly all our literati have found but one resource in this—which is in the ample scope afforded by periodicals—a kind of literary pride has prevented my father from mingling in these—and never having published any thing anonimously, he feels disenclined to enter on a to him new career.

I feel persuaded that he would render his proposed Lives of the Necromancers[2] a deeply interesting and valuable work—There is a life and energy in his writings which always exalts them above those of his contemporaries. If this subject, which seems to me a fortunate one, does not please you—there are many others which would offer themselves, were he certain that you would accede to them, and give him that encouragement which he has been accustomed hitherto to find. He had thought of the Lives of the English philosophers—I should certainly be glad that the Publisher of Byron and Moore, and all the best writers, added the name of Godwin to the list—and if upon consideration, you find that your views do not oppose an engagement with him, you will perhaps invite him to further communication on the subject.

Excuse my pressing this point—which after all must be decided by the laws of expediency, and believe me

Yours truly & Obliged
MWShelley

ADDRESS: For / John Murray Esq / 50 Albermarle St. POSTMARKS: (1) T.P / Duke St M.S; (2) 4. EVEN[. 4] / 4. MY / 1832. ENDORSED: 1832 May 4 / Shelley Mrs. PUBLISHED: Jones, #404. TEXT: MS., John Murray.

1. Jane Williams Hogg (see [?10 June 1832]).

2. Godwin's *Lives of the Necromancers* was published by Frederick J. Mason in 1834.

To [ALARIC A. WATTS] 33 Somerset St.   Portman Sq   14 May—1832

Sir

I do not know whether the enclosed drama[1] will suit your Annual[2] or whether it may be considered as more befitting the beautiful Juvenile One, edited by Mrs Watts[3]—If it should please you, I shall be glad that it appeared in either publication—& I refer to your usual terms, to arrange the question of remuneration

I am, Sir, Y^s Ob^ly MWShelley

I may mention that this drama has been seen & liked by two or three good judges whose opinion emboldens me to send it you

PUBLISHED: Jones, #405. TEXT: MS., The John Rylands Library.

1. *Midas* (see vol. I, 9 May [1824]).

2. *Literary Souvenir* (see vol. I, 30 October [1826] to Alaric A. Watts, n. 1).

3. Pricilla Maden (Zillah) Watts (1799–1873) edited the *New Year's Gift and Juvenile Souvenir* from 1829 to 1835 (for details of the lives of Alaric and Pricilla Watts see Alaric Alfred Watts, *Alaric Watts,* 2 vols. [London: Richard Bentley and Son, 1884]).

To JOHN GREGSON   33 Somerset St.   6th June / 32

Dear Sir—Will you be so good as to let me know when I may send for the cheque—If you wish to communicate with me—I shall be very glad if you will appoint a time when I can see you either in Bedford Row or Cumberland St—& I will call—I have made every arrangement to leave town for Sandgate in Kent which I hear is an healthy & cheap place—After the Summer holydays Percy goes to Harrow—He is to board with Mr Kennedy,[1] the Under Master—Dr Longley the head Master, not having a vacancy—I am very anxious that he should get as strong as possible by the seaside, before entering on a public School.

May I request an answer this Ev^g

Yours Ob^ly

MWShelley

ADDRESS: John Gregson Esq / 1 Cumberland St. ENDORSED: 6 June 1832 / Mrs Shelley. PUBLISHED: Jones, #406. TEXT: MS., Bodleian Library (MS., Shelley, Adds., c. 6, ff. 133–34).

1. Benjamin Hall Kennedy (1804–89; *DNB*), D.D. and classical scholar, was a master at Harrow from 1830 to 1836, and housemaster at the Grove, the house of Percy Florence Shelley, from 1831 to 1836 (information supplied by Rosemary Hudson, Vaughan Library, Harrow School). Kennedy, a member of the Cambridge Apostles (see 12 December [1838] to Edward Moxon, n. 4), went on to become headmaster of Shrewsbury School, regius professor of Greek at Cambridge, and canon of Ely.

To John Gregson   Saturday [?9 June 1832]   33 Somerset St.

Dear Sir

I enclose the receipt and will you be so good as to give the cheque to the Bearer.   I leave town with Percy in less than a fortnight, as soon as his holydays begin—I shall go to Sandgate in Kent—that being a quiet & healthy place. Percy has lately been taking riding lessons at the Knightsbridge Barracks.—It is arranged that he goes to Harrow after the Summer holyday—he will board with Mr Kennedy, the Under Master—Dr Longley, the Head Master, not having a vacancy—I called with him twice at your house, on our return from Church, but was not so fortunate as to find you—I am, d^r Sir

Y^s Ob^ly
MWShelley

ENDORSED: June 1832 / Mrs Shelley. PUBLISHED: Jones, #408. TEXT: MS., Bodleian Library (MS., Shelley, Adds., c. 6, ff. 135–36).

To John Murray   Sunday Morning [?10 June 1832]
Somerset St.

Dear Sir

The more I look over Lord Byron, the less do I see what I can say in illustration—historical, since the Life so copiously treats of them—for instance in Don Juan, the only things I can discover is in Canto IV CXI—
I knew one woman of that purple school
Which the Lady C. [*Charlemont*]¹ alluded to in the life—Vol II 268—But as Lady Charlemont would recognize herself in such an assertion, it would not be right to put it in—and in Canto XIV c. where the dangerous passion arising from a game of billiards alludes to Lady F.W.W. [*Frances Wedderburn Webster*] the Heroine of the Bride—and the Ginevra of the Sonnets—Of the Poems to tell you that Florence is Mrs Spencer Smith—is to tell you what you know already
          "When all around was dark & drear"²
Was to Mrs Leigh
          Thou art not false but thou art fickle
to Lady Oxford—
          "Though the day of my destinys over³
to Mrs Leigh
          Well Thou art happy & I feel
to Mary Chaworth
All this you know already—The feelings which gave rise to each poem, are so dwelt on in the Letters in Mr Moore's Life—that there seems nothing left to say on that subject.—and by printing the poems in a Chronological

order, you force on the readers apprehension his state of mind when he wrote them ⟨The elegance mingled with pass⟩ the difficulty of clothing well his ideas resulting from youth—though they forced expression—which made the Hours of idleness a failure. The depth of passion, nursed in solitude—and wild romantic scenery which breathes in his poems to Thirza[4]— Who she was I do not know—I believe a cousin—at any rate she was a real person <u>decidedly</u>—and his feelings of misery on her death most real—I have heard him express the sensations of acute despair that produced those poems—and those "on a Cornelian heart that was broken"—Alone in Greece— his imagination imparted its fire to his feelings—and encreased their impression on his own heart, as well as bestowing greater power of language and poetry—Returned to England & mingling with the world, a certain elegance mingled itself with his with his inspiration, and was diffused over his productions—remarkable especially in the "Bride"—Attached one after the other to women of fashion his heroines displayed the delicacy & refinement of civilization.

When he quitted England, feeling himself wronged—an outcast & a mourner—his mind took a higher flight—It fed upon his regrets—& on his injuries—& Manfred & the 3^d Canto of C.H [*Childe Harold*] bear marks of solitary ruminations in wild scenery—detached from the spirit of fashion & the world—The gaieties and incorrectness of his Venetian Life breathed their Influence in Beppo & D. [*Don*] Juan—while solitary Lido—the moon lit palaces—and the deserted ruined grandeurs of that city awakened the vein that displayed itself in the 4th Canto of C.H. in Mazeppa—in the Ode on Venice—

As his mind became more subdued—he became more critical—but his school of criticism being of the narrow order, it confined his faculties in his tragedies & Lord Byron became sententious & dull—except where character still shone forth—or where his critical ideas did not intrude to Mar— Sarcasm, before confined to his speech—now acquiring a sting from his susceptibility to the attacks made on him induced him to write the Vision— & the Solitude in which he lived at Ravenna gave birth to Deep thoughts— to Cain—and Heaven & Earth—

At Pisa he again belonged more to the English world—It did him little good—Werner he wrote chiefly because he had for many years thought it a good subject—He was very anxious to go on with D. Juan—and verging on the time when people revert to past feelings, instead of dwelling on the present—he amused himself by descanting on English fashionable life— The last Cantos of D.J. were written with great speed—I copied them[5] there were scarcely any erasures and his chief delight was in sending them to me, to date the beginning & end with the name of the same month—to prove how quickly they were composed—the opposition he met concerning the Liberal made him defy the world in D. Juan—Then it made him despise the Liberal itself, so that when he wrote expressly for it, he wrote tamely— as is the case with the Island—But, in the end, this war gave him a disgust to Authorship—and he hurried to Greece to get a new name as a man of action—having arrived at the highest praise as a poet.

I have thus run through his works, to shew you what I think and know of the periods of their composition and the moods of mind in which they were written. If you think that a few lines of their history appended to each (which you could alter & frame as you like) would be of use, you can judge by this sketch, what my view would be, & I should be happy to furnish them—but still I think, the life supplies the place of any such observations.

I write in haste. Next week I leave town for 3 Months—Would it not be better that I saw Mr Finden before I went? I have been reading Contarini Fleming—Who is the Author?[6] I like parts of it excessively—Especially the 1st Volume—Thanks for the 6th of the Life—Permit me to remind you that the copy you gave Mrs Williams needs also a 6th Vol.—I am, d^r Sir—Y^s truly MWShelley

ADDRESS: John Murray Esq /50 Albermarle St. POSTMARKS: (1) T.P / Duke St M.S; (2) [   ]NOON [   ] / [?10] JU / 1832. PUBLISHED: Jones, #407. TEXT: MS., British Library (Add. 38,510, ff. 56–60).

1. Details of Byron's association with all the women listed in this letter, with the exception of Lady Charlemont, are included in Marchand, *Byron*.

2. "When all around grew drear and dark," the first line of "Stanzas to Augusta."

3. "Stanzas to Augusta."

4. "Thyrza" was John Edleston (see Marchand, *Byron*).

5. See vol. I, 3 October 1818, n. 3, and 15 October 1822 through [2 April 1823].

6. Benjamin Disraeli, *Contarini Fleming,* 4 vols. (London: John Murray), published in May 1832 (William Flavelle Monypenny and George Earle Buckle, *The Life of Benjamin Disraeli,* 2 vols. [New York: Macmillan Co., 1929], I, 185, 194).

*To CHARLES OLLIER   Tuesday   11 June / 32   33 Somerset St.

Dear Sir—I enclose a note I have just received from the Author of the "Younger Son—"[1] I certainly did tell him that he should receive 1⟨6⟩2 copies—because I & my father, & every one I ever knew always received 12, and I could not guess that you would commence a system of stinginess with him—he has had only seven. I cannot imagine why you refuse to give him his MS.[2] which would be in <u>my</u> possession, if I had corrected the proofs, as I might—he desires nothing else from it but to collate it with the printed copy for his own satisfaction—it could not injure you   Let me hear from you or see you on the subject—& soon, as I leave town at the end of the week—I am, de^r Sir—Y^s truly

MWShelley

His second part is about Lord B—Shelley—his adventures in Greece &c &c he [*cross-written*] is employed in it now—

ADDRESS: Charles Ollier Esq / 8 New Burlington St. POSTMARKS: (1) T.P / Duke St M.S; (2) 12. NOON. 12 / 12. JU / 1832. UNPUBLISHED. TEXT: MS., Pforzheimer Library.

1. Trelawny returned to England early in May 1832 (Trelawny, *Letters*, p. 172). Trelawny's note, dated 1 June 1832, enclosed in this letter is in the holdings of the Pforzheimer Library.

2. His manuscript, in the hand of Charles Armitage Brown, is now in the Houghton Library, Harvard University (Trelawny, *Adventures*, xi, xiv).

*To John Hobart Caunter[1]   Sandgate—9th July 1832[2]

Dear Sir

According to my promise I send you a contribution for the Belle Assemblie—As my time has been a good deal taken up I have been scarcely able to find time to get it ready—but have adapted a tale written on the scenes it describes and finished it—and I hope it will answer your purpose— Though it is so long that it must be divided.[3] Have the goodness to direct your answer on the subject to me at my fathers in Gower Place, who will forward it me—And permit me to say that I shall be glad of an early communication

> I am, Sir—
> Yours Obbed[tly]
> MWShelley

ADDRESS: Caunter Esq / 36 Somerset St. / Portman Sq. UNPUBLISHED. TEXT: MS., Pforzheimer Library.

1. John Hobart Caunter (1794–1851; *DNB*], author and clergyman. Caunter was a frequent caller on Godwin and in 1835 adapted Godwin's *St. Leon* for the stage. Although no biographical reference links Caunter with the *Court Magazine and Belle Assemblée*, his connection is established by the contents of this letter and its address. *Boyle's Court Guide*, 1829, lists the Reverend J. H. Caunter at 36 Somerset Street.

2. Mary Shelley and Percy Florence spent more than three months at Sandgate, seventy-one and three-quarters miles east-southeast of London, beginning c. 15 June 1832 (see 11 June 1832; and MWS Journal, June–September 1832).

3. "The Pole," "by the Author of Frankenstein," was published in two parts in the *Court Magazine and Belle Assemblée* 1 (August 1832): 64–71; 2 (September 1832): 129–36. The story was written by Claire Clairmont, who sent it to Mary Shelley to correct, to "write the last scene of it," and to try to place it in the *Keepsake* under the signature "Mont. Obscur." Claire Clairmont also stated that should it be sold, half the money would belong to Mary Shelley (*S&M*, IV, 1159–60).

*To Frederic Mansel Reynolds   [Sandgate] Wednesday
                                             [26 July 1832]

This is not so very long[1]—though its shortness must make it a little abrupt— but to cure this, would have required another putting together of the parts of the story, which must have doubled its length. As I have now earned the cash I need so much—I hope M[r] Heath[2] will be so good as not to make any difficulty about giving a cheque, which you will oblige me by sending down here—I imagine that this will find you still in town—and I shall be glad to hear from you—The weather is delightful now, and this place as green and beautiful as possible

I scarcely know what I write I am so tired of scribling—

Y^{rs}

MS.

ADDRESS: F. Mansel Reynolds Esq / 48 Warren St. / Fitzroy Sq. POSTMARKS: (1) FOLKE-STONE / PENNY POST; (2) E / 26 JY 26 / 1832. UNPUBLISHED. TEXT: MS., Pforzheimer Library.

1. This letter follows the conclusion of Mary Shelley's "The Invisible Girl," published in the *Keepsake for 1833*, ed. Frederic Mansel Reynolds (London: Longman, Rees, Orme, Brown, Green, and Longman, [1832]), pp. 210–27. Also published in that *Keepsake* is Mary Shelley's story "The Brother and Sister" (pp. 105–41).

2. Charles Heath (see [?7 April–June 1829], n. 2). Heath contributed five engravings to the *Keepsake for 1833,* none of them related to Mary Shelley's works.

*TO CHARLES ARMITAGE BROWN   Somerset St.   27 July [?1832][1]

My dear Sir

Will you excuse me if I take a liberty I have not before taken, and present to you Mr Blair, a Gentleman about to have the happiness to visit the beautiful country you are so happy as to inhabit—You will much oblige me by shewing him any civility in your power.

I am yours truly

MaryShelley

ADDRESS: For / Charles Browne Esq / Florence. UNPUBLISHED. TEXT: MS., Pforzheimer Library.

1. From the time Mary Shelley moved to Somerset Street through part of April 1832, Trelawny resided in Florence. Almost certainly she would have sent this letter of introduction for Mr. Blair (unidentified) to Trelawny if he were still in Florence, rather than to Charles Brown, a comparative stranger. In April 1833 Mary Shelley moved to Harrow. Therefore, the most likely date for this letter is 27 July 1832, which means that it was written from Sandgate and that Mary Shelley used her home rather than her vacation address.

TO FREDERIC MANSEL REYNOLDS   Sandgate—Thursday
                                                [?2 August 1832]

Dear Fred

Many thanks for the cash—and tell Mr Heath that I am much obliged to him for sending it me so soon. There wanted a page of my story in the proof—I should like to have corrected that also—as it was the last & the most likely to be incorrect in the Manuscript—

I have taken your advice and Miss Trelawny is paying me a visit[1]—to make assurance doubly sure[2] her father has accompanied her—to be sure he stays only a few days.—

As to the question you ask me, after reminding you that friendship is but a name, I add also with the Poet

And love is still an emptier sound[3]

if it makes you thin, you find it worse than I do—for I am not thin—

Adieu I write in haste

Yours truly

MS.

ADDRESS: F. M. Reynolds Esqre. PUBLISHED: Jones, #409. TEXT: MS., British Library (Add. 27,925, ff. 125–26).

1. On 17 July 1832 Trelawny wrote to inform Mary Shelley that he was about to send his daughter Julia to Italy to be in the care of his friend Lady Dorothea Campbell. Lady Dorothea Campbell, a younger daughter of the first earl of Desart, married Sir James Campbell (?1773–1835; *DNB*) in March 1817 and had five children. Trelawny urged Mary Shelley and Claire Clairmont to become acquainted with Lady Dorothea Campbell when they had the opportunity, and both did. He requested that Julia reside with Mary Shelley during the period from the end of July until he could make the necessary arrangements for her journey. On 27 July 1832 Trelawny responded to Mary Shelley's letter (unlocated) to say that they would both arrive at Sandgate on 1 August (Trelawny, *Letters*, pp. 176–77; *S&M*, IV, 1162–63). On 1 September he requested that Mary Shelley take Julia to Dover for her departure for Calais (*S&M*, IV, 1166–67).

2. *Macbeth* 4. 1. 83.

3. Oliver Goldsmith, "A Ballad," line 77, in chapter 8 of *The Vicar of Wakefield*.

*To Teresa Guiccioli   Sandgate—15mo Agosto [August 1832]

Cara Contessina

Le vostre amabile premure mi sono assaissime grate—e mi dispiace tanto che vi ho veduto cosi poco—ma davero Cara Mia, che fare? Non posso godere niuno piacere sin tanto che sono cosi povera—quando il mio destino, se mai sara—cambiara, allora, certamente, cerchero anch'io di allegrare il vostro soggiorno in questo paese. La società è cosi stabilità in Inghilterra, che senza quattrini bisogna sottomettersi e sotterrarsi—non c'è rimedio. Il vostro progetto è molto amabile e carino—si vedra:—come dite voi, come si puo far progetti per un altro anno:—forse allora saro piu padrona di me stessa che non lo sono ora.[1]

Mi fece gran paura l'idea che Lady Blesinton[2] dovesse far menzione della Chiarina—Perche non solamente sarebbe un gran torto per lei e per me—ma poi Chiara ha degli Amici che sicuramente farebbe guerra, non con la memoria di Bÿron, ma con la bella Autrice—senza domandare consigli ne consentimento ne di Chiarina ne di me—e queste pettegollezze finirebbe con sommo dispiacere per ognuno—Scrissi adunque a M. Bulwer,[3] e Miledi mi ha assicurata che non parlera di quella poverina—cosa che mi fa contenta—Per altro non mi mischio—e non ho letto <u>gli Articoli</u> (di fede?) della Medesima. La ringrazio come ringrazierei uno che mi minacciava con uno stiletto, e poi mi risparmiava—non saprei se lei sarebbe contenta di essere paragonata a un tale—ma è giusto—è come!—

He who steals my purse
steals trash[4]

Per adoperare il linguaggio di Shakespear, ma chi publica intorno di me, mi fa un torto assai più grande, e io direi piu <u>scelerato</u>—ma queste son cose non da dire. Mi dicono che Medwin mi da lode[5]—ma non ho veduto nemeno quel che ha scritto lui.

Mi rallegro che avete veduto tanto i nostri nobili—e spero che sempre terrete caro gli Inglesi—Sicche quantunque le regole della società sono tiranniche e difficile, amo i miei compatrioti—e li credo stimabili. Ho avuto una lettera di Moore[6]—non è mai stato in Londra da che siete quà voi. Io saro di ritorno nel Settembre. Forse vi trovero sempre—ne saro felice—Ricordatevi di me—e credetemi pur sempre

V^r A. A^{ma}
MW. Shelley

E gli spropositi!!! ma scrivo con furia

[Translation]

Dear Contessina

Your gracious attentions are very pleasing to me—and I am very sorry that I have seen so little of you—but indeed My Dear, what is to be done? I cannot enjoy any pleasure as long as I am so poor—when my fate, if ever it will—shall change, then, certainly, I too will try to enliven your sojourn in this country. Society is established in such a way in England, that without money it is necessary to yield and to hide oneself—it cannot be helped. Your plan is very amiable and nice—we shall see:—as you say, how can one make plans for another year:—perhaps then I will be more my own mistress than I am now.[1]

It frightens me very much to think that Lady Blesinton[2] should mention Claire—Because it would be a great injustice not only for her and for me—but also Claire has some Friends who assuredly would wage war, not with the memory of Byron, but with the lovely Authoress—without asking advice nor consent from either Claire or myself—and this trivial gossip would end with the utmost displeasure for everyone—Therefore I wrote to M. Bulwer,[3] and Milady has assured me that she will not speak of that poor woman—something that makes me happy—For the rest, I am not getting involved—and I have not read <u>the Articles</u> (of faith?) of the Same. I am thankful to her as I would thank someone who had been threatening me with a stiletto, and then spared me—I don't know if she would be content to be compared with such a person—but it is fitting—and how!—

He who steals my purse
steals trash[4]

To employ the language of Shakespeare, but he who publishes on the subject of myself, does me a far greater injury, and I would say more wicked—but these are not things to speak about. They tell me that Medwin praises me[5]—but I have not even seen what he has written.

I am glad that you have seen so much of our noblemen—and I hope that you will always hold the English dear—So although the rules of the society are arbitrary and difficult, I love my countrymen—and I believe them to be estimable. I have received a letter from Moore[6]—he has never been in London since you have been here. I shall be returning in September. Perhaps I'll still find you there—I shall be delighted of it—Remember me—and believe me always

Your most affectionate friend

MW. Shelley

And the mistakes!!! but I'm writing in a frenzy

UNPUBLISHED. TEXT: MS., Pforzheimer Library. TRANSLATION: Ricki B. Herzfeld.

1. I.e., Sir Timothy Shelley might die.

2. Margaret Sally Power (1789–1849) married Charles John, earl of Blessington, in 1818, and became Marguerite, countess of Blessington. She was an author, an editor, and the center of a literary and social circle that included Bulwer and Benjamin Disraeli. Beginning in July 1832 and intermittently until December 1833, Lady Blessington published a series of articles about her friendship with Byron at Genoa in 1823 as a *Journal of Conversations with Lord Byron* in the *New Monthly Magazine,* then edited by Bulwer (Michael Sadleir, *The Strange Life of Lady Blessington* [Boston: Little, Brown, and Co., 1933], pp. 174–79).

3. Bulwer replied that only a few words about Mary Shelley were included in the July article by Lady Blessington, that they were complimentary in nature, and that nothing more would be written about her by Lady Blessington (Bulwer to Mary Shelley, 23 July 1832, MS., Pforzheimer Library). Although Lady Blessington refrained from further comment in print, she attacked and maligned both Mary Shelley and Claire Clairmont in conversation (see Lady Blessington, *Conversations of Lord Byron,* ed. Ernest J. Lovell, Jr. [Princeton: Princeton University Press, 1969], pp. 95, 99 and n.; 53, 156). Bulwer, a friend of Godwin's, had written to Mary Shelley prior to becoming editor of the *New Monthly Magazine* in November 1831 to ask whether she could supply him with any material about Shelley. The first line of that letter suggests that Bulwer had franked a letter for her (MS., Pforzheimer Library; Locke, *Godwin,* p. 318).

4. *Othello* 3. 3. 150.

5. Thomas Medwin's "Memoir of Shelley" was published in six weekly parts in the *Athenaeum,* from 21 July 1832 to 25 August 1832. It was immediately followed by Medwin's "Shelley Papers," published weekly until the issue of 6 October, which was entirely devoted to the death of Sir Walter Scott on 21 September 1832. Installments of the "Shelley Papers" resumed from 20 October through 8 December 1832; the final part appeared on 20 April 1833. These series were then compiled as *The Shelley Papers: Memoir of Percy Bysshe Shelley,* ed. Thomas Medwin (London: Whittaker, Treacher & Co., 1833). Mary Shelley is mentioned or alluded to in the *Athenaeum* articles of 28 July; 4, 11, 18 August 1832.

6. 23 July 1832 (Moore, *Letters,* II, 752–53). In this letter Moore stated he had not been in London since he and Mary Shelley had last met, which was on 1 April 1832 (Moore, *Journal*).

Our letters, dearest Friend, it would seem crossed on the road—the stupidity of the people of Somerset St—so arranged, it that I did {not} get yours till last Friday.—Not being in town and unable to hunt out & see people—the best thing I could do, as it appeared to me, was to enclose your <u>interesting</u> & <u>well written</u> letter to Dr Bowring, with whom I am acquainted. I have this moment got his answer—he is at Exeter—and he tells me that in a few days he will be at Plymouth,[1] & he adds—"I will then call on Mrs Gisborne, whom I have heard Bentham mention with tenderness—& whose visit to him was a great delight—" "I think Bentham mentioned the letter more than once" If you have not already seen Bowring, you will now expect him—and I write & send this letter immediately, that you may have previous intimation—How could you imagine that I should not be delighted to do any commission for you[2]—and this one was most easily executed.

Here I am still.—Trelawny & his daughter are still with me—thank God he remains—for I do not know how I should be able to support her frivolity, but for the aid of his more amusing company.—She is amiable lively & polite, but so unidea'd—so silly in her gaiety—so childish yet overgrown in her merriment, that it is hard to bear—never was there such an opposite to her father.—He talks of visiting Plymouth, & I shall make him call on you.—You must please him—for he loves good sense, liberality & enthusiasm, beyond all things—he is too violent in his politics for me—he is radical à l'outrance[3]—& altogether unprejudiced—to use the common phrase—& yet as full of prejudices as he can hold—which contradiction you will have no difficulty in understanding—If you have any <u>very</u> pretty girl among your acquaintance, enchant him by shewing her to <u>him</u>—he is sadly off here—I never found so great a dearth of female beauty as at Sandgate.

My Percy is gone back to school—I love the dear fellow more & more every day—he is my sole delight & comfort—On going away he insisted on having his supper alone in his room—telling me, to persuade me, that Sancho liked an onion behind a door,[4] & why might he not enjoy the pleasures of solitary fare?—I cannot tell you how much cleverer & more companionable he was than my present companion—We have had a good deal of rain & eternal wind; this one day has risen cloudless & breezeless on us—There is a want of wood here—but the sea is open—and the hills the most singular in the world—They are so precipitous, that they look mountains—yet three steps leads you to their summits—& when you get up one rather higher than the rest—you see them sprinkled about, in conical shapes, each distinct, with ravines between—but so low that you could almost step from one to the other—They are verdant, & covered with sheep & cattle. I am reading a little Greek—& amusing myself as well as I can—but I am very stupid—and not at all in an energetic mood—though not quite so languid as when I was in town—I am here, wishing for nothing but an exemption from pecuniary annoyances, both for myself & my father—unwilling to return to town, yet I must next Month tho' but for a short time only—I shall settle myself not far from Richmond.[5] Jane, Jeff & her children are al Solito[6]—Will any change ever come there? None, I imagine, but what grim Necessity may bring—& I hope that that will keep afar.

You do not mention the Cholera[7]—as with us in London, I suppose you hear less of it on the spot, than we do at a distance from you—Is it not strange that it should have got to New York? And reign there so violently—fear is its great auxillary—& as that ⟨I suppose⟩ seems very great among the Yankees, that will explain it. By the bye Trelawny is America-mad[8]—a feeling with which I have no sympathy—if you have, cela vous fera fortune[9]—Have you read his book? pray do— After all his going to Plymouth is very uncertain. Let me hear from you as often as you can. You write very good letters. As is often the case with those who possessing great talents, yet find difficulty in writing—for then they do not pay us with words merely—but with ideas, concisely & energetically clothed.—If you had not been in the midst of a great town like Plymouth—when I wanted the open country so much, I should have visited Devonshire, instead of coming here—Remember me with all kind{n}ess to Signor Giovanni [John Gisborne], who I hope is quite recovered—take care of your precious self—Maria Carissima & love ever

Your true friend MWShelley

ADDRESS: Mrs Gisborne / 17 Union St. / Plymouth / Devon. POSTMARKS: (1) FOLK[E]STONE / PENNY POST; (2) E / 25 AU 25 / 1832. ENDORSED: Sandgate 24th Aug. 1832 / re[ ] Do / Ans. / M. Shelley. PUBLISHED: Jones, #410. TEXT: MS., Bodleian Library (MS., Shelley, Adds., c. 6, ff. 137–38).

1. Plymouth, Devon, where the Gisbornes resided, two hundred fifteen and a half miles west-southwest of London.

2. Mary Shelley was assisting Maria Gisborne's unsuccessful efforts to publish some writing.

3. "To the extreme."

4. Though there are references to Sancho eating in *Don Quixote*, there appears to be no specific reference to his eating in private.

5. Ten miles west-southwest of London.

6. "As usual."

7. See [?18 November 1831–February 1832]. William Godwin, Jr., died of cholera on 4 September 1832 (Locke, *Godwin*, p. 333; *S&M*, IV, 1167–68). In her 20 August 1832 letter Maria Gisborne reported that cholera at Plymouth was on the wane but had taken upwards of five hundred lives (Abinger MSS., Bodleian Library).

8. Trelawny visited America from March 1833 through July 1835 (Paula R. Feldman, "Letters Unravel the Mystery of Trelawny's American Years," *Manuscripts* 32, no. 3 [Summer 1980]: 170, 183; see also [11 Januray 1833]). Although Mary Shelley states that she does not share Trelawny's enthusiasm for America, she sets part of *Lodore* in Illinois, which she describes in idyllic terms.

9. "That will make your fortune."

To ANNE FRANCES HARE   [?Sandgate ?September–October 1832][1]

Your accounts of your child (Francis)[2] give me very great pleasure. Dear little fellow, what an amusement and delight he must be to you. You do indeed understand a Paradisaical life. Well do I remember the dear Lucca baths,[3] where we spent morning and evening in riding about the country— the most prolific place in the world for all manner of reptiles. Take care of yourself, dearest friend. . . . Choose Naples[4] for your winter residence. Naples, with its climate, its scenery, its opera, its galleries, its natural and ancient wonders, surpasses every other place in the world. Go thither, and live on the Chiaja. Happy one, how I envy you. Percy is in brilliant health and promises better and better.

Have you plenty of storms at dear beautiful Lucca? Almost every day when I was there, vast white clouds peeped out from above the hills—rising higher and higher till they overshadowed us, and spent themselves in rain and tempest: the thunder, re-echoed again and again by the hills, is undescribably terrific. . . . Love me, and return to us—Ah! return to us! for it is all very stupid and unamiable without you. For are not you—

"That cordial drop Heaven in our cup has thrown,
To make the nauseous draught of life go down."[5]

PUBLISHED: Hare, *The Story of My Life,* pp. 30–31. TEXT: Hare, *The Story of My Life,* pp. 30–31.

 1. Augustus Hare noted that this letter was written to Anne Hare just before the birth of his sister, Anne Frances Maria Louisa, on 9 October 1832 (*The Story of My Life,* p. 30).

 2. Born 1830 (*The Story of My Life,* p. 27).

 3. See 4 December 1827, n. 1.

 4. The Shelleys had lived on the Chiaia at Naples from 1 December 1818 to 28 February 1819 (see vol. I).

 5. Unidentified.

To JOHN GREGSON   Sandgate—Kent 1 September—1832

Dear Sir

I send the receipt, will you have the goodness to send me the cheque in return to this place.

I have been spending the Midsummer holydays with Percy in this quiet watering place.—He is now returned to Mr Slaters, and enters at Harrow at Michaelmas[1]—by which time I shall be in town for the purpose of placing him there and I shall call on you with him, hoping to be more fortunate than hitherto, in finding you.

I was sorry to see poor Mr Whitton's death[2] in the papers. I hope you are quite well—

I am, Sir,
Yours Ob^ly
MaryWShelley

ADDRESS: J. Gregson Esq / 18 Bedford Row / London. POSTMARKS: (1) FOLKESTONE / PENNY POST; (2) E / 3 SE 3 / 1832. ENDORSED: 1 Sep 1832 / Mrs Shelley. PUBLISHED: Jones, #411. TEXT: MS., Bodleian Library (MS., Shelley, Adds., c. 6, ff. 139–40).

1. 29 September.
2. See 3 June 1831.

To John Gregson
Sandgate—5 Sep. 1832

Dear Sir

I have safely received the check for £100 & am much obliged to you— I think this place the healthiest in the world (though a little windy & cold) Percy learnt to swim,[1] and I sent him up to town quite robust & stout. He is a good boy & the greatest possible comfort to me—

I am, Dr Sir

Y^s Obl^y

MWShelley

ADDRESS: John Gregson Esq / 18 Bedford Row / London. POSTMARKS: (1) FOLKESTONE / PEN[NY P]OST; (2) [   ] / 6 SE 6 / 1832. ENDORSED: 5 Sep 1832 / Mrs Shelley. PUB-LISHED: Jones, #412. TEXT: MS., Bodleian Library (MS., Shelley, Adds., c. 6, ff. 141–42).

1. Unlike Shelley, who had never learned to swim.

To Edward John Trelawny
Somerset St.   Monday
[8 October 1832]

Dear Trelawny—I came home this Morning & am impatient to see you. I enjoyed myself at Harrow as much as the vile weather would permit. Percy is very happy—he likes his school and is delighted with the freedom & comfort he enjoys. There are 30 boys in the same House with him—only two of whom have the power of fagging[1]—so that he does not in the least suffer by the only evil of a Public School.

I send you Claire's Article with Mr Bulwer's note. Her Article is excellent & perfectly adapted, I should think for a Magazine. I have an idea that Lady Bles{s}in{g}ton is the person who is furnishing them with articles on Italy— & compared to Claire's they must be poor. Do let Marryatt[2] see them— and make him be pleased with them—print them in the No. for Novem-ber—& desire more. Take great care ⟨they are⟩ it is not lost & if he rejects ⟨them⟩ it let me have ⟨them⟩ it back immediately—as I must get it in some-where with as little delay as possible

I return to all my cares—which are sufficiently weighty—but when you call I will forget them—and for a short time enjoy a respite

Yours ever

MS.

Perhaps if M[r] M. [*Marryatt*] knew that the New Monthly were bringing out a series of Articles on Italy—⟨they⟩ he may be eager for rival ones for the Metropolitan

PUBLISHED: Jones, #413. TEXT: MS., Bodleian Library (MS., Shelley, Adds., c. 6, ff. 145–46).

1. Mary Shelley had told Hogg of Shelley's resistance and opposition to fagging, which was a part of Shelley's school days at Eton (Hogg, *Shelley*, I, 33; White, *Shelley*, I, 37, 570).

2. Frederick Marryat (1792–1848; *DNB*), naval captain and author, was editor of the *Metropolitan Magazine* from 1832 to 1835. On 1 September 1832 Trelawny had written to tell Mary Shelley that if "Bulwer makes any difficulty regarding the article written by Clare, I shall readily, if you like, try the 'Metropolitan,' which seems as good if not better" (*S&M*, IV, 1167). On 26 October 1832 Claire Claremont wrote asking Mary Shelley to thank Trelawny "for his kindness about the article" (*S&M*, IV, 1172). Claire Clairmont's article may be "Naples," published in the November 1832 *Metropolitan*, pp. 336–44, unsigned, which is critical of Byron and lauds Shelley.

TO JOHN GREGSON   33 Somerset St.   8 October—1832

Dear Sir

I should be glad if you will let Sir Timothy know that Percy has now been a fortnight at Harrow—I have been spending a week there on a visit to Lady Paul, and found my Son perfectly contented and happy. He is at the house of M[r] Kennedy.   the Under Master, who expresses himself pleased with his progress & his docility. Percy has been disappointed in not seeing his Grandfather this year and desires his duty & love to him. He is in the 2[d] Remove of the 4th Form—& will go higher before Xmas. As he went immediately from Kensington to Harrow I was unable to bring him to you as I wished.

                                        I am, dear Sir Yours Obli[ly]
                                        MWShelley

ADDRESS: John Gregson Esq / 18 Bedford Row. ENDORSED: 8th Oct—1832 / Mrs Shelley. PUBLISHED: Jones, #414. TEXT: MS., Bodleian Library (MS., Shelley, Adds., c. 6, ff. 143–44).

*TO CHARLES OLLIER   33 Somerset St.   Thursday   25 Oct [1832]

My dear Sir

Could you call some morning very soon between 12 & one—as I have several things I want to talk to you about—concerning the Younger Son, & other things—Have you any pretty book to lend me to read?—The New book by the Author of Hadji Baba[1]—the 5 & 6 Vol—<u>in French</u> of the

Memo{i}res of the Duchesse d'Abrantis[2] would be very acceptable—but
not the translation—or any other work you could recommend

I am dear Sir
Y[s] truly
MWShelley

ADDRESS: Chas Ollier Esq / 8 New Burlington St. UNPUBLISHED. TEXT: MS., Pforzheimer
Library.

1. *The Adventures of Hajji Baba, of Ispahan,* by James Justinian Morier (?1780–1849), 2
vols., was published by John Murray in 1818. Morier's *Zohrab the Hostage,* 3 vols., was published
on 21 September 1832 by Richard Bentley. After the dissolution of the partnership of Colburn
and Bentley in 1832, Mary Shelley, Godwin, and Medwin were published by Richard Bentley.
The reason for this may be that Charles Ollier continued with Bentley (until 1839) rather
than with Colburn, for whom Ollier had worked from 1823 (he had worked for both partners
from September 1829) (*SC,* V, 127).

2. Volumes 1 and 2 of the *Mémoires de la Duchesse d'Abrantès,* by Laure Sant-Marten (Permon)
Junot, duchesse d'Abrantès (1784–1838), were published in French in November 1831. The
original Paris edition, comprising 18 volumes, appeared almost simultaneously with Bentley's
eight-volume edition of 1831–35. Volumes 3–8 were published only in English (Bentley
publication lists).

TO JOHN MURRAY 33 Somerset St. Portman Sq 25 Oct. 1832

My dear Sir

I am very tardy in returning the Volumes of L[d] Byron's works—because
I felt that after all, I had little to say to any purpose. I send them now,—
but I am afraid you will be disappointed. May I ask for the Volumes of the
New Edition, which I have not received. The 6th was the last sent to me I
think—the last of the "Life" it was. I have not yet seen M[r] Finden to see
how he proceeds with the Engraving[1]—for I have not long returned to
town—and have been much occupied since I came back. I have placed
my Son at Harrow—& spent a week with some friends of mine, who have
a house there—The school is in excellent repute now—and Percy is very
happy there—I hope that you & your Family are quite well—I am, Dear
Sir

truly Y[s] Obliged
MWShelley

ENDORSED: 1832—Oct. 25 / Shelley Mrs. PUBLISHED: Jones, #415. TEXT: MS., Keats House,
Hampstead.

1. See 30 April [1832], n 2.

To John Gregson   33 Somerset St.   Saturday—1 Dec / 32(*a*)

My dear Sir

I send you the usual receipt. If you can give the bearer the cheque in exchange it would convenience me, as I am going out of town for a week on Monday or Tuesday & should be glad of it before I go. Otherwise perhaps you will mention when I can send again.

My Son comes home for his holydays on Dec. 11th & on the following Sunday, if agreable to you, I will call on you with him in Cumberland St. I am Dr Sir Y^s Ob^{ly}

MWShelley

ENDORSED: 1 Decr. 1832 / Mrs M. W. Shelley. PUBLISHED: Jones, #417. TEXT: MS., Bodleian Library (MS., Shelley, Adds., c. 6, ff. 147–48).

To John Gregson   [33 Somerset St.   1 December 1832] (*b*)[1]

Dear Sir

I send you the receipt as you desire—& will send early tomorrow morning for the cheque—When I shall be so glad if you will give it

Yours Ob^{ly}
MWShelley

ENDORSED: 2 Decr 1832 / Mrs M. W. Shelley. PUBLISHED: Jones, #419. TEXT: MS., Bodleian Library (MS., Shelley, Adds., c. 6, ff. 149–50).

1. The contents and endorsement of this letter, together with the previous letter, indicate that this letter was sent late on Saturday, 1 December, and received the next day (see the next letter).

To John Gregson   [33 Somerset St.]   Sunday   2 December 1832]

Dear Sir—I feel so ashamed to trouble you—but you quite forgot your promise yesterday—Perhaps you will be good enough to send to me to-morrow morning—Otherwise I shall send to Bedford Row early on Tuesday & hope that you will have left the cheque ready for my messenger   Y^s Obed^{ly}

MWShelley

ADDRESS: John Gregson Esq / 1 Cumberland St. ENDORSED: 3 Dec. 1832 / Mrs M. W. Shelley. PUBLISHED: Jones, #418. TEXT: MS., Bodleian Library (MS., Shelley, Adds., c. 6, ff. 151–52).

My dear Sir

The enclosed papers will in some degree explain to you the nature of my difficulties, & I hope excuse ⟨you⟩ me, for applying thro' you, to request Sir Timothy Shelley to afford me that assistance, without which, I, and, what is of more consequence, my Son will be placed in a situation of great embarassment.

The letter to Mrs Paul is one from Dr Longley, Head Master at Harrow, to whom she wrote last year, at my request, for particulars as to the expence of that school. It was upon the information contained in that letter, that I pressed Sir Timothy to arrange that his Grandson should go to it—he kindly complied, & afforded me the means.

On applying again to Dr Longley, his numbers were full, so I placed Percy with Mr Kennedy the Under Master, whose terms are higher than Dr Longley, but who said that the bills should not exceed £150 P ann.—which I hoped to be able to meet.

You may judge of my consternation on receiving the enclosed account for one quarter. Having had many things to provide for Percy on his first going to a Public School, I am not before hand with the world—I have many things to get for him on his return—he is at home for the holydays—and I have to provide for my own expences till next March—you may judge therefore that it is impossible for me to pay a bill of £75—which must be discharged before the 16 Jan^{ry} when the school reopens. I had expected to be called upon for rather less than half that sum—I have no resources except Sir Timothy's allowance; & have no possible means of meeting it. In this emergency I am forced to have recourse to Sir Tim^{thy}   I feel great pain in making this demand, & regret exceedingly having been led into false views with regard to the expence of the school, through the representations of its ⟨teachers⟩ Masters. But there is no use in regret—the bill must be paid. I do trust that Sir Timothy's interest in & kindness towards his Grandson will induce him to assist me on this occasion, & to excuse this inevitable request.

What is to be done for the future is another question—On examining Mr Kennedy's account I find that I may hope that the future quarterly bills <u>may</u> fall short of this by about twenty pounds—which yet leaves a sum of £55 which is beyond what I can meet—as thus Percy would cost me very nearly £300 P ann. including clothing, holydays at home &c. He must not be taken from Harrow—for having once entered a public School, he cannot leave it without a slur. There is one expedient, which, with Sir Timothy's leave, I shall adopt. You see that Dr Longley says that no objection exists against home Boarders—and Percy tells me that some of the best & most highly esteemed Boys in the school are Home Boarders. My design is therefore to go to reside at Harrow after the Xmas holydays—the school—the pupil room, which he must attend, books &c would limit the expences to about £50 per ann. and I could meet his other expences & my own with that respectability, which Sir Timothy must desire that his Grandson should enjoy. I should have to take a house there, & in some degree furnish it—however if the present bill be defrayed through Sir Timothy's kindness, and he does not object to the plan I mention, I have every hope that we shall go on well for the future, without again annoying him. If he objects, will he be so good as to direct me as to what I ought to do—as I shall myself be totally at a loss, & deeply anxious on the subject.

I enclose also a note from Mr Kennedy, concerning Percy's character & progress, which Sir Timothy will perceive to be a favorable report—Percy went to Harrow at Michaelmas.

I am, dear Sir,
Y^s Obed^{tly}
MWShelley

I write this letter fearing that I may miss you again. I ought to mention that the hosiers joiners &c mentioned in the bill—are for repairs & furniture for Percy's bed room & study—items I certainly had no idea of being called upon {to} defray.

It is impossible to say how excessively anxious I feel. To know that here is a debt I am unable to pay, is very painful, but the idea of any injury arising to Percy in the course of his education, is ten times worse—I hope Sir Timothy will consider these things, and prevent any real harm from occuring. Allow me to entreat you to use your influence in our behalf.

ADDRESS: John Gregson Esq / &c &c &c. ENDORSED: (1) 16 Decr 1832 / Mrs Shelley; (2) Copy sent to Sir Timy Shelley / 27 Decr 1832. PUBLISHED: Jones, #420. TEXT: MS., Bodleian Library (MS., Shelley, Adds., c. 6, ff. 153–55).

*To [FREDERICK MANSEL REYNOLDS]   33 Somerset St.   Thursday
[?December 1832][1]

My dear Fred.
You have received my letter for Mrs Paul has received her Keepsake—& Mr Heath is returned—I suppose he thinks that he ought not to pay because the story is not printed, but as it will be next year, I do not see why he should be so cross—I had no idea of an objection & have counted on it—or I should not be so troublesome—and he need not be so stingy—it is very unamiable—I wrote, in all hurry & expedition because you asked me—& so he rewards my complaisance—yet still I hope you will bring him to reason & I very much desire it—

One of the Keepsakes you sent me has pages omitted—& is turned topsy turvy in the binding—I sent it to a friend in the country who finds it a riddle-my-ree[2]

> Adieu
> Truly Yours
> Obliged
> MWShelley

UNPUBLISHED. TEXT: MS., Jean de Palacio.

1. The date [?December] is based on the contents of the letter, which indicate that a *Keepsake* that included work by Mary Shelley had recently been published. *Keepsakes* were published annually in November or early December. I place this letter in 1832 because the earliest Mary Shelley letter that I have located bearing the same watermark on the same stationery used for this letter ("J WHATMAN / 1830") is her letter of 8 October 1832 to John Gregson. The *Keepsake for 1833* (1832) contained two stories by Mary Shelley: "The Brother and Sister, An Italian Story" (pp. 105–41) and "The Invisible Girl" (pp. 210–27). The following year, "The Mortal Immortal" appeared in the *Keepsake* (pp. 71–87) (Lyles, *MWS Bibliography*, p. 29).

2. A variant of the phrases "riddle me a riddle" and "riddle my riddle."

*TO MARY WOOD   Somerset St.   Sunday   23 Dec [1832]

Dear Mrs Wood

My Father says that he & I are invited for the same Evening—but I fancy that you asked me to come on New Year's Eve—& he says that he is to be with you on New Year's day—I dare say that he is right—if he is—if I had not seen him, I should have come the day <u>before</u> the Fair; but as I feel doubtful, will you set me right, & tell me which day your party is fixed on[1]

I hope you are getting well & taking care of yourself

> I am Yours truly
> MWShelley

UNPUBLISHED. TEXT: MS., Houghton Library.

1. The party was on 1 January 1833 (see [1 February 1831] to John Howard Payne, n. 1).

TO JOHN GREGSON   33 Somerset St.   Portman Sq   2 Jan^ry 1833

Dear Sir

I hope you will not think me importunate ⟨when⟩ if I remind you that in a fortnight Percy's holydays end—and I must come to some decision, as well as pay his bill—I am not a little anxious to know the [re]sult of my application to Sir Timothy.[1]

> I am dear Sir
> Yours Obt^ly
> MWShelley

ENDORSED: 2 Janry 1833 / Mrs. Shelley. PUBLISHED: Jones, #421. TEXT: MS., Bodleian Library (MS., Shelley, Adds., c. 6, ff. 156–57).
    1. See 16 December 1832.

TO JOHN GREGSON   33 Somerset S^t   3 Jany 1833

My dear Sir

    Your note alarms me beyond measure. My childs respectability through life depends upon his going on fairly at his school. I will, if you will permit me, call in Bedford Row tomorrow between twelve & one and ask your advice as to what [   ] do. I do not ask this [?advi]ce for any common [?reas]on—& I must think that upon <u>some conditions</u> Sir Tim^thy will consent to give me a sum on which the education & welfare of his Grandson entirely depend—I have no other resource on Earth—

                                              I am dear Sir,
                                              Yours Ob^ly
                                              MShelley

ENDORSED: 3 Janry 1833 / Mrs Shelley. PUBLISHED: Jones, #422. TEXT: MS., Bodleian Library (MS., Shelley, Adds., c. 6, ff. 158–59).

TO EDWARD JOHN TRELAWNY   33 Somerset St.   Friday Ev^eg
                                              [11 January 1833]

My dear Trelawny

    I was very glad to get your letter.[1] I did not suspect your going so immediately—but as you did not come on Sunday, I sent to your lodgings, to ask you to dine on Wednesday with Papa & Jane—but you had disappeared—It is frightful to think of your exposing yourself to that ⟨fright⟩ miserable cold—but that you bear a charmed life, you must have died—considering your previous indisposition.—Nothing harms you however, which destroys others, and I do not doubt that you will return to find me a <u>Vecchiaccia</u>,[2] while you still are conquering hearts—& living, like a bee on sweets—What a pity you do not contrive a little wax as well as honey;—but that comes from other flowers—and except a Virginian Widow should cede her right of flogging & rearing tobacco, none of the Fredericas, Barbaras, or Katherines can furnish your hive, & turn the Wanderer into a lazy Gentleman in an easy chair.

    You will return with a whole life of new experiences—the tale of a thousand loves—the same, yet ever new—Dont let them (your Americans) spoil Lady Berghersh's—Lady Dorothea's[3] & the gentle Marchesa's[4] work—and rub off that polish which adorns so well the good strong metal. Jane, whom I saw today, says that she did not wish for a leavetaking, but wished much to see you again—She says she will write to you & meanwhile sends her love—She & M^r and Mrs Godwin dined here on Wednesday, & your absence was much lamented. The two ladies composed your Elegy—which was as laudatory as an Epitaph ought to be—While the wilds of America were destined to be your untimely grave   For Myself, I consign you to the elements you love, believing that they will return you again, all the better in health & spirits for their congenial ministrations.

I will give your message to Mrs Leicester Stanhope if ever I see her again— but it looks much as if I were going to take an everlasting adieu of London. This house is let—so I cannot prolong my stay—Sir John Paul in the kindest way, offers to furnish the house at Harrow for me. I do not like obligation yet should disoblige if I refused. What a strange position mine is—& how annoying—however as it might be worse I will not repine: While Percy continues [   ] the blessing & comfort to me that he is, I ough[   ]

I have heard & seen nothing of the [   ] or Beauclerks:—I cannot tell you how your lady pales and wanes—& becomes a skeleton. Did you really cause her to grow a little thiner; you would do her a greater service, than you did poor Frederica[5]—I think of going to Ditton[6] for a week or two. When in America you had better direct to me to the care of my father 44 Gower Place, Euston Sq.. Although few, & those slender, ties bind me to London, and I am surrounded by privation & mortification, I suppose I should have lingered on for ever but for the wreck of my finances— Reasonably & prospectively speaking, I do not regret going—& yet it is sad to change—to be cut off from the few one likes—It is different in travelling, when the excitement of something new prevents regret for the old.

Pray write again at the moment of sailing—Stay as short a time as you possibly can among the Yankees—so that you may not write "that was" of all your young womankind—nor find me with a mask on—for fear of shew-ing my face. All happiness be yours

Yours MWS.

ADDRESS: Edward Trelawny Esq / Mess. Ross & Brothers / 16 Harrington St. / Liverpool. POSTMARK: [   ] / JA 12 / 1833. PUBLISHED: Jones, #425. TEXT: MS., Bodleian Library (MS., Shelley, Adds., c. 6, ff. 165–66).

1. Trelawny wrote from Liverpool on 9 January 1833 informing Mary Shelley that he had left London on Saturday, 5 January, and was waiting for a ship that would take him to Savannah or Charleston. He noted that Charleston was blockaded at the time (MS., Huntington Library [HM 19632]; see also 16 January 1833, n. 8). Trelawny sailed on the *Tally-Ho* on 16 January (Trelawny to John Murray, MS., John Murray).

2. "Hag."

3. Lady Dorothea Campbell.

4. Jane Boccella.

5. Perhaps Frederica de Conroy, whose sister married William Perry, whom Claire Clairmont referred to as "our playmate" in her 2 June 1835 letter to Mary Shelley (Abinger MSS., Bodleian Library). Perry (1801–74), eventually a British consul at a number of posts (*Alumni*

Cantabrigienses), was the eldest of the eight children of James Perry (1756–1821; *DNB*), noted journalist, and his wife Anne Hull Perry (d. 1815).

6. Mary Shelley noted in her Journal entry of "October–November December 1832" that the Robinsons had moved to Thames Ditton, which is thirteen and a half miles southwest of London, in Surrey.

TO JOHN GREGSON   33 Somerset St.   13 Jan^{ry} [1833]

My dear Sir

The weather was so bad today that I did not fulfil my engagement—hoping to see you—and thinking also that by delaying a day, there was a greater chance of your being able to oblige me without inconvenience.—I will call tomorrow without fail, at half past one—in Bedford Row—as that is the last day of the holydays—

I am dear Sir
Y^s Ob^{ly}
MWShelley

ADDRESS: John Gregson Esq / Cumberland St. ENDORSED: 13 Janry 1833 / Mrs M. Shelley. PUBLISHED: Jones, #423. TEXT: MS., Bodleian Library (MS., Shelley, Adds., c. 6, ff. 160–61).

TO MARIA GISBORNE   33 Somerset St.   16 Jan^{ry} 1833

Dear Maria   I was very glad to receive the Signor Giovanni's [*John Gisborne's*] invelope (more by far than the enclosure—which did not amuse me in the least) & to hear that your silence was occasioned merely by your being the naughtiest person in the world, & not through any mishap—This being the case—& being assured that a letter from me will not bore you—I scribble a few lines, being ⟨assured⟩ secure of a frank tomorrow—If modesty on the score of postage prevents your writing, you may at any time direct to me under cover to Major Beauclerk[1] M.P. 12 Chester St. Grosvenor Place. London.

Never was poor body so worried as I have been ever since I last wrote, I think—Worries which plague & press on one, & keep one fretting. Money of course is the Alpha & Omega of my tale. Harrow proves so fearfully expensive that I have been sadly put to it to pay Percy's bill for one quarter (£80 soltanto)[2] & to achieve it, am hampered for the whole year—My only resource is to live at Harrow—for in every other respect, I like the school & would not take him from it. He will become an home boarder—& school expences will be very light   I shall take a house, being promised many facilities for furnishing it by a kind friend[3]—To go and live at pretty Harrow, with my Boy, who improves each day, as [*and*] is everything I could wish, is no bad prospect—but I have much to go through, & am so poor that I cannot turn myself—It is hard on my poor dear Father—And I sometimes think it hard on myself—to leave a knot of acquaintances I like—but that is a fiction—for half the times I am asked out, I cannot go, because of the expence—& I am suffering now for the times when I do go, and so incur debt.—No, Maria mine—God never intended me to do other than struggle through life—supported by such blessings as make existence more than tolerable—& yet surrounded by such difficulties as make fortitude a necessary virtue, & destroy all idea of great good luck—I might have been much worse off—and I repeat this to myself ten thousand times a day, to console myself for not being better—& it has now & then the desired effect. Had God meant me ever to be well off, he had taken Sir Tim to himself twelve years ago—if decently, ten—As it is I shall be imbrogliata—e non avrei da vantarmi mai—Pazienza—e basta.[4]

Poor Janey climbing up a pair of wooden steps "on household cares intent"—fell—or rather the steps came in two, & she & they came down by the run.—She escaped with only breaking the ligaments of her elbow joint, neither dislocating it, nor injuring the bone. It was an affair of a good deal of pain, & much inconvenience, it being her right arm—But she is now perfectly recovered. Jeff is well & flourishing—the Children well—Dina is a very nice girl indeed.

My Father's Novel is printed & I suppose will come out soon.[5] Poor dear fellow! It is hard work for him—I am in all the tremor of fearing what I shall get for my novel,[6] which is nearly finished—His & my Comfort depend on it—I do not know whether you will like it—I cannot guess whether it will succeed—There is no writhing interest—nothing wonderful, nor tragic— Will it be dull? Chi lo sa![7] We shall see—I shall of course be very glad if it succeeds.

Percy went back to Harrow today. He likes his school much—Have I any other news for you? Trelawny is gone—to America—he is about to cross to Charlestown—at the moment that there is a prospect of War.[8] War in America! I am truly sorry—Brothers should not fight for the different & various portions of their inheritance—

What is the use of republican principles & liberty, if Peace is not the offspring? War not Kings is the fleau[9] of the world—War is the companion & friend of Monarchy—if it be the same of freedom—the gain is not much to Mankind between a Sovereign & a president.[10]

The Countess Guiccioli is gone at last[11]—what she found to please her in this dingy land, I cannot guess—Not an Amante,[12] I believe,—as far as I could judge by the aspect of things. Still she did like it & was sorry to go.

I will write to you soon when I leave this place—Meanwhile you may enclose your letter to Major Beauclerk—writing my name in pencil on the enclosed letter—I may be, & probably shall, in Surrey and receive by the General Post—he will then frank it on to me—& will be sure to know my add   as I am in correspondance with his sister,[13] who writes to me in the same way.—

I wish I had more cheering news for you—But loneliness—My unsupported situation & the difficulties & annoyances that surround me are not rallegrante[14]—Will it ever be better? I despair for myself, & only live again in my Child, who is the delight of my heart.

Adieu, dear Friend—send me a few kind words—Present my regards to your Husband & believe me—Ever Aff[ly] Yours MWS.

ADDRESS: Mrs Gisborne / 17 Union St / Plymouth. POSTMARK: FREE / 19 [1] / 1833 London January nineteen 1833. ENDORSED: London 16th Jany 1833 / recd 21st Do / Ans 6th July 1834 / Mary Shelley. PUBLISHED: Jones, #424. TEXT: MS., Bodleian Library (MS., Shelley, Adds., c. 6, ff. 162–63).

1. Aubrey William Beauclerk (1801–54), M.P. for East Surrey 1832–37, major, 99th Foot, 1826, eldest brother of Georgiana Beauclerk Paul. Beauclerk married Ida Goring, fourth daughter of Sir Charles Foster Goring; she died on 23 April 1838. On 7 December 1841 Beauclerk married Rosa Matilda Robinson, one of Joshua Robinson's daughters (*Burke's Peerage*; see also vol. I, [19 February 1827], n. 1). From allusions to "A." in Mary Shelley's journal, together with her entries of "Farewell" on 13 February 1834 (the date Beauclerk married Ida Goring) and of "An Anniversary / Strange & sad!"———& bitter," on 13 February 1835, Emily W. Sunstein has conjectured that Mary Shelley was in love with Aubrey Beauclerk (Emily W. Sunstein, review of Jane Dunn, *Moon in Eclipse: A Life of Mary Shelley*, in *Keats-Shelley Journal* 29 [1980]:224). I am unaware of other evidence demonstrating the extent of Mary Shelley's relationship with Beauclerk.

2. "Only."

3. Sir John Paul (see [11 January 1833]).

4. "*Confused*—and I should never boast—Patience—that's enough."

5. *Deloraine*, 3 vols., was published by Bentley on 12 February 1833.

6. On 25 April 1833 Mary Shelley signed an agreement that Richard Bentley would publish 750 copies of *Lodore* in 3 volumes of 310 pages each and would pay her £100 in a bill twelve months from the agreement and £50 whenever the sale of the work reached 600 copies (Bentley Archives, British Library, Add. 46612, vol. 53, p. 7).

7. "Who knows."

8. On 12 November 1832 the South Carolina legislature adopted an Ordinance of Nullification which declared void the tariff laws of 1828 and 1832 opposed by slaveholders. On 10 December 1832 President Andrew Jackson issued a proclamation against the nullifiers. People became divided between nullifiers and unionists, and troops were readied for 1 February 1833, the date the Ordinance of Nullification would take effect. However, the issue was settled peaceably by the end of February through a compromise tariff bill and the repeal of the Ordinance of Nullification.

9. "Scourge."

10. The attitudes towards war and power expressed in this letter are central to *Perkin Warbeck* (see Betty T. Bennett, "Mary Shelley's Historical Novels," in *The Evidence of the Imagination*, ed. Donald H. Reiman, Michael C. Jaye, and Betty T. Bennett [New York: New York University Press, 1978]).

11. See 30 April [1832], n. 3.

12. "Lover."

13. Georgiana Paul.

14. "Cheerful."

33 Somerset St.   31 Jany 1833

My dear Sir

I send you my first vol. If you are not enclined to read it all—perhaps the most interesting portion of the present Vol. begins at Chapter 7—page 67—If you desire to see more you can have it—the whole only wants the filling up of a few omissions, of a page here & there, to be complete—& I could go to press almost immediately—

I do not know how briefly to give you an idea of the whole tale—⟨The⟩ A Mother & Daughter are the heroines—The Mother who after safrifising [*sacrificing*] all to the world at first—afterwards makes sacrifises not less entire, for her child—finding all to be Vanity, except the genuine affections of the heart. In the daughter I have tried to pourtray in its simplicity, & all the beauty I could muster, the <u>devotion</u> of a young wife for the husband of her choice—The disasters she goes through being described—& their result in awakening her Mother's affection, bringing about the conclusion of the tale—Perhaps a fitting motto would be Sir Walter Scot's well known lines beginning "O woman in our hours of ease &c'[1]

I hope the specimen will please you—I hope you will induce Mr Bentley to be pleased—and let me ask it of your kindness, to do your best for me, with as little delay as is practicable—I am, dear Sir

Yours truly
MWShelley

ENDORSED: 1833 / Mrs Shelley / Somerset St 31 Jany. UNPUBLISHED. Jones, #426, in summary. TEXT: MS., Keats-Shelley Memorial House, Rome.
  1. *Marmion* 6. 30.

To [CHARLES OLLIER]   33 Somerset St.   11 Feby 1833

My Dear Sir

Would it be possible for Mr Bentley or Mr Colburn to oblige me with a copy of any of my books—I have not one in the world—& wish to give them to a friend going abroad—If you can send me all or any—it must be directly, as my friend[1] Sails this week—

When shall I hear from you on the other subject?—soon I hope—as I want things to be settled before I leave town, Which I shall do almost immediately—So I commend me to your good offices

Yours truly
MWShelley

PUBLISHED: Jones, #427. TEXT: MS., Pforzheimer Library.
  1. Unidentified.

*To Charles Ollier   Saturday 2 March, 1833   33 Somerset St.

My dear Sir

Is it convenient for you to call here on Monday or Tuesday Morning? This delay is very sad—I suppose it cannot be helped—but I wish very much now to see you about my Novel, as something must be decided before I quit town—

Is not Deloraine[1] a beautiful book?

Yours truly
MWShelley

ADDRESS: Chas Ollier / 8 New Burlington St. POSTMARKS: (1) T.P / Duke St M[.S]; (2) 2. A. NOON. 2 / 2. MR / 1833. UNPUBLISHED. TEXT: MS., Pforzheimer Library.
    1. Godwin's *Deloraine* was published by Colburn and Bentley on 12 February 1833.

To John Gregson   2 March 1833 33 Somerset St. Portman Sq

My dear Sir

I enclose the usual receipt & will send on Monday Morning for the cheque—unless you could be so good as to send it me tomorrow

On writing to Mr Kennedy—he mentioned the Easter holydays as the period when I should be able to take Percy from his house—I shall at that time remove to Harrow. You may have seen in the Papers that there was a fire at the house of Percy's Tutor—which taking place in the Boy's bedrooms, destroyed them all—Most unluckily all Percy's clothes which I had just sent, were burnt, so that in addition to my other expences, I have had to refit him entirely.

I am, dear Sir,
Y^s Obl^y & Obliged
MWShelley

ADDRESS: John Gregson Esq / 18 Bedford Row. POSTMARKS: (1) T.P / Duke St M.S; (2) 2. A.NOON. 2 / 2. MR / 1833. ENDORSED: 2nd March 1833 / Mrs Shelley. PUBLISHED: Jones, #428. TEXT: MS., Bodleian Library (MS., Shelley, Adds., c. 6, ff. 167–68).

To [Charles Ollier][1]   33 Somerset St.   Monday   18 March [1833]

My dear Sir

Can I see you tomorrow morning at <u>twelve</u>?—or When do you think it likely that you can do me the favor to call? If not tomorrow, I hope some day early this week

I am Y^s truly
MWShelley

PUBLISHED: Jones, #429. TEXT: MS., Bodleian Library (MS., Montagu, d. 3, f. 97).
   1. A note on this letter states that it was addressed to Charles Ollier.

*TO [WILLIAM AND MARY JANE GODWIN][1]   [London or Harrow
                                                ?April or June 1833][2]

I shall be glad of good news of you both—You may consider me convalescent—but my spirit is tamed—& I shall take care of myself—I suffered
a martyrdom yesterday

                                                          Affl[y] Y[s]
                                                            MS

UNPUBLISHED. TEXT: MS., Pforzheimer Library.
   1. Godwin made notes on this letter for his *Lives of the Necromancers*, which he wrote from
18 October 1832 to 26 May 1834.
   2. Mary Shelley and Percy Florence had influenza in April 1833, and Mary Shelley had
influenza again in June 1833 (MWS Journal, 7 June 1833; 17 July 1834).

TO JOHN MURRAY   33 Somerset St.   15 April 1833

My dear Sir

   M[r] Finden has succeeded with the Engraving[1] far better than could have
been at all expected—If it is not every thing that one would wish a portrait
of Shelley to be, it is very far superior to any thing one could have hoped,
considering the picture.

   M[r] Finden mentioned to me your request that I should sit for the purpose
of an Engraving being made. There is no portrait of me—& it will be
neccessary that a drawing should be made. I do not quite like appearing in
public thus—Still I should be sorry to refuse any wish of yours. What artist
would you employ? I must tell you that I am (I don't know why) a very
difficult subject for the pencil.—There is also another difficulty. I leave
town on Monday 22[d][2] inst. for Harrow—& shall not be in town again for
several months—so that what is done must be done quickly.

   You told me to write to you if I did not receive the remaining Volumes
of your Edition of LordByron—I did so—but you have taken no notice of
my <u>flapper</u>[3]   I have only the first 6 volumes—you have never sent the rest.
I am the more disappointed because I meant to have asked for something
more. When I heard that you had given M[r] Trelawny the Landscape Illustrations,[4] I intended as soon as Shelley's portrait was finished, to ask you
to be equally generous towards me.

                                   I am, dear Sir
                                     Yours truly & Obligd
                                       MWShelley

ENDORSED: 1833—April 15 / Shelley Mrs. PUBLISHED: Jones, #430. TEXT: MS., John Murray.

  1. See 30 April [1832], n. 1.

  2. Godwin's Journal notes that he and Mary Jane Godwin called on Mary Shelley on 22 April 1833; that Mary Shelley and Percy Florence supped with him on 24 April; and that he called on Mary Shelley on 25 April. We may assume, therefore, that her departure for Harrow took place shortly after 25 April.

  3. Swift, *Gulliver's Travels* 3. 2. 17.

  4. Trelawny had supplied John Murray with anecdotes about Byron and drawings done by Captain Roberts. In return, Murray gave Trelawny a gift of Byron's works, as well as a copy of the *Illustrations* (unpublished letters from Trelawny to John Murray, October 1832, MS., John Murray; see 30 April [1832], n. 2).

*TO MARY GASKELL[1]   Harrow   Tuesday   [?May 1833–36]

Dear M[rs] Gaskell

  I grieve very much at the Contre-temps which prevented my receiving your kind & (had I been at home) most welcome visit.—I returned here on Saturday—but I returned with a friend who has a house near here & dined & spent the Evening with her—nor got your letter & card till my return home at eleven—Nothing could be so tiresome especially as I am afraid that you will not venture again—yet do try once more—I should be so very glad to see you & M[r] Gaskell—to whom present my best Compts—& ask him to be so good as to frank[2] & send the enclosed

  Beleive me, dear M[rs] Gaskell

                              Very truly Yours
                              MWShelley

UNPUBLISHED. TEXT: MS., Jean de Palacio.

  1. On 15 March 1832 Claire Clairmont wrote a letter to Mary Shelley introducing Daniel Gaskell (d. 1875), M.P. from 1832 to 1837, and his wife, Mary Heywood Gaskell (d. 1848), and asked her to introduce them to Godwin, with whom they also became friends (see *SC*, I, 153–54; Locke, *Godwin*, p. 318; [8] November 1835).

  2. Daniel Gaskell was one of several members of Parliament who obliged her by franking letters for her (see [5 May 1833], n. 6). Mary Shelley's letters of 11 June [1835] and [8] November 1835 bear Daniel Gaskell's frank.

*TO JANE WILLIAMS HOGG   Sunday   [5 May 1833]   Harrow

My dearest Jane—You are quite right—there is nothing so disagreable as having to buy & sell & others—I shirked this piano affair, till I almost offended Georgina[1]—so now I am in for it—but, dear, while we must bear being worried you by Clint[2]—& I by her—dont let us worry each other, but speak plainly & come to the point at on{c}e.

I shall write to Mrs Paul by this same post to tell her that her piano is coming & bidding her remit me the money—which will come by return of post—& w^d have been here I dare say by this time, but that I waited for your answer to write. You seem to say that Clint wants the money in hand before he will send the piano—but I think he will not behave in so ungentlemanly a way as to disappoint her when he knows that the money is on the road—I cannot get her answer before Thursday or Friday—& she had set her heart upon having her piano on Wednesday—because of some musical people being at the Aldridges[3] on that day—If I were in town I would pay Clint myself but she should have it—there is no doubt about his getting it as quickly as the post will allow—I shall take it ill of him therefore, if he does not send the piano on Tuesday—and I give him my word that he shall have the money by the end of the week—I will send you the money as you say—Ask him to make such a bargain about sending it—as shall prevent any exorbitant charge. It shall be guineas—tho I am afraid I said pounds.

Mrs Godwin acquiesced in my reasons—she is as artful as possible—I don't believe Claire will come—but it is their affair me ne lavo le mani[4]— She asked me, when I wrote, to express to her daughter all my objections to her coming—Which simply consist in this, that dependance in England is l'Inferno Stesso[5]—& that besides she has no friends here—Mrs G. [Godwin] talks of Mrs Gaskell[6]—but as that lady always dubs her my Sister that w^d be a hopeful recommendation—And, as I told her, she knew what giving dayly lessons is, as she has a young protegèe half killed by being too well off in that way.—

What Italian weather—the country here is all meadow so that the verdure is lovely—& the wide extent of prospect enchanting—& every place so quiet that it is like being in your own park—Many thanks for your kindness—One day next week I shall try to get to town to see my father. Percy is offered a bed in town—so whether I shall be able to prevent his peeping in on Edward some Saturday or Sunday, I doubt.—I wonder if it would inconvenience or annoy you much to deliver the enclosed yourself, to give further directions with it—I want, as you see, besides two P^r of White two P^r of other trowsers for Percy & these I want you to chose—something light—washable & cheap—if you do not like the job simply put the letter in the post—as with this weather he wants light things quickly: but I should be much obliged if you c^d chose them. Direct to me simply "Harrow"— basta cosi[7]—

It w^d be difficult not to be happy this weather, on ones own resources, if there was nothing outward to annoy. God grant no ill is coming—for things—since Papa is provided for,[8] seem all too favourable, almost—It is a great addition to happiness to know that there is affection & care for one in one heart, joined to some degree of power to make those things of avail—I hope things will turn out well—I trust they will—that is all I know. Adieu dearest—Take care of yourself   I shall be so glad when you can visit this beautiful spot—you will enjoy it much—Kindest regards to Jeff—A kiss my pretty Dina—I am

always Aff^y Yours
MWShelley

[*By Percy Florence Shelley*]
Dear Med[9]

I have got some mony so if you can get hold of any good play such as Maclin[10] with the book tell me quickly. I have got my stage painted

[*By Mary Shelley*]

These are my words to Georgina "I hear that your piano will {be} sent immediately—Will you send me the money by return of post—as I have promised it without delay"—

She may fancy, reasonably enough, that she will not be expected to send the cash till she receives the instrument—but really Clint should not make a question of a day or two—as if he were not treating with with gente di garbo[11]—

ADDRESS: Mrs Jefferson Hogg / 12 Maida Place / Edgware Road. POSTMARKS: (1) T.P / Harrow; (2) 12. NOON. 12 / 6. MY / 1833. UNPUBLISHED. TEXT: MS., Pforzheimer Library.

1. Georgiana Beauclerk Paul.

2. George Clint.

3. Caroline Anne Beauclerk (1804–69), one of Georgiana Paul's sisters, married Captain John Aldridge (d. 1871) in October 1829.

4. "I wash my hands of it."

5. "The Inferno Itself."

6. See Tuesday [? May 1833–36].

7. "That's enough."

8. On 15 April 1833 the Whig government offered Godwin the post of Office Keeper and Yeoman Usher of the Receipt of the Exchequer, a sinecure that carried a stipend of £200 per year and free accommodations at 13 New Palace Yard. The Godwins moved to New Palace Yard on 4 May 1833 (Locke, *Godwin*, pp. 334–35; Godwin, Journal).

9. Edward "Meddy" Williams.

10. Perhaps a reference to Charles Macklin (?1697–1797), actor and dramatist.

11. "Polite people."

*To [MARY JANE GODWIN]   [Harrow ?c. 11 May 1833][1]

Dear Mamma—I found the enclosed on my return. I have slipt {a} little note into the folds of your letter to tell M^{rs} P [*Paul*] that I got hers safe—

UNPUBLISHED. TEXT: MS., Pforzheimer Library.

1. After moving to Harrow, Mary Shelley first revisited London on 10 May 1833, when she dined and supped with the Godwins (Godwin, Journal). This letter was also used by Godwin to note his "Collections, Memoranda & Hints, for History of Necromancers" (see [?April or June 1833]).

Dear Mrs Stanhope

I hope you were amused at the debate—I forgot to tell you to be sure to go early—Did you listen? Or did any stray Members debate better up-stairs than those below? I am grieved to say that I was in town last week, & did not see you—I was there only for one day, & so harrassed—& my time so taken up, that I was not able to get to you—Yet I should have been very glad to have seen you & your Baby[2]—the next time I come I will be kinder to myself—but I do not think that will be while this Italian weather lasts—Which seems as if it would go on for ever—& yet alas! it will not—

I wish Mrs Elliot[3] every happiness—was she as quiet as ever at her wed-ding?—she is a nice gentle girl & will no doubt be happy—I wish both the others good husbands   Charles B[4]—I have heard, I think, is not in their vicinity but there is still the County Member[5] & Mr Rainie[6] & many many more—I wager Catherine is married before this time next year—& Helen[7] too if she likes—What an account 1 shall have to give Trelawny of his "Woman" as he calls them, what sad defoliation! I give the little Mc Eliney [McElkiney] joy of giving up Perry[8]—Trelawny was a better passion—for he thinks & speaks well of the sex—& however vain, is grateful for kindness, & knows how to understand the difference between masculine & feminine feelings, & to respect the latter—Perry, I guess—but I will not tell you what I guess, for I am afraid you would gossip—but pray cure your little friend of all les restes of per [her] predilection.

I am very stupidly placed here in lodgings in the town not having been able to get a house—If I find one to suit me I shall take it   if not I shall not remain here beyond the summer—Are there any pretty small detached cheap houses near Cedars[9]—or a little beyond towards Wimbledon Common[10]—Yet I shall be sorry to leave this place for my Percy's sake—who is so very happy—& so fat & so big I am quite ashamed of him. How very warm parties must be—I thought London looked odious during the few hours I was in it—but very full & very gay. When you are in Hanover Sq—I shall be ab[le] to get to you more easily when I come to town, as my piêd à terre is in Somerset St—Remember me very kindly to your Mother[11]—And to Colonel Stanhope—I wish there was to be a dissolution, he would be sure to be made M.P—& he ought to be it for the good of his Country—Don't tell my wish to Your Member,[12] for he will remember the 4000£ it cost him to get in & owe me a grudge—Write to me like [cross-written] a good girl—& get a very nice set of Beaus for me to flirt with when you give a party or I will flirt with————I won't tell you who—You jealous! That is affectation you would as soon think of calling this Winter as being jealous—Adieu   Yours ever

MWShelley

ADDRESS: The Honble / Mrs Leicester Stanhope / 6 Craig's Court / Charring Cross. POST-
MARKS: (1) Harrow; (2) 12. NOON. 12 / 18. MY / 1833. UNPUBLISHED. TEXT: MS.,
Pforzheimer Library.

1. In April 1831 Elizabeth Green (d. 1898) married Col. Leicester Fitzgerald Charles Stanhope, who became the fifth earl of Harrington in 1851 (*DNB*). Stanhope, an agent of the
London Greek Committee, joined Byron in Cephalonia in 1823, served with him in Greece,
and accompanied the poet's remains back to England (see Marchand, *Byron*, III, 1135–1260;
vol. I, [?24–31] May [1824], 22–27 February [1825]).

2. Anna Carolina Stanhope.

3. Jane Perry, daughter of James and Anne Perry (see [11 January 1833], n. 5), married
Thomas Frederic Elliot on 15 May 1833 (*The Register Book of St. George's Hanover Square,* ed.
George J. Armytage [London: The Harleian Society, 1897]), who became undersecretary of
state for the colonies from 1847–68 and was knighted (Frederic Boase, *Modern English Biography . . . 1851–1900,* 6 vols. [1892; reprint ed., New York: Barnes and Noble, 1965], I,
col. 979).

4. Perhaps Charles Robert Beauclerk (1802–72), a brother of Georgiana Beauclerk Paul.

5. Unidentified.

6. Unidentified.

7. Catherine and Helen Perry, daughters of James and Anne Perry (see n. 3 above).

8. Louisa McElkiney (d. 1841) and Thomas Erskine Perry (1806–82; *DNB*), judge, knighted
in 1841, were married on 16 September 1833 (*Register Book of St. George's*). Thomas Erskine
Perry was a son of James and Anne Perry (see n. 3 above).

9. The Leicester Stanhopes' home in Putney, seven miles southwest of London.

10. Eight miles southwest of London.

11. Anne Rose Hall Green.

12. Major Aubrey William Beauclerk (see 16 January 1833, n. 1). Beauclerk recorded that
he had spent almost £400 for his first election (letterbook of John Wilson, agent to Ogilvie
Estate, Ardglass, Public Record Office, County Down [T. 1546]). Mary Shelley's figure of
£4,000 may be an error of fact or a slip of her pen.

TO JOHN GREGSON   Harrow on the hill   1 June 1833

My dear Sir

I enclose you my receipt—will you send me the cheque—which will be
only for £75 I suppose—unless Sir Tim, who is in town I hear should hear
of my debt to you,[1] from you—& remit it to me. Harrow I find expensive—
though of course in the end I shall find living here the cheapest way of
going on—

                                        I am, dear Sir
                                        Ys Obl^ly & Ob^ly
                                        MWShelley

ADDRESS: John Gregson Esq / 18 Bedford Row. POSTMARKS: (1) T.P / Harrow; (2) 12.
NOON. 12 / 1. JU / 1833. ENDORSED: 1 June 1833 / Mrs Shelley. PUBLISHED: Jones, #431.
TEXT: MS., Bodleian Library (MS., Shelley, Adds., c. 6, ff. 169–70).

1. Mary Shelley's regular quarterly advance at this time was £100 (see 10 February 1832,
n. 1). In response to her letters to Gregson of 16 December 1832, 2 January 1833, 3 January
1833, and 13 January [1833], which pleaded for a further advance from Sir Timothy, John
Gregson, as this letter shows, personally loaned Mary Shelley £50, to be repaid at the June

and September quarterly advances. On 2 September 1833 Mary Shelley asks if she might postpone repayment of the remaining £25 until the December quarter.

To [?CECILIA GORE][1] Harrow Tuesday [?1833–36]

I hope your cold is better Percy will be quite ashamed to see you without a letter for his dear Henry[2]—He really loves him & looks forward with great delight to seeing him again

Ever Affectionately Y[s]
MWShelley

ADDRESS: [ ]e / [ ]r St. / [ ]osvenor Pl. POSTMARK: Harrow. ENDORSED: Mrs Shelley. PUBLISHED: Palacio, *Mary Shelley,* p. 611. TEXT: MS., Jean de Palacio.

1. Based on the fragmentary address on this letter, Jean de Palacio has conjectured that it was written to Cecilia "Cissy" Gore, one of the ten children of Catherine Frances Gore (Palacio, *Mary Shelley,* pp. 611–12). Godwin's Journal records that Miss Gore visited Mary Shelley on 2 September 1834.

2. Unidentified.

*To CLAIRE CLAIRMONT [?Harrow ?24–28] August 1833

[*Quotation*][1] Something will happen this year to me to change my fate, and as nothing can do that but my <u>obict</u> I expect it. I shall just be the age of my mother[2] and have arrived at my ⟨grand⟩ first climacteric[3]—next ⟨Sund⟩ Friday is my birth-day and before another comes I shall be translated to Paradise.

UNPUBLISHED. TEXT: MS., Claire Clairmont to Mary Shelley, 15 September 1833, Abinger MSS., Bodleian Library.

1. Claire Clairmont's letter containing this quotation, dated 15 September 1833 (supplied by Marion and David Stocking), expresses deep concern about the "melancholy predictions" made by Mary Shelley: "Would to God these visions you have may be the results of the typhus you have had. However it is, your letter made me wretched." Mary Shelley described her illness as an attack of influenza, not typhus, in her Journal and in her letter of 17 July [1834] to Maria Gisborne.

2. Mary Wollstonecraft Godwin was thirty-six when she died.

3. A critical stage in human life; a point at which a person was supposed to be specially liable to change in health or fortune. To some, all years denoted by multiples of seven, to others only odd multiples, were climacterics (*Oxford English Dictionary*).

To JOHN GREGSON 2 Melbury Terrace Dorset Sq.[1] 2 Sep. 1833

My Dear Sir

I send the usual receipt, to be exchanged for a cheque; which you will oblige me by sending by the 2[d] post to the above address, if you do not give it to the bearer.

I am going to make a request which, when I have explained the cause, I hope you will not think unreasonable—you will oblige me greatly if you can comply.

When I arranged to go to Harrow I could not immediately take my Son from the Boarding House—where I had placed him—this occasioned another heavy bill—which was not delivered to me till the beginning of the present holydays.—My moving & settling at Harrow cost me so much as to prevent my being able to reserve any portion of my income—Mr Kennedy's bill is £65—if I receive only £75 I shall experience very great inconvenience. At Xmas on the contrary—I shall have only the school bill, and be able to spare the £25[2] far more easily. If therefore you could make it convenient to yourself, to let me have my full quarter now—deferring the payment of the remaining £25 till December You would be extricating me from a great deal of difficulty—The bill at Xmas will not be more probably than £25. I shall be so much obliged if you can favor me as I ask.

Percy is quite well—Mr Kennedy expresses himself quite satisfied with his industry & on being removed to a higher form this quarter, he took a high place, although having had the Influenza twice (as well as myself) he was prevented attending the school quite regularly. I return to Harrow at the end of the holydays which conclude on the 18th

I am, Dear Sir,
Y^s Ob^ly
MWShelley

ENDORSED: 3 Sept 1833 / Mrs Shelley. PUBLISHED: Jones, #432. TEXT: MS., Bodleian Library (MS., Shelley, Adds., c. 6, ff. 171–72).

1. The Robinsons' address at Putney. Mary Shelley and Percy Florence spent most of August in London with the Robinsons. For three weeks in September Mary Shelley was with Julia Robinson at Putney but frequently visited London. She and Percy Florence returned to Harrow around 23 September 1833 (Godwin, Journal; MWS Journal; 17 July [1834]).

2. See 1 June 1833, n. 1.

*TO [WILLIAM GODWIN]   [Harrow]   Friday   [?27 September 1833][1]

My dear Father

I am come up (I write on board & the packet shakes not a little) to go to a party in Palace Y^d[2]   I return God willing tomorrow—will you go back with me? Pray do—I will breakfast with you at 8—we must be at the Tower by ⟨nine⟩ ten—Sunday There is no packet & I cannot wait longer away from Percy—If you cannot go with me—write me word—

Affec^ly Yours
MWS

But you will—wont you?—

UNPUBLISHED. TEXT: MS., Abinger MSS., Bodleian Library.

1. Godwin's Journal indicates that he went to Harrow on Saturday, 28 September 1833, and returned the following day. Godwin jotted notes on "Speculations ⟨Observations⟩ on Man his Faculties and Their Operation" on this letter.

2. The party was probably at the home of the Speaker and his wife, Charles and Ellen Manners-Sutton, who resided at St. Stephens Court, New Palace Yard.

*To Charles Ollier   Harrow.   10 Feb.   [error for
                                                        10 November 1833][1]

My dear Sir

I have heard nothing from you since I left town—and you must have thought me very rude not to have written to remind you of your kind promise of visiting me—but scarcely was I established here, than I got the Influenza again—so as to be confined to my bed a week or two & to the house for a much longer time—I did not recover till the Holydays when I went to Putney & got quite well—I am here again now—& if you feel enclined this cold weather to venture to our Hill—I shall be very glad to see you—only let me know a day or two before as I visit town now & then & it would be very annoying to miss you.

Do you know when my Novel[2] is to go to the press—I am ready whenever you are. Is Godolphin by Henry Bulwer?[3]   Pray tell me—Do you remember promising to lend me the newly published letters of Horace Walpole[4] when they came out?—⟨Now⟩ If you were very good & wished ⟨much⟩ to please me you would send them & ⟨Trevyllian⟩ Trevellian[5]—which I should like to read as being by the person who wrote Marriage in High Life[6]—for me to my Father (13 Palace Y^d) ⟨who⟩.   He is going to send me a parcel this week—& could include yours.

Do come here if you can find time & courage—I am in the town—any one can direct you to the house when you are here but we are too primæval for numbers

                                                        Yours truly
                                                        MWShelley

Address: Chas Ollier Esq / 8 New Burlington St. Postmarks: (1) T.P / Harrow; (2) 12. Noon. 12 / 11. No / 1833. Unpublished. Jones, #433, in summary. Text: MS., Keats-Shelley Memorial House, Rome.

1. The postmarks indicate that 10 February is an error for 10 November.

2. *Lodore.*

3. Edward Bulwer's *Godolphin* was published in 3 volumes by Richard Bentley in 1833. Henry Bulwer (1801–72), English diplomat and author, was Edward Bulwer's brother.

4. *Letters of Horace Walpole, Earl of Orford, to Sir Horace Mann,* ed. Lord Dover, 3 vols. (London: Richard Bentley, 1833).

5. Lady Charlotte Maria Bury, *Trevelyan,* 3 vols. (London: Richard Bentley, 1833).

6. "Lady Caroline Lucy Scott," *A Marriage in high life,* ed. the authoress of "Flirtation" (i.e., Lady Charlotte Maria Bury), 2 vols. (London: Henry Colburn, 1828).

*To [CHARLES OLLIER][1]   Harrow 21 Nov. 1833

Dear Sir

I send, not the whole of my M.S. but enough for the Printer to begin with—The conclusion of Vol I & the greater part of Vol II—I want to see how much it will make before I can decide as to the exact place where the second Vol. will end. The whole is ready however And the printer will not be kept waiting—It is very inconvenient to part with all the M.S. at once—as one wants continually to refer—and I do now as I have always done—sending the printer a portion at a time; and I hope I shall be permitted to do so in this instance. I mean the title to be "Lodore—a tale of the present time"—

You are very good to promise me the books. I shall be very glad of them, I am glad that you really intend coming here—if you put it off too long, I shall remind you again. Let me know a day or two before you come—as sometimes I go to town & should not like to miss you—it would be too provoking. I hope you will get the parcel safe—let me know of its arrival

Yours truly
MWShelley

UNPUBLISHED. TEXT: MS., Pforzheimer Library.
    1. See the previous letter.

*To [CHARLES OLLIER]   Harrow   Wednesday   [?25 November 1833]

Dear ⟨Papa⟩ Sir

I am glad that my book is printing at last—& at the very outset I am going to give you trouble. You see the motto to Chapter II
                    Tranquillity thou better name
                    Than all the family of fame
This is taken from a poem of Coleridge's[1] published in the Friend—I forget the following verses—two of them are
                    The bubble floats before
                    The shadow stalks behind
—I want the whole or greater part of them (the two standing alone as they do, are nonsense) as the motto—but I have not the Friend nor Coleridge's Poems—a friend of mine here has the former work, so I thought I could refer to it at any time—But when I sent for it, I found that his is the second edition, so <u>unamended</u> as to leave out most of the verses & especially thos[e] I want—Will you look in Coleridge's Poems for me & put in the verses as you find them but adapted—This is one of the evils of being out of town but I cannot help it. I am not sure that you will find the verses in the collection called the Sibylline Leaves but you will in Galignani Edition & the neighbourhood of Saunders & Ottley[2] will render it not very difficult I trust for you to assist me

--◆{ 196 }◆--

I shall be very expeditious in future in returning the proofs
I write in [   ] hurry
—& shall write again in a day or two.

Yours Obld^y
MWShelley

UNPUBLISHED. TEXT: MS., Harrow Education Department.

1. The lines, from Coleridge's "Tranquillity," were not used. Instead, "Settled in some secret nest, / In calm leisure let me rest; / And Far off the public stage, / Pass away my silent age," from "Senec. Traged. ex Thyeste Chor. 2," translated by Marvell, were substituted. I have found no information to indicate whether the change was Mary Shelley's.

2. Saunders and Ottley, publishers, were located at 50 Conduit Street, about two blocks from Colburn and Bentley, at New Burlington Street.

TO JOHN GREGSON   Harrow—2 Dec. 1833

My dear Sir

I send the receipt—will you be so good as to send the cheque—I shall be in town tomorrow & can get the cheque cashed there more easily than when I am here—will you be so good as to send it as soon as you can to me at 2 Melbury Terrace Dorset Sq. by the 2^d post—

Percy is very well indeed—& getting on very well—he is a good boy—& his Masters are quite satisfied with him

I am dear Sir
Y^s Ob^{ly}
MWShelley

ADDRESS: John Gregson / 18 Bedford Row. POSTMARKS: (1) T.P / Crawfo[r]d S[t]; (2) 12. NOON. 12 / 3. DE / 1833. ENDORSED: 2nd Decr 1833 / Mrs Shelley. PUBLISHED: Jones, #434. TEXT: MS., Bodleian Library (MS., Shelley, Adds., c. 6, ff. 173–74).

*TO F. MARRECO[1]   Harrow   17th Jan. 1834

Dear Sir

Absence from home prevented my receiving your polite note & must excuse this dilatory answer—Which I fear will come too late. The best portrait of Mr Moore is one in Mr Murray, the Bookseller's possession. It was the last work of our lamented Sir Thos Lawrence[2] and is a work of great genius & very like. Mr Moore's address is Sloperton—Devizes—Wilts— He must be gratified with the extension of fame you intend to bestow on him—& the best way I should think would be for you to write to him at once on the subject.

Mme d Andrada[3] has quite forgotten me. Nevertheless I rejoice in her good fortune—Her fortitude & praiseworthy endeavours deserve every reward. I saw the Misses Robinson the other day (who reside at 2 Melbury Terrace where you directed to me) they desire their best Compliments

I am Y^s truly

MWShelley

ADDRESS: F. Marreco Esq / 13 Old Fish St. / Doctors' Commons. POSTMARKS: (1) HARROW; (2) 7. NIGHT. 7 / 17. JA / 1834. UNPUBLISHED. TEXT: MS., Pforzheimer Library.

1. Unidentified. Godwin's Journal notes that Mary Shelley's guests on 1 August 1831 were himself, D'Andradas (see below), and Marreco.

2. See [25 January 1830](*b*).

3. Unidentified. Godwin's Journal records that he, Mary Shelley, and D'Andradas dined at the Robinsons' on 8 July 1831.

*TO EDWARD MOXON   Harrow—22 Jany 1834

Dear Sir

Your letter in some degree puzzles me—You say "if permission could be obtained"—I have always understood that the copyright of Mr Shelley's works belonged to me. Family reasons prevent my undertaking the republication of them at present.[1] When these no longer exist (& it is probable that they will not endure any very long time)—it is my intention to endeavour to arrange to republish them—with the addition of some letters & prose pieces in my possession. If it were then thought best to add a life—though I should decline writing it myself—I should wish to select the person I should wish to undertake the task—and whom I think I could induce to perforne [*perform*] it.

I am sorry for the delay, but it is not in my power to prevent it.—nor can I fix the term of its duration. But when I am free to follow my own wishes I shall be most happy to enter into any arrangement with you for their execution[2]   I am flattered by the offer you make & return my sincerest thanks

I am Sir

Your Ob^t Servant

MWShelley

ADDRESS: Edward Moxon Esq / 44 Dover St / Picadilly. POSTMARKS: (1) T.P / HARROW; (2) 12. NOON. 12 / 23. JA / 1834. UNPUBLISHED. TEXT: MS., Pforzheimer Library.

1. See vol. I, 18 September [1823]; [c. 3–4 August 1838].

2. Moxon again contacted Mary Shelley in 1835 about an edition of Shelley's works with a life and notes, for which he offered £600 (see 9 February [1835]). These proposals eventually led to Mary Shelley's 1839 editions of Shelley's works (see 7 December 1838). Moxon clearly felt a proprietary interest in this project, possibly based on this letter. On 6 March 1834 Godwin wrote to Moxon after consulting with Mary Shelley to say that she would be glad if Moxon could exert pressure to stop the publication of Shelley's works in numbers (MS., Pforzheimer Library). This probably refers to John Ascham's unauthorized 1834 edition of Shelley's works (Taylor, *Early Collected Editions*, pp. 26–27).

To CHARLES OLLIER   Harrow   Saturday   [15 March 1834]

My dear Sir

I wish the printers w[d] go on a little quicker—I only get two proofs a
week & am quite tried—especially as something might take me further from
town—I should like at least a proof a day—& so have done with it—will
you be so good as tell the Printers to be more expeditious

The Hamiltons[1] is very clever—& the character of Susan very sweet—
& true to nature & highly interesting—but how very political—& how very
radical—Nor did the Tory Ladies go out of fashion because the Whigs came
in—for there are very few ladies who are not Tories—

I like Godolphin[2] very much—It is like all His things in a high tone of
feeling & truth & beauty

                                        Ever Y[s] Obliged
                                        MWShelley

I wish you & M[rs] Ollier would contrive to come & see me soon—One day
next week if fine—Why not?—

ADDRESS: Chas Ollier Esq / 8 New Burlington St. POSTMARKS: (1) T.P / Harrow; (2) 7.
NIGHT. 7 / 15. MR / 1834. PUBLISHED: Jones, #435. TEXT: MS., Pforzheimer Library.
  1. Catherine Gore, *The Hamiltons*, 3 vols. (London: Richard Bentley, 1834).
  2. See [10 November 1833], n. 3.

*To CHARLES OLLIER   Harrow—Tuesday   [?18 March 1834]

Dear Sir

I am uneasy at not hearing from you & receiving no more proofs[1]—I
have had but two—as I do not know the reason—There need be no fear
of my delaying the printer—as I have very little to do—& shall do it all the
better—by receiving proofs at the same time   I send more copy of the 3[d]
vol & very much wish to know how much more is needed—Let me hear
from you

                                        Y[s] truly & Obl[y]
                                        MWShelley

I hope you received the packet of Copy, which I sent last week by the
coach, safely.

UNPUBLISHED. TEXT: MS., Pforzheimer Library.
  1. Of *Lodore*.

*To CHARLES OLLIER   Harrow—Thursday   [?20 March 1834][1]

Dear Sir

You frighten me very much—I told you I was afraid that the MS. would
be a little short—but not so much as you say. There has been so long a

delay that I forget the calculations I made. The first Volume <u>must</u> conclude as it does for the story's sake—I remember that I was uncertain about the 2nd not being sure how much it would make I imagine that what I now send up to p. 255 (256 is marked for Vol III) is all that I can give additionally to the second vol.

I have not now sent the whole of the MS. I was making an alteration at the conclusion when your letter cames—and I have kept back some to lengthen it somewhat if necessary Let me know how many more pages are necessary for the completion of the 3^d volume or whether with the addition of 100 more of my pages any thing more can be spared for the 2nd Let me hear from you soon—

I am Y^s truly
MWShelley

ADDRESS: Chas Ollier Esq. UNPUBLISHED. TEXT: MS., Pforzheimer Library.
    1. I have tentatively dated this Thursday letter from Harrow as 20 March 1834 because on Thursday, 6 March, Mary Shelley was in London (Godwin, Journal) and Mary Shelley's letter of Saturday, 15 March, to Ollier makes no reference to a lost manuscript (see the next letter).

*To Charles Ollier   Harrow—4 April [1834]

My dear Sir
    I am quite alarmed by a letter from the Printer mentioning a hiatus in copy—I have sent it in portions to you—I <u>can</u> have made no mistake—I have always kept all the Manuscript in the draw of my desk. You have received, you say up to 435——(I think the number is 455—but that is nothing)—the sequel up to 491 I sent in two thick letters by the post some weeks ago—directed to you at New Burlington St. As I am quite sure of this fact & have a perfect remembrance of it—pray make the necessary enquiries I am quite sure that it will all come right at last—and that these packets have been mislaid—I cannot be mistaken as I remember the whole circumstances of making up the two packets late at night to go by the morning's post—I should think as far as I can remember three weeks ago—and sending them to you.

I have sent to the Post office to make sure that there was no drawback from over weight—but had such a thing happened of course we should have heard of it—There can be no doubt that the letters were sent to Burlington St—& that they will be found—let me hear about this as soon a[   ] you can—as nothing is so worrying {as} a loss of copy—I have no second one of any kind

Yours truly
MWShelley

I go to town town tomorrow for 2 days so direct your answer to 2 Melbury Terrace Dorset Square—I hope the books you were so kind to lend me have been sent back—if not you shall receive them while I am in town—

You might send to Mr Smith the Comptroller of the 2^d post at gerard St—as it might happen that through some wonderful oversight that I misdirected <u>your street</u> but even then by this time we [   ]t have heard of it—2 packets at once by the 9 o'clock post from Harrow—as nearly as possible 3 weeks ago

ADDRESS: Chas Ollier Esq. / 8 New Burlington St. POSTMARKS: (1) Harrow; (2) 7. NIGHT. 7 / 7. AP / 1834. ENDORSED: Ansd / CO. UNPUBLISHED. TEXT: MS., Pforzheimer Library.

*TO [CHARLES OLLIER]   Harrow   30th April—1834

Dear Sir

I am totally at a loss what to do—I cannot be mistaken as to the packages I sent—I remember the whole circumstance of looking over the MS. for the last time, making up the packets & sending them—I cannot doubt as to the correctness of this statement—I have no copy at all—& should be obliged to rewrite it—at this moment I am engaged writing for Dr Lardner[1] & am very busy indeed.—I do not see therefore how I am to enable the Printers to proceed. I know that I sent the copy—It must have arrived at Burlington St & be mislaid—the mode in which I sent it—packets regularly paged, & going on without interruption, proves that there can be no omission on my part—I stated all this above a month ago, & received no answer, & consequently had no doubt that the packets were found:—as I said there were two, directed to you—sent at the same time—Has enquiry been made at the Post Office? I really am quite at a loss what to do—and I cannot see how it can devolve upon me to take all the trouble—I feel quite sure that if proper search were made they would be found in Burlington St.

Had I nothing else to do it were still rather hard to come upon me to rewrite a portion of Manuscript which, after I had done so with the utmost difficulty & annoyance, would be found in some odd corner of Burlington St—but as it is, I have engaged myself, as to time, & the whole thing is as impossible as it is vexatious—Pray let proper enquiries & search be made   I <u>know</u>—I could, as the vulgar people say <u>swear</u> that the copy was sent & therefore there can be no doubt that it will be found if looked properly for. I am truly pained at all this annoyance as I am sure that it must be vexatious to you, but pray let the packets be properly looked for—for I do assure you that they were sent—& there can be no doubt that they are mislaid unless the fault is in the Post Office—Truly Yours

MWS

The servants remember the fact perfectly. The maid gave them early in the morning to the boy here, who always puts my letters in—& he remembers taking them & one of the packets being too large to go into the hole, & taking it into the office—Be assured therefore that you have but to look to find.

Unpublished. Text: MS., Pforzheimer Library.

1. MWS, *Lives* (1835–37), for the Rev. Dionysius Lardner (1793–1859; *DNB*), literary and scientific writer. Lardner's Cabinet Cyclopædia series, 1829–49, was contributed to by many eminent figures of the day, including Sir Walter Scott and Thomas Moore, and ran to 133 volumes. *Lives,* vol. I, published c. February 1835, with essays by James Montgomery (1771–1854; *DNB*), poet and journalist, included essays on Dante, Petrarch, Boccaccio, Lorenzo de' Medici, Marsiglio Ficino, Giovanni Pico della Mirandello, Angelo Ferrara, Burchiello, Bojardo, Berni, Ariosto, and Machiavelli. Mary Shelley wrote the lives of Petrarch, Boccaccio, and Machiavelli; Montgomery, that of Dante. The other essays have not been attributed. *Lives,* vol. II, published c. September or October 1835, with essays by Montgomery and Sir David Brewster (1781–1868; *DNB*), scientist and author, included essays on Galileo, Guicciardini, Vittoria Colonna, Guarini, Tasso, Chiabrera, Tassoni, Marini, Filicaja, Metastasio, Goldoni, Alfieri, Monti, Ugo Foscolo. Mary Shelley wrote the lives of Metastasio, Goldoni, Alfieri, Monti, and Foscolo; Brewster, that of Galileo; and Montgomery, that of Tasso. The others have not been attributed (Lyles, *MWS Bibliography*, p. 37).

To Edward John Trelawny   Harrow—7 May—1834

Dear Trelawny—I confess I have been sadly remiss in not writing to you—
I have written once however, as you have written once (but once) to me—
I wrote in answer to your letter—I am sorry you did not get it—as it
contained a great deal of gossip—It was misdirected by a mistake of Jane—
who had your letter to me—& told me that the address given was Brown
& Barclay—do ask Brown & Brothers[1] to enquire after it—it was sent at
the end of last September to New York—I told you in that of the infidelity
of several of your womankind—how Mrs Robert Stanhope[2] was flirting with
Bulwer—to the infinite jealousy of Mrs Bulwer[3] & making themselves the
talk of the town—how your little Jewess Miss McEliney [*McElkiney*] was
desperately in love with & lately married to Erskine Perry—how Barbara
Cummings[4] was blooming & surrounded by admirers at Lady Thorolds'[5]—
how Catherine Perry shewed a soft inclination to the handsome Mildmay[6]
who never spoke to her—such & much more tittle tattle was in that letter—
all old news now. Mrs Erskine Perry has been in Italy with her husband &
returns in June to be confined—The Stanhopes (Captain Robert & wife I
mean) went to Paris & were ruined & are returned under a cloud, to rusticate
in the country in England—Bulwer is making the amiable to his own wife—
who is worth in beauty & wit all the Mrs R.S.s [*Robert Stanhopes*] in the
world—of Barbara I have no news just now. Jane Perry married Frederic
Elliot last summer—she has had the small pox since & says herself that she
has lost all her beauty—she is indeed sadly disfigured—but I hope it will
go off—Mrs Crawford[7] always asks most kindly after you—None of the
Perry girls liked Erskine's marriage indeed there were several things attendant on it ⟨arising from⟩ which made it disagreable—but he got a good
deal of money (for him—500 a year & 1500£) and he could not do better.
Mrs Leicester Stanhope is one of the Belles this season—she goes out a
great deal—acts charades & amuses herself & others—she is a good natured

clever woman besides being handsome & I like her very much—Louisa Robinson is married & just sailed to India—it was a very happy match; her husband[8] is a Major in the B.A. [*Bengal Army*] Company's service   he is a handsome man—of very good family tolerably well off & with great expectations—I liked him much & was sorry to lose them both. Claire is still in a situation at Pisa—she is in good health & grown fat   she always asks after you—she had formed acquaintance with Jane Bocella[9]—whom she likes—and describes as you used, as a most interesting & elegant person—She (Jane B) was just going to be confined of her first child, when Claire last wrote—she is not happy—Claire describes Zella as very handsome clever & spirited, & very charming when she likes—Laurette & Nerina Mason or Tighe are both married[10]   Laurette's marriage is not propitious, but Nerina appears matched delightfully to an amiable & cultivated & rich Italian.—Sir Tim was intended to die last November—being given over— but he has come out as fresh as ever, on a new lease, he has quarrelled with John,[11] won't see him, & is ruining him as he has done me, cutting down his timber &c—Georgina[12] is settled in a little cottage in Sussex—everyone visits her—yet her situation is a painful one—Jane has been a good deal indisposed & is grown very thin—Jeff had an appointment[13] which took him away for several months—& she pined & grew ill on his absence—she is now reviviving [*reviving*] under the benificent influence of his presence— I called on your Mother a week or two ago—she always asks after you with empressement & is very civil indeed to me—she was looking well—but Julia[14] tells me, in her note enclosing your letter, that she is ill of the same illness as she had two years ago—but not so bad—I think she lives too well.—Julia is expecting to be confined in a very few weeks or even days— She is very happy with Burley—He is a thoroughly goodn[a]tured & estimable man—it is a pity he is [?*not*] younger & handsomer; however she is a good girl & contented with her lot—we are very good friends.—I saw poor Lord Wenlock's[15] death in the paper a few days ago—he died at his Villa near Florence—I should like much to see your friend Lady Dorothea[16]— but though in Europe—I am very far from her. I live on my hill, descending to town now and then;—I should go oftenor if I were richer—Percy continues quite well & enjoys my living at Harrow—which is more than I do, I am sorry to say—but there is no help. My Father is in good health—Mrs Godwin has been very ill lately but is now better—I thought Fanny Kemble was to marry & settle in America—What a singular resemblance you have discovered—I never saw her except on the stage—So much for news—They say it is a long lane that has no turning; I have travelled the same road for nearly 12 years;—adversity poverty & loneliness being my companions—I suppose it will change at last—but I have nothing to tell of myself except that Percy is well—which is the beginning & end of my existence.—I am glad you are beginning to respect women's feelings—You have heard of Sir Harry's death.—Mrs Brereton[17] (who is great friends with Salisbury now Sir William, an MP.)[18] says that it is believed that he has left all he could to the Catholic members of his family. Why not come over & marry Letitia[19] who in consequence will be rich?—and I dare say still beautiful in your eyes, though 54—We have had a mild fine winter & the weather now is as warm sunny & cheering as an Italian May—We have thousands of birds—& flowers innumerable & the trees [*cross-written, p. 1*] of spring in the fields—Jane's children are well—The time will come I suppose when we may meet again more befriended by fortune—but youth will have flown—& that in a woman is something—I do not recommend you to marry because I do not think you would make a good husband—else surely—In marriage & its results we can only hope for happiness—I mean to marry when I find a person I should like to have—not very likely to happen in this place—& indeed I have always felt certain that I should never again change my name—& that is a comfort, it a pretty & a dear one—Adieu; Write to me often, & I will behave better & as soon as I have accumulated a little news write again

Ever Yours,
MWS.

ADDRESS: John Edward Trelawny Esq / care of / The Honble James Barber / ⟨Mess. Brown, Brothers & Co⟩ / Orange Co. ⟨New York⟩ / Barbersville / Virginia US. POSTMARKS: (1) PAID / 9 MY 9 / 1834; (2) 180 STRAND[   ]; (3) NEW—Y[ORK]— / JUN / 26. PUBLISHED: Jones, #436. TEXT: MS., Bodleian Library (MS., Shelley, Adds., c. 6, ff. 175–76).

1. See address of this letter.

2. Elizabeth Rosamund Ward married Captain Robert Stanhope (1802–39), a cousin of Leicester Stanhope, in March 1830 (*Burke's Peerage*).

3. Rosina Doyle Wheeler (1802–82) and Bulwer were married in 1829. Irreconcilable differences became apparent early in their marriage, leading to a legal separation in 1836. Rosina Bulwer, feeling wronged because of Bulwer's infidelities, spent the remainder of her life publicly maligning Bulwer (Second Earl of Lytton, *The Life of Edward Bulwer,* 2 vols. [London: Macmillan and Co., 1913], I, 245–342; Michael Sadleir, *Bulwer* [Boston: Little, Brown, and Co., 1931]).

4. Unidentified.

5. Unidentified.

6. An Edward Mildmay is included in Mary Shelley's address list at the conclusion of her Journal, though no address is given.

7. A Mrs. Crawford, 27 Wilton Crescent, is included in Mary Shelley's address list at the conclusion of her Journal.

8. Major Alexander Macdonald Lockhart Maclean (1804–40) (India Office Library).

9. Trelawny's letter to Claire Clairmont of 10 December 1833 from Charleston, South Carolina, mentions the friendship between Claire Clairmont and Jane Boccella (Trelawny, *Letters,* p. 186).

10. Laurette Mason, much against her mother's wishes, married Prince Adolfo Domenico Galloni d'Istria, of the French consular service, in November 1832. Nerina Mason (b. 1815) married Bartolomeo Cini, of a prominent Pistoian family, in January 1834 (McAleer, *The Sensitive Plant,* pp. 209–11; *S&M,* IV, 1168–70).

11. John Shelley (1806–66), Sir Timothy's second son (see vol. I, 4 March 1827, n. 4).

12. Georgiana Beauclerk Paul.

13. In 1833 Hogg received a temporary appointment as a member of the Royal Commission on Municipal Corporations. In 1833 and 1834 he also tried to improve his prospects through

attendance at the Durham and Newcastle assizes and was often away from home (Scott, *Hogg*, p. 200; Norman, *After Shelley*, pp. 72–87).

14. Julia Trelawny Burley, who married John Burley, the Trelawny family lawyer, in the summer of 1833.

15. Sir Robert Lawley, sixth baronet, Baron Wenlock (d. 10 April 1834) (*Burke's Peerage*).

16. Lady Dorothea Campbell.

17. Trelawny's mother.

18. Sir William Lewis Salusbury-Trelawny (1781–1856), M.P. for East Cornwall from 1832 to 1837, became eighth baronet on 24 February 1834, upon the death of his father, Sir Harry Trelawny (b. 1756), seventh baronet (*Burke's Peerage*).

19. Daughter of Sir William Lewis Salusbury-Trelawny.

---

*TO JANE WILLIAMS HOGG   [London]   Friday   [23 May 1834]

Dearst Jane—Mrs Bankhead[1] takes me back to Harrow tomorrow, so I am sorry to say I shall not see you till my next visit which will be speedy however, as Mr Gregson will oblige me to come on business[2] in 10 days or a fortnight—I am very glad to get home and quiet such creatures of habit are we—& then I am very very glad to get back to Percy

In haste   Affly Yours   MWS

[*P. 1, top*] I have had a letter from Claire—no news in it   her Mother will forward it to you   I heard from Dah[3]—on Friday that you were recovered

ADDRESS: Mrs Hogg / 12 Maida Place / Edgware Road. POSTMARKS: (1) T.P / [   ]; (2) 8. MORN. 8 / 26. MY / 1834; (3) 10. F.NOON. 10 / 26. MY 1834. UNPUBLISHED. TEXT: MS., Abinger MSS., Bodleian Library.

1. Maria Horatia Paul (d. 1866), daughter of Sir John Dean Paul and Frances Eleanor Paul, in 1825 married Charles Bankhead (d. 1870), who became secretary of the legation at Constantinople (*Burke's Peerage*).

2. Mary Shelley was attempting to renegotiate the amount of the allowance she received from Sir Timothy Shelley but was disappointed (see [?7 June 1834]). In May 1833 Sir Timothy had pointed out that the £6,000 he had agreed to advance her would soon be exhausted (Ingpen, *Shelley in England*, II, 614).

3. Nickname for Thomas Jefferson Hogg.

---

*TO THOMAS JEFFERSON HOGG   [Harrow]   Saturday Ev^g
                                                        [?7 June 1834][1]

Dear Jeff—I went to Mr Amory on Thursday to put things in train & he wrote to make an appointment with Mr Gregson—& receives for answer that since he last wrote to me he had had a letter from Sir Tim to say that at his advanced age he must decline further pursuing the subject[2]—I have gone through all this worry & expence for nothing!—such is life!—

⟨I want you to send me back the two⟩

I think I sent you Gregson's note contain{in}g his offers together with the statement of the state of the property in my note before leaving town— if I did will you return it to me—I want it—

Really Mr Gregson might just as well not have made the proposals to me, & given me so much trouble & worry untill he was authorized

Y^s truly
MWShelley

ADDRESS: To Jefferson Hogg. UNPUBLISHED. TEXT: MS., Abinger MSS., Bodleian Library.
1. Mary Shelley's letter of [23 May 1834] indicates that she planned to return to London in ten days or a fortnight.
2. On 4, 8, and 11 May 1834, Sir Timothy Shelley wrote to John Gregson inquiring about Mary Shelley's financial plans for herself and Percy Florence. In these letters he suggested that he wished to arrange for his wife to remain at Field Place for approximately three years after his death. He also wanted to know if Mary Shelley had a career selected for Percy Florence and whether she would be entitled to a "Valuation" of the property on Sir Timothy Shelley's land after his death. He stated that he would advance no further sums until these matters were settled and that he wished her to hire a respectable gentleman other than Hogg to represent her (Abinger MSS., Bodleian Library).

*To Charles Ollier   Harrow—10 June [1834]

Dear Sir

You seem to think that you gave me an easy task in rewriting that unlucky MS[1]—quite the contrary—I did it as soon as ever I could—and tried all I could to do it sooner. The fairies are at work most malevolently if by this time the Printers have not the whole—⟨as well⟩ as I sent the termination of the restoration on Saturday—in two packets; which I hope they received safely—I think there might be a page or two more than was lost—but cannot tell exactly—as I had no copy whatever. Give my compliments to Mr Bentl{e}y, & tell him I am very sorry, that like Don Quixote, an Enchanter meddles with my affairs—it is very disagreable indeed to me as well as to him— Yours truly

MWShelley

ADDRESS: Chas Ollier Esq / 8 New Burlington. POSTMARKS: (1) T.P / Harrow; (2) 7. NIGHT. 7 / 10. JU / 1834. UNPUBLISHED. TEXT: MS., Haverford College.
1. Of Lodore (see 4 April [1834]).

*To Charles Ollier   Harrow—23 June [1834]

Dear Sir

I send you the Title Page a copy of which I have sent to the Printer— Will it do?—⟨if you do not like it, wd⟩ at any rate you would oblige me by forwarding it to my Father & consulting him about it.[1] He has a very good judgement about Titles, & might make some lucky suggestion.—"A Tale of the Present Times" does not quite please me yet what exchange it for?—

I forget how many copies is written in our bond as coming to me—but I remember you said I should be indulged in having 12,—which I require—I should be much obliged to you if you would direct the printers to send me the fair sheets <u>here</u> by coach. I <u>promise</u> that they shall not go out of my hands—but there has been such interruption such accidents by flood & field that I shall not be easy till I read it over & find all right.—

Have you any pretty new book to lend me? If you have, how much you would oblige me by sending it—Is Mr Bulwer's book[2] out—can you so infinitely favor me as to lend me that—You know I admire & delight in his novels beyond all others—There is none comparable to them. I hear you have thrown poor St. Aubyn[3] overboard. He has given his novel to Mr Hogg to read—Do you not pity him?—

Lodore—Mr Bentley & yourself & my self have my earnest prayers—if it succeeds—it will please me that Mr Bentley is rewarded for his risk—yourself for your great kindness—myself for my industry & good intentions—Do, do me the favor not to be lazy, but to Deign to read it <u>all</u>—& let me know your opinion.

If Mr Bentley could let me have a copy of Deloraine he would oblige me much—a friend having appropriated mine, but I do not like to ask too much

Ever truly Yours
MWShelley

When do you mean to come over here the weather is fine, does it not tempt you?

ADDRESS: Charles Ollier Esq / 8 New Burlington St. POSTMARKS: (1) T.P / Harrow; (2) 12. NOON. 12 / 24. JU / 1834. UNPUBLISHED. TEXT: MS., Pforzheimer Library.

1. Godwin read *Lodore* on 25–28 July 1834 (Godwin, Journal).

2. *The Last Days of Pompeii,* 3 vols. (London: Richard Bentley), published in September 1834.

3. Perhaps Rev. John Henry St. Aubyn, a son of Sir John St. Aubyn. In 1826 Mary Shelley was a confidante of his about his unhappy love affair. Two letters from John Henry St. Aubyn to Mary Shelley express his intention to publish the story of this affair (Abinger MSS., Bodleian Library). On 11 October 1832 St. Aubyn had entered into a contract with Bentley to publish a novel called *Hugo the Fourth* in the autumn of 1833 (Bentley Record Book). I can find no actual publication of this novel. However, in 1837 Richard Bentley published a novel by St. Aubyn entitled *The Elopement; or, The Deadly Struggle.*

TO MARIA GISBORNE   Harrow—Middlesex   17 July [1834]

My dearest Friend—I have just received your agonizing & interesting letter. Often have Jane & I said: "When shall we hear from her again?—She forgets us!"—& last Spring we looked each day for your arrival. I cannot tell you of my delight in receiving tidings of you—sad as they are. How your letter reached me I cannot exactly say—you directed it to me to <u>the care of Major</u>

B [*Beauclerk*]—which destroyed the priviledge of franking—Pray do not direct to Chester St. again at all on any account—Write to me directly <u>here</u> your letters are worth far more than their postage—or if your extreme tenaciousness of cost prevent your writing on these terms write to me (<u>not</u> to the care of, but) <u>under cover</u>—no matter the weight of your letter—to The Speaker G.C.B.[1] New Palace Yard. Indeed I beg of you to write not, long letters to injure your delicate nerves—but news of your precious health.[2] May life be prolonged, dearest Maria:—for your husband's sake you must desire this. His affection is rare and admirable—you are most happy to possess it—You truly deserve it by your qualities, your talents—your devotion to him—still gratitude & constancy are infrequent and delightful to know of. Do write to tell us of your state—I answer your letter immediately to assure you of having received it—and how dearly I prize any communication from you. I will forward it to Jane, it will touch her to the heart. I congratulate you on your <u>Alentours</u>[3] Your Doctor[4] so virtuous—so attached & thank God so capable—your poor faithful. Elizabeth[5]—and I would express to S.G. [*Signor Giovanni, John Gisborne*] however feebly the respect I feel for his devotion & affection—What scenes! Gracious God—Wherefore do your creatures exist!—if not for another world wherefore?—how sure I feel that our being will continue yet how & where who can tell!—

I could go on long—remarking on each line of your letter, & dwell on the terrible narrative with all the interest & grief it excites—but it will please you more if I tell you of ourselves—Do you know of my taking up my residence at Harrow? In the Autumn of 1832 I placed Percy to board here—but found it so frightfully expensive, that I could only meet it by taking up my abode here & having him as a home boarder. I did this in April 1833—I am satisfied with my plan as regards him—I like the school, and, the affection thus cultivated for me will I trust be the blessing of my life. Still there are many drawbacks—This is a dull inhospitable place—I came counting on the kindness of a friend who resided here—but she died of the Influenza[6]—and I live in a silence & loneliness—not possible any where except in England where people are so <u>islanded</u> individually in habits—I often languish for sympathy—& pine for social festivity. Percy is much—but I think of you & Henry[7] & shrink from binding up my life in a child, who may hereafter divide his fate from mine—But I have no resource—Everything earthly fails me but him—except on his account I live but to suffer—Those I loved are false or dead—those I love absent & suffering—& I absent & poor can be no of no use to them—Of course in this picture I subtract the enjoyment of good health & usually good spirits—these are blessings—but when driven to think I feel so desolate, so unprotected, so oppressed & injured that my heart is ready to break with despair. I came here as I said in April 1833—and 9 June was attacked by the Influenza so as to be confined to my bed—nor did I recover the effects for several Months. In September during Percy's holydays I went to Putney & recovered youth & health—Julia Robinson was with me—we spent days in Richmond Park & on Putney Heath—often walking 12 or 14 miles—which I did without any sense of fatigue. I sorely regretted returning here—I am too poor to furnish—I have lodgings in the town—disagreable ones—Yet often in spite of care & sorrow I feel wholly compensated by my boy. I will try to describe him to you, though it is difficult—In person he is of a fair height & excessively fat—his chest would remind you of a Bacchus he has a florid complexion, blue eyes—like his father—& his looks & gestures & shape of his face would remind you of Shelley & his person before he grew fat—he is full of spirit & animation but proud & reserved with strangers—There used to { } a great want of sensibility—this lingers about him—but is rather concentrated that [*than*] slight—he loves me more than he knows himself & would not displease me for the world—if he sees me sad he does all he can to comfort me—& would give up any pleasure for my benefit—his temper is a little defective but he is neither violent nor sulky—but perfectly generous & true—he is trustworthy & thoughtful beyond his years—cautious tho' impetuous—& exceedingly constant, so that he now loves Edward & Dina better than any newer friends   He has the true Shelley hatred of society—he has no ambition & little emulation—yet attentive to his lessons & sufficiently diligent—he is the 20th boy in a form of 50 boys—he has a great respect for truth & good faith—One day I said to him—"Suppose when you grew to be a Man—you would leave me all alone"—"O Mamma," he said, "how do you think I could be so shabby:—that would be too bad!" To be <u>left all alone</u> seems to him the worst evil of all—he does not like any poetry except Percy's Ancient ballads[8] and Shelley's translation of Homer's Hymn to Mercury & the Cyclops—but he likes romances any marvellous tales & is a great story teller—he is a little bitten by metaphysics—he is always occupied. He is very handsome—& a perfect Child in all his notions & quite obedient—He is better to me than any one; for he has no notion of giving up any whim to any body but me,—besides being very incommunicative except to his intimates—God help me if any thing was to happen to him—I should not survive it a week   Besides his society I have also a good deal of occupation—I have finished a Novel—which if you meet with it—read—as I think there are parts that will please you—I am engaged writing the Lives of some of the Italian Literati for Dr Lardner's Cyclopedia[9]—I have written those of Petrarch Boccaccio &c & am I now engaged on Macchiavelli—This takes up my time & is a source of interest & pleasure.

My Father I suppose you know has a tiny shabby place under Government[10]—The retrenchments of Parliament endanger & render us anxious—He is quite well—but old age takes from his enjoyments—Mrs G. [*Godwin*] after the Influenza has been suffering with the Tic Douleureux in her arm most dreadfully—they are trying all sorts of poisons on her with little effect—Their discomfort & low spirits will force me to spend Percy's holydays in town to be near them. Jane & Jeff are well—he was sent last

Autumn &Winter by Ld Brougham as one of the Corporation Commissioners he was away for Months & Jane took the opportunity to fall desperately in love with him—She pined & grew ill & wasted away for him—The children are quite well   Dina spent a week here lately   she is a sweet girl—Edward improves daily under the excellent care taken of his education—I leave Jane to inform you of their progress in Greek—Dina plays wonderfully well—& has shewn great taste for drawing—but the last is not cultivated—I did not go to the Abbey—nor the Opera nor hear Grisi,[11]— I am shut out from all things—like you—by poverty & lonliness—Percy's pleasures are not mine I have no other companion—What effect Paganini would have had on you I cannot tell—he threw me into hysterics—I delight in him more than I can express—his wild etherial figure rapt look—& the sounds he draws from his violin are all superhuman—of human expression   it is interesting to see the astonishment & admiration of Lindley Spagnoletti & Mori[12] as they watch his evolutions.—Bulwer is a man of extraordinary & delightful talent—but spoilt by vanity disappointed ambition (for he wishes to be a Parliamentary leader[13] which his deafness entirely prevents) and a certain vulgarity of fashion, not acknowledged by supreme ton[14]—He went to Italy & Sicily last Winter & I hear disliked their inhabitants—to depreciate is his tone—& then a deaf man without a word of Italian to judge of Italians in a rapid journey of 5 months—si da retta a un tale forse![15]—Yet notwithstanding I am sure he will spread inexpressible & graceful interest over the Last Days of Pompeii[16]—the subject of his New Novel—Trelawny is in America—& not likely to return—Hunt lives at Chelsea and thrives I hear by his London Journal[17]—I have not seen him for more than {a} year—for reasons I will not here detail—they regard his family not him—Claire is in a situation at Pisa near Mrs Mason—Laurette & Nerina are married—the Elder badly to one who won her at the dagger's point—a sad unintelligible story—Nerina to the best & most delightful Pistoian, by name Bartolomeo Cini—both to Italians—Laurette lives at Genoa, Nerina at Livorno—the latter is only newly a Bride & happier than words can express—My Italian maid Maria[18] says to Claire—Non vedo l'ors to see Mi' Padrona ed il mi' Bimbo![19]—her Bimbo!—such a Bimbo as tall as I—& large in proportion or rather [   ]rger—He has good health with all—he had a blow [   ]n his knee which menaced a tumour but did not come to one, so I took him to Lawrence[20] in a fright (such a fright— tho groundless—as made me pass days of torture) over health he said was all his ailment so forbade him animal food—but the less he eats the more robust he grows—his contrast to Edward is whimsical—both in complexion & stoutness—their height is the same.—

I have written this letter immediately on receiving yours that you may be sure that it came safe—I direct it simply to Plymouth—I trust you will receive it duly—Pray write one word of information concerning your health— before I attributed your silence to forgetfulness—but you must not trifle now with the anxiety you have awakened—I will write again soon—With kindest regards to your poor good husband—the fondest hopes of hearing that your health is improved & anxious expectation of a letter   believe me ever

Affectionately Y^s

MWShelley

ADDRESS: Mrs Gisborne / Plymouth / Devon. [*In another hand*] Mrs Gisborne / Plymouth / ES Ruthven. POSTMARKS: (1) FREE / 19 JY 19 / 1834; (2) C4 / 19 JY 19 / 1834. ENDORSED: Harrow 17th July 1834 / recd 20th Do / Ans. 22nd Augt / M. Shelley. PUBLISHED: Jones, #437. TEXT: MS., Bodleian Library (MS., Shelley, Adds., c. 6, ff. 177–78).

1. Sir Charles Manners-Sutton, Knight Grand Cross of the Bath.

2. Maria Gisborne had been afflicted with dropsy for fifteen months and reported her doctor's belief that she was not expected to live very much longer (6 July 1834, Abinger MSS.).

3. "Neighborhood."

4. John Wreford Budd (b. 1805), physician, who closely attended Maria Gisborne during her illness (Maria Gisborne letters to Mary Shelley, Abinger MSS.; *Alumni Cantabrigienses*).

5. Elizabeth Rumble, the Gisbornes' companion-housekeeper, has been identified as the natural daughter of John Gisborne (see David M. Stocking and Marion Kingston Stocking, "New Shelley Letters in a John Gisborne Notebook," *Keats-Shelley Memorial Bulletin* 31 [1980]: 1). Elizabeth Rumble inherited John Gisborne's journals and all other papers belonging to him (see 5 April 1838).

6. Lady Paul had died on 15 April 1833.

7. After Henry Reveley's marriage in 1824 to Amelia Fielding, in 1826 they went to live in Capetown, South Africa, which they left in 1829 to help found a colony at the Swan River in Western Australia (later Perth). Henry Reveley has been credited with being the first engineer in Western Australia (*CC Journals,* pp. 469–70).

8. Thomas Percy, *Reliques of Ancient English Poetry* (London: J. Dodsley, 1765).

9. See 30 April 1834, n. 1.

10. See [5 May 1833], n. 8.

11. Guilia Grisi (1811–69), Italian soprano (*New Grove Dictionary of Music and Musicians*).

12. Robert Lindley (1776–1855), English violoncellist and composer; Paolo Spagnoletti (1768–1834), Italian violinist; Nicholas Mori (1796–1839), violinist and music publisher (*New Grove Dictionary of Music and Musicians*).

13. Bulwer was first elected to Parliament in April 1831. He served until 1841, when he lost his seat. In 1852 he was reelected and served until 1866, when he was elevated to the peerage.

14. "Manners."

15. "As if one listens to such a man!"

16. See 23 June [1834], n. 2.

17. *Leigh Hunt's London Journal*, a literary miscellany, published April 1834–December 1835.

18. Maria had been with the Shelleys from c. November 1819 or before until June 1823 (see vol. I).

19. "I can't wait" to see "my mistress and my child."

20. Dr. William Lawrence (see vol. I, [24 September 1817] (*a*), n. 2).

To DOUGLAS WILLIAM JERROLD[1]   13 New Palace Y^{d2}   9 Aug. 1834

Dear Sir

You would very much oblige me if you would give me admissions for 2 for Beau Nash[3] next Wednesday—If that day is not convenient any day next week—only letting me have them as soon as you can. Excuse the impertinence of this request—but a successful dramatic writer must make up his mind to be the victim of impertinence—as a philosopher he will forgive—as a Xtian he will return good for evil—and I shall get the orders

Dear Sir I am
Y^s truly
MWShelley

ADDRESS: Douglas Jerrold Esq / Chelsea / or at T. R. Haymarket. POSTMARKS: (1) Charing Cross / 2 py PA[   ]; (2) More / to Pay. 1d; (3) 10. F.NOON. 10 / AU. 9 / 1834; (4) 18. PAID. [   ]4 / AU. 9 / 8[—] 10NN. 8. PUBLISHED: Jones, #438. TEXT: MS., Keats-Shelley Memorial House, Rome.

1. Douglas William Jerrold (1803–57; *DNB*), journalist and playwright. Jerrold was a co-founder with William Godwin, Jr., of the Mulberries (see vol. I, 11 July [?1824–27], n. 2).

2. The Godwins' residence.

3. Jerrold's comedy *Beau Nash* opened at the Haymarket, Theatre Royal, on 16 July 1834 (Nicoll, *English Drama*, p. 332).

TO MARIA GISBORNE   7 Upper Eaton St.   19 August [1834]

Dearest Maria—I feel anxious to know whether you got my last letter safely[1]—& above all how you are—There was a little embroglio with your last, from the letter being too heavy for a frank—but if you enclose under cover to the Speaker, this need not disturb you—Do let me hear how your health is—and whether this warm weather has been too much for you—or revived you with a reflex of Italy.—Claire says that it is so hot at Pisa that existence is a burthen—here it is pleasant enough to exist, if one has nothing else to do.—

Mrs Godwin is gone to Herne Bay[2] to try to recover a little health after an attack of Influenza & tic douleureux—I am in town with Percy during his holydays—to keep Papa company on her absence—Papa likes the heat— & the few less warm days that interpose he calls quite wintry.—Percy is fat & blooming—the acquaintances of the Shelleys find him very like that family—Jane is quite well—She has dined with me frequently lately, to meet Papa with whom she is a great favourite   Dina is grown taller than Percy & is a very fine girl—Edward improves; under Jeff's care he must turn out well—I often wish I had a <u>Dah</u> for Percy, who is not quite amenable to feminine management—not that he is disobedient—& being very trust-worthy & childish no evil results as yet—but bad habits of imperiousness & thinking only of himself are difficult to be got over—& will be hurtful to him hereafter—and yet a <u>Dah</u> must be something very wonderful for him to respect & obey—& so perhaps it is best as it is—& as it is likely to be for evermore.

I went to the House of Lords the other Night & heard the Debate on the Tithe Question[3]—Is Lord Brougham a favourite of yours? <u>Buffone</u>

<u>sublime</u>[4] the Italians would call him—as with all his powers, he plays the Buffoon in the house.—His wit & sarcasms provoke laughter—but his want of dignity ill befits the Ld High Chancellor. I am very angry with him for his speech on the poor laws[5]—

What would I give could I see you again. If I were able to make a trip to Devonshire you would soon see me in your seclusion—sympathizing with Sig. G. [*Signor Giovanni, John Gisborne*] & trying to rally the spirit of life in you. Did I tell you of my misfortune, in my Aunt,[6] my Mother's surviving sister, coming over & settling at Pe{n}tonville—Everina was never a favourite with any one—& now she is the most intolerable of God's creatures. The worst is, that being poor & friendless, it is on my conscience to pay her attention—and she is so disagreable to me, that I know no punishment so great as spending an hour in her Company.—Dont let me lead you into a mistake—others might like her—for she can be amusing & means well—but her queerness—her assumption—the right that she thinks she has to annoy me, makes me deplore that I cannot <u>purchase</u> exemption from personal attentions—& I do as much as I can.—The many sorrows & cares I have—& the very little good that is sprinkled over my melancholy existence, renders me blameably intollerant of annoyance.

Adieu, my dearest Friend—pray write & let me know how you are—My Novel is not published yet & God knows when it will be—it is printed & that is all I know about it.—Jane & Papa send kindest messages—Make my kindest remembrances to Sig. Giov. & believe with—with the greatest anxiety to know how you are

Ever Affectionately Yours
MWShelley

ADDRESS: Mrs Gisborne / To the care of Dr. Budd / Plymouth / Devon. [*In another hand*] Mrs Gisborne / Plymouth / Devon / ES. Ruthven. POSTMARK: FREE / 19 AU 19 / 1834. ENDORSED: 7 Eaton Street / recd 20th Augt / 1834 / ansd 22nd Do / Mary Shelley. PUBLISHED: Jones, #439. TEXT: MS., Bodleian Library (MS., Shelley, Adds., c. 6, ff. 180–82).

1. Mary Shelley's 17 July [1834] letter and this one were replied to in Maria Gisborne's ?August–22 August 1834 letter (Abinger MSS., Bodleian Library). Both Mary Shelley's letters were franked by Edward Southwell Ruthven (1772–1836; *DNB*), Irish politician and M.P. Thomas Moore's 9–10 August 1834 *Journal* entry notes that Ruthven called on Mary Shelley.

2. A seaside resort eight miles northeast of Canterbury. Mary Jane Godwin was at Herne Bay from 6 August through 3 September (Godwin, Journal).

3. The debate, on 11 August 1834, dealt with the question of the payment of Irish tithes used to support the Episcopal Church, which angered Irish Catholics and led to a tithe war in 1831. In August 1833 an Irish Church temporalities bill was passed to relieve taxpayers from the burden of parish expenses for the Irish episcopate, but it failed to apply the savings to secular purposes, which brought another wave of outrage. The tithe issue was resolved in July 1838 by the conversion of tithes to fixed rent charges (Great Britain, *Hansard's Parliamentary Debates,* 3d ser., 25 [1834], cols. 1143–1207).

4. "Sublime fool."

5. The new Poor Law, debated on 11 August 1834, altered earlier relief legislation. The new law limited permitted charitable doles only to sick and aged paupers and established workhouses where able paupers were put to work. Brougham's arguments were taken largely

from Malthus (Great Britain, *Hansard's Parliamentary Debates*, 3d ser., 25 [1834], cols. 1207–24).

6. Everina Wollstonecraft (1765–1843), Mary Wollstonecraft Godwin's youngest sister.

To Maria Gisborne   Harrow   October 30   Nov. 7 [1834]

My dearest Maria—Thank you many times for your kind dear letter[1]—God grant that your constitution may yet bear you up a long time & that you may continue impressed with the idea of your <u>happiness</u>. Your expression is not ill applied—the object of tender solicitude—necessary & dear to one whom you love & esteem, you enjoy a greater portion of happiness than many whose lots are less beset by pain—To be loved is indeed necessary— sympathy & companionship are the only sweets "to make the nauseous draught of life go down"[2]—And I, who feel this, live in a solitude, such as since the days of Hermits in the desert, no one was ever before condemned to! I see no one—I speak to none—except perhaps for a chance half hour in the course of a fortnight. I never walk out beyond my garden—because I <u>cannot</u> walk alone:—you will say I ought to force myself—so I thought once, & tried—but it would not do—The sense of desolation was too oppressive—I only find relief from the sadness of my position by living a dreamy existence from which realities are excluded—but going out disturbed this—I wept—my heart beat with a sense of injury & wrong—I was better shut up. Poverty prevents my visiting town—I am too far for visitors to reach me—I must bear to the end—when & what will that be? You say truly that my father-in-law's prolonged life will ruin me—it has done so— twelve years have I spent, the currents of life benumbed by poverty—and meanwhile he does all he can to injure the future prospects of Percy & myself. Of him I think,—life & hope are over for me. You may guess that absorbed in him, I adhere to your advice of cultivating his affection—Fate shews her determination to drive me to him alone—she cuts me off from love, friendship, society, ambition; she gives me him alone—but there is no sympathy in a child—& though I look forward to reaping a subsequent harvest from my sacrifices (how likely to be blighted—he will marry—& there ends a Mother's happiness) yet for the present something more is needed—something not so <u>unnatural</u> as my present life. Not that I often feel ennui—I am too much employed—too much a being of dreams—but it hurts me—it destroys the spring of my mind; it makes me at once over sensitive with my fellow creatures, & yet their victim & dupe—it takes all strength from my character—making me, who by nature am too much so— timid. I need to have one resource, a belief in <u>my good fortune</u>; this is exchanged after twelve years of <u>One</u> Adversity, blotted & sprinkled by <u>many</u> adversities,—a dark ground with sad figures painted on it—to a perfect belief in my ill fortune—Percy is spared to me because I am to live—I should be free & die if———but no—He is a blessing; my heart acknowledges that he is perhaps as great a one as any human being possesses. & indeed, my dear friend, while I suffer I do not repine while he remains,— He is not all you say—he has no ambition—& his talents are not so transcendant as you appear to imagine but he is a fine, spirited, clever Boy— & I think promises good things—If hereafter I have reason to be proud of him—these melancholy days & weeks at Harrow will brighten in my imagination—And they are not Melancholy—I am seldom so—but they are not right—& it will be a good thing if they terminate happily soon   At the same time I cannot in the least regret having come here. It was the only way I had of educating Percy in a public school—of which institution, at least here at Harrow, the more I see, the more I like—besides that it was Shelley's wish that his son should be brought up at one. It is indeed peculiarly suited to Percy—and whatever he will be—he will be twice as much as if he had been brought up in the narrow confinement of a private school— The boys here have liberty to the verge of licence—yet of the latter, save the breaking of a few windows now & then, there is none. His life is not quite what it would be if he did not live with me—but the greater scope given to the cultivation of the affections is surely an advantage—Then it cultivates his hospitality, since his friends would rather dine badly with him than well at their tutors—He has two who frequent the house—he will not extend the number, for fear of their annoying me—but sometimes he gives breakfasts to 6 or 8—& so gets a portion of popularity, despite my poverty— this last has caused him to be quizzed now & then—the character I hear from others that he bears among his companions, is that he is very clever, & gives more help than any boy in the school, but is very haughty—it is odd that with me he is yielding either to persuasion or rebuke—but with his Boys—their utmost violence can never make him give in a jot—he can say <u>No</u>, which I cannot do—& has lively spirits—& is indeed a strange mixture of Shelley & I—he wants sensibility—but I fancy mine at his age was almost as covert—except that Mrs Godwin had discovered long before my excessive & romantic attachment to my Father—he is not cruel to animals, & he likes them but has no tender solicitude about them. But when he has suffered himself he will feel for others—May that day be far off!

Nov. 17

So much was written some time ago—& has been waiting for a frank—now I send it—You heard of the dreadful fire of the Houses of P. [*Parliament*][3]— We saw it here from its commencement blazing like a Volcano—it was dreadful to see—but fortunately I was not aware of the site—Papa lives close to the Speakers so you may imagine my alarm when the news reached me—fortunately without foundation, as the fire did not gain that part of the Speaker's house near them—so they were not even inconvenienced. The poor dear Speaker & Speakress have lost dreadfull[y]—what was not burnt is broken smoked & drenched—all their pretty things & magni[ficent] furniture & princely chambers—the h[ouse] was a palace—for the sake of convenience [   ] the Commons, they are to take up their abode among the ruins.

Why did not Sig. G [*Signor Giovanni, John Gisborne*] send his MS.[4] It is sure to interest from the very circumstance you mentioned of its being true. You have awakened my curiosity & I long to see it—Do, dear Signor G. send it!—Jane I believe has written to you—She talks of coming here for a day or two—You allude to Henry?—Have you news of him? What is he doing & where is he?

Now to your questions[5]—I am reading Caspar Hauser[6]—its being an invention takes from the interest—if it were true, it w^d be a deeply exciting work—It reminds me much of Calderon's La Vida es Sueño[7]—My book is called Lodore—I know nothing of when it is to be published—I have heard nothing of the Booksellers intentions since it was printed—but I suppose it must be published this winter—Papa's Necromancers was published last summer—has it not made its appearance in Plymouth—Percy likes animals & is not cruel—but there is a certain indolence in his disposition (which indeed pervades all his actions—except when he has a <u>desire</u> for a thing, & then he w^d go thro' fire & water—in this he is like me) that renders him inattentive to the wants of his pets—so I have reduced them to one dog—a smooth-haired terrier—ugly—except in face, sagacious & affectionate—Even with him I am obliged to attend to his wants.—Percy is now 15—

You are very good to write so often—I am always anxious to hear of your health & delighted to get your letters—Reading your letter again I fancy I ought to have sent to Mr Curtis's.[8] I have [*cross-written*] not done so but will—Signor G's keeping back his MS. made me neglect it—it was very wrong in him. Adieu my dear friend, God preserve you & diminish your sufferings—With Kindest wishes for you & Sig. G

Ever Aff^{ly} Y^s

MWShelley

ADDRESS: Mrs Gisborne / Plymouth / Devon. [*In another hand*] Mrs Gisborne / Plymouth / Devon / AW Beauclerk. POSTMARKS: (1) FREE / 19 NO 19 / 1834; (2) [   ] / 19 NO 19 / 1834; (3) 4. EVEN. 4 / NO. 19 / 1834. ENDORSED: Harrow 17th Nov / 1834 / rec. 20th Do / Ans. / Mary. PUBLISHED: Jones, #440. TEXT: MS., Bodleian Library (MS., Shelley, Adds., c. 6, ff. 183–85).

1. Dated 14 October 1834 (Abinger MSS., Bodleian Library).

2. See [?September–October 1832], n. 5.

3. Fire destroyed Parliament on 16 October 1834.

4. John Gisborne's "Evelina" was sent to Mary Shelley, but she was unable to arrange for its publication and returned it (Maria Gisborne to Mary Shelley, 20 October 1835, Abinger MSS., Bodleian Library).

5. Mary Shelley responded to all of Maria Gisborne's questions except "What do you intend to do with your beautiful Matilde?" (see vol. I, 28 August 1819, n. 5, and 2 June 1822, n. 8).

6. Anselm von Feurbach, *Caspar Hauser*, translated from the German (London: Simpkin, 1833), based on the life of Kaspar Hauser (?1812–33), a German who became the subject of a celebrated mystery. It was alleged that he was of German nobility. In 1828 he was left with the Nuremberg authorities, and the following year he was wounded by an unidentified assailant.

In 1832 he came under the protection of the fourth earl Stanhope, but in 1833 he died of a wound, perhaps self-inflicted. His story inspired many works, including: Philip Henry Stanhope, the fifth earl (1821–55), *Tracts Relating to Caspar Hauser* (1836), and Verlaine's poem *Sagesse* (1881).

7. Published in 1635 (see vol. I, [27–30 November 1819], 13 December [1820], and 4 April [1826], n. 1).

8. Maria Gisborne indicated that she had sent a small parcel for Mary Shelley in care of Stephen Curtis, No. 19 Coleman Street. Curtis was the brother of the Gisbornes' friend who was a seller of books and musical instruments at Plymouth (Maria Gisborne to Mary Shelley, ?August and 22 August 1834, Abinger MSS., Bodleian Library).

*To Richard Bentley   Harrow   17 Nov [1834]

Dear Sir

I hear nothing of the publication of "Lodore"—nor of the copies I am to have—Will you tell me when it is likely to be published & when I can have my copies (11—I have had 1—) & I will send word how I wish them to be distributed

                               I am Dr Sir
                               Y^s Ob^{ly}
                               MWShelley

ADDRESS: R Bentley Esq / 8 New Burlington St. POSTMARKS: (1) T.P / Harrow; (2) 7. NIGHT. 7 / NO. 14 / 1834. UNPUBLISHED. TEXT: MS., Pforzheimer Library.

*To Charles Ollier   Harrow   30 Dec. [1834]

My dear Sir

The World is turned topsy turvy I know—but are <u>you</u> turned with it? Where are you? Where is 8 New Burlington St? Where is lost Lodore? Do let me hear from you! If the season were more favourable, & you had leisure, I would ask you to pay me a visit; And if you can, shall be delighted to see you—Meanwhile do send me tidings of my lost Sheep—& if the copies can be distributed as I wish—& if any of us are alive & what doing?— You & yours I hope are well.

                             Ever truly yours
                             MWShelley

ADDRESS: Chas Ollier Esq / 8 New Burlington St. POSTMARKS: (1) T.P / Harrow; (2) 12. NOON. 12 / DE. 31 / 1834. UNPUBLISHED. TEXT: MS., Pforzheimer Library.

My Dear Friend

When you spoke in September of wishing to see me on business—I suppose it was concerning it—& S—& if I had had any thing agreable to say I would {not} have forestalled you. Even now I can say nothing to the purpose. You know a little better than a year ago I was in a most terrible predicament for want of money—I have been making some way since then—but this Xmas sees me very poor indeed—If absolutely necessary I could promise a little next Midsummer—and I hope to do better & better—I am economizing—living alone & with no extra expences—Except that Percy is a great & growing one—so I must be able to meet at last the bill of the year by next Xmas.

But I write to you now in a dilemma—Percy went to town on Monday Janʸ 5ᵗʰ & ordered a <u>coat</u>—now you must know that this coat is a matter of great importance—as Percy has just entered the 5ᵗʰ form—where a tailed coat is <u>de riguer</u>, & he cannot make his appearance at school—nor in Harrow, without it—He writes me word today "What I'm to do I don't know—for Aylieff² has not begun my coat, and says he dont know when he <u>can</u> begin it"—Does this <u>stop</u> arise from his wanting money first—I have not heard from him—& know nothing—but do you know any thing?—nothing can be more disagreable than the delay for school begins tomorrow—Will you let me know what is to be done—if it is mere delay & stupidity perhaps you would immediately write a note to Aylieff, telling him to send it out of hand—

Heaven help me—my life is hard work—& very different from any thing I anticipated—but believe me, I speak the simplest truth when I say, that my chief annoyance now is being obliged to worry you—& that false calculations & hopes should have thrown me so [*cross-written, p. 1*] back in money matters—I will do my best to arrange this better hereafter, meanwhile pray assist me on this occassion

I hope you & yours are well

Yours very truly
MWShelley

UNPUBLISHED. TEXT: MS., Pforzheimer Library.

1. The familiarity of the salutation of this letter and the letter's subject suggest that Thomas Love Peacock was the addressee. Peacock, as executor of Shelley's estate, often assisted Mary Shelley in business matters. Another letter on the same subject also dated 13 January 1835 and addressed to "My dear Friend" has come to my attention too late for inclusion in this volume. (It will appear in an appendix of additional letters in volume 3 of this edition.) The second letter seems to have been in response to a reply from the addressee to the letter here published. It indicates that Mary Shelley would engage to thenceforth pay Aylieff's bill regularly at Christmas, that she would prefer to retain Aylieff as Percy Florence's tailor, and wished the addressee to arrange these matters.

2. Joseph Aylieff & Co., tailors, located at 5 St. James's Square.

My dear Hunt

Thank you for your kind letter—I hope things are going on as prosper-
ously as you expected—I am glad to hear of dear Henry's destination[1]—
he was a very fine boy—when I saw him last—and no doubt still <u>tops</u> Percy—
though for size <u>round</u>, I am afraid he must yield.—

Beleive me I did not think of currying your public influence for my book
when I wrote, for valuable as that is—it did not enter my head—Where
the book is, I cannot even imagine—it has been printed these 10 Months
but I hear nothing of it & can extract no information from Burlington St—
which I strongly suspect, has become a Ward of S[t] Luke's.[2] A volume of
the Lives, is coming out directly. Is out that is on the 1st   Unfortunately
before I was applied to—some of the <u>best lives</u> were in other hands—The
Omnipresent M[r] Montgomery wrote Dante & Ariosto in the present Vol.—
the rest are mine.[3]

I wish I could look with the indulgence you do on Shelley's relations.
Sir Tim indeed, were he alone, I could manage—did I see him—violent as
he is—he has a heart & I am sure I could have made a friend of him. It is
Lady S—— who is my bitter enemy—and her motive is the base one of
securing more money for herself and her terror was great lest I should see
Sir Tim at one time now there is no fear since the old Gentleman never
comes to town. Besides the sacra auri fames[4] (is that right syntax—I wager
not) her conduct having been very open to censure,[5] she naturally attacks
me—because those kind of women love detraction.

Janey paid me a visit yesterday   she is looking very well—we talked
about you, you know how great a favourite you are with her. I had already
got the books you mentioned. However defective these lives are (& I am
far from satisfied) I spared no pains to get information & to do my best.

I have not been to town for Months, I have no idea when I shall visit it
again—I am quite a prisoner. I cant tell you how civil & Kind the Conservatives have shewn themselves about Papa's Place which was in jeopardy[6]—
The D. of W. [*Duke of Wellington*] of [*and*] Sir Robert Peel both have shewn
the greatest consideration, besides the <u>real good</u> of continueing him in it—
They have not the <u>Morgue</u>[7] of our Whigs.—Do write and let me know how
you all are. It is too late in the day to congratulate Thornton—but I <u>do</u>
wish him & Kate[8] all happiness with all my heart—They are both deserv-
ing—With love to Marianne & best wishes, I am dear Hunt

Sincrerly Y[s] Evr
MWShelley

I have mislaid your letter & forget the address—I fear <u>Chelsea</u>[9] w[d] not
be enough so send the letter to M[r] Hunters

ADDRESS: To be forwarded / Leigh Hunt Esq / Rowland Hunter Esq / St. Paul's Church Yd.
POSTMARKS: (1) T.P / Harrow; (2) 7. N[IGH]T. 7 / FE [   ] / 1835. ENDORSED: M Shelley.
PUBLISHED: Jones, #441. TEXT: MS., Huntington Library (HM 2756).

1. [James] Henry Sylvan Leigh Hunt seems to have been prepared to go abroad for a career, but instead, through his father he obtained a Treasury appointment in 1836, which he lost in 1852 (Brewer, *The Holograph Letters*, p. 216; *SC*, V, 261).

2. St. Lukes Hospital for the insane, founded 1751.

3. See 30 April 1834, n. 1.

4. "Cursed hunger for gold," Virgil *Aeneid* 3. 57.

5. Perhaps a reference to Shelley's belief that his mother had had an affair with Edward Fergus Graham (?1778–1852), who was employed by Sir Timothy Shelley (*Keats-Shelley Memorial Bulletin* (24 [1973]: 20–24).

6. On 14 October 1833 the Whig government decided to eliminate certain sinecures, Godwin's among them. Action on this was delayed and when, from November 1834 through April 1835, a Tory Ministry headed by Sir Robert Peel held power, the Tories saved Godwin's post (Locke, *Godwin*, pp. 337–38).

7. "Haughtiness."

8. A reference to the marriage of Thornton Hunt and Katherine Gliddon (see vol. I, 2–5 October [1823], n. 3).

9. The Hunts lived at No. 4, Upper Cheyne Row, Chelsea, from 1833 through the summer of 1840 (Hunt, *Correspondence* I, 267). Their neighbors and new friends were Thomas and Jane Carlyle, who lived at No. 5 (now renumbered 24) Cheyne Row.

*To Mary Ellen Peacock[1] [Harrow 3 February 1835]

My dear Ellen

Many thanks for your dear little note, which brought the very welcome intelligence of your Papa's being better[2]—I hope he is now quite convalescent—do let me know. I have a great inclination—if he is well enough to see any one, to drive over to see you—let me know whether my visit would please him.

Percy is indeed a big boy—but you also are grown into a young lady—I should like much to see you

Believe me, dear Ellen,[3]

ADDRESS: Miss Peacock / Lower Halliford / Esher / MS. Surrey. POSTMARKS: (1) T.P / Harrow; (2) [ ]X / 3 FE 3 / 1835; (3) 7. NIGHT. 7 / FE. 3 / 1835. UNPUBLISHED. TEXT: MS., Houghton Library.

1. Mary Ellen Peacock (1821–61), Thomas Love Peacock's eldest daughter. In January 1844 she married Lieutenant Edward Nicolls, who drowned in March 1844. She and her daughter, Edith Nicolls (afterwards Clarke) (1844–1926), went to live in London. There Mary Ellen Nicolls met George Meredith (1828–1909), poet and novelist, whom she married in August 1849. One son, Arthur Meredith (1853–90), was born of this marriage. In 1857 Mary Ellen Meredith left her husband and formed a liaison with the pre-Raphaelite painter Henry Wallis (1830–1916) (Van Doren, *Peacock*, pp. 229–31; for a detailed account of the life of Mary Ellen Peacock see Diane Johnson, *Lesser Lives* [New York: Alfred A. Knopf, 1972].

2. See 9 February [1835].

3. The signature has been cut away.

My dearest Friend—I am rendered anxious by your long silence I fear you suffer through the vile winter weather, yet we have not much cold—& it must be warmer in your Devonshire—Do write—I have no news—I have scarcely stirred from this place since I wrote—I confess that sometimes I am visited by fits of dreadful despair at my exile from all my friends—especially when any circumstance renders me anxious about any of them—& I hear nothing for days & days—& weeks—& sometimes not at all—It is too bad—could I get to town readily I would not mind—but it is always a matter of calculation & fear of spending money &c &c.

Percy is very well—he is in the 5 form, with a tailed coat & watch, & quite a man—his leg annoys me sometimes, and I think it very hard that I cannot get a horse for him. My father feels the cold weather, but is well. The Conservatives have been very civil & kind to him—And I feel that his income is safe while Sir Robert Peel is in—It is strange but so it is—Sir Robert wrote to him to say that a sense of justice as well as of gratitude from the pleasure he had received from his works would make him Do all he could—& he wrote to my friend The Speaker at the same time, to say that he did not doubt but that Papa's income would be secured to him. We had a very clever letter from Claire the other day—she describes the annoyances of of her life—& her rage at Church, when the Clergyman begins "We have followed too much the devises & desires of our own hearts—" "I," she continues, "who am always forced to do every thing that my heart detests."—Apropos of a little blasphemy, I must tell you of Ld Alvanley's[1] Môt on the grossesse of our gracious Adelaide;[2] He says that it reminds him of the psalm—Lord Howe[3] wondrous are thy works![4]—

I must tell you that I have had the offer of 600£ for an edition of Shelley's works with life & notes.[5] I am afraid it cannot be arranged yet at least—& the life is out of the question—but in talking over it the question of letters comes up—You know how I shrink from all private detail for the public—but Shelley's letters are beautifully written, & every thing private could be omitted—You must have many of them. Would you allow the publisher to treat with you for their being added to my edition?—If I could arrange all as I wish, they might be an acquisition to the book, and being transacted through me you could not see any inconvenance in receiving the price they w^d be worth to the bookseller. This is all in aria as yet—but I should like to know what you think about it.

Poor Peacock has been dangerously ill of an inflamation of his lungs. He is in the Country at Halliford, with his children—his wife in Stamford St.—is not this too good? she must be mad. You know I suppose that when his Mother died in 33, his wife played the same part—& though at the same time her children were ill of the scarlet fever, made her maid write word that she was too unwell to join them. I first heard of poor Peacock's danger in a note from his daughter—I told Jane—& Jeff wishing for news, wrote to Mrs Peaco[ck] directing to Stamford St—fancying that Peacock was there. He gets for answer from the <u>wife</u> dated Stamford Street "I am happy to inform that the accounts from Halliford are more favourable—& that our poor friend is pronounced out of danger"—And yet her husband is the person in the world she cares for <u>most</u>—Do you think that a very powerful magnifier c^d discern her heart?—I think not—

I write all this, yet very anxious to hear from you—never mind postage, but do write. Percy is reading the <u>Antigone</u>—but he has no talent for latin verses—he makes sad work—He has begun Mathematics—Mrs Cleveland & Jane dined with me the other day—M^rs C—[*Cleveland*] thought Percy wonderfully improved—he gets more <u>disinvo{l}tura</u>⁶ yet that is not his forte.—The Vol. of Lardner's Cyclopedia with <u>my lives</u> was published on the 1st of this Month—It is called Lives of Eminent literary men Vol. I— The lives of Dante & Ariosto are by the Omnipresent Mr Montgomery— the rest are mine—How is S.G. [*Signor Giovanni, John Gisborne*]? What are you doing—Do write, my dearest Maria, & believe me Ever & Ever

Affectionately Y^s
MWShelley

I have just begun the Adone⁷—& like it.

ADDRESS: Mrs Gisborne / Plymouth / Devon. [*In another hand*] Mrs Gisborne / Plymouth / Sir J Rickman. POSTMARK: FREE / 10 FE 10 / 1835. ENDORSED: Harrow 9th Feby—1835 / rec. 12th Do / Ans / Mary. PUBLISHED: Jones, #442. TEXT: MS., Bodleian Library (MS., Shelley, Adds., c. 6, ff. 186–87).

1. William Arden, second baron Alvanley (1789–1849), described by Frances Kemble as "the keenest wit and one of the finest gentlemen about town" (*Records of a Girlhood* [New York: Henry Holt & Co., 1884], p. 456).

2. Adelaide of Saxe-Meinigen (1792–1849), wife of William IV (1765–1837), who succeeded to the throne on the death of George IV, his brother, on 26 June 1830. Mary Shelley attended the coronation of William IV on 8 September 1831 (MWS Journal).

3. Richard William Penn Howe, first earl Howe (1796–1877).

4. Thomas Moore noted on 11 February 1835: "Letter from Mrs. Shelley—Joke current in town on the reported pregnancy of the Queen—'Lord Howe wondrous are thy works!' " (Moore *Journal*).

5. See 22 January 1834.

6. "Poise."

7. Giambattista Marino, *L'Adone* (1623).

*TO JOHN MURRAY   Harrow   10 Feb—1835.

My dear Sir

I live here so entirely out of the world that I never see you now—Which I regret—but hope you are well—& when I come to town should be very glad of a call. I will let you know when I am there.—

Will you send me your prospectus of your new Edition of Boswell's Life of Johnson—It is a book I long to possess—especially Mr Croker's¹ edition—the best of all editions of the most delightful book in the world—Now <u>pray</u> <u>pray</u> dont think I am fishing for a <u>present</u>—for I am not—I shall get it in exchange for some of my stupid pen & ink labors—but let me know all about it.—

I <u>do</u> <u>not</u> <u>fish</u> for it—if I <u>fished</u> for any thing it would be for the "Illustrations of Ld Byron"—which I <u>almost hoped</u> to have—especially when Trelawny got them[2]—but I was not so lucky—I suppose you <u>could</u> not & Finden <u>would</u> not—for I could not make up my mind to be exhibited among the portraits, I have such a dislike of display

I am dear Sir
Most truly Y^s
MWShelley

ADDRESS: John Murray Esq / 50 Albermarle St. POSTMARKS: (1) T.P / Harrow; (2) 7. NIGHT. 7 / FE. 10 / 1835. ENDORSED: 1835 Febry 10 / Shelley Mrs. UNPUBLISHED: Jones, #443, in summary. TEXT: MS., John Murray.

1. *The Life of Samuel Johnson by James Boswell*, a new edition with additions and notes by John Wilson Croker, 5 vols. (London: John Murray, 1831), was republished by Murray in ten volumes in 1835.

2. See 30 April [1832], n. 2; 15 April 1833, n. 4.

To JOHN MURRAY   Harrow—Friday [20 February 1835][1]

My dear Sir

Many Thanks for the Illustrations—which are so beautiful & interesting—I am delighted at the success of your publication   I have read Boswell I am sure ten times—& hope to read it many more it is the most amusing book in the world, besides that I do love the kind hearted wise & Gentle Bear—& think him as loveable a ⟨Man⟩ friend as a profound philosopher—I do not see in your list of Authors whence Anecdotes are extracted the name of M^{rs} d'Arblay—Her account of Dr Johnson Mrs Thrale &c in her Memoirs of Dr Burney[2] are highly interesting & valuable—

I am so unhappy that Sir C. Manners Sutton has lost his election as Speaker[3]—It is not that I am not a Whig—I suppose I am one—but I think the Whigs have treated him most shabbily—electing him themselves as they did last ⟨Par^t [*Parliament*]⟩ year—They will never have such a Speaker again. I feel particularly kindly towards the Conservatives also just now as they have behaved with the greatest consideration towards my father—preserving him in his place, which was about to be abolished by the Whigs & that with a <u>manner</u> as gracious as the <u>deed</u>. The Duke of Wellington & above all the [*cross-written*] Prince of our Orators Sir Robert Peel deserves my gratitude & has it—By the way what will the Whigs do for an orator in the Commons—I never heard Canning—& never heard any Speaker who I thought could claim the praise of a good Orator except Sir Robert Peel—

his speeches have all a beginning middle & end—he rises with his subject
& carries the hearer along with him—L. [*Lord*] Brougham I only heard in
the House of Lords & his want of dignity & his insolent sarcasm towards
the Peers annoyed me—

My boy is now in the 5th form & is very promising & clever & <u>good</u>—I
am dear Sir

Very truly Y[s]
MWShelley

PUBLISHED: Jones, #444. TEXT: MS., John Murray.

    1. See the previous letter and n. 3 below.

    2. Frances Burney, Madame D'Arblay (1752–1840; *DNB*), author, edited her father's *Memoirs* in 1832. Hester Lynch Thrale (1741–1821; *DNB*) was a close friend of Samuel Johnson's.

    3. Sir Charles Manners-Sutton's reelection, opposed by the Whigs, was lost on 19 February 1835. He was succeeded by James Abercromby (1776–1858; *DNB*), afterward Lord Dunfermline.

*To Mary Ellen Peacock   Harrow—7th March [1835]

My dear Ellen

I am much grieved to learn from M[r] Hogg that he had heard that your
dear Papa was not quite so well again—the weather being unfavorable—
You have been very good to answer my enquiries—but do, dear Ellen, write
by the earliest post—& tell me how he is <u>now</u>—I should be so glad to hear
that he is again better—so be a good dear girl & let me know as soon as
you can—& forgive me for troubling you—but I am sure you will—as your
Papa is almost my oldest Friend—and I cannot hear of his illness without
feeling very unhappy—

I hope you & your brother & sister[1] are well—Ever Affectionately Yours

MWShelley

Write me rather a longer note & tell me what the Doctor says—

ADDRESS: Miss Peacock / Lower Halliford / Esher—Surrey / MS. POSTMARKS: (1) T.P / Harrow; (2) EX / 7 MR 7 / 1835; (3) 7. NIGHT. 7 / MR. 7 / 1835; (4) 7. NIGHT. 7 / MR. 7 / 1835. UNPUBLISHED. TEXT: MS., Yale University Library.

    1. Edward Gryffydh Peacock (1825–67), first a midshipman in the Indian Navy, then a clerk in the Examiner's Department of the East India Company from 1844 to 1858. Following that, he was a solicitor. He married Mary Hall and had one son, Thomas Love (b. 1851). Rosa Jane Peacock (1827–57) married Henry Collinson and had two children, Margaret Ellen (1854–57) and Richard Vyse (1856–57) (information about Edward and Rosa Peacock supplied by Nicholas Joukovsky).

Percy Bysshe Shelley

Wash drawing and etching by John Taylor Wedgwood,
courtesy of the Humanities Research Center,
University of Texas at Austin

July 1814

This book is sacred to me and
as no other creature shall ever look
into it I may write in it what I
please — yet what shall I write
that I love the author beyond all
powers of expression and that I
am parted from him

Dearest & only love by that
love we have promised to each
other although I may not be your
I can never be another's—
But I am thine exclusi-
ly thine — by the kiss of love by
The glance none can beside
The smile none else might under—
The whispered thought of hearts allied
The pressure of the thrilling hand
I have pledged & my self to thee &
sacred is the gift—
I remember your words you
are now Mary going to mix with
many & for a moment I shall dep
but in the solitude of your chamb
I shall be with you — yes you are
ever with me sacred vision

Double-page opening of the inside back cover
of the copy of *Queen Mab* given by Shelley to Mary Shelley,
courtesy of the Huntington Library

But ah I feel in this was given
a blessing never meant for me
Thou art too like a dream from heaven
For earthly love to merit thee.

Thou see, Mary, I have
not forgotten you

Teresa Guiccioli

Engraving by Henry Thomas Ryall
from a drawing by William Brockedon,
courtesy of John Murray

John Howard Payne

Engraving by H. B. Hall and Sons,
courtesy of the National Portrait Gallery,
Smithsonian Institution, Washington, D.C.

Thomas Love Peacock

Portrait by Henry Wallis, courtesy of the
National Portrait Gallery, London

Mary Ellen Peacock

Portrait by Henry Wallis, courtesy of the
University of California Press

Thomas Moore

Portrait by Sir Thomas Lawrence,
courtesy of John Murray

Frances Wright

Engraving by Nagel and Weingaetner,
courtesy of the National Portrait Gallery,
Smithsonian Institution, Washington, D.C.

Prosper Mérimée

Portrait by Simon Jacques Rochart,
courtesy of the Bibliothèque Nationale

Caroline Norton

Detail from a group portrait by Frank Stone,
courtesy of the National Portrait Gallery, London

Lady Sydney Morgan

Portrait by William Behnes, courtesy of the
National Portrait Gallery, London

*To Charles Ollier   [Harrow]   25th March [1835]

My dear Sir

At length I see that poor Lodore is crawling into existence—Now do pray remember that though I believe that there are only 6 "in the bond"[1]— that you promised me 12 copies—As soon as they are ready will you send a copy to (from the Author

    T.L. Peacock Esq
       East India House
(from the Author
Mr Godwin 13 New Palace Y^d
To the Viscountess Canterbury[2]
    New Palace Y^d
To the Honble Mrs Leicester Stanhope
    6 Hanover Sq.
To Mrs Paul
  to the care of
    Captain Beauclerk[3]
    23   Belgrave Cottage
    Belgrave St. Grosvenor Place
And send the rest to me at Harrow

Lady Stepney's Novel[4] shall be returned to you in a day or two—It is very clever & amusing—

Dont forget your promise to visit me at Harrow when this vile East wind ceases to destroy us—and present my Compliments to Mrs Ollier & tell her how gratified I shall be if she will accompany you. Harrow is a pretty <u>sight</u> though a dull abode—Let me know a day before your visit to secure my being at home

I am dear Sir
Yours truly
MWShelley

ADDRESS: Chas Ollier Esq / 8 New Burlington St. POSTMARKS: (1) T.P / [   ]hapel St; (2) 7. NIGHT. 7 / MR. 25 /1835. UNPUBLISHED. TEXT: MS., University of Iowa Library.

   1. *The Merchant of Venice* 4. 1. 259.

   2. On 10 March 1835 Sir Charles Manners-Sutton was created Baron Bottesford of Bottesford and Viscount Canterbury.

   3. George Beauclerk (1803–71), son of Charles George and Emily Beauclerk, and a captain in the 23d Regiment Royal Welsh Fusiliers. George Beauclerk was another member of the Beauclerk family with whom Mary Shelley was particularly friendly (see George Beauclerk to Mary Shelley, ?July–September 1834, Abinger MSS., Bodleian Library).

   4. *The Heir Presumptive*, 3 vols. (London: Richard Bentley, 1835).

To Gabriele Rossetti[1]   Harrow, 3^{zo} Aprile 1835

Signor Pregiat^{mo}

Vuol Scusare colla solita sua bontà un incomodo che la reco intorno al mio vergheggiare?[2] Sto in questo momento scrivendo la vita dell'illustre suo compatriota Alfieri;[3]—e vorrei sapere se inoltre la vita scritta da se stesso, ve ne sono altre vite o altri saggii, che mi daranno notizie pregiabili intorno al medesimo; vuol favorirmi, gentillissimo Signore Rosetti con delle informazioni.

E poi—dopo Alfieri, devo scrivere la vita del Monti[4]—della quale si sa pochissimo qui—chi fra voi altri hanno composto la vita sua?—e dove troverò quelle notizie che mi faranno consapevole degli avenimenti a lui accaduti—lettere scritte da lui, ve ne sono publicate?

Abito sempre questo paesaccio col mio figlio—così non vedo nè Lei, nè nessun de'miei amici che così raramente, che mi fa proprio disperare. Spera intanto che lei goda una buona salute—e quella prosperità che merita i talenti ed egregii pregii suoi.

Scusa questo Italiano barbarico—non sento il linguagio—non le parlo mai mai ne leggo pur sempre—ma pero che vuole! C'è una certa inusitatezza nella mia mente che mi fa sempre dire cento spropositi, quando tento di esprimermi in una lingua forestiera—tanto ne possiedo, non di meno, che basta per assicurarla che mi repeto sempre

Ammiratrice e serva sua
M. W. Shelley

[*Translation*]

Most honored Sir

Will you excuse with your usual goodness my troubling you about my [?writing]?[2] I am at this moment writing the life of your illustrious compatriot Alfieri;[3]—and I would like to know whether besides the life written by himself, there are any other lives or other essays, which will give me valuable notices concerning the same; will you favor me, my dearest Signor Rosetti with some information.

And then—after Alfieri, I have to write the life of Monti[4]—of whom very little is known here—who among you people have written his life?—and where shall I find such notices as will acquaint me with the incidents which befell him—of the letters written by him, have any been published?

I am still living in this wretched town with my son—so I see neither you nor any of my friends except so rarely, that I am really in despair. I hope meanwhile that you are enjoying good health—and that prosperity which your talents and distinguished qualities merit.

Excuse this barbarous Italian—I do not hear the language—I never never speak it {but} I read it constantly—but after all what do you expect! There is a certain disuse in my mind which always makes me utter a hundred blunders, when I try to express myself in a foreign language—I know enough of it, however, as suffices to assure you that I am always

Your admirer and servant
M. W. Shelley

POSTMARK: 18 PAID 35 / AP. 3 / NIGHT. PUBLISHED: Jones, #445. TEXT: E. R. Vincent, "Two Letters from Mary Shelley to Gabriele Rossetti," *Modern Language Review* 28 (October 1932): 459–61. TRANSLATION: John P. Colella.

1. Gabriele Rossetti (1783–1854), Italian patriot, poet, and professor at King's College, London, and his wife Frances Mary Lavinia Rossetti, (nee Polidori) (see 20 April 1835, n. 1), were the parents of Christina Georgina Rossetti, (1830–94), Dante Gabriel Rossetti (1828–82), and William Michael Rossetti (1829–1919) (for details of the life of Gabriele Rossetti see E. R. Vincent, *Gabriele Rossetti in England* [Oxford: Clarendon Press, 1936]; and R. A. Waller, *The Rossetti Family, 1824–1854* [Manchester: University of Manchester, 1932]). Mary Shelley may have met Gabriele Rossetti through the Novellos; through Godwin, who notes calling on him on 1 September 1829 (Journal); or through the John Dean Pauls, at whose home Rossetti performed as an "improvisare one night" (MWS Journal, 24 September [1830]). It is believed that Mary Shelley gave her copy of Leigh Hunt's *Foliage* (1818), inscribed by Hunt "To Mary Wollstonecraft Shelley / from her affectionate friend the author," to Gabriele Rossetti, who in turn gave it to Dante Gabriel Rossetti (*Quaritch Auction Catalogue*, New Series, Bulletin 1 [1982]: 10).

2. "To flog." This is an error by either E. R. Vincent or Mary Shelley. The word meant was probably *vergare* ("to write").

3. Vittorio Alfieri (1749–1803), Italian dramatist (see MWS, *Lives* [1835–37], II, for the life of Alfieri).

4. Vincenzo Monti (1754–1828), Italian poet (see MWS, *Lives* [1835–37], II, for the life of Monti).

*TO [?CHARLES OLLIER][1]   Harrow   April 6—1835

Dear Sir

I have seen Lodore a good deal advertized[2] and therefore expected the publication.—I shall be very glad if it succeeds—for your sake as well as my own.

I have always received from you <u>twelve</u> copies of my books—and I hope you will not send me fewer now—as that will put me to great inconvenience—and it will oblige me greatly if you can let me have that number.— I have marked on the other side[3] the persons to whom I wish them to be sent in town—but there are some copies which I wish to send abroad—the remainder therefore of the number, you will oblige me by sending <u>here</u>, by the Coach—I thank you for your promise of sending the copies directly & am, Dear Sir,

Yours truly
MWShelley

UNPUBLISHED. TEXT: MS., Pforzheimer Library.

1. A letter from Mary Shelley to Charles Ollier, dated Harrow, 6 April 1835, is listed in the Puttick and Simpson sale catalog for Monday, 22 July 1878.

2. On 3 April 1835 Godwin noted that both the *Athenaeum* and the *Literary Gazette* had received copies of *Lodore* though he had not (William Godwin, *Memoirs of Mary Wollstonecraft*, ed. W. Clark Durant [London: Constable & Co., 1927], p. 334). The *Athenaeum* and the *Literary Review* favorably reviewed *Lodore* on 28 March 1835; almost all of the other contemporary reviews also praised this novel (Lyles, *MWS Bibliography*, pp. 179–81).

3. The list is unlocated but see Mary Shelley's list to Charles Ollier in her letter of 25 March [1835].

To Gabriele Rossetti   Harrow   il 20 de Aprile 1835

Gentil^mo Signor Rosetti

La ringrazio tanto per la sua amabile risposta e le di lei premure per la interpresa di una penna pur troppo indegna di quei bellissimi nomi che danno un tal lustro alla sua patria. Intanto ho da farla un'altra domanda—ma temo di mostrarmi poca discreta, e la prego di dirmi schiettamente il suo parere—non vorrei avere l'apparenza di far spropositi impertinenti, e se la mia idea le pare impracticabile, non ne dica una parola a nessuno—

Mi dice che il suo suocero, il celebre Polidori[1] può narrare molte circostanze interessanti intorno all'Alfieri. La vita che scrivo sarà stampata nella Ciclopedia del Dottore Lardner—così è corta assai, cioè può fare una settantina di pagine, non più. Però, se potessi introdurre qualche notizie non conosciute, ma degne da essere publicate, mi farà assaissimo piacere. Non saprei se il Polidori volesse darmi queste notizie. Per esempio vorrei sapere se veramente era così malinconico e silenziale come dice il Cavaliere Hobhouse nella sua opera 'Illustrations to the Fourth Canto of Childe Harold'[2]—se mostrava amare gli amici suoi, e se fu riamato caldamente da loro—qualche annedoti me sarebbero gradevoli—e poi qualche notizie sulla Contessa di Albany.[3] V'è l'affettazione di silenzio in quanto tocca ad essa in tutto quel che sia scritta finora sopra l'Alfieri ma sicchè è ormai morta, questo non è più necessario. Fuorono maritati? Se no—non sene dice nulla—ma se lo furono, sarebbe bene di dichiararlo.

Sarò in Londra la Domenica prossima, e mi tratengherò costà per parecchi giorni. Ma sto in un quartiere così lontano dal suo (7 Upper Eaton St. Grosvenor Place) che sarebbe indiscreta di chiedere una visita di lei—ed assai più indiscreta di dire che se il Signor Polidori me vorebbe far visita forse mi dirà più facilmente che scriverà alcune cosine, come dicono i Toscani. Lascio far a lei—farà lei tutto quel che sia convenevole—e mi renderà risposta consuo comodo.

Ripetendo le grazie tante dovute alla sua bontà, Credami

Serva sua obligat^ma
M. W. Shelley.

(P.S.) Per quel che ho sentito era intrinseco il Alfieri col Guiccioli di Ravenna essendo l'ultimo giovanotto—ed ebbero insieme l'idea e l'interpresa non riuscita possibile di stabilire un Teatro nazionale in Italia. Forse ne è consapevole di questo il Signor Polidori. Ce n'è qualche opera istorica dove si troverà notizie sugli ultimi anni del real marito della Contessa di Albany—non so io—e sono nel bujo—Fu lui l'ultimo dei Stuardi, non è vero fuorchè il fratello, il Cardinale York?[4] Ah che impegno le do per rispondermi—ne ho veramente una vergogna indicibile adesso—ma è così buone lei!—e poi la grammatica di questa lettera sarà come la Cleopatra del Alfieri.[5]

[Translation]

Dearest Signor Rosetti

Thank you so much for your amiable reply and your interest in the undertaking of a pen but too unworthy of those great names which give such luster to your country. Meanwhile I have another question to ask you—but I am afraid of appearing to have little discretion, and I beg you to tell me your opinion candidly—I should not like to seem to be absurdly impertinent, and if my idea seems to you impracticable, don't say a word about it to anyone—

You tell me that your father-in-law, the celebrated Polidori[1] can relate many interesting circumstances regarding Alfieri. The life which I am writing will be printed in Doctor Lardner's Cyclopaedia—so it is very short, that is, it can amount to seventy-odd pages, not more. But, if I could introduce some notices not yet known, but worthy of publication, it would give me very great pleasure. I don't know whether Polidori wants to give me such notices. For example I should like to know whether Alfieri was really so melancholy and taciturn as Sir Hobhouse says in his work "Illustrations to the Fourth Canto of Childe Harold"[2]—whether he appeared to love his friends, and whether he was warmly loved by them in return—some anecdotes would be welcome—and also some information about the Countess of Albany.[3] There is the affectation of silence as to what relates to her in all that has been written so far about Alfieri but since she is now dead, this is no longer necessary. Were they married? If not—one need say nothing about it—but if they were, it would be well to make it known.

I shall be in London next Sunday, and I shall remain there several days. But I am in a quarter so distant from yours (7 Upper Eaton St. Grosvenor Place) that it would be indiscreet to ask you for a visit—and much more indiscreet to say that if Signor Polidori should wish to visit me perhaps he can tell me more easily than in writing some cosine ["little things"], as the Tuscans say. I leave it to you—you will do all that is fitting—and you will give me a reply at your leisure.

Repeating the thanks so much due to your kindness, believe me

Your much obliged servant
M. W. Shelley.

(P.S.) From what I have heard Alfieri was intimate with Guiccioli of Ravenna when the latter was a young man—and together they had the idea and design which turned out not to be possible of establishing a national theater in Italy. Perhaps Signor Polidori knows about this. Is there some historical work containing notices about the last years of the royal husband of the Countess of Albany—I don't know—and I am in the dark—He was the last of the Stuarts, was he not except his brother, the Cardinal of York?[4] Oh what trouble I am giving you to reply—I am really inexpressibly ashamed of it now—but you are so good!—and then the grammar of this letter must be like Alfieri's Cleopatra.[5]

POSTMARKS: (1) HARROW / 3 py. P. Paid; (2) 18 PAID 35 / AP. 20 / Night. PUBLISHED: Jones, #446. TEXT: Vincent, "Two Letters from Mary Shelley to Gabriele Rossetti." TRANSLATION: John P. Colella.

1. Gaetano Polidori (1764–1853), Italian translator and author, the father of Rossetti's wife Frances Mary Lavinia and of John William Polidori, Byron's physician (see vol. I, 1 June 1816, n. 3). Gaetano Polidori had been Alfieri's secretary.

2. John Cam Hobhouse, *Historical Illustrations to the Fourth Canto of Childe Harold* (London: John Murray, 1818).

3. Louise Maximilienne Caroline, countess of Albany (1752–1824), married Charles Edward, "the Young Pretender," Stuart claimant to the British throne (1720–88), but they were formally separated in 1784. Alfieri and the countess of Albany met in 1777 and formed a lifelong liaison.

4. Henry (1725–1807), cardinal duke of York.

5. Alfieri's first play, produced in 1775.

*TO LADY SYDNEY MORGAN[1]   7 Upper Eaton St.[2]   Sunday Morn[g]
                                                    [?26 April 1835]

[*Fragment*]   I am
            Dear Lady Morgan
            Very truly Yours
            MWShelley

ADDRESS: Lady Morgan / 49 Grosvenor Place. ENDORSED: from Mrs Shelley / author of / Frankenstein. UNPUBLISHED. TEXT: MS., Duke University Library.

1. In the winter of 1835 Sir Charles (1783–1843; *DNB*) and Lady Morgan were in London, where they met Godwin at a party. Lady Morgan noted: "We got on the subject of his poor son-in-law, Shelley, and his daughter, whom I shall go and see as soon as she comes to town" (Lionel Stevenson, *The Wild Irish Girl* [New York: Russell & Russell, 1969], p. 294). Godwin noted in his Journal that he was at a party also attended by Lady Morgan on 10 March 1835, that Sir Charles Morgan called on him on 11 March, and that he and Mary Shelley were at a party also attended by the Morgans on 17 March. It is probable, therefore, that the party at which Godwin spoke of Mary Shelley was on 10 March and that Mary Shelley met Lady Morgan for the first time shortly thereafter, perhaps on 17 March. The friendship between Mary Shelley and Lady Morgan was lifelong.

2. In her 20 April 1835 letter, Mary Shelley mentioned that she would be in London at 7 Upper Eaton Street for several days. Although she also resided at that address from 29 July through c. 14 September 1834, this letter can be dated during her c. 25–c. 28 April 1835 stay because of her new friendship with Lady Morgan (MWS Journal; Godwin, Journal).

*To Lady Sydney Morgan   [?   ]   Saturday   [?April 1835–51]

Dear Lady Morgan
Expect me at 6 tomorrow—<u>With thanks</u>

Ever Y^{rs}
MShelley

UNPUBLISHED. TEXT: MS., Fales Library, New York University.

*To Elizabeth Stanhope   Harrow—Saturday   [?23 May 1835]

Dear Mrs Stanhope
   I have just been reading The Wife[1] which pleases me greatly. I do not know which story I like best—They both contain such true observations—thoughts that come home to one's heart, even till it aches, as shew the Authoress to have the greatest sensibility joined to her acknowledged talent.—Is she vexed by Brinsley's marriage.[2] I am very glad of it—as a rich Bride must be of service to his fortunes—& that Sir Colguhoun who never let his daughter speak to any thing but a Lord (àla M^r. Birkbeck)[3] desserves no better.
   London is very full & you of course very gay. I was in town a few days ago[4] & intended & very much wished to see you—but I was taken very indisposed, & returned here having seen no one. I am still low & uncomfortable in health, which makes me regret less London gaieties; I like society—but it becomes a great trouble if one is not in strong health—Will you remember me to your Mother & make my excuses for not joining her party, to which she was so good as to invite me.
   I can't tell you how good I think you to write to me as you do   Your letters always afford me the greatest pleasure—so pray continue so kind & good a habit—though I can only answer you in this stupid way—How Anna[5] must be grown since I saw her—dear little thing, kiss her for me—And beleive me

Dear Mrs Stanhope
Yours Ever Sincerely
MWShelley

UNPUBLISHED. TEXT: MS., Fales Library, New York University.
1. "The Wife" and "Woman's Reward," 3 vols. (London: Saunders & Otley), published in April 1835, written by Caroline Elizabeth Sarah Norton, nee Sheridan (1808–77), granddaughter of Richard Brinsley Sheridan. In 1836 Caroline Norton's husband George Norton (1801–75) sued Lord Melbourne (1779–1848), the prime minister, for "criminal connection" with Caroline Norton. Although George Norton lost in this first step in a divorce proceeding, Caroline Norton's reputation was greatly damaged. She and her husband (who had separated and reconciled earlier) now separated amid much public scandal, and in accordance with the law, her husband gained total custody of their three sons. For a period of four years she was

not permitted to see her children. As a result of this, she became an activist for women's rights for child custody, and had printed two tracts which she had written, *Observations on the Natural Claim of a Mother to the Custody of Her Young Children* (1837) and *A Plain Letter to the Lord Chancellor* (published under the nom de plume Pearce Stevenson) (1839), as part of her political agitation for a change in the child-custody laws. She succeeded in changing the law in 1839, and thereafter divorced or separated wives were permitted access to their children.

Mary Shelley and Caroline Norton's friendship may have begun on 26 May 1835, when they were both guests of Dr. Lardner (*The Diaries of William Charles Macready, 1833–1851,* ed. William Toynbee, 2 vols. [1912; reprint ed., New York: Benjamin Blom, 1969], I, 229). By late 1835 or early 1836 Mary Shelley and Caroline Norton were close friends; and during Caroline Norton's period of greatest social ostracism Mary Shelley was one of her confidantes and supporters (for a full biography which includes many letters from Caroline Norton to Mary Shelley see Perkins, *Mrs. Norton*).

2. On 18 May 1835 Richard Brinsley Sheridan (?1809–88), Caroline Norton's brother, eloped with Marcia Maria Grant, only daughter and heiress of Sir Colquhoun Grant (?1764–1835) (Perkins, *Mrs. Norton*, pp. 67–69).

3. Perhaps a reference to George Birkbeck, M.D. (see [1 February 1831] to John Howard Payne, n. 1).

4. From c. 12 May to c. 17 May 1835 (Godwin, *Journal*).

5. Elizabeth Stanhope's daughter.

*To [?   ]   [Harrow   ?29 May–2 June 1835][1]

If you do not go to the Derby—&—being the day of the Derby have no dinner on your hands will you dine here on Thursday at 1/2 6 o'clock
                                                        Yours truly
                                                        MWShelley
let me have an early answer
I was going to congratulate you on the rise of the Tories & am now obliged instead to congratulate myself on the restoration of the Whigs

UNPUBLISHED. TEXT: MS., Barring Brothers.
    1. This tentative date is based on references in the letter to the Derby and the restoration of the Whigs to power. The Derby was run annually on the Wednesday of the week preceding Whitsunday until 1837 (since then it has been run on the Thursday). The only crisis and subsequent restoration of the Whigs that occurred in an April or May during the period prior to 1837 when Mary Shelley might have written this letter, of which only a portion is extant, was in April 1835. Sir Robert Peel, the Tory prime minister, resigned on 8 April 1835, and on 18 April Lord Melbourne formed his second cabinet, which retained power until April 1839 (James Rice, *History of the British Turf* [London: S. Low, Marston, Searle, & Rivington, 1879], pp. 14, 375).

TO MARIA GISBORNE   Harrow—11 June [1835]

My dearest Friend—It is so inexpressibly warm, that were not a frank lying before me ready for you, I do not think I should have courage to write.

Do not be surprized therefore at stupidity & want of connection. I cannot collect my ideas—& this is a good-will offering rather than a letter.

Still I am anxious to thank S.G. [*Signor Giovanni, John Gisborne*] for the pleasure I have received from his tale of Italy a tale all Italy—breathing of the land I love—the descriptions are beautiful—& he has shed a great charm round the concentrated & undemonstrative person of his gentle heroine. I suppose she is the reality of the story.—Did you know her?—It is difficult however to judge how to procure for it the publication it deserves. I have no personal acquaintance with the Editors of any of the Annuals—I had with that of the Keepsake[1]—but that is now in Mrs Norton's hands—& she has not asked me to write—so I know nothing about it—But there arises an stronger objection from the length of the story—As the merit lies in the beauty of the details, I do not see how it could it [*be*] but cut down to one quarter of its present length, which is as long as any tale printed in an Annual   When I write for them, I am worried to death to make my things shorter & shorter—till I fancy people think ideas can be conveyed by intuition—and that it is a superstition to consider words necessary for their expression.

I was so very delighted to get your last letter—to be sure the Wisest of Men said no news was good news[2]—but I am not apt to think so, & was uneasy   I hope this weather does not oppress you—What an odd climate! A week ago I had a fire—& now it is warmer than Italy—Warmer at least in a box pervious to the sun, than in the stone palaces where one can breathe freely. My Father is well—He had a cough in the winter—but after we had persuaded him to see a Doctor it was easily got rid of—He writes to me himself—"I am now well—now nervous—now old—now young—"   One sign of age is that his horror is so great of change of place that I cannot persuade him even to visit me here.—One would think that the sight of the fields would refresh him—but he likes his own nest better than all— though he greatly feels the annoyance of so seldom seeing me. Indeed, my kind Maria—you made me smile when you asked me to be civil to the brother of your kind Doctor.[3]   I thought I had explained my situation to you—You must consider me as one buried alive—I hardly ever go to town— less often I see any one here—My kind & dear Young friends the Misses Robinson are at Brussels—I am cut off from my kind   What I suffer— What I have suffered—I to whom sympathy—companionship—the interchange of thought is more necessary than the air I breathe I will not say. Tears are in my eyes when I think of days, weeks, Months; even years spent alone—eternally alone—It does me great harm—but no more of so odious a subject—let me speak rather of my Percy—to see him bright & good is an unspeakable blessing—but no child can be a companion especially one whose fault is a want of quick sensibility—he is very fond of me—& would be wretched if he saw me unhappy—but he is with his boys all day long, & I am alone—so I can weep unseen—He gets on very well—& is a fine boy—very stout—this hot weather though he exposes himself to the sun—

instead of making him languid, heightens the color in his cheeks & brightens his eyes. He is always gay & in good humour—which is a great blessing.

You talk about my poetry[4]—& about the encouragement I am to find from Jane & my Father. When they read all the fine things you said they thought it right to attack me about it but I answered them simply: "She exagerates—you read the best thing I ever wrote in the Keepsake[5] & thought nothing of it—" I do not know whether you remember the verses I mean I will copy it in another part—it was written for music. Poor dear Lord Dillon spoke of it as you do of the rest—but "One swallow does not make a summer"—I can never write verses except under the influence of a strong sentiment & seldom even then. As to a tragedy—Shelley used to urge me— which produced his own.[6] When I returned first to England, & saw Kean, I was in a fit of enthusiasm—and wished much to write for the stage—but my father very earnestly dissuaded me[7]—I think that he was in the wrong— I think myself that I could have written a good tragedy—but not now—My good friend—every feeling I have is blighted—I have no ambition—no care for fame—Loneliness has made a wreck of me.—I was always a dependant thing—wanting fosterage & support—I am left to myself—crushed by fortune—And I am nothing.—

You speak of women's intellect—We can scarcely do more than judge by ourselves—I know that however clever I may be there is in me a vaccillation, a weakness, a want of "eagle winged{"} resolution[8] that appertains to my intellect as well as my moral character—& renders me what I am— one of broken purposes—failing thoughts & a heart all wounds.—My Mother had more energy of character—still she had not sufficient fire of imagination—In short my belief is—whether there be sex in in souls or not—that the sex of our material mechanism makes us quite different creatures— better though weaker but wanting in the higher grades of intellect.—

I am almost sorry to send you this letter it is so querulous & sad—yet if I write with any effusion—the truth will creep out—& my life since you went has been so stained by sorrows & disappointments—I have been so barbarously handled both by fortune & my fellow creatures—that I am no longer the same as when you knew me—I have no hope—In a few years when I get over my present feelings & live wholly in Percy I shall be happier. I have devoted myself to him as no Mother ever did—and idolize him—& the reward will come when I can forget a thousand memories & griefs that are as yet alive & burning—and I have nothing to do here but brood.—

Another word of Mr Budd—I should have been delighted to have been of use to him—[   ] can make no offers—prisoner as I am. Jeff [   ] flourish—She suffers from his reserves of cha[   ] but his real good qualities make up for it—Dina [   ] growing a fine girl—Edward as yet does not develope much—he is not physically strong.—How I should like to see you & talk to you—I sometimes fancy a journey to Plymouth—What would you say to seeing me pop in some day.—The Countell Gu{i}ccioli is in England[9]—I have such a dread of her coming to see me here—imagine

the talk.—Adieu—Do write—if you ever want a conveyance—enclose your letter to me (while the Session lasts) <u>under cover</u> to D. [*Daniel*] Gaskell Esq M.P. 5 Parliament St. but dont let it me [*be*] above franking weight— O the Heat!—how overpowering it is—Percy is gone 2 miles off to bathe— He can swim—& I am obliged to leave the rest to fate—It is no use coddling witness the fable[10]—yet it costs me many pangs—however he is singularly trustworthy & careful—Do you remember 16 years ago at Livorno[11]—he was not born then—Do write & believe me   Ever your truly attached
                                                            friend MWS.

I sent to Mr Stephen Curtis for you the 1st vol. of my Lives of Italian Poets—The lives of Dante & Ariosto are not mine return it when you have done with it; it belongs to Jane.—Do you not guess why these nor those I sent you w^d please those you mention. Papa loves not the memory of S— because—he feels he injured him;—and Jane—Do you not understand enough of her to unwind the thoughts that [*cross-written*] make it distasteful to her that I should feel—& above all be thought by others to feel & to have a right to feel—O the human heart—it is a strange juggle.—
[*P. 5, upside-down*]

A Dirge

I

This morn thy gallant bark, Love,
  Sailed on a sunny sea;
'Tis noon, & tempests dark, Love,
  Have wrecked it on the lee—

Ah Woe—ah woe, ah woe
  By spirits of the deep
  He's cradled on the billow,
  To his unwaking sleep!

2

Thou liest upon the shore, Love,
  Beside the knelling surge;
But sea-nymphs ever more, Love,
  Shall sadly chaunt thy dirge.

O come, O come—O come!
  Ye spirits of the deep!
  While near his sea-weed pillow
  My lonely watch I keep.

[*P. 6, upside-down*]

3

From far across the sea, Love,
  I hear a wild lament,
By Echo's voice for thee, Love,
  From Ocean's caverns sent

O list! O list! O list!
The Spirits of the deep—
Loud sounds their wail of sorrow—
While I for ever weep!

ADDRESS: Mrs Gisborne / Plymouth / D Gaskell. POSTMARKS: (1) FREE / 11 JU 11 / 1835;
(2) Harrow / [   ] py P.Paid; (3) F / JU 11 / 1835; (4) [   ]8.PAID [   ] / JU 11 / 7. NIGHT.
7. ENDORSED: Harrow 11th June / 1835 / rec. 12 Do / An 22 / Oct. 1835. PUBLISHED: Jones,
#448. TEXT: MS., Bodleian Library (MS., Shelley, Adds., c. 6, ff. 188–90).
   1. Frederic Mansel Reynolds.
   2. The translation of the Italian "Nulla nuova, buona nuova" is traced to James Howell
(?1594–1666), British diplomat, in his *Epistolae Ho-elianae: Familiar Letters* (London: H. Mose-
ley, 1645), letter II. xviii.
   3. In her letter of 11 April 1835 (Abinger MSS., Bodleian Library) Maria Gisborne had
asked if Mary Shelley might do anything for Dr. Budd's brother, who was about to settle in
London. John W. Budd was one of nine brothers, seven of whom went into the medical
profession. The Budd who went up to London at this point may have been George Budd
(1808–82), who became professor of medicine at King's College.
   4. In her letter of 11 April 1835 Maria Gisborne asked why Mary Shelley had allowed her
poetic talent to lie dormant and suggested that Mary Shelley write a tragedy.
   5. "The Dirge," written out at the end of this letter, was published in the *Keepsake for 1831*,
p. 85 and, somewhat revised, in Shelley, *Poetical Works* (1839), IV, 225.
   6. *The Cenci.*
   7. See vol. I, 9 February [1824], n. 5.
   8. Perhaps a variant of "eagle-winged pride," *Richard II* 1. 3. 129.
   9. Teresa Guiccioli reached London c. 29 May 1835 and took lodgings at the Hotel Saunay,
Leicester Square (MS., Pforzheimer Library).
   10. Aesop's fable "The Ape and Her Young Ones," which Godwin, under the pseudonym
Edward Baldwin, published as "The Ape and Her Cubs" in *Fables, Ancient and Modern, Adapted
for the Use of Young Children*, 2 vols. (London: Hodgkins, 1805), II, 105–11.
   11. See vol. I, 27 June 1819 through 27 September 1819.

To JANE WILLIAMS HOGG   [?Harrow   ?12 June–July 1835][1]

Dearest Jane—I send the fly[2] for you—Come to me immediately as you
love me. I may say that I send for you on a matter of <u>life</u> & <u>death</u>—Yet be
not alarmed—⟨this is⟩ my sending arises from p{r}ecaution more than necessity—yet you ⟨are⟩ indeed you must come.

Do not shew any alarm on arriving at this house—there is no occasion
for any—& you would <u>much gratify</u> me if you would shew none at <u>your
house</u>—but let it be only supposed that as I have talked of calling for you
in the Fly—that I send in consequence—I shall of course explain all when
I see you & you will understand my earnestness to have you here for a day
or two—as well as my wish to conceal that any thing extraordinary has
prompted me to send for you—till you yourself know the cause

But Come—My only Friend Come—to the deserted one—I am too ill
to write more.

ADDRESS: Mrs Hogg / 12 Maida Place / Edgware Road. PUBLISHED: Jones, #416. TEXT: MS., British Library (Add. 43,805, ff. 6–7).

1. This conjectural date is based on Mary Shelley's description of herself in this letter as "deserted" and "ill" and her urgent request for Jane Hogg's assistance. On 11 June [1835] she wrote to Maria Gisborne, "You must consider me as one buried alive—I hardly ever go to town—less often I see any one here—My kind & dear Young friends the Misses Robinson are at Brussels—I am cut off from my kind—What I suffer." In a letter dated [13 July 1835] she describes herself to Trelawny as "friendless alone & poor" and "very ill lately." On 13 October 1835 she recounts to Maria Gisborne that during her summer illness Jane Hogg took care of her: "I can never forget nor cease to be grateful to Jane, for her excessive kindness to me when I needed it most, confined as I was to my sopha, unable to move."

2. A one-horse covered carriage, such as a cab or hansom, let out for hire.

To Edward John Trelawny   Harrow Monday [13 July 1835]

Dear Trelawny

I am glad to hear of your safe arrival[1] & wish I could give you an happier welcome. You left me the victim of poverty—you return to find me the same; & in addition a prisoner. My life at Harrow,—friendless alone & poor, has nearly destroyed me—but there is no remedy. I do not repent having come—for it was, I still believe, the only thing I could do to give Percy a decent education & save myself from getting into debt, which seemed inevitable on my remaining in London. Still I wish this place were not so odious & that the want of money, always pressing me to the limits of existence, had permitted me to make a home of some comfort here; but every mitigation has been denied me in my exile. I write in low spirits—because I hate having to give a disagreable account of myself—& because I have been very ill lately & am still ⟨confused by⟩ suffering from the weakness that is its consequents.

Percy's holydays begin in a fortnight when if possible I shall get to town for a few weeks—Shall we meet then? I have a repugnance to your coming here, you would hate it so much—and I hate that a friend should do any thing disagreable. You will see Jane. ⟨She has removed to a house a little beyond the one she lived in before⟩ You will find her in the same house 12 Maida Place. Will you call on the Godwins? 13 New Palace Y^d Westminster—they will be delighted to see you.

Percy is grown of course—but you will despise him for he is <u>horrifically fat</u>—He is the best & dearest boy in the world.—I do not wonder at your hatred of this vile country. To the poor it is a place of perpetual torture—every wish of the heart is denied—every possibility of escaping from ills cut off—I had courage in adversity for a long time—it is gone now.

Adieu—pardon me for croaking & believe me

Ever truly Y^s

ADDRESS: E. J. Trelawny Esq / Colonnade Hotel / Charles St. [In another hand] Sir W. Trelawny / 8 Great George St / Westminster. POSTMARKS: (1) T.P / Harrow; (2) 12. NOON.

12 / 14. JY / 1835. PUBLISHED: Jones, #449. TEXT: MS., Bodleian Library (MS., Shelley, Adds., c. 6, ff. 191–92).
    1. From America, where he had been since 10 March 1833 (see [11 January 1833]).

*TO [MARY JANE GODWIN]   [?3 Alfred Place]   Friday
[c. August–September 1835][1]

Dear Mamma

I am sorry to say that Mrs Burley has made such engagements for me that I shall not be able to see you this week—I shall stay here I fancy a week longer—nevertheless I will contrive to get to you some day next week— though I fear it will be towards the end of it—

How does this cold weather agree with you & Papa? I suffer dismally from it—cold is the most hateful thing in the world—If you do not hear from or see me before expect me next Friday yet even then I dont think I shall dine but call at—Yet at any rate I will call some morning earlier next week—on Monday or Tuesday

Aff^y Yours
MWS.

UNPUBLISHED. TEXT: MS., Gene DeGruson.
    1. The contents of this letter indicate that it was written sometime between c. September 1833 (when Julia Trelawny married John Burley) and 7 April 1836 (when Godwin died), during a period in which Mary Shelley was on an extended stay away from Harrow. During Percy Florence's August–September holidays in 1833 Mary Shelley and Percy Florence were with the Robinsons; during the 1834 holidays they were in London. The most likely date for this letter is c. August–September 1835, when Mary Shelley was at Dover at the same time as Trelawny's mother and Julia Burley (see 22 September 1835, n. 2). Godwin's Journal records that Mary Shelley visited the Godwins on 29 July 1835, but not again until 6 September, after which she frequently visited them through 22 September (see [c. 14 September 1835], n. 1).

TO CHARLES OLLIER   3 Alfred Place   Dover   6 August. 1835

My dear Sir

My Aunt, Mrs Wollstonecraft[1] has never received Lodore. You would very much oblige me if you would see to this—as the neglect is a real annoyance to me.

In vain all this summer I have looked out for you. I myself have been very ill—& as I could not get well at Harrow, as soon as the holydays began, came here where I am fast regaining health & strength. I shall return to Harrow in September when perhaps the spirit may move you & Mrs Ollier to fulfil your kind promise.

What of Lodore—Do you remember that when 700 are sold I am to have £50—? Will 700 never be sold—I am very unlucky; praised & noticed as it has been. You promised me to look after my interests in this particular and I trust you, because I think you will ⟨find⟩ feel more sympathy with a poor Author than a rich Publisher. If therefore 701 are sold, have pity on me & let me know, that I may claim a sum, which will pay for my unlucky illness, & do me a world of good. Do pray attend to this, & I shall be so very much obliged—

I hope you are all well at home & am ever

Yours truly
MWShelley

My Aunt's Address is,—
Mrs Wollstonecraft
  19 White Conduit St.
    Pentonville

ADDRESS: Chas Ollier Esq / 8 New Burlington St. POSTMARKS: (1) T.P / [   ] St West; (2) 7. NIGHT. 7 /AU. 8 / 1835. PUBLISHED: Jones, #450. TEXT: MS., British Library (Add. 30,262, ff. 33–34).

  1. I.e., Everina Wollstonecraft, called Mrs. Wollstonecraft by the courtesy accorded to elders.

TO CHARLES OLLIER   [?London   c. 14 September 1835][1]

Dear Sir

I write this in case I do not find you at home. I perceive with a good deal of surprize an Edition of the Younger Son advertized for the Standard Novels—without any notice being given to me or Mr Trelawny.[2] The contract was that Mr Trelawny was to receive £100 more, when a 2^d Edition was printed.[3] Pray represent this to Mr Colburn or Mr Bentley—& let me or Mr Trelawny hear from you on the subject.

Mr Trelawny is at present at Brighton a letter would find him directed to 13 Cavendish Place Brighton   I heard the other day from him & he is particularly vexed that he was not applied to—as he wanted to make various corrections   As the contract was entered into between you & me it falls to me to remind you of the £100 & to beg of you to take care that it is properly arranged.

You have not answered my question about Lodore & the 700 copies— nor has Mrs Wollstonecraft ever received the copy you promised to send   I am returning to Harrow directly—so fear I cannot see you unless you will keep your often broken promise & come out there   I am anxious to send a satisfactory account to Mr Trelawny

Yours truly   MWS.

ADDRESS: Chas Ollier Esq / 8 New Burlington St. PUBLISHED: Jones, #451. TEXT: MS., Pforzheimer Library.

1. See the next letter. Mary Shelley was in London or in the vicinity from 6 to 22 September 1835. Godwin records being in her company on 6, 10, 13, and 18 September; he also notes that she slept at a hotel from 18 to 22 September (Godwin, Journal). This letter is dated c. 14 September because Mary Shelley says that she received Trelawny's 12 September letter "the other day."

2. In a letter to Mary Shelley of 12 September 1835 from Brighton Trelawny informed her of Colburn's advertisement in a newspaper of a second edition and expressed anger at not being notified of this edition (S&M, IV, 1204).

3. This agreement between Mary Shelley and Charles Ollier was made verbally. It was not kept, which led to negotiations that on 12 May 1836 awarded Trelawny £40 for the copyright of the second edition and any future editions of *Adventures* (British Library [Add. MS. 46,681, f. 60]; see also 12 October 1835).

TO EDWARD JOHN TRELAWNY   London 22 Sepr 1835

Dear Trelawny

I waited to see Ollier before I commenced your letter—for I was more surprized than you to find your book advertized for the Standard Novels without any application being made to either of us—I only contrived to see Ollier today—What you can do with these people I know not—and whether you could manage them if you were in town I know not—There was certainly a contingency of a further sum understood to come to you on a second edition—They say that if this contingency had been taken into consideration, they would never had [*have*] printed this edition—I think your claim might stand a lawsuit—& it is too much my fault that it was not put in a clearer shape—If they had applied to you before printing this edition, all had been well—As it is, you must judge what to do with them—The facts were these—Ollier wrote down the offer of £300—with a £100 more on a second edition—I accepted this—He drew out the contract & I signed it, and I am sorry to say without reading it—taking it for granted that the terms were the same which I had accepted. The £100 on the second edition had been left out—I discovered this & represented it to Ollier—He promised over & over again that no advantage should be taken of the oversight & that he would give evidence, in a court of justice, that such had been agreed upon—Now he says that this 2nd Edition would never have been printed if there had been £100 or even £50 to pay—as the 1st Edition did not pay its expences—But in honesty this ought to have been represented before instead of after publication—& perhaps by law they might be prevented selling this edition, or by fear of law make a compromise with you—All this pains me naturally more than I can say; since I was the person concerned in drawing up the agreement—were you in town, we might discuss all this—

With regard to alterations not many copies are yet printed off or sold, & they would willingly cancel any pages you wished to have altered—such a thing as the change in the spelling of a name (I know you wished Zela's name to be printed differently)[1]—could not be altered, because that goes through all the book—but any alterations that extended only to some pages (especially towards the end of the book which is not printed off{)} they would gladly adopt—They are to send you two copies this week—one interleaved with blank leaves—that you make the alterations as you go on— They have put a sort of preface to the book, which, if you are not pleased with, they will suppress—& print instead any thing you like—If in town do call there, or write yourself to Bentley or Ollier, & see if you can make any thing of them—& if you make alterations let them have them as soon as you can, that the printing may be gone on with—I go back to Harrow today—I am not well at all—& regret having left Dover so soon—I write in haste to save the post, that I may not keep you waiting any longer—

Your Mother talked of staying at Dover till towards the end of October[2]—

Bentley will be very tractable & civil about alterations—for he knows that he has acted if not dishonestly, yet very like it, & would be glad to mollify you in any possible manner—You might insert & add as much as you like—Adieu

Y[rs] ever
MWShelley

PUBLISHED: Palacio, *Mary Shelley*, p. 610 (three-quarters of letter); Jones, #453, in summary.
TEXT: MS. (copy), Abinger MSS., Bodleian Library.

1. On 19 July 1831 Trelawny wrote to Mary Shelley to ask that his daughter's name be spelled "Zellâ" (Trelawny, *Letters*, p. 170).

2. Trelawny had asked Mary Shelley if she knew how long his mother planned to remain at Dover (*S&M*, IV, 1204).

*To Charlotte Trevanion[1]   Harrow: Saturday
                                              [?26 September 1835]

Dear Mrs Trevanion

I shall be happy to join your party—You dine I suppose at five—I will be with you at a little after four. I am sorry to say that I am any thing but well—so that I may feel myself obliged to return home directly, if the theatre should knock me up for when I am ill, I can only bear to be in my hole. I hope however that things will be better—& I better.

I had no idea that Edward was in town[2]—I have not heard from him   Percy is in town today going to the play—which will satisfy him till after xmas— thank you for thinking of him

I am glad to hear you are looking well—take care of yourself & your spirits

With love to M[rs] Brereton & best wishes I am, dear M[rs] Trevanion
                                              Yours Aff[ly]
                                              MWShelley

UNPUBLISHED. TEXT: MS., Pforzheimer Library.

1. Trelawny's youngest sister, Charlotte Trevanion, who had married a distant cousin, John Charles Trevanion, in 1827 (Anne Hill, *Trelawny's Strange Relations* [Stanford Dingley: Mill House Press, 1956], pp. 32–33).

2. On 12 September 1835 Trelawny had informed Mary Shelley that he planned to remain at Brighton for approximately a fortnight (*S&M*, IV, 1204).

To EDWARD JOHN TRELAWNY   [Harrow ?26 September 1835]

Dear Trelawny

I have just had a note from Charlotte, that tells me you are still in town. I am going tomorrow to Cedars[1] for a day or two–On leaving Putney, I shall stop short at Brompton[2]—for a day or two, not more—On Monday I think I shall be there. Would it be possible that the tiresome business with Bentley could be arranged for next Thursday? as being in town, I can attend to it better. I must be back here on Friday or Saturday—being very busy. Percy is looking so well, grown thinner & taller: it is odd to mark the white down on his face, changing to mustachios the color of his father's hair—he has so much more of his father's blood in his veins than of mine—& yet in many things is so unlike both of us.

I shall hope to see you while I am in town. The journey here is too far & to drear to make for any except—

Adieu—it will be a great comfort to see you—for notwithstanding—tweedledum—I am truly & always attached to you—

MaryShelley

I had almost forgotten a message to you from Teresa, which she sent in a letter I got from her from Paris   She says "I beg you will say a thousand cordial things to Trelawny from me—since I really have a great esteem and liking for him—and tell him besides that I do not need the letter for Lady Blessin{g}ton, because I am almost sure that he would not make use of it."—

PUBLISHED: Jones, #452. TEXT: MS., Bodleian Library (MS., Shelley, Adds., c. 6, ff. 193–94).

1. The home of Col. and Mrs. Leicester Stanhope.

2. Trelawny's mother lived at 16 Michaels Place, Brompton (MWS, Journal, address list).

To JOHN BOWRING   Harrow—3 Oct. [1835]

Dear Doctor Bowring

You are very kind to answer my letter in the midst of all your important avocations. One great difficulty seems to be getting books—There is no Spanish Library[1]—& one wants to turn over so many that the Longmans would be tired of buying. I own that I depended much on yours—& am disappointed at what you say—is there no getting at them?—are the cases large & are all the Spanish books in one case?—Could indeed any but yourself touch them?—I do not mind trouble—but wish to do my task as well as I can—& how can I without books?—The difficulty seems to be that from slight biographical notices one can yet the book will be more of literature than lives—& I know not how Lardner will like that. The best is that the very thing which occasions the difficulty makes it interesting— namely—the treading in unknown paths & dragging out unknown things— I wish I could go to Spain.

Many thanks for the hints you give   I am, dear Dr Bowring

Yours truly

MWShelley

ADDRESS: Dr. Bowring M.P. / 1 Queen's Sq / Westminster. POSTMARKS: (1) T[.P] / Harrow; (2) 7. NIGHT. 7 / OC. 3 /1835. ENDORSED: (1) Mrs Shelley / 3 Octr 1835; (2) Lo[n]don Oct 1835 / Mrs Shelley. PUBLISHED: Jones, #455. TEXT: MS., Huntington Library (HM 2767).

1. Mary Shelley was preparing volume III of the *Lives* (1835–37), in which she wrote about Boscan, Garcilaso de la Vega, Diego Hurtado de Mendoza, Luis de Leon, Herrera, Francisco de Sá de Miranda, Jorge de Montemayor, Castillejo, Cervantes, Lope de Vega, Vicente Espinel-Esteban de Villegas, Gongora, Quevedo, Calderon, Ribeyra, Gil Vicente, Ferreira, and Camoens (Lyles, *MWS Bibliography,* p. 38). On 3–4 December 1835 Thomas Moore noted in his Journal: "Wrote to Lady Holland, at Mrs. Shelley's request, to ask for access to the Spanish Biography, for Lardner, and books on the subject being very rare in London. A long letter from Lady H. [*Holland*] explaining why Lord H. [*Holland*] could not infringe the rule he had laid down on this subject. This I had prepared Mrs. S. for." On 8 December 1835 Moore wrote in his Journal: "Letter from Mrs. Shelley on the subject of the refusal from the Hollands—quotes some foreigner who says that, in England, 'chaque individu est une Ile' ["each person is an island"] and adds that 'some even surround the island with martello-towers.' "

TO EDWARD JOHN TRELAWNY   Harrow   Oct 12 1835

Dear Trelawny

Do not I pray make any apologies for troubling me—I deserve it all for my folly—Ollier does not deny that the other £100 ought to have been in the contract—& he devoutly wishes, he says, that I had read it over—Jeff has not yet returned from the North—I am not sure that I would choose him—I should prefer Peacock[1]—if he would—because he is an Author accustomed to dealings with booksellers & would not lean to the strongest side, which Jefferson as a lawyer is inclined I think, to do—I prefer Peacock to my father—simply because you tell me to name the person—Had you named him it had been well—but it were more impartial in me, since I am so much implicated not to name so near a relative—Peacock is very much occupied & not in good health, but as this affair lies, as the lawyers say <u>in a nutshell</u>, I think his friendship for me will induce him to comply—I will write to him by todays post—

I own I am sorry you do not get to Dover for a week, as it was a promise—it is not too late now—I do not wonder at your not being able to deny yourself the pleasure of Mrs Nortons society—I never saw a woman I thought so fascinating—Had I been a man I should certainly have fallen in love with her—As a woman—ten years ago—I should have been spell bound & had she taken the trouble she might have wound me round her finger—Ten years ago I was so ready to give myself away—& being afraid of men, I was apt to get <u>tousy-mousy</u> for women—experience & suffering have altered all that—I am more wrapt up in myself—my own feelings—disasters—& prospects for Percy—I am now proof as Hamlet says both against man & woman[2]—There is something in the pretty way in which Mrs Norton's witticisms glide as it were from her lips, that is so very charming—& then her color which is so variable—the eloquent blood which ebbs & flows—mounting, as she speaks to her neck & temples—& then receding as fast—it reminds me of the frequent quotation of "eloquent blood"[3]—& gives a peculiar attraction to her conversation not to speak of fine eyes & open brow—Now do not in your usual silly way shew her what I say—She is despite all her talents & sweetness a London lady—She would quiz me (not perhaps to you—Well do I know the London <u>ton</u>) but to every one else in her very prettiest manner—

I was very ill indeed when I last wrote to you which caused me perhaps to fancy your letter angry—I am better now, but this place disagrees with me sadly   I mean to get away from it entirely next spring if possible—

Very truly Y^rs

MWShelley—

PUBLISHED: Jones, #454, in part; Jones, #456, in part. TEXT: MS. (copy), Abinger MSS., Bodleian Library.

1. On 2 October 1835 Trelawny wrote to Richard Bentley requesting the £100 for the second edition of *Adventures*. Richard Bentley met Trelawny's demands by an agreement to arbitrate the matter, and Trelawny selected Peacock as his representative (British Library [Add. MS. 46,681, f. 60]; see also [c. 14 September 1835]).

2. "Man delights me not, nor woman neither, though by your smiling you seem to say so" (*Hamlet* 2. 2).

3. *Alastor,* line 168.

TO MARIA GISBORNE   Harrow—13 Oct—1835

My dear Friend—I wrote you a long letter about a month ago, ready for a frank—& lo! when I w^d use it—it has disappeared, & I cannot find it any where;—this is tiresome—as there is nothing so annoying as <u>writing</u> a twice told tale—besides that writing is now a real labor to me—so you must be content with a scrap of a incoherent letter—but I cannot delay any longer asking how you are, & entreating you to let me have a few lines at least to inform us of your state, & that of S.G. [*Signor Giovanni, John Gisborne*]—

& also, permit me to say, of your dear good Elizabeth,[1] whom fidelity & zeal, renders very interesting.

I shall begin my own history in an Irish way—by commencing with Jane—for it will please & interest you to know that she expects to encrease her family in Feb^ry next[2]—She is frightened at danger & pain—& Jeff, I believe, at expence—but I think it is a good thing—especially if it is, as they <u>both</u> wish a boy—a girl, in going out into life, is the Mothers care—a boy the father's—Jeff, I think, will find new feelings—anticipations & even energies develope, when he has a son to think of & provide for. You or at least S.G. must have seen his name frequently in the papers—Ld Brougham sent him as one of the Corporation Commissioners—but his Tory, or as he calls them high Whig principles, betrayed themselves—he played the Conservative & brought himself into notice—I hope it will do him good in his profession—had the Tory Ministry remained in, it certainly would.—He is now gone on a visit home—a visit prolonged by the death of <u>Aunt Jones</u>[3] at Cheltenham—John & Prue[4] went to attend the funeral—he remained to console Mamma & Sarah[5]—which he says is like riding in a mourning coach all day long. Jane's children are well—Dina is a very interesting girl indeed—the talent she has developed for drawing, would be absolute genius, had she imagination & understanding to put soul in the eye she has for form—we shall see; I sympathize much in the pursuit She is nearly as tall as her Mother—Jane would be well, but that over activity & the want of a sopha (which Jeff cannot <u>afford</u>) threaten to make her suffer as she did with her last[6]—I preach & pray, but to little purpose.

Of myself—my dearest Maria—I can give but a bad account—Solitude—many cares—& many deep sorrows brought on this summer an illness from which I am now only recovering. I can never forget nor cease to be grateful to Jane, for her excessive kindness to me when I needed it most, confined as I was to my sopha, unable to move.[7] I went to Dover during Percy's holydays—& change of air & bathing made me so much better that I thought myself well—but on my return here, I had a relapse—from which now this last week I am, I trust, fast recovering—but I am obliged to take great care of myself—there is something the matter with my blood I fancy; bark & port wine seem the chief methods for my getting well—In the midst of all this I had to write to meet my expences—I have published a 2^d Vol. of Italian Lives in Lardners Cyclopedia—all in that vol. except Gallileo & Tasso are mine—The last is chief I allow—& I grieve that it had been engaged to the Omnipresent Mr Montgomery[8] before I began to write—I am vain enough to think that I should have written it better than he has done. I am now about to write a Volume of Spanish & Portugueeze Lives—This is an arduous task, from my own ignorance, & the difficulty of getting books & information. The Bookseller wants me to write another Novel—Lodore having succeeded so well—but I have not as yet stren{g}th for such an undertaking.

My Father is tolerably well—he is about to move to another public building[9]—& this is a great worry & labor to them both—M[rs] G—[*Godwin*] was excessively kind to me in my illness. Percy is much grown & very big— he goes on much the same; but I think of taking him from Harrow, as soon as I can find a tutor—In the first place—I am being killed by inches here— And then he as a home boarder is not enough with other boys—& con- sequently does not take exercise enough—I shall place him with a tutor who has four or five other boys.   I shall leave this place at Easter I think— but poor as I am, a move is a great anxiety.—Sir Tim is quite well & nearly doting.—Claire is at Florence; expecting, poor dear, most firmly to die of Cholera.[10] It is very bad at Leghorn—20,000 people fled from the town— the Doctors could afford no help; one, Punta, faceva fiasco;[11] the people rose on him, & he ran for his life—the common people expect to be poi- soned. At Florence one Man, taken to the hospital, refused every remedy, even a cup of camomile tea—& died of Cholera in 2 hours—At Florence they take every precaution to conceal the state of the disease—& it seems milder than at Leghorn—The Granduke is exerting himself in the most exemplary manner goes into every squalid hovel—& himself overlooking the cleanliness of the Streets.—Poor Claire's state {of} mind is very sad— the family[12] she is with remain at Florence, so she does,—fully expecting to die.—Jane has seen Weale[13] once or twice—dined there once with Jeff— Mamina[14] flourishes—Trelawny is in England. in America he was en- chanted with Fanny Kemble[15] here he is enchained by M[rs] Norton—I do not wondr at the latter—she is a wonderful creation possessing—wit, beauty & sweetness at their highest grade—they say a stony heart withal—so I hope she will make him pay for his numerous coquetries with our sex—I have not seen Peacock for some time   His wife lives in town—She is quite mad—his children in the country all by themselves except for his weekly visits—His eldest girl educates herself & reads Paul de Kock's[16] novels in all innocence   Adieu—my dear friend—pray write soon & beleive me ever Affectionately Y[s]

                                                                    MWShelley

ADDRESS: Mrs Gisborne / Plymouth / Devon. [*In another hand*] Mrs Gisborne / Plymouth / England / ES Ruthven. POSTMARKS: (1) FREE / 22 OC 22 / 1835; (2) GREY ABBEY. EN- DORSED: Harrow 13 Oct / 1835, / rec. 23 Oct / Ans. / M. Shelley. PUBLISHED: Jones, #457. TEXT: MS., Bodleian Library (MS., Shelley, Adds., c. 6, ff. 195–96).

    1. Elizabeth Rumble.

    2. Prudentia Sarah Hogg was born on 4 February 1836 (d. 1897). She married first Thomas James Arnold (d. 1877), a London magistrate, and second John Lonsdale (d. 1886), recorder of Folkestone (Norman, *After Shelley*, p. xxxvii; *S&M*, IV, 1207).

    3. Thomas Jefferson Hogg's mother's sister (Scott, *Hogg*, p. 14).

    4. John Hogg (1800–1869), barrister at law, and Prudentia Ann Hogg (1796–1851), Thomas Jefferson Hogg's brother and sister (*SC*, III, 4).

    5. Elizabeth Sarah Hogg (1798–1863), Thomas Jefferson Hogg's sister (*SC*, III, 4).

    6. See vol. I, 28 July 1827, n. 2.

    7. See [?12 June–July 1835], n. 1.

8. See 30 April 1834, n. 1.

9. On 6 November 1835 the Godwins moved to the Exchequer Building in Whitehall Yard (Godwin, *Journal*).

10. Claire Clairmont's letter of 1 September 1835 describes the effects of cholera at Florence and expresses her fear for her own life (*S&M*, IV, 1197–1203).

11. "Was a complete failure."

12. Henry Grey Bennet (1777–1836), second son of the fourth earl of Tankerville, and his wife Gertrude Francis Bennet (d. 1841). Claire Clairmont was governess to their daughters, Charlotte Emma, who married Fitzstephen (Patrick) French in November 1839, and Gertrude Francis, who married Hamilton Gorges in August 1839 (*Burke's Peerage*).

13. In 1822 Mary Diana Dods, as David Lyndsay, instructed William Blackwood to write to her in care of a James Weale, 19 York Buildings (Blackwood MS., National Library of Scotland).

14. Mrs. Cleveland, Jane Williams Hogg's mother.

15. See 15 December 1829, n. 9.

16. Charles Paul de Kock (1793–1871), prolific and popular French novelist and dramatist, wrote about all aspects of society. Some of de Kock's works were considered licentious. Mary Ellen Peacock may have been introduced to his fiction by her father, who planned to write a major work about him (Van Doren, *Peacock*, pp. 204–7).

To Maria Gisborne   Harrow   [8] Nov. 1835

My dearest Friend

You are very good to write, but indeed it would be too cruel to deprive us of intelligence about you. The prolongation of your sad disorder—& your prolonged life are matters of the deepest anxiety & interest to us all— to me in particular—for I always fancy something of relationship between us. I wish I could see you. I often dream of a journey to Plymouth—but alas! the operations of the poor are soon stopt.

I fancy our last letters crossed but I do not remember the date of mine— which I sent to Ireland for a frank[1]—as this will go to Yorkshire—Away from town, I cannot catch the passing Members as they fly—& therefore use those who are fixtures in their country residences during the recess. The M.P. & his wife[2] to whom this will go are curious people in their way— They are Liberals—have been to Italy (where they formed Claire's acquaintance & got an introduction to me) knew your friend Bentham[3] & are allied to all the ultra Radical party—but they are Country folks in core— he—a plain silentious but intelligent looking man of fifty she the Beau ideal of a Country Blue grafted on a sort of lady Bountiful—Unitarians in Religion—They do a great deal of good in the country about them—& he looks as if he could feel—while she talking of enthusiasm—benevolence & the poor, bears a face, all the time in which such gentle feelings have made small traces—You esteem but cannot love her—and pretention, harmless indeed, but still pretention animates her to perpetual talk.—The moment the reform bill past the people of Wakefield chose him for their MP. He attends the house night after night & dull committees & likes it!—for truly after a country town & country society, the dullest portion of London life seems as gay as a masked ball.

I fancy Jane intends to write. She has made herself ill by walking & exerting herself about her brother's children—I think this a great weakness on her part—but preach in vain—J.C. [*Jesus Christ*] says "Do unto others as you would they should do unto you"—it may seem an extension of such charity to say "Do unto others as they would that you should do to them.{"} Yet sometimes it is a narrowing of it—in the present instance Major Cleveland would certainly prefer that Jane should not injure her health & fret her temper about saving him sixpences when he is spending en Prince. When she has her baby this will stop. Her goodness to me in my illness I shall never forget—and I feel the utmost gratitude to her for it. The Godwins are in the act of moving which is a most troublesome affair tho' with them the use of Government conveniences facilitates their arrangements.

Did I not write to you about the Literary Lives—You guessed right as to the sex of Dante's Life; it was written by the Omnipresent Mr Montgomery—as well as Ariosto's—with Evelina,[4] in a few days, I will send you a 2^d vol—the life of Gallileo is by Sir David Brewster[5] that of Tasso by Mr Montgomery[6]—the rest are mine & so ends the Italian lives; for which I am sorry. The Spanish & Portugueeze will cost me more trouble, if I can do them at all—There is no Spanish Circulating Library—I cannot while here, read in the Museum[7] if I would—& I would not if I could—I do not like finding myself a stray bird alone among Men even if I know them— Nothing could make me voluntarily go among strange men in a character assimililating [*assimilating*] to their own—One hears of how happy people will be to lend me their books—but when it comes to the point, it is very difficult to get at them; however as I am rather persevering, I hope to conquer these obstacles after all.

My health has improved much since I last wrote—and I hope to get away from this detestable place in the spring—Liking society as I do—& too much given in the happiest situations to devour my own heart—I endure torture while day after day books & my own sad thoughts are my only resource [   ] Percy grows—he is taller than I am—& very sto[ut] If he does not turn out an honor to his parents [   ] be through no deficiency in virtue or talents—[   ] from that dislike of mingling with his fellow [   ] except in the two or three friends, he cannot [   ] without, which he has in common with all the m[   ] Shelleys. He may be the happier for it. He has a good understanding & great integrity of character.

How I feel for dear good S.G. [*Signor Giovanni, John Gisborne*] in all his anxieties & fears—his attentions to you & affection make him an object of great interest—for as I grow older I look upon fidelity as the first of human virtues—& am going to write a novel[8] to display my opinion. The publishers pleased with the success of Lodore want me to write another—and I want money to get away from here. Have you read Lodore—& can you get it.

If not let S.G. or yourself write me three lines <u>immediately</u> you can send it (take care it is not too heavy for a frank) & enclosed to D. Gaskell Esq. M.P. Lupzet Hall, Wakefield, Yorkshire & if you write directly I shall I hear before I send the parcel to Mr Curtis & will include Lodore in it.—If you did read it, did you recognize any of Shelley's & my early adventures— when we were in danger of being starved in Switzerland—& could get no dinner at an inn in London?[9]

Remember how anxious we are about your health and write when you can. Your remarks about Bulwer, who is my acquaintance but not my friend,—are just. Vanity is his marked characteristic & this is disappointed— in Literature, he wanted to be a Novelist philosopher & poet—in the last he failed. He wishes to be a leader in Politics & fashion—for the last he is voted vulgar—for the first he can neither acquire confidence nor influence— He is distrusted I know not why—for both he is much disqualified by a considerable deafness. He is ill tempered thro' disappointment—& he disliked the Italians in the true wise English way—who could not speak a word of the language—I could tell you much more of his flirtations &c by which 2 years ago he rendered himself tres ridicule—I am angry with him—I admired his novels so much, I wanted him to be a great man but he is envious as well as vain—after all I am [*partially cross-written*] not a fair judge—I know him too little; [   ] I judge him by his actions & his conversation & books—& not by the inner man, [   ] which intimacey only reveals to one. Adieu, dear Maria   with best & earnest wishes Ever

Aff^ly Yours
MWS

ADDRESS: Mrs Gisborne / Plymouth / Devon. [*In another hand*] Mrs. Gisborne / Plymouth / Devon / D Gaskell. POSTMARK: WAKEFIE[I·D] / NO 8 / 1835. ENDORSED: Harrow Nov / 1835 / recd 11 Nov / Ans / M Shelley. PUBLISHED: Jones, #458. TEXT: MS., Bodleian Library (MS., Shelley, Adds., c. 6, ff. 197–99).

1. Her letter of 13 October 1835, franked by Edward S. Ruthven.

2. Daniel and Mary Heywood Gaskell.

3. Maria Gisborne wrote to Mary Shelley on 1 August 1832 asking if her (Maria Gisborne's) letter had been read to Bentham before his death.

4. John Gisborne's manuscript.

5. See 30 April 1834, n. 1.

6. See 30 April 1834, n. 1.

7. The British Museum records indicate that unlike William Godwin and William Godwin, Jr., Mary Shelley was never a reader there (information supplied by K. J. Wallace, Archivist, British Museum).

8. *Falkner*, 3 vols. (London: Saunders and Otley, 1837), was Mary Shelley's sixth and last novel.

9. See Dowden, *Shelley*, I, 436–38; MWS, *Lodore*, II, 256–95.

*TO THOMAS JEFFERSON HOGG [London ?18 January–
2 April 1836][1]

Dear Jefferson

Have you heard of the St. Mary{le}bone Bank[2]—it is a new Bank insti-
tuted on the system of the Scotch Banks—of course you, who know all
things, are fully acquainted—how Sir Robert Peel—threw some cold water
on ⟨these⟩ it—& how—if it ⟨they⟩ suc{c}eed, it ⟨may⟩ must from ⟨their⟩ its
nature—the goodess of the security &c swallow up every other bank—

I tell the tale as it is told to me—You must judge—a million is wanted,
& several hundred thousand already subscribed—They are now making out
a list of Directors—& they want some, who are Gentlemen of character, &
yet who will work—the first is easily got—the second more difficult   A
director ought to attend several hours two days in the week & will receive
£300 pr annum—he must become a shareholder to a certain extent.

If the Bank succeeds there is no doubt that the Directorship will not
only be a very good thing in itself—but afford a geat influence ⟨for patronage
& so⟩ & enable a Director to help on his family &c—As to the success you
must judge—& you must judge whether you would like to be a Director.
If you would—or would enquire & consider, will you call on Alfred Robinson 17 Orchard St. Portman Sq. between 11 & 4 tomorrow. They are
in a hurry to get out a list of Directors so you must not delay. He is the
Solicitor—& can shew you all that has been done.—They are in treaty to
take (but this is a secret) the D. of R's[3] house in Cavendish Square—The
projector is a Mr Dove[4]—

I really think you had better enquire before you decide.—it might be an
opening for your brother[5]—& Edward.[6] It was I who mentioned your name—
I hope I did not do wrong—but as I know Leicester Stanhope is a Director
of the Irish Bank—&—in fact on the whole I felt sure that if you judged
well of the success of the undertaking that the employment would ⟨not⟩
suit you. I am going out today or I would have called this evening to have
told you this

Yours very truly   MS.

ADDRESS: T. J. Hogg Esq. UNPUBLISHED. TEXT: MS., Abinger MSS., Bodleian Library.

1. The contents of this letter indicate that it was written not too long before the opening
of the Marylebone Bank (see n. 2 below) and while Mary Shelley remained more than one
day in London. She was in London from 18 to 23 January 1836 and again on 23 March 1836,
which probably marks her permanent return from Harrow to London (see [5 February 1836],
n. 2). Mary Shelley notes that Godwin was confined to his bed for five days before his death
on 7 April 1836 and that she was in close attendance (see 20 April 1836). It is unlikely that
this letter was written after Godwin's death, because it is not written on mourning stationery,
which she used through August 1836. Therefore, this letter probably was written sometime
between 18 January and 2 April 1836.

2. The St. Marylebone Bank was established in 1836 and failed in 1841. It opened for
business on 5 September 1836 at 9 Cavendish Square and in 1838 moved to 17 Cavendish
Square. Leicester Stanhope was one of the original directors of the bank; Alfred Robinson

was its solicitor, later replaced by Richard Roy. The bank's manager, David Hannay, embezzled the capital of the bank, thereby causing its failure and entangling Leicester Stanhope and the other directors of the bank in a chancery suit. It was held that the directors had committed acts of gross mismanagement of the bank's affairs (The Archives Department, Westminster City Libraries). Whether Hogg was interested in becoming a director is unknown; however, he is not listed as one of the directors.

3. Perhaps an error for the "D. of L's," that is, the duke of Leed's, since the duke of Leeds lived at 9 Cavendish Square.

4. James Dove was the original secretary of the St. Marylebone Bank.

5. John Hogg (see 13 October 1835, n. 4).

6. Edward Williams.

*To Charles Ollier   Harrow—25 Jan^{ry} 1836

Dear Sir

Mr Trelawny left town for Brighton a few days ago. Before his departure he sent me the enclosed note. Being in town last week I called in Burlington St. to deliver it, & to ask you whether there was any chance of bringing this disagreable question[1] to a speedy termination. Mr Peacock's inability to attend to this business on any day but Thursday, may, I fear, prolong the suspense. Mr Trelawny suggested the naming another arbitrator—but I thought that so doing might appear capricious, besides that I do not know any one so well fitted.

This delay with regard to Mr Trelawny's business has prevented my saying anything further on your proposal that I should write another Novel.[2] Till you spoke I had no intention of writing another—but in consequence of what you said, I began to reflect on the subject—and a story presented itself so vividly to my mind that I began to write almost directly—and have finished one volume—the whole will be ready in the Autumn. It is in the style of Lodore, but the story more interesting & even, I should think, more popular. I am afraid you cannot negociate about it for Mr Bentley, till Mr Trelawny's affair is settled—and yet it is very necessary for me to know what I have to depend upon.—I received almost nothing for Lodore[3]— but I cannot part with this under a fair price. I would at once name one, but cannot with any propriety under the present circumstances.

Any Thursday that is named for the matter of the reference—I will see Mess. Peacock & Knight[4] at the India House. When that is over—I may hope also to see you here—but you must be quick as I leave this place finally in March.

I am, dear Sir,
Yours truly
MWShelley

Unpublished. Text: MS., Pforzheimer Library.
1. The arbitration about the money due to Trelawny for the second edition of *Adventures.*

2. *Falkner* (see [8] November 1835).

3. See 16 January 1833, n. 6.

4. Charles Knight (1791–1873; *DNB*), author and publisher. On 13 April 1836 Charles Knight wrote to Richard Bentley to discuss his role as an arbitrator (Bentley Archives, Part II, Reel #39, University of Illinois).

To Maria Gisborne   Harrow—Friday [5 February 1836]

Dearest Maria—I enclose a note I got today from Jeff[1]—you will rejoice that all is happily over—Jane had been so weak that I much feared a bad time—I shall go up in a day or two to see her—but as I can only go for a few hours I think it best to leave her quiet for a few days

I have not been very well since I wrote. My fate is so unchangeably sad, that I have not spirits enough to get well after being ill. I leave this place at Easter[2]—having found a tutor[3] for Percy—and I think the change will prove beneficial to him. For myself I hope nothing. The moving will be full of difficulty an [*and*] annoyance my residence in London dreary & mortifying; I am friendless & alone!—

I long to hear how you are. We had a little severe weather about Xmas—but otherwise a mild winter—I am busy writing another novel—but the exertion, though necessary to my purse—& not difficult, since my story writes itself—yet is not beneficial to my languid irritable state.—

My Father is quite well—& dearest Percy also.—The Cholera has disappeared from Florence & Claire escaped—she gives a frightful account of the effects that panic produced.

I have written to Dr Budd[4] but not seen him—I am not well enough to make myself agreable to a stranger & this place being so far—& so odious in winter—& I am so soon to migrate to London, I thought it best to defer his visit till that time—I never see any one here for I am domiciled miserably—

Do let me hear how you are—it is so long since you have written—I hope S.G. [*Signor Giovanni, John Gisborne*] continues well—his asthma mitigated—God bless you

Ever Aff^ly Yours

MWShelley

ADDRESS: Mrs Gisborne / Plymouth / Devon. [*In another hand*] Mrs Gisborne / Plymouth / Devon [?M Dahlehern].POSTMARK: FREE / 15 FE 15 / 1836. PUBLISHED: Jones, #459. TEXT: MS., Bodleian Library (MS., Shelley, Adds., c. 6, ff. 200–201).

1. The announcement, dated 4 February 1836 (*S&M,* IV, 1207), of the birth that day of Prudentia Sarah Hogg (see 13 October 1835, n. 2).

2. Easter was celebrated on 3 April in 1836. On Wednesday, 23 March, Mary Shelley and Percy Florence dined with Godwin (Godwin, Journal). The fact that Percy Florence was in London on a weekday suggests that the Easter holiday had begun and that Mary Shelley had given up her Harrow residence by 23 March.

3. Archibald Charles Henry Morrison (1794–1866) (see 1 March 1836).
4. See 11 June [1835], n. 3.

To John Gregson   Harrow—1 March 1836

Dear Sir

I enclose the receipt—will you be good enough to send the cheque to me at W. Godwin Esq—Exchequer Whitehall Yard—as thus I shall receive it sooner, & get the cash more readily.

I must now mention a change that I have arranged with regard to Percy & his education. At Easter I shall place him with a Tutor. I should have written before, had I believed it possible that Sir Timothy would make any objection. But I feel sure that he will approve this step—which several circumstances render eligible.

I think Percy has been the better for being at a Public School:—but Home-boarders—& he is one—labor under disadvantages, which encrease as they rise higher in the school.—And besides it were as well, since he is now sixteen, that he should be under the care of a Man, & at a greater distance from town. I have nothing to complain of in my Son—he is obedient & trustworthy—his faults are rather negative than absolute—I think he will exert himself more under a private tutor.

I think I am fortunate in my selection of one. Mr Morrison is Vicar of Stoneleigh, near Leamington; in Warwickshire.[1] He has been highly recommended to me. The Head of his College, Wadham[2] of Oxford—speaks in the highest terms of his classical attainments. Lady Dorme & Mr Chandos Leigh,[3] his neighbours, give the very highest testimonials of his temper—morals—& the esteem in which he is generally held. Mr Chandos Leigh in particular will be very kind to Percy.—Mr Morrison has five pupils besides Percy—The son of Sir Guy Skipwith formerly M.P. for Warwick Sh. the son of Lady Chamberlayne—the son of Lady Maxwell—who was at Harrow—these boys are of Percy's own age—there are two younger boys, named Barrett. Percy has been 3 years & a half at this school. At Easter he takes his place in the highest form but one in the school—in another year he would in the usual course of things leave it—I think his going to a tutor now, under all the circumstances to be preferred—I think Sir Tim^{thy} and yourself will agree with me. I may add that Mr Morrison's terms are moderate, and within my means.

Percy is in robust health—well grown—he has good spirits & a good temper. I wish Sir Tim. would see him before he goes. It is hard that going to another County, where I am promised that he shall be kindly received—that he should go without any mark of kindness from his Father's family—who were not always so estranged from him. He himself remembers that his Grandfather was at one time kind enough to notice him—& wonders why there should be a change now—when the notice would benefit him more.

I will if you please call on you with him before he goes to Warwick Shire.
I am dear Sir Yours Ob^{ly} MWShelley

ENDORSED: 1 March 1836 / Mrs Shelley. PUBLISHED: Jones, #460. TEXT: MS., Bodleian Library (MS., Shelley, Adds., c. 6, ff. 202–3).

1. Ninety miles north-northwest of London.

2. Morrison matriculated at Wadham College in October 1811 and received his B.A. in 1815 and his M.A. in 1820. In 1845 he became the rector of Sezincote and vicar of Longborough, Gloucester (*Alumni Oxonienses*).

3. Chandos Leigh (1791–1850; *DNB*), in 1839 first baron Leigh, author. Chandos Leigh's father, James Henry Leigh, nephew of the duke of Chandos, had been privately educated by Isaac Hunt, Leigh Hunt's father, who named his son after his pupil [Blunden, *Leigh Hunt,* p. 6).

TO MARIA GISBORNE   Harrow—4th March [1836]

My dearest Friend—I cannot express the deep concern I feel at the sad intelligence. Poor dear S.G. [*Signor Giovanni, John Gisborne*] The devoted husband—the kind friend! For him it is a mercy not to have survived you—but for you with your passionate attachments—with your nervous sufferings I know & feel what you must be enduring I long to be able to hasten down to you—Alas! poverty is a curse indeed when it prevents all possibility of being of use & comfort to those we love. Your good Elizabeth[2] will I trust write to me again. You have a treasure in her—which while it cannot soothe your regrets, yet in part diminishes the so to speak, bodily wretchedness attendant on your loss. She will wait on you & take care of you.

What she tells me of Mrs Hale[3] is exactly what one might have expected— What right have <u>they</u> to interfere in a question that concerns Henry[4] wholly?— But vulgar spirits are never easy except when they are making their odious influences felt. Elizabeth proves her extraordinary worth by her conduct on this occasion—and Henry I dare say will act as he ought—But that she refers by giving up her claim to him, to one as near & dear to you as your son & one of generous feelings—I should had advised her only giving up part of the legacy[5]—she never can be called upon to relinquish the whole. And do not you save & injure yourself by privation—to save for her—for Henry will assuredly do all that he ought. Meanwhile Elizabeth has the strongest claims on your friends—& I do beg she will regard me as one most anxious to serve her—Now my means are limited indeed but it is to be hoped that by & bye I can give more than words to prove my sense of her fidelity.

Jane goes on well. Jeff idolizes his baby—so that Jane says she wonders how he can have endured life so long without one. I envy her even to bitterness in the possession of a little girl. I am not well—but I hope to become so when I leave this place—where my spirits suffer so much & I have no refuge from melancholy thought. Percy is well—and My Father—

You must indeed let me hear often <u>of</u> you, if not <u>from</u> you—By & bye avoiding a subject which I <u>know you</u> will never be able to touch upon you can write to me of your health & other things. Is there any thing I can do for you?—

Ah dearest Maria What a thing life is! Do you remember our Italian summer—Villa Valsovano[6]—the stream of life runs on us—for us not calmly & kindly, but destructive & turbid, wrecking & leaving us solitary & desolate—Yours is indeed a bitter fate—would I could be with you to try to comfort you—Adieu—I shall count the days till I hear again from Elizabeth—She will always find a friend in me

Ever Affectionately Yours,
MWShelley

Jane sends her love & every kind & regretful message—She begs that Elizabeth will call on her if ever she comes to town

[P. 1, top]   Direct to me at Jane's

    13 Maida Vale
    Edgware Road

as I leave this place shortly—I will write soon again & tell you my new address

ADDRESS: Mrs Gisborne / Windsor Place / Princess Square / Plymouth [In another hand] Mrs Gisborne / Windsor Place / Princess Sq. / Plymouth / W. S. Trelawny. POSTMARK: FREE / 5 MR 5 / 1836. PUBLISHED: Jones, #461. TEXT: MS., Bodleian Library (MS., Shelley, Adds., c. 6, ff. 204–5).

    1. Of the death of John Gisborne, who was buried at Plymouth on 16 January 1836. Maria Gisborne survived her husband only a few months. Her burial was on 16 April 1836, also at Plymouth (Gisborne, Journals and Letters, p. 11).

    2. Elizabeth Rumble.

    3. Unidentified.

    4. Henry Reveley.

    5. John Gisborne bequeathed his papers to Elizabeth Rumble (see 5 April 1838, n. 1).

    6. See vol. I, 27 June 1819, n. 1.

*TO CHARLES OLLIER   Harrow—7 March—1836

Dear Sir

    I wrote to you some time ago & have received no answer—no intimation with regard to M[r] Trelawny's affair—no word by which I can judge if it will ever be terminated.

    I told you then that having at your suggestion begun another novel, I had hit upon a story that pleased me so much, that I wrote with a rapidity I had never done before—& had reason to believe that it would succeed far better than Lodore—being also of the present times—but with a much more interesting story. Nor could I part with it under fair price—but could make no offer in the present state of things.

I cannot however remain any longer in the suspense in which your silence throws me—and if this delay continues I may find myself obliged to dispose of it to another publisher[1]   I wish therefore for an immediate decision.

I would not thus urge you but it is six Months since the arbitration was agreed upon—& it being no further advanced than at the first day, it appears likely never to come to a conclusion.

You yourself & Mr Bentley must at once perceive that I cannot treat with you till it is decided. Let me hear from you directly on the subject as I shall be forced to understand your silence as a change of mind with regard to my novel—which I shall be sorry for—but wish to know the worst at once   I am in my third volume. Will you represent these things to Mr Bentley

I am, dear Sir

Yours truly

MWShelley

Why should not the arbitrators meet at the India House next Thursday? I would go up to town & meet them there on that day.

ADDRESS: Chas Ollier Esq / 8 New Burlington St. POSTMARKS: (1) T.P / Harrow; (2) 7. Nt. 7 / MR. 7 / 1836. UNPUBLISHED. TEXT: MS., Pforzheimer Library.

    1. On 18 March 1836 Godwin wrote to the Rev. John Hobart Caunter about negotiations with a Mr. Churton for the publication of *Falkner* (MS., Pforzheimer Library). Mr. Churton may have been Edward Churton (d. 1885), bookseller and publisher, 26 Holles Street, Cavendish Square.

To John Gregson   14 North Bank   Regent's Park[1]   8 April 1836

Dear Sir

Will you have the goodness to communicate to Sir T^thy & Lady Shelley the melancholy event of my dear Father's death—it occurred yesterday evening at seven after an illness of ten days—of a Catarrhal fever

Percy is quite well. He was to have gone to Warwick to his Tutor next Monday   His going must now be deferred till after the funeral[2]

I am, dear Sir,

Your Ob^ly

MaryW. Shelley

ENDORSED: 8th April 1836 / Mrs Shelley. PUBLISHED: Jones, #462. TEXT: MS., Bodleian Library (MS., Shelley, Adds., c. 6, ff. 207–8).

    1. Mary Shelley moved to this address c. 23 March 1836 (see [5 February 1836], n. 2).

    2. Godwin's funeral, on 14 April, was attended only by Percy Florence Shelley, James Kenney, Thomas Campbell, Dr. David Uwins, Rev. John Hobart Caunter, and Trelawny (Locke, *Godwin,* p. 345). In accordance with his wishes, Godwin was buried in the churchyard of St. Pancras as close as possible to the remains of Mary Wollstonecraft Godwin. In February 1851 their remains were removed to St. Peter's Churchyard, Bournemouth, and were interred with the remains of Mary Shelley, who died on 1 February 1851 (Paul, *Godwin,* II, 332–33; Jane, Lady Shelley to Alexander Berry, 7 March 1851, MS., Mitchell Library, New South Wales).

To John Corrie Hudson[1]   [?14 North Bank]
                                                      Friday [8 April 1836]

Dear Mr Hudson
    Relying on your often proved goodness & needing a friend I am come
to you on a very sad affair—My poor dear Father is gone—I am at the door
in a fly—pray come out to me—I want to take you to Mrs Godwin—who
prefers consulting you on several things to any one else—if you can give
her some portion of your valuable time—
    I am now waiting.

                                                      Yours truly
                                                      MWShelley

ADDRESS: J. C. Hudson Esq / Legacy Duty Office. PUBLISHED: Jones, #464. TEXT: MS.,
Huntington Library (Rare book 90327).
    1. Godwin's friend John Corrie Hudson, of the Legacy Office, was appointed by Godwin
as the sole executor of his will (Ingpen, *Shelley in England,* II, 611).

*To Edward John Trelawny   [?14 North Bank]
                                                     Sunday [10 April 1836]

Dear Trelawny
    I have no idea how you feel as to the question of attending my dear
Father's funeral. If you wish to go, I can arrange it—In that case leave a
note tomorrow directed to ⟨Mrs Godwin⟩ J. C. Hudson Esq saying that you
shall be glad to go—leave or send this with a card for Mrs Godwin at the
Exchequer <u>before twelve</u> tomorrow morning—as at that hour Mr Hudson
will be with M^rs G—[*Godwin*] making final arrangements
    At any rate leave your card tomorrow on Mrs Godwin—
                                                 In haste   Y^s truly
                                                             MS
    My Father is to be buried at St. Pancras.—Could you go with the Un-
dertaker to fix on the spot—"the nearest practicable to my Mother's tomb"—
if you can, mention this in your note tomorrow morning—& offer to go.
    I am ashamed to ask you all this—but are you not the best & most constant
of friends

UNPUBLISHED: Jones, #463, in summary. TEXT: MS., Keats-Shelley Memorial House, Rome.

To Mary Hays[1]   14 North Bank   Regents Park   20th April 1836
Dear Madam
    Having for some months been somewhat of an invalid—the extreme
fatigue and anxiety I went through while attending on the last moments of

my dearest Father have made me too ill to attend to any thing like business. By my Father's will his papers will pass thro' my hands,[2] & your most reasonable request will be complied with. There is nothing more detestable or cruel than the publication of letters meant for one eye only. I have no idea whether any of yours will be found among my Father's papers—any that I find shall be returned to you.—But my health is such that I cannot promise when I can undergo the fatigue of looking over his papers.

You will be glad to hear that one whom you once knew so well, died without much suffering—his illness was a catarrhal fever, which his great age did not permit him to combat—he was ill about 10, & confined to his bed 5 days—I sat up several nights with him—& Mrs Godwin was with him when I was not—as he had a great horror of being left to servants. His thoughts wandered a good deal but not painfully—he knew himself to be dangerously ill—but did not consider his recovery impossible. His last moment was very sudden—Mrs Godwin & I were both present. He was dosing tranquilly, when a slight rattle called us to his side, his heart ceased to beat, & all was over. This happened at a little after 7 on the Ev^g of the 7 ins. .

My dear Father left it in his will to be placed as near my Mother as possible. Her tomb in St. Pancras Church Y^d was accordingly opened—at the depth of twelve feet her coffin was found uninjured—the cloth still over it—& the plate tarnished but legible. The funeral was plain & followed only by a few friends—there might have been many more, but being private, we restricted the number. My Son, now sixteen, was among the Mourners.—

I have written these few particulars as they cannot fail to interest you.— I am obliged to you for your kind expressions of interest—your name is of course familiar to me as one of those women whose talents do honor to our sex—and as the friend of my parents—I have the honor to be, dear Madam

Very truly Yours
MaryShelley

ADDRESS: Miss Hays / 11 Grosvenor Place / Camberwell. POSTMARKS: (1) T.P / Newstead; (2) 7. Nt. 7 / AP. 20 / 1836. PUBLISHED: Jones, #465. TEXT: MS., Pforzheimer Library.

1. Mary Hays (1759–1843), author, was the close friend of both Godwin and Mary Wollstonecraft (Locke, *Godwin,* pp. 112–14).

2. Godwin had willed: "It is further my earnest desire that my daughter would have the goodness to look over the manuscripts that shall be found in my own hand-writing, & decide which of them are fit to be printed, consigning the rest to the flames." He wished her also to judge if any of the letters received by him would "be found proper to accompany my worthier papers" (Ingpen, *Shelley in England,* II, 611–12, a copy of Godwin's will).

To Edward John Trelawny   [?14 North Bank]
Saturday [14 May 1836]

Dear Trelawny

I send you a letter just received from Claire. If you think any thing can be done I should recommend its being placed at once in Mrs Norton's hands. It speaks for itself—& will excite her sympathy more than any other representation can do.[1] I do not think it impossible to do something—though I do not clearly see what.

Claire always harps upon my desertion of her—as if I could desert one I never clung to—we were never friends[2]—Now, I would not go to Paradise, with her for a companion—she poisoned my life when young—that is over now—but as ⟨I never⟩ we never loved each other, why these eternal complaints to me of me. I respect her now much—& pity her deeply—but years ago my idea of ⟨an agreable world⟩ Heaven was a world without a Claire—of course these feelings are altered—but she has still the faculty of making me more uncomfortable than any human being—a faculty she, unconsciously perhaps, never fails to exert whenever I see her—

Send me back her letter unless you send it to Mrs Norton as upon the whole I think her Mother had better see it—Yours MS.—

I shall see you tomorrow, by the by—we can talk about it then

ADDRESS: E. Trelawny Esq / 1 Duke St. St. James's. POSTMARKS: (1) T.P / Cra[wf]ord [St]; (2) 4. Mg. 4 / MY. 14 / 1836. PUBLISHED: Palacio, *Mary Shelley*, p. 613. TEXT: MS., Jean de Palacio.

    1. This may refer to Claire Clairmont's plan to become a housekeeper, perhaps for someone in England, which Trelawny refers to in his 14 May 1835 letter (Trelawny, *Letters,* p. 200).

    2. See vol. I, [24 April 1815], n. 4, and 19 July 1820, n. 13.

To Henry Crabb Robinson   14 North Bank—Regent's Park
27 May—1836

Dear Sir

I am, for the benefit of Mrs Godwin, who is left unprovided by the unfortunate death of my dear Father[1]—engaged in collecting his papers for publication[2]—There is a portion of autobiography & some interesting Correspondance—Could you assist me in augmenting the latter. It strikes me that there may be many interesting letters to Mess. Coleridge, Wordsworth & yourself—which no one would object to seeing published—I have no acquaintance with Mr Wordsworth nor the Executors of Mr Coleridge—Would you kindly interest yourself on the subject—& if there exist letters that would interest the public & annoy no one to see in print, would you endeavour to procure them for me

I take a great liberty in asking you—but am induced by the long intimacy that subsisted between you & my father & Mrs Godwin & my belief that you would willingly to [*do*] the latter a service

I am, dear Sir
Your Ob^t Servant
MaryShelley

ADDRESS: Henry C. Robinson Esq / 2 Plowden Buildings / Temple. POSTMARKS: (1) Park Terrace / 2D. PAID; (2) 7 N[n] 7 / MY 28 / 1836. ENDORSED: 27 May 1836 / Mrs Shelley, / Autograph / No publication took place—All the letters I was in possession of were applications for money—I wrote in reply that I had none but on business. PUBLISHED: Jones, #466. TEXT: MS., Dr. Williams Library (H. C. Robinson's letters, volume for 1836–37, f. 131).

1. In order to provide for Mary Jane Godwin, Mary Shelley, with Caroline Norton's assistance, applied to Lord Melbourne for a continuation of Godwin's annuity. Melbourne declined the annuity but instead granted a present of £300 from the Royal Bounty Fund. The extant letters from Caroline Norton to Mary Shelley written during this period suggest that the two had become friends (24 August 1836; Abinger MSS., Bodleian Library; Perkins, *Mrs. Norton,* pp. 89–91). An application for funds from the Royal Literary Fund on Mary Jane Godwin's behalf was endorsed by the Rev. John Hobart Caunter. On 10 May 1836 this Fund granted her £50, which she received on 16 May 1836 (MSS., Royal Literary Fund).

2. On 19 July 1836 Henry Colburn contracted to pay Mary Jane Godwin 350 guineas for Godwin's memoirs and correspondence, to be edited by Mary Shelley (Jones, #470, n. 1). Mary Shelley began this project, which she never completed, by organizing the three chapters of memoirs written by Godwin and collecting, organizing, and commenting on copies of his letters. Her notes are extensively quoted in Paul, *Godwin* (Abinger MSS., Bodleian Library). For these memoirs Mary Jane Godwin borrowed from Sir Charles Aldiss (?1775–1863; *DNB*), surgeon and antiquary, a copy of Godwin's *Sketches of History in Six Sermons* (1783). Aldiss noted that Mary Shelley "declared she did not know he had ever written any" (MS., Pforzheimer Library). Among others whom, like Henry Crabb Robinson, Mary Shelley unsuccessfully solicited for Godwin's correspondence was Bulwer. On 8 August 1836 he informed her that he possessed only a few scanty notes from Godwin and that he could not find them because of his change of residence (MS., University of Kansas).

*To [?   ]   [?14 North Bank   ?May–June 1836][1]

[*Fragment*]   I hope you are well—Percy writes me very satisfactory letters   Adieu

Ever Most truly Y^s MWShelley

UNPUBLISHED. TEXT: MS., Pforzheimer Library.

1. Because this fragment is written on black-bordered mourning stationery (which Mary Shelley stopped using by September) and refers to letters written by Percy Florence, the letter was probably written sometime after Godwin's funeral, when Percy Florence went to live at his tutor's home at Stoneleigh, near Leamington, and before 2 July 1836, when he returned to Mary Shelley for his holidays.

To JOHN GREGSON   14 North Bank   Regents Park   1 June 1836

Dear Sir

I send the receipt   will you send the cheque to me here.

I have frequent letters from Percy. He seems to be getting on very well—
& Mr Morrison says that in a twelvemonth he will be fit for colledge—I
have reason to be pleased with my selection of a tutor—& also—with Percy's
improvement & good qualities His holydays begin 2^d July[1]

> I am dear Sir
> Y^s Ob^ly
> MWShelley

ADDRESS: John Gregson Esq / 18 Bedford Row. POSTMARKS: (1) T.P / Park [Terr]; (2) 10
[F]n 10 / JU 2 / 1836. ENDORSED: 1 June 1836 / Mrs Shelley. PUBLISHED: Jones, #467.
TEXT: MS., Bodleian Library (MS., Shelley, Adds., c. 6, ff. 209–10).

1. Archibald Charles Henry Morrison's letter of 27 June 1836 informed her that Percy
Florence's holiday would extend from 2 July through 18 August 1836. Although his acquaintance with Percy Florence was brief, Morrison also expressed his pleasure at Percy Florence's
conduct and application to studies; indicated that he had found a violin master for him, if
Mary Shelley approved of the fee of three shillings; and enclosed an account of Percy Florence's
expenses for tuition, supplies (including fishing tackle, knife, pencil, toothbrush, sealing wax,
silk handkerchief), shoemaker, and tailor, which amounted to £34.5.1 [Abinger MSS., Bodleian
Library).

To JOHN GREGSON   14 North Bank   Regent's Park   6 June 1836

Dear Sir

Have you quite forgotten me?—I would not write to remind you that I
sent the receipt on the 1st but that if any accident has happened to the
cheque it ought to be discovered—

> I am dear Sir
> Y^s Ob^ly
> MWShelley

ADDRESS: John Gregson Esq / 18 Bedford Row. POSTMARKS: (1) T.P / Park Ter; (2) [10 F]n
10 / [J]U 6 / 1836. ENDORSED: 6 June 1836 / Mrs Shelley. PUBLISHED: Jones, #468. TEXT:
MS., Bodleian Library (MS., Shelley, Adds., c. 6, ff. 211–12).

To THOMAS LOVE PEACOCK   14 North Bank   Regent's Park
                                Monday Mor^g   [6 June 1836]

My dear Friend

Your naming Thursday's only as a visiting day is very provoking—Next
Thursday I expect a friend from the Country, who will prevent my reaching
the I.H [*India House*]—the first Thursday I can command you shall see me.

Will you put the enclosed in the post

I am ever very truly Y[s]

Turn over

Upon second thoughts let me say a word about Jeff[2]—Do you not think that you do wrong do [*to*] decide so determinately against being of service to a friend—a man of honor, integrity & talent? His judgement, I should consider, sound in most cases—his industry unwearied—The objection against him is only that he is odd—odd in appearance—A gentleman he is in feeling & conduct—if your Grandees think him <u>too odd</u> at first sight there is an end—but it is not every day one can serve a friend materially—nor help fortune to raise one, who has many claims to the sympathy of his friends— What say you? Will you reconsider?—

ADDRESS: T. L. Peacock Esq / East India House. POSTMARKS: (1) T.P / Park Ter; (2) [10] Fn. 10 / JU 6 / 1836. PUBLISHED: Peacock, *Works*, VIII, 478–79. TEXT: MS., Pforzheimer Library.
1. Thomas Jefferson Hogg.

TO [HENRY COLBURN] 14 North Bank—Regent's Park ⟨Tuesday⟩
Wednesday ⟨7⟩ 8 June [1836]

Dear Sir

I have heard that there has been, thro' M[r] Ayrton,[1] some communication made to you—with regard to the intended publication of my Father's Autobiography letters &.[2] I should be glad to see you & converse with you on the subject—Can you call tomorrow before two—or the next day—but tomorrow would suit me best—I am, dear Sir

Yours Ob[y]
MWShelley

PUBLISHED: Jones, #469. TEXT: MS., Pforzheimer Library.
1. William Ayrton (1777–1858; *DNB*), music critic and friend of Charles Lamb.
2. See 27 May 1836, n. 2.

*TO THOMAS ABTHORPE COOPER[1] 24 August—1836.
4 Lower Belgrave St.

Dear Sir

You will have heard by the public papers of the death of my dear Father, M[r] Godwin, which took place on the 7 April last. His strength had been failing for some months—but I thought him destined to live several years longer. His illness was a catarrhal fever—it lasted only about a week—he did not suffer much & his last moment was unaccompanied by any struggle or pain. You who knew him in his best days, will be interested in these details.

He enjoyed as I suppose you know, a small office in the pay of Government—this expired with him. Mrs Godwin is left without any resources, & my situation is such that I can do little for her. I applied for a continuance of my father's annuity for her—but his place being abolished Lord Melbourne contented himself by a present of £300. from the Royal Bounty Fund.

My father left his Autobiography up to his twentieth year—& a considerable Mass of letters & papers—I am employed in arranging these for publication for the benefit of Mrs Godwin   In my father's early journals I find mention of letters to you, particularly on theatrical subjects at the time of your first appearance as an actor in 1792—It is probable that among the accidents of a various life you have not preserved any of these but if any do exist, may I request that you will kindly furnish them for the publication I mention, to which they will add value.

You will scarcely remember me—It is many many years since I have seen you[2]—but you will remember my father and I dare trust to your kind recollections inducing you to comply with my request, if it is in in your power.

Believe me, dear Mr Cooper,
Ever truly Yours
MaryW. Shelley

Direct to me at Hookham's Library 15 Old Bond St. London.

ADDRESS: To be forwarded immediately / Thos A. Cooper Esq. / ⟨To the care of / Stephan Esq / Park Theatre / New York. U.S.⟩ [*In another hand*]. BRISTOL / Penna [   ]. POSTMARK: NEW YORK / OCT / 14. UNPUBLISHED. TEXT: MS., Pforzheimer Library.

1. Thomas Abthorpe Cooper (1776–1849), the son of William Godwin's mother's first cousin, was Godwin's ward and pupil from 1788 to 1792. In 1796 Cooper went to America, where he became a highly successful actor (Locke, *Godwin*, 33–34, 38–39; *SC*, V, 355–57; Elizabeth Tyler Coleman, *Pricilla Cooper Tyler and the American Scene, 1816–1889* [University, Ala.: University of Alabama Press, 1955]).

2. Cooper was in London from c. 9 December 1827 through c. 23 January 1828. On 17 December he played in *Macbeth* at Drury Lane. However, he was not well received by London audiences, and by March 1828 he was back on the American stage. During this London visit, he and Mary Shelley met at least once, on 23 January 1828, in the company of Godwin and John Howard Payne (Godwin, Journal; Fairlie Arant Maginnes, "A Biography of the Actor Thomas Abthorpe Cooper, 1775–1849" [Ph.D. diss., University of Minnesota, 1971]).

*TO [JOSIAH] WEDGWOOD[1]   4 Lower Belgrave St.   Belgrave Sq
                                                    9 Sep. 1836

Sir

On the lamented event of my dear Father's death, which occurred last spring, it has fallen to me to prepare his Memoirs & letters for the press—

—⋅◄{ 275 }►⋅—

it is my chief wish of course to do his Memory honor—besides this, he has left his Widow without any resources, & as my situation is such that it is not in my power to do much for her it becomes my duty to bring out this work for her benefit.

My father, Mʳ William Godwin was intimate with your Brother Mʳ Thomas Wedgewood[2]—if you have any letters—especially early letters, from my father to Mʳ Wedgewood you would greatly serve & oblige me by giving me such as you deem fit for publication[3]—I am sure there can be none that would not do your Brother honour as I suppose a more excellent & generous Man never existed

Excuse me for this request & I have the honor to remain

Your Obediᵗ Servant
MaryShelley

ENDORSED: Mrs Shelley / 9 Sept 1836. UNPUBLISHED. TEXT: MS., Pforzheimer Library.

1. Josiah Wedgwood, Jr. (1769–1843), second son of Josiah Wedgwood (1730–95; *DNB*), founder of the Wedgwood pottery works at Etruria, one hundred fifty miles north-northwest from London. Josiah Wedgwood, Jr., continued the pottery works after his father's death.

2. Thomas Wedgwood (1771–1805; *DNB*), pioneer in photography, spent part of the fortune he inherited from his father in aiding men of genius, including Coleridge and Godwin (Locke, *Godwin*, pp. 64–65, 191, 220).

3. Josiah Wedgwood, Jr., complied (see the next letter). The correspondence between William Godwin and Thomas and Josiah Wedgwood, Jr., preserved in Abinger MSS., Bodleian Library, includes seven letters from Godwin, four from Thomas Wedgwood, and five from Josiah Wedgwood, annotated for publication by Mary Shelley.

*To Josiah Wedgwood   4 Lower Belgrave St.   London
[c. 11 September 1836]

Sir

I thank you very much indeed for your promptitude & kindness in acceding to my request. The best way to forward the letters to me will be, I imagine by the Coach or Mail—directed to me either to my house, or to. me at Hookham's Library, 15 Old Bond St. London.

I will certainly send you copies of such letters of your Brother's as I wish to publish—& shall be grateful to you for your remarks. From all I have heard & know nothing can be said of your late lamented Brother that is not highly to his honor[1] As I suppose a better man never existed. It is against my wish & principles to publish any thing that could reasonably pain any relative of a correspondant of my Father

I shall anxiously expect the letters you are good enough to promise & before very long will send you those you ask for

I am, Sir
Yours Obliged & Obˡʸ
MWShelley

ADDRESS: Josiah Wedgewood Esq / Mari / Newcastle / Staffordshire. ENDORSED: Mrs Shelley /
Sep^tr 1836. UNPUBLISHED. TEXT: MS., Wedgwood Manuscripts 10098–11, Messrs Josiah
Wedgwood & Sons Ltd., Barlaston, Stoke-on-Trent, and Keele University Library, where the
manuscript is deposited.

1. Mary Shelley notes in reference to Thomas Wedgwood's 9 November 1795 letter to
Godwin which urges Godwin to accept Wedgwood's gift of £100: "Wedgwood's reply is so
full of good sense & ingenuous & upright feeling that I give it entire. We have here the sincere
confession of a modest & generous nature such as best depicts the amiable writer" (Abinger
MSS., Bodleian Library).

TO WILLIAM HAZLITT, JR.[1]   4 Lower Belgrave St.   10 Oct—1836

Sir

I am at this moment occupied in editing the Memoirs & Correspondance
of my Father, Mr Godwin. If among your Father's[2] papers, you found any
letter or notes of his, you would confer an obligation on me by letting me
have them. I have a few notes from Mr Hazlitt to my Father, which I will
look out & send you if you wish.

I wish I may perform my task as well as you have done yours   I read
your Memoir of your Father with great pleasure.[3]   Mr Talfourds Essay is
very beautiful & worthy its subject.

As I am leaving town will you direct to me at Hookham's Library 15 Old
Bond St. & oblige me by an early answer

I am, Sir
Your Ob^t Servant
MaryShelley

PUBLISHED: Jones, #470. TEXT: MS., Pforzheimer Library.
    1. William Hazlitt, Jr. (1811–93), registrar of the Court of Bankruptcy and man of letters.
    2. William Hazlitt.
    3. William Hazlitt had died on 18 September 1830. William Hazlitt, Jr., published a number
of his father's works, including the *Literary Remains of the Late William Hazlitt, with a Notice
of his Life, by his Son, and Thoughts on His Genius and Writings*, by E. L. Bulwer and Sergeant
Talfourd, 2 vols. (London: Saunders & Otley, 1836). Thomas Noon Talfourd (1795–1854),
knighted in 1849, author, lawyer, M.P., was a friend of many literary figures, including Hazlitt,
Lamb, Godwin, Coleridge, and Bulwer (*DNB;* Merriam, *Moxon,* pp. 150–54).

TO EDWARD JOHN TRELAWNY   Brighton—3^d Jan. [1837]

My dear Trelawny—This day will please you—it is a thaw—what snow we
have had—hundreds of people have been employed to remove it during
the last week—At first they cut down deep several feet as if it had been
clay—& piled it up in glittering pyramids & masses—then they began to
cart it on to the beach it was a new sort of Augean Stable—a never ending
labor—Yesterday when I was out—it was only got rid of in a very few &

very circumscribed spots—Nature is more of a Hercules—she puts out a little finger in the shape of gentle thaw—& it recedes & disappears—

When I got your letter I looked & rubbed my eyes & looked again for the little speck you mention—but no it was gone absolutely gone—& how much I miss the dear entity I need not tell—since you know what a dear thing she is—She has left behind a microscopic something that she calls a Mustachio comb—I wish I could send it you—it is delicate & immaterial as if made by Queen Mab—how she could fancy that it would suit the shaggy hairs of a wolf[1] I do not know—but even now she insists that it will meet with your approbation—We shall see.

Percy arrived only yesterday—having rather whetted than satisfied his appetite by going seven times to the play. He plays like Apollo on the flageolet—& like Apollo is self taught—Jane thinks him a miracle; it is very odd—he got a frock coat at Mette's[2] & if you had not disappointed us with your handkerchief he would be complete—he is a good deal grown—though not tall enough to satisfy me—however there is time yet—he is quite a child still—full of theatres & balloons & music—yet I think there is a gentleness about him which shews the advent of the reign of petticoats—How I dread it—I hope you will be useful to me when it begins—& let him into a few of those secrets—which, as he has a horror of risking health or comfort, will I hope keep him right—

Poor Jane writes dismally—She is so weak that she has frequent fainting fits. She went to a physician who ordered her to wean the child—& now she takes 3 glasses of wine a day—& every other strengthening mendiament—but she is very feeble—& has a cough & tendency to inflamation on the chest—I implored her to come down here to change the air—Jeff gave leave & would have given the money—but fear lest his dinner should be overdone while she was away—& lest the children should get a finger scratched makes her resolve not to come—what bad logic is this—if she got stronger here how much the better they would be in consequence   I think her in a very critical state—but she will not allow of a remedy. Claire's direction is 11 Queen St. Mayfair—Mrs Bennett is better & Claire also. Do write to her.[3]

I have no other news for you—no news from Mrs N— [Norton] or Mrs G— [Godwin][4]   The day before you left Brighton Caroline Aldridge came to it—she staid a week—She was looking very handsome indeed—& her daughter of 6 years old you would have idolized—a little fair fairy thing, as gay as a lark—She called on me—& I was glad to see how well, happy, & handsome she looked.

Poor dear little Zella—I hope she is well & happy—We are such wandering Tartars that we can be of little comfort to her—Thank you for your offer about money—I have plenty at present—& hope to do well hereafter—you are very thoughtful—which is a great virtue—I have not heard from your Mother or Charlotte[5] since you left—A day or two afterwards I saw Betsey Freeman—she was to go to place the next day—I paid her for her work—she looked so radiantly happy that you would have though{t} she was going to be married rather than to a place of hardship—I never saw any one look so happy—I told her to let me know how she got on & to apply to me if she wanted assistance. Jonathan still sails in stately size along the Parade—I am glad you are amused at your Brother's[6]—I really imagined that Fanny Butler[7] had been the attraction, till sending to the Gloucester, I found you were gone by the Southampton coach—& then I suspected another Magnet—till I find that you are in all peace—or rather war—Sherfield House—Much better so.—

I am better a great deal—quite well I [   ] believe I ought to call myself—Only I feel a little [   ] odd at times—I have seen nothing of the Smiths[8] I have met with scarce an acquaintance here—which is odd—but then I do not look for them, I am too lazy—Adieu—I hope this letter will catch you before you leave your present perch   Believe me always

Yours truly

MWShelley

Will this be a happy New Year? Tell me—the last I cant say much for—but I always fear worse to come—Nobody's Mare is dead[9]—if this frost does not kill—My cure (such as it will be) is far enough off still.

[*P. 1, top, by Trelawny*]   it is hard pleasures come singley Misfortunes in batallions[10]

ADDRESS: Edward Trelawny Esq / Sherfield House / Romsey-Hants. POSTMARK: BRIGHTON / JA 3 /1837. PUBLISHED: Jones, #471. TEXT: MS., Bodleian Library (MS., Shelley, Adds., c. 6, ff. 213–14).

1. A wolf was on the Trelawny family's crest (see *SC*, V, 325–26).

2. Mette & Co., 14 Sackille Street, Piccadilly.

3. Claire Clairmont's letter of 19 October 1836 informed Mary Shelley of her arrival, with the Bennets, at Paris. She noted that she was still uncertain about when she would arrive in London and encouraged Mary Shelley to go to the sea for her health rather than wait in town to receive her (Abinger MSS., Bodleian Library). Trelawny wrote to Claire Clairmont on 10 February 1837 asking her to write the review of Mary Shelley's *Falkner* that he had promised for the *Westminster Review* (Trelawny, *Letters*, pp. 205–6); however, no review of *Falkner* appeared in the *Westminster Review*. Falkner received a largely favorable reception from the critics (Lyles, *MWS Bibliography*, pp. 181–83).

4. Trelawny had interested himself in obtaining funds for Mary Jane Godwin after Godwin's death. He credited himself for obtaining Caroline Norton's efforts on behalf of Mrs. Godwin (Trelawny, *Letters*, pp. 199–201).

5. Charlotte Trevanion, Trelawny's sister.

6. Harry Trelawny (b. 1792), Trelawny's older brother.

7. Fanny Kemble Butler visited England from the beginning of December 1836 through 13 September 1837 (Frances Anne Kemble, *Records of Later Life*, 3 vols. [London: Richard Bentley & Son, 1882], I, 70–112; Armstrong, *Fanny Kemble*, pp. 197–201).

8. The Horace Smiths, who lived at Brighton from 1827 until Horace Smith's death in 1849 (unpublished letters of Horace Smith, Pforzheimer Library; Beavan, *James and Horace Smith*, p. 267).

9. *Henry IV, Part II* 2. 1. 38. "How now? Whose Mare's dead? What's the matter?"

10. *Hamlet* 4. 5. 78–79. "When sorrows come, they come not single spies, / But in battalions!"

*To Charles Ollier   Rock Gardens—Brighton   7 Jan^{ry} 1837

Dear Sir

You will have seen my New Novel[1] advertized by Saunders & Otley. I offered it thro' you to Mr Bentley, but you would not treat till it was finished. My necessities forced me to conclude with a publisher who did not object to advances—which were the more necessary—as ill health delayed my finishing till now.

You said a New Novel might cause the remainder of Lodore to be sold— I hope still you will reap that benefit from it—Are you sure 700 are not sold & that £50 is not due to me?[2] It would be very welcome & considering the very insignificant sum which you gave & the fair success it had—I own I think it is a little hard that the sale should stick just a few copies this side of 700—or 600 or whatever the number was—But I trust to your kindness— & sympathy with a poor Author to get me the £50 when it is possible—

I hope you are well & flourishing—I have been seriously indisposed— & came here for air & am much better

Believe me Dear Sir
Very truly yours
MWShelley

Address: Chas Ollier Esq / 8 New Burlington St / London. Postmarks: (1) [BRI]GHTO[N] / [JA] 8 / [1837]; (2) [   ] / PAID / 9 JA / 1837. Unpublished. Text: MS., Pforzheimer Library.
    1. *Falkner*.
    2. See 16 January 1833, n. 6.

To Edward John Trelawny   Brighton—Thursday
                                           [26 January 1837]

Dear Trelawny—I am very glad to hear that you are amused & happy— fate seems to have turned her sunny side to you—& I hope you will long enjoy yourself—I know but of one pleasure in the world—sympathy with another—or others—leaving out of the question the affections—the society of agreable—gifted—congenial-minded beings is the only pleasure worth having in the world—My fate has debarred me from this enjoyment—but you seem in the midst of it.

With regard to my Father's life—I certainly could not answer it to my conscience to give it up—I shall therefore do it—but I must wait. This year I have to fight my poor Percy's battle—to try to get him sent to College without further dilapidation on his ruined prospects—& he has to enter life at College—that this should be undertaken at a moment when a cry was raised against his Mother—& that not on the question of <u>politics</u> but <u>religion,</u> would mar all—I must see him fairly launched, before I commit myself to the fury of the waves.

A sense of duty towards my father, whose passion was posthumous fame makes me ready—as far as I only am concerned, to meet the misery that must be mine if I become an object of scurrility & attacks—for the rest—for my own private satisfaction all I ask is obscurity—What can I care for the parties that divide the world—or the opinions that possess it?—What has my life been what is it Since I lost Shelley—I have been alone—& worse—I had my father's fate for many a year a burthen pressing me to the earth—& I had Percy's education & welfare to guard over—& in all this I had no one friendly hand stretched out to support me. Shut out from even the possibility of making such an impression as my personal merits might occasion—without a human being to aid, or encourage or even to advise me—I toiled on my weary solitary way. The only persons who deigned to share those melancholy hours, & to afford me the balm of affection were those dear girls whom you chose so long to abuse[1]—Do you think that I have not felt, that I do not feel all this?—If I have been able to stand up against the breakers which have dashed against my stranded wrecked bark—it has been by a sort of passive dogged resistance, which has broken my heart, while it a little supported my spirit. My happiness, my health, my fortunes all are wrecked—Percy alone remains to me & to do him good—is the sole aim of my life. One thing I will add—if I have ever found kindness it has not been from liberals—to disengage myself from them was the first act of my freedom—the consequence was that I gained peace & civil usage—which they denied me—More I do not ask—Of fate I only ask a grave—I know what my future life is to be—what my present life is—& shudder—but it must be borne—& for Percy's sake I must battle on.

If you wish for a copy of my Novel you shall have one—but I did not order it to be sent to you because being a rover all luggage burthens—I have told them to send it to your Mother—at which you will scoff—but [   ] was the only way I had to shew my sense of her kindness. You may pick & choose those from whom you deign to receive kindness—You are a Man at a feast—Champagne & comfits your diet—& you naturally scoff at me & my dry crust in a corner—often have you scoffed & sneered at all the aliment of kindness or society that fate has afforded me—I have been silent—the hungry cannot be dainty—but it is useless to tell a pampered Man this.—Remember in all this, except in one or two instances—my complaint is not against <u>persons</u> but <u>fate</u>—fate has been my enemy throughout—I have no wish to encrease her animosity or her power, by exposing more than I possibly can to her rancourous attacks.

You have sent me no address—so I direct this to your Mother's—Give her & Charlotte[2] my love—& tell them I think I shall be in town at the beginning of next Month—My time in this house is up on the 3^d and I ought to be in town with Percy to take him to Sir Tim's Solicitors—so to begin my attack

I should advise you, by the bye—not to read my novel—You will not like it—I cannot <u>teach</u>—I can only <u>paint</u>, such as my paintings are—& you will not approve of much of what I deem natural feeling because it is not founded on the New light.—

I had a long letter from M^{rs} N— [*Norton*]³ I admire her excessively & I <u>think</u> could love her infinitely—but I shall not be asked nor tried, & shall [*cross-written*] take very good care not to press myself—I know what her relations think

[*P. 1, cross-written*] I shall soon be in town I suppose—<u>where</u> I do not yet know. I dread my return—for I shall have a thousand worries. Despite unfavourable weather—quiet & care have much restored my health—but mental annoyance will soon make me ill as ever—Only writing this letter makes me feel half dead—Still to be thus at peace is an expensive luxury, and I must forego it for duties, which I have been allowed to forget for a time—but my holyday is past. Happy is Fanny Butler if she can shed tears & not be destroyed by them—this luxury is denied me—I am obliged to guard against low spirits as my worst disease—& I do guard—& usually I am not in low spirits—Why then do you awaken me to thought & suffering by forcing me to explain the motives of my conduct   Could you not trust that I thought anxiously—decided carefully—& from disinterested motives—not to save myself but my child from evil—Pray let the stream flow quietly & as glittering on the surface as it may [*p. 2, cross-written*] do not awaken the deep waters, which are full of briny bitterness—I never wish any one to dive into the secret depths be content if I can render the surface safe sailing that I not annoy you with clouds & tempests but turn the silvery side outward, as I ought, for God knows I would not render any living creature as miserable as I could easily be—and I would also guard myself from the sense of woe which I tie lead about & sink low low—out of sight or fathom line

Adieu Excuse all this; it is your own fault—speak only of yourself— Never speak of me & you will never again be annoyed with so much stupidity.

Yours truly
MS

[*P 4, cross-written*]   If you are still so rich & can lend me £20 till my quarter I shall be glad—I do not know that I absolutely want it <u>here</u> but may run short at last—so if not inconvenient—will you send it next week—

ADDRESS: Edward Trelawny Esq / 16 Michael's Place / Brompton / London. POSTMARKS: (1) BRIGHTON / JA 26 / 1837; (2) T.P / Rate 2d; (3) A / 27 JA 27 / 1837; (4) 10 Fn 10 / JA 27 / 1837. PUBLISHED: Jones, #472. TEXT: MS., Bodleian Library (MS., Shelley, Adds., c. 6, ff. 215–16).

1. In Trelawny's 8 April 1831 letter to Mary Shelley (in a passage omitted in Trelawny, *Letters*), he had written: "You must indeed be hard pressed for companions when, with such a mind as yours, you can lower yourself to the level of such animals as these. In truth you have fallen from the high estate (I mean in respect of companionship) in which I first knew you—the Robinsons and the chaffy set with which they are allied, and then such straw stuffed idols as these Hares that you appear to idolise. God forgive you, for you have much to answer for" (Grylls, *Mary Shelley*, p. 220).

2. Charlotte Trevanion, Trelawny's sister.

3. Caroline Norton's letter of 5 January 1837 concerns itself largely with her views in support of the rights of divorced women to their children; her completion of her pamphlet *Obervations on the Natural Claim of a Mother to the Custody of Her Children;* and her intention to influence Parliament to change the law as it then stood. She also comments on a letter (unlocated) from Mary Shelley about the pamphlet: "It was a great triumph to me to see how <u>alike</u> what I had written & part of your letter were (what very awkward prose!) I improved the passage materially by your observation on <u>what was permitted to women, or rather excused in women when they receive any rudeness</u>: but as you are to have the trouble of reading it in print, I will not say more about it now. Perhaps you will not think I have gone far enough" (Abinger MSS., Bodleian Library; Perkins, *Mrs. Norton,* p. 133).

*To Mr. Macpherson   11 Queen Sreet   May Fair,[1]
                                                    Thursday   Feb—8th 1837

Mrs Shelley will feel obliged to Mr Macpherson to give to the Bearer of this note, a parcel of Books that was left for her to his care a considerable time ago.

ADDRESS: Mr Macpherson / Bookseller / Middle Row / Holborn. ENDORSED: Shelley Mrs / Feb. 8th 1837. UNPUBLISHED. TEXT: MS., Historical Society of Pennsylvania.

1. Claire Clairmont's residence (see 3 January [1837]). Mary Shelley's Journal entry for 2 February 1837 indicates that she had arrived that day from Brighton "to a comfortless No-home" and that she was "somewhat recovered" from her illness but suffered from "mortification, desolation & loneliness" and wanted to "hope or arrange a home of quiet comfort."

*To Thomas Abthorpe Cooper   [London   ?February–March 1837][1]

Dear Mr Cooper
    When I received your kind letter I was ill at Brighton & very little capable of writing—Since then I have been moving about—yet I ought to have written to you before to thank you for your prompt answer & kind invitation [   ] My work has been suspended by my illness—& it is only just now that I am getting to it again.[2] I do not think that it will be published till next winter—The profits will belong to Mrs Godwin—Could I encrease these—& could you facilitate my so doing by any arrangement made before hand with an American bookseller, you would confer an obligation on us.[3]
    I am a prisoner in this island—unable even to visit the Continent—far less able to wander away to the New World for a year—or your invitation would tempt me—& the Cities & Wilds of America excite wishes in one who has a passion for travelling—ingrafted early—& these [   ]iated.[4] I was left, as you may recollect, very young [a widow with] an only son, to whose education & welfare [I dedicate] myself. We are wholly dependant on my husband's [father during] his life & he is narrow-minded & niggardly—[Therefore my] life has been by no means an easy one—[When he

dies] Percy & I shall be well off—but he continues to live & may for years longer—While he lives I must remain here—When he dies the thousand cares attendant on our embarrassed property will still retain me. Percy is now seventeen—he is all I could wish—but I would not separate from him for the world—& his education must be finished at one of our universities. He will not be unworthy either of his Grandfather[5] or father—his understanding is clear—& his integrity & steadiness singularly great—joined as these qualities are to a high spirit & great cheerfulness of disposition—I do not much expect him to make a figure—for he has no ambition—but I feel certain that he will be a happy & a good Man—With such a tie you will perceive that a voyage across the Atlantic is beyond the bounds of possibi[lity]

Not the less Do I thank you for your hospitable offer—I grieve for the loss you have had[6]—but with so numerous a family[7] you must have a cheerful home. Mr Trelawny, whom you may remember seeing in America, tells me how highly considered & [sta]tioned you are in your adopted country [I hope] you long enjoy the blessings of competen[ce   ] midst of your family—It will alway[s give me] great pleasure to hear from you & [I remain]

Ever truly Yours
MaryShelley

As my stay in town is uncertain—my best direction will still be at Hookham's Library—15 Old Bond St.—London

My father's Memoirs—Consisting of a portion of autobiography regarding his early years—a great many letters from & to him—with notes by myself to connect & explain—will be in two Octavo Volumes[   ] I would send over one Volume as soon as p[ossible] if by so doing you could secure any price [   ] left as Mrs Godwin is with nothing except a [   ] from Government of a few hundred pounds wo[uld] be a benefit to us all.

ADDRESS: Thos A. Cooper Esq— / Bristol / Buck's County / Pennsylvania U.S. POSTMARKS: NEW-YORK / SHIP /APR / 16. UNPUBLISHED: Quotation in Coleman, *Pricilla Cooper Tyler*, pp. 55–56. TEXT: MS., Fairlie Arant Maginnes.

1. Mary Shelley returned to London from Brighton on 2 February 1837 (MWS *Journal*). The 16 April postmark indicates that this letter was written sometime in late February or early March.

2. The life of Godwin.

3. In 1817 Godwin had asked Cooper to arrange for publication of *Mandeville* in America (*SC*, V, 354–59).

4. The words are faded from an almost two-inch-square block in the lower lefthand corner of page 1 and the reverse side of the letter. Words supplied in square brackets in this letter were taken from previous transcriptions by Elizabeth Tyler Coleman and descendants of Cooper, including Fairlie Arant Maginnes, the letter's present owner.

5. Godwin.

6. Cooper's wife, Mary Fairlie Cooper, died on 19 March 1833 at the age of forty-three (Coleman, *Pricilla Cooper Tyler*, p. 26).

7. The Coopers had five daughters and one son.

*To [CHARLES OLLIER]   24 South Audley St.[1]
                                        Tuesday   21 March [1837]

Dear Sir

As you did not answer me in any way when I last wrote to you—will you now tell me whether the number of Lodore is sold—& whether I am entitled to the £50—considering all I ever got for that book was £100—it seems hard to get no more—Will you do me the favour to enquire about it & to speak to Mr Bentley—it would be a great comfort to me if you can arrange this little affair for me & I shall feel obliged

                                        I am, dear Sir,
                                        Yours truly
                                        MWShelley

UNPUBLISHED. TEXT: MS., Pforzheimer Library.
    1. Mary Shelley resided at 24 South Audley Street from March 1837 to November 1837.

*To CHARLES OLLIER   24 South Audley St   5 April 1837

Dear Sir

I have not heard from you as I hoped—As I am not far off—perhaps you would call some morning—I have not seen you a long time—& we might talk—of the subject of my last note—& other Matters—Dear Sir
                                        I am yours truly
                                        MWShelley

ADDRESS: Chas Ollier Esq / 8 New Burlington St. UNPUBLISHED. TEXT: MS., Fitzwilliam Museum.

*To LEIGH HUNT   24 South Audley St.   26 April [1837]

My dear Hunt

I ought to have answered your kind letter long ago—and having thus acknowledged my duty, & confessed having failed in it, I will not fill up a page with reasons & excuses, none of which are sufficing—though from day to day they have led me on. I am much flattered & pleased by your praise of my book—the more so that I have heard dispraise—Trelawny does not like it—but as I fancy I can detect the causes of his distaste—& do not when I write, think of pleasing him (though I always do whether you will approve or not) I do not so much mind—Jane also says that she liked the Last Man better—for myself I own it is a favourite of mine—yet I can see its defects—I had a vivid conception of the story & wrote with great speed— It wanted afterwards I believe, a sort of softening in the tone, & something to diversify the continual pressure on one topic—but I fell into ill health & was obliged to let the pages go to the press, in a cruder state than I generally permit.

Trelawny ⟨told⟩ tells me that he met a very handsome son of yours a few evenings ago—whom I presume to be Henry—His encomium of his personal appearance was very energetic—You do not mention him in your letter, nor what he is doing—& to do—The account you give me of your present situation is very pleasing—I hope its comforts will continue & encrease. I hope one day to visit Marianne & see how you are—But in this large town there is nothing so difficult as for a woman to get to the verge of the radii, to see those who fly off from the centre—You ought to call on me, & I shall hope to see you—though changed as I must be, after a lapse of years—after a great deal of ill health (a new thing for me—but not the most disagreable part of my fate—it was rather an amusement) & many struggles & sorrows—which still continue, alas! for mine is not a path of roses.

At Easter I went on a visit to a friend of mine in Sussex[1]—the gentry there are very willing to be civil to me—Every one hating the Shelley's so much—not Sir Tim exactly—who though something of a fox, is more of a fool—but Lady Shelley is so illnatured, the girls so arrogant & disagreable, that they are very generally disliked. It is they say, & truly, a pleasure to be praised by the praiseworthy—& certainly it is gratifying to find one's enemies unworthy & generally disliked. I am now trying to impel his Grandfather to pay Percy's expences at College[2]—I do not know whether I shall succeed. Percy writes me word that he wants to get his university education soon over that he may devote his time to music instead of the classics—he says "Perhaps it is all humbug but Elston (his Master) says that I shall be a good flute player"—& he is to take to the piano also when in town—he has the power of attention & industry in his amusements, which promises well.

Write—if you do not call—& tell me what you are all doing. Give my love to Mary & tell her how sincerely I wish her all happiness[3]—I am looking for a permanent lodging in town—at present I am in an inconvenient one—yet convenient in as much as it is near several people I know & like—& if one is to have <u>any</u> society, I find one must tend towards the centre & not emerge towards the circumference of wide London besides the expence to a poverty stricken being to see one's friends only when they make a pilgrimage.

My best love to Marianne—I hope Thornton finds his lucubrations profitable[4]—their hard name & I believe dry meaning rather frighten me. Have you Vincent with you again?—Hampstead is a dear place—I sometimes visit the Heath—& not long ago descended into the Vale of Health[5]— How altered, how bepainted & becocknified are its little Cottages—& all the old washerwomen's cots turned into <u>villinas</u> & a Villa—most resplendant of all—the very incarnation of the spirit of ignorant finery sprung up be-

hind—But there are the Heath—the fields—the truncated Avenues & em-
bowering limes just the same as ever, & it is a very pretty place.—
Adieu—I shall hope to see you, & am always

Affectionately yours

MaryShelley

Trelawny wrote down your address in his pocket book & vows to make
an invasion on your territories

UNPUBLISHED. TEXT: MS., Pforzheimer Library.

1. Possibly Georgiana Beauclerk Paul.

2. Percy Florence Shelley was admitted pensioner at Trinity College, Cambridge, on 7 July
1837. His attendance began with the Michaelmas term, 10 October 1837, and he was awarded
a B.A. on 23 January 1841. His tutor at Trinity was Thomas Thorp (1797–1877), who
eventually became archdeacon and chancellor of Bristol (information supplied by Rosemary
Graham, Trinity College Library).

3. Almost certainly a reference to the marriage of Mary Florimel Hunt and John Gliddon
(see vol. I, 2–5 October [1823]; SC, V, 258–60). Thornton Hunt had married Katherine
"Kate" Gliddon, John Gliddon's sister, in 1834. About 1849 Thornton Hunt formed a permanent liaison with Agnes Jervis Lewes (1822–1902), the wife of George Lewes (1817–78;
DNB). Thornton and Kate Hunt had ten children; he and Agnes Lewes had four. The relationship between Hunt and Agnes Lewes eventually led to George Lewes's union with Mary
Ann Evans, the future George Eliot (Tatchell, Leigh Hunt, pp. 59–71; SC, V, 260).

4. Thornton Hunt became a successful journalist (DNB). He wrote about many subjects
but gained a reputation particularly in the area of art criticism. Mary Shelley's comment in
this letter may refer to the article that he wrote for the Constitutional on the disposal of
colonial lands (Blunden, Leigh Hunt, p. 277).

5. The Hunts lived in the Vale of Health when the Shelleys first knew them (see vol. I, 5
December 1816, n. 6).

To Edward John Trelawny   [?24 South Audley Street]
                                 Friday   [?May–July 1837][1]

Dear Edward

I have heard from Charlotte[2] & agreed to dine at Brompton[3] on Monday.

I have not yet called on Mrs Butler—How can I without a carriage? It is
too hot to walk—I will on Monday if possible. Send me her address, for I
do not know it

Yours Ever

MWS

PUBLISHED: Jones, #474. TEXT: MS., Pforzheimer Library.

1. See 3 January [1837], n. 7. Until c. 26 July 1837, Frances Kemble Butler resided with
her parents in their London home, 10 Park Place. After that she traveled in England until her
departure (Kemble, Records of Later Life, I, 73–84). The date of this letter is based on Mary
Shelley's comments that she is within walking distance of Frances Kemble and that the weather
is hot. This would suggest that the letter was written after Mary Shelley took up her residence
at 24 South Audley Street (March 1837) but probably not before May.

2. Charlotte Trevanion.

3. Trelawny's mother's home (see [?26 September 1835] to Charlotte Trevanion, n. 2).

*To Claire Clairmont   [24 South Audley Street]   2 May—1837

My dear Claire

I enclose you an Autograph of Shelley's as you requested—I hope the person to whom you give it will appreciate it as it deserves—or I should not like to part with it—

I am, dear Claire

Ever Affectionately Yours
MaryShelley

[P. 2, Shelley's autograph]

Yours ever faithfully
Percy B Shelley—

UNPUBLISHED. TEXT: MS., Jean de Palacio.

To John Bowring   24 South Audley St   1 June [1837]

Dear Doctor Bowring

Many thanks for the Del Rios,[1] which is of the greatest assistance—would it be quite impossible for you to lay your hands on any other of Cervantes's works—I remember you lent me some several years ago—Pellicers' book[2] I want much

Do not forget your promised call—a conversation with you would doubtless be a great help to me, and I count on it—though it is trespassing on very valuable time

Ever truly Yours
MWShelley

ENDORSED: (1) Mrs Shelley / 1 June 1837; (2) June 1 1837 / M. Shelley. PUBLISHED: Jones, #475. TEXT: MS., Huntington Library (HM 2768).

1. Vincent de los Rios, "Análisis del Quijote," in Miguel de Cervantes, *El ingenioso hidalgo Don Quijote de la Mancha* (Madrid: Real Academia Española, 1780), I, pp. xliii–clxiv, referred to in MWS, *Lives* (1835–37), III, 121.

2. Juan Antonio Pellicer y Pilares, *El ingenioso hidalgo Don Quijote de la Mancha, compuesto por Miguel de Cervantes Saavedra* (Madrid: Real Academia Española, 1782), referred to in MWS, *Lives* (1835–37), III, 121.

To Leigh Hunt   Rock Gardens, Brighton   June 20, 1837

[*Quotation*]   I was an exile at Harrow for several years—a more dreary life than that which I lived there cannot be imagined—however, I did not grudge it for Percy's sake.

PUBLISHED: Jones, #476. TEXT: Jones, #476.

*To Edward John Trelawny   17 or 24 South Audley Street
                                                        [30 June 1837]

Dear Trelawny—I send you the autograph   Mad^m B— [?*Boccella*]¹ number Claire thinks (She has not been there yet & Mad^m B has been out of town) is 40 Curzon St.
      Percy has come much improved & very nice & dear—It is a great comfort
                                                        In haste Y^s truly

[*Enclosure, Shelley's autograph*]

      Believe me
      affectionately your's
B. Shelley

ADDRESS: E. Trelawny Esq / 1 Duke St. / St. James's. POSTMARKS: (1) S. Audley St. / 2D. PAID; (2) PAID / 2 An A / JU 30 / 1837 / 2 An 2. UNPUBLISHED. TEXT: MS., Pforzheimer Library.
      1. Claire Clairmont refers to Trelawny's friend Jane Boccella as Madame Boccella in her letters to Mary Shelley (Abinger MSS., Bodleian Library).

To John Bowring   17 South Audley St.   Monday   3 July [1837]

Dear Doctor Bowring
      Your labours in P^t [*Parliament*] are closing for the moment—shall I not see you before you quit town—is there the slightest hope of your being able to get at any other Spanish books for me   And will you tell me what papers you have written in what Reviews on Spanish literature & if there exist any translations by you of Spanish poets besides the volume which I am well acquainted with.¹ Will you tell me if any where I can meet with any translations from Boscan, Garcilaso de la Vega, Herrera, Mendoza² &c &c—Do let me have an answer to this question directly—
                                    I am dear Dr Bowring
                                    Ever truly Y^s
                                    MWShelley

ENDORSED: (1) July 3 1837 / MWShelley; (2) Mrs Shelley / 3 July 1837. PUBLISHED: Jones, #477. TEXT: MS., Huntington Library (HM 2769).

1. *Ancient Poetry and Romances of Spain*, ed. and trans. John Bowring (London: Taylor and Hessey, 1824).

2. See 3 October [1835], n. 1.

TO JOHN BOWRING   24 South Audley St.   Thursday   13 July [1837]

Dear Doctor Bowring

Your note made me Melancholy to think how you should be drawn from the studies you loved & adorned to the arid business of life. Thanks for all the hints you have given me[1]—I have got Wiffin's Garcilaso[2]—He mentions in that that he meant to publish a Spanish Anthology—did he ever?—or can you tell me if any where I can find translations from Boscan & Hurtado de Mendoza[3]—Did you ever in any Article? Your translations are best of all—they are so easy flowing & <u>true</u>.

Would You be so good as to frank & send the enclosed today if possible if not tomorrow

> Ever truly Y^s
> MWShelley

ENDORSED: (1) Mrs Shelley / 13 July 1837; (2) July 13 1837 / Mrs Shelley. PUBLISHED: Jones, #478. TEXT: MS., Huntington Library (HM 2770).

1. Mary Shelley also sought information from other sources. On 7 October 1837 Robert Southey wrote a letter, believed to be to Dionysius Lardner, containing information about Southey's article in the *Quarterly Review* which discusses Macedo's attack on Camoens. A note on this letter reads: "Sent Mrs Shelley the information" (MS., Pforzheimer Library). MWS, *Lives* (1835–37), III, 333, refers specifically to Robert Southey and his article in the *Quarterly Review*.

2. *The Works of Garcilaso de la Vega*, trans. Jeremiah Holmes Wiffen (London: Hurst, Robinson and Co., 1823).

3. See 3 October [1835], n. 1.

TO BENJAMIN DISRAELI[1]   24 South Audley St.   Friday
                                        [?15 November–7 December 1837][2]

Dear M^r D'Israeli

I send you a letter to frank—I hope it will not inconvenience you—but let it go as soon as you can.

Winter has come hard upon the heels of summer: I detest winter & all its belongings—And the cold dispirits one sadly—Are you meditating your Maiden speech? I wonder if you <u>will be</u> what you <u>can be</u>.—Were your heart in your career it would be a brilliant one

> Beleive me yours truly
> MaryShelley

The enclosed is for

> Miss Robinson[3]
> Ardglass Castle
> Down

PUBLISHED: C. L. Cline, "Two Mary Shelley Letters," *Notes and Queries* 195, no. 22 (28 October 1950): 475–76. TEXT: MS., Bodleian Library.

1. Benjamin Disraeli and Mary Shelley may have been introduced by Mary Anne Evans Lewis (1792–1872), who, along with her husband Wyndham Lewis (1778–1838), politician, befriended Disraeli in 1832. After Wyndham Lewis's death, Mary Anne Lewis and Disraeli were married, on 28 August 1839 (for an account of her life see Mollie Hardwick, *Mrs. Dizzy: The Life of Mary Anne Disraeli Viscountess Beaconsfield* [New York: St. Martin's Press, 1972]). Mary Shelley probably met Mary Anne Lewis through George Beauclerk, with whom Mary Anne Lewis had a three-year love affair (Hardwick, *Mrs. Dizzy*, p. 65; see also [?19 March 1838]). Godwin's Journal records that Mrs. Wyndham Lewis visited Mary Shelley at 7 Upper Eaton Street on 25 August (with George Beauclerk) and 2 September 1834. Godwin's Journal also records visits to him by Disraeli, who admired Godwin; thus it is also possible that it was Godwin who introduced Mary Shelley to Disraeli.

2. This letter was written sometime between 15 November 1837, when Disraeli took his seat in Parliament, and 7 December 1837, when he gave his maiden speech (Cline, "Two Mary Shelley Letters," p. 475, n. 2).

3. Although it has been thought that the Miss Robinson referred to was Rosa Robinson, who later married Aubrey Beauclerk, it is more likely that this letter was directed to Julia Robinson. On 2 February 1837 Mary Shelley noted in her Journal: "But I will not complain—I write this but as a landmark—on Xmas Eve J— [*Julia*] left me for A [*Aubrey or Ardglass*]." On 31 December 1837 Mary Shelley wrote in her Journal: "Time passes—my correspondance with Julia prevents my wish to overflow in this book."

*TO THOMAS LOVE PEACOCK   41[D] Park St.[1]   Grosvenor Sq
                                               5 Dec. [1837]

My dear Friend

I was agreably surprized by a visit from Mary:Ellen yesterday   She is a very fine girl—& her pretty face indicates intelligence. Pray send her to call on me whenever she is in the humour for so long a walk—It will give me great pleasure to have her with me for a few days—I explained to her how I had no spare bed at present—but in a few weeks I hope she will favour me with a visit. I have moved since I last wrote—I got frightened about my house—& the money I counted on for entering was mostly spent on Percy—& I could not anticipate on the future   With the possibility of having to pay Baily[2] besides.—

Claire will be in town at Xmas—you & your daughter must come & meet her here at that time. I expect Percy from Cambridge on the 15[th3]   Nothing is settled about him   I suppose it will be this Xmas—

Get the enclosed (<u>seal it</u>) franked & sent as soon as you can—It had better go by sea—It was a very stupid mistake on the part of M[rs] Maclean[4]

directing to me at the I. H— [*India House*] but she is now aware & wont
do so again—If any letter comes under cover to you for me let me have it
by the 2ᵈ post—

I am very truly Yˢ
MWShelley

UNPUBLISHED. TEXT: MS., Houghton Library.

1. Mary Shelley lived at 41d Park Street until c. 28 March 1839.
2. Unidentified.
3. Percy Florence left Cambridge on 18 December 1837 (Trinity College Exit Book).
4. Louisa Robinson Maclean, who had gone to India in 1834, died at Arakan on 15 December
1837 (India Office Library; see also 7 May 1834). The letter Mary Shelley refers to was
probably from Julia Robinson, who was in regular correspondence with her sister and brother-
in-law. Lockhart Maclean's 10 August 1837 letter to Juila Robinson informed her of the
death of the Macleans' daughter, their expectation of another child in January, and the difficulties of adjusting to the climate in Calcutta. In this letter he also sent kind remembrances
to Mary Shelley (Abinger MSS., Bodleian Library).

*TO LEIGH HUNT   Park St.   [?December 1837–March 1838] (*a*)¹

My dear Hunt—The book you mention is packed with many others in a
case at Kentish Town²—I could not get at it now by any means—I am very
sorry.

I am always glad to see your hand writing—I ought to have thanked you
for your agreable present³ & I meant { } have replied to it unworthily
by my Lives of the Spanish poets—In writing of Cervantes so much reminded me of you that I thought it would please you but I have learnt to
procrastinate & you must forgive me.

If you wᵈ name an evening when you would meet Jane at my house we
should rejoice—Would not Marianne accompany you?—think of this—I
am delighted to think that you do not forget me Jane & I often talk of
you—& did we wear trowsers instead of petticoats should attempt
Chelsea We have neither of us been well however this dreary weather. I
did not see Henry—Trusting that some fair sun smiles on you & cheers
your warm heart—whether self created or ⟨heave⟩ earth [*cross-written*] born—
some sun of prosperity & enjoyment—& with love to Marianne I am Dear
Hunt

Yours Ever
MS.

Look at my seal—Mʳˢ Norton gave it me⁴—is it not pretty? & not pert—
since a gift

UNPUBLISHED. TEXT: MS., Pforzheimer Library.

1. This date is based on Mary Shelley's residence at Park Street and the contents of this
letter, which suggest that it was written relatively soon after the publication of Mary Shelley's
Spanish *Lives,* c. September or October 1837 (see the previous letter).

2. Mary Shelley resided at Kentish Town from June 1824 through July 1827.

3. Perhaps a reference to *The Book of Gems,* edited by Samuel Carter Hall (1838), a compilation of poetry which included five poems by Hunt as well as his brief sketches of Keats, Shelley, and Tennyson.

4. The seal is missing from the letter and is not otherwise identified.

TO LEIGH HUNT   41d. Park St.   Saturday
                                          [?December 1837–March 1838](*b*)

My dear Hunt

Your promise for May[1] is very kind & pleasant—though so far off—I shall remind you of it be assured & Jane & I shall be delighted once again to see our unforgotten & dear friend. I am sorry that Marianne cannot join us. I hope all coughs & illness will be well then—You are good & right to be careful—for Jane especially—as. she has a little baby.

I hear that some friends Talfourd[2] & Bulwer are trying to get a pension for you[3]—God grant they succeed—no one deserves it more. I am trying to get a small one for Mrs Godwin[4]—poor as I continue to be through circumstances never changing, I have it much at heart to succeed.

I will tell Dr Lardner to cause the Lives of the Spanish Poets to be sent directed to you at Hookhams—some day next week send for it—I am sure that of Cervantes will come home to you. Camoens was more unfortunate than he—but does not <u>come home to you</u> in the same manner   I am now writing French Lives[5]—The Spanish ones interested me—these do not so much—yet it is pleasant writing enough—sparing one's imagination yet occupying one & supplying in some small degree the <u>needful</u> which is so very needful.

With love to Marianne believe me Y^s Ever Truly

                                                    MWShelley

PUBLISHED: Jones, #474. TEXT: MS., British Library (Add. 38,523, ff. 106–7).

1. See the previous letter for Mary Shelley's invitation to Hunt.

2. See 10 October 1836, n. 3.

3. Leigh Hunt did not receive a pension until 22 June 1847, when he was awarded £200 yearly from funds of the Civil List (Blunden, *Leigh Hunt,* p. 297).

4. Caroline Norton's letters to Mary Shelley during this period indicate that she was again assisting Mary Shelley's efforts to obtain a pension for Mary Jane Godwin (Abinger MSS., Bodleian Library; Perkins, *Mrs. Norton,* pp. 141–43).

5. *Lives* (1838–39) was published in two volumes. Volume I, published c. July 1838, includes essays on Montaigne, Rabelais, Corneille, Rouchefoucauld, Molière, La Fontaine, Pascal, Madame de Sévigné, Boileau, Racine, and Fénélon. Volume II, published in 1839, includes essays on Voltaire, Rousseau, Condorcet, Mirabeau, Madame Roland, Madame de Staël (Lyles, *MWS Bibliography,* pp. 38–39).

*To Charles Ollier   41d Park St.   Monday Mor^{ng}
                                              [December 1837–March 1839]

Dear Sir
   I am obliged to go out this morning—so do not call at 12   I will call on
you between 1 & 2—or will you call between 3 & 4—

                                                       Yours truly
                                                       MWShelley

ADDRESS: Chas Ollier Esq / 8 New Burlington St. UNPUBLISHED. TEXT: MS., Pforzheimer
Library.

To Lady Sydney Morgan   41 d. Park St.   Wednesday
                                            [December 1837–March 1839][1]

Dear Lady Morgan
   As you return none of my calls I suppose {you} cut me—which I think
cross.—I send you the _relic_[2] & you may say that I have never parted with
one hair to any one else. You will prize it—Poor dear fellow—he was very
nice the evening I cut it off—which was in August 1822—with love to Miss
Clarke[3]

                                       Yours Ever   MShelley

ENDORSED: (1) 1840 note from Mrs Shelley The Author of Frankensten on [?sending] me a
lock of Lord Byrons hair—; (2) Mrs Shelley / Author of / Frankenstein. PUBLISHED: Jones,
#482 (half of letter). TEXT: MS., Pforzheimer Library.
   1. The date 1840 in the endorsement is in error, since Mary Shelley moved from 41d Park
Street at the end of March 1839.
   2. A lock of Byron's hair (see endorsement). In July 1832 Lady Morgan requested and
received a lock of Byron's hair from Teresa Guiccioli, but on 30 January 1836 Lady Morgan
wrote in her journal that she had lost the lock (_Lady Morgan's Memoirs,_ 2 vols. [London: Wm.
H. Allen & Co., 1863], II, 345, 412).
   3. Josephine Clarke (later married to Edward Geale), Lady Morgan's niece, who accompanied
Sir Charles and Lady Morgan when they removed permanently from Ireland to England on
20 October 1837 (_Lady Morgan's Memoirs,_ II, 427).

*To Mary Gaskell   41d Park St   Friday
                                       [?15 December 1837–18 March 1839]

Dear Mrs Gaskell
   Will you & Mr Gaskell & Miss Hill[1] favour me by drinking tea with me
on Monday Evening 18th at 1/2 past nine

                                                       Yours truly
                                                       MWShelley

UNPUBLISHED. TEXT: MS., Pforzheimer Library.

1. Unidentified.

*To [?ERSKINE OR WILLIAM] PERRY   41D Park St.   Thursday
                                        [?19 December 1837–March 1839][1]

Dear Mr Perry

Percy is out—but I know that he is engaged today to a young friend who sets off for Paris tomorrow—Julian is at Thames Ditton[2]—he returns Saturday. Some day early next week if convenient to you Percy will be delighted to attend your hospitable table—am I never to see you again? It is an age since you charmed me by a call

                                                            Yours Ever
                                                            MWShelley

UNPUBLISHED. TEXT: MS., Pforzheimer Library.

1. This letter was written sometime after 18 December, when Percy Florence joined Mary Shelley at 41d Park Street during his holiday from Cambridge (Trinity College Exit Book), and before c. 28 March 1839, when Mary Shelley removed from 41d Park Street.

2. Julian Robinson (1818–99), a son of Joshua Robinson. Julian Robinson became a clergyman and was stationed in India (India Office Library). The Robinsons had moved to Thames Ditton in October 1832 (MWS Journal, October 1832).

To EDWARD BULWER   41^d Park St.   Sunday
                                        [?19 February–March 1838]

Dear Mr Bulwer

Do excuse my writing a few lines to say how very much the Lady of Lyons[1] pleased me. The interest is well sustained—the dialogue natural— one person answers the other—not as I found in Werner & Sardanapalus, each person made a little speech a part; or one only ⟨spoke⟩ speaking that the other might say something—the incidents flow from the dialogue, & that without soliloquies, & the incidents themselves flow naturally one from another—There is the charm of nature & high feeling thrown over all.

I think that in this play you have done as Shelley used to exhort Ld Byron to do—left the beaten road of old romance—so worn by modern dramatists & idealized the present—& my belief is that now that you have found the secret of dramatic interest, & to please the public—you will, while you adhere to the rules that enable you to accomplish this necessary part of a drama, raise the audience to what height you please. I am delighted with the promise you hold out of being a great dramatic writer.—But (if I may venture to express an opinion to one so much better able to form them— an opinion springing from something you said the other night) do not be apt to fancy that you are less great when you are more facile—it is not always the most studied & (<u>consequently</u>) the favourite works of an author that are his best titles {to} fame—the soil ought to be carefully tended, but the flower that springs into bloom most swiftly is the loveliest. I have not read your play—I would not till I saw it—for a play is a thing for acting not the closet

I hope you will remember your promise of calling on me some Evening & believe me

Y^s truly

MWShelley

PUBLISHED: Jones, #479. TEXT: MS., Hon. David Lytton Cobbold, on deposit at the Hertfordshire County Record Office.

1. Bulwer's play *The Lady of Lyons* was first produced by William Charles Macready (1793–1873; *DNB*), actor and manager, on 15 February 1838 at Covent Garden and was highly successful. The published edition, dedicated to Thomas Noon Talfourd, was in its second edition before 11 March 1838 (Lytton, *Life of Bulwer*, I, 534–36).

TO ANDREW SPOTTISWOODE[1]   4 March [1838]   Park St

Sir

I sent you the other day the life of Rousseau[2] from p. 1 to p. 31.

When you returned the pages of copy before sent, (while the life of Voltaire[3] was printing) you kept back p. 4   I was afraid it was lost, & rewrote it. All you have to do is to cancel p. 4 in the copy I sent you the other day, & to substitute p. 4—that originally belonged to it, now enclosed—which—as marked by the printer you will find connects itself with what is already printed, & then go on to page 5—

Why you send me p. 31—the last page of copy I sent I cannot guess—I sent the whole life regularly from 1 to 31.—

Yesterday I sent from 31 to the end.

Y^s Ob^y

MWShelley

If you find difficulty you had better send me the last sheet of the life of Voltaire containing the beginning of Rousseau & the whole of my copy—together with these two pages & I will explain it in a moment   no difficulty really exists & why you send me p. 31 I cannot guess.

ADDRESS: Mr Spottiswode / Printer / New St. Sq. POSTMARKS: (1) T.P / Oxford St W; (2) 10 Fn 10 / [M]R 4 / 1838. PUBLISHED: Palacio, *Mary Shelley*, p. 612. TEXT: MS., Pforzheimer Library.

1. Andrew Spottiswoode (1787–1866), printer, then a member of the firm of Bradbury and Evans, printers to Queen Victoria (1819–1901), who succeeded to the throne on the death of William IV, her uncle, on 20 June 1837 (Boase, *Modern English Biography*, III, col. 692).

2. See [?December 1837–March 1838] (*b*), n. 5.

3. See [?December 1837–March 1838] (*b*), n. 5.

To George Beauclerk   41—d. Park St.   Monday Ev^g
                                              [?19 March 1838]

Dear Captain Beauclerk

Many thanks for your letter & your account of poor Mrs Lewis—the
melancholy scene having drawn to a close I shall hope to see her[1]—She
must deem herself lucky that she has passed so many years happily—I think
of my own tragedy—compleated so early—so disastrous in its consequences
& feel the more for her—though she will not have to struggle as I have
done through long years of poverty & solitude. I am glad she has so true
a friend as you near her—I verily beleive in your disinterestedness & have
that opinion of your friendly feelings & capacity for giving good advice that
if I needed the counsel or active kindness of a friend, I should apply to
you with every feeling of Confidence

Mrs Goring[2] has returned to New St.—But more of that when I see you—
I rejoice at her return, for I think under all the circumstances a separation
would have caused her great misery—happiness she cannot expect married
as she is—but must take a lesson in the difficult art you mention of resignation to ill—

I have very agreable letters from Percy—which is a great happiness—if
he does not break the promise his early good dispositions make, I shall be
a happy woman & a lucky one yet—I am

                                        Dear Captain Beauclerc
                                        Yours Ever
                                        MWShelley

PUBLISHED: Cline, "Two Mary Shelley Letters," p. 476. TEXT: MS., Bodleian Library.
    1. A reference to the death of Wyndham Lewis on 14 March 1838 (see [?15 November–
7 December 1837], n. 1).
    2. Augusta Dent Goring (d. 1875) temporarily returned to her husband Harry Dent Goring
(1801–59), later eighth baronet (*Burke's Peerage*). She and Trelawny met in 1838 and by August
had formed a liaison. Their first child, Edgar (registered as John Granby), was born on 5
August 1839. In June 1841 Goring divorced his wife by act of Parliament, and Augusta Goring
and Trelawny married. They settled at Usk in Monmouthshire, one hundred forty-four miles
northwest of London, and had two more children, Laetitia and Frank. In 1858 Trelawny brought
a young woman home as his mistress, precipitating the breakup of the marriage (St. Clair,
Trelawny, pp. 165–69).

*To Elizabeth Rumble   41.D. Park St.   Grosvenor Sq   5 April 1838

Dear Elizabeth

You must think me the most negligent person in the world—I am afraid
to think how long it is since I wrote to you—& indeed forget. All last winter
I was at Brighton for my health—& when I came back I found the journals[1]
for which I am much obliged to you—You wrote to me some weeks ago—
mentioning a mode by which I could return them. But I was very ill of the

influenza at that time & could not attend to it & have mislaid your letter; so you must let me know again. I should be obliged to you if you would take care hereafter that these journals do not fall into the hands of strangers. You are likely to outlive me—but if you should not will you take care that they come back to me.

What news have you of the Reveley's? How are you yourself?—tolerably well, I hope & your house succeeding.

Mrs Hogg & her family are well as well as I & my son—though we all suffered a great deal from Influenza during this hard winter. Let me hear from you—& never make apologies for writing. Be assured, for your own sake, as well as those of our lost friends, I shall always be glad to hear from you—Believe me

Ever truly Y^s
MWShelley

UNPUBLISHED. TEXT: MS., Pforzheimer Library.

1. Taped to this letter is a note which reads: "Mr Gisborne's Journal, and all other papers belonging to him, was left to me by his Will. Mr Reveley was very angry with Mary Shelley for asking me to let her have them on my death. Mr Reveley was not pleased with me for lending them to her (as I did) for more than two years. Mary Shelley knew that by my Will I left every thing that I possessed to Henry Reveley, son of Mrs Gisborne / E Rumble."

*To [?   ]   41d Park St.   June—Tuesday [1838]

[*Fragment*]   Would it be possible for you to call at the time I mention. Are you acquainted with Mr Murchison a friend of Mr Sedgwick[1] a name well known in Geology—living in Eccleston Place?—

I am dear Sir

Y^r Ob^t Servant
MaryShelley

UNPUBLISHED. TEXT: MS., Pforzheimer Library.

1. Adam Sedgwick (1785–1873; *DNB*), geologist, who collaborated with Roderick I. Murchison on a number of studies and papers.

TO JOHN GREGSON   [41d Park Street   c. 3–4 August 1838][1]

When I returned to England nearly fifteen years ago, Sir Timothy made it a condition with me that I should not publish Shelley's Poems. I complied. His motive was that he did not wish his poetry republished; but this has not prevented the publication, but only prevented me from receiving any benefit from it. Many pirated editions[2] have been published. There is now a question of another edition, which if I were allowed to carry on myself would be very advantageous to me. I wish therefore to learn whether I might.

PUBLISHED: Ingpen, *Shelley in England,* II, 618. TEXT: Ingpen, *Shelley in England,* II, 618.

1. John Gregson's letter to Sir Timothy Shelley of 4 August 1838 quotes the passage given here and supports Mary Shelley's request for permission to publish Shelley's poems. Sir Timothy acceded to this request on the condition that no memoir would be published with the poems (Ingpen, *Shelley in England,* II, 618–19). Although she agreed to this condition, Mary Shelley largely circumvented this stricture by her lengthy, biographical notes to the poems, which have remained one of the valuable sources of information about Shelley's life.

2. At least five unauthorized editions of Shelley's poems, including the Galignani edition which Mary Shelley directly aided, were published between Mary Shelley's 1824 and 1839 editions of Shelley's poems (for a discussion of these editions see Taylor, *Early Collected Editions,* pp. 11–33).

To RICHARD ROTHWELL   41d Park St.   Friday Ev^g [5 October 1838]

Dear Mr Rothwell

Will you go to Drury Lane with me & a party tomorrow[1]—If you will, be here at six—or join us at Drury Lane any time in the Evening—going to the Private Door—& asking for the Duke of Bedfords'[2] box—Eliza Robinson will be with me—She considers that she requires another lesson on the art of [?Singing in Public] &c & docility in yielding to the requests of others—You giving an example by joining our party at the theatre tomorrow—

> Beleive Me
> Y^s truly
> MWShelley

ADDRESS: Richard Rothwell / 31 Devonshire St. / Portland Place. POSTMARK: 12 Nn 12 / OC 6 / 1838. PUBLISHED: Jones, #481. TEXT: MS., Luther A. Brewer Collection, University of Iowa.

1. *Don Juan* and *The Devil on Two Sticks* played at the Drury Lane on 6 October 1838.

2. Francis Russell, seventh duke of Bedford (1788–1861), was the husband of Anna Maria Stanhope (d. 1857), Col. Leicester Stanhope's sister (*Burke's Peerage*).

*To WILLIAM HAZLITT, JR.   41d Park St.   5 Nov [1838]

Sir

Many thanks for the Paper[1] It is astonishing to me how much can be got for 2^d—I must have every Wednesday enlivened by your sheet—& should be obliged to you to give orders that it should be sent me. I am flattered by your reprinting my Tale. Bentley & Colburn bought the Copy right of Frankenstein when it was printed in the Standard Novels.[2] Frankenstein was first published in 181⟨9⟩8[3] I think so perhaps the book is common property—but I do not know what the laws are.

Wishing you every success
I am, Sir,
Y^s Ob^{ly}
MWShelley

UNPUBLISHED. TEXT: MS., Lockwood Memorial Library, State University of New York at Buffalo.

1. William Hazlitt, Jr., edited *The Romancist, and Novelist's Library: The Best Works of the Best Authors,* published weekly on Wednesdays. At twopence a copy, its objective was to present literature to a wide audience. The first number included Mary Shelley's "A Tale of the Passions" (see vol. I, 6 November 1822), pp. 14–16; the tenth number reprinted Shelley's *Zastrozzi* (London: G. Wilkie and J. Robinson, 1810), pp. 145–56. The weeklies were collected into a volume in 1839 and published by J. Clements. The second collected volume, published in 1840, included Shelley's *St. Irvyne; or the Rosicrucian* (London: J. J. Stockdale, 1810), pp. 113–26, as well as works by Leigh Hunt, Washington Irving, William Hazlitt, and Charles Lamb.

2. See [?February–10 March 1831], n. 1.

3. This date is corrected several times and remains unclear. Its alterations include 1817, 1818, and 1819. *Frankenstein* was published in January 1818, but a few copies were distributed in December 1817 (*SC,* V, 366, 393 ff.).

*To EDWARD MOXON   41 D Park St.   7 Dec. 1838

Dear Sir

It gives me great pleasure to publish Shelley's poems with you,[1] ⟨& I am⟩ as I believe the publication will have justice at your hands. I am content with your offer of £200 for the edition of 2,000—but I should be glad to dispose of my entire interest & for that I think I ought to have £500[2]   I feel sure among other things that the copy right of the Posthumous Poems must be entirely mine. The M.S. from which it was printed consisted of fragments of paper which in the hands of an indifferent person would never have been decyphered—the labour of putting it together was immense— the papers were in my possession & in no other person's (for the most part) the volume might be all my writing (except that I could not write it) in short it certainly stands to reason, & I should think that it is law that a Posthumous publication must belong entirely to the editor, if the editor had a legal right to ⟨poss⟩ make use of the MS.—

I think that £500 is not too much to ask for the entire copy rights which I will take pains to render as valuable as I can. I hope you will agree to this additional sum in which case we might at once conclude.   the agreement being ⟨subject⟩ founded as you said on the present laws—⟨& to be⟩

I am dear Sir
Y^s truly
MWShelley

UNPUBLISHED. TEXT: MS., Pforzheimer Library.

  1. The first volume of Shelley, *Poetical Works* (1839), dedicated on 20 January 1839 to "Percy Florence Shelley, / The Poetical Works / Of His Illustrious Father / Are Dedicated, / By His Affectionate Mother, Mary Wollstonecraft Shelley," was published late in January 1839. The remaining three volumes appeared at approximately monthly intervals, the fourth in May (Taylor, *Early Collected Editions,* p. 34).

  2. Moxon agreed to £500 (see 12 January 1839; 4 March 1839; 4 April 1839; and 27 May 1839).

*TO THOMAS JEFFERSON HOGG[1] 41 d Park St. 11 Dec 1838

Dear Jeff—

Jane has told you I suppose that I am about to publish an Edition of Shelley's Poems—She says you have not a Queen Mab—yet have you not? Did not Shelley give you one—one of the first printed.[2] If you will lend it me I shall be so very much obliged & will return it safely when the book is printed. I want your opinion on one point. The Bookseller (Moxon) has suggested leaving out the 6th & 7th parts as too shocking & atheistical What do you say? I dont like mutilations—& would not leave out a word in favour of <u>liberty</u>. But I have no partiality to irreligion & much doubt the benefit of disputing the existence of the Creator—give me your opinion.[3] Will you lend me your Alastor also—it will not go to the printer—I shall only correct the press from it. Sir Tim forbids biography—but I mean to write a few notes appertaining to the history of the poems—if you have any Shelley's letters you would communicate mentioning his ⟨author⟩ poetry I should be glad & thank you.[4] I am Yˢ Ever MWShelley

UNPUBLISHED: Abridged and mutilated text, Jones, #483. TEXT: MS., Pforzheimer Library.

  1. An altered and abridged text of this letter was published by Hogg in his *Life of Percy Bysshe Shelley,* 2 vols. (London: Edward Moxon, 1858), and reprinted by Jones. Omitted are the lines "I want your opinion" through "Give me your opinion." Added in Hogg's text after "Sir Timothy forbids biography" is "under a threat of stopping the supplies. What could I do then? How could I live? And my poor boy!"

  2. On 12 December 1838 Hogg responded that he had loaned it to someone who had failed to return it (draft of Hogg's letter, written in Taylor's system of shorthand on verso of last leaf of Mary Shelley's 11 December 1838 letter to him, MS., Pforzheimer Library). After a number of unsuccessful attempts, Mary Shelley was able to borrow *Queen Mab* from Harriet de Boinville, who sent it from Paris on 26 January 1839 (*S&M,* IV, 1221).

  In July 1814 Shelley had given Mary Shelley a copy of *Queen Mab,* in which he had written on the inside cover, "Mary Wollstonecraft Godwin, P.B.S.," and inside the other cover, "You see Mary, I have not forgotten you." On the dedication page he wrote, "Count Slobendorf was about to marry a woman, who attracted solely by his fortune, proved her selfishness by deserting him in prison." This is believed to be a reference to Count Gustav von Schlabrendorf, a Silesian, who was a friend of Mary Wollstonecraft. He was imprisoned during the Terror in Paris in 1793, but evidence shows that it was he, not his fiancée, who broke their engagement (Eleanor Flexner, *Mary Wollstonecraft* [New York: Coward, McCann & Geoghegan, 1972], pp. 180, 297). Mary Shelley wrote on the end papers of this copy of *Queen Mab (see illustrations and endpapers):*

July 1814 This book is sacred to me and as no other creature shall ever look into it I may write in it what I please—yet what shall I write that I love the author beyond all powers of expression and that I am parted from him

Dearest & only love by that love we have promised to each other although I may not be yours I can never be another's—

But I am thine exclusively thine—by the kiss of love by
    The glance none saw beside
    The smile none else might understand
    The whispered thought of hearts allied
    The pressure of the thrilling hand
I have pledged myself to thee & sacred is the gift.

I remembor your words you are now Mary going to mix with many & for a moment I shall depart but in the solitude of your chamber I shall be with you—yes you are ever with me sacred vision
    But ah I feel in this was given
    A blessing never meant for me
    Thou art too like a dream from heaven
    For earthly love to merit thee.

The first quatrain, slightly misquoted, is from Byron's "To Thyrza"; the second quatrain is from Byron's "If Sometime in the Haunts of Men."

This signed copy of *Queen Mab,* as well as others with Shelley's notes in them, were left at Marlow when the Shelleys went to Italy in 1818 and were retained by the Shelleys' landlord, Robert Madocks, who claimed the Shelleys owed him money. Mary Shelley, through Peacock, unsuccessfully attempted to have these items returned, which explains why she had neither her personal copy nor any of the other copies of *Queen Mab* owned by Shelley. Her copy, sold at Sotheby on 13 August 1879, is now at the Huntington Library (see vol. I, 29 September 1822, n. 4; *SC,* II, 898–99, IV, 488–91; H. Buxton Forman, *The Shelley Library* [London: Reeves and Turner, 1886], pp. 44–46; and Huntington Library *Queen Mab* [HM 114869]).

3. Edward Moxon asked for these omissions in order to protect his copyright, which he could lose if *Queen Mab* were judged, under the law, as blasphemous. Hogg said he had "no recollection of the parts" referred to by Mary Shelley, but he said that he "would omit whatever I honestly believed he would omit himself if he were—how I wish that he were—now living: whatever is shocking and irreligious, of course" (Hogg's letter draft [see n. 2 above]). Mary Shelley finally agreed to Moxon's request that the atheistical passages be removed and omitted part of canto 6 and all of canto 7. She also omitted the dedication to Harriet Shelley because she believed that was Shelley's preference (see 11 February [1839], n. 1). In mid-November 1839 (but bearing 1840 as publication date) a one-volume edition of *Poetical Works* was published by Moxon, with the omitted passages of *Queen Mab* restored (Taylor, *Early Collected Editions,* pp. 48–49; Ingpen, *Shelley in England,* II, 620–22; Dunbar, *PBS Bibliography,* p. 37). Also added in this edition were *Peter Bell the Third,* previously unpublished, and *Swellfoot the Tyrant,* published in 1820 but immediately suppressed.

4. Hogg wrote that he had no letters that would suit Moxon, and also commented: "As to biography and the history of his studies, the less said the better. It would not be expedient to tell the truth at present, and it can never be expedient to tell anything else" (Hogg's letter draft [see n. 2 above]). In her preface to *Poetical Works* (1839), Mary Shelley echoed this opinion. She wrote: "This is not the time to relate the truth; and I should reject any colouring of the truth" (I, vii).

41d Park St. 12 Dec. [1838]

Dear Sir

I have failed in procuring a copy of Queen Mab. I think Mr Southey[1] may have one—will you ask for the loan.—but it must be quick. I have asked Mr Hookham[2] to let you know, if he can, who printed it—& you might get it from the printer.[3] I should much like to get hold of the original edition—but if I cannot for this edition I must do my best & get it for the ⟨second⟩ next. I had no idea we should have so much difficulty

Talking of our Edition with Mr Milnes[4]—he said the whole <u>poem</u> of Q.M. [*Queen Mab*] ought to be printed but not notes. I dislike Atheism but I shrink from Mutilation—I have not yet decided.

Will you send over the enclosed to Mr Hookham

Let me have a copy of Alastor of the first edition if you can

I am Y^s Ob^ly
MWShelley

Is Mr Milnes in town do you know? I have a notion that the Chancery Lane Main Archives may have a copy of the original edition—Could you find out & procure it.—

Are you sure Mr Rogers[5] has not a copy—Shelley sent a copy to all the great Poets of the day—will you enquire—I am <u>sure</u> he sent one to Southey— for he was acquainted with him.

[*On inside flap of envelope*] Would you let me have copies of your Edition of Wordsworth Southey & Coleridge[6]

ADDRESS: Edward Moxon Esq / Dover St. POSTMARK: 1838 / DE 13 / 8 [   ] 8. UNPUBLISHED. TEXT: M.S., Fales Library, New York University.

   1. Shelley at one time admired Southey and sent him copies of *St. Irvyne* and *Alastor* (Ingpen, *Shelley in England*, I, 124; II, 358–59, 464). Later Shelley was attacked by Southey for his religious and political views, and Shelley, in turn, attacked Southey (Cameron, *The Golden Years*, pp. 31, 436–38). Southey was not among the known recipients of *Queen Mab* (White, *Shelley*, I, 653, n. 11).

   2. Thomas Hookham, Jr.

   3. Unidentified.

   4. Richard Monckton Milnes (1809–85; *DNB*), in 1863 created first baron Houghton, politician and author. Milnes was a member of the Cambridge Apostles, an association of gifted young men which included Tennyson, Arthur Hallam (1811–33), and Thackeray. Milnes knew many of the same people that Mary Shelley knew, and they may have met through any number of mutual acquaintances, including Edward Moxon, who published ten of Milnes's books, beginning with *Memorials* in 1834 (Merriam, *Moxon*, pp. 54–56). In 1838 Milnes wrote to J. W. Blakesley, another Apostle, to inquire on behalf of Mary Shelley about a private tutor for Percy Florence Shelley (MS., Trinity College, Cambridge).

   5. Samuel Rogers (1763–1855; *DNB*), a renowned poet of the era and a major figure in literary circles, who counted among his friends Thomas Moore and Byron. Rogers and Shelley met first in 1817 (*SC*, V, 241 ff.) and then at Pisa in 1822 (*Table-Talk of Samuel Rogers*, ed. Morchard Bishop [London: Richards Press, 1952], pp. 194–95). Mary Shelley may have known Rogers earlier, perhaps through Godwin, whom Rogers knew and admired (*Table-Talk of Samuel Rogers*, pp. 205–6), but the first mention of him in her letters or Journal is the 30 June 1838 Journal entry in which she records that she and Rosa Robinson enjoyed one of Rogers's

famous breakfasts. Sutton Sharpe, who brought some of Mérimée's correspondence to Mary Shelley, was Rogers's nephew (see [?October 1828] [*a*], n. 1).

6. *The Poetical Works of William Wordsworth, A New Edition,* 6 vols. (1836–37, reissued in 1839); Southey, *The Doctor,* 3 vols., reprinted (1839); *Letters, Conversations, and Recollections of S. T. Coleridge,* 2 vols. (1836; see 2 May [1839]).

TO LEIGH HUNT   41 Park Street   December 12, 1838

My dear Hunt,—I am about to publish an edition of our Shelley's Poems, Sir Tim giving leave if there is no biography. I want a copy of the original edition of Queen Mab to correct the press from—it must be the original— it would not go to the Printers, but only [be] used to correct from. Have you one—or do you know who has—Has Miss Kent? I should be so grateful for the loan. Moxon wants me to leave out the sixth part as too atheistical. I don't like Atheism—nor does he now. Yet I hate mutilation—what do you say? How have you been, and when does your Play[1] come out? With love to Marianne,

Yours ever,
M. W. Shelley.

Let me have the book quickly—if you have it—as the press is waiting.

PUBLISHED: Jones, #485. TEXT: Ingpen, *Shelley in England,* II, 619–20.

1. *A Legend of Florence,* successfully produced at Covent Garden on 7 February 1840 (Blunden, *Leigh Hunt,* pp. 279–81).

TO [?CHARLES OLLIER][1]   41d Park St.   12 Dec [1838]

Dear Sir

You would oblige me very much if you could inform me whether you have, or any friend of yours has, a copy of the original edition of Queen Mab. And if it could be sold or lent to me—as I am publishing an Edition of Shelley's poems & wish to correct the press by the original edition & cannot find a copy. You would greatly favour me—I would take every care of the book & return it.

I am, dear Sir
Yours truly
MWShelley

PUBLISHED: Jones, #484. TEXT: MS., bound in *The Poetical Works, Letters and Journals, of Lord Byron: With Notices of His Life,* ed. Thomas Moore, Esq., 44 vols. (London: John Murray, 1844), XXXVIII, 22.

1. See [?15 December 1838].

To Leigh Hunt   41d Park St.   Friday   [14 December 1838]

Dear Hunt

Many thanks for your kind note—I have not yet made up my mind. Except that I do not like the idea of a mutilated edition, I have no scruple of conscience in leaving out the expressions which Shelley would never have printed in after ⟨life Life⟩ I have a great love for Queen Mab—he was proud of it when I first knew him—& it is associated with the bright young days of both of us.

Thanks for your very kind offer of assisting me in my note. But it must rest on myself alone. ⟨I do not⟩ The edition will be mine—& though I feel my incompetencey—yet trying to make it as good as I can, I must hope the best. In a future edition if you will add any of your own peculiarly delightful notes it will make the book more valuable to every reader—but ⟨your⟩ our notes must be independant of each other—for as no two minds exactly agree, so (though in works of imagination two minds may add zest & vivacity) in matters of opinion—we should perhaps only spoil both—

Will you look in on me on Tuesday—with love to Marianne

Ever Yours
MWShelley

I will give your message to Jane but to poor pedest{r}ian ladies Chelsea is <u>very</u> far—especially in winter—or we should have called before.

PUBLISHED: Jones, #486. TEXT: MS., Huntington Library (HM 2751).

To Abraham Hayward[1]   41d Park St.   Friday   14th Dec [1838]

Dear Mr Hayward

Will you do me the pleasure to drink tea with me on Tuesday next— Will you ask Mr Sumner[2]—if you think he would like to come

Yours truly
MWShelley

ADDRESS: A. Hayward Esq / Athenaeum Club / Pall Mall. POSTMARKS: (1) T.P / Lr Brook S[t]; (2) 4 Eg 4 / DE 15 / 1838. PUBLISHED: Jones, #487. TEXT: MS., Houghton Library.

1. Abraham Hayward (1801–84; *DNB*), lawyer and author and a friend of many literary figures, including Caroline Norton and Samuel Rogers (see 12 December [1838] to Edward Moxon, n. 5).

2. Charles Sumner (1811–74), U.S. statesman. In the course of a tour of Europe (December 1837 through March 1839), Sumner visited London from 31 May 1838 to 21 March 1839. His absence from London for trips to Oxford and Cambridge from 7 December through 28 December 1838 precluded his acceptance of this invitation (Edward L. Pierce, *Memoir and Letters of Charles Sumner,* 2 vols. [Boston: Roberts Brothers, 1893], I, 213, 298–300; II, 23–

34). Charles Sumner and Mary Shelley met on 3 December 1838 at a party given by Lady Morgan. Sumner wrote of Mary Shelley on 4 December 1838: "I talked a good deal with Mrs. Shelley. She was dressed in pure white, and seemed a nice and agreeable person, with great cleverness. She said the greatest happiness of a woman was to be the wife or mother of a distinguished man. I was not a little amused at an expression that broke from her unawares, she forgetting that I was an American. We were speaking of travellers who violated social ties, and published personal sketches, and she broke out, 'Thank God! I have kept clear of those Americans.' I did no seem to observe what she had said, and she soon atoned for it" (Pierce, *Memoir and Letters of Charles Sumner*, II, 21). Lady Morgan's party was also attended by Samuel Rogers (see 12 December [1838] to Edward Moxon, n. 5).

To [?CHARLES OLLIER] 41d Park St   Saturday   [?15 December 1838][1]

Dear Sir

I am sorry I could not see you today—Your friend is very vexatious—any one else w^d prefer assisting me in giving out a perfect ⟨copy⟩ edition—The press has been waiting some days—and I know not what to do—I have no friend on whom I can put this sort of job—which I wish to do myself—so the agreable result of your friend's want of courtesy is that ⟨I shall⟩ his offer is of no use at all.—Who is <u>Brookes</u>[2]   The press is waiting & all delay is too tiresome rending success in the end of no avail—Do tell me who & what Brookes is that I may apply—two persons so uncivilized as to refuse to lend the book to <u>me</u> for <u>such a purpose</u> cannot exist.

If you will call tomorrow at twelve I will see you—& you will be very obliging—if you cannot, pray let me know who Brookes is.

You do not even tell me who your friend is & where he lives—so that could I send,—this disastrous delay still goes on—Perhaps the Publisher w^d go & look at the copy—did I know where it was to be found—I am heartily vexed that a copy should have got into such churlish hands—

I beg your pardon—but I am vexed & with cause—

> Yours truly
> MWShelley

[*Cross-written*]   I <u>must</u> send the proofs back <u>early</u> on Monday Morning—I would give any thing to see the original tomorrow—

It is <u>too bad</u>

I shall be at home this Evening if you called—<u>do</u> help me—I know <u>you</u> w^d if you could. If I cannot get the book tomorrow—it will be welcome at any time to correct the latter proofs or for our erata—but [*p. 1, top*] the sooner the better

PUBLISHED: Jones, #491, TEXT: MS., British Library (Add. 30,262, ff. 35–36).

1. A slip of woven paper, lighter weight than the stationery on which the letter is written, bears the endorsement "1835 / Mrs Shelley / Park S^t 13 Dec^r." This letter was sold at the Puttick auction on 19 July 1877, listed as addressed to Charles Ollier. Since Mary Shelley did not live at 41d Park Street in 1835, it is almost certain that the endorsement document and the letter are unrelated. The contents of this letter strongly suggest that it refers to Shelley,

Poetical Works (1839), which would place it in December 1838 through mid-January 1839 at the latest.

2. Probably a reference to John Brooks, who published a pirated edition of *Queen Mab* in London in 1829 (Taylor, *Early Collected Editions*, p. 28).

TO THOMAS JEFFERSON HOGG   41d Park St.   12 Jan^y / 39

My dear Jefferson

I hope you will not consider me indiscreet in asking your opinion & aid in a point very material to me. Moxon has offered me £500 for the copyright of Shelley's poems. ⟨Till the will is proved I cannot prevent⟩ Till the will is proved my claim to them is not established—so Moxon wanted Peacock to sign the agreement also as Shelley's Executor. Peacock said he could not without incurring indefinite risks. So I agreed that in the agreement I should pledge myself to indemnify Mr Moxon if any one else claimed the copyright as inheriting it from Shelley. Percy could be the only person. In the agreement however it is mentioned that I am to indemnify him for any expences incurred in resisting piracies—which is out of the question—for Moxon is aware, having years ago taken an opinion, that till the will is proved I cannot get an injunction from Chancery.

I enclose you my letter to him dissenting from this clause. Would you very kindly look over the agreement & see if any other objection arises. Mr Proctor[1] is Mr Moxon's legal adviser—perhaps it would be best to see him—but I must not give you too much trouble. Let me know what you think as soon as you can. Gregson would not I think refuse to see Moxon's Adviser & tell him that I am the personal representative of Shelley when the will is proved—& that Percy is such until then.

I am dear Jeff
Y^s truly
MWShelley

PUBLISHED: Scott, *New Shelley Letters*, pp. 168–69. TEXT: MS., Pforzheimer Library.
1. I.e., Bryan Waller Procter ("Barry Cornwall").

TO THOMAS JEFFERSON HOGG   [41d Park Street]   Sunday E^g
[?13 January 1839]

Dear Jefferson

Thanks for the trouble you have taken—I beg your pardon for giving you so much you need not fear more.

You seem to forget that on my legal title, imperfect as it is, to what I am hereafter to inherit under Shelley's will, I have existed all this time—Sir Tim has given me nothing except as dependant on that, & I should have starved had I not availed myself of it. The reasons for making use of such title as I have to the copyrights is far more obvious. Since in a very few years they will expire & so much property be entirely lost without advantage to anyone.

I shall not sign any paper the prudence of which is problematic. I cannot tell how this affair may end—but if end as I wish, I shall be able to have a house of my own a few miles from town & I think that that will be a more <u>suitable</u> & <u>modest</u> style of life than the lodgings to which I have hitherto been doomed

With many thanks for your good wishes—which accept on my part for you & yours I am

Y^s truly

MWShelley

PUBLISHED: Scott, *New Shelley Letters*, pp. 167–68. TEXT: MS., Pforzheimer Library.

TO CHARLES SUMNER   41d Park St.   Monday   [?14 January 1839][1]

Mrs Shelley's Compts to Mr Sumner & requests the pleasure of his company at tea on Thursday at 5 o'clock

ADDRESS: Charles Sumner Esq / 2 Vigo St. / Regent St. PUBLISHED: Jones, #490. TEXT: MS., Houghton Library.

1. On 23 January 1839 Sumner wrote: "A far different person from Lady Morgan is Mrs. Shelley. I passed an evening with her recently. She is sensible, agreeable, and clever. There were Italians and French at her house, and she entertained us all in our respective languages. She seemed to speak both French and Italian quite gracefully" (Pierce, *Memoir and Letters of Charles Sumner*, II, 46). Sumner's comments may refer to the invitation in this letter. Since he indicates that he had recently spent an evening at her house, it is probable that the evening was sometime after 17 January, when he returned from an approximately two-week trip out of London (Pierce, *Memoir and Letters of Charles Sumner*, II, 34–37).

TO THOMAS MOORE   [41d Park Street   c. 18 January 1839][1]

[*Fragment*]   I cannot help writing one word to say how mistaken how [*you*] are. Shelley was too true a poet not to feel your unrivalled merits—especially in the department of poetry peculiarly your own, songs and short poems instinct with the intense principle of life and love. Such, your unspeakably beautiful poems to Nea—such, how many others! One of the first things I remember with Shelley was his repeating to me one of your <u>gems</u> with enthusiasm———In short be assured that, as genius is the best judge of genius, those poems of yours which you yourself would value most were admired by <u>none</u> so much as Shelley. You know me far too well not to know I speak the exact truth.

PUBLISHED: Jones, #492. TEXT: Moore, *Journal.*
    1. On 13 December 1838, apparently in response to a request from her, Thomas Moore wrote to Mary Shelley to inform her that he had never received an original *Queen Mab.* On 18–19 January 1839 Moore wrote in his journal: "Received a letter one of these days from Mrs. Shelley, who is about to publish an Edition of Shelley's works, asking me whether I had a copy of his Queen Mab as originally printed for private circulation; as she could not procure one & took for granted that I must have been one of those persons to whom he presented copies. In answering that I was unluckily <u>not</u> one of them, I added in a laughing way that I had never been much in repute with certain great guns of Parnassus, such as Wordsworth, Southey, her own Shelley &c.—Received from her, in consequence, a very kind & flattering reply, in which she says. . . ." Following this is the quotation from Mary Shelley's letter.

To Mary Ellen Peacock   41d Park St.   Tuesday   [22 January 1839]

Dear Mary

Engagements of one sort or another have sprung up with the week, so that I find Friday is my only day. I expect Mrs Hogg & a few people on that day—if you will join us I shall be very glad, at dinner. I dine at ⟨past⟩ six—but come when you like

Yours Aff^y
MWShelley

ADDRESS: Miss Peacock / XVIII Stamford St. / Blackfriars. POSTMARKS: (1) Park St GS; (2) 6 EV 6 / JA 22 / 1839. PUBLISHED: Jones, #493. TEXT: MS., Pforzheimer Library.

*To Thomas Jefferson Hogg   [41d Park Street]   11th Feb— [1839]

Dear Jefferson

My motive for the omission[1] was simply that when Clarke's edition appeared, Shelley rejoiced that it was omitted—& expressed great satisfaction thereon. It <u>could</u> be nothing to <u>me</u> but matter of pleasure to publish it. My motive was the purest & simplest that ever actuated any one. If convinced that I am in the wrong, it shall be restored in the next edition[2]

I thank you for your kindly expressed insinuations. I began to be fed on poison at Kentish Town[3]—it almost killed me at first—now I am used to it—& should have been heartily surprised not to have been supplied with a large dose on the present occasion you have mixed the biggest you possibly could & I am proportionately obliged to you

Yours truly MS.

ADDRESS: T. J. Hogg Esq. UNPUBLISHED. TEXT: MS., Pforzheimer Library.
    1. See 11 December 1838. The reviews of volume I in *The Spectator* (12, no. 552 [26 January 1839]: 88–89) and *The Examiner* (no. 1618 [3 February 1839]: 68–70) both criticized Mary Shelley for her omissions. *The Spectator,* which generally attacked Shelley, also complained that Mary Shelley's preface "is rather a panegyric than a judgment." In contrast, the

Examiner complained of a "cold and laboured effort" in her preface and notes. Mary Shelley expressed her response to Hogg's and others' criticism for the omissions in her Journal, 12 February 1839:

> I <u>much</u> disliked the leaving out any of Queen Mab—I dislike it still more than I can express—and I even wish I had resisted to the last—but when I was told that certain portions would injure the copyright of all the volumes to the publisher, I yielded. I had consulted, Hunt Hogg & Peacock. they all said I had a right to do as I liked & offered no one objection. Trelawny sent back the volume to Moxon in a rage at seeing parts left out. How very much he must enjoy the opportunity thus afforded him of doing a rude & insolent act. It was <u>almost</u> worthwhile to make the omissions if only to give him this pleasure.
>
> Hogg has written me an insulting letter because I left out the dedication to Harriet. Poor Harriet to whose sad fate I attribute so many of my own heavy sorrows as the atonement claimed by fate for her death.
>
> Little does Jeff—how little does any one know me! When Clarke's edition of Q.M. came to us at the Baths of Pisa Shelley expressed great pleasure that these verses were omitted—this recollection caused me to do the same—It was to do him honour—What could it be to me?—There are other verses I should well like to obliterate for ever—but they will be printed—& any to her could in no way tend to my discomfort; or gratify one ungenerous feeling. They shall be restored; though I do not feel easy as to the good I do S—

William Clark's pirated 1821 edition did reprint the dedication to Harriet, but it was missing from some copies, including the one that reached Shelley (Ingpen, *Shelley in England,* II, 621).

2. See 11 December 1838, n.3.

3. A reference to Jane Williams Hogg's disloyalty (see vol. I, 22 August [1827] to John Howard Payne; [?14 February 1828]).

*To [CHARLES OLLIER]   41 d Park St.   13 Feb 1839

Dear Sir

You may remember when Hellas was published[1] certain verses & a portion of a note were omitted.[2] A few copies containing these were struck off—four you sent to Italy—I have given or lent them & do not possess a perfect copy—Do you? If you do & would lend it me <u>immediately</u> I should feel very greatly obliged

Yours truly   MWShelley

ENDORSED: [*on separate slip of paper*] 1839 / Mrs Shelley / Park St 13th Feby. UNPUBLISHED. TEXT: MS., Pforzheimer Library.

1. See vol. I, 30 November 1821, n. 5.

2. Omitted in the 1822 edition were lines 1091–93, "more bright and good / Than all who fell, than One who rose, / Than many unsubdued," and the part of note 8 which elucidated those lines: *"The One, who rose,* or Jesus Christ, at whose appearance the idols of the Pagan world were amerced of their worship" and "The sublime human character of Jesus Christ was deformed by an imputed identification with a power, who tempted, betrayed, and punished the innocent beings who were called into existence by his sole will; and for the period of a thousand years, the spirit of this most just, wise, and benevolent of men, has been propitiated with myriads of hecatombs of those who approached the nearest to his innocence and wisdom,

sacrificed under every aggravation of atrocity and variety of torture." The lines and note were restored in *Poetical Works* (1839) (see *PBS Letters*, #697, #698; Taylor, *Early Collected Editions*, pp. 58–61). Also omitted from the first edition was the penultimate paragraph of Shelley's preface, which begins: "Should the English people ever become free they will reflect upon the part which those who presume to represent their will, have played in the great drama of the revival of liberty. . . ." The paragraph was restored by H. Buxton Forman in the 1892 Aldine Edition of Shelley's *Poetical Works* (Shelley, *Poetry and Prose*, p. 410).

To Edward Moxon   41d Park St.   4 March 1839

Dear Sir

Thanks for the Second £125—which I have received—

I have heard much praise of the mode the book is got up—but regrets <u>from all parties</u> on account of the omissions in Q.M. [*Queen Mab*][1]   I trust you will not think it injurious to the copyright to insert them in the next edition   I think it would improve the sale—

Thanks for the books—have you sent 2^d Vols to those who read the 1st I am, dear Sir

Y^s truly,
MWShelley

PUBLISHED: Jones, #494. TEXT: MS., Bodleian Library (MS., Shelley, Adds., c. 6, ff. 217–18).

   1. See 11 December 1838, n. 3; 11 February [1839].

To Edward Moxon   41 d Park St   5 March 1839

Dear Sir

Pray do not believe that I intended to express any discontent about the omitted passages—All I mean is—that as they have been published several times, I should prefer their being published in your edition—unless your doing so injured your interests.

You were quite right in not sending Mr Trelawny a copy of the 2^d Vol[1]— I did not mention it—but of course understood that you would not.

Yours truly—MWShelley

PUBLISHED: Jones, #495. TEXT: MS., Bodleian Library (MS., Shelley, Adds., c. 6, ff. 219–20).

   1. See 11 February [1839], n. 1. On 30 June 1841 Trelawny wrote to Moxon praising the inclusion of the omitted passages in the one-volume edition and offering his assistance to Moxon, who was prosecuted by the government for that version of *Queen Mab* (British Library [Ashley MS. 4137]). Moxon was found guilty but received no punishment (Merriam, *Moxon*, pp. 101–3).

*To William Brownsword Chorley[1]   41D. Park St.   Grosvenor Sq
18 March 1839

Mrs Shelley Compliments to Mr Chorley & would be much obliged to him if he would lend her (<u>as soon as he possibly can</u>) for an hour or two the Annual containing her drama of Proserpine which he edited some years ago. Mrs Shelley would be much obliged to Mr Chorley for an early answer

UNPUBLISHED. TEXT: MS., Pforzheimer Library.
   1. William Brownsword Chorley, M.D. (b. 1800), was the brother of Henry Fothergill Chorley (1808–72; *DNB*), author and critic, who also contributed to *The Winter's Wreath*, in which Mary Shelley's *Proserpine* had been published (see vol. I, 9 May [1824], n. 1).

*To Edward Moxon   ⟨41d Park St.⟩   Layton House   Putney[1]
28 March [1839]

Dear Sir
   I send on the other side the list of persons to whom I wish copies sent out of my 20.[2] The rest may be sent here per carrier. I have sent the contents of the 4th Vol. to the Printer. I think the 4th vol. will prove thicker than the 3^d   Thanks for the proofs of the print—they are beautifully got up.

                                        I am dear Sir Y^s truly
                                        MWShelley

UNPUBLISHED. TEXT: MS., Pforzheimer Library.
   1. Mary Shelley moved to Layton House, Putney, seven miles west-southwest of London, after 18 March 1839 and remained there until 25 March 1840.
   2. Unlocated.

*To Marianne Hunt   Putney   Wednesday
          [?March 1839–March 1840; September 1843–March 1846][1]

Dear Marianne
   I am sorry Hunt is so unwell—does he wear flannel under his shirt?— These last autumns I have always had rhumatic pain, which has disappeared when I have put on flannel.
   The Cicale begin in July—when the heats begin—The Italians say summer is really come when the cicale are heard.
   Percy is waiting for Moonlight—I do not like his walks alone in dark nights—He has no finery about him

                                        In haste
                                        Ever truly Y^s

UNPUBLISHED. TEXT: MS., Pforzheimer Library.
1. In September 1843 Mary Shelley again lived in Putney, this time at White Cottage, where she remained until March 1846.

TO MARY ELLEN PEACOCK   Layton House   Putney   30 March [1839]

Dear Mary

You Will think me very rude not having answered your kind considerate note—But I have been ever since that time so very much indisposed—& as my illness was nervous, could not write. Even now I can only send a shabby letter. The poor girls were quite overwhelmed by the dreadful blow[1] & are by no means recovered from it. Rosa sends her love & thanks you very much for your kindness.

I have got away from town at last & am so very glad. I have taken a furnished house on the Upper Richmond Road very near Putney—& if we have a fine summer I hope to enjoy myself greatly. Julia is with me. Percy rows in his boat to Kew[2] & fetches Rosa & Eliza—I hope you will join us in the summer for some days—Meanwhile write & let us know how you get on—& if I am not able to write in answer, Rosa will for me.

Thanks for the Misfortunes of Elphin[3]—Percy claims Melincourt as promised & wants it very much so if you find a copy pray let him have it. He deserves it—as he knows your father's Novels nearly by heart.

Your "Childhood's friend"—has been very ill—indeed poor Girl—she was very ill the day you saw her—She had afterwards an inflamation of the chest—but is now quite recovered   Adieu, dear Mary—Remember me to your father—I am

Ever truly Y[s]
MWShelley

ADDRESS: Miss Peacock / Lower Halliford / Esher. POSTMARKS: (1) PUTNEY / [   ] / MR 30 / 1839; (2) G / MR—30 / 1839; (3) 4 Eg 4 / MR 30 / 1839. PUBLISHED: Jones, #496. TEXT: MS., Huntington Library (HM 12874).
1. Unidentified.
2. The Robinsons had moved to Kew, nine miles southwest of London.
3. Peacock's *The Misfortunes of Elphin* (London: T. Hookham, 1829).

TO [EDWARD MOXON]   Layton House   Putney   4 April / 39

Dear Sir

Thanks for your parcel & the £125—which I received. The 3[d] vol is thin—& I have an idea that the 4th will be a good deal thicker; but I could not get the Printers to calculate exactly—& did not like to trust to my own idea—We shall see—I sent a week ago the order of the ⟨proof⟩ remaining poems to the printer & am in daily expectation of proofs. I told them to send them to me two at a time by the 2ᵈ post.—

Thanks for Miss Martineau's book[1] with which I am highly delighted Her pictures are so graphic & true to nature that they interest highly. Hester is I think very finely drawn indeed. Without Miss Austen's humour she has all her vividness & correctness. To compensate for the absence of humour she has higher philosophical views It is a very interesting & very beautiful picture of life.—I say this having read only two volumes.

I hardly like asking you for books—but if I am indiscreet you must let me know. I should like Campbells works[2]—& Philip Von Artevelte[3]—If you can easily spare them, ⟨if you can⟩ send them to me to the care of Miss Bennet[4] 2 Wilton St. Grosvenor Sq—& they will be brought to me on Saturday.

I am dear Sir Yˢ ⟨truly⟩ Obˡ
MWShelley

PUBLISHED: Jones, #497. TEXT: MS., Duke University Library.

   1. *Deerbrook,* 3 vols. (London: Edward Moxon, 1839).

   2. Thomas Campbell, *Poetical Works* (London: Edward Moxon, 1839).

   3. Henry Taylor, *Philip Van Artevelde: A Dramatic Romance* (London: Edward Moxon, 1834). Pages xxi–xxvi contain evaluative criticism of Shelley.

   4. See 13 October 1835, n. 12; 3 January [1837], n. 3.

To Elizabeth Stanhope   Putney   Friday   [5 April 1839]

Dear Mʳˢ Stanhope

If you go to town tomorrow & it is not inconvenient to you would you call at 2 Wilton St. / Mʳˢ Bennet[1] & ask for some books left there for me[2] I am very rude to ask you to take so much trouble—if inconvenient you will not do it, of course—

I wanted much to call, but have been very unwell.

Eᵛ Ys
MWShelley

ADDRESS: Honble / Mrs Stanhope / Cedars. PUBLISHED: Jones, #498. TEXT: MS., Montague Collection, New York Public Library.

   1. Gertrude Francis Bennet (see 4 April 1839, n. 4).

   2. Mary Shelley now lived near Elizabeth and Leicester Stanhope, whose home, Cedars, was in Putney.

*To Elizabeth Stanhope   [?Putney ?April 1839–March 1840;
                                            September 1843–March 1846][1]

Dear Mrs Stanhope
    Would you be so very good as to call in John St. at the Stationers for
the books I left to be bound.
                                                          Y^s Evr
                                                          MWShelley

Unpublished. Text: MS. The Johns Hopkins University.
    1. The contents of this note suggest that Mary Shelley wrote it while residing near Elizabeth
Stanhope at Putney (see [5 April 1839], n. 2).

To Edward Moxon   Putney—2 May [1839]

Dear Sir
    There was some delay at the beginning of April through my being too
ill to write at all—The Printers were very impatient then—Latterly they
have been slower when I was ready. In a few days now all will be finished   I
very much hope the book will have great success. Remember when you
think of another edition to let me know—as for several reasons I shall wish
it to pass through my hands.
    In a short time I should like to see you with regard to {a} volume of
Letters & other prose essays[1]—which I beleive that the public will warmly
welcome. I will call in Dover St. Some day when in town
    With regard to the books you will deduct the price out of the sum I next
receive. Certainly I did not know that Southey's[2] would be so voluminous
& cost so much—& would return them but have cut open two volumes
which I fear will prevent your being able to return them—& you must not
lose—if their being cut open makes no difference I will return them—but
keep the Wordsworth & Coleridge
    I send a fresh list for distribution. I should have accepted your kind offer
& delayed finishing till I was quite well—But my illness being chiefly produced by having to think of & write about the passed [past]—it would have
revived when I return to it—and I felt that at no time could I do better
than I have done now. It has cost me a great deal.
    With fervent wishes for success I am, dear Sir
                                                          Y^s truly
                                                          MWShelley
    I have done as you asked with regard to mentioning the suppressions[3]—
You will find one or two new poems added.

Address: Edward Moxon Esq / Dover Street / Piccadilly. Postmark: T.P / Putney. Published: Jones, #499. Text: MS., Henry W. and Albert A. Berg Collection, New York Public
Library.

1. Mary Shelley's edition of Shelley, *Essays, Letters,* was published in mid-November 1839.

2. See 12 December [1838] to Edward Moxon.

3. See 11 December 1838, n. 3. In a postscript to her preface to the one-volume edition, Mary Shelley wrote: "At my request the publisher has restored the omitted passages of Queen Mab.—"

*To Edward Moxon   Putney—Monday   27 May 1839

Dear Sir

Thank you for the last cheque of £123 which you sent me. I send the packet for Mr Smith but I forget his exact address—if you were to send it with the books to Horace Smith Esq care of Mr Bentley 8 New Burlington St. & put to be forwarded directly that would be best.

I send the Southey. I have not yet been able to put together & think of the prose but some time next Month early I will ask you to come down here to talk it over.

I trust you will find our book succeed to the utmost of our expectations— And with many thanks I am Y^s truly

MWShelley

UNPUBLISHED. TEXT: MS., Pforzheimer Library.

*To Lady Sydney Morgan   Putney—Saturday   [July 1839]

Dear Lady Morgan

I intended doing myself the pleasure of hearing your delightful music yesterday—though it is the only Ev^eg Party I went to since in a happy hour I escaped from Babylon—but having spent all Thursday in town I was so knocked up that I could only keep quiet—

It is long since I saw you—& now that summer is really come I wish you could contrive to spend a day here—do fix one when you can <u>all</u> come, when you can—

Ever truly Y^s
MWShelley

ENDORSED: 1839 July / Mrs Shelley / Frankenstein. UNPUBLISHED. TEXT: MS., Pforzheimer Library.

*To [?Andrew Spottiswoode][1]　　　　　Putney　20 July [1839]

Sir

The volume will finish with Madame de Stael.[2] It is to come out 1st
August so there must be no delay in sending me revises & getting it complete

Y^s ob^{ly}

MWShelley

Will you communicate with Mr Matthews[3] 9 G^t Queen St—about the
Index if there is to be one.

UNPUBLISHED. TEXT: MS., Yale University Library.

　1. See 4 March [1838].

　2. Volume II of *Lives* (1838–39).

　3. Probably a professional indexer. Volume II of *Lives* (1838–39) does contain an index.
In addition, "The Analytical and Chronological Tables and Index to the Series of Lives of
Eminent Literary and Scientific Men of Italy, Spain, and Portugal" *Lives* (1835–37)] are given
at the end of this volume.

*To Mary Ellen Peacock　　　　　Layton House—Putney
　　　　　　　　　　　　20 July [1839]　Saturday

My dear Mary

Last Tuesday Percy went with Mess. George Robinson & Campbell[1] to
Oxford; they are to return in a boat & fish by the way. Percy will call on
you.—If you & your Papa think you may trust yourself (Percy w^d be very
good Chaperon) come down with them—they can easily pull in one day
from Halliford, & spend a few days with me. If you think this would be
too frisky, pray fix some time soon to spend a few days here—⟨Any day
after⟩ If you dont come with them, let it be Monday 30 July, if you can.
What an odious summer! You will find Rosa Robinson with me—

　Edward Williams says that your Sister Rosa is the prettiest & nicest girl
he ever saw. I should much like to see her—

I am Y^s Ever　　MWShelley.

Will you remind your Papa that I want the Symposium & Defence of
Poetry,[2] of which he has the M.S. If they are at Halliford will you bring
them with you. If in town will you ask him to have them at the I.H. [*India
House*]—& I will call there one day soon.

ADDRESS: Miss Peacock / Lower Halliford / Esher. POSTMARKS: (1) T.P / Putney No; (2) O /
JY—20 / 1839. UNPUBLISHED. TEXT: MS., Pforzheimer Library.

　1. William George Campbell (?1810–81), Percy Florence's friend, was the son of William
George Campbell of Inverary. In November 1832 the younger Campbell was admitted to the
Middle Temple, and he was called to the bar as a barrister in January 1836. He was a
commissioner in lunacy from 1845 to 1878 (The Library, Inner Temple; Boase, *Modern English
Biography*, I, col. 535).

　2. For her edition of Shelley, *Essays, Letters*, I, 1–57, 70–163 (see [?26 July 1839]).

*To Leigh Hunt   Layton House—Putney   20 July [1839]

Dear Hunt

I believe you would never seek me by letter or visit did I not seek you—which is unchivalric   Perhaps you are angry that I have made no explanation of the passage to which you objected.[1] I regret that it inadvertently slipt in—& will alter it in another edition. But we have all our theories, I suppose, as to what we like to do in print—and I cannot bear in my own person explanations to the public—or rather to critics—& therefore could not bring myself to explain & so attract attention to that which I beleive—like all else I do, attracted no attention. In fact my notes on Shelleys poems have met with no remark, except a little ill nature from the Examiner[2] & therefore ⟨I must repeat that⟩ what they contain seems of little consequence. I had several very painful & vexatious things occur about them but of kindness & encouragement not an atom from any one. Yet I did my best—though in truth the best was not my best—for publishing the book writing the notes & receiving disagreable letters had so violent an effect on my health that I really felt in danger of losing my senses. My physician ordered me opium.   I took about a hundreth part of what I was ordered & it certainly strengthenyed my head, which had gone far astray—you have suffered these things & will understand the sort of unspeakable sensation of wildness & irritation. I ordered myself the country & took a house here where by degrees I have recovered my general health though my head will not bear much work still.

I expect Jane to spend two days with me next week—Will you join us on Tuesday or Wednesday?—let me know which. I have a piano harp flute—&c for Percy's musical propensities collect music in plenty—Percy himself is on a river expedition   He is the dearest treasure ever Mother was blest with   I wish he would study more—that is all of defect I see—he is passionately fond of Metaphysics—Sir Tim had two severe attacks this spring & summer—given ⟨up⟩ over in both—but recovered—He will last yet a year a [or] two—When he does go I shall have the comfort of being of some use to you.

I live very quiet & see very few people—it is my fate to have a few friends about me which prevents me from being able to afford acquaintance   I prefer the friends—but should be glad of both. I like acquaintance; they serve as flying gibs & top royals to make one speed gaily over life—they are not necessary it is true like the mainsail.

How is Marianne & the rest of your family—Well I trust. Poor Jane is not well—She has stuck on a <u>Rock</u> it seems, nor do I see how she can be got off—though in some danger of being battered to pieces

    With love to Marianne   Ever Y^s
              MWShelley.

[Cross-written]   When you have crossed Putney brid [bridge] walk up the town till you come to cross roads—turn to the right & find a very ugly house—which is mine. It is better than it looks outside.

[*P. 1, top*] Trelawny lives at Mr Leaders[3] not far off—but I never see him He has a theory that absence is the fosterer of friendship. You will guess there is cause for this theory—⟨he does not⟩ however we are good friends & never see each other.

UNPUBLISHED. TEXT: MS., Pforzheimer Library.

1. Perhaps Leigh Hunt had objected to Mary Shelley's reference to his failure to publish Shelley's *Masque of Anarchy* until 1832 or her description of Hunt's connection with the *Liberal* (Shelley, *Poetical Works* [1839], III, 205–6; IV, 153–54).

2. "The Literary Examiner," *The Examiner,* no. 1618 (3 February 1839): 68–70; no. 1634 (26 May 1839): 323–26.

3. In 1839 Trelawny moved to Putney Hill Villa, the home of his friend John Temple Leader (1810–1903; *DNB*), political radical. Augusta Goring was then living at Leader's Farm Cottage on the Upper Richmond Road, near Putney. The cottage and the villa were separated by a field, which Trelawny could cross in private to be with Augusta Goring. It was at Putney that their first child was born (see St. Clair, *Trelawny,* p. 164; [?19 March 1838], n. 2).

*To Leigh Hunt   Putney   Wednesday   [?24 July 1839]

Dear Hunt—Let it be next Wednesday ⟨after next⟩   I hope it will be fine— but it <u>will</u> not be fine this summer   Tell me if you like dining early—if you do we will dine at two if not my hour is 6—but 2 is equally convenient if you will only let me know.

I wish you would let me see your last play, written last year[1]—Bulwer praised it so very much to me.

I am the most stay at home person in the world as far as visiting goes— for this reason that going out costs money—& I have only enough, with great care, to have a comfortable home & be useful to those about me—

Let me hear from you about the dinner hour. With love to Marianne

        Yours Ever
        MWShelley

UNPUBLISHED. TEXT: MS., Pforzheimer Library.

1. Leigh Hunt wrote *A Legend of Florence* in 1838 but revised it a number of times before its 7 February 1840 production at Covent Garden, which starred Ellen Tree (1805–80; *DNB*) as Ginevra (Blunden, *Leigh Hunt,* pp. 279–81).

To Leigh Hunt   Putney—Friday   [?26 July 1839]

Dear Hunt—

I am about to publish a vol. of Prose of Shelleys—This will please you I am sure—& it will not be painful to me as the other was. But I want your advice on several portions of it—especially with regard to the translation of the Symposium. I want also to know whether you would assent to the letters you published in your recollections[1] being joined to such as I shall publish—I expect you on Wednesday & will dine at 5—but if you could a little earlier to discuss these things I shall be glad. Do not disappoint me on Wednesday or you will disappoint M[r] Robinson who <u>almost</u> worships you—besides two pretty daughters who have inherited his feeling—You need not be at the trouble of answering this letter—I only write that you may come, if you can, a little earlier, for the reason I have mentioned.

I have read your play   It is admirably written. It is full of beautiful & elevated & true morality clothed in poetry—Yet I can under understand Macready's[2] not liking to identify himself with Agolanti—his conduct—true to nature & common, being redeemed by no high self forgetting passion would not I think interest in representation as much as in reading. I long to hear of your new play[3]—

Ever truly Y[s]
MWShelley

PUBLISHED. Jones, #502. TEXT: MS., Huntington Library (HM 2757).

1. In *Lord Byron and Some of His Contemporaries* (see 14 November [1839], n. 1).

2. On 1 August 1839 Hunt wrote of Macready: "I am expecting to send you news daily from Macready, who said he would write to me, and of whom I have still hopes, and <u>greater</u> ones, though no certainty. He would not hear me read more than one act. He says that every word requires weighing, step by step, and that he shall perhaps read the play three times over! I am told, however, by his friends, that this looks well. He was very kind and hospitable; and I floundered in a luxurious down bed, grateful and sleepless" (Hunt, *Correspondence*, I, 315). The role of the jealous Agolanti was finally declined by Macready and was performed by a Mr. Moore.

3. During this period Hunt wrote at least four plays (Hunt, *Autobiography*, II, 226). Of these, only *A Legend of Florence* and *Lover's Amazements*, a seriocomic play given at the Lyceum Theatre in January 1858, were produced (Blunden, *Leigh Hunt*, pp. 283, 330).

*TO LEIGH HUNT

Putney   Thursday
[?August 1839–March 1846] (*a*)[1]

My dear Hunt

It is very difficult to arrange the various appointments of two persons it seems—Percy now tells me he is engaged on Tuesday—Can you come on Monday at 5 o'clock—or 4

Y[s] truly   MS.

UNPUBLISHED. TEXT: MS., Pforzheimer Library.

1. Mary Shelley's letter to Hunt of 20 July [1839] indicates that she and Hunt had not earlier corresponded since she had moved to Putney. We may assume, therefore, that this letter was written at the earliest in August 1839 but before 9 October, when Percy Florence returned to Trinity College for the Michaelmas term. It might also have been written sometime from 14 December 1839 through 12 January 1840, when Percy Florence was again at Putney; or as late as September 1843–?March 1846, when Mary Shelley and Percy Florence also lived at Putney.

To Leigh Hunt   [?Putney]   Monday
                                          [?August 1839–March 1846] (b)[1]

Dear Hunt
    When I told Percy you were coming next Thursday he said "what a bore!"
He being engaged to dine out that day in town—Can you make it Friday?
If not let it still stand for Thursday—but let me know how it is decided—
It was a most lovely night—I hope you got home well—With love to
Marianne

                                                   Ever Y[s]   MWS

PUBLISHED. Jones, #509. TEXT: MS., Henry W. and Albert A. Berg Collection, New York
Public Library.
    1. See [?August 1839–March 1846] (a), n. 1.

To Elizabeth Berry[1]   Putney—3 August 1839

My dear Cousin
    M[r] Charles Robinson carries with him a recommendation to you from
our Aunt Everina.—I will add that I have known him from boyhood that
he is most honourable kind hearted excellent young man—he goes out for
the purposes of advancement & any advice & kindness you & M[r] Berry
shew him will oblige me deeply—& be well bestowed.
    I saw our Aunt yesterday—she is infirm—but is tolerable health—she is
with very good people & well taken care of. I wish I could do more for
her—I do what I can, but while my father-in-law lives I have little to
command.   Charles Robinson will describe us to you—he knows Percy
well, so if you have any curiosity about us, you have but to see & question
him. I am sure you will like him—every body does—for he deserves it. He
has a good mercantile connection in this country & if put in the right way
will I hope get on. Ever, Dear Cousin

                                                   Truly Y[s]
                                                   MaryShelley
[P. 1, top]   If you write to me direct to me at Hookham's Library—15 Old
Bond St. London

ADDRESS: Mrs Berry. PUBLISHED: Jones, #501. TEXT: MS., Alexander Hay Collection,
Mitchell Library, Sydney.
    1. Elizabeth Berry (d. 1845), Mary Shelley's cousin, was the daughter of Edward Wollstone-
craft (b. ?1758), Mary Wollstonecraft Godwin's oldest brother. Sometime between 1815 and
1819 Elizabeth Wollstonecraft married Alexander Berry (1781–1873), who became the business partner of Edward Wollstonecraft (1783–1832), Elizabeth's brother. In 1819 the three
went to Australia, where they established a highly successful business in Sydney. Eventually
the government of New South Wales granted Wollstonecraft 500 acres and Berry 10,500
acres. By the time Alexander Berry died, he owned 65,000 acres, an area of one hundred
square miles (MWS Letters, II, 135).

*To Elizabeth Rumble   Layton House   Putney   19th August [1839]

Dear Elizabeth

Mrs Williams[1] called on me   She seems a most amiable & agreable lady. I should wish to have been of use to her; but I live in such retirement & so far from town, that I could do nothing. I gave her Mrs Hogg's address.

I should be glad to have the copies of letters[2] you mention, & thankfully accept your offer of sending them to me. I want you also to do me another favour: among the papers of our lamented friends you will find a manuscript in Italian of an account of the death of the Cenci family[3]   If you would send me this immediately by coach I should be much obliged to you. I will take every care of it & return it very soon.

Have M^r & Mrs Reveley arrived?[4] I am anxious to hear how they are. I was glad to hear from Mrs Williams that you were getting on very well   Take care of yourself & dont be snapt up by an unworthy man. I am always glad to hear from you. We are all well—I am Ever

Sincerely Y^r friend
MShelley

UNPUBLISHED. TEXT: MS., Houghton Library.
    1. Unidentified.
    2. See 5 April 1838, n. 1.
    3. Mary Shelley wrote in her "Note on the Cenci": "When in Rome, in 1819, a friend put into our hands the old manuscript account of the story of the Cenci" (Shelley, *Poetical Works* [1839], II, 274).
    4. From Australia (see 17 July [1834], n. 7).

To Mary Ellen Peacock   [15 Old Bond Street][1]
                                                Thursday   29 Aug [1839]

My dear Mary

This letter is more for you Papa than you—but I want an answer—& that is not to be hoped for from him—& so I trespass on your good nature to make you read my letter & get you to answer me. In the first place is there any chance of my getting the papers I so much want[2]—I should have thought that all <u>my</u> papers would have been together & form a largish packet easily discernible   I should be <u>so</u> glad of them.

I must tell you that this being Thursday I have been to the India house hoping to find your father   I got there by 2—but the bird had flown—I wanted to speak to him about the plans & prospects of a young friend[3] of Percy—who thinks of trying his fortunes in the Military service of India— I wanted to know whether your father could & would serve him—even advice is service—so if you & yours do not object Percy will take him down to Halliford on Sunday or any day when your father is there & introduce him. He is English but has been educated in France—he is a good fellow

& I should be very glad to serve him. Let me have an answer about this visit by return of post—as Percy thinks it would be to intrusive to take down a stranger without previous permission

I write in a hurry in Hookham's shop—Rosa[4] talks of writing to you every day—Mr Campbell[5] is in Wales—we went to Kew the other day & were caught in the storm. Adieu dear Mary—I wish we were nearer & that you could pop in on us now & then. Percy was enchanted with every thing at Halliford except the Cats—In haste

Y^s Ever
MWShelley

ADDRESS: Miss Peacock / Lower Halliford / Chertsey / M.S. POSTMARKS: H / AU—29 / 1839. PUBLISHED: Jones, #503. TEXT: MS., Bodleian Library (MS., Autogr. c. 9, ff. 143–44).

1. The text of this letter indicates that it was written from Hookham's Library.
2. See 20 July [1839] to Mary Ellen Peacock, n. 2.
3. Unidentified.
4. Rosa Robinson.
5. William Campbell.

TO GIDEON ALGERNON MANTELL[1]

Layton House   Putney
Sep. 5—1839

Sir

I am going to publish some prose Works of my husband which will include some letters. Mr H. [*Horace*] Smith tells me that some time ago he gave you one of Shelley's letters, & he gives me leave to ask you for a copy of it—You will very much oblige me by letting me have it—& it will add to your kindness if you will let me have it soon.

As Mr Smith says that you are an enthusiastic admirer of Shelley—I am sure these volumes will please you. The first piece A defence of poetry, is the only entirely finished & corrected prose essay left by him—it is truly magnificent & places him very high in the scale of prose writers. Its diction is exquisitely harmonious & the imagery grand & vivid.[2]

Hoping soon to hear from you—I am

Your Ob^t Servant
MaryW Shelley

PUBLISHED: Jones, #504. TEXT: MS., Alexander Turnbull Library, Wellington, New Zealand.

1. Gideon Algernon Mantell (1790–1852; *DNB*), physician, naturalist, and author. For further information about the friendship of Mantell and Mary Shelley see Dennis R. Dean, "Mary Shelley and Gideon Mantell," *Keats-Shelley Journal* 30 (1981): 21–29.
2. Mary Shelley elaborated on this description in her preface to Shelley, *Essays, Letters,* I, vi–vii.

Dear Sir

I have received some proof of the new edition of poems from the printer
& find some of the notes to Queen Mab are still omitted. In my observation
on the omissions & restorations I have said that "I was glad to restore them
as to omit them seemed to me disrespectful towards the author"—I cannot
say this if there are still to be omissions.

We do not print these portions of Queen Mab and the notes because
they contain truths—or because Shelley continued to maintain these opinions—but because the poem & notes are already printed & published—
they cannot be cancelled, & the omissions only render our editions imperfect & mutilated. I have other reasons I own in not wishing a word he ever
wrote to be lost—& above all that I should not cast a slur on them—but
the first reason suffices you cannot suppress what you disapprove—why
not put your edition on a par with all others by making it entire—pray give
orders accordingly to the Printer

I am Yours truly
MWShelley

ADDRESS: Edward Moxon Esq / Dover St. POSTMARKS: (1) 12 Nn 12 / SP 8 / 1839; (2)
PUTNEY / MG / SE [   ] /1839. UNPUBLISHED. TEXT: MS., Pforzheimer Library.

TO GIDEON ALGERNON MANTELL   Layton House   Putney
                                                   18 Sep. [1839]

Sir

I must appear very rude—but it was only on returning from Sussex today,
after nearly a fort night's absence that I found your very acceptable present[1]
& note. The books are delightful—of course I have only <u>looked</u> into them
yet—but they treat on a subject, which has always greatly interested me.

I am sorry for your Son's departure[2]—& regret the absence of the letter—
perhaps some time hence both may be restored. I will take an early occasion
of asking your acceptance of the volumes of Shelley's poems published by
me.

If ever you come this way I hope you will kindly call on me

I am dear Sir
Y^s truly
MaryShelley

PUBLISHED: Jones, #505. TEXT: MS., Alexander Turnbull Library, Wellington, New Zealand.
    1. Possibly Mantell's *Wonders of Geology* (2 vols. [1838]) or *Thoughts on a Pebble* (1836) (see
Dean, "Mary Shelley and Gideon Mantell," p. 24). Among other subjects about which Mary
Shelley offered to write for John Murray was a geological study of the history of the earth
(see 8 September 1830).

2. Walter Baldock Durant Mantell (1820–95), scientist, explorer, government administrator, and pioneer, in January 1840 arrived in New Zealand, where he spent the rest of his life except the years 1856–59, when he returned to England. During this visit he and Geraldine Jewsbury formed a lifelong friendship (Howe, *Geraldine Jewsbury*, pp. x, 147–60).

TO EDWARD MOXON   Putney   30 Sep^br [1839]

My dear Sir

Will you dine with me next Wednesday at 5 o'clock   I expect Leigh Hunt—& I have asked Mr Campbell[1]—persuade the latter to come—& tell him how to find my house.

I have told the printer to send me the proofs in slips[2] at first to save expence from alterations—I got a note from them as if they meant to be furiously quick—& they sent with it a proof without copy—so I am waiting for the copy to come before I return it

Yours truly
MWShelley

PUBLISHED: Jones, #506. TEXT: MS., Pforzheimer Library.
   1. Thomas Campbell, with whom Moxon had a close relationship. Moxon republished Campbell's *Poetical Works* in 1839 and a smaller less expensive edition ten years later, as well as a new collection, *The Pilgrim of Glencoe and Other Poems*, in 1842 (Merriam, *Moxon*, p. 128).
   2. A proof taken before the matter is made up into pages, usually about eighteen inches long. When the corrections are likely to be numerous, proofs in this form allow alterations to be made much more cheaply (F. Howard Collins, *Authors and Printers Dictionary* [London: Humphrey Milford, 1905]).

*TO LEIGH HUNT   Putney   Saturday   [?5 October 1839]

Dear Hunt

Will you read the enclosed & tell me whether you object to its being printed. I do not like it I own for I do not think it in good taste—but Percy says if you do not dislike it, it ought to be printed. It is the dedication to Peter Bell.[1] If you could return me the Symposium with annotations before next Saturday I should be glad—but that day will do if you cannot be quicker—I mean to publish the letters appended to the 6 weeks tour—the question is whether the 6 weeks tour itself shall be printed—it was printed & corrected by Shelley though written by me[2]—& being once published— as a part of his life might as well appear again—What do you say?

I hope when I see you next to be in better spirits—The state I fell into last Winter too often returns on me—& I have not spirits unluckily to appear other than I am when melancholy—this is a great fault & has injured me much through life but I cannot help it but I am better now I trust—

Ever Your
MS.

Send me back these papers Michi{n}g Mallico³ safe—I have no other copy—
& send them <u>as quickly</u> as you can

UNPUBLISHED. TEXT: MS., Pforzheimer Library.

1. Shelley's satire is dedicated "To Thomas Brown, Esq., The Younger, H.F," i.e., Thomas
Moore, who had written the satires *The Twopenny Post-Bag* (1813) and *The Fudge Family in
Paris* (1818) under the name Thomas Brown, the Younger, H.F. (Historian of Fudges) (see
vol. I, 22 January 1819, n. 8, 30 November 1821, n. 11; 11 December 1838, n. 3). Following
the dedication, Shelley's preface explicitly satirizes William Gifford, editor of the *Quarterly
Review*, and John Murray, publisher of the *Quarterly Review*, for that publication's attacks on
Leigh Hunt. In the course of this satire, Shelley humorously depicts the *Quarterly*'s view of
Hunt as a "murderous and smiling villain" and a "monkey suckled with tyger's milk, this odious
thief, liar, scoundral, coxcomb and monster." These lines were omitted, one may conclude,
at Hunt's request and not, as has been suggested, because Mary Shelley was fearful of attacking
John Murray (see Shelley, *Poetry and Prose*, p. 322). The entire Preface was first published in
Shelley, *Poetry and Prose*, pp. 323–24.

2. *Six Weeks' Tour* was included in Shelley, *Essays, Letters*.

3. *Hamlet* 3. 2. 149. Shelley had signed *Peter Bell the Third* as written "By Miching Mallecho,
Esq."

TO LEIGH HUNT   Putney   Sunday   [6 October 1839]

Dear Hunt

I send you the rest of the Devil¹ that you may judge better—You see I
have scratched out a few lines which might be <u>too shocking</u>—and yet I hate
to <u>mutilate</u>. Consider the fate of the book only—if this Essay is to preclude
a number of readers who else would snatch at it—for so many of the religious
particularly like Shelley—had I better defer the publication, till all he has
left is published—Let me hear what you think as soon as you can

Remember Wednesday   Yˢ   MS.

Remember <u>I</u> do not enter into the question at all. It is <u>my</u> duty to publish
every thing of Shelley—but I want these two volumes to be popular—&
would it be as well to <u>defer</u> this Essay? Send back the slips.

ADDRESS: Leigh Hunt Esq / 4 Upper Cheyne Row / Chelsea. POSTMARKS: (1) Putney S[   ] /
3py P.Paid; (2) 4 Eg / PD / OC 7 / 1839 / 4 Eg. ENDORSED: Mary Shelley. PUBLISHED: Jones,
#507. TEXT: MS., Huntington Library (HM 2758).

1. Shelley's essay "On the Devil and Devils," written in ?1819–21, was not included in
Shelley, *Essays, Letters* (see the next letter). For discussions of the date the essay was written
see Cameron, *The Golden Years*, p. 602; and Stuart Curran and Joseph Anthony Wittreich,
Jr., "The Dating of Shelley's 'On the Devil, and Devils,' " *Keats-Shelley Journal* 21 (1972), 22
(1973): 93.

*To Edward Moxon   Layton House—Putney
                                         Tuesday   8 Oct. [1839]

My dear Sir

After printing an Essay I mentioned to you on the Devil & Devils, I have changed my mind & will not include it in this publication. I think it would excite a violent party spirit against the volumes which otherwise I beleive will prove generally attractive   The printer therefore must cancel the pages.

When this Edition is sold I think of ⟨bringing⟩ printing all Shelley's prose, which I think will make two volumes similar to the poetical works—in that this Essay will of course appear. If you read it I am sure you will approve of my leaving it out of the present publication the volumes will be large enough without—10 sheets each I trust.[1]

I wish some fine day you would bring Mrs Moxon[2] & the children to luncheon here—just let me have a line to say when—if she would do me the pleasure to come

                                                    Yours truly
                                                    MWShelley

UNPUBLISHED: Quotation, Anderson's Auction Catalogue, April 1925, p. 35. TEXT: MS., Pforzheimer Library.
    1. Volume 1 of Shelley, *Essays, Letters,* contains 243 pages; volume 2, 248 pages.
    2. Emma Isola (?1809–91), an orphan who was informally adopted by Charles and Mary Lamb in 1821, married Moxon on 30 July 1833 (Lamb, *Letters* [Lucas], II, 290–91; Merriam, *Moxon,* p. 195).

To Leigh Hunt   [Putney]   Thursday   [?10 October 1839]

Dear Hunt

You have puzzled me much. What you said convinced me. You said: "Do as Mills,[1] who has just phrased it so that the common reader will think common love is meant—the learned alone will know what is meant." Accordingly I read the Phædrus & found less of a veil even than I expected— thus I was emboldened to leave it so that our sort of civilized love should be understood—Now you change all this back into friendship—which makes the difficulty as great as ever. I wished in every way ⟨to leave⟩ to preserve as many of Shelley's own words as possible—& I was glad to do so under the new idea which you imparted—but your alterations puzzle me mightily—I do not like not to abide by them—yet they destroy your own argument that different sexes would be understood, & thus all is in confusion

Accordingly I have left some & not others—where you seemed very vehement—& your p. 192 I have altered & omitted as you mention—but I could not bring myself to leave the word love out entirely from a treatise on Love. With regard to your verbal corrections—this was no hasty translation—Shelley read it over aloud several times[2]—so some things that look uncouth, I suppose he thought, as you phrase it—more Greek—and I like to leave it as he left it as much as possible.

After all the beauty of the piece consists in Agathon's, Socrates, & Alcibiades speeches—the rest are of minor importance. It is puzzling—That's a fact as the Americans say.

I shall have other sheets so—so hope you will come to look at them   Will you dine here next Wednesday—or Thursday—if Thursday write directly if I dont hear from you I shall expect you on Wednesday.

Ever truly Y^s
MWShelley

PUBLISHED: Jones, #508. TEXT: MS., Luther A. Brewer Collection, University of Iowa.

1. John Stuart Mill's translations, with notes, of Plato's *Protagoras, Phaedrus, Gorgias,* and *Apology of Socrates* were published in the *Monthly Repository* in 1834–35. Of *Phaedrus,* Mill commented: "The dialogue derives an additional interest, from its containing, in the form of an allegory, those doctrines, or rather ideas, on the subject of love which, by giving rise to the vulgar expression 'Platonic love,' have made the name of Plato familiar to the ear of thousands" (*Four Dialogues of Plato,* trans. with notes by John Stuart Mill, ed. Ruth Borchardt [London: Watts & Co., 1946], p. 67).

2. Shelley read the *Phaedrus* on 4–5 August 1818, Mary Shelley on 4 August 1818. On 2 May 1820 Mary Shelley indicates that "Shelley finishes Phædrus" (MWS Journal).

*TO EDWARD MOXON   Putney—Friday Ev^g   11 Oct. [1839]

Dear Sir

I am under the necessity of consulting a Plato—& not having one, am put to inconvenience. The dialogue I must see is entitled Ion[1]—Could you borrow, & let me have for a day, the volume of Plato's works containing this dialogue—let it have a latin translation appended. Pray oblige me as I cannot correct the press without it—& the press is waiting for the correction—so I am in a hurry.

I count on yours & Mrs Moxon's[2] promised visit during this second summer—

Y^s truly
MWShelley

UNPUBLISHED. TEXT: MS., Brigham Young University.

1. "Ion; or, of the Illiad; translated from Plato" appears in Shelley, *Essays, Letters,* I, 273–98.

2. See 8 October [1839], n. 2.

TO LEIGH HUNT   Putney—Wednesday   [23 October 1839]

Dear Hunt

I heard from Mrs Carlyle[1] that your play was accepted[2]—but your note gives me the further pleasure of the agreableness of its reception—the

Green Room,—that purgatory before bliss or the other thing, to Saturnine & umbrageous spirits, will be a milky way, all sprinkled with dancing stars to your free hearted disposition & witty mind—God Speed you through all

I send you a ⟨note⟩ letter I got from Percy today[3]—He thinks the Pit the most influential position I fancy. Rothwell resolves to go & to give the aid of his Irish enthusiasm—You must & will succeed.

I will let you know about Claire when the time comes. I delight in your having got among these kind friends but dont wonder—Carlyle[4] says you read your play so exquisitely, so much better than any one ever read before, that you must enchant—

Let me hear how you progress & beleive me   Your truly

MWShelley

Percy when he says he was bigotted means that he would not be persuaded to have any more lessons from Nichols[5] having spent so much already—

ADDRESS: Leigh Hunt Esq / 4 Upper Cheyne Row / Chelsea. POSTMARKS: (1) T.P / Putney N.O; (2) 12 Nn 12 / OC 24 / 1839; (3) 2 An 2 / OC 24 / 1839. ENDORSED: Percy & Mary / Shelley. PUBLISHED: Jones, #510. TEXT: MS., The Charnwood Loan, British Library.

1. Jane Baillie Welsh Carlyle (1801–66; *DNB*, s.v. "Carlyle, Thomas").

2. That is, accepted to be read before the management of Covent Garden Theatre in their Green Room (a room in theaters for the accommodation of actors and actresses when they are not required to be on stage). The theater was managed by Lucia Elizabeth Mathews, Madame Vestris (1797–1856; *DNB*), an actress credited as the first female theater manager, who was the wife of Charles James Mathews (1803–78), actor, the son of Hunt's friend Charles Mathews (for Hunt's account of his reception see Hunt, *Autobiography,* II, 225–26). Hunt had already successfully read *A Legend of Florence* to a group of his friends, including James Sheridan Knowles (1784–1862; *DNB*), dramatist and actor; Bryan Waller Procter; Charles Dickens; and Carlyle (Blunden, *Leigh Hunt,* pp. 278–79).

3. Percy Florence indicates in his letter that if Hunt's play was to be performed before his vacation time, he would "come up to go in the pit." He also asks Mary Shelley to send him "those two works of my father's directly you can, do not delay it, two of each" and other items along with the forthcoming editions (MS., W. Hugh Peal, 22 October 1839).

4. Mary Shelley and the Carlyles almost certainly became acquainted through Hunt. On 3 December 1839, in response to a request from Mary Shelley (unlocated) about a quotation from Carlyle's *Wilhelm Meister's Apprenticeship and Travels* (from the German of Goethe, a new edition, rev. [London: James Fraser, 1839]), to be used as a motto for *Essays, Letters,* Carlyle wrote saying that he could not clearly remember the lines she referred to but would that day have a copy of *Wilhelm Meister* sent to her (Marshall, *Mary Shelley,* II, 292). The volume is autographed: "To Mrs Shelley / with kind regards. / T. C." (*The Library of Jerome Kern,* auction catalogue, The Anderson Galleries, 21–24 January 1929, item 231). Carlyle's lines, which follow Mary Shelley's preface, read: " 'That thou, O my Brother, impart to me truly how it stands with thee in that inner man of thine; what lively images of things past thy memory has painted there; what hopes, what thoughts, affections, knowledge, do now dwell there. For this, and no other object that I can see, was the gift of hearing and speech bestowed on us two.' Thomas Carlyle."

5. Percy Florence's flute master.

*To [EDWARD MOXON]   Putney Nov. 11 [1839]

Dear Sir

A thousand thanks for your valuable present which I like very much indeed.[1] I am afraid that I gave the printer some trouble about the poems—but was earnest to have this edition complete & you cannot imagine how confusing & tantalizing is the turning over Manuscript books—full of scraps of finished or unfinished poems—half illegible—I am sorry he found the MS. for the 2[d] Vol so incomplete—it was complete but copied variously at different times by different persons.—The letters read beautifully. In about a week you will be able to judge of the publication as a whole & you must come & dine here & make final arrangements. I will write again when I see land.

Thanks for "Love"[2]—Know[l]es is the finest poet of these latter days—& his dramatic genius inspiring situations founded on passion & sentiment—not melodramatic effect, is full of power & beauty. I hope to get to town soon to see his play.

Pray do me a service   in page 160 of the proof I send there is mention of Guido & his mistress[3]   her name is illegible in the original, & here I have no book to refer to for the right one—Would you look at some biographical dictionary & put in the right name

I am Yours truly
MWShelley

UNPUBLISHED. TEXT: MS., Pforzheimer Library.

   1. The one-volume edition of Shelley's *Poetical Works.*

   2. *Love,* by James Sheridan Knowles, was first produced at Covent Garden on 4 November 1839.

   3. Elizabetta Sirani (Shelley, *Essays, Letters,* II, 160).

TO LEIGH HUNT   Putney   14 Nov. [1839]

Dear Hunt

I have desired to fix a day when you will meet Claire but have not yet been able—I hope I shall soon—Meanwhile I wish much to hear of your play—& when it will appear—Percy is very anxious to learn.

I see a few asterisks & omissions in the letters of Shelley you published[1]—were these wholly private & indifferent or did some temporary or modest personal reason cause them   If the latter pray let me replace them—let me have the originals for a few days—but then it must be <u>directly</u>—as they are printing fast off—tomorrow it ought to be   I hope you have been quite well all this time—

Yours truly
MWShelley

PUBLISHED: Jones, #511. TEXT: MS., Huntington Library (HM 2750).

1. Of the six Shelley letters Hunt published in *Lord Byron and Some of His Contemporaries* (I, 383–406), three, dated 22 March 1818, 15 August 1819, and 26 August 1821, are republished in Shelley, *Essays, Letters* (II, 110–11, 220–23, 325–27), as Hunt gave them; the letter of 27 September 1819 has passages added to it in *Essays, Letters* (II, 226–29); and the letters of 2 December and 23 December 1819 are not included. Hunt informed Mary Shelley that he was unable to find the letters (see [?26 July 1839]; and 22 December [1839] to Leigh Hunt).

Mary Shelley also obtained Shelley's letters to Horace Smith, who gave permission to publish them, with the provision that one of them not be associated in any way with his name (Horace Smith to Mary Shelley, 9 November 1839, Duke University Library). Mary Shelley included four letters from Shelley to Horace Smith in Shelley, *Essays, Letters,* two given as addressed to him (II, 328–32, 346–53) and two addressed to "C. T., Esq." (II, 341–44, 353–55). For the complete texts of these letters see *PBS Letters,* #699, #719. In a letter of 21 December 1839 Horace Smith thanks Mary Shelley for her gifts of a copy of the one-volume edition of Shelley's *Poetical Works* (1839) and a copy of Shelley, *Essays, Letters* (MS., Duke University Library).

To Leigh Hunt   [Putney   c. 15 November 1839]

Dear Hunt

I write in haste—will you come here & talk over your finale with me[1]— flint & steel knocking a dormant spark may come out

I send you a book[2] you will be glad to have—Let me have the letters[3] as soon as you can even if too late for this—they will only be <u>time enough</u> for another edition—so let {me} have them <u>as soon</u> as you can—I have it at heart to replace these passages.—why not—we wish to shew <u>him</u> not ourselves—& each word of <u>his</u> is <u>him</u>—besides one does not get so much earthly honey to spare confessing that a bit of ambrosia was once on a time put in ones cup by heaven

Y^s MS.

PUBLISHED: Jones, #512. TEXT: MS., British Library (Add. 38,524, ff. 201–2).

1. Madame Vestris had suggested that Hunt change the ending of *A Legend of Florence* and return Ginevra to her husband Agolanti, but Hunt refused (Blunden, *Leigh Hunt,* p. 279).

2. The one-volume edition of Shelley's *Poetical Works.*

3. Mary Shelley believed that a second edition would rapidly follow. However, the second edition was not published until 1845, and the third edition was published in 1852 (see [?26 July 1839]; 14 November [1839]; and 22 December [1839] to Leigh Hunt).

To Charles Ollier   [?Putney   November–December 1839][1]

My dear Sir

Have you any letters addressed by Shelley to you which you could let me have to publish—You will see that I have published such as I have been able to collect and I should like to add in any that you will furnish me with.

I asked you to ask Mr Bentley to give me a copy of Lodore—if he will will you send it to the care of Honbl. Mrs Stanhope—at Mrs Woods—27 Charlotte St Portland Place

Would Mr Bentley like to include Valperga in his standard novels? that novel never had fair play; never being properly published[2]—I would write a preface for it—

Y^s truly   MWShelley

Could Mr Bentley also let me have a copy of Frankenstein published in the standard Novels?

PUBLISHED: Jones, #516. TEXT: MS., Huntington Library (HM 10797).

1. The contents of this letter indicate that it was written soon after Shelley, *Essays, Letters,* was published and in anticipation of a second edition (see [c. 15 November 1839], n. 3). Ollier noted on this letter, at the top of page 1: "I did not accede to this request, because no money was offered me, and I felt the letters were valuable to me."

2. Perhaps a reference to the manuscript changes made by Godwin (see vol. I, 7 March [1823], n. 10) or to the fact that *Valperga* was brought out by a small publisher who could not advertise it much.

---

*TO MARY ELLEN PEACOCK   Monday—Putney [9 December 1839]

My dear Mary

You promised a visit to Putney—When will it be?—Will you dine here next Monday—let me have an immediate answer. Percy will be back[1]— spend a long day here   Rosa[2] is now with me   Would your father come with you—Y^s Affl^y MWShelley

ADDRESS: Miss Peacock / 18 Stamford St. / Blackfriars. POSTMARKS: (1) NO Putney / 1py. P.Paid; (2) 12 Nn / PD / DC 9 / 1839 / 12 Nn. UNPUBLISHED. TEXT: MS., Houghton Library.

1. The Michaelmas term officially ended on Monday, 16 December 1839, but the Trinity College Exit Book shows that Percy Florence left on Friday, 13 December.

2. Rosa Robinson.

TO EDWARD MOXON   [Putney] Dec. 19, 1839.

The Examiner was really good—very—the Athenæum creditable.—But— the Spectator![1]—its editor must be both a goose and a coxcomb—the notion that L[ord] B[yron] had any hand in the Peter Bell is half-witted—the incapacity of appreciating the Defence of Poetry betrays a degree of ig- norance rarely to be parelleled in the whole circle of criticism—to so foolish and uneducated a person the Fragments of Metaphysics must indeed appear devoid of meaning—he does not know his a.b.c. of the language in which they are written.

PUBLISHED: Jones, #514. TEXT: Forman, *The Shelley Library,* p. 121.

1. The *Examiner*, no. 1663 (15 December 1839): 788–89, review of Shelley, *Essays, Letters,* agrees with the opening statement of Mary Shelley's preface that "these volumes have long been due to the public" and states that "if the publication before us is an instalment only, it is a rich one, and the public have reason to be thankful." The review lauds Shelley but makes no comment on Mary Shelley's editing. The *Athenaeum*, no. 633 (14 Decembe 1839): 939–42, review of the one-volume *Poetical Works* and *Essays, Letters* notes that the poems published in the four-volume edition with omissions now appear whole and that *Peter Bell the Third* and *Swellfoot the Tyrant* are also included. The review is critical of Mary Shelley for not publishing everything Shelley wrote and suggests that the letters should have been woven in with the poetry rather than published separately. A second review of *Essays, Letters* in the *Athenaeum,* no. 635 (28 December 1839): 982–85, declares that it now realizes that much was omitted by Mary Shelley and "since we can still only have a portion of Shelley, we do not think that the intrinsic merits of the present selection demanded their separate publication." The *Spectator* 12, no. 598 (14 December 1839): 1186–87, review of *Essays, Letters* sharply attacks Mary Shelley: "The time has been when a literary executor examined the papers of the dead with some degree of critical care, to prevent the publication of any thing inconsistent with the reputation of the deceased, or that respect which is due to the public taste, at least from third parties. But circumstances have changed all that; and now the chief consideration with any one possessing manuscripts seems to be whether the author's name is enough to sell them. This remark applies to a good part of the volumes before us, except in so far as it may be modified by Mrs. Shelley's relation to the writer, and the circumstance of her taste harmonizing with the weakest and most defective parts of his mind." It dismisses the essays and translations as incomplete or too visionary, and the *Defence of Poetry* as "scarcely needed now." Perceiving merit in the letters, it suggests that they might have been published as a supplement to the poems.

*To Leigh Hunt   Putney—22 Dec. [1839]

Dear Hunt

I am glad you are pleased with the preface—it is a comfort to get a little praise—I am sorry we have not seen you so long—I wish you could dine here the day after Xmas day—Thursday—I shall not be long in this house— a house is a blessing I never possessed long at a time—& this one costs too much—I leave in the Spring   I have ⟨I wish⟩ done something in it regaining health & spirits which lodgings in London destroyed

I wish you could find the letters—that they might be given perfect—The Examiner this time speaks as it ought of Shelley[1]—

How are you all? Remember me to Marianne   Ever Ys

                                                             MWShelley

UNPUBLISHED. TEXT: MS., Pforzheimer Library.
    1. See 19 December 1839, n. 1.

To Abraham Hayward   Putney   22 Dec. [1839]

Dear Mr Hayward

I give you great credit for your tact yesterday, in disclaiming the con-oisseurship you possess[1]—Thus you enable me to look back on past dinners without too much dismay—to future ones without overwhelming terror. You give proof of a friendship rare & to be valued in thus trying to decrease rather than encrease my anxiety when I may have the pleasure of entertaining you. I will try to reward it in some measure—Alas—I am an Ignorama—In my father's house we might eat—but were never allowed to talk of eating—Shelley had no dislike to seeing women eat (with moderation) but he thought it a blot on Julie's[2] character to be gourmande & was himself so very abstemious that I could never exert more cookery for him than making a pudding—I really scarcely knew what a dinner was till with a very few years—& now am at once dazzled & confounded by any display of learning; but as far as a partridge pie—with beefsteak over as well as under, the birds placed with their breasts downwards in the dish (469) a Surrey Capon (466) (apropos to that page—Hat Joliffe[3] says that pheasants to be good—and no bird is so variable—ought to feed on hurtleberries) or any little esoteric but simple dish you may communicate—I will try that you shall be pleased.—And are you not pleased with the promise—Do you go to Brighton?—

I send you the books[4]—You ought to like them—Pray let me have the Articles & Faust[5]—take care of yourself—I hope you got home well yesterday. It is an act of friendship to come all this way for a call—You ought to have preferred my simple dinner to Lockharts[6] when you were here

Y^s truly   MWShelley

ADDRESS: To Hayward. ENDORSED: M. Shelley. PUBLISHED: Jones, #515 (almost complete). TEXT: MS., John Murray.

1. Hayward's articles "Gastronomy and Gastronomers" and "Walker's Original," published in the *Quarterly Review* (no. 107 [July 1835]; no. 110 [February 1836]) and eventually collected and published as *The Art of Dining* (London: John Murray, 1852) established him as an expert on dining (*A Selection from the Correspondence of Abraham Hayward, Q.C.*, ed. Henry E. Carlisle, 2 vols. [New York: Scribner and Welford, 1887], I, 53–54).

2. A reference to Rousseau's *Julie ou la Nouvelle Héloise*.

3. Unidentified.

4. Probably a reference to one or more of the 1839 editions of Shelley.

5. Possibly Hayward's articles about dining. His translation of Goethe's *Faust* was published in 1833 by Edward Moxon.

6. Between 1834 and 1842 Hayward was a frequent contributor to the *Quarterly Review*, which John Gibson Lockhart edited (*A Selection from the Correspondence of Abraham Hayward*, I, 68).

*To Leigh Hunt   [Putney   c. 23 December 1839][1]

My dear Hunt

I am very much puzzled to know how to answer your friend. Of course I wish in every way to write pleasingly to a man of whom you have a good opinion—& who as you say worships Shelley. But I do think his request indiscreet   That I—who if I wished to write a biographical notice of the lost one would do it—any one may guess; the reasons that prevent me & will prevent me are so tragical—that I could never bring myself to converse on them to my nearest friend—& to a stranger it is quite out of the question.

I think he applies to too near a relation—as to making communications of facts &c I am totally averse—since in my own time I should put them in my own light. As to verifying ⟨of course⟩ this seems easy but it is far from being so—I must thus perhaps give to discouragement to what I disapprove—which in a <u>philosophical</u> life may be a great deal—which may only differ in views—in as much as it is <u>impossible</u> that a stranger & myself could agree, I feel certain, about inner views of Shelley—& if I do not dissent, I am said to give my assent & that may not at all suit me.

Time may flow on—but it adds only to the keeness & vividness with which I view the past—adds, how much: for when tragedies & most bitter dramas were in the course of acting I did not feel their meaning & their consequences as poignantly as I now do—I cannot write or speak of Shelley to any purpose according to my views without taking a seal from a fountain, that I cannot bring myself yet to let flow. And I think a stranger asking me for communications beyond verifying displays a deplorable want of knowledge of the fitness of things—& ⟨commits⟩ even the <u>verifying</u> is an act I must decline—

I enclose my answer which I hope you will ⟨not⟩ think as it ought to be. It is a most difficult to deny & appear an obstacle to a good intention—but I do not think that I ought to comply—and I am sure I could not.

I hope your play will indeed come out in Jany We long to see you—Will you dine here New Year's day—& if not on that day the previous Monday 30th Dec. at 4 o'clock

Will you forward my note. I thought it best to send it to you that you might see what I say—

Ever Yours

MWShelley

UNPUBLISHED. TEXT: MS., Keats House, Hampstead.

1. On 21 December 1839 George Henry Lewes enclosed a letter for Mary Shelley to Leigh Hunt with the request that Hunt forward it and "say a word" to her on his behalf. Lewes's intended biography of Shelley, whose work he greatly admired, had been advertised in 1838 in the *National Magazine and Monthly Critic*. Because of Mary Shelley's refusal of assistance, he instead wrote a number of positive critiques including: a review of the *Poetical Works* (1839); *Essays, Letters; Die Cenci*, trans. Felix Adolphie (Berlin, 1838); and *Adone. Nella Morte di Giovanni Keats. Elegia di P. B. Shelley*, trans. L. A. Damaso Pareto (Geneva, 1830), in the *Westminster Review* 35, no. 69 (April 1841): 303–44; "Shelley, Percy Bysshe," in *The Penny Cyclopedia of the Society for the Diffusion of Knowledge* (London: Charles Knight and Co., 1832–45), XXI, 374–76; and "Shelley and the Letters of Poets," *Westminster Review*, n.s., no. 2 (April 1852): 502–11 (White, *Shelley*, II, 402–3; Donald H. Reiman, "Shelley in the Encyclopedias," *Keats-Shelley Journal* 12 [1963]: 57–59; and Lewes to Leigh Hunt, 21 December 1839, MS., British Library).

*To Edward Moxon   Putney—6 Jan^y [1840]

Dear Mr Moxon

Many thanks for the papers—The Atlas[1] is very good—& sensible—I am very much obliged to you also for the books Campbell's poems[2] is a valuable present & I fell on his Soldiers dream & the Gentlemen of England & other old favourites with extreme delight—The former of these I think possesses the most simple homefelt pathos of any poem in the world—at the same time that it is so exquisitely melodious in its versification.

I hope our book goes on well—& that this New Year will in every way prosper with you.

With regard to our accounts could you let me have half the sum mentioned in the course of this week—the other half I do not want till March—You will oblige me by sending the sum in two cheques—one for £50 the other for £20.[3]

I am dear Sir
Yours truly
MWShelley

Could you make up for me the fair sheets sent—I have all but the title pages contents preface & odd parts of sheets

UNPUBLISHED. TEXT: MS., Pforzheimer Library.
    1. *The Atlas, a General Newspaper and Journal of Literature* 14, no. 706 (23 November 1839), included a favorable notice in a survey review of seven poets, among them Goethe and Thomas Percy (pp. 750–51).
    2. See 30 September [1839], n. 1.
    3. Almost certainly for Shelley, *Essays, Letters.*

*To Edward Moxon   Layton House—Putney   11 Jany 1840

Dear Mr Moxon

I have received the cheques for £70[1] & thank you. I regret your account of the sale—It seems strange that the most beautiful book that has been published in England for many a long year, should not be read eagerly—I hope it will go better soon

Y^s truly
MaryW. Shelley

UNPUBLISHED. TEXT: MS., Massachusetts Historical Society.
    1. See 6 January [1840], n. 3.

*To Leigh Hunt   Friday [?17 January 1840][1]   Putney

Dear Hunt

   No tickets are come for us—so I suppose we do not go—
   I was not well on Wednesday & quite unable to be good company—It
was very mortifying to me but these fogs & damps— — —never mind you
made up for all   You enchanted Percy's friends & I have heard of nothing
since from Knox[2] but his admiration of your wisdom your mi{r}th—& the
good of all kinds to be derived from hearing you talk—

                                              Yours Ever
                                              MShelley

UNPUBLISHED. TEXT: MS., Pforzheimer Library.
   1. The date of this letter is based on Mary Shelley's indication that she had not yet received
tickets for *A Legend of Florence*. It is likely that the tickets were not issued until the latter part
of January, as Mary Shelley acknowledged receipt of hers on [30 January 1840].
   2. Alexander Andrew Knox (1818–91) attended Trinity College, where he and Percy Florence became friends. Mary Shelley was particularly fond of Knox and assisted his efforts to
become a writer. He achieved success, first as a journalist, writing for the *Times* (London)
from 1846 to 1860, and then as a police magistrate (he had been called to the bar, Lincoln's
Inn, in 1844). In 1857 Knox married Susan Armstrong (*DNB;* Mrs. Andrew Crosse, "Alexander Knox and His Friends," *Temple Bar,* April 1892, pp. 495–517).

To Leigh Hunt   [Putney]   Thursday [30 January 1840]

My dear Hunt

   If possible Percy will stay till After Wednesday—rather than journey to
& fro from Cambridge. If however by any chance your play is put off longer
than one day next week let me know as soon as you possibly can
   Many thanks for the tickets.[1] Will not Henry[2] come to see us—

                                              Yours Ever
                                              MWShelley

ADDRESS: Leigh Hunt Esq / 4 Upper Cheyne Row / Chelsea. POSTMARKS: (1) Putn[ey SQ] /
1py PPa[id]; (2) PUTNEY / [   ] / JA 30 / 1840; (3) 8 NT / JA 30 / 8 NT / 1830. PUB-
LISHED: Jones, #517. TEXT: MS., Huntington Library (HM 11633).
   1. See [?17 January 1840], n. 1.
   2. Henry Hunt, Leigh Hunt's son.

*To Leigh Hunt   [Putney]   Sunday [2 February 1840]

   "Vaulting ambition o'eleaps itself, & falls on the other side"[1]—trying to
be too right makes one in the wrong. I grieve, dear Hunt, that so it should
be—It was necessary for Percy to appear at Cambridge <u>yesterday</u> or to lose
the term—it seemed foolish to go, to return on Wednesday—so I wrote to

one of the Heads of his College to ask as a favour to me a few days grace without losing term—leave came for him to stay till next Saturday—but after this he will not be able to come away in middle of term—and he is full of disappointment that thus he will not be at your First Night—His only consolation is, he says, that he knows it will succeed & so he will see it when he comes up.—now had I, with philosophic indifference let things alone—he would have gone yesterday, & have come up when summoned— Do get it played before Saturday, if you can, & then there will be no regrets—

I trust to your kindness to take care that I shall be present with a few friends

Ever Y^s
MWS

ADDRESS: Leigh Hunt Esq / 4 Upper Cheyne Row / Chelsea. POSTMARKS: (1) Putney SQ / 1py PPaid; (2) PUTNEY / MG / FE 3 / 18[4]o; (3) 2 An 2 / FE 3 / 1840; (4) 12 Nn / PD / FE 3 / 12 Nn / 1840. ENDORSED: M Shelley. UNPUBLISHED. TEXT: MS., Pforzheimer Library.
  1. *Macbeth* 1. 7. 27–28.

*To LEIGH HUNT   [Putney]   Monday [3 February 1840]

My dear Hunt—We are so charmed with your news[1]—Percy thinks Friday must be lucky—since it brings such good luck to him on this occasion. Rothwell[2] came in this evening & claimed our long standing promise to dine with him on the eventful day & go from his house to the Theatre— Are we {to} have a private box?—but then it must not be too high—the dress circle were better for hearing. if you send us orders—will you take care that we have good places for 5—let me know;—if we have <u>orders</u>— then send some to Claire (her address is Lansdowne Hotel Dover St.)— that she may make a party for herself but if it be a private box she had better go with us—Will you not send orders to Jane—

Dont worry yourself—⟨but the sooner⟩ you will of course let us know in time, that we may ask some friends <u>men</u> if to a Private Box. My fair friends are full of resolution that it <u>shall</u> succeed—and I know that it <u>will</u>.

God bless you

Y^s Ever
MS.

ADDRESS: Leigh Hunt Esq / 4 Upper Cheyne Row / Chelsea. POSTMARKS: (1) [P]utney S[Q] / 1py PPaid; (2) PUTNEY / MG / FE [4] / 1840; (3) [2] An 2 / FE 4 / 1840; (4) 12 Nn / PD / FE 4 / 12 Nn / 1840. ENDORSED: Mary Shelley. UNPUBLISHED. TEXT: MS., Pforzheimer Library.
  1. That *A Legend of Florence* would have its first performance on Friday, 7 February 1840.
  2. Richard Rothwell.

*To Leigh Hunt [Putney] Wednesday [5 February 1840]

My dear Hunt—⟨How⟩ What do you do about orders—If you have any to spare, I should like to distribute them among a few men—your admirers—if you are limited yet perhaps you can let me have one or two to give away. I shall hope soon to know what you have done about US.

Your Ever
MWS.

ADDRESS: Leigh Hunt Esq / 4 Upper Cheyne Row / Chelsea. POSTMARKS: (1) Putney SQ / 1py PPaid; (2) PUTNEY / [   ] / [FE] 5 / [1840]; (3) [8 Nt] / PD / FE 5 / 8 Nt / 1840. ENDORSED: Mary Shelley. UNPUBLISHED. TEXT: MS., Jean de Palacio.

*To Mary Ellen Peacock Putney—21 Feb. [1840]

My dear Mary—Percy tells me that he has got a dog for you, & asks whether he shall send it now—or bring it with him. I think you had better decide on the latter. But if you think otherwise & wish for it now, write to him yourself at Trin. Coll. [Trinity College] Cambridge.

I am anxious to learn whether you have found the M.S. book of the Banquet of Plato[1]—or any other of my stray papers. And also whether your father will let me have to read the letters you mentioned—or some among them.

This fearful weather makes a desart of Putney—I hope you are amusing yourself in town. My friends send their love—Ever dear Mary

Yˢ truly
MWShelley

ADDRESS: Miss Peacock / 18 Upper Stamford St. / Black Friars. POSTMARKS: (1) Putney Sq / 1py PPaid; (2) 8 NT / PD / FE 21 / 8 NT / 1840. UNPUBLISHED. TEXT: MS., Houghton Library.

1. This was among the manuscripts Mary Shelley agreed to put in Peacock's keeping when Shelley's *Posthumous Poems* were suppressed in 1824 (see vol. I, 18 September [1823], n. 2; [?10 October 1839]).

*To Mary Ellen Peacock [Putney 22 February 1840]

My dear Mary

I sent you a hurried line yesterday with a message from Percy—asking you to answer his—on second thought you had better send your message through me—for after all it is not proper for a young lady to write to a young Gentleman—any thing beyond an invitation in their Papa's or Mamma's name—I always forget that Percy is grown up.

Tell me therefore what you decide about the dog

Y^s in extra Haste
MS.

ADDRESS: Miss Peacock / 18 Upper Stamford St / Black Friars. POSTMARKS: (1) T.P / Putney S[Q]; (2) 4 Eg 4 / FE 22 / 1840; (3) [   ] / FE [ ] / 18[40]. UNPUBLISHED. TEXT: MS., Houghton Library.

TO LEIGH HUNT   Putney—Thursday   [27 February 1840]

My dear Hunt

Thanks for your beautiful play[1]—so full of poetry & philosophy and all the loveliest things of this (when you write about it) lovely world.

Could you manage that I should see it again. Mrs Stanhope[2] borrowed her sister-in-law's, the Duchess of Bedford's box last Saturday to see it— & then was grievously disappointed that it was not acted. Could you ask your Charming Manager (gress[3] I mean) to give her & me a box some day next week[4]—the one she gave us the first night was perfect—It will be very kind of her—& you—& very delightful to us.

Will you also put down the name of Mrs Larkins[5] & 4 friends (five persons altogether) for any day next week when your play will <u>certainly</u> be played—

And let me have as <u>early</u> notice <u>as possible</u> of both things—especially the <u>box</u>, as I shall ask two or three friends to go with me who will appreciate your merit

Adieu dear successful

    Dramatic—Poet

Ever Yours truly
MWShelley

Tell Marianne how I sympathize in her pleasure on this occasion—when are we to see you [*p. 1, top*] not this week—but some day next—

PUBLISHED: Jones, #518. TEXT: MS., University of Iowa Library.

   1. The published text of *A Legend of Florence* (London: Edward Moxon, 1840).
   2. Elizabeth Stanhope.
   3. Madame Vestris (see [23 October 1839], n. 2).
   4. See 3 March [1840].
   5. Mrs. Larkins took care of the elderly Everina Wollstonecraft (see the next letter).

TO EVERINA WOLLSTONECRAFT   Putney—1st March [1840]

My dear Aunt

The name of Mrs Larkins with 4 friends—5 in all—is down on the free list for Tuesday night 3^{d} March. Let her know this.

I will see you if possible this week—God bless you

Yours affly

MWShelley

PUBLISHED: Jones, #519. TEXT: MS., Eton College Library.

To Abraham Hayward   Putney,   March 3 [1840]

[*Quotation*] Will you join me at Covent Garden tomorrow. Leigh Hunt
has sent me a box.

PUBLISHED: Jones, #520. TEXT: Jones, #520.

*To Jane Williams Hogg   [Putney]   Tuesday—10 March [1840]

Dearest Jane—I believe you know me well enough to be aware that when
I am happy I seek my friends—when harassed & uncomfortable I shut
myself up in my shell. The idea of leaving this house—& the poverty to
which I have reduced myself by not being as wise as some people & only
caring for my own dinner, is in itself so much of care that I am quite
oppressed—other circumstances have occurred also—I have been engaged
& absorbed by the distress of a friend[1] (no one you know) you know it is
my Star to have unfortunate friends—no one ought to know me

  I should like to see you—to feel the repose of your gentleness—the
comfort of your sympathy   I cannot promise Dina a Beaux—But if you &
she will come & spend a day & night here this week I shall be delighted   I
long to hear news of you—I never see Claire—I feel wrecked again & tossed
on the waves of life—my own fault this time   I might have "kept it when
I got it" & still have had money in my purse—But I have not spent it on
myself,

  God bless you—Write a line—

Ever Thine

ADDRESS: Mrs Hogg / 12 Maida Vale / Edgware Road. POSTMARKS: (1) Putney Sq / 1py PPaid;
(2) 4 Eg / PD / 4 Eg / MR 11 / 1840. UNPUBLISHED. TEXT: MS., Abinger MSS., Bodleian
Library.

  1. Possibly Jeremiah Ratcliffe, born in Manchester in 1794, a lieutenant colonel who served
with the 6th or Inniskilling Dragoons. He entered the military in 1811 and became unattached
on 17 July 1840 (Public Record Office, Kew). An unpublished letter from Augusta Goring
to Mary Shelley of 7 November 1837 indicates that Goring and Ratcliffe were friends. In this
letter, Goring says that Ratcliffe asked to be "kindly remembered" to Mary Shelley (Abinger
MSS., Bodleian Library). Ratcliffe was also a friend of Thomas Moore, who responded on 7
April 1840 to a letter (unlocated) from Mary Shelley: "I had already seen the accounts of
poor Ratcliffe in the newspaper—and they at once explained to me the change of manner I

had observed in him. Indeed I had been so unjust to my own dear country as to think he had been spoiled in Ireland. Your account of him interested us all very much" (Moore, *Letters*, II, 854). On 19 February Moore noted that Ratcliffe had just come from Ireland; on 20 or 21 February, that he dined at Samuel Rogers's "to meet Mrs. Shelley, the two Miss Robinsons and Ratcliffe" (Moore, *Journal*).

*TO MARY ELLEN PEACOCK   Putney   Tuesday   [10 March 1840]

Dear Mary—I should have answered your note before but I have been occupied nursing a sick friend[1] & not had a moment to spare—There was no need to be so uncomfortable about so mere a trifle

I am on the point of leaving this house. Julia & Rosa[2] (I said nothing to them about your note as it was marked <u>private</u>) will be at Kew & within your reach—my destination is yet uncertain—I will let you know when I know myself. I hope you are well & amusing yourself—give my love to <u>Pop</u>

Ever Yours
MWShelley

ADDRESS: Miss Peacock / 18 Upper Stamford St / Black Friars. POSTMARKS: (1) Putney Sq / 1py PPaid; (2) 4 Eg / PD / MR 11 / 4 Eg / 1840. UNPUBLISHED. TEXT: MS., Houghton Library.
    1. See 10 March [1840] to Jane Williams Hogg, n. 1.
    2. Julia and Rosa Robinson.

*TO LEIGH HUNT   Putney   Thursday   [?12 March 1840]

Dear Hunt

It gave me such true pleasure to find that our pretty little Queen ordered your play & went to see it again[1]   God grant, my friend, that this piece of late justice & sweet taste of late prosperity encrease & continue & spread a cheering influence over a life spent too much in adversity & struggle.

I should have written to you before—but ever since that night when I saw your play last[2] I have been painfully occupied—it is my fate that my friends should be unfortunate.[3] I am not strong & my health is now suffering from a good deal of agitation the disasters of a friend have occassioned. I leave this house on the 25—my plans are unsettled—but I wish you would come here before I go—will you fix a day soon.

Percy says "Make great thanks to Hunt for his play. I like it very much."

God bless your
Ever truly Y[s]
MWShelley

ENDORSED: Mary Shelley. UNPUBLISHED. TEXT: MS., Pforzheimer Library.

1. Queen Victoria (Blunden, *Leigh Hunt,* p. 283).
2. See 3 March [1840].
3. See 10 March [1840] to Jane Williams Hogg, n. 1.

*To JOHN HOBART CAUNTER   3 The Rise   Richmond   Thursday
                      12 o'clock   [?26 March–c. 5 June 1840][1]

Dear Mr Caunter—I will call on you at 12 on Saturday if you please & are
disengaged—that I may confer with you on the subject of my publication[2]—
which Mrs Godwin & myself both so much wish you to as you are good
enough to offer arrange—I hope this hour & day will suit you—

                                      I am Yours truly
                                      MWShelley

UNPUBLISHED. TEXT: MS., Princeton University Library.
   1. Mary Shelley left Putney on 25 March and went to Richmond, where she remained until
c. 5 June 1840 (see [?12 March 1840]; and 6 June [1840] to Abraham Hayward).
   2. Unidentified.

*To DR. THOMPSON[1]   Richmond   Thursday   [?26 March–
                                          c. 5 June 1840][2]

Dear Dr Thompson
   How very kind you are. I shall be in town early on Saturday Mor^g—my
cook shall come with me & call at your house between 11 & 12—If that
will d^o—if she ought to see about the place tomorrow instead, pray let me
have a line to say so, & she shall attend
   With a thousand thanks

                                      Ever yours
                                      MWShelley

UNPUBLISHED. TEXT: MS., Pforzheimer Library.
   1. Unidentified.
   2. See [?26 March–c. 5 June 1840] to John Hobart Caunter, n. 1.

*To MARY ELLEN PEACOCK   Richmond   Tuesday   [31 March 1840]

My dear Mary
   Percy wishes to know whether you still desire to have the dog you asked
for—& if you do, where & how he is to send it when he comes to town—
let me know as soon as you can.

My time being up at Layton House I am come here, during the Easter vacation. Percy wishing to be near the river—& I wishing to have him with me.[1] Claire tells me you expect him to pay you a visit at Halliford at Easter—but that was projected, I fancy, under the idea of my being in Paris—As it is having come here on purpose to have him with me, I shall not part with him if I can help it—

I am at a very small house in the town of Richmond—Our friends the R—s [*Robinsons*] are at Kew—I hope you are amusing yourself & going to the Opera—I and amusement have I think shaken hands, & bid each other an ever lasting Adieu—I cant say I like the dull life I lead; but pleasure costs money, & I have none—

Let me have a line about the dog—& believe me dear Mary

Y[s] truly
MWShelley

Will you be so good as to ask your father if he will learn for me to what <u>Native Regiment</u> Col. Home[2] belongs to—& whether he is full Colonel or Lieutenant Colonel. He is stationed at Madras—& will you let me know as soon as you can

ADDRESS: Miss Peacock / 18 Upper Stamford St. /Black Friars. POSTMARKS: (1) Richmond / 1D. PAID; (2) [8 NT] / PD / AP 1 / 8 NT / 1840; (3) RICHMOND / EV / [AP] 1 / 1840. UNPUBLISHED. TEXT: MS., Houghton Library.

   1. See [6 April 1840], n. 1.

   2. Robert Home (1784–1842), of the Madras Army, was promoted to the rank of full colonel on 23 January 1841, and to major general on 23 November 1841 (India Office Library and Records).

TO LEIGH HUNT   Monday Ev[g] [6 April 1840][1]
3 The Rise Richmond

Dear Hunt

Could you without inconvenience get the name of M[rs] Blood[2] & two friends 3 in all—put down on the free list of C.G. [*Covent Garden*] any day <u>before Friday</u> & let me know in time.

I expect Percy tomorrow—when shall we see you—

With love to Marianne Y[s] truly

MWShelley

If pressed for time write in a note "M[rs] Blood & two friends are put on the free list of C.G.—for <u>such a night</u>"—& send it directed to

M[rs] Wollstonecraft
12 Copenhagen St.
Pentonville

this will save your note coming first to me & then going to town.

PUBLISHED: Jones, #521. TEXT: MS., Huntington Library (HM 12361).
1. In the text of this letter Mary Shelley states that she expects Percy Florence to join her the next day. The Trinity College Exit Book indicates that Percy Florence left college for his Easter holiday on 7 April 1840, which means that this letter was written on Monday, 6 April.

2. Perhaps the wife of George Blood, the brother of Mary Wollstonecraft Godwin's beloved friend Fanny Blood (for details of their friendship see Ralph M. Wardle, *Mary Wollstonecraft* [Lincoln: University of Nebraska Press, 1951]).

*To Mr. Meymott[1]   Richmond   1ˢᵗ May [1840]

Dear Mʳ Meymott

The welcome gift has come at last—& I thank you very much both for the trouble you have taken & your kind compliment in inscribing it to me. I shall never be happy now till it is published. It will be appreciated & liked I am sure—I think Novello would be very glad to publish it[2]—Do let me see it in print—though in print it will never look so pretty as in your elegant Manuscript.

Richmond is looking so beautiful now, that I hope some day you will be tempted to ride up here again—& that we shall have the pleasure of seeing you

I am, dear Mʳ Meymott

Yˢ truly
MaryShelley

UNPUBLISHED: Jones, #447 (quotation). TEXT: MS., Pforzheimer Library.
1. Unidentified.
2. No mention of a song by Mr. Meymott exists in the archives of Novello & Company. Their publishing records for the mid-1800s, however, are very incomplete.

To Marianne Hunt   Brighton   6 June [1840]

Dear Marianne—It was you wrote to me last—so I write to <u>you</u>. Henry[1] told me that Hunt talked of calling on me at Richmond—but lo! I am here— whisked off—It seems as if I were never to be stationary—I, who long so for a home. I am going for a few months abroad with Percy[2]—perhaps as far as Milan   I shall be back in the Autumn.

How delighted I was at the success of <u>The Play</u>—The Players I hear did not take to his comedy—I think there ought to be a dash of romance in all Hunt writes—he being so romantic—so let him not cast aside pretty names— romantic adventures & the adjuncts that enliven his imagination. The piece of which he sketched the plot to me would I am sure delight his Audience.

May you & he prosper! It is a hard world—& there are some Immortals in it—yet, as I wrote word to Jane today the Strulbrugg Lady Cork is dead at ⟨85⟩ 95—so I have only 8 years more to wait[3]—Meanwhile Percy is the comfort & charm of my life—& if my friends were well off I should deem myself happy.

Adieu, dear Marianne

Ever Yours
MWShelley

PUBLISHED: Jones, #522. TEXT: MS., British Library (MS., Shelley, Adds., 38,523, ff. 219–20).

1. Henry Hunt.

2. This is the first of two Continental tours that Mary Shelley and Percy Florence, accompanied by friends of Percy Florence, took between 1840 and 1843. Details of the journeys are found in Mary Shelley's letters of that period and in MWS, *Rambles in Germany and Italy.* Mary Shelley and Percy Florence left England in mid-June and arrived at Paris on 22 June. There they were met by their traveling companions, Julian Robinson and George Hibbert Deffell (1819–95), a schoolmate of Percy Florence. Deffell received his B.A. in 1842, his M.A. in 1845, and was called to the bar in 1846. He went on to become a judge of the supreme court in Sydney, New South Wales (Mary Shelley to Everina Wollstonecraft, 20 July 1840 [vol. 3]; *Alumni Cantabrigienses*).

3. The Struldbrugs were a people endowed with immortality in *Gulliver's Travels,* bk. 3. Mary Monckton, afterwards countess of Cork, born 1746, died on 30 May 1840 (*DNB*). If Sir Timothy, born 1753, lived eight more years, he, too, would be ninety-five.

*To ABRAHAM HAYWARD   20 Rock Gardens   Brighton   6 June [1840]

Dear Mr Hayward

I was so sorry not to see you again at Richmond; tho' indeed I did not expect so to do as it is to far from town for a mere ride—I have just left it for this place—whence I cross, as soon as Percy joins me,[1] to Dieppe—Paris—perhaps Milan is my next destination—I shall return, I fancy, in October[2]—If you know any agreable foreigners to whom to introduce me pray send me some letters—

I own that it pains me to exile myself from the circle of London society—but it cant be helped—poor as I am I only involve myself—for in London one cannot see ones friends without expence—However it is useless regretting what one cannot obtain—Write me a line & tell me how you are

Ever Yours truly
MWShelley

Count Guiccioli being gone to the other world,[3] Teresa will be well off—I wonder whether I shall see her this summer

ENDORSED: Shelley. UNPUBLISHED. TEXT: MS., Pforzheimer Library.

1. Percy Florence left college for his summer holiday on 6 June 1840 (Trinity College Exit Book).

2. See 6 June [1840] to Marianne Hunt, n. 2.

3. Count Alessandro Guiccioli died on 21 April 1840 at the age of seventy-nine and left a will that excluded Teresa Guiccioli, from whom he had been separated many years. Subse-

quently, she brought a lawsuit against Count Guiccioli's heirs, and lengthy negotiations resulted in a compromise between the parties (Origo, *The Last Attachment,* p. 392; see also vol. I, 30 November 1821, n. 4).

*To Edward Moxon   Brighton   6 June [1840]

Dear Mr Moxon

I should have liked to have seen you before I left the neighbourhood of town—but was not able. I fear I should have had no good news of my dear Book[1]—which would have vexed me heartily.

Sometimes Authors have sent me their works through you—& I am so rude I do not think I have ever thanked them. The truth is that since my illness, on bringing out the poems, I have felt the slightest penmanship an intolerable task—& so put off all note writing—till too late—If you ever do receive works for me, if you will send them to me, Care of Miss Robinson, Kew Green—they will be taken care of. I am myself about to cross to France, for a little tour, during Percy's Long Vacation. I shall be back in the Autumn.[2]

> I am, dear Sir,
> Yours truly
> MWShelley

UNPUBLISHED. TEXT: MS., Pforzheimer Library.
   1. Shelley, *Essays, Letters.*
   2. See 6 June [1840] to Marianne Hunt, n. 2.

Index

Shelley, ed.), 271, 272n, 274, 274n, 275,
277, 280, 281, 283, 284, 284n; sinecure,
189, 190n, 209, 211n, 219, 220n, 221, 223.
Works: *Caleb Williams,* 128n; *Cloudesley,*
105, 105n, 108, 108n; *Deloraine,* 183, 184n,
186, 186n, 207; *Fables, Ancient and Modern,
Adapted for the Use of Young Children* [pseud.
Edward Baldwin], 248n; *Lives of the Nec-
romancers,* 160, 160n, 187n, 190n, 216;
Mandeville, 284; "On Phrenology," 123n;
Sketches of History in Six Sermons, 272n;
"Speculations (Observations) on Man His
Faculties and Their Operation," 195n; *St.
Leon,* 165n; *Thoughts on Man,* 110, 110n,
123n. *See also* Godwin, William and Mary
Jane
Godwin, William, Jr., 44, 45n, 171n, 212n,
261
Godwin, William and Mary Jane, 38, 146,
181, 190n, 259n, 260, 272; letter to, 187
Goethe, 336n
Goldoni, 202n
Goldsmith, Oliver: *The Vicar of Wakefield,* 167,
167n
Gongora, 255n
Gore, Catherine Frances, 193n. Works: *The
Fair of May Fair,* 158, 158n; *The Hamiltons,*
199, 199n; *Pinmoney,* 142, 143n; *The Tuil-
leries,* 135, 136n
Gore, Cecilia, 193n; letter to, 193
Gorges, Hamilton, 259n
Goring, Augusta, 297, 297n, 319nn, 341n
Goring, Sir Charles Foster, 184n
Goring, Harry Dent, 297n
Goring, Ida, 184n
Graham, Edward Fergus, 220n
Granby, John, 297n
Grant, Sir Colquhoun, 243, 244n
Greece, 192n
Green, Anne, 191, 192n, 243
Gregson, John, 153, 153n, 156n, 192n, 205,
206, 206n, 299n, 307; letters to, 153, 155,
156(2), 157(3), 161, 162, 172, 173, 174,
176(3), 177, 179, 180, 182, 186, 192, 193,
197, 265, 268, 273(2), 298
Grey, Charles, second earl, 127n, 146n
Grisi, Guilia, 210, 211n
Guarini, 202n
Guicciardini, 202n
Guiccioli, Count Alessandro, 240, 241, 346,
346n, 347n
Guiccioli, Countess Teresa, 3, 38n, 51, 52n,
53, 134n, 159, 159n, 183, 246, 248n, 254,
294n, 346, 346n; letters to, 18, 35, 76, 167
Guido, 330

Hale, Mrs., 266
Halifax, Viscount. *See* Wood, Charles
Hall, Samuel Carter: *The Book of Gems* (ed.),
293n
Hallam, Arthur, 303n
Hallam, Mr., 40n
Hannay, David, 263n
Hardings Library, 42, 43n
Hare, Anne Frances, 106n, 128, 128n, 132,
133n, 134n, 142n, 144n, 146, 146n, 149,
172n; letter to, 172

Hare, Augustus, 172n
Hare, Francis, 106n, 146n
Hare, Julius Charles, 142, 142n
Hare, William Robert, 146, 146n
Hares, the, 282n
Harrington, fifth earl of. *See* Stanhope, Leices-
ter
Harrow, 177, 182, 194, 203, 208. *See also
under* Shelley, Percy Florence
Hastings, 42, 43n, 53
Hauser, Kaspar, 216n
Haymarket Theatre, 58, 59n, 60n, 81n, 84,
85, 85n, 87
Hays, Mary, 270n; letter to, 269
Hayward, Abraham, 305n; letters to, 305, 333,
341, 346. Works: *The Art of Dining,* 334n;
"Gastronomy and Gastronomers," 334n;
Goethe's *Faust* (trans.), 334, 334n; "Walk-
er's Original," 334
Hazlitt, William, 277, 277n, 300n
Hazlitt, William, Jr., 277n; letters to, 277,
299. Works: *Literary Remains of the Late
William Hazlitt* (ed.), 277, 277n; *The Ro-
manticist,* 299, 300n
Health, Vale of, 286, 287n
Heath, Charles, 74, 75n, 165, 166, 166n, 178
Heath's Book of Beauty, 1835, 147n
Henry Colburn and Richard Bentley, 98n,
105n, 108, 128n, 129, 133n, 138, 139n,
145n, 149, 150, 151, 175n, 186n, 197n,
251, 299; letters to, 105, 107, 117. *See also*
Bentley, Richard; Colburn, Henry
Herrera, 255n, 289
Hervieu, Auguste Jean Jacques, 16n
Hill, Miss, 294
Hobhouse, John Cam: *Historical Illustrations
to the Fourth Canto of Childe Harold,* 240,
241, 242n
Hogg, Elizabeth Sarah, 257, 258n
Hogg, James, 263
Hogg, Jane Williams, 2nn, 3n, 6, 8n, 19, 21,
23, 24n, 26n, 36, 37, 40n, 43n, 81, 82, 83n,
94, 95, 132, 146, 147n, 148, 149, 159,
160n, 164, 171, 180, 181, 183, 202, 203,
204, 207, 209, 212, 213, 216, 219, 221,
222, 246, 247, 249, 249n, 257, 260, 264,
266, 267, 278, 285, 292, 293, 298, 305,
309, 310n, 318, 322, 338, 345; letters to,
1, 8, 14, 25, 34, 38, 41(2), 47, 50, 53, 55,
188, 205, 248, 341. *See also* Hogg, Thomas
and Jane, letter to
Hogg, John, 257, 258n, 262
Hogg, Mary Prudentia, 19, 21, 21n, 34, 36,
37, 47
Hogg, Mrs., 257
Hogg, Prudentia Ann, 257, 258n
Hogg, Prudentia Sarah, 143n, 257, 266, 278,
293; birth of, 258n, 264, 264n
Hogg, Thomas and Jane: letter to, 147
Hogg, Thomas Jefferson, 6, 7n, 9, 15, 19, 21,
34, 42, 52, 53n, 54, 55, 117, 132, 171,
174n, 183, 190, 203, 204n, 205, 205n, 206n,
207, 209, 212, 221, 224, 246, 255, 257,
262n, 264, 266, 274, 274n, 301n, 302n,
310n; letters to, 205, 262, 301, 307(2), 309.
Works: "An Introductory Lecture in the
Study of Civil Law," 48n; *Leonora,* 117n;

Moore, Thomas (*continued*)
106n, 110, 111n, 113, 127, 131, 160, 168, 169, 169n, 202n, 222n, 255n, 303n, 309n, 326n, 341n, 342; letter to, 308; portrait of, 197. Works: Byron's *Letters and Journals* (ed.), 3n, 93, 93n, 101, 328; *The Fudge Family in Paris,* 326n; *The Twopenny Post-Bag,* 326n
Morgan, Mr., 127n
Morgan, Lady Sydney, 113n, 127n, 242n, 294nn, 306n, 308n; letters to, 242, 243, 294, 316
Morgan, Sir Thomas Charles, 127n, 242n, 294n
Mori, Nicholas, 210, 211n
Morier, James Justinian: *The Adventures of Hajji Baba, of Ispahan,* 174, 175n; *Zohrab the Hostage,* 175n
Morning Post, 119n
Morrison, Archibald, 265, 265n, 266n, 268, 273, 273n
Morton, fifteenth earl of, 7n
Mount Cashell, earl of, 55n
Moxon, Edward, 198nn, 301, 301n, 302n, 303n, 304, 307, 325n, 327n; letters to, 198, 300, 303, 311(2), 312, 313, 315, 316, 324, 325, 327, 328, 330, 332, 336(2), 347; prosecution of, 311n
Moxon, Emma Isola, 327, 327n, 328
Mulberries, The, 212n
Murchison, Charlotte, 127n; letters to, 127, 128
Murchison, Roderick, 106n, 127n, 128, 128n, 298, 298n
Murray, John, 33n, 88, 89n, 91n, 110n, 115, 116n, 127n, 131, 132, 188n, 197, 324n, 326n; letters to, 27, 56, 59, 89, 91, 93, 97, 101, 102, 103(2), 104, 105, 110, 113, 116, 121, 144(2), 159(2), 162, 175, 187, 222, 223
Murray, John III, 116, 116n, 117n; letter to, 115
My Absent Son, 61n

Naples, 172, 172n
Napoleonic Wars, 96n
Nashoba, 4, 5n, 16n, 123n
National Magazine and Monthly Critic, 335n
Neale, William Johnson: *Cavendish,* 151, 151n, 152
New Harmony, 5n
New Harmony Gazette, 123n
Newman, A. K., 108
New Monthly Magazine, The, 49, 63, 126, 129, 129n, 135, 136n, 152, 169n, 174
New Palace Yard, 194, 195n
New Year's Gift and Juvenile Souvenir, 161, 161n
New York, 171
Nichols, Mr., 329, 329n
Nicholson, William, 123n
Nicolls, Edith, 220n
Nicolls, Edward, 220n
Niobe, 6, 7
Norfolk, dukes of, 19, 20
Norfolk, twelfth duke of, 2, 2n, 6

Normanby, first marquis of: *The Contrast,* 158, 158n
Norton, Caroline, 244n, 245, 256, 258, 271, 272n, 278, 279n, 282, 283n, 292, 293n, 305n. Works: *Observations on the Natural Claim of a Mother to the Custody of Her Young Children,* 244n, 283n; *A Plain Letter to the Lord Chancellor,* 244n; *The Wife,* 243, 243n; *Woman's Reward,* 243, 243n
Norton, George, 243
Nothing Superfluous, 85n
Novello, Mary, 54, 55n
Novello, Vincent, 53, 54, 55n, 345; letter to, 28
Novellos, the, 239n

O'Hara, Barnes and Abel. *See* Banim, John and Michael
Ollier, Charles, 101, 101n, 175n, 200n, 252, 252n, 253, 255, 306n; letters to, 33, 62, 63, 65, 68, 80, 92, 96, 97, 98, 100, 121, 125, 126, 128, 129(3), 130, 135, 142, 144, 145, 148, 149, 150, 151(2), 152, 158, 164, 174, 185(2), 186(2), 195, 196(2), 199(3), 200, 201, 206(2), 217, 237, 239, 250, 251, 263, 267, 280, 285(2), 294, 304, 306, 310, 331
Ollier, Mrs., 199, 237, 250
Owen, Robert Dale, 5n, 17n
Owen, Robert Dale, Jr., 4, 5n, 16n, 17n, 123n; letters to, 16, 122
Oxford, Lady, 162, 164n

Paganini, Niccolo, 136, 136n, 210
Palmer, Henry, 132, 134n
Papal government, 19, 20
Pareto, L. A. Damaso: *Adone. Elegia di P. B. Shelley* (trans.), 335n
Paris, 41, 44, 46, 47
Parliament, houses of, fires at, 215, 216n
Parry, Sir William Edward, 62; *A Narrative of an Attempt to Reach the North Pole . . . in the year 1827,* 62n
Pascal, 293n
Pater, Mr., 111n
Paul, Aubrey John, 156n
Paul, George Robert, 106n
Paul, Georgiana, 133, 134n, 154, 155, 156n, 177, 178, 184nn, 188, 189, 190, 190n, 192n, 203, 204n, 237, 239n, 286, 287n
Paul, John Dean, 106n, 156n, 239n
Paul, Sir John Dean, 106n, 148, 148n, 149, 149n, 181, 184n, 205n
Paul, Lady, 174, 205n, 208, 211n
Payne, John Howard, 10n, 12n, 59n, 60, 61n, 127n; letters to, 3, 9, 11, 12, 13, 15, 18, 21, 22(2), 23(3), 24, 30(2), 31, 44, 58, 60(2), 61(3), 64(2), 65, 68(2), 69(2), 71(2), 73, 75, 81, 84(2), 85, 87, 90, 98, 118, 126, 136. Works: *Fricandeau,* 136, 136n; *The Two Galley Slaves; or, The Mill of St. Aldervon,* 81, 81n, 85, 85n, 90, 90n; *Virginius,* 68, 68n, 69
Peacock, Edward Gryffydh, 221, 224, 224n
Peacock, Jane Gryffydh, 221, 222, 258
Peacock, Mary Ellen, 220n, 221, 258, 259n, 291; letters to, 220, 224, 309, 313, 317, 322, 332, 339(2), 342, 343

THE JOHNS HOPKINS UNIVERSITY PRESS

This book was composed in Garamond text and display type by
FotoTypesetters, Inc., from a design by Susan Bishop. It was printed on
S.D. Warren's 50-lb. Antique Cream paper and bound in Joanna Arrestox
linen cloth by the Maple Press Company.

July 1814

This book is sacred to me and as no other creature shall ever look into it I may write in it what I please — yet what shall I write that I love the author beyond all powers of expression and that I am parted from him

dearest & only love by that love we have promised to each other although I may not be yours I can never be another's —

But I am thine exclusively thine — by the kiss of love by

The glance none can beside
The smile none else might understand
The whispered thought of hearts allied
The pressure of the thrilling hand

I have pledged & myself to thee & sacred is the gift —

I remember your words you are now Mary going to mix with many & for a moment I shall depart but in the solitude of your chamber I shall be with you — yes you are ever with me sacred vision